Early Arizona

Early Arizona

Prehistory to Civil War

Jay J. Wagoner

THE UNIVERSITY OF ARIZONA PRESS
Tucson, Arizona

About the Author ...

Jay J. Wagoner, southwestern historian, has been interested especially in the political and ranching history of Arizona. Author of *The History of the Cattle Industry in Southern Arizona, 1540–1940,* and *Arizona Territory, 1863–1912: A Political History* (U. A. Press), he also has had published numerous articles in historical journals. He holds an M.A. degree in history from the University of Arizona and has pursued additional studies at UCLA and at Stanford, Columbia, and American universities. Fulbright scholar to Brazil in 1960, he also has traveled world wide. After joining the Phoenix Union High School system in 1949, he later became head of the Social Sciences Department at East Phoenix High School.

Third printing 1983
THE UNIVERSITY OF ARIZONA PRESS

L.C. No. 73-76307
ISBN 0-8165-0501-2

Contents

MAPS

ILLUSTRATIONS

Preface

FOR NEARLY A CENTURY, archaeologists have been carefully collecting information on prehistoric life in Arizona. Through the use of tree-ring dating, radioactive carbon 14, and a new process called archeomagnetism, scientists have shown that man inhabited this area at least 11,000 years ago, and probably earlier. The evidence indicates that the first people were hunters and that they gradually evolved into three distinct sedentary cultural groups by the beginning of the Christian era: the desert Hohokam in the river valleys of southern Arizona, the mountain-dwelling Mogollon on both sides of the present Arizona-New Mexico line, and the Anasazi on the Colorado Plateau in northeastern Arizona. By the time the Spanish arrived in the 1500s, however, all of these groups had completed the world-wide pattern of the rise and fall of ancient societies; they had either declined or disappeared from the Arizona scene. Today the Pimas and Papagos can trace their ancestry back to the Hohokam, and the Hopis are descended from the Anasazi, but no modern tribe can be identified as the progeny of the Mogollon. The Apaches and Navajos who figured so prominently in Arizona history during the Spanish, Mexican, and early American periods, were latecomers who did not begin arriving in this area until the sixteenth century.

The primitive people of Arizona did not have a system of writing and so it has been the task of the archaeologists to piece together the history of the forgotten Americans of Precolumbian times. Fortunately, however, the pioneers of New Spain, who next appeared on the stage of Arizona history, not only recorded their own experiences in the "rim of christendom" but also described the Indians with whom they associated for nearly 300 years. Beginning with Coronado's trek across the state in 1540 in search of the fabulous seven cities of Cíbola, every Spanish expedition had at least one diarist, usually a missionary. The men of the cloth, who followed in the paths of the gold-seeking conquistadores to spread the gospel and establish missions, were especially well-qualified by education and training to describe what they observed at the outposts of civilization. The letters and diaries of such missionaries as the padres Kino and Garcés have given us a good picture of Arizona in the seventeenth and eighteenth centuries. The soldiers who came in the latter century to build presidios from which they could protect the missions and settlements — as well as conduct campaigns against the hostile Apaches — also kept records that are invaluable today for understanding the history of Spanish Arizona. One of the best collections of Spanish and early Mexican colonial materials, most of it on microfilm, is now available at the Arizona Historical Society in Tucson. The documents have been catalogued and many of them donated by Father Kieran McCarty, a very capable Franciscan historian.

In preparing this narrative on early Arizona, the author has made extensive use of land grant records accumulated from the archives of Spain and Mexico by investigators for the Court of Private Land Claims. More is known about the ranchers who occupied the land grants than about the miners who prospected for precious metals because the ranchers bothered to petition for deeds to their vast estates. The era of the land grants began in the last decades of Spanish rule — the "golden age" of Hispanic Arizona. During that period, settlements along the Santa Cruz and elsewhere in southern Arizona reached a zenith of prosperity. Cattle ranches and mines were developed and new mission churches were constructed as settlers took advantage of a lull in the Indian maraudings. The Apaches had been subdued and placated by a Spanish policy inaugurated in 1786 that combined military pressure and a dependency system whereby the Indians were promised regular gifts when they settled on reservations near the presidios. This Spanish program was not dropped after the Mexicans gained independence in 1821, but the officials of the new nation lacked the interest and money to carry out effective pacification of the natives in the remote northern provinces. Though titles to most of the land grants in Arizona were secured during the first part of the Mexican period, the 1820s and early 1830s, the Apaches renewed their assaults in the 1830s and succeeded in destroying almost every trace of European-type civilization in this region. The new Mexican republic was so beset with internal troubles that it paid little attention to the northern frontier settlements and the hostile Indians eagerly took advantage of the situation.

The first Anglo-Americans to enter Apachería — a term which applied to almost all of Mexican Arizona but the white settlements at Tubac and Tucson — were the fur trappers. Almost as Indian-like in appearance and habits as the Apaches themselves, this reckless breed of men moved into the Gila Valley as early as 1826 to trap beaver. Men like "Old Bill" Williams, the Patties (father and son), Jedediah Smith, Ewing Young, and Kit Carson returned to New Mexico with pelts to sell. They also told stories about Arizona that were passed on by merchants and traders to easterners. The mountain men, as the trappers were called, blazed the trails for the United States in the Southwest and their ventures helped to whet the appetites of Anglo-Americans who believed that it was the manifest destiny of the United States to expand to the Pacific Ocean. The expansionists wanted a chance to tame the wilderness that had vexed the Spaniards and Mexicans for the greater part of three centuries. As tension mounted on the Southwest frontier in the 1830s and 1840s, war between the United States and revolution-plagued Mexico seemed inevitable.

The clash came in the struggle over Texas, but quickly spread to California and ended with the Mexican cession of the vast Southwest — including Arizona north of the Gila River — to the United States. The accounts written by military men and members of the Mormon Battalion en route to California during the war give us a glimpse of sparsely settled Arizona at that time. To their observations were soon added the personal accounts kept by the gold-hungry "Forty-niners" as well as the official reports of the boundary commissioners who surveyed first the Gila route and then the present inter-

national line after the Gadsden Purchase of 1853. Volumes
of information were compiled also by Army explorers who
traversed most of the newly acquired lands in the 1850s.

Migration from the States came slowly, however, despite
the ambition of Southern leaders for a transcontinental railroad across the Gadsden Purchase and the hope of mine
developers for a bonanza in Arizona. Yet, the constructive
work done by the pioneer merchants, miners, stock raisers, and
roadbuilders during the 1850s seems remarkable when one
reads in their personal papers and the contemporary periodicals
about the handicaps under which they operated — in particular
the hostility of the Apaches and the absence of any effective
local government. From 1850 to 1863 Arizona was administered as a part of the Territory of New Mexico, and the settlers,
who lived mainly south of the Gila, felt isolated and remote
from the territorial government in Santa Fe. They resented
the condition appropriately described as "no law west of the
Pecos," and began asking Congress to create a separate territory. But all their efforts were doomed to failure until the Civil
War made Arizona a pawn in the struggle for control of the
western territories. The South was first to pick up the thread
of Arizona's territorial aspirations by creating, on February 14,
1862, the Territory of Arizona, comprising the southern half
of both present-day Arizona and New Mexico and extending
from Texas to California.

Confederate control of this region was short-lived, however, and on February 24, 1863, President Lincoln signed the
Organic Act creating a separate territory with the present
boundary lines of the State of Arizona, except for the northwest
corner (Pah Ute County) chopped off by Congress and transferred to Nevada in 1866. In his book entitled *Arizona Territory, 1863–1912: A Political History,* this author traced the
history of the territory. This companion volume is intended
as a comprehensive history of Arizona prior to the creation of
the territory in 1863.

It takes the assistance and cooperation of many people to
bring a book of this size to reality. I am especially indebted to
the following individuals who graciously consented to read one
or more chapters related to their special interests and who

made valuable suggestions for improvement of the manuscript:
Dr. Emil W. Haury of the University of Arizona whose archaeological projects and voluminous writings are landmarks for
studies on prehistoric Arizona; Sidney Brinckerhoff, Director
of the Arizona Historical Society, who has written some excellent books and articles on the Spanish period of Arizona history;
Father Kieran McCarty, Franciscan historian at Mission San
Xavier del Bac and authority on the church and public archival
records of Sonora; Frank Brophy, owner of the Babocomari
(also Babacomari) land grant whose interest in Arizona's past
has found an outlet in a number of books and articles; Mrs.
Constance Altshuler, author of *The Latest From Arizona: The
Hesperian Letters, 1858–61* and scholar on the early American
period of the state's history; and the late B. Sacks, a recognized
expert on the history of Arizona in the 1850s, who wrote
Be It Enacted: The Creation of the Territory of Arizona and
several well-researched articles on this era. I am also indebted
to Don Bufkin for cartography. Finally, I feel a deep sense of
gratitude to the University of Arizona Press, especially to
Marshall Townsend, Elizabeth Shaw, Elaine Nantkes, Doug
Peck, Erwin Acuntius, and Barbara Vigil for their various contributions in bringing the book into being.

The depositories of historical materials listed below have
been used during the fifteen years that this book has been in
preparation and the assistance given me by the personnel in all
of them is sincerely acknowledged: Arizona Historical Society,
Tucson; University of Arizona Library and Special Collec-
tions, Tucson; Arizona State Museum at the University of Ari-
zona, Tucson; Arizona Department of Library and Archives,
Phoenix; Arizona Corporation Commission, Phoenix; Charles
Trumbull Hayden Library and Special Collections, Arizona
State University, Tempe; Arizona Historical Foundation,
Tempe; Phoenix Public Library, Arizona Collection; offices
of the county recorder and the county assessor in the counties of
Cochise, Pima, Santa Cruz, and Yavapai; Transamerica Title
Insurance Company in Bisbee and Prescott; Sharlot Hall
Museum, Prescott; Museum of Northern Arizona, Flagstaff;
United States General Land Office, Phoenix; Library of Con-
gress, Washington, D.C.; National Archives, Washington, D.C.,

and the Washington National Records Center, Suitland, Maryland; Federal Records Center, Bell, California; State of New Mexico Museum, Collections and Library, Santa Fe; State of New Mexico Records Center, Archives Division, Santa Fe; University of New Mexico Library, Special Collections, Albuquerque; California State Library, Sacramento; Bancroft Library, University of California, Berkeley; Henry E. Huntington Library, San Marino, California; Los Angeles County Museum of Natural History, History Division; Southwest Museum, Los Angeles; San Diego Historical Society and Junipero Serra Museum; San Diego Public Library; Archivo del Gobierno del Estado de Sonora, Hermosillo, Sonora, Mexico; Biblioteca, Universidad de Sonora, Hermosillo; and Archivo General y Público de la Nación, Mexico City.

J.W.

PART ONE

GEOGRAPHY AND PREHISTORY

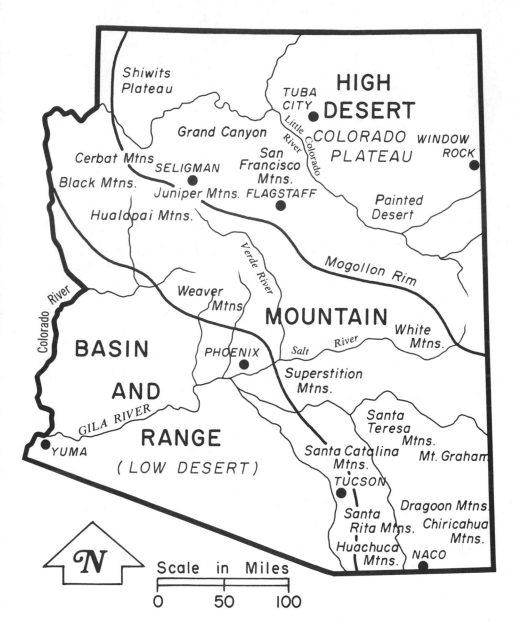

Arizona: Physiographic zones

Chapter I

Geographical Background

MUCH OF THE AREA that now comprises the state of Arizona is arid, but it has not always been that way. During most of the time since the earth was formed several billions of years ago, this region was under water. Inland seas laid down thousands of feet of limestone which interbedded with lava heaved up from the cooling depths of the earth's interior. Geologists say that gradually, beginning about 170 million years ago, the seas dried up and left great sand deposits. Then, after a tremendous upward surge of the Colorado Plateau about 30 million years ago, and some volcanic action and erosion in later times, the modern face of Arizona began to take its present shape.

The state is divided into three physiographic regions, each of which has its own climate, flora, and fauna. The high northern plateau, mantled with juniper and piñon, is separated from the hot southern deserts by a mountainous section which traverses the state diagonally from northwest to southeast. The northern section is part of the high Colorado Plateau. Cut by innumerable deep canyons which have made north-south travel very difficult, this region to a large extent has been isolated and pastoral. Scenic though it is and swarmed by tourists coming to view such natural wonders as the Painted Desert, Meteor Crater, and the Petrified Forest, the northern area has not been easily connected with the rest of the state by modern surface transportation. Surrounded by mountains and elevated far above the canyon streams and the underground water table, much of this area is dry and lacking a cheap source of water. The Colorado River, a blessing to desert regions downstream, serves up north only to divide the plateau into subsections

San Francisco Peaks, near Flagstaff, Arizona
(Photo by Barry Goldwater, 1950)

— the sparsely settled Northeast which contains the huge Navajo and Hopi reservations and the even more remote land north and west of the Grand Canyon.

In the walls of this magnificent canyon one can see huge horizontal layers of limestone and sandstone, which make up most of the plateau except for mountains that were formed by volcanic eruption of molten lava. The best examples of the latter are the White Mountains in the eastern part of the state and the San Francisco Peaks north of Flagstaff (including Humphreys Peak which at 12,670 feet is the highest point in Arizona). In between these two mountainous areas is an escarpment called the Mogollon Rim which is the southern edge of the plateau. In contrast to the more barren land of scant rainfall north of the Little Colorado River, there is a great belt of pine forest along the Rim and mountainous edges of the plateau.

In addition to the volcanic mountains, Arizona has a broad band, 70 to 150 miles wide, of nearly parallel and broken mountain ranges running from Mohave County in the northwest to Cochise County in the southeast. These formations were made millions of years ago by the folding of the earth's rocky crust. Internal pressures uplifted and tilted underlying sedimentary rocks to form such spectacular mountains as the Junipers, Weavers, and Bradshaws in Yavapai County; the Superstitions east of Mesa; the Santa Catalinas and Santa Ritas in the vicinity of Tucson; and the Chiricahuas and Huachucas in the southeast. The highest peak in the Mountain Zone is Mount Graham in the Pinaleño range; it is 10,713 feet above sea level and nearly eight thousand feet above the town of Safford in the Gila Valley. Mount Lemmon in the Santa Catalinas has an elevation of 9,150 feet while Mount Wrightson in the Santa Ritas rises to 9,432 feet. Chiricahua Peak in the southeast part of the state is 9,795 feet high.

The third part of Arizona is classified as the Basin and Range (or Low Desert) area. Short ranges of low mountains in this zone rise abruptly from broad, level, arid plains. Many of the mountains appear to be partially buried, which, in fact, is the case. The broad desert plains have been formed from material washed down from mountains protected only by sparse

The desert near Yuma, Arizona

vegetation. Many of the mountain ranges are mineral bearing and have played an important part in the economic life of Arizona. Some of the sediment-filled plains and valleys have been irrigated to produce high-grade cotton and other crops. Cattle have also flourished where sufficient grasslands could be found to support them.

Cartoonist Reg Manning briefly described the three physiographic divisions of Arizona in his book, *What Is Arizona Really Like?* "If you were a giant and wanted to eat the state of Arizona," he wrote, "you would find that, roughly, it would make three large and widely different mouthfuls."

Starting at the northeast corner (the only point in the United States where four states meet — Utah, Colorado, New Mexico and Arizona) you would bite out a large quarter circle, sinking your teeth in to encompass the Little Colorado River. This corner takes in the vast Navajo and Hopi Indian Reservations — a wildly beautiful land where prehistoric dinosaurs roamed and left their footprints in the sands — where Indians dwell in picturesque canyons and atop high plateaus. It includes the Painted Desert — eroded bluffs of colored sand and clay following the curve of the Little Colorado in a 150-mile-long "rainbow." And it takes in the famous Petrified Forest.

The second mouthful of your mythical meal would be the "greens" course. Here you would chew off a huge crescent consisting almost entirely of virgin forest — the largest unbroken expanse of Ponderosa pine in America. It would also include, slashing across the northern tip of the crescent, one of the world's great wonders, the Grand Canyon.

The remaining bite would be your dessert — or properly the desert. Almost all of it, from the Hoover Dam country in the northwest corner, to the Mexican border region on the south, and bordered on the west by Nevada and California, is in the "cactus-belt." It's the portion of Arizona which most folks think of as "typical" — the warm dry land which travel agents call the "winter playground." Here are great irrigated valleys, and booming cities, where every home is air conditioned, and most of the orange groves have been sub-divided. Not far from modern skyscrapers you can visit Spanish Missions built when America was young.

GEOGRAPHIC KEYS TO ARIZONA'S HISTORY

The Basin and Range Zone, which dips down to a low elevation of 137 feet at Yuma, is one of the four geographic keys to understanding the history of Arizona. This area, an extension of the long, narrow, west coast plain of Mexico, is

the part of Arizona first known in recorded history. Though
undoubtedly used earlier by prehistoric Indians as a trade and
migration route, it is revealed in Spanish documents as a highway of conquest, conversion, and commerce, beginning in the
sixteenth century. Conquistadores, missionaries, soldiers, and
settlers traveled along the corridor into Arizona — the chief
routes following the north-flowing Santa Cruz and San Pedro
rivers. A more difficult alternate trail, known as the *Camino del
Diablo* or Devil's Highway, ran through Arizona's southwest
corner to the juncture of the Gila River and the Colorado. The
Hispanic influence in Arizona began with the visits of men like
Coronado, Kino, Garcés, and Anza; it is still very much a part
of the state's cultural heritage.

It would be difficult to interpret Arizona's history without
consideration of the Colorado Plateau, the second geographical
key. The plateau and adjacent mountains constituted a physical
barrier to northward expansion of Spanish settlement from
Mexico and seemed at first to be a bleak, unattractive region to
early white visitors. It was the heartland of the early Anasazi
Indians, however, and the home of the Hopi and Navajo in
later times. And in the nineteenth century the discovery of
excellent grazing lands, fine timber land, and mineral deposits
made parts of the area more desirable to Caucasians. Despite
the hostility of the Apache and Navajo tribes, Mormons penetrated the plateau from the north, and eventually the transcontinental railroad entrepreneurs built the Santa Fe line across
the area from the east. While settlement and development were
late in coming, the northern region had long been passively
determining Arizona's history in another sense; it furnished a
big part of the topsoil and water for the more habitable part
of the state. This phenomenon gives us the third geographical
key to the past.

Through the centuries, the Colorado River system, which
drains or waters most of Arizona, carried silt from the highlands downstream to the desert valleys. The rain-swept mountains and verdant edges of the plateau have provided tangible
surface water for the dry but rich agricultural lands of the
Salt and Gila river valleys. Long before the arrival of Anglo-
American farmers and urban dwellers in central Arizona,

sedentary agricultural Indians realized the possibility of harnessing the water for irrigation. Ruins of their villages and canals in the vicinity of Phoenix indicate that the natives successfully tilled the soil until driven out by unpredictable and prolonged drought as well as the maraudings of more predatory tribes. Today, agriculture flourishes anew and the population is booming because the precious water is stored in reservoirs behind huge dams on the Gila River and its tributaries. The motto of the Salt River Valley Water Users' Association, "Where water flows, Arizona grows," is certainly an appropriate summary of the influence of the Colorado River system on the progress of Arizona.

The fourth and last geographical key to an understanding of Arizona's history involves another path of entry — this one through the pass where the Rio Grande River crosses a low break in the continental backbone between the Rockies and the Mexican highlands. From this point, known as El Paso del Norte, Anglo-Americans moved westward through New Mexico into Arizona over routes originally used by the Spaniards. Military expeditions during the Mexican War years, federal exploring and boundary survey parties, and Forty-niners went through the pass, as did Texas cattle drivers. Less than a decade after James A. Gadsden was sent to purchase what is now southern Arizona, the Confederates came over this route to occupy Tucson during the Civil War. Still later, the Southern Pacific railroad was built through the same country from California. Many of the travelers who entered were passing through and lingered only briefly; others stayed, however, and helped to civilize the Arizona frontier.

Chapter 2

Prehistoric Animals and Early Men

MORE THAN 200 MILLION years ago — and for a subsequent 140 million years — much of northern Arizona was swampland, lower in elevation than present-day southern Arizona. This was the Mesozoic Period — the fourth geologic age of the earth. Giant reptiles roamed through the "dinosaur belt" that stretched eastward from present-day Kingman to the Four Corners area and beyond. Many of their huge, three-toed footprints were subsequently fossilized. Today these tracks are visible in such places as the Dinosaur Canyon north of Flagstaff and on the Hopi reservation near Tuba City.

Though there must have been many reptiles ranging back and forth across northern Arizona, most of the skeletal remains which have been discovered were found in one quarry in Dinosaur National Park near Vernal, Utah. From this site alone, Carnegie Museum scientists excavated bones belonging to no less than 300 dinosaurs and assembled two dozen mountable specimens representing the best collection of reptilian monsters in the world.

The disappearance of the prehistoric reptiles may have been caused by the new climate and vegetation that resulted from tremendous geological changes. At present no one really knows. Even during the Mesozoic Period the earth's crust folded and tilted to form the Sierra Nevada and the California Coast Range. In the following age, the Cenozoic, a similar upheaval raised the Colorado Plateau and created the Rocky Mountains.

After the prehistoric animals became extinct, approximately 60 or 70 million years ago, Arizona became arid for millions of years. But during the Ice Age, from about one million to 10,000 years ago, a gigantic glacier covered most of the northern hemisphere four times and the climate became much cooler and more moist than it is today. After the last glacier started retreating north — about 18,000 years ago — the present period of mild climate began, and Arizona became a land of lakes, streams, and green valleys. Annual rainfall up to forty inches produced an abundance of vegetation for animals. The mammoth, which resembled the modern elephant, thrived on verdant grasslands, along with other now-extinct animals such as primitive horses, four-pronged antelope, bison, and camels. The carnivorous dire wolf preyed upon the hairy ground sloth, tapir, deer, and wild pig.

Wherever game ventured, man was sure to follow. Most archaeologists believe that prehistoric hunters migrated to North America from Asia. During glacial periods, when a vast amount of the earth's water was frozen in ice masses, men could wander freely across the Bering Strait land bridge from Siberia to Alaska. Once in Alaska, however, man's southward advance was blocked by a great continental glacier; he had to wait for a warm period, when the glaciers melted and filled the seas again, before pushing into the interior of North America. One such interglacial period is thought to have occurred about 40,000 to 25,000 years ago, and as mentioned above, the present one began about 18,000 years ago. Though there were undoubtedly Indian migrations to the Southwest during the first of these periods, it is uncertain when man first came to what is now Arizona. A small amount of evidence that has been uncovered and dated by the carbon 14 technique, however, would indicate that he was definitely living in this area at least as early as 11,000 years ago.

The early people were nomadic hunters who left behind only occasional traces of camp sites and the remains of animals. Some of the early inhabitants may have depended almost entirely upon game for food. It seems likely that they formed some sort of group organization in order to kill large animals with spears and other weapons. The prey was usually slain at regular kill-sites, such as bogs or watering places, and butchered on the spot. This theory was corroborated in 1951 when the

State Museum, University of Arizona

Early hunters probably disabled their prey by cutting the tendons of the hind legs with stone knives, then completed the kill by spearing the animal. At the Naco and Lehner ranch archaeological sites in southern Arizona, the remains of now extinct mammoths have been found along **with weapons and butchering tools.**

bones of an extinct Columbian mammoth *(Mammuthus columbi)* with eight spear points lodged in his head and rib cage, were unearthed along Greenbush Creek, near Naco on the Arizona-Mexico border. Evidently the early hunters used a detachable foreshaft on each point; this method allowed the recovery of the main shaft and made it difficult for the wounded animal to work an embedded point from his body. The thirteen-foot-high Naco elephant was killed on the sandy bank of the stream and remained excellently preserved for an estimated 11,000 years because it was covered with clay and silt soon after death.[1]

In 1955, another important discovery was made in the same vicinity, at the Lehner Ranch on the west bank of the San Pedro River. At a site that was once a watering hole, archaeologists from the University of Arizona excavated the remains of nine elephants, ranging in age from adolescents to young adults. At the same place were recovered the bones of extinct forms of the horse, bison, and tapir. Also significant in the Lehner Ranch discovery were the fluted spearheads and the cutting and chopping tools which were found with the bones. The ashes from two fires — probably for roasting meat — made it possible for the scientists to date the killings, like those at Naco, at about 11,000 years ago.

At best, the early hunters must have had a hand-to-mouth existence. But even harder times faced them when the ice cap melted away and the climate of this region started to dry out again. They continued to hunt, however, but for deer, elk, bighorn sheep, and smaller animals; the bigger animals virtually disappeared because of climatic changes and slaughter by man. The main characteristic, however, of the people who inhabited southern Arizona in the centuries just prior to 500 B.C. was not hunting. The extensive use of grinding stones suggests that these Indians were dependent upon the gathering of wild grains, nuts, and roots for much of their food. They were known as the Cochise people because many of their remains were first brought to view in present-day Cochise County when flood waters cut deep into arroyos and valleys in the late nineteenth century. These ancient inhabitants were one link between the earliest elephant hunters and later Indians of the Christian era.*

Unfortunately, we know little about the physical appearance, housing, clothing, or burial customs of the Cochise people; but the culture of these gatherers and grinders of natural wild foods makes the subsequent development of agriculture and pottery more understandable. Indeed, the Cochise people themselves added a new plant to their economy after about 2000 B.C. From the natives of Mexico they learned to grow a small type of corn with each kernel on the cob sheathed in its own husk. Though true farming was still a long way off, the Cochise people of southeastern Arizona had taken a step toward making the transition from a hunting and food-gathering subsistence to sedentary agriculture. In the last centuries B.C. they learned from Mexico how to make a brown and red pottery which has conveyed to archaeologists the thought that the eastern Cochise group became the Mogollon culture of later times.

The difficult task of identifying and establishing the sequence of prehistoric Indian cultures in Arizona was facilitated in the 1940s with the excavation of Ventana Cave on the Papago Reservation west of Tucson.† In this high and dry cave, archaeologists worked for several years digging carefully down through fifteen feet of trash which had accumulated for more than 10,000 years. The record of habitation in the cave before 8000 B.C. began with the Ventana hunting culture, identified by the stone tools and bones of now-extinct animals recovered from the lowest deposits. The subsequent Amargosa culture, approximately 8000 to 7000 B.C., was also based upon hunting

---

*For an early description of these early pre-pottery Indians, see E. B. Sayles and Ernest Antevs, *The Cochise Culture*. Globe, Arizona: Gila Pueblo, 1941. On the basis of artifacts found at sites along the Whitewater Creek in southeastern Arizona, these archaeologists tentatively divided the Cochise culture into three stages: Sulphur Springs Stage — before 8000 B.C. (10,000 years ago); Chiricahua, from 8000 to 3000 B.C.; and the San Pedro Stage, between 3000 to 500 B.C. Refinements in these dates were made possible by later discoveries at other sites, especially the Ventana Cave.

† Even after the discovery of Ventana Cave, archaeologists still did not have enough information to establish exact dates for the different stages of the Cochise culture. See Emil W. Haury, *The Stratigraphy and Archaeology of Ventana Cave Arizona*. Tucson and Albuquerque: University of Arizona Press and University of New Mexico Press, 1950, pp. 521–48.

Ventana Cave, where a 10,000-year record of man was found

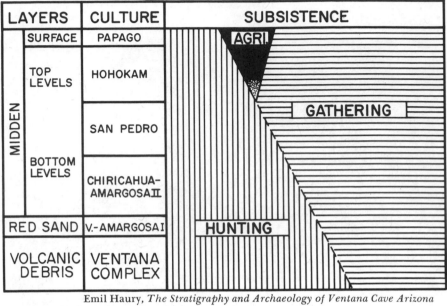

Emil Haury, *The Stratigraphy and Archaeology of Ventana Cave Arizona*

Schematic representation of changes in subsistence patterns of the Ventana Cave occupants

along with some gathering; animals and native plants, similar to types that still grow in the desert, supplied the food. During the Chiricahua period, 7000 to 3000 B.C., there was a mingling of two cultures: the hunting Amargosa people of the desert country to the west and the food-gathering Cochise people of eastern Arizona described above. The inhabitants of the cave during the later Cochise era, also called the San Pedro period, from 3000 B.C. to A.D. 1, had a plant and animal food supply sufficiently stable so that they could occupy one place for extended periods of time. More is known of the desert Hohokam, A.D. 1 to 1400, than of all earlier occupants of the cave. Village dwellers and irrigation farmers, the Hohokam may have been ancestors of the present-day Papago and Pima Indians. Unfortunately, the Ventana Cave debris did not shed any light on the period from A.D. 1400 to 1700 about which historians still know very little.

Chapter 3

Prehistoric Indian Cultures

THE THREE MOST IMPORTANT Precolumbian tribal groups in Arizona were the Hohokam, the Anasazi, and the Mogollon. Though their origins are unknown, it is logical to assume that some of their roots lead back to the Cochise people. All three groups raised their standard of living by cultivating new crops, using new agricultural methods, and developing new arts such as pottery making. Obviously they learned many of these things from the more advanced Mexican cultures through trade contacts; but it is interesting also to note the influence of geography on these prehistoric cultural groups. Each developed in its own section and intermingled with the others only after mastering the local environment. The Hohokam lived in the desert regions of southern Arizona; the Mogollon centered in the mountain belt; and the Anasazi inhabited the Colorado Plateau.

HOHOKAM

Hohokam (pronounced ho-ho-kam) is a modern Pima Indian word which means "all used up" or "those who have vanished." The forgotten Americans of pre-Spanish times, it almost seems as if the Hohokam planned it that way. They cremated their dead, much to the inconvenience of today's anthropologists, and thus prevented posterity from forming a clear picture of their physical appearance. The Hohokam became skilled workers in stone and clay, but in most cases deliberately smashed the most beautiful of their artifacts — vessels, figurines, and ornaments. Few examples of their architecture were left, and their amazing irrigation canal systems were nearly all concealed by the desert sands. Fortunately,

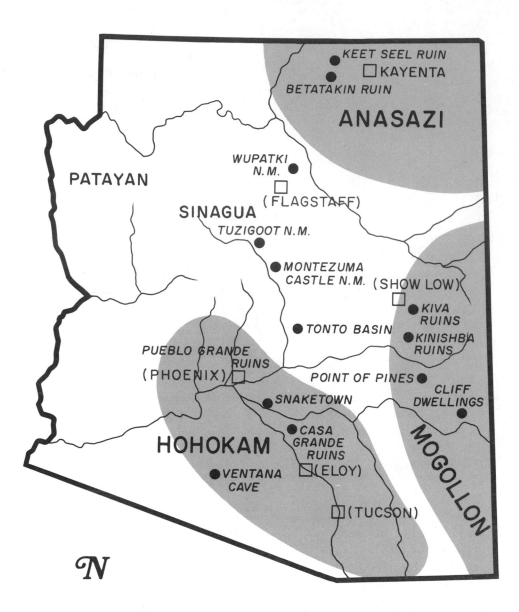

Arizona: Principal prehistoric Indians

patient archaeologists and allied technicians have been able to piece together material objects such as pottery, to excavate ancient watercourses and villages, and thereby to construct part of the history of an ancient agricultural civilization which fell into near oblivion. The origin of the Hohokam remains uncertain. Evidence uncovered at Ventana Cave led archaeologists to believe that both the Hohokam and the Mogollon descended from the Cochise people. More recent findings, however, indicate that the Hohokam migrated to the Southwest from Mexico.

The Hohokam pioneered the Gila Valley before the beginning of the Christian era in Europe. Their long habitation in the desert can be divided into four periods: Pioneer, Colonial, Sedentary, and Classic. Our knowledge of the Pioneer Period (about 300 B.C. to A.D. 500) is largely based upon excavations such as the one at Snaketown, situated near the Gila River southwest of Chandler, Arizona.[1] Here the people dwelled in pithouses which were sunk at least a foot below ground level. The walls of these homes were probably constructed of poles and brush with mud chinked into the holes. The roofs, which were supported by vertical posts, consisted of brush and mud piled upon cottonwood or mesquite rafters. Since there were no windows, the houses were dark inside and such tasks as pottery making, weaving, and grinding of corn were done outdoors under a ramada. It is believed that the dog was the only domesticated animal that one might have found near these houses or in the surrounding fields.* Careful exploration of the Snaketown area in 1964–65, by a team of archaeologists and Pima Indian helpers, revealed that irrigation was practiced there as early as 300 B.C. With a system of hand-dug, gravity-fed canals the villagers grew corn to supplement a diet of cactus fruits, mesquite beans, fish, deer, and rabbit meat. Cotton may have been cultivated as early as the Pioneer Period, and textiles woven from the fiber.

Other crafts and arts also had their beginning at this time. The Hohokam used the "paddle and anvil" technique in making pottery. The potter held an anvil inside the vessel and

---

* Evidence uncovered at Ventana Cave indicates that the dog existed in Arizona as early as 7000 B.C., long before Europeans came to the Southwest.

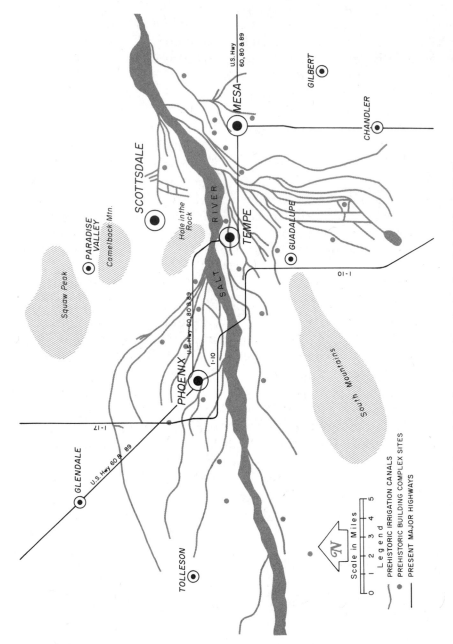

Prehistoric irrigation canals in the Salt River Valley

moved it around as he shaped the soft clay with a paddle applied on the outside; the product was then placed in an oven to be fired. Starting with a plain brown ware, the Hohokam eventually developed a type of red-on-buff polychrome decoration. Another craft which the early Hohokam perfected was stone working. They made stone axes with wooden handles, manos and trough-shaped metates for grinding corn, bowls for their food, and an assortment of other tools and weapons: arrowheads, palettes for compounding pigments, drills, scrapers, reamers, and anvils.

During the Colonial Period (A.D. 500 to 900) the Hohokam continued digging irrigation canals — their greatest achievement economically.* About 200 miles of these canals have been traced in the Salt River Valley, some as wide as thirty or forty feet and as much as fifteen feet deep. Such a watering system was a tremendous accomplishment for a primitive people who had no beasts of burden or earth moving equipment other than stone or wooden tools for digging and baskets for hauling. Even the modern engineers who surveyed the present-day Grand Canal found that they "couldn't gain an inch in a mile" to improve the old Hohokam arterial that followed approximately the same route. What is more significant, this unequaled prehistoric irrigation system made it possible for the people to settle in permanent villages. With the ability to grow and accumulate surplus food, some of the people had time to play ball. Like the Mayans and Toltecs, from whom the Hohokam probably learned the game, they excavated a court about five feet below the ground and approximately 60 by 180 feet in size. The object of the sport was evidently to get a rubber ball (a similar ball was found in a pottery jar dug up near the present town of Eloy) through rings made of twisted grass or other perishable material and set vertically in the middle of the sides of the court. Such large projects as ball courts and

---

* According to archaeologists, the Hohokam started irrigation during the Pioneer Period and, in fact, had a knowledge of canal building at the time they migrated from Mexico. For a description of a Colonial Hohokam site farther up the Salt River see Emil W. Haury, *Roosevelt: 9:6: A Hohokam Site of the Colonial Period.* Medallion Papers No. XI, Globe, Arizona: Privately printed by The Medallion Gila Pueblo, 1932.

More battle than sport, a Hohokam ball game at Snaketown probably resembled ancient Mexican contests described by the Spanish. Forbidden to throw or kick the rubbery ball—made from guayule, a desert bush—players tried to knock it through rings with their hips, knees, or elbows. There was little scoring, but when a goal was made the victors could claim the jewelry and clothing of the spectators—if they could catch them! (From a painting by Peter Bianchi)

canals could have been planned only by an exceptional social organization. But, unfortunately, we do not know what kind of society or government the Hohokam had.

Further refinement of the Hohokam culture was characteristic of the third, or Sedentary Period (A.D. 900 to 1200). The people began to move from outlying areas and congregate in larger villages, which were sometimes enclosed by adobe walls as "compounds" for protection against marauding tribes.* The canal system supplying water to thousands of cultivated acres surrounding the villages was enlarged and improved. And the arts were also refined. The potters, for example, made huge jars and bowls with capacities as large as thirty gallons. Designs resembling a textile weave pattern were often applied to the pottery; some authorities feel that this decoration, done in red on a buff background, was superior to any other ceramic work

---

* The multi-storied housing complex, however, was more characteristic of the next, or Classic, period.

found in the Southwest. The Hohokam may have traded their
pottery and other products to Mexican Indians for such items
as little copper bells. They were also known to have brought
shells from the Gulf of California to make into ornaments with
etched designs. This etching was perhaps the most startling of
their artistic achievements. Over 300 years before European
craftsmen learned a similar process for decorating medieval
armor in the 1400s, the Hohokams were fashioning delicate
designs on seashells with acid. The technique involved the use
of pitch to shape an animal such as a toad or snake on the shell;
when soaked in a weak acid solution — probably the fermented
juice of the saguaro cactus fruit — the unprotected surface of
the shell was eaten away, leaving the raised design. In addition
to their development of ceramics and etchings, the people of
the Sedentary Period also made baskets, figurines, and fine
cotton textiles. Little is known, however, about the physical
characteristics of the craftsmen who produced these artifacts or
the farmers who irrigated small and often irregularly shaped
fields. Cremation was still the accepted method of disposing of

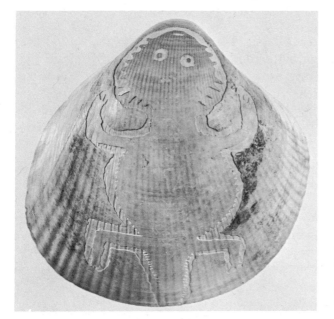

*Hohokam
etched shell*

State Museum,
University of Arizona

Ancient decorated Hohokam pottery and figurine

the dead, and only a few unburned bones, some in urns with offerings, have been found.

In the final, or Classic Period (A.D. 1200 to 1400), the Hohokam lands were invaded by at least two groups of the northern pueblo Indians. One group, the Salado people, were probably impelled by the great drought beginning in 1276 to move from the Tonto Basin area in east-central Arizona. Before about A.D. 1100, they had lived farther north near the Little Colorado River. Another group, some Sinaguans, came from northern Arizona, perhaps for the same reason. It was not long before these pueblo-dwelling Indians made an impact on the culture of their Hohokam hosts; the groups lived together peacefully and gradually merged into one society. As a result of the influx of new blood, the Gila Valley villages soon showed the influence of a new style of architecture, namely the multi-storied house with many rooms.* The ruins of such fine struc-

---

* Scientists do not agree on the main source of influence that brought about the construction of the adobe walled-compounds during the Classic Period. Some archaeologists and anthropologists believe that the new architecture had its origin in Mexico. Adherents to this theory diminish the role played by the Salado and the Sinaguan Indians in changing the culture of the Hohokam. See Alfred E. Dittert, Jr., "They Came From the South," *Arizona Highways,* Vol. XLVIII, No. 1 (January, 1972), p. 38.

tures as the Pueblo Grande in east Phoenix and the Casa Grande north of Coolidge can still be seen.

The famous Casa Grande, America's first skyscraper, is a four-story housing complex built about A.D. 1300. Forty feet high, it dominated the village in which it was constructed and served as a watchtower. From its top, sentinels could observe outsiders approaching from as far away as ten miles and warn the field laborers by smoke signal. To support the weight of the upper stories, builders made the walls four feet thick at the base, filled in the first floor with earth, and carried only the central room to the four-story height. The walls were built in 25-inch layers of wet caliche, a cement-like clay containing a large percent of lime that is found abundantly beneath the desert topsoil in Arizona. The upper floors were supported by logs brought down the Gila River from the mountains. Considering the building materials available, this early "apartment house" was well built and was used until the surrounding farm lands

Casa Grande ruins as photographed in 1878. The Hohokam made a living by irrigating the desert around this imposing Casa Grande.
National Archives

were deserted, about 1450.² Signs of habitation — cooking vessels, sleeping mats, corncobs, fragments of cloth and other household articles — have been found in the eleven large rooms which help to tell the story of the final years of the Hohokam culture. For some mysterious reason, the Casa Grande and other large villages were abandoned in the fifteenth century.

What caused the disintegration of the pueblo-type communities between 1400 and 1450? What happened to the Hohokam? The answers to these questions remain in obscurity though there are many hypotheses. The farmland may have become waterlogged as the water table rose; or possibly the land was exhausted by centuries of cultivation and laden with alkali from silt brought in by irrigation water. Perhaps devastating floods, occasionally washing out the laboriously constructed brush, rock, and dirt dams, contributed to the departure of the "vanished ones." It is very likely that the Hohokam remained in the desert country of southern Arizona and were the ancestors of the present-day Pimas and Papagos. Instead of living in large villages, however, they scattered and reverted to the old-style pithouse and the simple life of their ancestors. The Piman culture — including house construction, irrigation techniques, and pottery — suggests Hohokam influence in many respects. But whatever happened to the Hohokam, the Gila Basin of southern Arizona was definitely the scene of the rise and fall of a great culture, one which endured approximately 1700 years.

ANASAZI

At the same time that the Hohokam were irrigating the desert valleys, another people were living on the Colorado Plateau. Though we do not know what they called themselves, the modern Navajo who now live there refer to them as the Anasazi, meaning "the ancient ones" or the "old peoples."³ The known cultural sequence of the Anasazi is a continuous one and can be traced back about 2000 years. Unlike the Hohokam, they buried their dead, thus giving modern scientists an opportunity to study dozens of preserved bodies which have been exhumed — along with mortuary offerings such as baskets, food, weapons, and sundry personal possessions. So today we

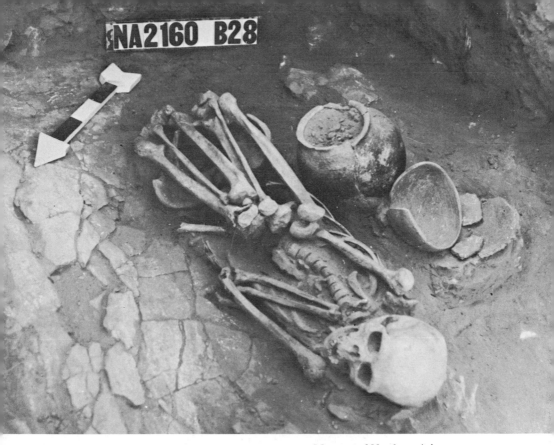

An Anasazi burial at Inscription House

not only know about the arts and crafts of the Anasazi, the food that they ate, the clothes that they wore, and their homes, but also their general appearance and physique.

The culture of the Anasazi can be divided into two main periods: the Basketmaker and the Pueblo. The first evidence of the early Basketmakers was revealed in 1893 when the remains of ninety bodies, along with many finely woven baskets, were found in a cave in Butler Wash in southeastern Utah. From this discovery, and later ones in the red sandstone cliffs of the Four Corners area, the short, slender, long-headed, broad-nosed Basketmakers were identified as a people who preceded the builders of the cliff houses.*

*Archaeologists once believed that the early Basketmakers were a partly Negroid people who migrated from what is now western Texas. This idea has been discredited by more recent evidence.

The atlatl, *a spear thrower, was used before the bow and arrow were known in America. It served as an extension of the arm, permitting its user to hurl a spear with greater force.*

These early colonists, who started one of Arizona's first real estate booms, were called Basketmakers because of the great number of baskets found at their sites. While the men were out hunting, the women skillfully wove a variety of containers. Using native fibrous materials, they fabricated parching trays, bowls, trinket baskets, and carrying baskets; some of the latter were made water-tight and sealed with mud or pitch made from piñon gum to keep the soft fibrous materials from rotting. Their smoothly woven, square-toed sandals were made from yucca fiber and are greatly admired today as examples of intricate finger weaving and for the elaborate patterns which were stitched into the soles. Round, seamless, multicolored bags were beautifully woven from vegetal fibers. And in addition to these articles, the weavers also made belts out of white dog's hair and braided rope with human hair.

To provide the hair fiber the women usually lopped off their locks to within two or three inches of the scalp, thus giving them a hairdo shorter than that of the men. The latter often wore a bob of hair on each temple and a Manchu-like, braided or tied queue down the back; occasionally the top of the head was shaved to give a baldpate or wide part effect. The clothing found in the caves with the mummified Basketmakers would indicate that these early Anasazi dressed very scantily. The main item in their wardrobe appeared to be ornamented sandals which were tied to the ankles with cords running from the toes and heel. Summer clothing, when worn, consisted of a woven loin cloth (more commonly called a "gee string") for the male and an apron for the female; the apron was a hula-like skirt made by attaching a fringe of cedar or yucca fiber to a waist cord. During the colder months, of course, the people had to dress more warmly. Some covered themselves with a tanned deerskin robe, while others wore blankets woven from strips of rabbit fur wrapped around cords.[4]

To kill rabbits the men used a curved wooden club, shaped something like an Australian boomerang, but nonreturning. The main weapon used in hunting, however, was the *atlatl*, a kind of throwing stick with which a spear or dart could be hurled with great force.[5] Though inferior to the bow and arrow, which was not used by the earliest Basketmakers, the *atlatl* was a remarkable invention; it produced the same effect as would lengthening the arm of a man by about two feet. Armed with this weapon and a stone-pointed spear, the native hunter could bring down the larger game, including deer, mountain sheep, and the mountain lion. Once killed, the animals were skinned with a wooden-handled stone knife. The meat was either eaten raw or cooked by roasting or boiling — the technique for the latter being very tedious, at least by modern standards. Heated rocks were dropped in a clay-covered basket of water and replaced with others as they cooled. There is no evidence that pottery or metal pots, which can be exposed directly to fire, were used in the early part of the Basketmaker period.[6]

In addition to meat, other wild foods were an important part of the diet. Seeds were gathered from various grasses and shrubs, notably sage. The gatherers used a saucer-like tray basket to shake off the dry hulls. They then transferred the harvest to a carrying basket shaped to fit on their backs. By walking several miles a person might acquire the protein equivalent of several loaves of whole wheat bread. The food gatherers also dug up edible roots, such as wild onions, with a sharp-pointed digging stick. Thus, with their meat, cereals, wild vegetables, berries, piñon nuts, and possibly honey on occasion, the pioneer Basketmakers had a variety of food.

Several changes occurred in the Anasazi culture between approximately A.D. 500 and 700, an era which is classified as the Modified Basketmaker Period. During this time the people became more sedentary and made improvements in housing. There are several reasons why they abandoned their caves for snug little round huts. First, they desired better protection from the cold weather. Then the cultivation of crops — corn, squash, and finally beans — and the domestication of wild life, such as the turkey, gave the people an opportunity to settle in one locality for a longer time. Imitating the gophers and the prairie dogs, they dug pithouses, three to five feet deep. At first the houses were circular in design. The roof was built cone-shaped by setting poles in the earth at the edge of the excavation and leaning them toward the center in such a way that smoke could escape through a hole in the middle. The framework was covered with brush and plastered over with mud. The doorway was usually placed on the east side to catch the morning sun rays. The hardened clay or stone slab floor had a firepit in the center. *Metates* for grinding corn were usually on the south side of the pit, suggesting that this may have been the women's part of the house. On the other side of the room there was a small hole, known as the "Sipapu," which represented the mythical place of emergence of the first people from the underworld. Later on, oval and rectangular pithouses, in that order, replaced the circular type. But whatever the architectural style, the people tended to congregate into villages with houses grouped close together, but not adjoining.

In addition to permanent houses, several other cultural changes came during the Modified Basketmaker Period. One significant sign of progress was the making of pottery. Though at first they had only crude, undecorated containers made by lining baskets with clay to hold water, the Anasazi eventually developed pottery, using the coiling technique; for decoration, designs in black on a white or gray background were affixed to the coiled clay before firing. Also, the bow and arrow replaced the *atlatl;* improved stone tools and weapons, including notched axes with better cutting edges, were developed, and new foods — including several varieties of corn, beans, and domesticated turkeys — were added to the diet. These changes laid the foundation for a golden age in Anasazi culture several centuries later.

Starting about A.D. 700, the Anasazi entered into the second major subdivision of their culture, the Pueblo, that was to continue for about 600 years. Until recently the long-headed Basketmakers and the broad-headed Pueblo people were considered to be entirely different racial types. And some scientists hold to the theory that the early Pueblos were outsiders who invaded the Colorado Plateau area, assimilated some of the Basketmakers into their own culture, and either exterminated or drove others into peripheral areas. More detailed studies of skeletal remains, however, now suggest that the Basketmakers and Pueblos were basically the same people. Rather than a mass invasion of racially different conquerors, it is more likely that any new migrants who arrived were amalgamated with

the Basketmakers and peacefully influenced the evolution
of the new Pueblo culture. One custom of the Pueblo people
which made them appear to be racially different was their
practice of artificially flattening the rear portion of the skull.
It was the fashion to strap babies tightly against hard cradle-
boards so that the backs of their soft heads were flattened,
the resulting deformity giving the effect in later life of a
broader skull.

There were significant changes in the Basketmaker culture
which began to develop during the transition era, the so-called
Developmental Pueblo Period (A.D. 700 to 1100). Some of the
more important innovations were in the realm of architecture
since many of the people abandoned the pithouse dwelling for
surface structures. In the course of time, floors became less
depressed and multiroomed unit houses were built of stone or
adobe, the walls being strong enough to support roof timbers
covered with clay or mud. The unit house usually had six to
fourteen rooms, all in one story. A storeroom, safe from storm
and rodents, was usually attached to each main room. Each unit
was inhabited by the members of a matriarchal clan, typically
consisting of a woman, her husband, and her daughters with
their families.

It is interesting to note, in connection with the new architectural styles, however, that the pithouse style did not
completely disappear. Just as in modern times, religious architecture was more traditional and lagged behind secular building. The Pueblo people continued to erect the subterranean,
circular pithouse, called the "kiva," as a ceremonial chamber
where religious rites were performed by the males of a class.
Eventually, the still-popular communal "Great Kivas," as large
as seventy or eighty feet in diameter, were constructed for use
by an entire village.

Just as in architecture, there were changes in the crafts
during the Developmental Pueblo Period. Sandals were still
being woven, but with rounded instead of square or scalloped
toes. Fur and feather robes, particularly the latter, were still
used, but blankets and clothing made from cotton came into
use for the first time during this era; kilts, or short skirts, were
made for the men and aprons for the women. After learning

how to grow the cotton, the Pueblos developed primitive techniques for spinning thread and looming it into fabrics. Cloth manufacturing, as well as improved methods for making pottery, greatly reduced the importance of basketmaking. In brief, the basic traits of the Pueblo culture were developed and spread during the transitional period prior to A.D. 1050. During the ensuing years one of the most advanced aboriginal cultures in North America blossomed in the Four Corners area.

Perhaps more definite information has been obtained concerning the "golden age" of the Pueblo culture (approximately A.D. 1050 to 1300) than about any pre-European period in the history of the Southwest. During this era, also known as the "Classic" or "Great" Period, impressive communal houses were built in caves (cliff houses) and on the tops of mesas. Not only have these sites yielded much archaeological "loot" to be studied, but most of the ruins have been accurately dated through the tree-ring science of dendrochronology which was developed by Professor A. E. Douglass of the University of Arizona. After discovering that the annual rings of trees vary in width according to the amount of rainfall, Douglass constructed a chart showing the pattern and sequence of the rings over hundreds of years. With this chart, the beams found in the pueblos could be dated and the effects of climatic fluctuations on the movements of the people could be studied.[7]

The greatest change from the preceding Developmental Period was in architecture. There were still many scattered one-story clan houses, where a large percentage of the people continued to live, but huge apartment houses were also built. In these structures, hundreds of rooms were stacked four or five stories high with plazas for easy access. Unfortunately, we do not know why these large compact houses were built. Defense does not seem to have been a primary motive since the complexes were not hurriedly, but rather carefully and painstakingly constructed; also, most of the Anasazi continued to dwell in smaller houses at some distance from the main centers, and there is little evidence of extensive violence or bloodshed in the area. Furthermore, aside from location, most of the defensive features of the big houses appear to have been an afterthought and were the result of remodeling. Whatever the

Betatakin (A.D. 1242 to A.D. 1277), in one of the short branches of Tsegi Canyon in northeastern Arizona, was discovered by Byron Cummings in 1909 and later became a national monument. The name "Betatakin," meaning "side hill house," was inspired by the fact that the rooms of the ruin were anchored to the steeply sloping rock floor of the cave.

reason, there was a general tendency for large groups of people to congregate and to cooperate in community living in three localities of the San Juan River basin: Mesa Verde in southwestern Colorado, Chaco Canyon in northwestern New Mexico, and Kayenta in northeastern Arizona. The two best thirteenth-century cliff houses in the latter area — the 350-room Keet Seel (Navajo for "broken pottery") and the 200-room Betatakin ("side hill house") — can be seen today on the grounds of the Navajo National Monument.

The people who lived in these houses, in the Arizona part of the Colorado Plateau, were not as advanced in some respects as were their neighbors farther east. The Kayenta houses, as well as the nearby kivas, were inferior in construction to the

Pueblo Bonito in New Mexico and the Mesa Verde dwellings, and some of the Kayenta pottery differed from that found in the eastern sites. The corrugated culinary pieces, made by spiraling coils of unsmoothed clay, especially showed poorer workmanship and less graceful shapes than examples from the Chaco Canyon and Mesa Verde. On the other hand, the Kayenta black-on-white ware contained elaborate patterns and was excellent by comparison. Also, the polychrome — black, red, or white on a base color of orange or yellow — was a distinctive pottery made in the Arizona villages. Many of the bowls and jugs which have been uncovered are adorned with broad, red bands outlined in black or black and white.

The high level of perfection attained in architecture and pottery making, as well as in the other arts and crafts, during the Pueblo "golden age," is well known. There is still an aura of mystery, however, concerning the sudden departure of the prehistoric Pueblo Indians from their homes. During the thirteenth and fourteenth centuries the villages and cultural centers of the Pueblo Period were abandoned and one can

Interior of Keet Seel (also Kiet Siel), the largest cliff city in Arizona

Museum of Northern Arizona

only guess what happened. The arrival of the hostile Athapascan Indians (Apache and Navajo) may have hastened the
decline of the Pueblo culture but did not initiate it. A better
explanation is needed and at present it would seem that the
twenty-three-year drought (A.D. 1276 to 1299) was the most
impelling cause for the exodus. Some of the villages were
abandoned prior to this drought, however, indicating that
there may have been other causes as well for the end of the
"golden age" of the Pueblos. Whatever the motivation, the Anasazi began migrating, some eastward to present-day New Mexico and others southward to the land of the Hohokam and the
Mogollon. No doubt many of the migrants integrated with
their hosts. And descendants of some of these people returned
to their homeland in the Four Corners area by A.D. 1500. The
modern Hopis, for example, can trace their ancestry back to
these returnees.

MOGOLLON *

The modern progeny of another prehistoric group, the
Mogollon, are not so clearly identified. Classified until recently
with their better known neighbors, the Anasazi and the
Hohokam who greatly influenced them, the Mogollon are now
considered to have been a separate and distinct people. Though
they were of indefinite origin, archaeological studies of their
pottery, tools, and limited agriculture indicate that the Mogollon evolved from the Cochise seed gatherers. Unfortunately,
not enough is known about them yet to divide their culture
into clear-cut chronological periods, as has been done for the
desert and plateau groups. Often described as a drab, simple people, the round-headed, medium-built Mogollon were
among the first people in the Southwest to make pottery and
grow corn. As early as the first or second century B.C. they were
producing an unpainted ware which later showed a Mexican
Indian influence as well as a local tribal distinctiveness. A kind
of coiled pottery, which was sometimes scraped and decorated
with red designs on a brown base, was probably traded to the

---

* Mogollon is usually pronounced "mug ee *yown*," though residents along the
Mogollon Rim often say the first syllable with a long "o." The name comes from that
of Juan Ignacio Flores Mogollon, governor of New Mexico, 1712–1715.

Hohokam and has been found in the most ancient Pioneer level of debris at Snaketown. The Mogollon planted corn even before they manufactured pottery. Farming, however, was very rudimentary and never became a dominant phase of the economy. The people subsisted mainly on the wild game which they hunted and on berries, roots, and nuts which they gathered.

A typical early Mogollon community which has been excavated in Arizona is Bear Ruin, located in the Forestdale Valley about eight miles south of Show Low.[8] Through the study of pottery, as well as tree rings in several beams found there, archaeologists have set the time of occupation as A.D. 600 to 800. Bear Ruin is historically significant because it shows the dominating influence of Anasazi traits. Most of the pithouses clustered in the village, for example, are similar to those built

A Mogollon kiva uncovered at the Point of Pines site by University of Arizona archaeologists

State Museum, University of Arizona

farther north at early Anasazi sites. And a large Anasazi-like kiva near the edge of the village was undoubtedly used by inhabitants in the practice of some form of ceremonial worship. On the other hand, the cooking done at Bear Ruin was probably derived from the Cochise culture. It was done over large rock hearths, in or near the houses. The food was insulated with some material such as grass, placed in a pit, and then covered with hot rocks and earth.

Materially, the Mogollon culture revealed at Bear Ruin and at other sites, was not very advanced. Among the stone articles which have been found are rough tools, small bowls, and *metates;* many of the latter were no more than unshaped stone blocks for grinding corn. Tubular stone pipes, technically a difficult kind to make, were probably used for ceremonial smoking. Bone was also used in making a few simple tools such as awls; gambling pieces cut from bone have been found too, indicating at least one social diversion of the people. Cotton was utilized in the looming of cloth, and baskets were woven in the later years of the culture. Finally, a reddish-brown type of pottery has been found at all Mogollon sites.

As in the case of the Anasazi, the most rapid progress in Mogollon culture was made outside the present bounds of Arizona — particularly in the Mimbres Valley of southwestern New Mexico. Here, approximately between the years A.D. 1000 and 1200, a kind of hybrid society developed as Anasazi and Hohokam practices were adopted. Architectural styles, for example, shifted from the pithouse to masonry buildings erected above the surface in Pueblo-type clusters of rooms.

One interesting custom of some of the Mimbrenos was the practice of burying their dead under the house floors with some of the most beautiful and intriguing prehistoric pottery that has been found anywhere in the Southwest. Skillfully executed, surrealistic designs furnish us with information on the appearance, customs, and daily life of the people. Scenes portray such activities as men fighting bears, setting snares, dancing, and picking bugs from corn plants. The men were shown wearing breech-cloths while the women wore fringed sashes, sandals, and sometimes blankets. Jewelry, *metates,* and *manos* were often placed in women's graves along with the pottery. Each of these objects was "killed" ceremoniously before burial to release the soul or spirit which was thought to be part of the maker. This was done by chipping the object or punching out a hole in the pottery.

Eventually, the Mogollon deserted the fertile Mimbres Valley as well as villages in what is now Arizona. There is no evidence of warfare or any indication of a hurried departure. All we know is that they picked up their belongings and abandoned their homes. Some archaeologists think they may have migrated to Mexico where they were assimilated with the natives. It may not be just coincidence that many of the Mimbres burial customs, pottery-making techniques, and other influences began appearing in Chihuahua about A.D. 1200, the very time of the mysterious Mogollon exodus from the Southwest.

SINAGUA

Another prehistoric people who lived in Arizona were the Sinagua. At first thought to be part of the Anasazi culture or a branch of the Mogollon, the Sinagua lived near the San Francisco Mountains north of modern Flagstaff, and, later, in the Verde Valley. From their brown pottery made by the paddle and anvil technique, it has been determined that the Sinagua were occupying the first area during the sixth and seventh centuries A.D. They lived in both round and rectangular pithouses with center firepits; the roof consisted of sloping poles covered with earth and the entrance was a long ramp facing east. Later, this style was replaced by the timber pithouse. The walls in this type were made of upright poles fastened together between larger corner poles which supported the roof platform.[9] The entire structure was covered with grass or bark and banked over with earth, giving good protection from the weather. Eventually the east ramp was used as a ventilator and entry was through the roof. Where drainage was poor, however, surface or near surface houses were constructed. Rectangular in shape, these homes were entered through a small extended alcove. Surface storage granaries made from timber were also used since the Sinagua did some farming and apparently lived a sedentary life, enjoying peace and prosperity.

Wupatki, near Flagstaff, was a thriving community in the 1100s.

Their way of life was changed late in 1064 or early 1065, however, with the eruption of the volcano known today as Sunset Crater. The Sinagua may have interpreted the disaster as having been caused by the wrath of supernatural powers. At first they were frightened and fled, but eventually drifted back and had cause to rejoice when they found that the soil had been enriched by the volcanic overflow. Traders carried the word of the black earth to other parts of the Indian world and soon other people moved in. The resulting blend of different cultures can be seen today in the form of Hohokam ball courts and new architectural styles. Before long, the Sinagua people began building multi-room surface pueblos with masonry instead of timber. Typical Sinagua villages, inhabited during the twelfth and thirteenth centuries, have been preserved at the Wupatki National Monument. Ruins of pueblos, a ball court, and an open-air amphitheater presumably used for religious ceremonies have been found there.

The Wupatki pueblos and others in the Flagstaff area were evacuated because of the twenty-three-year drought (1276–1299) which turned the region into a dust bowl. Many people moved south into the Verde Valley where they joined Sinaguans who had migrated earlier and adopted the Hohokam system of irrigation. The two main population centers were Tuzigoot, near present-day Clarkdale, and Montezuma Castle, near Camp Verde, Arizona.

Tuzigoot Pueblo, near Clarkdale, Arizona, was a fortified pueblo constructed on a defensible promontory.

The latter is one of the best-preserved cliff dwellings in America. Constructed between A.D. 1100 and 1400 by the Hohokam and Sinagua people, Montezuma Castle was so skillfully engineered that most of the structure is still intact. The walls of the four-story building are twelve inches thick and are curved to conform to the arc of the cave in which the castle rests. The average size of the nineteen rooms is about 100 square feet and there are two storage rooms in the basement. The doors appear to be low enough for pygmies though the male residents averaged about five feet four inches tall. The openings were made small, however, so that the rooms would be warmer. Also, a family could quickly strike down any invader who would have to stoop over and enter head first.

The forty or fifty people who lived in the castle worked their irrigated farm land and supplemented their diet with wild game, berries, and nuts. They wove cloth, mined salt, fired a finely-polished red-ware pottery, and, in general seemed to be secure in their way of life. Yet, sometime about 1400, the Sinaguans suddenly left the Verde Valley. The scientists are at a loss to explain the exodus, but it is not likely that there was a single catastrophe such as drought. Overcrowding and the resultant intra-pueblo discord, disease, and water pollution are possible causes. Whatever the reasons for their departure, many of the Sinaguans probably went to Hopi country. The modern Hopi people have a legend about some dark-skinned people having joined them from the south. The Verde cliff dwellings were left to the buzzards and the occasional influx of the nomadic Yavapais.

PATAYAN

West and north of the Sinaguan homeland along the Colorado River, lived another prehistoric people — the Patayan, or "old people." Little is known about the Patayan (or "Prehistoric Yuma" as they are sometimes called) because, in the years before Hoover Dam was built, flood waters of the Colorado annually washed away or covered up remnants of their culture. A few accessible sites in northwest Arizona indicate that for at least 1500 years they were both sedentary farmers and nomadic hunters or food gatherers. Their culture

Montezuma Castle, one of the best-preserved cliff dwellings

is perhaps best known today for a distinctive pottery which was made by the paddle and anvil method. Eventually the archaeologists may uncover information in the valley of the Colorado and adjoining areas which will furnish an interesting chapter in Arizona's prehistory. It is possible that the ancestry of the modern Yuma, Mojave, Cocopa, Walapai, Havasupai, Yavapai, and Maricopa may be traced back, at least in part, to the Patayan.[10]

PART TWO

THE SPANISH IN ARIZONA

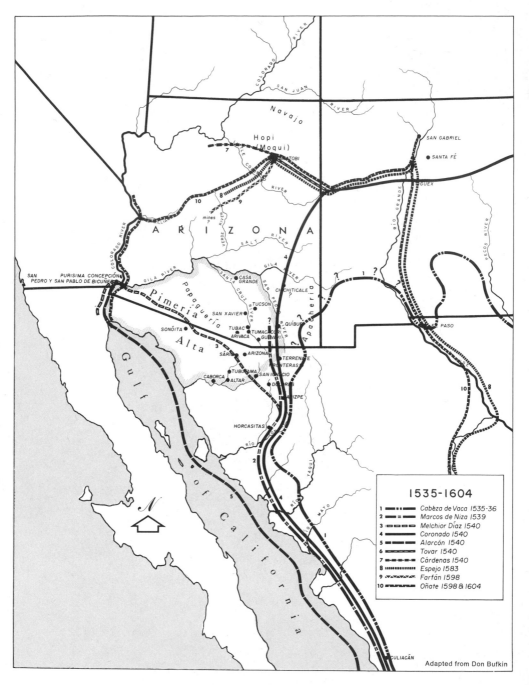

Routes of the early Spanish explorers

Chapter 4

Spanish Explorers in the 1500s

THE SPANIARDS WERE THE first Europeans to come into contact with the Indians of the Southwest; and for nearly three hundred years they were about the only white men who entered this region. Within half a century after the initial voyage of Columbus, adventurers from Spain colonized the West Indies, firmly established the authority of Emperor Charles V in Mexico, and laid claim to the New World as far north as the Grand Canyon. Spurred on by fabulous tales of untold riches and myths of golden cities, the conquistadores swiftly expanded the frontier of New Spain, enslaving the natives of Mexico for work in the mines and on the ranches or farms that supplied the mining camps with food. By 1531, an outpost had been built at Culiacán, in the Mexican state of Sinaloa. And within the next decade, the area that now comprises the state of Arizona was traversed for the first time by non-Indians.

The honor for making the earliest *entrada* probably belongs to a dark-skinned Moorish slave named Estevanico, who accompanied two different groups through the Southwest, at least one of which entered Arizona.* On the second journey in 1539, he served as a guide for Fray Marcos de Niza and crossed the southeastern part of the state en route to the

---

* There has been some question about the racial origin of Estevanico (also Estebanico or simply Esteban or Estevan) because the Spanish word *negro* is used to designate both the black people of sub-Saharan Africa and the Moors or Arabs. Marcos de Niza referred to Estevanico as a "negro," but Cabeza de Vaca, who was associated with him for about nine years, said that he was an Arab from Azamor, on the Atlantic coast of Morocco. Castañeda, a diarist with the Coronado expedition, also knew Estevanico and said that he was a *moreno*, or brown man. Despite his large size, he was called Estevanico (Little Stephen), which is the diminutive form of Estevan.

Seven Cities of Cíbola in present day New Mexico. Less than
four years earlier, Estevanico was with a small party led by
Álvar Núñez Cabeza de Vaca. His travels on that occasion were
important in the state's history, even though it is doubtful that
he was far enough north to be in Arizona.

Vaca, Estevanico, and two Spaniards named Alonso del
Castillo and Andrés Dorantes (Estevanico's master) were
among the survivors of the Narváez colonizing expedition that
escaped from hostile Indians in Florida, in 1528, only to be
shipwrecked in the Gulf of Mexico. Captured by natives in
Texas, Vaca and his companions endured nearly eight years
of hardship, most of that time in slavery. Eventually, however,
they were accepted as medical wizards who could perform
minor surgery and bring about magical cures with gourd
rattles and the sign of the cross. Followed by crowds of Indians
clamoring for attention, the castaways were permitted to
migrate from tribe to tribe until they finally reached Culiacán
in 1536. Unfortunately, the route which they followed was
only vaguely described by Vaca in the narrative which he
wrote after returning to Spain. Most scholars on the Spanish
Southwest, who have studied the topography, flora, and fauna
to which Vaca now and then referred, believe that he crossed
northern Mexico, coming only close enough to Arizona and
New Mexico to hear rumors of rich Indian cities in those
areas.[1]

The only thing about which we can be sure is that Vaca
and his men told fantastic stories that they had heard from
Indians along the way. These tales of great wealth whetted
the appetites of the gold-hungry opportunists of New Spain
and commanded the attention of the viceroy, Don Antonio de
Mendoza. Too canny to start a mad gold rush, however, Mendoza publicly discounted Vaca's reports while quietly organizing an expedition to explore the fabled region. He tried
unsuccessfully to induce Vaca or Dorantes to lead the reconnaissance. But he was able to purchase Estevanico and assigned
him to guide an unostentatious exploration led by Fray Marcos de Niza, a thirty-eight-year-old missionary-adventurer who
had already served fearlessly among the Indians of Guatemala
and Peru. So, while Cabeza de Vaca returned to Spain and
accepted an appointment as governor of the settlements on the

La Plata River in South America,[2] Estevanico became the first non-Indian to definitely enter Arizona.

Early in March, 1539, the small exploring party left Culiacán. Besides Fray Marcos and Estevanico, there were Indians to carry supplies and another Franciscan, Fray Onoroto, who fell ill after a few days and turned back. At Vacapa, Estevanico was sent ahead on the trail with instructions to send back Indian couriers to keep the friar informed on what he found. Since Estevanico could not read or write, a simple system of communication was devised. If the land ahead was moderately important, he should send a messenger back with a small cross the size of a man's hand; if of exceptional importance, a cross as large as two hands; and "if it were something greater and better than New Spain, he should send a large cross." One can imagine Fray Marcos' surprise several days later when natives arrived at Vacapa bearing a cross as high as a man. Estevanico had heard about the legendary "Seven Cities of Cíbola" and urged the friar to hurry.

Proceeding northward free from authority, the giant guide flaunted his new-found power with childlike vanity. To impress the natives along the route, he bedecked himself with bright cloths and brilliantly colored feathers; bells and tortoise rattles dangled from his limbs. Acting the part of a medicine man who supposedly possessed invulnerable strength, he sent ahead his magic gourd, filled with pebbles and adorned with red and white feathers, to announce his approach to villages. The Opata Indians of Sonora and the Pimas of Arizona were overawed by the gourd and by the strutting Estevanico's magnificence. The native escort accompanying him grew to several hundred in number and included a harem of Indian maidens. Until he reached Háwikuh, in present-day New Mexico, he was treated like an oriental despot. But there the normally peaceful Zuñi felled him with a shower of deadly arrows and sent his Indian companions scurrying to relate the murderous incident to Fray Marcos.

The friar, who had been following his guide at a leisurely pace, was shocked at the news. His Indian followers were frightened, and only after being bribed with gifts and threatened with punishment would they continue the journey with him to Cíbola. But in spite of the disaster, at least according

to his own account which is yet to be verified, Fray Marcos
was determined to see Háwikuh, which he took for granted was
Cíbola, and moved on until he came within sight of the settlement. Fearing to enter because of possible hostility on the part
of the natives, he at best got a distorted glimpse of the place
which he later described as larger than Mexico City. After
viewing the sun-drenched village from a distance, he purportedly erected a cross claiming the region for Spain and then
began a hasty retreat to Culiacán and Mexico City, where he
gave an overly enthusiastic account of the country to Viceroy
Mendoza.[3] He optimistically told how the tribes of these cities
used gold or silver utensils, decorated their houses with tur-
quoise, and wore giant pearls, gold beads, and emeralds. The
fact that Fray Marcos had observed the riches of the Incas,
when he was in Peru, probably helps to explain why he was
so susceptible to the fantastic stories which he heard about the
Seven Cities.

CORONADO

Obviously his encouraging words fell upon receptive ears
and the public mind of New Spain reached a high pitch of
excitement. Viceroy Mendoza lost no time in organizing a
large military expedition to take possession of a new dominion
that promised to supply the coffers of Spain with more precious
metals. Lured by riches and glory, men of all walks of life
clamored to join the expedition which was to be led by the
Viceroy's friend, Francisco Vásquez de Coronado. Given the
title of Captain-General, Coronado set about organizing the
venture. His enthusiasm was dampened only by the thought of
being separated from his lovely wife, Doña Beatriz, whom he
had recently married.

February 22, 1540, was a great day in the Pacific town of
Compostela. Viceroy Mendoza had traveled from Mexico City
to review the troops of the thirty-year-old Coronado. What a
gorgeous spectacle it must have been! Some of the bluest blood
of Spain was represented in the army that paraded before the
Viceroy. Castañeda, one of the expedition's diarists, observed
the large number of men of great distinction and wrote that
he doubted if "there were ever assembled in the Indies so

many noble people in such a small group of three hundred men."[4] Though there was a sprinkling of veterans, most of the adventurers were in their twenties; more were in their teens than over thirty.

According to the muster roll there were some 225 of them riding on the finest horses in Mexico. A few wore coats of mail though most of them were only partially equipped with European armor such as breastplates and helmets. Many of them had donned an assortment of more comfortable buckskin war dress, called *cueros de anta.* As befitted his rank, Coronado wore a gilded armor with a plumed helmet which was later to single him out for many a hard knock in the Pueblo Indian country. The lack of uniformity distracted little from the pageantry. With lances held high and swords rattling on their thighs, the *caballeros,* as the horsemen were called, presented a fine martial appearance.

Behind them came over sixty foot soldiers in iron pot-helmets or headpieces of bullhide. Some bore pikes and others had either a great two-handed sword or a short sword and shield; occasionally a soldier carried a crossbow or a harquebus. Native Aztec Indian weapons were also in evidence. Next in line came about a thousand Indian allies; the warriors were in full war regalia — brilliantly decorated with feathers and flesh-daubed paint and equipped with bows, arrows, slings, or flint-edged wooden maces. The Indian servants and Negro slaves proudly pulled a half dozen cannon. They tended nearly six hundred saddle and pack horses as well as thousands of cattle, sheep, goats, and swine which would insure a food supply on the journey. Little did these sixteenth-century cowboys know that their trail drive across present-day Arizona would be the first significant event in the livestock history of the Southwest. Nor could the brown-clad Franciscan friars who shuffled along in the procession realize the salient role that their brethren would play in the annals of this region.

Altogether, the expeditionary force which was reviewed that day represented the largest enterprise ever attempted by the Spanish in the New World. The Viceroy's pride in the organizational work which had required so much of his time and money was exceeded only by his anticipation of the benefits to the crown and to the church that would result from a successful expedition. He had planned well and also generously. Each horseman was given an advance of thirty pesos and each foot soldier twenty pesos. Every European, including a handful of non-Spaniards in the group, was promised a land grant and was provided with livestock.

On February 23, 1540, Coronado set forth amid the clank of armor, high-spirited shouts, and the bellowing of cattle to conquer the Seven Cities of Cíbola. The army's progress through the broken, hilly country was slow and laborious; it took a month of difficult travel to reach the farthest northern outpost, Culiacán, some 350 miles away. Straying livestock and heavily-loaded pack animals delayed the march. These animals could not be hurried and several days were lost in transporting them one by one across the alligator-infested Rio Santiago. The patience of the anxious *caballeros* was thoroughly tested. Unused to the hardships of pioneering, they suffered from the rough going. They were further discouraged by an event at Chiametla, a deserted Spanish village about 200 miles along the route. The army halted here and a foraging party was sent out to the mountains to replenish the fast-diminishing food supply. Not only was the party unsuccessful but the popular commander, Lope de Samaniego, became the expedition's first mortality when his eye was pierced by an Indian arrow. Even though several natives were hanged for the crime a gloom was cast over the travelers.

Another circumstance also dampened enthusiasm for the adventure. Melchior Díaz and Juan de Zaldívar, who had been sent northward the previous autumn to check the stories of Fray Marcos, arrived in camp with bad news. The scouting party of fifteen horsemen and a troop of Indians had traveled 220 leagues (approximately 660 miles) to Chichilticale, near the Gila River in what is now eastern Arizona. The Indians here gave them no encouragement and freely contradicted the friar's alluring story about gold and other rich minerals that could be found in Cíbola. Disappointed, the party returned to report and, despite Coronado's efforts to keep the disheartening news secret, it leaked out. Fray Marcos, knowing that the soldiers were disturbed, preached an eloquent sermon to allay their suspicions and hostilities. They accepted his explanation that the scouts had not gone far enough, and all was well again.

Coronado delayed nearly a month at Culiacán to gather new supplies for the long march and to rest and perhaps build up the morale of the men. He decided to go ahead with a small contingent of cavalry and infantry in order to relieve the main army of unnecessary risk and uncertainty. This plan seemed wise since Díaz had reported a scarcity of provisions and a scattered native population along the rough road. On April 22, Coronado departed with a select vanguard of about one hundred picked men, together with friars and a large party of Indians. The largest part of the army was left to advance more slowly under the command of Tristan de Arellano and did not get underway until May 9.

Coronado followed a route which had been marked by De Niza and Díaz. Traveling over difficult Indian trails, he finally reached the fertile valley of the Sonora River which he followed to its source. About thirty miles south of the present boundary he moved east to the northward-flowing San Pedro and down that stream to a point just below the present site of Benson. It was now July and the expedition was among primitive but friendly Pima people called the Sobaípuris. Leaving the San Pedro, or Nexpa as the Indians called it, the army apparently marched a little east of north through the Galiuro Range and across Aravaipa Valley to the foot of Eagle Pass, the opening between the Pinaleño and Santa Teresa mountains in modern-day Graham County. Here was Chichilticale where Díaz and his companions had shivered through part of the previous winter. The "Red House," as it was called, may well be one of the extensive pueblo ruins which can be seen today on the 76 Ranch. Originally this structure was a large earth-walled fortress, daubed with ochre, which had been built by civilized people from Cíbola. But Coronado's men were disappointed to discover that the vaunted Chichilticale was merely a roofless ruin of mud walls. It had been destroyed by a nomadic Gila River tribe which dwelt among the ruins in isolated huts. The scouting party, however, was happy to rest here for a few days. The horses were exhausted from bearing heavy loads over the rough mountains. Food supplies were also running low and the roasted piñon nuts presented by the natives tasted delicious to the half-starved cavaliers.

Having been proved wrong in his praises of Chichilticale Fray Marcos was now questioned on another point. He had reported that the sea could be seen from this village. Upon investigating, Coronado made the bitter discovery that the coast was at least ten days away. It was not surprising that the disillusioned soldiers spat at Marcos as he passed their camp-fires, for Coronado's interest in the Western Sea was no idle concern. He had hoped to get supplies from the three ships that Viceroy Mendoza had sent up the Gulf of California to cooperate with the land expedition. But the captain of the naval flotilla, Hernando de Alarcón, was at least 200 miles to the west and of little use in alleviating the hunger pangs of the Cíbola-bound gentlemen.

Meanwhile, however, Alarcón was making history. On August 26 he reached the head of the Gulf and observed the mighty Colorado River which he named Buena Guía, or "Unfailing Guide," a phrase that was used in the motto on the coat of arms of Viceroy Mendoza. After failing to navigate his sailing vessels against the rushing river current, Alarcón made anchor and proceeded upstream with twenty men and some small cannon in two launches. Thus the determined captain became the first white explorer to sail the turbulent Colorado River and the first European to visit among the tall Yuman (Cócopa) Indians who lived along its banks. With some difficulty Alarcón convinced the Indians that he came peace-fully and persuaded them to lay down their primitive weapons. The natives were impressed by his gifts, especially the little holy crosses, but accepted his contention that he was the "Son of the Sun" only after considerable questioning. Though later informed by Viceroy Mendoza that he was guilty of heresy for taking advantage of the natives because they worshipped the sun, Alarcón reported that he laid the groundwork for the conversion of these people to Christianity. He received corn and other provisions from them but learned nothing concern-ing the whereabouts of Coronado's army until he was farther up the river.

After many inquiries through his interpreter who knew the Yuman speech, he was finally informed that Coronado had arrived at Cíbola; but Alarcón was unable to find a volunteer, either Spaniard or Indian, to make the long journey to the Captain-General. Displeased because of his failure to make contact with Coronado, he reluctantly decided to retrace his course, but only after reaching a point somewhere north of the Yuma Crossing. In his first-hand account of the expedition Alarcón wrote that he erected a tall cross near the mouth of the river now known as the Gila and that he buried a message summarizing his discoveries at the foot of this marker. Promising the Indians that he would return, Alarcón then went downstream to his ships and reached the port of Colima by early November.

While Alarcón was exploring the Colorado and Coronado was pushing toward Cíbola, the main army under Arellano had camped in the Sonora Valley (in Mexico) to await further orders. From this valley Arellano sent a small party of men to the Gulf in search of Alarcón's fleet. The ships were nowhere in sight, but there were plenty of tall Indians. Shortly after this search detail returned to Sonora, Fray Marcos and Melchior Díaz arrived with instructions for the army to proceed at once. Díaz was commissioned to take charge of the small detachment remaining at San Gerónimo and to outfit an exploring party to find the elusive ships.

Toward the end of September, 1540, Díaz set out in a northwesterly direction with twenty-five picked Spanish soldiers and several Indian guides. The group moved slowly because a flock of sheep was taken for fresh meat. Apparently the route of march was over the Devil's Highway, a terrible desert trail across what is now southwestern Arizona that was later followed by Sonora forty-niners in the California gold rush. After traveling an estimated 150 leagues, Díaz reached the Colorado River near its junction with the Gila, where he found one of the Yuman tribes that Alarcón had visited. These Indians were exceedingly tall and strong. One of them easily picked up a log that six soldiers were unable to lift. They lived in communal huts that often held a hundred persons and in cold weather carried firebrands to warm their naked bodies.

Hence came the name Río de Tizón, or Firebrand River, which the soldiers gave to the Colorado.

Díaz was excited to learn from the Yumans that Alarcón had been seen downstream a few weeks before. In great suspense, he hastened south in search of the sea captain. About half way down to the Gulf, according to a second-hand account written later by Castañeda, he found a tree upon which these words were inscribed in Spanish: "Alarcón came this far; there are letters at the foot of this tree." Obviously, the Alarcón and Castañeda narratives differ as to the type of marker and its location; both agree, however, on the message that the sea captain buried and Díaz found in a sealed jar. In this document Alarcón explained how he had discovered that the Gulf of California was a bay and not a strait. He related the story of how, after waiting for many days without news from Coronado, he had been obliged to return to New Spain because the ships were being slowly eaten away by the *teredo,* or marine worm.

The disappointed Díaz retraced his steps back to the Yuma Crossing and, after a skirmish with the Indians on the California side of the river, started the homeward march to the Sonora Valley. On the return journey Díaz was wounded in the groin when he fell upon his own lance while galloping after a greyhound which was molesting the sheep. He was carried on a litter for twenty days but died and was buried before reaching the settlement of San Gerónimo. Of all the brave men who participated in the Coronado expedition, perhaps few played a more gallant role that did Melchior Díaz, who was officially the mayor of Culiacán.

Continuing with the story of Coronado we find that by July 7, 1540, the weary and discouraged Spaniards had reached Cíbola. The party spent fifteen days crossing the uninhabited wilderness from Chichilticale to about the present location of Bylas and then across the rugged mountains of eastern Arizona to the Little Colorado River. This 150-mile stretch was one of the most difficult of the entire journey. Not only was the terrain almost impassable but there was a shortage of provisions and the men and animals were in worn-out condition. No grass was found until they reached the fresh waters of the White River, near the site of present-day Fort Apache. The pine nuts which were found in this region helped to alleviate, but failed to solve, the food problem.

Before long, famine and death stalked the expedition. Near a spring in the vicinity of modern McNary, a Spaniard named Espinosa and several others died from eating poisonous herbs after their rations gave out. Starvation was so close at this point that the tired adventurers were probably thinking more of food than of fabulous riches. The two-day march from the "Camp of Death" to the Little Colorado near its junction with the Zuñi River was an anxious one. A messenger from the advance scouts under García López de Cárdenas reported that four Indians from Cíbola had appeared to welcome the Spaniards. Needless to say, the famished soldiers were over-joyed upon hearing that the natives had promised to supply the visitors with food. They were impatient, however, with the slow pace ordered by Coronado.

The general was trying to avoid a surprise ambush and his caution seemed to be justified when the advance guard was attacked one night by Cíbolans while encamped at Bad Pass, a narrow, rocky defile near the present Arizona-New Mexico line. Cárdenas had tactfully tried to avoid a conflict by giving presents and a cross to the Indians, bidding them to go home and tell their people that the Spaniards were coming on a "peaceful errand." The natives were skeptical of this con-tention, however, and after dark they moved to a position close to the camp where they began yelling and shooting arrows among the Spaniards. According to an account written by the diarist Castañeda, some of the greenhorns panicked, a few of them being so excited that they tried to put the saddles on their horses hind side before. With the steadying influence of the veterans, however, the Spaniards charged the nocturnal raiders and put them in flight.[5] Nevertheless, the retreat was orderly and the Spaniards were soon to learn that the Indians would fight in defense of their homeland.

When Coronado reached the pass the next day, he decided to hasten forward because of the military crisis and the hunger of his followers. Ascending the Zuñi River, he led his exhausted treasure seekers to the crumbling pueblo. And what a shock it was! The Spaniards were both amazed and enraged

Murals by Gerald Cassidy in the post office at Santa Fe depict the first meeting of the Europeans (above) and Indians (facing page) at Háwikuh. Coronado is shown in full armor ready for battle. When not fighting, especially when traveling across the burning deserts of the Southwest, the Spaniards usually carried their "hot suits" on horseback.

not to see golden walls and turquoise-studded doors. Here they were at the end of the rainbow and there was no pot of gold. In only one respect had Fray Marcos been accurate in his reconnaissance report: the stone houses were several stories high. The men felt bitter about having staked their lives and fortunes in pursuit of the will-of-the-wisp fantasies that the padre had "heard." It is not surprising that Fray Marcos, now broken in spirit and in ill health, was sent back to Mexico in August with the military party that took Coronado's report to Viceroy Mendoza.

No one was more disheartened than the friar. Hardship and physical suffering eventually nearly paralyzed his aged body and he never fully recovered his vigor, though he lived until 1558. He died in a convent in Mexico after attempting to seek relief in the delightful climate of Jalapa. Despite the fact that he was much slandered in his lifetime by no less a

public figure than Hernando Cortés and by others, Fray Marcos, nevertheless, had made his niche in history. He was the first of a host of priestly explorers who were to venture unarmed into the interior of the continent. Footsore, but fearless, he walked through the unmarked deserts of Mexico and the Southwest long before English colonists appeared at Jamestown or Plymouth. It is true that his veracity, if not his honor too, has been much questioned. Some writers have even concluded that his reconnaissance expedition in 1539 went no further than the Gila ruins, the rest of the journey being imagined. There is evidence to the contrary, however. Coronado, who showed no reluctance in criticizing Marcos on the accuracy of his reports, did not seem to doubt that the friar journeyed all the way to Cíbola. This is perhaps the best proof that the Italian-born priest was not only the first European to enter Arizona but that he also reached the land of the Zuñi, both in 1539 and again with Coronado a year later.

Although Coronado was disappointed in not finding the riches in Háwikuh that he had anticipated, he tried in vain to win the friendship of the inhabitants. The women and children, as well as all movable possessions, had been taken to a place of safety in the cliffs. Arrayed in front of the city were several hundred warriors who made hostile gestures with bows, arrows, and war clubs. They ordered the Spaniards not to cross the lines which they drew with sacred corn meal. The Zuñi did not fear the strange horses and armored soldiers; anyone could tell that both the men and animals were starving. And when the Indians let go with a shower of arrows, peace was beyond the question.

Shouting "¡Santiago y a ellos!" ("St. James and at them!"), the famous Spanish war cry, the angered soldiers charged with a zeal born of hunger. In the ensuing battle, Coronado, in his gilded armor, was a special object of the native wrath. Twice he was knocked down by rocks hurled from the top of the pueblo. He was fortunate to escape with bruises and an arrow wound in the leg. His men, however, easily proved the superiority of guns and military skill over the primitive weapons. Though outnumbered, they forced the Zuñis to abandon the pueblo after struggling for less than an hour. And then the famished conquerors wasted no time preparing to feast upon the beans, maize, and fowl which were found in the deserted houses. How they gorged themselves in eating their first square meal in months! At the time even the long-sought silver and gold would have been less welcomed.

In the weeks to follow, Coronado made every effort to conciliate the natives, assuring the chiefs, who came to confer with him, that their people would receive good treatment and safety. After recovering from his wounds he visited the other pueblos of Cíbola and then settled down to direct the exploration of the surrounding country. Two of his side expeditions were important in the history of Arizona. The first was led by Pedro de Tovar to a province about seventy-five miles to the northwest called Tusayán. In search of villages where the modern Hopi towns are now located in Arizona, Tovar took about twenty soldiers and Juan de Padilla, a Franciscan friar who had not forgotten his military training as a youth. Marching across the painted desert the party surprised the people of Awátovi with their presence. The Hopis had heard of how "Cíbola had been conquered by fierce men who rode animals that ate people" and were in a hostile spirit. As was their custom, they drew battle lines with corn meal and warned the white intruders to stay away. The patience of ex-soldier Padilla grew thin as his leader parleyed for peace. Finally he said to Tovar, "Indeed, I do not know what we have come here for."[6]

It was a short battle that followed. With ecclesiastical approval the Spanish horsemen charged the Indians and soon had them scurrying for their mesa-top homes. To avoid a slaughter the native head men surrendered and promised Tovar the obedience of the province of Tusayán. As peace offerings the Indians brought presents of cotton cloth, corn meal, dressed skins, piñon nuts, and fowl. The Spaniards were pleased to accept these gifts as well as the submission of the Hopi villages. They showed even keener interest, however, in what the natives had to say about a large river farther to the west. But since Tovar was not commissioned to go beyond Tusayán, the party returned to Háwikuh with this news.

Coronado was excited about the report of a deep gorge and decided to send a second expedition into what is now northern Arizona. He was curious to learn if the mysterious river had any connection with the Strait of Anían, a legendary waterway through North America. Correctly assuming that the river flowed into the Gulf of California, he hoped that a party of men following its course downstream might get in touch with Alarcón's fleet. Perhaps a rumor of giants to the west helps to explain why he placed Captain Cárdenas, his right hand man and a hard-fisted soldier, in charge. Cárdenas led twenty-five horsemen by way of Tusayán where he was well-received. The natives furnished him with Indian guides and plenty of provisions for the march across the dry plateau country. Traveling over the still-visible Moqüi trail, the explorers reached the rim of the Grand Canyon in about three weeks. Here, within a few miles of the present Bright Angel and Grand View trails, they gazed down upon one of the world's greatest scenic wonders.

To the Spaniards the stream at the bottom of the huge arroyo looked no more than six feet across and they were surprised when the guides told them that it was actually a wide river. After searching three days for a place to descend, Captain Pablo de Melgosa, Juan Galeras, and one other agile man spent most of a day going down about one-third of the distance to the bottom. From this vantage point these pioneer Arizona mountain climbers could verify the geographical information given to them by the natives. But frustrated in their attempt to reach the river, and lacking a supply of drinking water, the Cárdenas party returned to Háwikuh. They were the first white men to discover the Grand Canyon. After their departure it was a half century before Europeans again saw the Colorado.

Most of the remainder of Coronado's story, though interesting, does not particularly concern Arizona. Extending his conquests eastward across present day New Mexico, he took possession of the Tiguex Indian pueblos found along the Rio Grande in the Albuquerque-Bernalillo area. The severe winter of 1540 was spent in homes from which many of the natives had fled in fear for their lives.* While at Tiguex, Coronado and his men listened to a slave from nearby Cicúye. Nicknamed "El Turco" because of his appearance, this strange Indian was probably ordered by the natives to tell fanciful stories about a rich land to the east called Gran Quivira. The Spaniards rose to the bait and in the spring of 1541 the search for the phantom gold began again. At the instigation of the Indians, El Turco led the army on a wild goose chase across the plains of Texas. Finally discouraged and distrustful of his guide, Coronado sent the main body back to Tiguex and continued with a small group of thirty horsemen. Another dream was shattered when these gold seekers arrived at Quivira.

This city turned out to be a group of miserable Indian villages in what is now Kansas. Disgusted with what they

---

* Before Coronado arrived at Tiguex with the main body of the army in the autumn of 1540, several outrages were committed. On one occasion, for example, Cárdenas ordered a group of rebellious Indians burned at the stake as a lesson for their neighbors. Prior to this event some of the soldiers had been forcing the pueblo people to give up their best blankets and clothing; and one Spaniard had molested an Indian woman after forcing her husband to hold his horse. On the other hand, an Indian raid on a Spanish horse herd may have contributed to the hostilities. See "Translation of the Narrative of Castañeda," in George W. Winship, *The Coronado Expedition, 1540–1542.* Reprinted in Chicago: Rio Grande Press, Inc. 1964, pp. 218–25.

found, the adventurers turned their wrath upon El Turco whom they promptly garroted after exacting a confession. Following a month in Quivira, Coronado returned to Tiguex for another dismal winter of quarrels with the Indians and mutinies among some of the soldiers. With trouble continuing to grow, the weary and disappointed Captain-General finally announced in the spring that the entire expedition, except for the friars who volunteered to remain only to suffer martyrdom later on, would return to New Spain.

It was April, 1542, when the tattered remains of the magnificent army, which had left Culiacán two years before, started home. En route Coronado found Cíbola pacified and calm. At Háwikuh the soldiers equipped and provisioned for the journey through the rugged, uninhabited country of eastern Arizona to Chichilticale. Two days beyond this village, near the San Pedro River, Coronado met Captain Juan Gallego coming with supplies from New Spain. Reinforcements encouraged some dissenters to rebel against continuing on home. Even Gallego favored going back to the pueblo country. But the homesick rank and file had seen too much hardship and too little gold and would not agree to anything except to return to New Spain. After resting in Culiacán, Coronado continued his journey to Mexico City, leaving the men who did not wish to follow along the way. Less than a hundred of the faithful were with him when he arrived to report to Viceroy Mendoza.

Coronado's contemporaries wasted no time in denouncing him as a failure.[7] It is true that his expedition did not discover the fabulous riches which were sought but it accomplished things of much greater significance to later generations. From Coronado's reports the Spanish gained a geographical knowledge of much of the great Southwest, including the Gila Valley and the Colorado Plateau regions in Arizona. We also have a vivid description of the Indians in this region as the white men first found them. Unfortunately, however, Coronado's reports were so discouraging that forty years were to elapse before another white man actually entered Arizona.

ESPEJO

Coronado's failure to find gold, combined with another event in 1542 — the discovery of the rich silver mines at Zacatecas, Mexico — put an end to extensive exploration in Arizona until the 1580s. The new *entrada* in the latter decade was inspired by missionary zeal and came this time by way of the central plateau of Mexico and the Rio Grande Valley of New Mexico. In 1582, the Franciscans at Santa Bárbara, in Mexico, were fearing for the lives of three of their brethren, including Fray Agustín Rodríguez, who had journeyed to the pueblo villages near modern Albuquerque.* A rescue party was organized, financed, and led by the wealthy Antonio de Espejo. Reaching the Rio Grande country, the Espejo expedition learned that the friars had become martyrs to their cause.

Too late to serve the church, Espejo and his soldiers decided to explore the country in hopes of making or increasing their fortunes. By March, 1583, they were in Háwikuh and other Zuñi pueblos listening to the tales of some Mexican Indians who had been left behind by Coronado. Naturally, Espejo was excited at reports of rich mines to the west. With nine adventurous soldiers and about 150 friendly Zuñi Indians, he penetrated what is now Arizona, traveling first to the Moqüi, or Hopi country. Here the Spaniards spent nearly a week claiming the villages for his majesty and taking advantage of the native hospitality. They quickly accumulated a large stock of blue and green ores, tasseled towels, and blankets. On one occasion they were given four thousand *mantas* made of both white and multicolored cotton. Before departing from the Hopis, Espejo designated five men to transport the loot

---

*In 1580, Friar Agustín Rodríguez asked Viceroy Condé de Coruña of New Spain for permission to explore the new country in what is now New Mexico. With two Franciscan brothers, Francisco López and Juan de Santa María, a small escort of soldiers, and some Indian servants, Rodríguez left Santa Bárbara, the center of a rich mining district in southern Chihuahua, on June 5, 1581, and visited most of the pueblos along the Rio Grande and its branches. Father Santa María was killed when he ventured out alone to find a new route back to Mexico. Rodríguez and López were murdered by hostile natives at Puaray after the soldiers, under the command of Francisco Sánchez (called "Chamuscado" because of his red beard), returned to Mexico. See J. Lloyd Mecham, "The Second Spanish Expedition to New Mexico, An Account of the Chamuscado-Rodríguez Entrada of 1581–1582," *New Mexico Historical Review*, Vol. I, No. 3 (July, 1926), pp. 265–91.

Museum of Northern Arizona

Oraibi, shown in the 1920s, is considered to be the oldest continuously inhabited town in the United States. Pottery sherds indicate occupancy since about A.D. 1150. The old town is atop a mesa, while the newer Oraibi is at the foot and about two miles away on the modern highway. The Espejo expedition was at Old Oraibi in April 1583.

back to Zuñi. He was concerned about Hopi stories of barbarous Indians in the area of the mines and, in event of his death, hoped something would be salvaged from the expedition.[8]

Fortunately, however, Espejo and his four companions arrived safely in the vicinity of Jerome, east of modern Prescott, and discovered the mines which they sought.[9] As luck would have it, the warlike Indians were frightened by the neighing of the white man's strange animals. Not only did these mountainous people flee, but they kept a respectable distance along the entire route. Nevertheless, Espejo and his men did not linger. Their objective having been reached, they hastened back to Zuñi where they joined the remainder of the party. By September, 1583, the expedition reached San Bartolomé, near Santa Bárbara in the Conchos Valley. Espejo's silver ore specimens and the story which he had heard about a lake of gold northwest of Zuñi rekindled an atmosphere of excitement along the northern frontier. But it was not until the last years of the century that another official expedition was sent into the closely associated regions of New Mexico and Arizona.

OÑATE

As early as April 19, 1583, King Philip II of Spain had let a royal contract to anyone who might undertake the conquest of the pueblo country at his own expense. More than ten years elapsed, however, before the wealthy Juan de Oñate was awarded the coveted patent. Oñate, whose wife was the granddaughter of Cortés and whose father was a discoverer of the bonanza silver mines at Zacatecas, was granted special privileges as Governor and Captain-General of the enterprise. With 400 men, 130 women, a number of children, and 7,000 cattle, sheep, and goats, his expedition started north on February 7, 1598, from the Conchos River Valley. Pushing ahead with sixty *caballeros* after reaching what is now the city of El Paso in west Texas, Oñate established his headquarters at the Indian pueblo of Caypa, about forty miles northwest of modern Santa Fe. He quickly brought the Indians under control. When the settlers arrived in August the colony of New Mexico settled down and the missionaries began to convert the nearby pueblo dwellers.

Not satisfied with his early remarkable success as a colonizer, Oñate turned his attention to exploration and within a period of six years he made two notable treks into Arizona. The attractions which motivated him were Espejo's mines and the possibility of discovering the South Sea, over which his colony could trade with Peru, New Spain, and China. While resting at Zuñi in October, 1598, he sent Captain Marcos Farfán on a short *entrada* into the state in search of a salt spring. Farfán found a huge saline deposit just as the Indians said he would. Yet no one has been able to identify the exact site of the discovery. On November 8, Oñate's entire party left the Zuñi country for the Hopi villages. Even though they were unmolested by the Indians, both the soldiers and animals suffered from the severe winter weather and a scarcity of water. To avoid submitting the entire group to further hardship, Oñate delegated eight men under the command of Farfán to search for the mines.

While the Governor returned to Zuñi, Farfán and his companions traveled westward. Authorities do not agree on the exact route he took. Nor is there agreement on the precise sites where Farfán staked out claims to the mines which he discovered. At any rate he found some rich silver ore in the vicinity of Prescott near either the Rio Santa María or the Big Sandy River, and left posterity with a good description of a land inhabited by peaceful Indians, abounding in game and in tall pines and fertile valleys. Hurrying back to Zuñi, Farfán found that Oñate was deeply pleased with the results of his journey.[10] The Governor was especially interested in what the Indians at the site of the mines had to say about the great river and a sea to the west. Not until 1604, however, was he able to leave more pressing problems in the Rio Grande Valley to seek the South Sea.

In October of that year Oñate led thirty soldiers, some Indian servants, and two Franciscans (Juan de Buenaventura and Francisco Escobar) across northern Arizona. Reaching the fork of the Bill Williams River, the party followed the river to its junction with the Colorado, named Rio de Buena Esperanza (Good Hope) by the leader. Near the mouth of the Gila they left some twenty horses to graze and get in condition for the return trip to New Mexico.

Following the Colorado the explorers arrived at the Gulf of California on January 25, 1605. In the name of King Philip III they claimed possession of what was described as a splendid harbor.

Though disappointed in not having found the South Sea and the lustrous pearls which they sought, the men heard many exciting stories from the Indians which Escobar recorded in his diary. The Mojaves, in the vicinity of Needles, spoke about a great Lake of Copalla where the natives wore gold bracelets. Supposedly, the Aztecs of Mexico had migrated from these shores. There was another account of a rich island of bald-headed men ruled by a fat woman with big feet. Then there was the tale of a nation of people whose ears were so huge that five or six persons could stand under each ear. Nearby were natives who purportedly slept under water, a tribe whose people had only one foot, and still another group that slept in trees. Furthermore, the Spaniards were told that there were Indians in the Colorado region who lived solely on the odor of food and still others who slept standing up. Unbe-

lievable as these stories were, the friar wrote them down merely
as a matter of record.

Unfortunately, his diary was not so complete in covering
events of the arduous return journey to the Rio Grande. The
Indians had eaten about half of the horses which had been
left near the Gila River junction. And by the time San Gabriel
was reached on April 25, 1605, the Spaniards had been forced
to eat the remainder of the animals. With Oñate's return to
New Mexico the first great period of exploration (1540–1605)
came to a close.

In retrospect we see that Oñate traveled farther in Arizona than did Coronado or Espejo. And even though his explorations were not followed up immediately by colonization,
Oñate did more to advertise the region's mineral wealth and
to make this area known to Europeans than did any previous
visitor.

Chapter 5

Missionaries in the 1600s

THE DOMINANT POSITION of Spain in the New World at the end of the sixteenth century was truly remarkable. Whereas two-thirds of the Western Hemisphere was then Hispanic, no other European nation except Portugal had yet established a permanent settlement in the Americas. After the dawn of the seventeenth century, Spain's rivals began to colonize, first in the Caribbean and then on the North American continent. During the 1600s the French and English joined the Spanish in the struggle for vast empires and developed their own peculiar frontier institutions that transformed the Indian way of life. In New France the fur trader and missionary penetrated the wilds of the continent, one in the search of beaver and the other in quest of souls to save; each in his own way extended the French domain and attempted to establish friendship with the Indians. In the English colonies the fur trader blazed the trails and was followed by the backwoods settler who cleared the forests and drove back the Indian with whom he did not readily mingle. In New Spain the task of civilizing and holding the frontier, which sixteenth century conquistadores had explored in search of gold, was given to the missionary and the presidial soldier.

There was little Spanish contact in the 1600s with the lands that now comprise the state of Arizona after the round-trip journey of Governor Juan de Oñate in 1604–1605 from New Mexico across Arizona to the Colorado and down that river to the Gulf of California. The northward advance of Spanish civilization in Mexico during the seventeenth century was steady but slow and followed three different routes from Mexico City. One of these went up the coastal corridor west

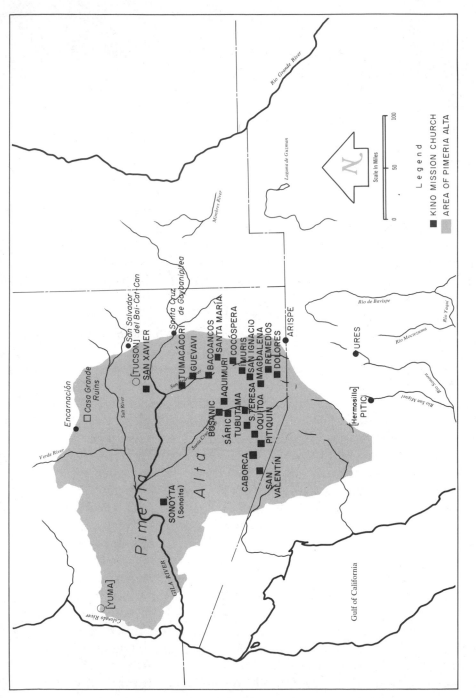

Missions of Kino's Pimería Alta

of the Sierra Madre range to Sonora, and finally into southern Arizona to the Gila River, beyond which lay the broken mountains of the Mogollon Rim; Coronado, in 1540, followed this route from Compostela through Pimería, crossed the depopulated region of east-central Arizona and penetrated the Mogollon mountain barrier to reach the Pueblo people of New Mexico. A second route paralleled the first from 100 to 200 miles to the east along the relatively high plateau of Mexico to the Rio Grande into New Mexico. An extension of this route went west from New Mexico across northern Arizona to the Colorado River. A third route that did not involve Arizona went up the east coast to Texas.

When Oñate was banished from New Mexico, in 1609, after being charged with nearly thirty offenses — including the mistreatment of Indians — he left behind a permanently established province that jutted hundreds of miles farther north than any other settled portion of New Spain. In the century following his departure, a few Franciscan missionaries from time to time expanded their activities westward from the pueblos in New Mexico to the Hopi villages in what is now northeastern Arizona; but it was not until the last decade of the seventeenth century that another European, Father Eusebio Kino, reached the Gila and began converting the Pimas in southern Arizona. The Jesuit order to which he belonged had been establishing missions in Sonora since 1613. In that year, Father Pedro Méndez, with the protection of thirty soldiers commanded by Captain Diego Martínez, established a mission settlement on the Mayo River, the first in Sonora. By the time Father Kino arrived in the province in 1687, dozens of other missions had been built and thousands of natives baptized. Kino established his home mission at Nuestra Señora de los Dolores on the San Miguel, and, in the tradition of his Jesuit predecessors in Sonora, advanced the Spanish frontier northward. In the next quarter century he extended the "rim of christendom" down the Santa Cruz and San Pedro valleys beyond the present international boundary to the Gila River.

The more valuable parts of the Spanish empire, which the frontier mission and presidio were designed to protect, lay in the settled mining, ranching, and agricultural areas where the *encomienda* system could be used to control a docile native population. By this system the land and Indians were divided among Spaniards known as *encomenderos,* or trustees, who exploited their wards and exposed them to European culture. Spain was forced to colonize with aborigines because her own population was small and little of it could be spared to people the New World. But the *encomienda* system was successful only where the Indians lived in fixed villages and were used to labor. The wilder tribes on the northern borderland were often harder to control and it was among these natives that the value of the missionary as a frontier agent was recognized — not only to spread the faith and induce the Indians to live at peace in pueblos near the missions, but also to serve the political and economic ends of the state.

Though the missionary was usually accompanied in his travels by a small military escort, he sometimes went unmolested, and without arousing suspicion or hostility, into districts where the soldier was not welcome. By education and training he was exceptionally well-qualified to record what he saw in new lands; hence some of the best diaries of early exploration in Arizona and the Southwest were written by missionaries. And even more important, the padres were often able to deter their neophytes from attacking interior settlements and to obtain their aid in holding back more distant tribes. Father Kino, for example, was considered to be worth more than a whole company of soldiers in the defense of Sonora because of his influence with the Pimas, a friendly tribe whose services he enlisted against the Apaches. Occasionally, however, the missionaries were victims of rebellions by neophytes. Franciscans who were killed during the seventeenth century while trying to convert reluctant Pueblo Indians in the Hopi villages were the first Christian martyrs to die on Arizona soil.

FRANCISCAN MARTYRS IN THE LAND
OF THE HOPIS

Despite the fabulous stories of rich mines, it was the missionary who next appreciated and advertised present-day Arizona. In attempting to convert the Indians to Christianity, the pious men of God concentrated their activities among the Hopis, then called Moqüi,* in the northeastern part of Arizona. These Indians were more easily contacted because they lived in permanent houses and towns. In another sense, however, the Hopis were less desirable as potential converts in that their villages were remote and the inhabitants very suspicious of Christianity. The medicine men had been successful in discrediting the strange religion of the friars. So the first attempt at religious conquest of the Hopis in 1629 was a daring undertaking. In that year three Franciscans detached themselves from the relative comfort of established churches in New Mexico and ventured into the Moqüi villages. Francisco de Porras, Andrés Gutiérrez, and Cristóbal de la Concepción, accompanied by twelve soldiers, reached Awátovi† on August 20. They named the mission San Bernardo de Aguatubi (Awátovi) in honor of the saint on whose day they had arrived.

The missionaries quickly detected an atmosphere of hostility which was to be changed only by a miracle. The natives were probably inhospitable because of rumors brought to them by an apostate Indian who had entered the village a short time before. Supposedly, the Spaniards had come to burn their villages, to behead the children, and to kill all who were submissive by means of a ceremony which involved sprinkling water on the head. The friars tried to break the ice by presenting trinkets to their hosts, but the ill feeling lingered. A change came only when Friar Porras healed a blind boy, an event

---

*Moqui (pronounced Mó ke) literally means "dead people" or "stinking people" and is offensive to the Hopi. The correct term was *Mó ok wi* which the Spanish appropriately rendered as *Moqüi*. Unfortunately, it was carelessly written *Moqui* and hence the opprobrious connotation. See Watson Smith, *Seventeenth-Century Spanish Missions of the Western Pueblo Area. The Smoke Signal,* Tucson Corral of Westerners, No. 21 (Spring, 1970), pp. 4–5.

† The attempts of the Spaniards to reproduce the native name for this town resulted in varied spellings. These include: Abattobi, Aguato, Aguatobi, Aguatubi, Aguatuby, Aguatuvi, Aguatuya, Aguitobi, Ahuato, Ahuatobi, Ahuatu, Ahuatuyba, Ahuzto, Ahwat-tenna, Aoátovi, Aquatasi, Aquatubi, Atawobi, Aua-tu-ui, Awatobi, Awá-to-bi, Awatúbi, Vattobi, Waterby, Zagnato, Zaguate, and Zuguato. Archaeologists often use the most popular Spanish form — Aguatubi. The Navajos and Hopis usually refer to it today as Tallahogan. See Ross G. Montgomery, Watson Smith, and John O. Brew, *Franciscan Awátovi . . . Papers* of the Peabody Museum of American Archaeology and Ethnology, Harvard University, Vol. XXXVI, Cambridge, Massachusetts, 1949, p. xxii.

Montgomery, Smith, and Brew *Franciscan Awátovi*

A conjectural restoration of San Bernardo de Aguatubi (Awátovi). The ruins of several Franciscan buildings at Awátovi were excavated by archaeologists from the Peabody Museum, Cambridge, Massachusetts. This restoration of one of the churches — two were completed and a third one started — was done by Ross Montgomery from data gathered in the actual digging.

which the Franciscans considered a miracle.* Evidently the Indians were also convinced and within a short time there were hundreds of converts to the Christian faith. Naturally this success angered the Hopi shamen who awaited an opportunity for revenge against the healer who had caused them to lose face. That day came on June 28, 1633, when Porras became the first martyr of the cross in Arizona after eating food which had been poisoned by the Indians of Walpi. It is not known what happened to the other two friars who accom-

---

*Fray Alonso de Benavides, *Benavides Memorial of 1630*, translated by Peter P. Forrestal, C. S. C. Washington, D.C.; Academy of American Franciscan History, 1954, pp. 32–34; also in Lansing B. Bloom, "Fray Estevan de Perea's *Relacion*," *New Mexico Historical Review*, Vol. VIII, No. 3 (July, 1933), pp. 230–32. Father Estevan de Perea described the pueblo of St. Bernard (Awátovi) as follows: "It is eighty leagues from the *Villa* of the Spaniards [Santa Fe], a more temperate country and like that of Spain in the fruits and grains which grow here. Much cotton is harvested; the houses are of three stories, well planned; their inhabitants are great laborers and solicitous in their work. Among them the vice of intoxication is a great reproach. For amusements they have their appointed games, and a race which they run with great speed . . ."

panied Porras to the Hopi country. There is evidence, however, that other Franciscans came to the Moqüi village from
time to time during the next half century. By 1675 there were
missions at Shungopovi (also spelled Shongopovi or Xongo-
pabi) and Oraibi as well as at Awátovi. At least two *visitas,*
one at Mishongnovi and another in the vicinity of Walpi, were
established.

Then in 1680 disaster struck. On August 9, the Pueblo
Indians of Arizona and New Mexico revolted in unison. They
had long been discontented under the Spanish rule, not only
because their pagan religious ceremonies had been repressed,
but because of the tribute and personal service which was
exacted from them. A medicine man named El Popé became the
symbol of the resistance. This native leader had been embit-
tered by his imprisonment for witchcraft. After his release from
jail he began playing upon the causes of unrest and secretly formulated plans for the extermination of all the Spanish colonists. The revolt resulted in the slaying of some 400 settlers.

State Museum, University of Arizona

Ruins of Awátovi

Moqüi village of Walpi in 1877

Most of the remainder assembled in Santa Fe from which they retreated to the vicinity of El Paso. Only eleven of thirty-three friars escaped martyrdom. At least three of the four missionaries then on Arizona soil in the Moqüi villages were murdered: Fray José de Figueroa at Awátovi, José de Trujillo at Shungopovi, and José de Espeleta at Oraibi.[1] Another missionary at Oraibi, Augustín de Santa María, may have been enslaved by the Indians and used as a beast of burden — an object of scorn and ridicule; if so, his death was a slow one. Fearful of Spanish vengeance for these murders, the Hopis moved the villages at the foot of the mesas to more easily defended positions on the summits.

Twelve years elapsed after the tragedy of 1680 before the newly appointed and very able Governor Diego de Vargas reconquered, at least in part, the frontier province of New Mexico. In November, 1692, he reached the Hopi settlements with a select group of sixty-three soldiers and two missionaries. At first hostile, the Indians observed the friendly manner of Vargas's well-armed troops and, with the exception of the inhabitants of Oraibi, professed a willingness to live in peace with the Spaniards. However, the Hopis had no intention of keeping their promises. They resisted throughout the next century and often allied with the Navajos, the Utes, and the Pueblos of New Mexico to attack their Spanish rulers.

During the early 1700s the Hopis were joined by a large number of Tanos, Tewas, Jemez, and Santo Domingan Indians from the Rio Grande Valley. Known as "apostates" for having rejected Spanish control, these Pueblo people were regarded as a menace for their influence on the Hopis. So, in 1716, Governor Phelix Martínez sent an expedition to take them back to their villages in New Mexico.[2] This force destroyed maize fields, killed a large number of livestock, killed several natives, but was only partially successful in its mission. Some of the apostates agreed to be escorted back. The Tewa-speaking Tanos, however, who had settled at Hano on the First Mesa near the village of Walpi, defiantly refused to go and remained with their Hopi hosts. The refugees undoubtedly influenced the Hopis, most of whom continued to prefer their own way of life to that of the Spanish. And for the next century and a half the Hopis remained united, with little effective Spanish interference in their affairs.

FATHER EUSEBIO FRANCISCO KINO

Missionaries were successful in converting and influencing the more docile Indians of Pimería Alta. This region extended northward from the Altar River in Mexico to the Gila River and eastward from the Gulf of California and the Colorado River to the San Pedro River. Of some 30,000 Indians living in this area, the Pima tribe was the most numerous. There were several branches of this loosely organized and scattered people in what is now Arizona.

A line drawn from Tubac on the Santa Cruz through Fairbank on the San Pedro approximates the boundary between the Pimas proper to the south and the Sobaípuris to the north. The Sobaípuris were divided into three groups: one lived on the San Pedro north of Fairbank, another on the middle Santa Cruz between San Xavier del Bac and Picacho, and a third on the Gila River from the Casa Grande westward nearly to Gila

Bend. The latter were also called the "Gila Pimas" and occupied a region roughly corresponding to the present day Pima
Reservation.* During the eighteenth century after Kino
departed, the eastern Sobaípuris were all either destroyed or
driven westward from the San Pedro by the Apaches. Their
descendants today, and the descendants of the Sobaípuris on
the Santa Cruz, are to be found mainly on the Pima and the
San Xavier reservations. West of the Santa Cruz River in
the arid region centering around modern Ajo were the less-
cultured Papagos, a name meaning "the Bean Eaters." They
lived in scattered villages in the same general area where the
modern Papagos live today, having been the least disturbed
by the white man. The Pimas proper, the Sobaípuris, and the
Papagos were all of the Piman stock and spoke the same tongue;
all were classified as Upper Pimas.

The Pimas were essentially sedentary and irrigated their
cultivated fields. In comparison to their neighbors they
were also peaceful; harassed by the wild, mountain-dwelling
Apaches, their desire for military protection might have made
them more receptive to Christian teachings. Certainly it was
among the Piman people that Arizona's most important missions were established. The Spanish had little contact with the
non-Pima Indians who resided in the Arizona part of Pimería
Alta. These were mainly Yuman tribes: Cocomaricopas along
the lower Gila River and the Yumas, Quíquimas, Cócopas,
and others along the lower Colorado River. The Yuman people spoke a language altogether different from the Piman
tongue and farmed without irrigation.

It was to the thinly populated homeland of all these tribes,
though mainly to the Pimas, that Father Eusebio Francisco
Kino came in the 1690s. He was priest, explorer, ranchman,

---

* The nomenclature relative to the Pimas is confusing because modern ethnologists
designate the Gila Pimas — the best known group today — as the Pimas proper,
whereas Kino called them "Sobaíporis," spelling the name with an "o" instead of a
"u" in the next to last syllable. See Kino's 1701 map opposite p. 44 labeled "Passage
Par Terre a la Californe," and his 1702 map labeled "Tabula Californiae" between
pp. 46 and 47, in Ernest J. Burrus, S.J., *Kino and the Cartography of Northwestern
New Spain.* Tucson: Arizona Historical Society, 1965. See also Herbert E. Bolton, *Rim
of Christendom:* a Biography of Eusebio Francisco Kino Pacific Coast Pioneer. New
York: Russell and Russell, 1960, pp. 246–49. See also Charles DiPeso, *The Sobaípuri
Indians of the Upper San Pedro River Valley, Southeastern Arizona.* Dragoon, Arizona: The Amerind Foundation, Inc., 1953.

astronomer, cartographer, defender of the frontier, all in one. For almost a quarter of a century this "apostle to the Pimas" was the outstanding figure in the advancement of the Spanish frontier into what is now Arizona.

Born in the small mountain town of Segno in northern Italy in 1645, Kino went to college at a Jesuit school in Hall, near Innsbruck, Austria, where he contracted a serious illness.* While miraculously recovering his health, he decided to become a foreign missionary and joined the Society of Jesus. At first wishing to work in the Orient, he entered several excellent German universities to study mathematics and map making, because the Chinese had favored Jesuits who were skilled in these subjects. Fortunately for Arizona and the Southwest, however, he was sent to the New World. In 1681, the thirty-six-year-old padre arrived in Mexico. He spent six months in Mexico City where he published an essay on the comet of 1680 and demonstrated a good knowledge of astronomy. Late in 1681 he was assigned as map maker, geographer, and missionary on an expedition sent by the viceroy to colonize Baja California. After his first visit to that region he returned to the capital city with his commander, Admiral Isidro Atondo y Antillón.

In 1687, Kino was appointed missionary to the Pimas, and in March he established a mission on the upper San Miguel River which he named Nuestra Señora de los Dolores. This site, approximately seventy-five miles south of the modern city of Nogales, was his headquarters until his death in 1711. During a period of some twenty-four years, Kino embarked upon at least fifty major journeys by horseback to the native settlements in Pimería Alta. He often traveled alone, though occasionally a few Indian converts and one or two Spanish officers accompanied him. Since he was working for the crown,

---

*Eusebio Kino was born August 10, 1645, in Segno, the son of Franciscus Chinus and Donna Margherita. In his early manhood, Eusebio usually wrote his name Chinus or Chino, pronounced "Ke nus" or "Ke no." When he went to Spain, however, he found that Chino meant "Chinaman" and in Mexico the name was applied contemptuously to persons of mixed and low caste. To avoid ambiguous connotations and yet preserve the Italian sound of his proud old family name, the missionary wrote his name "Kino" in Spain and in Mexico. Today he would have other problems since Kino is now the German word for "movie" and the name of a gambling game (Keno). See Bolton, *Rim of Christendom*, pp. 28–29.

Donald B. Sayner Collection

Map made by Kino in 1702

as well as for the church, the government of New Spain sent soldiers to mission Dolores. Lieutenant Juan Mateo Manje accompanied him on nine journeys from 1694 to 1701 and proved to be an ideal companion. Like the hard-riding padre, he was also a superb diarist and, in this capacity, left posterity a wealth of information on the history of Kino and southern Arizona.

On many of the trips to his missions and *rancherías,* Kino drove cattle, sheep, and horses from the Dolores ranch to supply his Indian friends.[3] A model missionary, he fully realized that the natives could best understand the gospel of love if it were demonstrated with better living conditions. For that reason he attempted to assure his converts a regular food supply by instructing them in the best methods of crop raising and animal husbandry. Kino believed in the "Give us this day our daily bread" part of the Lord's Prayer as well as "Hallowed be thy name." Each mission station was a complete community, no scattering of spiritual or material seed but a well-preserved, active center of Christian life.

After establishing a chain of missions and branch missions, or *visitas,* in Sonora, Father Kino went north into what is now Arizona. Sobaípuri messengers bearing crosses had invited the padre to visit their villages in the Santa Cruz Valley. Accompanied by Father Juan Salvatierra, he journeyed as far as Tumacácori and visited Guevavi * in January, 1691. Pleased with the industriousness and friendliness of the natives, Kino returned the following year. This time he visited the more populous *rancherías* of Bac, near modern Tucson on the Santa Cruz, and Quíburi, on the San Pedro. Kino found the 800 inhabitants of Bac so eager for religious instruction that he named the village San Francisco Xavier del Bac after his patron. He hoped to make it his next headquarters but was later to be disappointed when he could not gain permission to transfer from Dolores. At Quíburi he was cordially

---

* Since "v's" and "b's" are interchangeable in Spanish, the word Guevavi is sometimes written Guebabi, Guebavi, or Guevabi in the documents. The accent is on the second syllable and, in accordance with the rules of Spanish pronunciation, no accent mark is needed.

received by Chief Coro, the Apache-fighting warrior who became the padre's fast friend though he remained a pagan.[4]

During the next year, Kino was occupied in expeditions to the Gulf in the company of Captain Manje. But in November, 1694, he made another *entrada* into Arizona, this time in search of the famous Casa Grande near the Gila River. Stopping en route at San Xavier, he made the first recorded visit to the ancient ruin near modern-day Coolidge on November 27. While in the area, he said mass at El Tusónimo, a village on the Gila near Sacatón which he renamed La Encarnación. As on later trips to the Gila — including one by way of the San Pedro with Manje in 1697 — he did not go beyond the river, but sent messengers to the north with friendly greetings and assurances that he came in peace and in the true spirit of Christianity. Wherever he went, accompanied only by native converts, Kino was welcomed. He returned to Dolores convinced that a missionary could travel unharmed in the Pima country.[5]

Unfortunately, however, not all of the official representatives of the Spanish crown conducted themselves as wisely as did Kino. His courage was put to the test in April, 1695, when a band of Indian malcontents rose in rebellion at Tubutama and brought about a general uprising in the Altar Valley that spread to other parts of Pimería Alta. The revolt was a culmination of events starting with the assault of a Spanish employee — an Opata chief herdsman named Antonio — upon a Pima overseer. The savage instincts of the only partially Christianized Indian workers were aroused by the *hechiceros,* medicine men who resented the threat to their tribal power and superstitious practices. Aided by hostile Indians from other tribes, the Pimas began to stampede cattle, burn missions, and to kill white people. The climax of the rebellion came on April 2, when the youthful Father Saeta was murdered at Concepción del Caborca, a new mission which he and Father Kino had established less than six months earlier. A party of Indian renegades ruthlessly filled the kneeling priest's body with arrows, killed his assistants, vandalized the mission, and stampeded the livestock.[6] Soldiers from General Domingo Jironza's

Flying Company rode into Pimería Alta and, unfortunately, began a bloody and indiscriminate slaughter of the guilty and innocent alike. The frontier soon exploded into open war between the cavalry and Indians who dashed, in guerrilla fashion, from mountain strongholds to ravage the Christian settlements. For several months peace on the "rim of christendom" seemed like an impossible dream.

Perhaps the best testimony to Kino's respected position with the Indians is the fact that his mother-mission at Dolores was the only one untouched in this freak war. He was able to use his influence to bring the warring factions together for a conference. In a meeting with the Spanish officials, the Pimas agreed to turn over the principal malefactors, including the murderers of Father Saeta, for punishment. In an act of mercy these guilty ones were pardoned. Thus ended the only serious difficulty that developed between the Pimas and the Spanish during Kino's time. It is regrettable that he, instead of the military, was not called upon in the beginning to settle the disturbance. Bloodshed probably would have stopped with the martyrdom of Father Saeta.

To satisfy his superiors that all was quiet on the frontier, Kino again rode his tough little mustangs on extended journeys to the north. In December, 1696, he visited his friend El Coro at Quíburi and showed his confidence in the natives by leaving a few cattle and horses for the beginning of a church ranch. In January, Kino went down the Santa Cruz to San Xavier, distributing livestock there as well as at Tumacácori and at Bacoancos. Wherever he visited, the "Padre on Horseback" looked after the spiritual welfare of the natives and asked them to be prepared at all times to accompany the soldiers on an expedition against their enemies — the Jocomes, Janos, Sumas, and Apaches. Slowly the Spanish authorities began to acknowledge his success with the Indians. He proved that they were not only law-abiding and trustworthy but that they could also be useful as allies in the struggle against the Apaches.

In March, 1698, for example, El Coro led his armed Pimas against the five or six hundred Apaches, Jocomes, Sumas, and

Mansos who had sacked the *rancheria* of Santa Cruz on the San Pedro River.* An unusual event followed. The natives engaged in a type of combat that one would expect to occur more in a medieval tournament than on the Arizona desert. The outnumbered Apache chieftain, El Capotcari, proposed a fight of ten of his warriors against ten Pimas, each side to be divided into two battle lines of five men each. The Pimas accepted and quickly showed their good shooting and greater dexterity at parrying arrows. They defeated their adversaries with El Coro completing the triumph by dashing Capotcari's head with stones. The frightened enemies fled and the Pima braves followed, killing and wounding more than 300. The remainder eventually surrendered to the Spanish soldiers.

When many people in New Spain still refused to believe that the Pimas were friendly and considered the Indian report of this engagement an exaggeration, the fifty-three-year-old Kino saddled his best mustang and rode more than 100 miles to the battlefield. His investigation and account of the gruesome episode vindicated the Pimas and served as evidence of their loyalty. So effective had the padre become in associating the Pimas with the Spanish objectives that he was said to be equal to a garrison of soldiers on the frontier.[7]

Aside from saving souls, Kino's chief interest after 1699 was to find a land route to California so that he could supply the missions of his friend and fellow Jesuit, Father Salvatierra. Although he never found a route, Kino pointed the way for later explorers and proved that Baja California was not an island. He had begun doubting the island thesis when the Yuman Indians presented him with some blue shells. He learned that these abalone shells were valuable in trade because they were not obtainable along the Colorado River nor the Gulf of California. Kino had seen such shells on the shore of the Pacific Ocean in 1685 and began to wonder how desert

---

*The Jocomes, who lost their identity in the eighteenth century, were a nomadic, Apache-speaking group that roamed south of the Gila across southeastern Arizona, New Mexico, and Chihuahua. The Sumas and Mansos were nomadic groups that lived mainly in Chihuahua. Kino referred to these bands, as well as the Apache-speaking Janos, as separate tribes which were associated with the hostile Apaches. The latter lived mainly along the upper Gila River and in the Chiricahua Mountains, but made raids into the surrounding country. See Edward H. Spicer, *Cycles of Conquest*. Tucson: University of Arizona Press, 1962, pp. 231–37.

Indians could acquire them. He decided to do some scientific sleuthing and asked all the tribes of Pimería Alta to help in the investigation. A council meeting of chiefs was held in April, 1700, at San Xavier del Bac. After several night conferences with these Indian leaders under the beautiful Arizona skies, Kino concluded that the blue shells came from the Pacific slope of California by a land route.[8]

This assurance was the inspiration for several journeys to the vicinity of the Yuma crossing. Finally, in November, 1701, the priest-explorer sat in a basket on a leaky raft as swimming Indians towed him across the Colorado River. On the California side he was befriended by the Cutgane tribe. These Indians presented him with more blue shells and explained that the ocean was only an eight- or ten-day journey westward. On a second trip in 1702 he went far enough around the head of the Gulf to satisfy himself that the "island" was in reality a peninsula. But Kino did not fulfill his ambition to open a road to the Pacific because he wished to return to Dolores with his ill traveling companion, Padre Manuel González.[9] On a hurried trip across the deserts of present-day Arizona and Sonora, González died. The expedition was far from a failure, however. Scholar that he was, Kino wrote a treatise verifying the peninsular theory that was sent to Mexico City for publication.

Meanwhile Kino had been establishing three missions in the Santa Cruz Valley. The turn of the century brought the founding of the first and principal mission in Arizona, San Xavier del Bac. Prior to building the church he had made preparations for the material well-being of the converts there. His Indian cowboys rounded up 1400 cattle on the ranch at Dolores, half of which were to be driven to Bac where corrals had already been constructed. After his arrival, Kino described the economic situation in his diary on April 26, 1700. He wrote that the natives were tending 300 beeves, forty head of sheep and goats, and a small drove of mares. They also had a good field of wheat beginning to head and were planting a large field of maize.[10]

Only a church was needed to make San Xavier a full-fledged mission. The foundations for this structure were begun on April 28. Stone, called *tezontle* by Kino, was carried from a nearby hill and water for the mortar was drawn from irrigation ditches. The exact location of the church is not known since extensive archaeological work has failed to disclose any remains of it.* The beautiful "White Dove of the Desert" — the name that Kino gave to his mission — was constructed by the Franciscans in the latter part of the eighteenth century.

Farther south, up the Santa Cruz, Kino built the mission San Gabriel de Guevavi with a *visita*, San Cayetano (now San José) de Tumacácori, in 1701.[11] The adobe walls of the mission buildings erected by the Pimas at these sites long ago deteriorated. The important thing, however, is that Kino was the first missionary to bring the story of the cross to these people and to give them the self-sufficiency that they needed to maintain the faith. For each mission and its branches, he sent herds of cattle and sheep. The livestock drive to Tumacácori serves to illustrate Kino's success as a missionary, for the herdsmen were the same Indians who had risen in revolt and killed Father Saeta in 1695.

After continual pleading Kino was given two resident priests in 1701 for his Arizona missions. Father Juan de San Martín was assigned to establish Guevavi with *visitas* at Tumacácori and Bacoancos. Evidently his stay was short because by March, 1704,· he was at Pitic — now Hermosillo — in Mexico. The sojourn of Father Francisco Gonzalvo at San Xavier del Bac was also short. Although he converted and baptized many Indians he felt compelled to leave in 1702. The church records show that he rode to San Ignacio where he died that summer of pneumonia at the age of twenty-nine.[12] Manje explained the departure, however, as being due to a revolt of nearby villages, one of which was Tucson. The Pimas began to kill the drove of mares and the cattle herd. Evidently they were either not as gentle as expected or Gonzalvo was no Kino.

---

* Bolton, *Rim of Christendom*, p. 507. There is no evidence that the church for which Kino laid the foundations was ever finished. Dr. Bernard L. Fontana of the University of Arizona expressed doubt after having some letters — written in 1732 by Father Segesser, a German Jesuit who served in Arizona — translated by an expert in a now archaic Swiss-German dialect. "The impression you get from reading Segesser's letters," Fontana said, "is that either Kino's church was not in existence or was in such a state of ruin that it wasn't worth mentioning." *Arizona Daily Star*, May 30, 1969.

Arizona Historical Society

Ruins of Mission Los Santos Angeles de Guevavi in 1889

Whatever the cause for the setback, the Father Visitor, Antonio Leal, was disappointed. Earlier, on a trip to the Santa Cruz Valley with Kino in 1699, he had expressed high hopes for the future of this area. He believed that the valley served by the mission at Bac could easily support 30,000 people in "another city like Mexico" because of the fertility of the soil, the many irrigation ditches, and the extensive ranges for cattle.[13] Of course it would be an understatement to say that in modern times his prophecy has more than been fulfilled by the growth of Tucson into a large city.

One of the great sorrows in Kino's optimistic life was that no Jesuit was ever sent to relieve him at Dolores so that he could become the resident missionary at San Xavier.[14] Three "black robes," including Gonzalvo, died on the frontier in 1702. No replacements came from Europe since Spain was too involved in the War of the Spanish Succession (1701–1714) to be concerned about the work of a saintly missionary in the remote province of Pimería Alta. So Kino was left to carry on and, even though his main work in his later years was in Sonora where he established more churches, he never forgot San Xavier del Bac. He returned there in 1702 after Gonzalvo's departure to work on the church.[15] Though this visit to Bac was the last one of which there is any record, the pioneer padre did not disappear from Arizona history at that time.

The Apache outbreak of 1703 had given Kino an opportunity to suggest to Spanish authorities that a mission be established east of San Xavier on the San Pedro, with a fortification for its defense.* He argued that El Coro's Sobaípuri Pimas in that area were the most reliable and competent ally that the Spaniards had. A fortified mission at Quíburi would serve to protect Sonora from further inroads of Apaches, who were becoming bolder as they penetrated deeper and deeper into the Spanish provinces. In *Favores Celestiales,* a kind of autobiography and chronicle of his missionary work through 1706, and also in a special letter to the King in 1710, Kino optimistically envisioned the reduction and conversion of Apachería. With the Apache land subdued, the gate would be open for contact with New Mexico and beyond. How different might the history of Arizona have been if Kino's plan had been carried out! Perhaps El Coro, not General George Crook and General Nelson Miles, would have subjugated the defiant Apaches. Who knows but what Baicatcan or Quíburi, probably with an Anglicized name, would be one of Arizona's big population centers today.

Another unfulfilled plan of Padre Kino was the idea of establishing a large Spanish *villa,* or city-type of colony, on the Colorado River.[16] This outpost was to have served as a base of operations from which the Spanish temporal and spiritual authority might be extended to the hitherto uncon-

---

* On the Spanish maps, the San Pedro River was usually designated as Río de Quíburi or Río San José de Terrenate. In 1703, Kino listed San Salvador del Baicatcan, a *ranchería* which had been deserted in 1696, as the site of a new town. In 1706, he asked for a missionary at Santa Ana del Quíburi, the fortified home of Chief Coro, up the San Pedro River and south of Baicatcan. See Bolton, *Kino's Historical Memoir of Pimería Alta,* Vol. II, p. 182, and *Rim of Christendom,* p. 582. Other locations for new "flourishing" towns mentioned in the 1703 letter to the viceroy were Rosario on the San Pedro north of Baicatcan, Tusonimo on the Gila River northwest of the Casa Grande, and Oyadoybuise, located in the vicinity of the Cocomaricopas west of the Casa Grande on the Gila River at the southern extremity of the Gila Bend Mountains. Kino also listed six towns or stations already established that needed missionaries: San Xavier del Bac and San Gabriel del Guebavi in present-day Arizona; Búsanic and Tucubabia (*visita* of Búsanic), as well as Sonóydag (Sonoita) just south of the present international line; and Cabotca (Caborca) and Tubutama in Sonora. See letter of Kino from Nuestra de los Dolores, February 5, 1703, to the Viceroy of Spain, Mexico City, in Ernest J. Burrus (trans. and ed.), *Kino's Plan.* Tucson: Arizona Historical Society, 1961, pp. 30–31.

quered regions of the north and northwest. By 1706 the civil and military leaders were also eager to plant a strong Spanish settlement in western Pimería Alta. General Juan Fernández de la Fuente, Captain Juan Díaz de Terán, and Kino's friend Manje, all wrote letters to Kino in that year congratulating him for his work in bringing the Colorado River Indians into the Christian fold and submission to Spanish authority. Manje also wrote to the Viceroy in support of Kino's request for more missionaries and the founding of a *villa* to serve as a stronghold for the reduction of the Moqüis and Apaches. Fuente anticipated a great migration of people over the land route to the Californias. Manje believed that a good prospect for minerals would increase the Spanish population in the Yuma area.

But Spain's wealth and energy were fully committed to her affairs in Europe. By 1707 Padre Kino was so discouraged that he ceased recording his activities in detail in his diary. Not until his report to the King in 1710 did he again set forth the advantages to be gained by conquest and conversion of Upper California and other unknown arcas in the northwest.[17] He urged the King to establish the New Kingdom of New Navarre out of this region. In this kingdom he envisioned, among other things, the subjugation of the Apaches, the development of a trade route across Hopi country between Santa Fe and Upper California, and the establishment of a port at San Diego where scurvy-ridden sailors of the China trade could pick up fresh fruit and vegetables.

Kino proceeded in his letter to describe the temporal means whereby his dream could become a reality. His description of the Pima missions and their resources was in some ways actually a summary of his own achievements in transmitting European culture to the deserts of Pimería Alta. Among the assets at hand to help in achieving his vision, he even listed the humble cabbage and the lowly garlic. In his own words, "There are already very rich and abundant fields, plantings and crops of wheat, maize, frijoles, chick peas, beans, lentils, bastard chick peas, etc. There are good gardens . . . vineyards for wine for masses, and cane-fields of sweet cane for syrup and panocha, and with the favor of heaven, before long for sugar.

There are many Castilian fruit trees, such as fig trees, quinces, oranges, pomegranates, peaches, apricots, pears, apples, mulberries, pecans, tunas, etc.; all sorts of garden stuff, such as cabbage, melons, watermelons, white cabbage, lettuce, onions, leeks, garlic, anise, pepper, mustard, mint, Castilian roses, white lilies, etc."[18] He also wrote of the mineral resources, livestock, and the industrious, well-disposed natives. And in the role of the Southwest's first chamber of commerce he enthusiastically reported that the climate of the area was pleasant and mild. He was convinced that this region was the heart of North America.

In light of Kino's vision and practical energy it is interesting to speculate on how different Southwestern and Arizona history might have been if the Spanish authorities had been able to support him in carrying out his suggestions. His proposals anticipated the founding of a city where Yuma is now located, 140 years before it came into being. The Yuma Revolt of 1781 that resulted in the martyrdom of Father Garcés and his companions on the Colorado probably would not have occurred.

The ports of San Diego and Monterey would have been opened two generations sooner and a land route from Sonora across Arizona into California would have been established a half century earlier. But Kino was in advance of his time. Starved for funds to carry on his work, his final years were filled with heartache. He died at Magdalena in 1711 before the war in Europe was finished. His dreams had to be fulfilled by other builders of souls and empires.

In a lifetime covering two-thirds of a century, Kino crowded the achievements which will make him outstanding for all time in the pioneer history of Arizona and the Southwest. For twenty-four continuous years the padre on horseback crisscrossed the burning deserts, through both friendly and hostile Indian lands, spreading his good words and good deeds. First and foremost a black-robed man of God, he was also an enthusiastic doer of earthly things. He blazed trails which civilized man had either forgotten or never trod. His route from Sonoita (near the present Arizona-Mexico border) to the Colorado River, for example — later known as *Camino del*

Diablo, or Devil's Highway — went through a waterless wasteland which through the years became the graveyard of dozens
of thirsty travelers who lacked Kino's pioneering skill. The
cattle and sheep that the padre drove over the trails were used
to introduce stock raising to Arizona and the Southwest. Not
only was he the first great missionary, explorer, and ranchman
of Pimería Alta, but his manuscripts and maps have also given
us the best contemporary record of this relatively unknown
region at the merging of the seventeenth and eighteenth centuries.

However, little can be gleaned from his writings about
the man himself. For an intimate picture of what manner of
man he was, we are indebted to his successor, Padre Luis
Velarde.[19] According to Velarde, Padre Kino never smoked
or took snuff, never drank wine except to celebrate mass, or
had any other bed except the sweat blankets of his horse for
a mattress. He never had more than two coarse shirts because
he preferred to give everything as alms to the Indians. He was
charitable to others but cruel to himself. When he publicly
reprimanded a sinner he showed signs of being hot-tempered.
But if anyone showed him personal disrespect he not only
restrained his temper but exalted whomever had mistreated
him with expressions of courtesy and gratitude. His food was
taken without salt and was mixed with herbs to make it more
distasteful. And one night Velarde saw him whipping himself
mercilessly in the church. Is there any wonder that such an
ascetic, self-effacing man could endure the hardships of pioneering over the deserts of the Southwest?

He died as he had lived, with extreme humility and in
poverty. His deathbed consisted of two calf skins for a mattress,
two Indian blankets for covers, and a pack saddle for a pillow.
He was buried in the chapel of San Francisco Xavier in Magdalena, which he had just dedicated before falling ill. A year
later, in 1712, Padre Agustín de Campos, had the bodies of
two other missionaries — Manuel González and Ignacio Itur-
mendi — exhumed at Tubutama, and reburied them on either
side of Kino. In the ensuing years the adobe walls of the
chapel deteriorated and the burial place of the priests was
forgotten and lost. There was naturally great excitement in

both the United States and Mexico in May, 1966, when a team of historians and archaeologists from both countries succeeded in locating and identifying the remains near the Magdalena City Hall.* After a century of searching, the grave of Kino had been found at last! The Mexican people were especially delighted since they could now share in Kino's fame. Just a year before, Arizona had stolen the limelight by unveiling a statue of the famous padre in the Capitol at Washington, D.C.

Since each state is entitled to only two statues in the Statuary Hall collection, the Arizona legislature in 1961 had bestowed great honor on Kino by asking Congress for permission to erect one of him in recognition of his contributions to the state's history.

Congress approved, probably unaware of a regulation in the 1864 law that provided for the Hall but did not permit imaginary conceptions of historical persons. As it turned out, there was no known portrait of Kino. No one knew what he looked like, how he wore his hair or whether he might have been bald. What was the shape of his nose? Was he tall or short? A committee which collected photographs of descendants of Kino's family (now called Chini), found an amazing resemblance persisting through several generations. Working from one of the photographs, a Tucson artist, Mrs. Frances O'Brien, painted a portrait in 1962 that turned out to be a remarkable likeness of the venerable missionary.† Nearly four years later, historians and scientists who discovered Kino's remains at Magdalena compared the painting with Kino's skull and were astounded at the almost perfect physical correspondence. Meanwhile, twenty-six sculptors submitted models based upon this picture and other pertinent facts on Kino, the winning

---

* The Mexican government expedited the search for Kino's remains, hoping that the site would become Mexico's most stirring historical and tourist attraction at the time of the 1968 Olympic games in Mexico City. For a detailed account of the search see James M. Murphy, "The Discovery of Kino's Grave," *The Journal of Arizona History*, Vol. VII, No. 2 (Summer, 1966), pp. 89-95; see also "Introduction" by Barry Goldwater in Smith, Kessell, and Fox, *Father Kino in Arizona*, pp. xiii-xvi.

† *Arizona Daily Star*, May 16, 1971. At first Mrs. O'Brien described her portrait of Kino as a composite of the features shown in photographs of twenty-one of Kino's relatives.

*Frances O'Brien's concept
of Father Kino*

Arizona Historical Society

entry being designed by Madame Suzanne Silvercruys of Connecticut and Tucson.

At the dedication of the completed copper statue on February 14, 1965, Father Ernest Burrus, from the Historical Institute of the Jesuits in Rome, traced the career of one of the most outstanding figures in Arizona's glorious past. He concluded with these words of praise:

> We can feel justified in dedicating this statue not merely to the memory of one man, however great he may be; we dedicate it to all Americans who would share Kino's high ideals, lofty aspirations, and his bold vision of the future to bring together all peoples in true understanding and in abiding communion of spirit; we dedicate this statue to the citizens, present and future, of Arizona whose pioneer founder he was.[20]

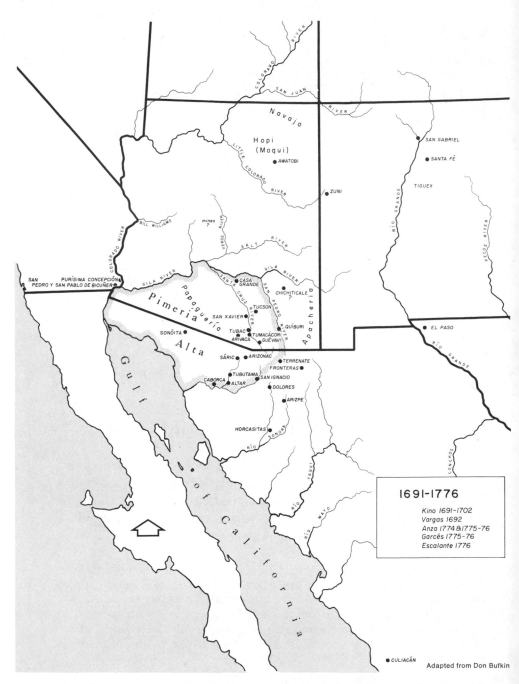

Spanish exploration routes in Arizona

Within the map:

Navajo

Hopi
(Moqui)

• SAN GABRIEL

• SANTA FÉ

• AWATOBI

• ZUNI

TIGUEX

mines
?

BILL WILLIAMS

SAN
PEDRO Y SAN PABLO DE BICUÑER
PURÍSIMA CONCEPCIÓN

Pimería
Alta

Papaguería

CASA GRANDE

CHICHITICALE
?

TUCSON

SAN XAVIER

QUÍBURI

SONÓITA
TUBAC
ARIVACA
TUMACÁCORI
GUÉVAVI

Apachería

• EL PASO

SÁRIC
ARIZONAC
TERRENATE
FRONTERAS

TUBUTAMA
CABORCA
ALTAR
SAN IGNACIO
DOLORES

ARIZPE

HORCASITAS

Gulf of California

1691-1776

Kino 1691-1702
Vargas 1692
Anza 1774 & 1775-76
Garcés 1775-76
Escalante 1776

• CULIACÁN

Adapted from Don Bufkin

Chapter 6

Missionaries and Soldiers in the 1700s
Relations With the Pimas, Yumas, Apaches, and Hopis

FOR MORE THAN TWENTY YEARS after the death of Padre Kino, Arizona was neglected by both Spanish officials and missionaries. It was not until the 1730s that Spain recovered sufficiently from her European wars to again devote some attention to Pimería Alta. In that decade the Jesuits began returning to the once prosperous missions of the Santa Cruz Valley. Among the new padres were several who had been recruited in the German states — Father Johann (Juan) Grazhoffer who was assigned to Guevavi, Father Phelipe Segesser who came to San Xavier, and Father Gaspar Stiger. Stiger ministered to the needs of neophytes first at San Xavier and then at Guevavi before being ordered in 1736 to take over the head mission at San Ignacio in present-day Sonora.

Grazhoffer, a forty-two-year-old Austrian, was the first of the German Jesuits to reach what is now Arizona. After completing his apprenticeship at Tubutama, where he nearly died of a fever, Grazhoffer was sent to Guevavi, arriving there on May 4, 1732, with an escort of soldiers under the command of Captain Juan Bautista de Anza. Hundreds of Pimas, dressed in their best blankets and feathers, gathered to receive gifts and to enjoy the pageantry of the occasion. Captain Anza ceremoniously introduced the natives to their padre with a symbolic replanting of the Holy Cross and the firing of muskets. The Indians reciprocated with races, dancing, and singing. After Don Eusebio Aquibissani — an old Christian named after Father Eusebio Kino — was chosen as the native "governor," Anza moved on down the Santa Cruz to San Xavier. Father Grazhoffer was left with the problem of building a new mission and serving an estimated 1400 souls at Guevavi and its four *visitas:* Sonoita, Arivaca, Tumacácori, and Tubac.

Grazhoffer was soon to learn that the Pimas were not exactly the people Father Kino had described. Kino emphasized only those good qualities that would most likely influence the Spanish government to send additional missionaries to Pimería Alta; he failed to mention such things as their drinking orgies, thievery, and polygamy. For the most part, his visits had been short, and the Pimas got the idea that Christianity involved little more than a few symbolic gestures for which they were rewarded with presents. But the Indians reacted differently to Father Grazhoffer because he moved into the village as a resident missionary and represented authority. His Ópata and Yaqui assistants assumed some control over them too, causing further resentment. Unwilling to give up many of their native customs and to become full-fledged Christians, some of the Pimas tried to relieve their frustrations by putting poison into Grazhoffer's food. The padre died on May 26, 1733, in the arms of Father Segesser who had stopped at Guevavi while traveling between San Xavier and San Ignacio.[1] Not many months after he buried Father Grazhoffer, Segesser himself became sick — probably of malaria — and was carried on the shoulders of the Pimas to the mission at Cucurpe. After an illness lasting five months he returned to Guevavi, only to fall ill again. This time he made his final exit from Arizona, being assigned to a mission in Lower Pimería where he ultimately regained his health and wrote a classic description of the Pimas in 1737.[2]

Though impressed by the generosity and willingness of the Pimas to share food and clothing, and by their skill in fabricating wool and cotton sashes, fiber baskets, and other products, the priest was chagrined at their polygamy and communal drinking. When Segesser tried to persuade some of the men living with wives other than their own that they were sinning, they answered: "Don't you see that the rooster has more than one hen, a stallion more than one mare? And you say that we shouldn't have more than one wife!"[3] And Father Segesser was no more successful in curbing the drinking habits of his neophytes, though he chose to be lenient with them on this point. On one occasion he rode to Sonoita to find that some Pima workers who were supposed to be clearing brush from land at Guevavi were instead having a drinking bout. "... one should have seen the capers they cut!" he wrote. "Some who could not even walk on their quaking knees, were dragged up by the others, and all shouted very tearfully: 'Father, the drink is good! Get off your horse and join us, the wine is good!'"[4] The Pimas made wine from the fruit of the giant saguaro cactus and from other edible fruits such as the mulberry. They also fermented a kind of brandy from roasted mescal. Drinking these intoxicants was part of the Pima traditional way of life that they refused to give up. As more and more of them died of disease or became culturally disoriented, they seemed to resort to drinking even more frequently. And if the Jesuits tried to forbid either this habit or their nightly dancing, the Indians threatened to return to the mountainous wilds where they could do as they pleased.

Segesser wrote about the evils of nocturnal dancing, as well as the lack of cleanliness, in this passage:

Cleanliness is not found among them, rather the opposite. When a cow is slaughtered they besmear themselves completely with its blood. Others paint themselves with yellow, red, or white paint so that they more resemble spectres than human beings. They paint themselves in this way especially when they dance. Dances occur in Upper Pimería every night, accompanied by singing or yowling with no articulated words, until the father rings *satis* ["enough!"] with the church bell. The nightly dances make most Pimas lazy and inactive and they lounge about unless the father drives them to work like donkeys, whereas other Indians like the Opatas and Yaquis are very little behind the Spanish people in industry and at times even excell [excel] them in diligence and skill.[5]

Father Segesser also wrote that the Pimas loved their children "as do monkeys their young." He said that the mothers seemed to have "no more important occupation than that of catching the children's lice, which they do not throw away but bite and then eat." When questioned about why they did this, the women asked the padre if he hadn't noticed that "hens also eat their lice."[6]

Segesser described several other activities of the women. They did a war dance, for example, when the men returned from a campaign against the Apaches. With the tokens of victory — hair, hands, and feet of the dead enemies — hoisted on poles, the Pima women danced jubilantly and went from house to house in the village to receive donations. Women also gathered to dance when a girl's father arranged a marriage for her. On some occasions three girls would dance and the one who had the most endurance would be taken home by the groom. These "wedding" dances often continued throughout the night.

Of course the women also cooked the food, maize being the usual fare. The favorite dish served in the mission pueblos was *posoli* — flour cooked in a kettle with ox flesh. Another dish that they enjoyed was made from mescal roots roasted to a yellow color on red hot stones and then ground into a sweet porridge. Edible fruits supplemented the diet, especially when grains were not available. The Pimas and their brethren, the Papagos, also ate roasted mice and boiled snake meat. They loved horsemeat when it was available, but did not eat the flesh of the dog, chicken, or birds of any kind. They killed the latter, however, with the bow and arrow for the feathers.

Another custom of the Pimas was to place food on the graves of their dead in the belief that the deceased would eat in the other world. After a death the survivors covered their faces, except for the eyes and mouth, with a thick layer of porridge. And for at least six months after the burial they made horrible wailing noises three times a night. The relatives set free any horse that was used to carry the dead person, who was wrapped in covers rather than placed in a box, to his grave. They also burned the house of the deceased, believing that a ghost returning for his horse or house might take back with him one of the living. When a chief died he was buried in the center of the village and the whole village was then deserted. While Segesser was still at San Xavier, for example, he visited Tubac on one occasion, only to find all the houses either burned or vacant; the magistrate had died and the people moved to a new location out of fear.

The Pima converts continued many of their old ways and sometimes returned to the hills, especially when the padres were absent. In 1734, for instance, when both Segesser and Stiger were away from their missions for awhile, the natives of

Guevavi departed with all the horses and cattle. At San Xavier the neophytes broke into the padre's house and stole everything, including the vestments which they shattered; they used two chalices for their festive drinks and slaughtered all the livestock for food. Supposedly, the revolt was caused by a false rumor that Captain Anza was coming to kill all the Pimas. Order was restored with the arrival of Anza on the scene and through the kind persuasion of Segesser and Fathers Stiger and Ignacio (Ignatius) Keller, who accompanied him in seeking the fugitive Indians. The natives of Guevavi returned from the mountains while those at San Xavier brought back all the stolen property. Not all the Pimas were completely pacified, however. The native shamans (*hechiceros,* or medicine men) at San Xavier attempted to cast a curse on Father Stiger; they also gave him poison from which he suffered ill effects the rest of his life. But after the final departure of Segesser, Stiger continued to minister to the needs of the neophytes at both San Xavier and Guevavi until the spring of 1736. At that time the tall, dark-haired, Swiss-born padre was ordered to San Ignacio to replace Kino's aging protégé, Father Agustín de Campos.[7]

All of northern Pimería then fell to Father Keller, a tough and zealous missionary like Kino who often preferred to go it alone. Perhaps he and Father Jacobo Sedelmayr are the best-known German Jesuit missionaries. Both men were ambitious to discover new lands and peoples on the northern frontier of New Spain. While Sedelmayr was still at Tubutama converting Indians, condemning witchcraft and polygamy, erecting churches, and dodging the poisoned arrows which jealous medicine men shot into his home at night, Father Keller was appointed to undertake a journey to the Moqüi (Hopi). He was chosen for this trip because of his previous explorations. In 1736 he had journeyed down the Santa Cruz Valley to Casa Grande and the Gila River. The next year he followed the San Pedro to the Gila and observed the deserted *rancherías* that had been depredated by the Apaches. With these experiences behind him Father Keller eagerly set forth for Moqüi country in September 1743. With an inadequate escort of nine soldiers he ventured for a few days beyond the Gila. Unfortunately, the expedition was attacked at night by

Indians, probably Apaches bent upon robbery, and was lucky to escape back to the home mission at Santa María Suamca, on the Santa Cruz River south of the present international boundary.[8]

Keller was naturally disappointed by his failure, and more so when he was refused an escort for a second try. Father Sedelmayr was appointed to undertake the trip and spent five years exploring in the Colorado and Gila river regions in preparation for his assignment. Even though his superiors canceled the expedition in 1749 because the Franciscans had taken charge of the Moqüi, Sedelmayr worked diligently to advance the frontier and hardly deserved the obscurity into which he has fallen.[9]

In 1743, prior to his Moqüi appointment, Sedelmayr twice journeyed through the deserts of Papaguería converting the Indians. On the second trip he also visited the Cocomaricopa *rancherías* on the Gila, presenting ribbons, knives, and other gifts to the natives who seemed delighted to greet him. The next year he set forth from Tubutama with intentions of going all the way to the land of the Moqüi. On this occasion he stopped at the Casa Grande and preached a sermon against witchcraft. He then visited other Pima villages and asked for volunteer guides to lead him northward to the Moqüi. Refused in this request, he went downstream to the country west of the juncture where the Salt River flows into the Gila. Here he prevailed upon the Cocomaricopas for help but found that they were also reluctant to furnish guides. Though naturally disappointed, Sedelmayr visited some forty-one of the Cocomaricopa villages and then left the Gila at Agua Caliente, setting out in a northwestward direction to a point where the Río Azul, known today as the Bill Williams River, joins the Colorado River. No other explorer since Oñate had ventured so far north and west from New Spain. The Indians in the vicinity presented the Sedelmayr party with watermelons, muskmelons, squash, beans, and maize. They willingly furnished the missionary with information about the Moqüi. Sedelmayr, however, was unable to proceed further because he didn't have the guides, messengers, and military escort that he wanted and because several Indians in his party were sick.[10]

After his return to Sonora from his trip in 1744, Sedelmayr had an opportunity to make a plea for greater Spanish commitment to the development of the region now comprising Arizona. Advised of a new royal *cedula* wherein the King asked for reports on conditions in the northern lands of New Spain, he decided to present firsthand information to the civil authorities. On a trip to Mexico City in 1745 he not only gave a complete account of his explorations but also recommended the founding of new missions, at Casa Grande and for the pagan Cocomaricopas, Pimas, Yumas, and other tribes along the Gila and Colorado rivers. He urged also the placing of a presidio on the Gila somewhere east of Casa Grande in order to check Apache raids. Many of his suggestions for the salvation of souls and expansion of the royal domain were repeated in a letter to the viceroy in 1751.[11] In this message he again stressed the possibilities of converting Upper California and reconquering the province of the Moqüi, once the fertile lands along the rivers of central and western Arizona were secured. Thus, in going beyond his request for eleven or twelve new missionaries, Sedelmayr indicated a broad understanding of the military, political, and commercial — as well as the religious — advantages to be obtained from the permanent occupation of the land.

Sedelmayr's last important trip into Arizona was made in 1750, a few months before he wrote to the viceroy. At that time he attempted to explore the region near the mouth of the Colorado River. With a military escort, he went from Tubutama to Sonoita and across the Papago country to the juncture of the Gila with the Colorado, probably following Kino's old trail much of the way. But after moving for some distance downstream, the expedition stopped when the hostile Quiquimas threatened to attack. A skirmish followed in which the soldiers were forced to defend themselves from arrows and clubs. Sedelmayr's ensign wrote in his diary on December 3 that thirteen of the Indians were killed and others wounded.[12] To prevent further trouble Sedelmayr decided to turn back. Giving up his plans to explore the Gulf, he was in Caborca ten days after the unfriendly encounter on the Colorado. Returning to Tubutama, he then wrote his optimistic letter to the viceroy, only to be shocked by the Pima uprising five months later. Narrowly escaping martyrdom at the hands of the suddenly violent Pimas, Sedelmayr and other Jesuits became involved in a bitter controversy with the civil authorities after peace with the Indians was restored in 1752.

Falsely accused by Governor Parrilla of Sonora of causing the revolt by cruel treatment of the natives, the Jesuits diverted energies from their main work for five or six years to refute the spurious charge. Sedelmayr entered the dispute in 1754 by writing a letter to his superiors in which he emphatically denied that the missionaries were guilty of injustice toward the Indians. Eventually the Jesuit case was presented to the viceroy and the "Black Robes" were exonerated. Unfortunately for them, however, the Society of Jesus was considered a political threat by King Charles III and was ordered expelled from the Spanish colonies.

Still robust in constitution, Sedelmayr was able to withstand months of deprivation and confinement in a warehouse at the seaport of Guaymas, as well as a long sea voyage to San Blas and an overland march to Vera Cruz for deportation to Spain in 1769. Of the fifty-plus fathers who were arrested and rounded up by the dragoons in Sonora and Sinaloa, twenty died on the march because of sickness resulting from bad treatment and lack of medication. Among the survivors, Sedelmayr finally reached Spain where he died at the age of 76 in Aldea de Ávila on February 12, 1779.[13]

SILVER STRIKE AT "ARISSONA"
AND THE PIMA UPRISING OF 1751

Aside from missionary activities there were two notable events in the history of Arizona between the death of Kino in 1711 and the expulsion of the Jesuits in 1767. One relates to the discovery of silver a few miles south of the present international boundary. The other was the Pima revolt of 1751 mentioned above. In October, 1736, a Yaqui miner named Antonio Siraumea discovered some chunks of silver lying close to the surface between the mission at Guevavi and the *ranchería* of Arissona, a *visita* of the mission of El Sáric. As the story of this event spread, many hopeful Spanish prospectors rushed on the scene and began searching the hills. The surrounding area became known as Real (mining town) de Arissona. Reportedly, it soon had several thousand inhabitants, enough for the rush to be ranked as one of the early booms of the West.

Captain Juan Bautista de Anza, father of the founder of San Francisco, hastened from the nearby presidio of Terrenate to make an official investigation of the mine, which was called Las Bolas or Las Planchas de Plata. Most of the silver had already disappeared when the captain arrived. He learned that no less than four thousand pounds of silver — in the form of large balls and slabs — had been picked up in a relatively small area; one slab weighed over a ton and had to be broken into manageable pieces. To protect the interests of the monarchy, Anza ordered an embargo on all the silver. Under Spanish law the crown was entitled to its *quinto,* or king's fifth, if the silver was the product of normal mining operations. If the metal were a treasure trove left by the Aztecs on their way to the Valley of Mexico, as many people believed, then the state could claim all of it. But the miners cared little for legal technicalities and succeeded in evading the tax collectors. Nor were they excited when frustrated officials closed down all mines in the area by royal order in 1741. By that time the mines were nearly exhausted and the prospectors had spirited away most of the precious lode.

Nevertheless, hardy frontiersmen continued to come, even after the Real de Arissona became a ghost town and then vanished altogether. They secretly combed the rough country of Sonora and the area that is now in southern Arizona, hoping to discover more fabulous balls of silver. No reliable records were kept of the occasional strikes but it is certain that there was sufficient activity to justify the presence of traders and herdsmen during the decades prior to the Pima uprising of 1751. The musical name of "Arissona" remained on the tongues of adventurers and, as a result, was eventually identified with the forty-eighth state. Some authorities believe that the word was a softened spelling of "Arizonac" which was derived from the Papago Indian words *ali* (small) and *shonak* (place of the spring). Whatever the origin, the Spaniards applied the name to the *ranchería* located on a small stream in Mexico about twenty-three miles southwest of the modern twin cities of Nogales. The lure of silver gave the name its permanence.

The silver strike also contributed to the antagonism that developed between the Indians and the rough, impatient miners and other frontiersmen in Pimería Alta. The specific incidents that caused the usually peaceful Pimas and Papagos to revolt against Spanish rule in 1751 are not very clear. It is known, however, that their leader, Luis Oacpicagigua of Sáric, was very ambitious to drive out the white men and to rule Pimería Alta himself. He started agitating for revolt at least a year before the uprising actually occurred and even changed his name to Bacquioppa, which in Piman meant "Enemy of Adobe Houses."[14] The Spaniards unintentionally had helped to whet his appetite for power when they appointed him native governor with the title of captain-general as a reward for his help against the rebellious Seris to the south. The failure of the Spaniards to subdue the Seris showed a weakness which emboldened Luis to carry out long-harbored intrigues. To stir up unrest among his people and to discredit the padres who would no doubt attempt to thwart his rebellious plot, Luis fabricated stories that the missionaries were cruel, crafty, and tyrannical in their treatment of the Indians. The natives were secretly promised the mission's possessions as well as the loot from the mines and ranches, once the few hundred Spaniards and their sympathizers were driven from the land.[15]

Father Sedelmayr sensed trouble when he heard that an unusually large number of pagans had been gathering at the *visita* of Sáric. He sent Father Nentuig there with instructions to convert the Indians or at least to prevent sedition. Luckily, however, Nentuig was summoned back to Tubutama just before the Pimas rose in rebellion. Shortly after the padre's departure from Sáric, Luis, under the ruse that the Apaches were about to attack, gave refuge to some twenty persons on the evening of November 20, 1751. After entertaining his "guests," whose number included Spaniards and several of Nentuig's Indian servants, Luis set fire to the house. The trapped occupants either perished in the flames or were killed trying to escape.[16]

At Tubutama the forewarned Sedelmayr assembled as many settlers and soldiers as he could and took refuge behind the mission walls. Hostile rebels appeared and laid siege to the mission for two days. But in the company of a few loyal natives and a handful of Spaniards, Nentuig and the badly wounded Sedelmayr were able to escape from the burning mission under the cover of darkness to safety at Santa Ana. Other white men and Spanish sympathizers were not so fortunate. More than a hundred settlers, miners, and herdsmen were slain in the course of a few days. Among the victims were two Jesuits, Fathers Tomás Tello at Caborca and Enrique Ruhen at Sonoita. The latter mission, just south of the present Arizona-Sonora line, had been reestablished by Sedelmayr in May, 1751, as a forward base for further exploration of the Colorado River area and to prepare the Papagos for Christianity. However, these Indians — though later remorseful — were persuaded by the Pimas to participate in the 1751 uprising against the Spaniards. The natives at both Caborca and Sonoita were aroused because of the cruel reputations of their missionaries. Tello was a hated user of the stocks at Caborca, and Ruhen's penchant for corporal punishment had resulted in the infliction of indignities on neophytes at Sonoita.

The killing and plundering were not confined to Sonora. Rebellion spread slowly to the scattered missions and ranches of the Santa Cruz Valley. Father Francisco Xavier Pauer at San Xavier and Father Joseph Garrucho at Guevavi anticipated trouble in time to flee toward the presidio of Terrenate.* En route, their small party of soldiers and loyal Indians was joined at Suamca (also Soanca) by Father Keller. The abandoned missions were ravaged by the riled Pimas. At Guevavi a band of rebels held a *tlatole,* or native rally, and let off steam. They ransacked Father Garrucho's house and then went to the church where they smashed the tabernacle and abused the few remaining santos; they also killed all of Garrucho's pigeons and chickens. At San Xavier del Bac the destruction was even more complete. The Padre's house and the roof of the ramada were totally demolished.[17] In addition to ravishing the mis-

---

* Pauer, a Moravian baptised Franz Bauer, was born in 1721. He was described as "not well proportioned, having clean swarthy skin, a thick nose, and brown hair." Garrucho was a slender Sardinian born in 1712. John L. Kessell, *Mission of Sorrows: Jesuit Guevavi and the Pimas, 1691–1767*. Tucson: University of Arizona Press, 1970, pp. 87, 130.

sions in southern Arizona, the Pima renegades also burned a church and the padre's house at Tubac and attacked the Spanish *visita* and farms at Arivaca where they slaughtered eleven Spaniards and several natives. Among the dead were two farm supervisors from Tubac. One was Father Garrucho's general foreman, Juan María Romero, whose wife and child were also murdered; the other victim was José de Nava.

Both of these men were disliked by the Tubac-area Indians, partly because of their participation in the "Squash Squabble" a short time before the November revolt. It seems that Romero, Nava, and one Manuel Bustamante were sent by Father Garrucho to the native *ranchería* near the Tubac mission ranch to arrest and imprison three native men, including a father and son, and four women who had supposedly trespassed on the mission lands. After taking the prisoners, Romero saw a squash vine and ordered the Indians to cut some. The young Pima replied that the squash were still green and explained that the riper ones were stored in the huts. But at this point communication failed. The foreman, thinking that his will had been questioned, began caning the youth. The boy's father, seeing his son mistreated, grabbed his bow and shot an arrow toward Romero, missing his mark in the excitement. Meanwhile, the third Indian man became involved, only to be lanced and wounded by the mounted Nava. The ultimate incarceration of the Indians only added one more frustration leading up to the Pima revolt.

For some time, the northern Pimas had suffered psychological stress resulting from what they considered the unpredictable and capricious behavior of the Spanish settlers and missionaries in authority. For example, a former native governor of Tubac, a Piman named José, was flogged in 1748 for disobeying Father Garrucho's order forbidding him to leave Tubac to participate in a Pima campaign against the Apaches. Garrucho accepted a trophy of the Pima victory, an Apache leather suit of armor, but then proceeded to beat the governor with a stick as though it were a crime to pursue the mutual enemy of both the Pima and the Spanish. The Indians resented the father's "justice" and applauded José for following the dictates of his upbringing by fulfilling his military obligation to the native tribal authority. As might be expected, the stalwart warrior and governor was a prime mover in the 1751 uprising at Tubac and the natives took out some of their spite by putting the torch to Spanish possessions.

For the time being, the sacked churches and buildings in Arizona and Sonora seemed to stand as abandoned monuments to a lost cause. Over three months elapsed before the military brought the rebellious Indians in line. The man of the hour was Governor Diego Ortiz Parrilla of Sonora and Sinaloa. He was advised of the uprising and dispatched an army north to quell native resistance. Establishing his headquarters at San Ignacio, he sent Captain José Díaz del Carpio of the presidio of Terrenate to pursue Luis and the fleeing Pimas, with instructions to bring the rebel leader to San Ignacio for a conference. The Governor was willing to forgive the Indians if they returned peacefully to their homes. Since many of them had concentrated in the valley of the Santa Cruz and in the mountains of what is now southern Arizona, Díaz made Tubac the base for his operations in March, 1752. Here he had pasturage for his horses and a good supply route from Terrenate. Learning that Luis was in the Santa Catalina Mountains, Díaz sent an Indian scout to warn him of the Spanish intent to squelch the rebellion by force of arms if the Governor's terms were not accepted. This threat, and perhaps the pangs of hunger, had some effect; the Pima chief humbled himself and arrived at Tubac on March 18, agreeing to live in peace. He returned to the Catalinas to inform his people and came back on March 22 prepared to meet with Parrilla. On the same day Díaz and his men left with their Indian prisoner for San Ignacio where final peace terms were negotiated.

After putting down the Pima rebellion of 1751, the Spaniards began making preparations to protect themselves against possible future uprisings of the Pimas and against the raids of the constantly warring Apaches. Two military garrisons were established in 1752. One was located on the Altar River in present-day Sonora and the other on the Santa Cruz River at Tubac, until then a *visita* of Guevavi. The early history of Tubac is significant for several reasons. It became the first Spanish presidio in Arizona when fifty soldiers were assigned there under the command of Captain Tomás de Belderrain, an officer who knew the country and had proven himself in the recent uprising. Very soon a settlement arose around the walls of the fort and evidently the populace felt relatively safe, for the first white women to touch Arizona soil arrived at Tubac in 1752. The town continued to grow, reaching a population of more than four hundred, including the garrison, by 1757. Except for brief stretches when the whites were driven away by raiding Apaches, Tubac has been inhabited and is said to be the oldest continuous white settlement in the state.

Despite the efforts of the Spanish officials to prevent a recurrence of Indian outbreaks, however, the adverse effects of the Pima uprising in 1751 were never really erased. The final days of the Jesuit period were filled with bickering and quarreling between the missionaries and the Spanish civil authorities. Even though the Jesuits had been outspoken against the enslavement of their converts in the Spanish mines and on the ranches, they could not offer the Indians much more in the mission system of communal labor. Shocked by Governor Parrilla's charge that the Jesuits had caused the revolt by appropriating lands of the Pimas and by severely punishing wayward Indians, Father Keller personally presented a defense to the viceroy in Mexico City in August 1752. He blamed the Governor for having granted so many honors to Luis of Sáric and for slowness and numerous military blunders in suppressing the uprising.* As this battle of words continued, Father Nentuig also entered the civil-ecclesiastical dispute and explained that it was Luis who had too much land at Sáric, not the church. He also accused Luis of leading his people into the hills for drunken orgies and for encouraging one Pedro de la Cruz to continue living a scandalous life apart from his deserted wife in Sáric. Finally, after years of investigation by many officials, the new governor of Sinaloa-Sonora, Colonel Don Juan Antonio de Mendoza, was requested by Viceroy Marqués de las Amarillas to make a confidential report

---

* Favoring aggressive military protection of the missions, Nentuig (Nentvig) wrote; "... it is not reasonable to remain content with our prayers and await to be freed by miracles ..." See Albert Francisco Pradeau, "Nentuig's 'Description of Sonora'," *Mid-America*, Vol. 35, No. 2 (April, 1953), p. 84.

on the revolt. Mendoza traveled the length and breadth of Pimería Alta and formed his opinion. He wrote that the Pimas had not risen against the Spaniards because of a dislike for the Jesuits, but because of the Indian's "natural inconstancy, love of liberty, and savage passion for living unrestrained according to his appetites." Amarillas was satisfied with Mendoza's findings and declared the dispute officially closed in 1758.[18]

Despite the extended dispute and the demoralization of the uprising itself, the padres assigned to Pimería Alta continued to minister to the needs of the neophytes at San Xavier and Guevavi in Arizona and at Suamca, Sáric, Tubutama, Caborca, San Ignacio, and Santa Teresa del Addi (Atil) in Sonora. The Jesuits went on with their mission work despite many obstacles, not the least of which was lack of support from the civil government. Jesuit persistence is described in *Rudo Ensayo* (Rough Essay), an anonymous account written in 1762 or 1763 and later realized as the work of Juan Nentuig. Describing San Xavier del Bac as the northernmost and last mission among the Pimas, Nentuig wrote:

... It is bounded on the west by the ranches of the Papagos who rove about this bleak wilderness; on the east by the Sobahipuris; and on the north, at a distance of about thirty leagues, by Casas Grandes and Pima of the Gila. At a distance of three leagues North ... lies the Post of Tucson with sufficient people and conveniences to found another Mission. Father Alphonsus [sic] Espinosa is the Minister of San Xavier, and he has to attend to more people than there are in all the other Missions. Many of the old people are new in the Faith, and he has to work hard with them to instruct them and keep in obedience; for such is their character that the Opatas, when they are advised by the priest to be obedient and gentle, say: "Are we perhaps Papagos?" *

Father Espinosa, mentioned in this passage, arrived at San Xavier early in 1756, after stopping at Guevavi where he baptized a native boy at the invitation of Father Pauer (also Paver) and signed the mission book on December 31, 1755.

---

* *Rudo Ensayo*. Tucson: Republished by Arizona Silhouettes, 1951, p. 110. The Opatas, an Indian group farther south in Sonora, were not as docile as the Papagos. The Papagos were classified by Kino as one of the four divisions of the Pimas. See Edward H. Spicer, *Cycles of Conquest*, Tucson: University of Arizona Press, 1962, p. 119.

For nearly twenty years the more populous mission of San
Xavier had been administered as only a *visita* of Guevavi. But
now, with the installation of Espinosa as a resident padre,
hundreds of heathens and marginal Christians, whether they
liked it or not, were to be provided with a chance for salvation.
Governor Mendoza, who accompanied Espinosa northward
with soldiers and toured Pimería, was determined that the
natives of Bac and Tucson, the "gateway to the Gila," should
be Christianized.[19] But Jabanimó, or "Crow's Head," the old
chief of the Gila Pimas, wanted no part of salvation and tried
to persuade the people of Bac and Tucson that they should
resist conversion. Espinosa himself probably contributed to a
native rebellion by trying to "purify" the traditional wine
feast that followed the cactus fruit harvest. Each year the
Indians celebrated this occasion with rain dances and a ceremony that resulted in the intoxication of the participants. Espinosa wished to eliminate these native elements of the event in
order to prevent drunkenness and to integrate the festival into
the church calendar as a Christian celebration. But the natives
wanted their centuries-old customs and rebelled against the
ecclesiastical restraints. Jabanimó and his warriors, including a
few Papagos and some of San Xavier's own neophytes, were
intent upon killing Father Espinosa. They ransacked and
pillaged the mission house and the huts of the loyal natives.
Espinosa managed to escape to the presidio of Tubac, however,
where word of the outbreak had been carried to Ensign Juan
María de Oliva. With only fifteen soldiers, Oliva rode to the
smoldering Bac and put the lingering enemy in flight.

Colonel Mendoza was not one to tolerate such an outrage
and wanted Jabanimó punished. He organized a punitive expedition of soldiers from the various presidios and recruited a
contingent of Indian auxiliaries. With himself at the head of
this force and Captain Francisco Elías González of Terrenate
second-in-command, Mendoza rode north in November. At
San Ignacio he acquired the services of a newly arrived German
Jesuit and cartographer named Bernardo Middendorff as chaplain. En route to the Gila the Governor also picked up Espinosa and reinstated him at San Xavier. From that point the
rebels were tracked to the Gila River and downstream to

the vicinity of modern Gila Bend where a battle was fought and the natives routed with a loss of fifteen killed. The revolt suppressed, Mendoza returned to San Xavier and laid the first stone for a church that Espinosa intended to build. Middendorff, who had been waiting at San Ignacio for an assignment at the time he joined Mendoza's Gila expedition, was designated to build a *cabecera* (head mission) at San Agustín del Tucson.[20]

The following excerpts from the first letter ever sent from Tucson was written in Latin by Middendorff to Father Juan Balthazar, procurator or treasurer of the missions, about two months after the Tucson project got under way. The letter gives a good picture of the situation in Arizona in 1756 and 1757:

That I have sent Your Reverence no letters in such a space of months, has not come about through forgetting of my duty or heedless will, but for this reason, that from this outmost boundary of Christianity (for my station is a day-and-a-half's journey from the Gila River) there is no one who might reliably carry letters down, and it is not known from any other place, if anyone live elsewhere, to whom they could be entrusted. In November and December I accompanied as Chaplain, the Lord Governor de Mendoza, who was conducting a Royal campaign of war against rebel Papagos and Cocomaric-Oopas, who had already before this started a war and thought to sate their savage rage by killing Father Alphonso Espinosa, and thought to wipe out in deadly destruction the Mission of San Xavier. But by the help of God fifteen of the enemy fell; the rest, whose number under the leadership of Gabanimo easily rose to fifty, the chief led off, in flight trackless in the mountains and hidden in the canyons.

... Your Reverence of your charity will not find it a burden to send me what I ask in the Memorandum; but what will be right to release as an alms to be sent hither, will see fit to release in Mexico. I pray Your Reverence not to send less than I ask, even though as to some items it seem a lot: it certainly will not be, for by having chocolate I can buy meat, which either I shall not eat this year or, if I do eat, it is already rancid, for I am 60 leagues distant from the Mission of San Ignacio, and Father Gaspar is my sole benefactor. Now I have not even wine for Mass nor anything to eat but grain. For the meat I cannot taste without nausea...

Your Reverence's
3 March 1757   least servant in Christ,
Bernard Middendorff
S.J.[21]

San Agustín, the first and only head mission in Tucson, existed for only about four months. When Middendorff arrived in January with an escort of ten soldiers, he had neither house nor church. He erected a brush and willow hut for lodging and celebrated Mass under a matting or cover of rushes and reeds which had been raised on four poles in the field. He had to instruct the natives, whose friendship he won with gifts of dried meat, through an interpreter. At first the people reciprocated with devotion and with gifts of birds' eggs and wild fruits. But the mutual affection was abruptly ended in May, 1757, when the rustic mission was attacked in the night by "about 500 savage heathen." Middendorff, who can be called Tucson's first bona fide European pioneer, escaped with his soldiers and the loyal families of San Xavier del Bac. And so ended abruptly the mission of San Agustín (St. Augustine) de Tucson. The post reverted back to the status of a *visita,* leaving Espinosa with the responsibility of both San Xavier and Tucson.

Remembering his unsuccessful attempt in 1756 to change the native wine festival into a Christian holiday, Espinosa learned to be patient with the Pimas. Even though their uncertain temper made it difficult for him to continue his missionary work, he proceeded to construct a church and bring in more livestock. He often found it necessary to call upon the commander at Tubac, a young officer named Juan Bautista de Anza, for military protection, but the soldiers were never near when needed. The Apaches, Seris, and even the Pimas themselves, raided the herds, driving off all the horses and reducing the number of livestock from a thousand to 200 head. Despite his problems, however, Espinosa stayed on the job to complete the church which he adorned with paintings and a candelabra brought from Mexico City.*

---

*For years no one seemed to know what happened to Espinosa's church which was located just west of the present San Xavier Mission. The mystery was finally solved by Bernard L. Fontana, ethnologist of the University of Arizona. In the process of excavating the site, Fontana found a row of pedestals running the length of what was a narrow twenty by eighty-five foot structure. He reasoned that Espinosa was unable to bring in logs from the Santa Catalina or the Santa Rita mountains because of the danger of Apache attack, and, therefore, hewed short ten foot beams, called *vigas,* from available mesquite trees. The twenty foot roof gap was bridged by using two short *vigas* supported by a post in the middle. Later, in the 1770s, the Franciscan priests dismantled the church and used the materials to build the *convento* wing on the other side of San Xavier. The *convento* is still used by resident priests at the mission. So Espinosa's church was never lost, but had to be recognized for what it was by an astute scholar of the mission.

After 1762 Espinosa had the added responsibility of assisting a new *ranchería* in the vicinity of the old mission of San Agustín. Several hundred Sobaípuri Pimas, who had been exposed to Apache raids in their homes along the San Pedro River, were escorted to the Santa Cruz by Captain Francisco Elías González, the commander at Terrenate who accompanied Mendoza on the Gila campaign in 1756. Elías named the new settlement San José del Tucson because the first group arrived on the holy day of that patriarch. The name of "San José" soon passed from use, but the *ranchería* was established, and by 1763 Father Espinosa was trying to change the economic base of the community by introducing cattle and sheep. The Indians, however, would have nothing to do with livestock, even though their native leader consented to the new enterprise. They preferred to work in their irrigated fields and then migrate to gather wild foods or to hunt after the harvest season.

Frustrated by this heathen vagabondage, Espinosa wrote in July, 1764: "All of them are an unsettled *ranchería*. At this time they live in their fields, and at the termination of what they have, in other towns in the mountains. Perhaps with the coming of the priest, supported by a good escort, they may be able to confine themselves to living like Christians in their town, which I have been unable to attain with all my diligence."[22]

Beginning with Father Kino in the 1690s, the Jesuits had been bringing Christianity to Tucson for about seventy years. But their efforts had been too intermittent to have much effect on the Indians beyond a superficial compliance. The *visitador,* Father Aguirre, visited in 1765 and reported that only a few of the 220 people in Tucson and 270 at San Xavier received the Eucharist sacrament. The sacrament of penance, however, was being received by 210 at Tucson and 240 at San Xavier. The hard-working Espinosa was in ill health and was replaced in 1765 by twenty-six year old José Neve who was the priest in charge when the expulsion order came from the king two years later.[23]

Though a native of New Spain, Neve was sent with the other surviving Sonoran missionaries to Spain and died in a hospital at Cadiz in 1773. Espinosa spent his last seventeen years in a monastery at El Yuste in western Spain, dying in

1786. Another padre who served in Arizona was Ignaz Pfeffer-korn, a German Jesuit who was at Guevavi in 1763. He was held in Spain for eight years after the expulsion and was permitted to leave for his native Germany only after Max Ferdinand, the Elector of Cologne, interceded with King Charles to secure his release. Pfefferkorn later wrote a valuable history of Sonora that he dedicated to the Elector.[24]

While Charles III expelled about 5,000 Jesuits from Spain, he refused to let most of the padres who had served in Sonora leave the country. It is possible that he foresaw war with the British Empire and believed that the missionaries who had served near the peninsula of California had knowledge that might be useful to a rival seapower. Whatever the reason for the King's change in attitude toward the Jesuits and his decision to expatriate some and not others, the effects were clear. The arbitrary decree of 1767 was vigorously enforced by the King's minions. The good fathers meekly submitted to the royal wish, and the work of the Society of Jesus, which stretched back over two centuries in Arizona, was suddenly ended.

THE FRANCISCANS: FRAY FRANCISCO GARCÉS

The more humble and tractable gray-robed friars of St. Francis came in June, 1767, to face the problems which had developed with the departure of their black-robed predecessors. They found that the formerly docile Pimas had become haughty and independent during a year of freedom from missionary control. Most of the mission establishments were in a decadent condition and subject to frequent attacks by the Apaches. The latter Indians were disdainful of all religious orders and presented at least one newly arrived Franciscan with an unwanted housewarming in his first year of residence. They swooped down upon San Xavier del Bac late in 1768 to pillage and destroy a part of Espinosa's adobe building while the little garrison of soldiers at Tubac, some forty-five miles away, stood helplessly by. But despite the insolence of the natives, the great distances between missions, and the need for additional missionaries to instruct the neophytes,

*King Charles III
of Spain.
(Painting in the
Prado Museum,
Madrid, Spain)*

Library of Congress

the Franciscans hastened to make the most of circumstances. At first they criticized their predecessors for not having taught the Indians to speak Spanish, but when the new fathers acquired sufficient knowledge of the Indian language, they had the good sense to instruct in it too. Despite the obstacles and the martyrdom of some good fathers, the Franciscans made progress, especially in the building of churches. Extensive explorations were made in the north with the view of expanding the mission field. By working industriously, the friars succeeded in bringing back much of the order and prosperity so long enjoyed under the Jesuits.

Fray Francisco Garcés, the Franciscan who was left with Father Espinosa's damaged mission at San Xavier, was ill at Guevavi at the time of the attack. He had taken charge on June 30, 1768, when San Xavier was the northernmost outpost of the Spanish empire and the least defended against incursions of the angry Apaches. The raids of these Indians continued until 1772, at which time the population of nearly 300 was able to stand off the invaders. Yet, Garcés was undaunted by the desolation and plunged cheerfully into his work of providing for the spiritual welfare of the people. The thirty-year-old native of Aragón was well suited for his chosen career and quickly found Indian assistants. One of his contemporaries wrote that Garcés was almost like an Indian himself. He would squat cross-legged with them in great serenity, and eat their coarse food, apparently enjoying every minute.

Within six months after reaching San Xavier, Garcés, who is sometimes called "the Kino of the Franciscans," journeyed to villages on both sides of the Gila and explored most of southwestern Arizona. In 1770, he repeated this junket in response to appeals from the Pimas. On this second visit to the more populous *rancherías* of the Gila, he ministered to the sick who were suffering from an epidemic of measles and baptized many of the Indians, some of whom were so eager for his teachings that they tried to detain him when he had to move on. In his discussions with the people he met — and he learned to speak the Pima tongue fluently — Garcés found that they had an idea of supreme beings to whom they prayed when they planted their fields or were sick. But he felt sure that their gods were the sun and the moon. Most pleasing to him about his second trip was the influx of a large number of Papagos to join the mission at San Xavier and his *visita* of San Agustín del Tucson, where a chapel and a fortified hacienda were constructed west of the river near Sentinel Peak (later called "A" Mountain) in the early 1770s.* Because of severe colds, fever, and several deaths in their new location, however, the superstitious Papagos became frightened and stopped coming. Consequently, Garcés wrote a long report in 1770 about his whole tour and explained the need for the establishment of new missions where the Indians had not seen sickness and suffering. His superiors had confidence in his plans and encouraged him to obtain further information.

---

* These structures were the first substantial buildings in Tucson. The chapel and a *convento* erected later in the mission period were still standing in 1852 when John Bartlett, the boundary commissioner, made a sketch of Tucson.

His third *entrada,* then, was more significant than the first two in that he was authorized to look for desirable mission sites. Also, in view of interest aroused in Mexico over the Spanish occupation of Monterey, Garcés was anxious to find a land route to California. With this twofold purpose in mind, he started out on August 8, 1771, with only three Indian guides to accompany him and a horse to carry equipment for saying mass. Traveling west over Kino's old trail, the *Camino del Diablo,* he reached the Yumas who welcomed him and showed an eagerness for conversation. Crossing the Colorado River near its mouth into present-day California, he ventured out over the Yuma desert and skirted the Cocopah Range in Baja California to its terminus at Signal Mountain. After recrossing the desert, a feat which Kino had tried in vain, Garcés learned that a state of war existed between the Yumas and the Gila tribes and decided to return to San Xavier by way of Sonoita. He arrived at his home mission on October 27, having traveled a total of 300 leagues, or 780 miles. Even more important, his heroic, lonely journey of nearly three months over mud flats and sand dunes was a link in the chain of forward moving events. His exploration convinced the Spanish authorities that an overland route could be opened to California. And his position as a dynamic factor in the frontier expansion of New Spain was firmly established. For the next decade his career was closely intertwined with that of a soldier, Captain Bautista de Anza.*

---

*The joint efforts of Fray Garcés and Captain Anza to advance the Spanish frontier may have been largely an alliance of convenience because the Captain questioned the effectiveness of the mission system in assimilating the natives into the ways of civilization. In his reports to Viceroy Antonio María Bucareli y Ursúa, Anza chided Garcés for promising missions to the heathens with whom he came in contact in his travels and explained that the mission had failed as an economic institution, partly because the Indians resented the amount of work and discipline expected of them by resident missionaries. He wrote that the missionaries were too paternalistic and criticized them for trying to establish little cities of God on earth where the natives were isolated from Spanish colonists and forced to work for the community instead of for themselves. Anza believed that the padres should concentrate on their spiritual ministry and leave the administration of political, vocational, and commercial activities to temporal authorities. See John L. Kessell, (ed.), "Anza Damns the Missions: A Spanish Soldier's Criticism of Indian Policy, 1772," *The Journal of Arizona History,* Vol. 13, No. 1 (Spring, 1972), pp. 53-62.

OVERLAND ROUTE TO CALIFORNIA

On his fourth entrada, Garcés accompanied an expedition headed by Captain Anza, commander of the presidio of Tubac and third generation Sonoran officer to bear that name. Anza had offered his services to Antonio María de Bucareli y Ursúa, the farseeing new viceroy at Mexico City who advocated the settling of Upper California. Commissioned by the viceroy to search for a feasible overland route from Sonora to the California missions, Anza began gathering horses, mules, and supplies. His departure scheduled for December 1773, was postponed when the Apaches swooped down on his *caballada* one night and stole 130 head, including many choice animals. Plans had to be changed. Originally intending to assemble the expedition at San Xavier and go by way of the Gila Pimas, Anza decided to turn around and go through Sonora via Caborca and Sonoita to avoid further Apache incursions on his herd. When Garcés rode the thirty miles from his mission to Tubac on January 6, everything was astir in final preparation for the journey. A year and a half had elapsed since Anza wrote his letter to Viceroy Bucareli and four months since the project was approved in Mexico City. Finally, on January 8, 1774, the interesting caravan which the captain had assembled got underway.

Besides Garcés the party included Padre Juan Díaz; Juan Valdés, a California guide and courier who was the "Kit Carson" of the expedition; twenty volunteer soldiers from the presidio of Tubac, one of whom carried a violin which proved useful in entertaining the Indians; Sebastián Tarabal, a runaway mission Indian who had been over the route from the Altar Valley to Yuma; an interpreter of the Pima tongue who is not named in any of the diaries; a carpenter; five muleteers; and two of Anza's personal servants. Well equipped with cattle and horses, the expedition traveled to the Sonoran missions and then meandered in a northwestward direction over *El Camino del Diablo*. This desert route was dangerous because of a scarcity of water, but winter was the best season in which to travel and there were no marauding Apaches with which to contend.

California State Library

Juan Bautista de Anza, commander of the presidio at Tubac, led two expeditions to California and founded San Francisco in 1776. This drawing is based on an original oil painting by Fray Orsi.

After reaching the Colorado River near the site of present-day Yuma, Anza lingered awhile to cultivate the friendship of Chief Olleyquotequiebe (the Wheezer), better known as Palma. This man's good will was needed since he ruled the Yumas and they in turn controlled the ford across the Colorado near its juncture with the Gila. Diplomatically Anza got off on the right foot when he assembled the tribe around

his tent and dramatically presented the chief with a silver medal embossed with the head of Charles III. The Indians cheered as Anza strung the gift on a red ribbon and placed it around Palma's neck. Presents for the tribe and a speech by Anza completed the ceremonies; everybody was happy and the Spanish leader trustingly decided to leave some of his supplies and animals with the Indians for use on the return trip. The next day, February 8, the native people guided the expedition across the Gila River near the original townsite of Yuma and also assisted in fording the Colorado the following day without wetting anything of importance. The Anza luck was holding out since the spring floods had not yet begun and the streams were at low water.

Leaving the Yuma area, the expedition traveled downstream for three days to a point called Santa Olaya. Then, on February 13, Anza said goodbye to Palma, who had accompanied the expedition thus far, and set forth westward. The arduous journey across the Colorado Desert in Baja California and through the mountains to San Gabriel was completed by March 22. Garcés guided the military command as far as San Gabriel, on this first overland expedition to reach California from Pimería Alta, and then returned to the Yuma crossing while Anza moved on to Monterey. Garcés, two muleteers, and nine soldiers remained with the Yumas to await the com-

Diorama showing the expedition of Captain Juan Bautista de Anza having difficulty crossing the sand dunes near the Salton Sea west of the Colorado River in California in 1774.

Los Angeles County
Museum of Natural History

mander. But another hero of the desert drama, Valdés, continued on across the *Camino del Diablo* accompanied by only two soldiers to Horcasitas. From there the "Castilian Kit Carson" continued alone carrying the precious diaries and letters to Mexico City.

Captain Anza reached San Dionisio (Kino's name for the junction of the Colorado and Gila rivers) on May 10, and again there was a jubilant display of friendship between the Spaniard and Indian. Chief Palma regretted telling Anza that the Spaniards who were left with him had departed, but explained that he turned over the cattle and provisions left in his charge to Garcés. Because the rivers were now rising, the Yumas made a large raft for the Anza party. The chief himself carried Anza and Father Díaz to the raft. "On it I crossed the rivers which must be six hundred varas wide,"* Anza wrote in his diary, "but I felt so secure that in all my life I have never crossed another river with greater confidence, since even though the craft might have capsized I had close by me more than five hundred persons ready to rescue me . . . At five o'clock in the afternoon I reached the camp where Father Garcés and the soldiers who had come ahead were awaiting me, and they confirmed the reports already related. . . ."[25]

---

* The *vara* measurement mentioned by Anza was slightly less than a yard in length.

Anza decided to return to Tubac by way of the shorter Gila River route instead of by Caborca. Supplies requested by Garcés from the governor of Sonora were coming over the latter route, but they were not needed and Anza was doubtless thinking of future journeys to the Colorado. The captain and the chief then said goodbye. In gratitude for a pledge of loyalty and fidelity to the king, Anza presented his Yuma friend with his own bastion, four beeves, and some articles of clothing. "I should have been glad," he wrote, "to be able to still further reward this heathen barbarian, whose equal perhaps is not to be found among people of his kind."

Confident that the strategic Yuma crossing was in cooperative hands, Anza pushed on up the Gila with his reunited party. For him it was new ground, but Garcés was well acquainted with the region and guided the group eastward as far as the Cocomaricopa settlement of San Simón y Judas de Upasoitac where the town of Gila Bend is located today. From this point, reached on May 21, Anza proceeded on his own to Tubac while Garcés detoured north of the Gila to determine if he could send a letter to the friars in New Mexico by means of the intervening tribes. He had been specifically instructed to search for another route to California, this one from New Mexico across the present state of Arizona. Leaving the Pimas on May 24, he was accompanied by two Jalchedunes who had offered to guide him to their people who lived on the Colorado River below the Bill Williams Fork. Among the Jalchedunes* he observed better fields and other advantages which these people had over Palma's people farther south. They planted cotton and made better arrows. Living in a cooler climate, most of them dressed in blankets and blue cloth from the Moqüi villages and from Pimería. Their enemies were the Mojaves to the north and for that reason they refused to join Garcés in his wanderings upstream where he visited with some Yavapais. But the Jalchedunes did promise to deliver his letter to New Mexico after the mesquite beans ripened and also provided him with information that was useful for later explorations in

---

* The Jalchedunes (also spelled Halchidomas today) were a Yuman people who were driven eastward in the late 1700s and early 1800s by the Mojaves; they settled along the Gila and merged with the tribe known today as the Maricopa.

northern Arizona. They told him of the Moqüi five days to the east, of the New Mexican friars seven days to the east, and of traders who came from the northeast wearing ribbons in their hair. Thankful for this knowledge as well as for the provisions which they furnished him, Garcés departed for San Xavier, leaving his letter to the Franciscans with the Indians and to providence.

The Jalchedunes offered him several servants but since he had nothing with which to repay them he chose only one who accompanied him part of the way as a cook. As the friar rode along wearing his flat hat and his cape flowing in the June breezes, the Jalchedune walked behind. Appreciative of the man's attention, Garcés wrote about him:

. . . He carried a firebrand in one hand all the way, and it did not go out. In the other hand he carried a stick with which to drive the horse, which could not hurry for lack of shoes, especially where there were stones. And besides all this he carried a jug of water on his head, enduring thirst in order that I might not suffer, and all this with a smiling face. Who will say that this Indian is a savage? And who will not praise a service of such qualities?"[26]

Returning to Upasoitac, Garcés ascended the Gila with Cocomaricopa guides who escorted him to his old friends the Pimas. This visit only confirmed the friar's conviction that the latter Indians could be the most meritorious in the king's realm if given the proper attention. Well supplied with food from irrigated fields, and eager for missionaries to baptize their children, the Pimas were ideally located and suited for assisting in the "subjugation of the Apaches and for direct transit to Monterey and New Mexico." A tempting prospect, indeed, and it must have been in Garcés's thoughts as he rode into San Xavier on June 10, 1774, after six months in the wilderness. Little did he know at the time that his request for missions on the Gila would have to take a back seat to Captain Anza's proposals for missions and presidios on the Colorado and especially to the Viceroy's plan to develop Upper California first.

After Anza left Garcés at Upasoitac, he cut across the Gila Bend and hurried back to Tubac in five days. He stopped at the site of the Sutaquison ruins at Vah Ki, located approximately where the Interstate 10 freeway now crosses the Gila, and appointed a governor for the 2,000 people who had a good wheat crop about ready for harvest. Here he was told that the Apaches had recently raided the village, killing sixty persons. Farther upstream at Uturituc, between Vah Ki and modern Sacatón, he found 3,000 frightened people living close together for defense against the Apaches. These people were as industrious as the natives of Vah Ki. Anza wrote that "the fields of wheat which they have at present are so large that, standing in the middle of them, one can not see the ends, because they are so long. Their width is also great, embracing the whole width of the valley on either side, and their fields of maize are of corresponding size."[27] Father Díaz was amazed too, commenting that the only implement used in cultivating the vast fields was a wooden stick, with which to make holes in the ground for seed. The still larger settlement around the Casa Grande ruins was mentioned by Anza, but to save time he left the Gila before reaching it and traveled directly over the waterless route to Tuquisón (Tucson). The next day, May 26, he was home in Tubac after an absence of four and a half months. But disappointment awaited. Orders to report to Adjutant Inspector Antonio Bonilla at Terrenate for temporary service at that presidio forced him to postpone a trip to Mexico City. It was not until November that he was able to deliver his complete diary to Viceroy Bucareli and report in person on the success of his California project. Anza's fame preceded him, however. On October 4, King Charles had promoted him to lieutenant-colonel of cavalry and granted each soldier who accompanied him on the expedition — except for three who deserted their posts at Yuma — a pay bonus of one extra *escudo* (gold coin) a month for life. Furthermore, he selected Anza to lead a colonizing expedition to San Francisco. Pleased though he was with his new assignment, Anza was disappointed that consideration of his proposals for a mission and a presidio at the Yuma crossing would have to be postponed. The quiet Friar Díaz supported his argument that any mission located among the Yumas would be free from Apache raids and would supplement the presidio in helping to keep the peace and in insuring the safety of California-bound travelers. The Viceroy appeared to be convinced but emphasized that his first objective was to colonize

Upper California. The Yuma settlement could be established later.

Eager to get underway, the newly promoted lieutenant-colonel set about making the necessary preparations for the difficult journey. After recruiting settlers and soldiers in Sinaloa and Sonora, Anza assembled his colonists at the presidio of San Miguel de Horcasitas. The male members were armed and taught how to shoot. Each person was given new clothing and shoes. Cattle were purchased to furnish a food supply. Three casks of brandy were taken in event of snakebite or, according to Anza's requisition, for other needs that might arise. Satisfied with the personnel and equipment, Anza led the party from Horcasitas to Tubac. At the latter place, Anza was disappointed to learn that the Apaches had raided the corrals of the presidio and driven off many of the good horses upon which he had counted for the remainder of the trip. He replaced as many as possible and by October 23, 1775, the expedition was ready to move. This time Anza chose the better-known and easier Gila route since the colonists were inexperienced. The caravan that marched out of Tubac down the Santa Cruz Valley included 240 persons, a majority of whom were women and children. All but one of the thirty soldiers had his wife with him and most of the colonists had their families.* Along with the party went Fray Garcés and Fray Thomas Eixarch who had been selected to establish missions at the mouth of the Gila. Another friar, Fray Pedro Font, was to continue on to California as diarist and chaplain for the expedition. There were more than 1000 head of stock, including nearly 700 horses and mules in addition to 355 cattle to be used either for food along the way or for breeding animals in California. In the luggage there was an ample supply of tools and tents as well as 350 pounds of tobacco and free food for the

---

* The wife of Lt. José Joaquin Moraga was ill and did not go at this time. Moraga was left in charge of the presidio at San Francisco when Anza returned to Tubac. Soldiers from Tubac who accompanied the expedition were: Corporal Marcial Sánchez, Juan de Espinoza, Joseph Marcos Ramírez, Juan Antonio Valencia, Joseph Torivio Coróna, Juan Joseph Rodríquez, Joseph María Martínez, Joseph Pablo Corona, Francisco Figuroa, Juan Martínez, Joseph Antonio Acedo, Ysidro Martínez, Joseph Antonio Romero, Pasqual Rivera, Juan Miguel Palomino, Joseph de Ayala, and Juan Angel Castillo. See "Correspondence," in *Anza's California Expeditions*, Vol. V. Translated from the original Spanish manuscripts by Herbert Eugene Bolton. New York: Russell & Russell, 1966, p. 203.

Indians. A supply of extra clothing included four pairs of stockings and six yards of ribbon for each woman. With 1000 miles of desert and mountains over which to drive, water, and feed the unwieldy herd — not to mention the responsibility of caring for 240 human beings — Anza had a job ahead of him.

The men of the cloth were kept busy from the beginning. The first night out from Tubac, Señora Félix died at La Canoa giving birth to her eighth child. With a party of four soldiers, Garcés took her body to San Xavier for burial. The next day, at the same mission, Fray Font baptized the new baby boy and solemnized three marriages of members of the expedition. Font also started his diary. Summarizing the first stage of the journey from Tubac to the Gila, a 100-mile dusty trail down the Santa Cruz past Red Rock and Picacho Peak, he wrote, "In all this land of the Papaguería which we have passed through I did not see a single thing worthy of praise . . ."[28] And in sizing up the Pimas he was not much more enthusiastic. Whereas Garcés was especially happy to be among these people, Father Font's interest in them went little beyond their salvation. Describing them as corpulent, very ugly and black — especially the women — he attributed their appearance and offensive odor to a coarse diet of grass seeds and *pechita,* which is the mesquite pod ground into atole. Font did concede, however, that the Pimas covered their bodies more decently than did Anza's favorites, the Yumas. And despite his prudish and overly critical attitude toward the natives, the diarist had a keen eye and gathered some enlightening data on the Gila Pimas, or Gileños as he called them. For example, he observed that while missions for this country were desirable because the people were self-supporting and gentle, there were two drawbacks. First, the Gileños were so harassed by Apaches that a presidio would be needed for protection. And, second, a presidio would be difficult to maintain because pasture land on which to support military horses or to raise cattle was scarce.

The slow trip down the Gila Valley by way of the Opa and Cocomaricopa settlements was in many ways uneventful. Babies were born and baptized. Families gathered together each night and cooked meals of beans and tortillas over campfires. Father Font, in spite of an affliction of the fever, kept watch over the manners and morals of his flock, reprimanding jealous soldiers who forbade their wives to talk to anybody or to attend mass. Anza had his troubles too. Cattle meandered away into the brush along the river and turned wild. Horses died from drinking salty water or were abandoned because of exhaustion. Saddles grew hard and feet heavy. The glistening alkali of the desert flats caused eyes to smart and throats to burn. Emigrants grew weary. But no one turned back and if Anza became impatient he did not show it in his diary.

Late in November the Spaniards reached the Colorado country and renewed friendships with Chief Palma. Anza was embarrassed to explain that the settlers and padres in his party were not the ones which had been promised to the chief. Palma was disappointed but treated his guests cordially. Beans, grains, and watermelons were provided. The melons were a welcomed out-of-season dessert that puzzled the Spaniards until they learned how the Yumas buried them in the sand. Anza estimated that at least 3000 melons were served. With all the shouting, dancing and hullabaloo, the picnic along the Colorado must have been a festive occasion.

Anxious to continue the journey, Anza declined Palma's offer to build rafts on which to move the Spaniards and their possessions to the opposite side of the river. With a little searching and the help of a soldier "of spirit," he found a place where the Colorado spread out 300 or 400 yards in width and ran in three channels making two islands. A ford having been found, the commander sent men with axes to open a road through the brush so that a crossing could be made the following day, November 30. Most of the men waded while the women and children were transported on the tallest horses guided through the waters by Indians. The friars were offered horses, but Garcés did not trust them and was carried over on the shoulders of three Yumas, his body stretched out face up as if he were dead. Font got his knees wet even though he rode a tall mount; three naked servants accompanied him, one in front guiding the horse and one on each side to keep him from falling. He complained, however, because the muleteers were careless with his belongings. The only pack that got wet was the one containing his holy oils and the vestments. "This is because so little attention was paid to me and to what I said . . .," he wrote.

With the Spaniards safely on the California side, the Indians were rewarded with presents of beads and tobacco. Palma donned the gala outfit which Anza brought him as a gift from Viceroy Bucareli. It consisted of a jacket with a yellow front and some decorations, blue trousers, a gold-braided blue cape, and a cap of black velvet adorned with imitation jewels and a palm-like crest. The chief's new clothes and the gifts which the other Yumas received made the successful river crossing a happy occasion for all. The next day, work started on a cabin for Fathers Garcés and Eixarch; Anza set aside a supply of provisions to sustain them for four months and gave them a bottle of sacramental wine for the mission. Before the dwelling was completed, however, he once again hit the trail with a soldier counting off the distance — 4000 weary paces to the league. Crossing both the desert and snow-covered mountains was a severe test of endurance. But the hardy band, with a boost in morale from the brandy kegs at Christmas time, arrived at San Gabriel on January 3, 1776, with four births having increased the size of the caravan.

Soon the colonists continued north to the San Francisco Bay area. After selecting a site for the colony, where the city by the Golden Gate now stands, Anza turned over his command to Lieutenant José Joaquín Moraga. Accompanied by Fray Font and a dozen mounted soldiers, he hurried back to the Yuma crossing in ten days. There he found only Eixarch performing his missionary tasks; the peripatetic Garcés was out on the trail for the second time since Anza's departure from the Colorado.

During December, 1775, Garcés had explored the lower Colorado region. Always in search of souls, he carried his famous linen print with the Virgin Mary holding the child Jesus on one side and the picture of a lost soul on the other. Presented with this simplified visual story of salvation, the Indians were more easily converted. They usually told Garcés that they would accept padres and Spaniards to live among them. Father Font, who often doubted the sincerity of the Indian converts, nevertheless appreciated Garcés's way with the natives. He wrote that Garcés was so well fitted to go among them that he appeared to be but an Indian himself. He was "phlegmatic" like the Indian, sat in a circle with them for hours, and ate their "nasty and dirty" food with great gusto saying that it was good for the stomach. "In short," said Font, "God has created him, as I see it, solely for the purpose of seeking out these unhappy, ignorant, and rustic people." [29]

In January, 1776, Garcés returned to the Yuma villages for a few days before embarking on another journey, this time up the Colorado. He visited the Mojaves, who were then called Yamajabes (or Jamajabs), and certain neighboring Indians including the Yavapais. After securing information from these people about the northern region of present-day Arizona, the friar made a quick trip back to visit the faithful Eixarch. But always restless, he set forth in the middle of February upon one of his most ambitious explorations. Hoping to find a shorter route from the Colorado River to Monterey or San Luis Obispo and eventually to mark out a direct trail from Santa Fe to the California presidio, he traveled northward to a point near the modern city of Needles, California. Turning westward he reached the San Gabriel mission on March 24, having followed the approximate route over which the Santa Fe Railroad was built through the Mohave Desert to Los Angeles a century later. On the way back to Arizona, Garcés went north across the San Bernardino Mountains and Tehachapi Range to the upper San Joaquín Valley. By May 30, he was again in the Mojave villages near the Colorado, two weeks after the departure of Anza and Fray Font from Yuma for Mexico.

Encouraged by the Walapai and the other northern Arizona Indians, Garcés decided to blaze a trail to the Hopi country. On this venture he traveled with Walapai guides into an unknown wilderness among strange savages. Leaving the Mojave villages on June 4 he passed through the site of modern Kingman and visited the Havasupais at the Grand Canyon. On July 2 he reached Oraibi, now considered to be the oldest continuously inhabited community on the North American continent. But since the Hopi were very unfriendly and uninterested in his pictures of heaven and hell, he spent only two days among them. They would not invite him into their homes nor accept his gifts. One elderly man did kiss his "el Cristo" and received tobacco and shells in return, but otherwise Garcés was repudiated and made to feel unwelcome.

The natives looked upon him as a spy from the Yumas, Pimas, and other enemies of the Hopis. They also feared that the Spanish wished to conquer and humiliate them. Not since the rebellion of 1680 had they been friendly to the white man. Thus the information about the Hopis that Garcés was able to garner and record in his diary was very limited. In regard to their clothes he wrote that the women wore blankets. The men had leather jackets, trousers, boots, and shoes when outdoors but donned black blanketing and moccasins while inside their pueblos. Concerning agriculture, the unwanted visitor reported that he saw peach orchards, herds of sheep, and garden plots near the springs. And as he huddled in a corner of the village at night, he heard singing, flute playing, and loud talking from the crowds which gathered on the roof tops to cool off.

On July 3, Garcés wrote a letter to Fray Silvestre Vélez de Escalante, the missionary at Zuñi, stressing the importance of a northern route from New Mexico to Monterey. He had no way of knowing that Escalante was at that very moment preparing for a journey in an attempt to do exactly what was urged in the letter. Nor could Garcés have known about the great event across the continent in Philadelphia the next day (July 4, 1776) when he wrote the following passage in his diary:

July 4. As soon as day broke I heard singing and dancing in the streets; the rout (el bayle) passed by the (place) where I was, and then only did I see that some of the Indians were painted red, with feathers and other decorations on the head, beating the sound of the dance on a kind of drum (batea) with two small sticks, to which the flutes played an accompaniment; and many persons kept time to the music (seguia el baile mucha gente) as well through the streets as on the house-tops. I observed that in some places the procession paused. The sun having now risen, I saw coming nigh unto me a great multitude of people (the sight of) which caused me some fear of losing my life. There came forward four Indians who appeared to be principals, of whom the tallest one asked me with a grimace (*risueño*), "For what hast thou come here? Get thee gone without delay — back to thy land!" I made them a sign to be seated, but they would not. I arose with the Santo Cristo in my hand, and partly in Yuma, partly in Yabipai, and partly in Castillian, with the aid of signs, which are the best language to use with Indians, I explained to them my route, naming the nations whom I had seen, those who had kissed el Cristo; I told them that all these had been good to me, that I also loved the Moqüis, and for that reason I came to say to them that God is in the sky, and that this señor whom they saw on the cross was the image of God, Jesu-Cristo, who is good. To this responded an old man in Castillian language and making a wry face, "No! No!" Then I said, "Fetch my mule!" After a little the Yabipai youth appeared with her, and having arranged my things I mounted on her back, showing by my smiling face how highly I appreciated their pueblo and their fashions.[30]

If Garcés had failed as a missionary to the Hopis, he had at least succeeded as an explorer. In proving the feasibility of a northern overland route to the west coast, he had traveled the entire distance, except for the already well-known eastern section between Oraibi and Santa Fe. From Hopiland he retraced his steps back to the Mojave villages and down the Colorado to the Yumas where he arrived on August 27. Three weeks later he was once again at his mission of San Xavier del Bac. In the wilderness almost continuously for nearly eleven months, he had traveled more than 2000 miles and opened up trails that are now traversed by highways and railroads.

Meanwhile, Colonel Anza had gone to Mexico City where he received a hero's welcome. Praise was heaped upon him for opening the king's highway to the Pacific. But, unfortunately, his advice that missions and presidios be established at the all-important Yuma crossing went unheeded for three years. Even the presence of Chief Palma and three other Indian chiefs from the Colorado who had accompanied him to the capital city had little effect. The Indian leaders came with Anza to Mexico City to meet Viceroy Bucareli and to present a petition in behalf of the Yumas.[31] While in the city Palma received instruction in Christianity. In the presence of his godfather, Juan Bautista de Anza, he was baptized in the imposing Cathedral of Mexico as Salvador Carlos Antonio Palma. The chief was then sent back to his people with a silver-headed cane, a symbol of Spanish trust in him, and with glowing promises of missionaries and settlers to come. Supposedly, there would be plenty of beads, tobacco, bright-colored cloth, and blankets for everyone.

Why the Spanish government failed to follow up its advantage with the Yumas is none too clear. Spain's traditional attitude of procrastination in capitalizing on her explorations, the expensive Apache warfare, the promotion and transfer of the capable Anza to the governorship of New Mexico, and the possible involvement of Spain in the American Revolution have all been given as reasons to explain why nothing was done. In March of 1778, Chief Palma made a trip to Altar to find out what was holding up the missions. Stalled again, Palma returned home to await the fulfillment of promises, only to see another year elapse. His people began taunting him, saying that he had been stuffed with lies. Such indignities caused the chief to journey again to Altar. This time the report of his visit was sent to the Comandante General of the Internal Provinces of northern New Spain, Teodoro de Croix, who began immediately to expedite the project.

THE YUMA MISSION-PRESIDIO

At long last, Garcés was given the go-ahead to establish a mission at the mouth of the Gila. Eager to get started, he did not wait for the complete escort to be assigned to him, but proceeded to the Yuma crossing with two soldiers in August, 1779. A worse time to start a mission among the Yumas could not have been chosen. The summer was abnormally dry and hot in Papaguería and the Indians were tired of waiting for the Spanish promises to be fulfilled. The two military escorts did not help the situation when they returned to Sonoita bearing messages of distress to the remainder of the party — Father Juan Díaz and ten rebellious, poorly equipped men from the presidios of Altar and Tucson. Though urged to abandon the Yuma project, Díaz overcame the reluctance of the soldiers and led the motley cavalcade to the Colorado, arriving on

October 2. There, despite the uncooperative soldiers, inadequate supplies, and the growing hostility of the natives, the two friars set about establishing a mission on the California side of the river. The Indians were disgusted with the petty nature of the missionary project and made no pretense to hide their resentment. Expecting lavish gifts, they were not satisfied with the beggarly kit brought by the friars. The fact that the holy men lacked the means for their own subsistence only added to the ill-feeling.

After several months, the hostile atmosphere became almost untenable and Díaz was sent to Arispe in Sonora to plead with Croix for aid. The *Comandante* sent him back with a plan that had little chance of succeeding. Two hybrid-type establishments were to be set up in the Yuma country. Designed to save money, both units would be a combination mission-presidio-settlement with the military in charge. Each would have two missionaries, nine or ten soldiers, ten families of colonists, and a half-dozen laborers.[32] Croix was severely criticized for his "mongrel" settlements. Anza, for example, felt that the experiment was doomed from the first without the protection of a strong presidio. His objections went unheeded, however, and the missionaries went ahead with their work as best they could.

In all fairness to Croix, some explanation of his position is in order. Prior to 1776, the northern frontier of New Spain was governed by the viceroy in Mexico City who had neither the time nor the experience to direct the defense of the distant borderlands. When Visitor General José de Galvez toured the area in 1769 he found it much neglected. He reported that disaster, if not depopulation, was imminent unless administrative changes were made. The Royal Regulations of 1772 brought about some of the recommended changes. But whereas Galvez had recommended that an independent office of commander-general be created, the Regulations provided only for an inspector-general to operate under the supervision of the viceroy. In 1776, however, a commander-general was appointed who had complete authority in the Internal Provinces, though he was still dependent upon the viceroy for troops and supplies.* Teodoro de Croix, long recognized for his distinguished service and the nephew of a former viceroy of New Spain, was the first appointee. By 1780 he had greatly improved the defense forces along the frontier. His failure to give adequate support to the Yuma project must be considered in light of the total demands for protection of a frontier that extended almost 2000 miles and the necessity placed upon Croix by King Carlos III for keeping expenses at a minimum. Besides, Garcés and Díaz assured him that the proposed plan could be made to work.

The two mission-presidio colonies got underway in the fall of 1780. La Puerta de la Purísima Concepción was located across the Colorado, on an elevation called Mission Hill, opposite the old Yuma territorial prison. There, Garcés and Father Juan Barraneche (or Barrenche), the young missionary sent to assist him, directed the construction of a church out of logs and mud. Nearby, the soldiers built a guardhouse and one-room cabins where they would live when their wives and children arrived. The other establishment, called San Pedro y San Pablo de Bicuñer, was about twelve miles up the Colorado in the vicinity of Laguna Dam with Díaz and Fray Matias Moreno in charge. The latter arrived in June, 1781, just in time to become a martyr.†

Despite the zeal and hard work of the missionaries, tension with the Indians continued to mount. The arrogant

---

* The Interior Provinces under Croix's jurisdiction eventually included Nueva Vizcaya, Sonora, Sinaloa, the Californias, New Mexico, Coahuila, Chihuahua, Texas, Nuevo Léon, and Nuevo Santander. See Alfred B. Thomas (translator and editor). *Teodoro de Croix and the Northern Frontier of New Spain, 1776-1783*. From the Original Document in the Archives of the Indies, Sevillle. Norman: University of Oklahoma Press, 1941, p. 17. See also Herbert I. Priestley, *José de Galvez: Visitor General of New Spain, 1765-1771*. Berkeley: University of California Press, 1916, pp. 293-95. For a description of the military frontier and the reorganization of the Spanish Empire in the 1760s and 1770s, see Sidney B. Brinckerhoff and Odie B. Faulk, *Lancers for the King: A Study of the Frontier Military System of Northern New Spain With a Translation of the Royal Regulations of 1772*. Phoenix: Arizona Historical Foundation, 1965.

† Concepción was definitely on present-day Fort Yuma Hill (Mission Hill), but the location of Bicuñer has been in doubt. Though most historical maps show it downstream from Yuma in the vicinity of Pilot Knob, there is good evidence that the exact site was upstream, south of Laguna Dam on the California side of the Colorado River. For an analysis of the relevant records see Richard Yates, "Locating the Colorado River Mission San Pedro y San Pablo de Bicuñer," *The Journal of Arizona History*, Vol. 13, No. 2 (Summer, 1972), pp. 123-29.

soldiers, who lacked the kindliness of the friars, jeered the natives for their primitive method of planting — punching a hole in the soil with a stick and dropping in the seeds. They also crowded the Indians out of the missions and confiscated the better farm lands. Little attention was paid to the rights of the aborigines, whose little *milpas* (cornfields), if spared at all in the formal distribution of lands, were rendered useless by the livestock of the colonists. The overuse of the whipping post and the stocks by Lieutenant Santiago de Islas, resident comandante at Concepción was especially galling to the Indians. And worst of all, the Spaniards grazed their horses on the beans of the dense mesquite trees which covered the banks of the Colorado. The Yumas used these beans very much as other tribes used wheat or maize. Ground into flour, roasted, or boiled, the beans furnished a nourishing food supply. When the wanton foraging continued, even Chief Palma turned against the Spaniards and began plotting to drive the white men out. Alarmed by the chief's defection, the Spaniards sent a military party in June, 1781, to mission San Gabriel in California for reinforcements.

About the time that the military messengers returned with only clothing and money, there arrived from Sonora, via Tucson and the Gila route, a large party of recruits and a few experienced soldiers headed for the California settlements. The party had more than forty soldiers, thirty of whom were accompanied by their wives and children. Led by the arrogant, blundering lieutenant-governor of Baja California, the once-competent but now aging Captain Javier Fernando de Rivera y Moncada, the party brought a *caballada* of nearly 1000 head of horses and mules. Needless to say, the Yumas were alarmed by this new transgression. Not only did the Spaniards fail to bring gifts but they fanned the fires of discontent by letting their animals browse in the mesquite groves. Furthermore, Rivera, who had been excommunicated for cruelty to an Indian when he was the comandante in upper California, quickly showed his contempt for the lowly Yumas by announcing a new deal for the crossing. He refused to recognize either the authority of the padres or the Indian ownership of lands. His whipping of several Yumas for stealing Spanish property did not improve matters, especially since the natives were in some cases simply retrieving their own horses which the Spaniards had taken. Bad as it was, the situation could have been worse. Most of the company of soldiers commanded by Ensign Andrés Arías Caballero, of the presidio of Tucson, promptly returned home after traveling with the Rivera caravan to the crossing. And another party which met Rivera at Yuma to escort him to San Gabriel consisted only of Sergeant Juan José Robles and six men. Finally, in his one act of wisdom, Rivera dispatched a party to San Gabriel.[33] Included were all the married men with their families, Ensign Cayetano Limón and nine soldiers from the Tucson detachment, Lieutenant Diego González and Ensign José Darío Argüello,* who was at later periods to serve as governor of both Baja and Alta California. All the animals able to travel were sent with this party to California.

To find better pasturage for the remaining animals, Rivera crossed to the eastern bank of the river with about a dozen men, including Sergeant Robles and five or six soldiers from the California presidios. Camping in an Indian field near the present site of downtown Yuma, he intended to remain long enough to restore the horses and cattle to their proper condition before continuing on to San Gabriel. Having no respect for the Yuma Indians whom he described as being dirty and lazy, Rivera refused to believe warnings that they were plotting rebellion. It was inconceivable to him that

---

* A native of Querétaro, New Spain, José Darío Argüello worked his way up from the ranks in the army. He first went to California with the Rivera expedition in 1781 and eventually became a temporary governor of Alta California (1814-15) when his friend, Governor José Joaquín de Arillaga, died. In 1815, Argüello was chosen governor of Baja California, a post which he held without pay until 1822. His greatest distinction, perhaps, is that he had two famous children. His son, Luis Antonio Argüello, was the first popularly elected governor of Alta California after Mexico achieved independence from Spain. José's daughter, Concepción, created quite a stir in Spanish California when she fell in love with Nikolai Petrovich Rezanov, a chamberlain of the Czar who came to San Francisco in 1806 in search of food to supply the Russian colony of Sitka. Leaving his bride-to-be in California, Rezanov sailed away with a laden ship, promising to go to Madrid after his return to St. Petersburg to smooth over misunderstandings between the two Pacific Coast powers. After years of waiting for news of Rezanov, Señorita Argüello, who took the vows of the Dominican order in 1850, finally learned that he had died in Siberia on his way home. See Charles E. Chapman, *A History of California: The Spanish Period.* New York: The Macmillan Co., 1939, pp. 439-40; Ralph J. Roske, *Everyman's Eden: A History of California.* New York: The Macmillan Co., 1968, p. 153; and Andrew F. Rolle, *California: A History.* 3rd ed. New York: Thomas Y. Crowell Co., 1970, pp. 106 and 133-38.

these creatures of the desert would consider fighting during the dreadful heat of summer. He did not even bother to post a guard or to maintain contact with the soldiers at Concepción.

This was the situation when the storm burst upon the unsuspecting Spaniards on July 17, 1781. First a mob of angry Indians struck the mission of San Pedro y San Pablo and killed both Father Díaz and Father Moreno, beheading the latter with an ax. Most of the male inhabitants were murdered. But for some reason, unique in the annals of Indian rampages, a few of the men and all of the women and children were spared and later put to work, but not mistreated.* Some of the survivors were compelled to cast all the sacred icons and altar vessels into the river. To complete the destruction, fire was set to the church and the Spanish dwellings. A few hours later at Concepción, the yelling Indians surrounded the church where Garcés was giving mass. Commander Islas rushed out and was clubbed to death and the intrepid friar who dashed out to give him absolution barely escaped back into the church. Not as thorough here in their diabolical fury as at Bicuñer, the attackers ransacked the dwellings of the Spaniards, killed most of the white men working in the fields, threw the commander's body in the river, and departed without molesting the few people who took refuge in the church. The next morning, however, the aroused Indians carried their bloody work to the Arizona side of the river where Rivera put up a gallant but futile defense. One by one all the men fell before the Indian arrows and clubs. Then the marauders returned to complete the holocaust at Concepción. After plundering and destroying the chapel and homes of the Spaniards, the more vicious Yumas began searching for Garcés and Barraneche, who were finally found on July 19 and beaten to death with clubs and sticks. Friendly Indians who had sheltered the two fathers reverently buried the bodies after the departure of the murderers.

---

* The men who survived the so-called Yuma Massacre were José Reyes Pacheco, Pedro Solares, and Miguel Antonio Romero, soldiers; Matías de Castro, Juan José Miranda, José Ignacio Bengachea, and José Urrea, settlers.

So it happened that the only Spanish missions ever established on the Colorado were founded in blunder and ended
in blood. All totaled, about fifty Spanish men were brutally
killed in the three-day Yuma revolt. When Ensign Limón
rode into Bicuñer, en route to Tucson from San Gabriel late
in August, he found the buildings burned and saw the decap-
itated body of Father Moreno. Limón himself was attacked
and wounded but managed to escape and hurried back to
San Gabriel to report the massacre. Refused troops to strike
the Yumas, he took a southern route to Sonora where he
found Croix, already informed, preparing to send a punitive
force to the Yuma crossing to rescue or ransom the captives.

The enraged Commander-General did send several expeditions to avenge the victims of the Yuma uprising. On September 16, 1781, the hard-riding Lieutenant Colonel Pedro
Fages departed from Pitic, now Hermosillo, with about 100
Spanish soldiers. En route he enlisted a complement of Pima
and Papago allies. His orders were to bargain for the return
of the captives, recover the bodies of the dead padres, and kill
the chiefs responsible. And when Fages rode up to the Colorado on October 18, he began negotiating almost immediately
with Chief Palma. Lined up on the opposite bank were some
500 braves armed with bows, arrows, spears, and some with
captured guns. Fages offered blankets, beads, and tobacco for
the captives and secured the release of forty-eight men, women,
and children. Failing to secure release of all the captives in
this way, he tried an old Anza trick of sending gifts to Palma:
a silver-decorated hat, a shirt, and some small boxes of cig-
arettes. Wiser from experience, the chief sent back a gift of
watermelons, squashes, maize, and beans instead of the remaining captives. On the same day of these exchanges, the bodies of
Rivera and his companions were found and buried with military pomp.[34] Three days later, Fages called a retreat and
escorted the ransomed people to Sonoita before returning for
another attempt to complete his mission.

Back at the crossing on November 30, the Spaniards,
more daring than before, camped at Concepción. From this
site Fages led a party of volunteers on December 7 to Bicuñer
where the remains of the July 17 victims were found. The

bones of Father Díaz and the headless Moreno were placed in a leather sack while the other skeletons were cremated and the ashes collected. A few days later back at Concepción the bodies of Fathers Garcés and Barraneche were found under a mound of fragrant camomile. All four martyrs were eventually buried together in one grave at Tubutama.[35] Before leaving the Yuma crossing, however, Fages secured the release of the last captives, including a woman named Juliana Sambrano and her newborn child. An attempt of the Spaniards to ambush Palma and his men went awry when the drummer prematurely sounded the signal to fire. But fifteen Yumas were killed in a later skirmish between the soldiers and a band of warriors assembled by the vengeful chief. One soldier encountered Palma on the latter occasion and would have shot him except for a pistol that misfired three times. He did have the consolation, nevertheless, of seeing Palma run away, leaving his horse and the gallooned hat that Fages had presented to him. Except for this small engagement and a joint campaign from Sonora and from California in the fall of 1782, the Yumas were never subjected to punishment for their crimes. The ringleaders were not captured nor the tribe subdued, and peace with the Yumas was not obtained. For many years afterward, the Yumas remained hostile and effectively blocked the overland route to California. Without control of the Colorado crossing the California colony became dependent upon coastwise shipping from New Spain, the interior being scarcely touched. The Yuma massacre did not bring the mission era to a close, but it did end the career of the last dynamic pioneer padre, Father Garcés, who belongs alongside such greats as Coronado and Kino in the annals of Arizona.

The preoccupation of Spanish officials with problems having much higher priority had resulted in the tragedy at the crossing and also made the recovery of the Colorado region unlikely. In 1786 all missionary and military activity among the Yumas ceased when the viceroy in Mexico City gave priority to the conquest of the Apaches. The Spanish dream of a northern trail across Hopiland was also abandoned at that time. The vast territory north of the Gila remained unsettled except by the Indians. The independent Hopi and Navajo continued with their time-honored religious practices and primitive agricultural methods, little affected by European contact. For the remainder of the Spanish period, efforts to maintain an outpost of civilization in what is now Arizona were concentrated along the southern tributaries of the Gila, in the valley of the Santa Cruz.

THE PRESIDIO AT TUCSON

The presidio for the protection of the Santa Cruz Valley had been moved from Tubac to Tucson in 1776. This change was part of an overall master plan of the Spanish government to provide a better line of defense against Apache penetrations in New Spain. Unlike previous policies that gave the military and church a shared responsibility for controlling the hostile Indians, the Royal Regulations of 1772 clearly put the burden on the military. Based upon an extensive inspection tour from Texas to Sonora made by the Marqués de Rubí, between 1766 and 1768, and another tour of the borderlands in 1769 by José de Galvez in his capacity as visitor general, the "Regulations" identified the implacable Apache as the enemy to be exterminated or forced to surrender unconditionally.* In accordance with Rubí's recommendation, they provided for a reorganization of the presidial line so that a cordon of fifteen forts scattered from the Gulf of Mexico to California could adequately accomplish this objective efficiently and economically. To carry out the huge task outlined in the royal orders, Viceroy Bucareli appointed Colonel Hugo O'Conor, a redheaded Irish mercenary long in the Spanish service, as *comandante-inspector*. The new distribution of presidios was to be in harmony with the best interests of Spain without regard to

---

*Whereas Rubí, whose full name was Don Cayetano María Pignatelli Rubí Corbera y San Climent, recommended changes in the presidial system and the Spanish Indian policy, Galvez was concerned mainly with the administration of this policy. He wanted an army commander with headquarters on the frontier and the authority to take quick action without having to consult first with the viceroy. See Kessell, *Mission of Sorrows*, pp. 173–80, and Bernardo de Galvez, *Instructions for Governing the Interior Provinces of New Spain, 1786*. Translated and edited by Donald E. Worcester. Berkeley: The Quivira Society, 1951, p. 7.

any particular locality. Defense against the raiding Apaches was to be made more effective and to O'Conor fell this responsibility. He was occupied for several years in campaigning against Apaches in Texas and in locating the best sites for forts on the eastern frontier. Not until 1775 was he able to give personal attention to the western sector of the defense line.

There were four presidios in Sonora that Rubí thought should be relocated: Tubac in present-day Arizona as well as Altar, Terrenate, and Fronteras south of the border.* All the presidial changes were effected except Altar. Terrenate was moved north to a location known as Santa Cruz (Quíburi) near the present town of Fairbank, Arizona, on the San Pedro River. Fronteras was moved north into the San Bernardino Valley just below the Arizona border. Both transfers were made in 1775, but Indian attacks became so severe that Fronteras was returned to its former site and Terrenate was moved first to Nutrias and then to the abandoned mission of Suamca in Sonora. To find a more desirable site nearer the Gila to replace Tubac, O'Conor inspected the Tucson area. On August 20, 1775, in the presence of Father Garcés, he·personally chose and marked off the site for the location of the future Royal Presidio of San Agustín, across the river from the Indian village and Garcés' mission of the same name, San Agustín del Tucson.† Though north of Rubí's recommended defense line, the new site was well situated to protect Anza's overland route to California and to defend the mission at San Xavier. O'Conor reported that the "requisite conditions of water, pasture, and wood occur, as well as a perfect closing of the Apache frontier."

---

*After visiting Tubac in December, 1767, Rubí concluded that the garrison there should be moved to a new location somewhat to the southwest. He explained that many settlers had come to Tubac because of the reputation of Captain Juan Bautista de Anza as a fair administrator and that there was sufficient population to defend itself. See Lawrence Kinnaird, *The Frontiers of New Spain, Nicolas de LaFora's Description, 1766–1768.* Berkeley, California: The Quivira Society, 1958, pp. 23–24, 108–109, 127–28.

† The Indian mission and village lay west of the Santa Cruz River at the foot of "A" Mountain. The Spanish settlement and presidio were east of the river. See Luis Navarro García, *Don José de Galvez y la Comandancia General de las Provincias Internas del Norte de Nueva España.* Sevilla: Publicaciones de la Escuela de Estudios Hispano-Americanos de Sevilla, 1964, pp. 238, 262, 326–27.

In 1776 the garrison at Tubac was transferred to Tucson, leaving the few settlers of the region exposed to Apache depredations. They were forbidden to leave by instructions which Viceroy Bucareli prepared supplementary to the Royal Regulations of 1772 for former presidio sites. The Tubac residents sent petitions to the central government asking for the restoration of the presidio; eventually the post was regarrisoned with friendly Indians under Spanish officers. Near the presidio was the mission of Tumacácori which kept the spark of Christianity alive.

Due to the absence of Colonel Anza, who was involved in the California project, Lieutenant Juan María de Oliva was in charge of the Tubac garrison at the time of its relocation. Oliva, though illiterate, had risen through the ranks after coming to Tubac in 1752 when that presidio was started. He had his problems since Anza had taken the best personnel. The only ensign left, for example, was an inefficient "fancy dan" named Juan Felipe Belderrain, who got his position only because his father founded the Tubac fort and because Anza was his godfather. The first permanent commander of the Tucson presidio, however, was a nobleman of exceptional ability, Captain Don Pedro de Allande y Saabedra, who took command in February, 1777. A veteran of wars in Europe and Mexico, though still in his mid-thirties, Allande was destined to play a prominent role in securing peace in Arizona. He was a "spit and polish" officer and deplored the sad condition in which he found the new post — located east of the Santa Cruz River in the vicinity of the present-day Pima County courthouse. Finding little more than a campsite, he directed the construction of a temporary palisade of rough logs that enclosed the magazine, guardhouse, ramparts for two cannon, and some of the dwellings. The permanent presidio, with adobe walls so characteristic of early Tucson construction, took several years to complete.

When Adjutant Inspector Roque de Medina visited the fort in the spring of 1779, he found that it was only about half finished and blamed the lack of progress on poor financial management by Ensign Belderrain. According to Medina:

An artist's concept of the Royal Presidio of Tucson

"Only on two walls is the material structure of this *presidio* to the height of a scant yard and a half, and it is of adobes." As the quartermaster in charge of accounting, Belderrain reported that over 1800 pesos had been expended. Belderrain, whose love of gambling, dancing, and fancy clothes preceded his Tucson assignment, lacked experience in handling finances and was squandering the building funds. Despite selling his own property to pay off his total debts, he still owed over 6,000 pesos at the time of Medina's visit, and eventually wound up occupying the guardhouse.

The fort was finally finished in 1783 but almost too late. The one gate, on the west side, was built of heavy mesquite wood; it opened onto what is now Main Street, then the *Camino Real* — the last lap of the King's Highway from Mexico City. There is some question about the exact height of the adobe walls, but they were twelve feet high according to one account. Archaeologists digging at the site in 1955 discovered that parts of the north and east walls were over three feet wide at the base. The original church of the presidio abutted the east wall, facing a small area called the *Plaza Iglesia.* The stables were located along the north wall near another open space called the *Plaza Militar.* The living quarters of the soldiers were on the south side looking out upon the largest open space, the *Plaza de las Armas.* These quarters were built against the walls with roofs sloping slightly inward that doubled as a rampart from which the troops could fire at attacking Indians. Filling out the fort were a jail, cemetery, and a granary. By the 1850s there was also a mescal saloon run by Juan Barruel inside the walls.[36] When the presidio was inspected in 1779 it had four bronze cannon and sixty-six balls ready for use. The powder magazine near the fort contained 694 pounds, an ample amount. Twenty-five pounds had been sold to the settlers at Tubac and only 140 pounds had been used in three years for target practice and actual engagements.

In addition to working on the presidio and performing the routine duties of guarding horse herds and protecting the settlements of Tucson, Tubac, and San Xavier, the soldiers also accompanied Captain Allande on several sorties. The first major contact with the Apaches came on November 6, 1779, when an Indian force, estimated at 350 in number, approached the presidio itself. With only fifteen men, out of his total command of about eighty, Allande engaged the enemy and drove them off. During the battle the captain cut off the head of a slain chieftain, stuck it on a lance, and waved it disdainfully at the Apaches. Then, except for an occasional Apache attempt to steal sheep or to stop a supply train, the Arizona frontier was relatively peaceful until Sunday morning, May 1, 1782, when several hundred Apaches boldly attacked the Tucson stockade.[37] The battle was noteworthy in that it marked a divergence from the customary Apache practices of ambushing only small parties of troopers and of raiding to acquire livestock or goods of immediate economic value. Luckily, the surprised garrison was not all inside the unfinished presidio. While the Indians were trying to concentrate against the open entrance of the fort, Lieutenant Don José

María Abate provided a tactical diversion by firing down on them from a nearby parapeted roof top. Abate's servant also sent a few savages scurrying for cover with his bow and arrows. Ensign Usarraga, Belderrain (now serving in the ranks shorn of his commission), and another soldier happened to be on the opposite side of the Santa Cruz; they defended the bridge on that river and may have kept the Apaches away from the Pimas at the Tucson mission near Sentinel Peak. Despite a bad leg wound, Captain Allande himself led a valiant stand at the entrance of the stockade. In the face of superior Spanish firepower and the unforeseeable dispersion of their forces by the sharpshooting roof-top lieutenant, the Apaches sheathed their arrows and departed, even though their casualties were relatively light.

One result of the surprise attack was the completion of the adobe fortification around the presidio in 1783, making it more secure. The May Day assault may have been prompted by the weakness of the post as well as its forward position relative to the other frontier presidios in the Rubí line. This vulnerability forced Captain Allande to limit his fighting to defensive actions during 1782. The May Day affair and another engagement in December were the best examples of the type of activities in which the troops were involved. On Christmas Day, cattle were run off by the Apaches. In retaliation, the captain dispatched a force that not only succeeded in recovering the livestock but also beheaded six of the renegades who were caught.

No effective aggressive probing into Apacheland was possible until 1783. Beginning in that year, and until his promotion to lieutenant-colonel and his transfer to another post in 1786, Allande harassed the Apaches in the field. In 1783 he conducted at least three campaigns in search of Apaches in the Gila country, the last being in December and the following January. In reporting on this winter expedition, Commander-General Felipe Neve — the former governor of Alta California who was appointed to succeed Croix when the latter was promoted to the position of viceroy in Peru — had only the highest praise for Allande and his men. After mentioning the harsh weather, he wrote:

... On the 5th he attacked two *rancherías* near the Gila River with
the death of five Apaches, four women, and capture of twenty-four prisoners of both sexes, recovery of one female captive, recapture of five
riding animals and destruction of everything in their miserable habita-
tions. He returned to his presidio on the 8th in order not to mistreat his
troop and mounts further, since the legs of the latter were swollen from
the intense cold and snows which they suffered ... [38]

Neve recommended Captain Allande, Ensign José Tona,
and Ensign Usarraga, hero of the May Day bridge defense, for
promotion. While his dispatch was winding its way through
the Spanish administrative machinery to the King, the frontier
soldiers continued their bloody struggle with the Apaches.
Usarraga died from his wounds and was replaced by Juan
Carrillo. At daybreak on March 21, 1784, Ensign Carrillo was
in command of the guard at the horse corral of the Tucson
presidio when the Apaches attacked and succeeded in stamped-
ing most of the herd, leaving five soldiers dead and one
wounded. Without wasting any time, an expedition quickly
organized to bring back the herd. The troopers who had
mounts were joined by thirty Pimas from Tucson and San
Xavier as well as five citizens. Led by Lieutenant Tomás Egu-
rrola, the mixed force caught up with the herd. Though
greatly outnumbered, they courageously attacked, killed Chief
Chiquita and several of his braves, and put the enemy in flight.
Seventeen heads of Apaches who died that day were carried
back to the presidio, but only twelve of the horses were
recaptured. In his report on the episode, Commander-General
Neve, who believed that Croix's frontier defense preparations
had reached the point where the Apaches could now be exterminated, wrote that the battle was among "the most distinguished and advantageous skirmishes that has occurred in
the Provinces." Explaining that Tucson was the presidio on
the Sonoran frontier that was most often struck by the vengeful
enemy, Neve said that in four months the Apaches had lost
thirty-seven killed, including four women, and thirty-three
prisoners. He added that many of the Apaches killed in the
skirmish of March 21 were uncounted. "... A great many
more were slain," he said, "until the party of troops grew tired
of lancing the great number of enemies who traveled on
foot." [39]

Neve's account emphasizes the importance of the cavalry lance as the most effective weapon of the Spanish soldier on the Sonoran frontier, once he got the enemy Indians in the open. As a matter of fact, it was the only weapon with which the Tucson company was completely equipped. According to the Regulations of 1772, each soldier was supposed to have been armed with a regular musket (*escopeta*) or with a short-barreled carbine (*carabina*), two pistols, a bullhide shield, and an arrow-proof jacket of six-ply heavy leather (*cuera*), in addition to the lance. Also, each soldier was to have six serviceable horses, one colt, and one mule as well as a *vaquero* style saddle.[40] The report of Adjutant Inspector Lieutenant Colonel Roque de Medina in 1785 revealed that all but one of the 73 men at the Tucson presidio possessed a lance, but there was a shortage in other items. Of the company's 64 muskets, nine were of small caliber; several of the carbines were almost worn out and nearly half of the pistols were too poorly manufactured to be serviceable. There were only twenty-one leather jackets, none of them reinforced. The fort itself was armed with four brass cannon mounted at the corners of the walls and supplied with 78 four pound balls and adequate powder; yet no artillerymen were assigned to the post. The animal herd numbered 356 horses and 51 mules, shy 82 and 22 respectively.[41]

Some of the other presidios were not as well equipped as the one in Tucson. But Commander-General Neve felt confident that a massive strategic offensive against the Apaches in the upper Gila River region would go a long way toward subduing them. Accordingly, as part of a planned five-pronged invasion of Apachería, Captain Allande led a company from Tucson in April, 1784, to probe through the Babocomari and other mountains into the Apache stronghold from the southwest. Other expeditions in 1784 and 1785 involved the Tucson garrison in sorties into southeastern Arizona and into the Gila River area.

As valuable as the combined probes from all the presidios were in making the hostile Indians throughout Apachería aware of the Spanish presence, it was obvious by 1786 that certain alterations in the Indian policy were needed. Warfare alone would not restrain the natives from raiding the Spanish settlements. Some 3200 officers' and men, organized into twenty-four presidios, ten *compañías volantes* — light-horse or "flying" companies, most of which operated in Nueva Vizcaya, perennially the major target of Apache attacks — and two companies of Spanish regulars, had only enabled the Spaniards to hold their own. The Indians were fighting on familiar terrain and using cunning methods hardly acceptable to the Marquis of Queensberry, all of which gave them the advantage over the troops. The military operations, far from reducing the raids, served only to elevate the natives from petty thieves to astute warriors. It was evident that the Apaches had perfected a unique way of life which called for no increase in their own territory and no desire to engage the Spaniards in open battle to determine power in European style. Though culturally and linguistically the Apaches constituted a single nation, politically they did not. The Spanish arbitrarily classified the western Apaches into five principal tribes, of which three were in Arizona: the Chiricahua in the general area of southeastern Arizona, the Tontos in central Arizona, east of the juncture of the Salt River with the Gila, and the Gileños in the mountainous upper Gila region of eastern Arizona.* But most of these subdivisions broke up into virtually autonomous bands which were united by kinship and controlled by a chief, at least in wartime. When convenient the Apaches preferred to be independent to roam about at will.

Physically robust, agile, indefatigable, and always in harmony with the environment, they moved continuously in search of new game and wild foods for subsistence. With the coming of the Spaniard, a new source of food supply was

---

*The Gran Apachería, as the Spaniards called it, stretched for 750 miles from the Santa Cruz River in Arizona to the Colorado River of Texas. Besides the three Western Apache tribes in Arizona there were two others, the Mimbreños and Navahos, west of the Rio Grande River in present-day western New Mexico. The Eastern Apache tribes were the Faraones, the Mescaleros, the Llaneros (Natagées, Lipiyanes, and Llaneros proper), and the Lipanes. The Apaches were linguistically of Southern Athapascan stock. The Navahos, who speak a dialect of the same language, were related to the Gila Apaches. By the end of the eighteenth century, however, the Navahos had settled down to farm and raise livestock; they were subsequently distinguished as a separate nation. See Daniel S. Matson (translator) and Albert H. Schroeder (annotator), "Cordero's Description of the Apache — 1796," *New Mexico Historical Review*, Vol. XXXII, No. 4 (October, 1957), pp. 335–56.

available for the shifting camps in the mountains of Arizona and New Mexico. The Apaches could now maintain themselves by hit and run raids to drive off the stock and plunder the settlements. They were not primarily interested in killing people since it was to their advantage to have the settlers producing the grains, cattle, and horses that were desired. When chased, the crafty Indians either skillfully lured their pursuers into ambush or fled with amazing speed across rugged mountains and waterless deserts to a secluded camp to avoid capture. The Spaniards who moved in to colonize this desolate land, and to subdue the Indians who thwarted them, were also a hardy breed. But after years of bloody effort they were still unable to crush the elusive resistance of the Apaches. A technologically advanced military power was frustrated by primitive guerrilla warfare. Finally, a Spanish official concluded that if the Indians could not be converted to Christian ways or defeated militarily, they might be conciliated with annual presents of such value that they would prize peace more than war.

In 1786, the new viceroy, Bernardo de Galvez, formulated a practical Indian policy and clearly laid it down in his detailed Instrucción to the new commander-general, Jacobo Ugarte y Loyola. Extermination of hostile Indians was still the incessant goal and each tribe would be forced to sue for peace unconditionally. But for the first time, treaties were to be permitted, and as long as these were observed, the natives were to be treated kindly. They were to be encouraged to establish settlements near the presidios and taught to be dependent upon Spanish friendship for food rations and intoxicating liquors. As part of the program to weaken their native culture, they were to be given firearms of poor quality. Galvez did not expect that the subdued Indians would always abide by the treaties and wanted to be sure that their weapons were inferior. Until the advent of the metallic cartridge in the nineteenth century, the bow and arrow was actually more deadly than the firearms in a sustained encounter. "Would to God," Galvez wrote, "that the Indians may not use the bow and arrow; then . . . we would have all the advantages, the functions of warfare would be less mournful, and the pacification of the Provincias Internas would be quicker and easier."[42]

Following the Instructions of 1786, the presidio commanders waged vigorous campaigns against the Apaches all along the Sonoran frontier. The Spanish troops probed quite deep into enemy territory and made 1788 an especially uncomfortable year for the Apaches. Captain Manuel de Echeagaray of the Santa Cruz *presidio,* just south of the present border, assembled a force of 186 men, including thirty from Tucson and a few from the re-established garrison of Tubac. In a hard riding campaign during January, Echeagaray led his command as far east as the Rio Grande in New Mexico, killing twenty-seven Apaches and capturing sixteen more. Over forty horses were recovered. Then, during the early summer, Allande's successor at Tucson, Captain Pablo Romero, took a 208-man force into Apachería, killing fifteen Apaches including Chief Quilcho, and capturing thirty-four men and women. Most of the captives were taken in a battle at a *ranchería* in the Pinal Mountains (north of the Gila and south of the present-day towns of Miami and Globe). Ensign Don Joseph Moraga distinguished himself for bravery in this conflict by killing an Apache in hand-to-hand combat. Captain Echeagaray took the field again during October and November, with over 400 men as part of a large scale surrounding maneuver against the Indians on the Sonoran frontier. Fifty-four Indians were killed and 125 were captured. But more important, fifty-five Apaches accepted peace and served as guides in helping the Spaniards locate *rancherías.*

By all indications, the Galvez plan was succeeding. By 1788, several Apache bands were coming into Bocoachi, Santa Cruz, and Fronteras. The first settlement of Apaches at Tucson began sometime during the early 1790s when the Aravaipas who had lived in the San Pedro Valley started receiving supplies of meat, corn, tobacco, and candy. The peace-at-a-price system seemed to be working, and yet there was articulate opposition to it. The Franciscan missionary, Father Diego Bringas de Manzaneda criticized the corruption of the dependency system and requested permission from the commander-general to send missionaries to several settlements, including Tucson, and to supply the Apaches at Tucson with the implements of farming. He advocated more missions and presidios instead of feeding stations as the best means of subjugating the Indians. The military, however, was not willing to relax its control over the Apaches. And even the new vices which the Indians picked up from the Spaniards were defended as being a part of Galvez's policy. Though he never specifically advocated such vices as cardplaying, gambling, prostitution, and cussing, he very specifically instructed that they be taught to drink liquor. "After all," he wrote in the *Instructions*, "the supplying of drink to the Indians will be a means of gaining their goodwill, discovering their secrets, calming them so they will think less often of conceiving and executing their hostilities, and creating for them a new necessity which will oblige them to recognize their dependence upon us more directly."[43] The system was definitely corrupting, expensive for the crown, and required constant vigilance. But it brought peace and prosperity to the frontier during the final years of New Spain — 1790–1821 — and the first decade of the Mexican period.

The commander of the Tucson post during most of the "golden years" of this region was the former acting commandant at San Diego, Captain José de Zúñiga. Unlike his predecessors, Romero and Don Nicolás Soler who were killed fighting the Apaches, Zúñiga survived several expeditions and lived to grow up with the country. In 1795, the year after he took command at San Agustín del Tucson, he was selected by Commander-General Pedro de Nava to make an important exploration of the upper Gila region in search of a direct trade route between Sonora and Santa Fe. The trade route was the most important object, but Zúñiga was also ordered to be diligent in punishing the Apaches, both coming and going. Leaving Tucson on April 9, he united his party of 143 troopers and eight Apache scouts at the abandoned *presidio* of Santa Cruz (near the present-day town of Fairbank) and marched out of the San Pedro Valley into the Little Dragoon and Pinaleño Mountains. The route led through the heart of Apachería and several small skirmishes were fought before the force reached Zuñi, in New Mexico, on May Day. Runners were sent by the Franciscan friar at Zuñi to the governor of New Mexico at Santa Fe with news of the party's arrival, and then Zúñiga turned back. In this way (by relays actually) the

Arizona Historical Society

Sabino Otero and Charles Poston in Chicago in 1888

first trip on record was made between Tucson and Santa Fe. But Zúñiga was disappointed at not having encountered more Apaches and wrote accordingly in his journal: "... I am ashamed of the very small results of my campaign."[44]

Perhaps the captain took more satisfaction in the economic growth of Tucson and upper Sonora. Under a Spanish settlement law of 1791, four square leagues (over twenty-seven square miles) were put at the disposal of each *presidio* commander to assign settlers.* Under this plan, both Tucson and

*One of the best known settlers was Reyes Pacheco who was given possession of lands near the presidio in 1802 by Mariano de Urrea, the commander at that time. In 1815, Pacheco transferred his title to Pedro Villaescusa. A descendant of the latter, a widow named Manuela Villaescusa de Marquez, and George Hill Howard, who bought an interest in several land grants in Arizona, filed suit for confirmation of title to the Pacheco grant before the Court of Private Land Claims in 1893. The court, however, was not authorized by the Gadsden Treaty to confirm presidial grants or any title "not located or duly recorded in the archives of Mexico," and, in 1899, rejected the claim. See report of U.S. Attorney Matt. G. Reynolds, Court of Private Land Claims, on the Reyes Pacheco Grant, Case No. 132: Manuela Villaescusa de Marquez, et al., vs. United States, from Santa Fe, New Mexico, June 20, 1899. In Matt. G. Reynolds Correspondence, Record Group 60: Department of Justice Files. See also *Tucson Daily Citizen,* June 15, 1899.

Tubac began to develop. Zúñiga reported in 1804, for example, that there were thirty-seven Spanish settlers and more than 200 Indians living in the pueblo of Tucson and engaging in farming. Dependent Apaches were being fed from a herd of some 4000 cattle and surplus hides were being sold as far south as Arispe, then the capital of Sonora. There were hundreds of sheep on the grasslands nearby and a horse herd of 1200 was available to the garrison. A lime mine in the hills north of town gave the town some occupational diversity.

The commander at Tubac reported similar activity in that area. In 1789, for example, a title to the first Spanish land grant in Arizona was given to Torbio (also Torevio) de Otero by the commander at Tubac, Don Nicolás de Erran. The small Otero grant was made in accordance with a provision of the Regulations of 1772 whereby persons who wanted to cultivate sowing lands and agreed to keep arms and horses for the defense of the country were encouraged to settle on lands near the presidios. The grant was occupied almost

Arizona Historical Society

Mission of San Cayetano del Tumacácori after restoration c. 1920

San Xavier del Bac, 1881

continuously for more than a century by Otero and his descendants.*

The new church construction was also symbolic of the peace that prevailed during the golden age. The mission of Tumacácori kept the spark of Christianity alive in the Tubac area. When Padre Kino's Guevavi was abandoned in the 1770s, the status of Tumacácori was raised from *visita* to an independent mission. Despite a lack of funds, a larger church with a domed roof was gradually constructed during the early 1800s. With new adobe houses protected by a wall, for the neophytes, Tumacácori prospered until Mexican Independence in 1821. After that, the Mexican government began expelling the Spaniards, including most of the frontier Franciscans.

A new church at San Xavier was erected by the Franciscans and still stands as one of the most beautiful and best preserved Spanish missions in North America, due to Papagos

---

* In 1858, the Otero heirs purchased the small adjacent grant of José Martínez who had been given a title in 1838. Then in 1893, Sabino Otero and other heirs relinquished their claim to the Otero-Martínez grants. Wishing to avoid the cost of having the claim confirmed by the Court of Private Land Claims, they hoped to homestead the land once it was restored to the public domain. Steps to acquire this entry were never completed. See Dockets, Court of Private Land Claims, General Land Office Records, Record Group 49, National Archives.

who cared for the building in later times. For years historians believed that the present magnificent edifice was commenced by Fray Balthasar Carrillo and finished by his assistant, Naciso Gutiérrez. These priests, however, were at Tumacácori. It was Fray Juan Bautista Velderrain (also Belderrain), brother-in-law of Juan Bautista de Anza, who actually began the San Xavier Mission. About 1783 he borrowed 7000 pesos from Don Antonio Herreras. Evidently the priest was quite a salesman, since crops of unplanted wheat were his only collateral for the loan. Velderrain died about 1790 and was replaced by Fray Bautista Llorenz who finished the church before the turn of the century.[45] Many people who visit the magnificent "white dove in the desert," as the San Xavier church is called, are surprised to learn that the present structure is Franciscan, though it was built on the site that dates back to the Jesuit period. The Franciscans also built a two-story *convento,* or residence for the missionaries, near the base of Sentinel Peak in Tucson about 1800; the adobe walls of this structure gradually deteriorated but the foundations have been discovered under a Tucson city dump.[46]

View of Tucson from Sentinel Peak ("A" Mountain), showing the Francisco convento *in the center, about 1890*

Library of Congress

In brief, the decades following 1790 were characterized by a relative degree of peace and prosperity. Not all of the previously occupied areas were resettled during this period, but the settlements along the Santa Cruz and elsewhere in southern Arizona reached the zenith of prosperity. Cattle ranches and mines were developed as settlers took advantage of the lull in Indian wars and branched out southeast and southwest from Tucson. The ruins of some establishments can still be seen not only in the Santa Cruz Valley but also in the San Pedro Valley which was not occupied in earlier Spanish or later Mexican times.

PART THREE

MEXICAN-ANGLO TRANSITION

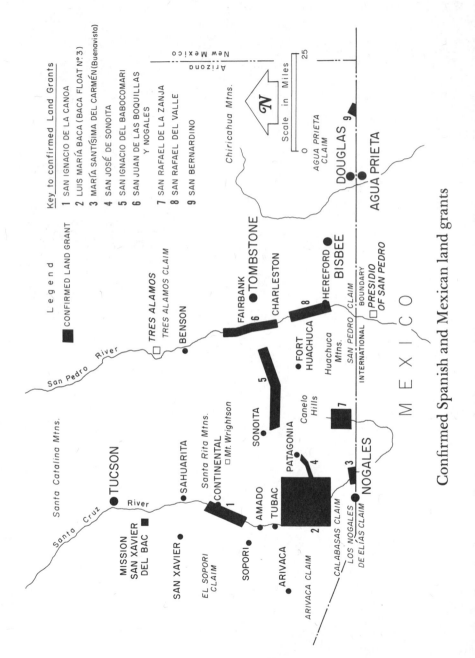

Legend

■ CONFIRMED LAND GRANT

Key to confirmed Land Grants

1 SAN IGNACIO DE LA CANOA
2 LUIS MARÍA BACA (BACA FLOAT N° 3)
3 MARÍA SANTÍSIMA DEL CARMÉN (Buenavista)
4 SAN JOSÉ DE SONOITA
5 SAN IGNACIO DEL BABOCOMARI
6 SAN JUAN DE LAS BOQUILLAS
   Y NOGALES
7 SAN RAFAEL DE LA ZANJA
8 SAN RAFAEL DEL VALLE
9 SAN BERNARDINO

Scale in Miles

0   25

Arizona
New Mexico

Confirmed Spanish and Mexican land grants

Chapter 7

Spanish and Mexican Land Grants

DURING THE GOLDEN DECADES of comparative peace with the Apaches, there was more economic activity in what is now southern Arizona than in previous years of Spanish occupation. Though mineral development in this area was never extensive at any time during the Spanish period — at least by modern standards — gold and silver mines were opened and ores found that were rich enough to be treated by simple amalgamation processes.* Most of the old workings which have been rediscovered and operated in recent times can be traced back to around 1800, and many of the ruins and prospectors' holes bear testimony to the mining activity at that time.

More is known about the livestock industry during the late Spanish and early Mexican period because stock raisers bothered to petition the government for titles to the land which they occupied. From the land records and also from accounts of early American travelers, such as boundary surveyor John R. Bartlett, one gets some idea who the *rancheros* were as well as the extent of their operations. Though Mexico became independent from Spain in 1821, the land laws remained fundamentally the same.

The ranchers not only grazed their stock on land granted to them by the Spanish or Mexican government but were allowed to occupy surrounding lands known as "overplus."

---

*There was nothing in the Spanish era to compare with the great copper mining enterprises in Arizona today. Except for the deposit at Ajo, copper has been found mainly in the wild, rough country that was controlled by the Apaches. Furthermore, the smelting processes and modern uses for copper that make the industry so profitable today, were unknown then.

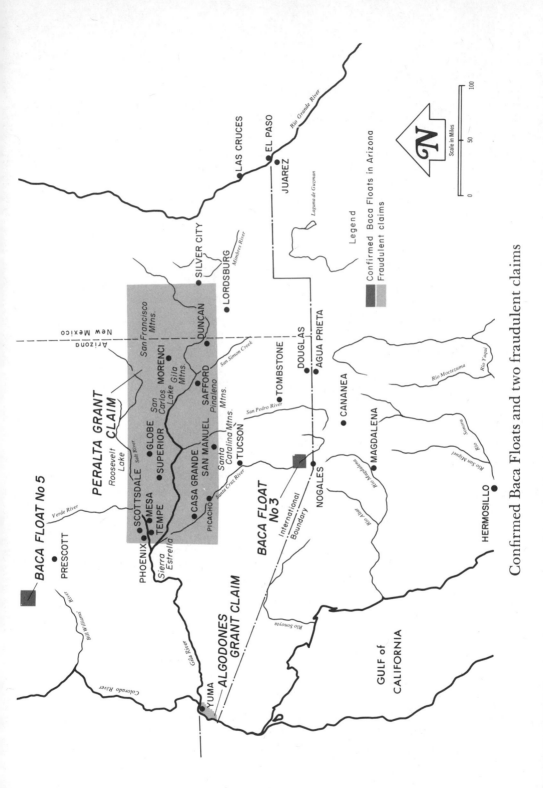

Confirmed Baca Floats and two fraudulent claims

All grants had to be marked with monuments of mortar and stone and generally were to revert back to the public domain if abandoned for more than three years. An exception was made if the abandonment of a site was due to encroachment by Indians. As it turned out, most of the nineteenth-century grants were on lands where the eighteenth-century missionaries had established *visitas* and *rancherías;* and just as their predecessors were driven away by Apaches, so were these later ranchers.

According to the land-grant records, stockmen were still active all along the present international boundary and as far north as the presidio of Tucson, as late as the 1830s. In the Santa Cruz Valley, the Ortiz brothers had spreads on the Canoa and Arivaca ranches. The Tuvera family was farther south on the Buenavista land, and the Romeros were occupying San Rafael de la Zanja. In the Sonoita Valley the León Herreras family was grazing large herds. Along the San Pedro and its tributaries were the vast holdings of the Elías González family on the Babocomari, Agua Prieta, and other grants. And in the extreme southeastern part of Arizona the Pérez family controlled the vast San Bernardino holdings which extended across the modern international boundary. Along with other large owners in southern Arizona, these stockmen were leaders in advancing the northern frontier.

They had had some cause for concern when their military protection was weakened as a result of the movement for Mexican independence. The number of ranches carved out of the public domain during the 1820s, however, is evidence that the Apache ravages were not unbearable until the following decades. Most of the claims to the Santa Cruz Valley grants were filed from 1820 to 1833, and with one exception, the San Pedro titles were issued between 1820 and 1831. The fact that few petitions were presented after that time would indicate that Indian raids discouraged settlements. The San Pedro Valley apparently was deserted completely and remained so until the 1870s and 1880s.

The presidios of Tubac and Tucson were protected by small detachments of soldiers. But for the most part, Mexican authority outside of these settlements existed in name only, after the 1830s. The Apache Indians were able to extirpate almost every trace of Spanish and Mexican civilization. They roamed largely unmolested with only token opposition. In April, 1845, Colonel José María Elías González made a full report on this state of affairs in the northern reaches of Mexico. The following summer he organized a large force for a grand campaign against the Apaches. In violation of a last minute summons to march south and support the Sonoran governor in putting down a revolution, Colonel Elías called a council of war in Tucson. The records show that Captain Comadurán of the presidio, with 155 men under his command, killed six Apaches.

From 1821 to 1848 — the year in which the region north of the Gila River was ceded to the United States — Arizona was legally a part of Mexico. The section south of the Gila remained under Mexican control until 1856 when United States troops took official possession of the Gadsden Purchase lands. But the actual political status of Arizona under Mexican rule is not so easily determined. The National Republican Congress at Mexico City in 1824 combined the provinces of Sonora and Sinaloa under the name Estado Interno de Occidente (Interior State of the West). Thus, Arizona south of the Gila became a part of this new state. But in 1830, the congress divided Occidente; Sonora, including southern Arizona, was again independent. Meanwhile, the forbidding land of rugged mountains and inhospitable Indians north of the Gila was only a place on the map described as "Los Yndios Gentiles" (the heathen Indians). Vaguely claimed by both the Mexican territory of New Mexico and that of California, it was colonized by neither. With practically no civilian rule and little military protection from the unstable, revolution-plagued Mexican government in the capital, it is little wonder that nobody in Arizona really knew who governed. Except for securing legal title to lands south of the Gila, the ranchers and miners who ventured northward were hardly concerned with the state boundary lines which were drawn by the authorities in the capital city.

When in 1854 the United States government accepted the purchase treaty that James Gadsden had secured from Mexico the previous year, it agreed to recognize the validity of Mexican and Spanish titles to land grants in the area transferred — provided that the lands had been "located and duly recorded in the archives of Mexico." At the time of the treaty, however, most of the *rancherías* in the purchase area had been abandoned, some for a second time; little value was placed upon them until the Apaches were brought under control by the U.S. cavalry in the 1870s and 1880s. Speculators, mostly from California, eagerly sought out the heirs and purchased the rights to the lands for a mere song. When Anglo-American settlers began moving into southern Arizona, they were disappointed to find that the choice sites along the San Pedro, Santa Cruz, and other streams were held by absentee owners and not subject to settlement by virtue of treaty commitments on the old grants. Unfortunately, no time limitation was specified for the United States government to confirm or reject claims. As it turned out, the complicated task of searching for evidence of authentic titles and of discriminating between the bona fide and fraudulent claims took half a century.

Adjudication of the Spanish and Mexican titles in the Gadsden Purchase got off to a slow start because no procedure was established whereby official acceptance could be given to each foreign title. Congress did not extend the method of examining claims provided for in the Mexican Cession of 1848 to the newly acquired area south of the Gila.[1] By this process, the surveyor general of the territory or state involved was charged with the responsibility of investigating each claim and rendering a decision on both the validity of the title and the physical limits of the grant; then a report was submitted to the General Land Office. Arizona was part of the surveying district of New Mexico until 1867 — even though it had been created as a separate territory in 1863 — and was then attached to the surveying district of California; in 1867, all the pertinent archives were transferred from Santa Fe to San Francisco. Because of the Indian hostilities prevailing in Arizona and the great distance from both of these cities, not even the basic surveys of public lands got under way. Consequently, even if the law of 1854 — applicable only to the Mexican Cession portion of Arizona north of the Gila — had been extended to the land grants south of the

river, it is doubtful if anything would have been done by the
surveyor general of New Mexico or of California to speed
up litigation.

In 1870, Congress authorized the surveyor general of
Arizona "to ascertain and report [to the Secretary of Interior]
upon the origin, nature, character and extent of the claims
to lands in said Territory, under the laws, usages, and customs
of Spain and Mexico."[2] When the Secretary approved a claim,
he submitted a recommendation to Congress, which was vested
with final authority for validating Spanish or Mexican grants.
Some of the surveyor generals who served in the Territory of
Arizona were reluctant to exercise the quasi-judicial duties
conferred upon them; they hoped that Congress would create
a special commission in each territory with full power to make
decisions on the basis of the evidence uncovered. But Congress
hesitated to act, and the responsibility for determining the
validity of claims remained in the hands of the surveyor
general until 1891. Reporting on some of the frustrations
involved, Surveyor General Royal A. Johnson wrote in 1884
that "letters are frequently months in being answered. Photographs of printing, writing, autographs, seals, etc. are not
infrequently sent to both Spain and the interior of Mexico
for comparison with authentic records, and every step of the
investigation . . . is laborious and requires time."[3]

Experts like R. C. Hopkins, who came from California
to assist Surveyor General John Wasson, were often absent
for months examining ancient documents in remote places.
Even measuring land was complicated by the descriptions
given in the *expedientes*. While most of the titles to grants
in Arizona specified a definite amount of land, sometimes only
indefinite natural boundaries were designated. As mentioned
above, a grantee customarily occupied lands in excess of the
stipulated grant, and under the Mexican laws, title could be
acquired to this additional land. In many cases, American
purchasers followed suit and claimed both the original grants
and the overplus. Thus, most of the preliminary surveys
were defective, not only because boundary descriptions were
vague but also because deputy surveyors often depended on
informal statements of persons in the vicinity, some of whom
may have wanted legal grants cut down in size.

Surveyor General John Hise summarized the situation in 1887 in his report to the Commissioner of the General Land Office:

The investigation I have thus far made leads me to believe that the great majority of these grants were abandoned in good faith for a period of from ten to twelve years by the original grantees, and that no value was attached to them by the principals or the heirs in Mexico.[4]

Hise said that speculators gained control of the titles and were asking the government to confirm their ownership in the grants. "The files are crowded with ancient documents, time-worn and almost defaced," he wrote. "and upon thorough investigation may be found to have been manufactured for the occasion and presented to verify doubtful records."

Despite handicaps and uncertainties, the surveyor generals had reported on all but a half-dozen claims by 1888 — thirteen favorably and two unfavorably. Congress, however, delayed in acting upon the recommendations. Legislative committees were simply not organized to give each claim the kind of painstaking scrutiny and legal acumen that it needed. Yet, each year's delay imposed new difficulties and added to the risk of confirming unfounded claims, and as long as the land grants remained in litigation, settlement of the areas in question would be retarded. President Benjamin Harrison stressed this in his annual message to Congress in 1889: "Provision should be made by law for the prompt trial and final adjustment before a judicial tribunal or commission of all claims based upon Mexican land grants."[5]

After many years of being pressed to do something, Congress turned the problem over to a special Court of Private Land Claims. Created in 1891, with sessions to be held in Denver and in Santa Fe, the court assumed the responsibility of determining the validity of the grants in New Mexico and Arizona.* In December, 1892, a separate district was estab-

---

*The five judges appointed by President Harrison were: Chief Justice: Joseph R. Reed of Iowa; Associate Justices: Wilbur F. Stone of Colorado, Henry C. Sluss of Kansas, Thomas C. Fuller of North Carolina, and William W. Murray of Tennessee. *New York Times,* June 14, 1891. Other officials were: Matt. G. Reynolds, U. S. Attorney; James H. Reeder, Clerk; Ireneo L. Chaves, Deputy Clerk; R. L. Long, Deputy Clerk for Arizona; and E. L. Hall, U.S. Marshal.

lished at Tucson to hear only the Arizona claims. Twenty cases, involving the confirmation or rejection of seventeen grants in Arizona, were filed with this court. The famous Peralta-Reavis claim was transferred to the court at Santa Fe, but each of the others was given a full hearing in Tucson. Most of the decisions were eventually appealed to the Supreme Court and either upheld or remanded to the Court of Private Land Claims for reconsideration. The legal entanglements were drawn out and complicated. But by 1904 — fifty years after the Gadsden treaty was signed — the work of the court was finished. Titles to 116,540 acres out of 837,680 acres claimed in Arizona, were validated and the surveys were approved by the court.* It was a long process to search the archives of Mexico and Spain to check the authenticity of titles; it took time to record the eyewitness testimony of pioneers who were on the Arizona scene in the 1850s. But in doing this work, the surveyor generals and the court accumulated and preserved volumes of invaluable historical data on the Spanish and Mexican periods of Arizona history that might never have been recorded otherwise.

CONFIRMED GRANTS

Although the full story of the land grants goes beyond the intended scope of this book, the author has chosen to bring the history of each of the grants up to date in order to give the reader a better perspective.

The Canoa Grant

One of the oldest and most interesting land grants is San Ignacio de la Canoa, located between picturesque mountain ranges in the fertile Santa Cruz Valley south of Tucson. The Canoa ranch was probably given its name because of a hollowed-out cottonwood log — resembling a canoe — that was

---

*By way of contrast, in California there were 588 grants totaling over twelve million acres, of which more than 8,850,000 acres (nearly 14,000 square miles) were confirmed. These California grants comprised nine percent of the total land surface of the state and were located in what is now the most populous and highly developed regions. See Frank Lounsbury, "Mexican Land Claims in California," mimeographed publication in the National Archives, RG 60: Department of Justice.

used as a watering trough. The Anza expedition stopped there in 1775 on its first night out of Tubac en route to California; both padres Font and Garcés mentioned Canoa and noted the existence of a Papago *ranchería* there. Military parties led by Captain Allande and other commanders from the presidios of Tucson and nearby Tubac sometimes camped at that site. It was not until September, 1820 — a year before Mexico gained independence — that Tomás and Ignacio Ortiz, residents of Tubac, petitioned the *intendente* of Sonora and Sinaloa for four *sitios** of grassland around La Canoa for the purpose of raising cattle and horses. In accordance with the Spanish law, the land had to be measured, appraised, and auctioned before a title could be granted. The survey was made under the supervision of Ignacio Elías González,† com-

---

*A *sitio* is a square league containing 4,338.464 acres. Four *sitios* would be the equivalent of more than 27 square miles or sections. In 1786, Mexico was divided by royal cedula into twelve provinces called intendancies. This order was put into effect in 1788, Sonora and Sinaloa being one of the twelve units. The man in charge of each was called *gobernador intendente,* or simply *intendente.*

† Ignacio Elías González (1776–1842) was the last commander of the royal fort of Tubac and the father-in-law of Tomás Ortiz. In 1821 — the same year in which his daughter, Josefa Clemente Elías González, married Ortiz — Ignacio supervised the survey of the Canoa, Sonoita, and San Rafael de la Zanja grants. Ignacio himself was later given title to the Babocomari and was a part owner of the San Juan de las Boquillas y Nogales grant. He was one of the illustrious sons of Francisco Elías González, a wealthy mine owner, and grandson of Francisco Elías González de Zaya, a Spanish-born military officer who once commanded the post at Terrenate. Ignacio's older brother, Símon (1772–1841) preceded him in command at Tubac (1807), having begun his military career in the presidio of Tucson at the age of fifteen with a special non-commissioned rank reserved for the élite. Following the achievement of Mexican independence Símon, in 1825 and 1826, was governor of Sonora and Sinaloa — officially called *Estado Interno de Occidente* (Interior State of the West) from 1824 to 1831; he was later a governor of Chihuahua too. Another brother of Ignacio was Rafael (1774–1840), who headed the government of Sonora for awhile in 1837 and owned several land grants, including the San Rafael del Valle in Arizona; Rafael was the great grandfather of General Plutarco Elías Calles, twice governor of Sonora at the time of World War I. Other brothers were Juan José (1779–1869), a priest, and José María (born 1793), a prominent military commander in Sonora who strengthened the Tucson presidio's defenses at the time of General Kearny's conquest of the Southwest during the Mexican War. A sister, Gertrudis Elías González, was married at Arispe in 1796 to Mariano de Urrea, then a lieutenant stationed at the Tucson presidio. A son born in Tucson of this marriage, José Cosme Urrea, was a general in the Mexican army at the battle of the Alamo in Texas and served twice as governor and military commander of Sonora between 1842 and 1845. As leader of the state's rights federalists he fought a bloody civil war against Manuel María Gandara, who then favored more power in the hands of the central government in Mexico City. See Francisco R. Almada, *Diccionario de Historia, Geografía, y Biografía Sonorenses.* Chihuahua, Chihuahua, Mexica: n.p., 1952, pp. 239–43; Henry F. Dobyns, "Tubac Through Four Centuries," Vol. 2, The Arizona State Parks Board, 1959, typescript, pp. 339–40; and Robert C. Stevens, "Mexico's Forgotten Frontier: A History of Sonora, 1821–1846." Ph.D. dissertation, University of California, Berkeley, 1963, pp. 84–85, 132, 138, 142, and 144–74.

mander of the Tubac garrison who wrote that the vast domain stretched from Tubac on the south to "Saguarita" on the north; he described the vegetation as consisting of "mesquites, china trees, tamarisks, palo verdes, giant cactus and few cottonwoods and willows." The appraisers set the value of the land at only $30 per *sitio* since there was no running water except when the arroyos and the Santa Cruz flowed during the rainy season.*

At the first publicized sale, on July 12, 1821, in Tubac, Fray Juan Bano (curate of the San Xavier Mission) bid $210 in behalf of Ygnacio Sanches and Francisco Flores, residents at the mission. The proceedings were transferred to the capital at Arispe, south of the present U.S.-Mexican border, and the final auction was held on December 13, 14, and 15. Interested people were called by the beating of a drum to the office of the *intendente*, and the auctioneer, Loreto Salcido, asked for bids. On the third day the property went to the Ortiz brothers for $250 — about nine dollars per section. By that time, the Spanish colonial government had been overthrown in Mexico and no *título* to the land was issued. In 1849, however, the brothers presented themselves at Ures, in Sonora, and were given a title for their own protection.

Apache depredations were now wreaking havoc on the Arizona frontier and most of the ranches had been abandoned. A census report in September, 1848, showed that the people were concentrated in two places: Tucson had a population of 760 and Tubac 249; but after an Apache attack on Tubac in December, resulting in the deaths of nine persons, the residents deserted the town for awhile and lived in Tucson. During the 1850s, Apache warfare extended west of Tucson and the Santa Cruz into the Papago country. The system of *establacimientos de paz,* by which the Spaniards kept the

---

*The legal history of the Canoa grant is summarized in the Report of the U.S. Attorney, Matt G. Reynolds, Court of Private Land Claims, Arizona District, Maish and Driscoll, Plaintiffs, vs. United States, et al., Defendants, from Santa Fe, New Mexico, June 2, 1899, in RG 60: Department of Justice, National Archives. See also Decree of Confirmation of the San Ygnacio (or Ignacio) de la Canoa Grant, Frederick Maish and Thomas Driscoll, plaintiffs, vs. The United States and the Sopori Land and Mining Co. (Impleaded), in the United States Court of Private Land Claims Sitting at Tucson, Arizona, January Session, 1899. National Archives RG 49: Records of the General Land Office (GLO), Arizona Private Land Claim #5.

Indians pacified with food, firewater, and inferior guns, deteriorated under the Mexicans. The efficiently operated presidios of the golden years were also a thing of the past, and faraway leaders in Mexico City were too preoccupied with the problems of organizing a new nation to devise a plan to bring lasting peace to the fringes of Apachería.

The Gadsden Purchase and American occupation of the region south of the Gila did not change the situation very much. La Canoa was still in the hands of the Ortiz brothers, though Anglo-Americans occasionally settled on parts of the huge grant. Apaches continued their raids on the ranch during the 1850s, driving off livestock and murdering the settlers. One day in 1857 the Apaches murdered a gang of lumbermen who had built a house and corral on the Santa Cruz. These men were employed whipsawing lumber in the Santa Ritas for the Heintzelman mines. Charles Poston, who first came to Arizona in 1854, rode over from Tubac and viewed the carnage the day after the attack. "When we reached the Canoa, a little after sunrise," he said, "the place looked like it had been struck by a hurricane. The doors and windows were smashed, and the house a smoking ruin. The former inmates were lying around dead, and three of them had been thrown into the well, head foremost. We buried seven in a row in front of the burnt houses."[6] In the same raid, 280 head of animals were taken from Canoa and adjoining ranches.

The first Anglo-American to bring cattle to the Canoa was Bill Kirkland; he drove 200 head from Sonora in 1857, but they were apparently stolen in 1860. Another famous pioneer who lived on the ranch was a Kentuckian named Pete Kitchen. Stubbornly defying the Apaches who frequently attacked, he fortified his ranch houses with adobe walls, first on the Canoa where he lived from 1855 to 1862 and later at the Potrero, near Nogales. Kitchen was about the only settler to hang on after the American troops withdrew during the Civil War. He curtly described the road through the desolated country between the walled pueblo of Tucson and Sonora with the phrase, "Tucson, Tubac, and to Hell."

After the war, despite incessant Apache hostilities, fresh attempts were made to reoccupy the stockless ranges. Among

Pete Kitchen

Arizona Historical Society

the new migrants to Arizona were Frederick Maish and Thomas Driscoll, who bought a controlling interest in the Canoa from the Ortiz heirs. The surveyor general recommended confirmation of their title but Congress took no action. Maish and Driscoll started their ranching about 1870 with some 300 head of long-horned Texan cattle bought from emigrants at $15 apiece. In an interview, several years later, Maish commented, "It went very slow. The first three years we did not make our salt. The Indians stole us blind. Afterwards we had smooth sailing." By 1884, the firm was grazing 10,000 head on the Canoa and adjacent public ranges — twenty miles up and down the Santa Cruz and about twenty-five miles from mountain to mountain. "We have eight different camps in the stretch of territory," Maish said. "The river furnishes abundant water and there is always plenty of gramma grass." [7] The first profits were made from a government contract in 1874. In accordance with this contract, beef was supplied at 12½ cents per pound dressed. In 1884, Maish sold 2,600 head for $65,000, mainly for the San Carlos Indian Reservation, but also at markets in Tombstone and Los Angeles. The firm's capital of $75,000 was invested in livestock including 400 Durham and Devon bulls, steam pumps, about 500 horses, houses, and corrals. Land was no problem until the government forbade all enclosures of the open range in 1885. With fencing of the public domain prohibited, the overplus lands seemed more desirable.

In 1893 a claim for 46,696.2 acres — considerably more than the four *sitios* (17,353.84 acres) in the original grant — was brought before the Court of Private Land Claims. This court confirmed the larger amount, which included overplus lands, but the federal government appealed the case and the U.S. Supreme Court reversed the decision of the lower tribunal in these words: ". . . . we think that the grant should be sustained for the four *sitios* purchased, petitioned, and paid for, and for no more." After an official survey, the title of Maish and Driscoll was confirmed for 17,208.333 acres, slightly less than the four square leagues in the 1821 grant.*

The Canoa changed hands several times. Just before World War I, it was purchased by an energetic Mississippian named Levi H. Manning for a reported $165,000. Under his management, the Canoa became the nucleus for a sprawling enterprise that grew to encompass thousands of acres of patented and leased lands. Manning sold the north half of the original Canoa grant during the first World War to the

---

*The official measurement was 17,203.214 acres. See Descriptive Notes of the Survey of the San Ignacio de la Canoa Private Land Grant, U.S. Surveyor General for the Territory of Arizona, Hugh H. Price, June 13, 1902, in RG 49, GLO, Arizona Private Land Claim #5. See also Decree of Confirmation of the San Ignacio de la Canoa Grant, Maish and Driscoll vs. U.S. et al., U.S. Court of Private Land Claims, Tucson, Arizona, January Session, 1899, RG 49, GLO, Arizona Private Land Claim #5. See also United States vs. Maish, 171 *U.S. Reports,* pp. 242–43.

The U.S. Court of Private Land Claims records are scattered, most of them being in the National Archives in Washington, D.C., and its branches in Suitland, Maryland, or Bell, California. The records for claims in Arizona that were once in the General Land Office in Phoenix were transferred to the National Archives, but the New Mexico records — including the Baca Float documents that concern Arizona — formerly in the possession of the Bureau of Land Management in Santa Fe, are now deposited in the State of New Mexico Records Center, Archives Division, Santa Fe. The dockets for the Arizona claims brought before the court, except for the Peralta-Reavis case, are on microfilm at the Arizona Historical Society in Tucson and the proceedings of the court are on microfilm in the Arizona Department of Library and Archives in Phoenix.

Continental Rubber Company which tried to grow guayule for the manufacture of synthetic rubber. About the same time, the McGee colony of Mormons was permitted to settle on tillable lands. In 1953, approximately 200 sections (128,000 acres) of leased and deeded lands outside of the original grant were transferred or sold by Howell Manning, Levi's son, to Kemper Marley of Phoenix for approximately $600,000. Other cattlemen, farmers, and real estate promoters, including the developers of the town of Green Valley, now own a share of the old San Ignacio de Canoa. Many changes have taken place on the old grant, and it probably would be as difficult for a modern visitor on the Tucson-Nogales highway to imagine what Canoa will be like in the mid-twenty-first century as it might have been for the Ortiz family to foresee the varied economic activities underway there today.

Buenavista Grant
(María Santísima del Carmén or Buena Vista)

The Buenavista land grant, located east of Nogales on both sides of the present international border, is another Spanish stock ranch that was abandoned in the eighteenth century and then reoccupied in the early nineteenth century. The lands on the Arizona side were acquired in 1881 by the enterprising Canoa claimants, Maish and Driscoll. They paid $4,000 for rights to the grant and were allotted 5,733.41 acres by the Court of Private Land Claims. The court traced the grant back to 1826, when Francisco José de Tuvera petitioned for the deserted *rancho,* then called "María Santísima del Carmén." He died during the proceedings and the application was then sought in the name of his widow, Dóna Josefa Morales. A title was not issued until 1831 because there were defects in the original measurements of the four *sitios* and the land had to be resurveyed. The grant was purchased at the appraised price of $190 and occupied for stockraising by Tuvera's heirs until 1851, when it was sold to Hilario Gabilando. In 1872, the tract was transferred to José María Quiroga for the sum of $500. He in turn sold it nine years later to Maish and Driscoll, making an eight-fold profit on

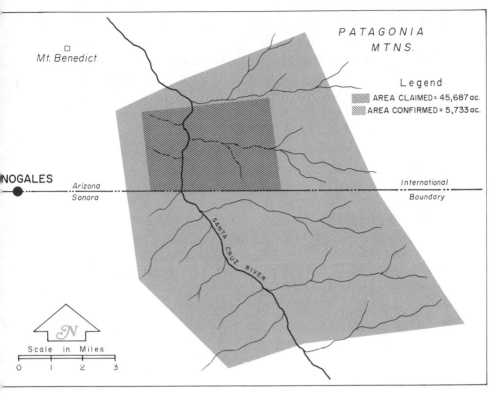

Buenavista grant

his investment. The modern Arizona real estate boom was obviously being nurtured years ago.

In 1882 the grant was surveyed by George J. Roskruge, and the surveyor general of Arizona, John Wasson, recommended confirmation of the title for 5,060 acres. But Congress took no action and the grant was finally confirmed by the Court of Private Land Claims in 1899; the amount of land approved by the surveyor general was increased to 5,733.41 acres.* Undoubtedly the most interesting and novel feature connected with this tribunal was that its proceedings and

---

*"Surveyor General's Descriptive Report on survey of the María Santísima del Carmén, alias Buena Vista, private land claim situated in Santa Cruz County, Territory of Arizona, and containing 5733.41 acres," witnessed on May 2, 1904, Frank S. Ingalls, U.S. Surveyor General for the Territory of Arizona, in RG 49, GLO, Arizona private land claim #6½.

decisions were governed primarily by Spanish and Mexican laws, even though it was a fully constituted United States court. The following copy of the transcript of the Buenavista case not only reviews the history of this particular claim but also illustrates the type of evidence considered by the court in all of the land grant suits:

In the United States
Court of Private Land Claims
Sitting in Tucson, Arizona
January Session, 1899

Frederick Maish and Thomas   Number 6½—María
Driscoll, Partners as Maish   Santísima Del Carmén
and Driscoll   Alias Buenavista Grant

vs.

The United States and
Santa Cruz Water Storage
Company, a Corporation

This cause having heretofore come on for hearing upon the pleadings and upon the evidence taken on behalf of claimants and defendants, the Court after considering the evidence submitted in the case hereby adjudges and decrees as follows, to-wit:

I

That a grant was made on the 24th day of October, 1831, by José María Mendoza, Treasurer General of the Sovereign State of Sonora, and in its name, unto Doña Josefa Morales, of a tract of land known as the rancho María Santísima del Carmén, alias Buenavista, consisting of four leagues of land, situated within the jurisdiction of the presidio of Santa Cruz and now situated partly in the State of Sonora, Mexico, and partly in the County of Santa Cruz, Territory of Arizona, the part in which County is more particularly hereinafter described.

II

That the said grant was an auction sale of said tract made by the Treasurer-General of the State of Sonora to the said grantee for the price of Sixty Dollars ($60.00) each for three of said *sitios*, and Ten Dollars ($10.00) for the remaining one, which price, amounting to One Hundred and Ninety Dollars ($190.00), was paid therefore by the said grantee named unto the Treasurer of the said State.

III

That said sale and grant were so made under and in pursuance of that certain law generally known as Decree Number Seventy of the General Congress of the United States of Mexico, issued on the 4th of August,

1824; and also under Law Number Thirty of the 20th of May, 1825, enacted by the Constituent Congress of the then United States of Sonora and Sinaloa, and also under other decrees and succeeding legislation relative thereto, authorizing such grant and sale to be made by said Treasurer General, all of which laws are hereby referred to as being those under which such grant is confirmed. And reference is hereby made to that certain treaty made between the United States and the Republic of Mexico on the 30th day of December, 1853, under which, as well as said laws before referred to, such confirmation is made.

IV

That at the trial of this cause the petition herein upon full hearing was sustained by legal and satisfactory proofs, and it was also shown that said grant and sale of the tract therein described constituted a valid title lawfully and regularly derived from the Government of Mexico and from the State of Sonora in said Republic of Mexico, having lawful authority to make the same, and that the said title was perfect and complete at the date of the acquisition of the Territory of the United States and that said grant and sale to said grantee constitutes such a valid title that the United States are bound upon the principles of public law and by the provisions of the treaty of Cession to respect it as a valid, complete and perfect title at said date.

V

That no part of the premises for which confirmation is made as hereinafter described has been disposed of by the United States.

VI

That at said trial it was made to appear that every condition and requirement stated in said grant as incumbent upon said grantee to be performed was performed within the time and in the manner stated in said grant.

VII

That the confirmation of the said grant herein decreed shall not confer any right or title to any gold, silver or quicksilver mines or minerals contained in such lands, but all such mines and minerals shall remain the property of the United States with the right of working the same, which fact shall be stated in any patent issued under this decree.

VIII

That this confirmation is made subject to all of the limitations and terms of the act of Congress of March 3, 1891.

IX

The claimants have acquired an interest in said lands hereinafter described by conveyances executed to them by the heirs at law of the original grantee herein before named.

X

Now, therefore, in consideration of the premises and by virtue of
the power vested in this Court by the provisions of the Act of Congress
approved March 3, 1891, confirmation is hereby made and decreed of
the title of said Doña Josefa Morales, and of her heirs, successors in
interest and assigns, in and to so much of the said tract María Santísima del Carmén, alias Buenavista as is situated in the County of Santa
Cruz, Territory of Arizona, and is particularly described, located and
bounded as follows, to-wit:

Beginning at the point marked "Las Casas Viejas de Buenavista," as
the same appears on the map filed in this Court and cause on February
13, 1899, which map is entitled "Map of the María Santísima del
Carmén, alias Buenavista, Private Land Claim, located in Arizona,
U.S.A., and Sonora, Mex., surveyed by George J. Roskruge Feb. 1893;"
running thence north Six Degrees 20 minutes west One Hundred and
Thirty-eight cords or Nineteen Thousand and Thirty-seven and One
Tenth feet; from the termination of said line running at right angles
easterly One Hundred and Six cords or Fourteen Thousand, Six
Hundred and Twenty-two and seven tenths feet to North-east corner;
from this point run southerly parallel to the line first described till such
parallel line intersects the International Boundary Line at the southeast
corner; from the termination of the line first described, run westerly at
right angles fifty cords or six Thousand Eight Hundred and Ninety-
seven and five tenths feet to Northwest corner, and from the termination
of this line run southerly parallel with the line first described till such
parallel line intersects the International Boundary Line at the southwest corner, thence run east along said International Boundary Line
to the point where the East line of the tract herein described intersects
said International Boundary Line at the southeast corner.

And the claim of claimants to all other land not so confirmed is
rejected.

Done in open court at Tucson, Arizona Territory, this 27th day of
November, A.D. 1899.

> (Signed) Joseph R. Reed
> Chief Justice Court of Private
> Land Claims.*

---

* Decree of Confirmation of the María Santísima del Carmén alias Buena Vista Grant
(#6½), Frederick Maish and Thomas Driscoll, partners as Maish and Driscoll, vs.
The United States et al. in the U.S. Court of Private Land Claims, Tucson, Arizona,
November 27, 1899, in National Archives RG 49, GLO, Arizona private land claim
#6½. The opinion was given by Associate Justice Stone. Justices Murray and Fuller
dissented on the ground that the grant was not located within the terms of the
Gadsden Treaty. See Report of U.S. Attorney Matt. G. Reynolds, CPLC, in the case
of Maish and Driscoll, plaintiffs, vs. United States and the Santa Cruz Water Storage
Company, defendants, Buena Vista Grant, from Santa Fe, March 15, 1900, in RG 60:
Department of Justice, National Archives.

After its confirmation by the court, the Buenavista changed hands many times, but remained intact until 1934. In that year, Karl and Delbert Peterson ended eleven years of joint ownership, dividing the grant by an east-west line that was surveyed by W. H. Roper, the Santa Cruz County Engineer.[8] A month after the partition papers were recorded in the courthouse at Nogales, Delbert sold his share, consisting of the southern portion along the international border, to Thomas F. Griffin. In 1937, Griffin deeded this property to Neilson Brown who, in turn, transferred it to Victor R. Weiss in 1957. Desert Diet Corporation of Miami, Florida, acquired title in 1959 and began subdividing the land to sell in smaller tracts.[9]

The larger northern portion of the partitioned grant was eventually purchased by movie actor James Stewart Granger. In 1969, however, Granger sold all but 119.4 acres of his ranch to Inverurie Realty, Inc., which had plans for developing a luxurious residential area similar to the Rio Rico project on the Baca Float No. 3.[10] Inverurie secured a license to do business in the state from the Arizona Corporation Commission and changed its name to Kino Springs, Incorporated.[11] The company's extensive advertising campaign to sell lots at Kino Springs — as the northern part of the grant is now called — focused nationwide attention on the Buenavista.

San Rafael de la Zanja

One of the more controversial land grants was San Rafael de la Zanja. Located east of Nogales in the headwaters of the Santa Cruz and between the Patagonia and Huachuca Mountains, it attracted competition for ownership from the beginning. A cattleman named Manuel Bustillo, who resided in the presidio of Santa Cruz, first petitioned for the grant on July 19, 1821. Explaining that he possessed considerable livestock and needed more grazing lands for their maintenance, he asked the *intendente* at Arispe to take the necessary legal steps to secure a title. The land was measured at the chosen site, under the supervision of Captain Ignacio Elías González, the commander of the *presidio,* and appraised. After asking the appraisers to consider that the land was close to Apache country, Bustillo was satisfied with their evaluation of three *sitios* with running water at $60 each and a fourth which contained no water at $30 — a total of $210 for more than 27 square miles of land. But at the public auction on January 8, 1822, Don Ramon Romero, in behalf of himself and residents of Santa Cruz, bid against Bustillo and bought the land for $1200 plus $97 in fees connected with the sale. During the course of the proceedings, Mexico gained her independence from Spain, causing an interesting novelty in the *expediente* given to Romero and other citizens.* The title issued at Arispe on May 15, 1825, by Commissary General Juan Miguel Riesgo was in the name of the Republic of Mexico but in accordance with the Spanish law of 1754 concerning such grants. One change from previous titles was a provision that the land would revert to the public domain if abandoned for one year, except for reason of Apache invasion; the usual time period was three years.

Romero lived well into the American period, dying in 1873. On his deathbed he gave the names of his legal heirs to his son Innocencio. But the young Romero apparently misplaced his father's legal papers for awhile, causing no small degree of consternation to American claimants who were trying to buy up all the rights to the San Rafael de la Zanja. Dr. Alfred A. Green gained possession of the papers in 1886 and relentlessly, though unsuccessfully, pressed his claim through the courts. Six years earlier, on June 20, 1880, however, he had signed a deed assigning his rights to the San Rafael to Rollin Rice Richardson, formerly in the oil business in Pennsylvania. Richardson owned the San Rafael for

---

*Confusion arose later over the meaning of the word *parcioneros* since the grant was not made to Romero alone but to "*Ramos Romero y parcioneros, sus hijos herederos y sucesores,*" i.e., "Ramon Romero and associates, their children, heirs and successors." The other citizens, or *parcioneros*, were not specifically named and hence there could be no deraignment of title from the original grantees to later owners. But there was a large number of persons who claimed to be heirs of the *parcioneros* and who claimed an interest in the land. Romero himself had three sons (Francisco, Pedro, and Innocencio) and two daughters (Juana and Dolores) as heirs. After 1853, the grantees paid taxes to the U.S. government. See "San Rafael de la Sanja (Zanja), Surveyor General's [John Wasson] Opinion and Recommendation in the Case," Tucson *Citizen*, May 1, 1880. See also, "Transcript of Proceedings Before the U.S.S. Gen'l. for Arizona in the Matter of the Rancho 'San Rafael de la Sanja' claimed by Ramon Romero et als.," RG 49, GLO, Arizona Private Land Claim Docket No. 9.

three years, during which time he poured $40,000 into the ranch for improvements. He was to become one of the biggest ranchers in southern Arizona, owning most of the land in the vicinity of old Fort Crittenden and Patagonia, a town which he founded in 1896. But in 1883 he chose to sell the San Rafael to Colin Cameron, who promptly chartered the San Rafael Cattle Company, under the incorporation laws of New Jersey, with a capital stock of $150,000. During the next twenty years Cameron became the epitome of enlightened self-interest among cattlemen in the Arizona territory. Not only did he improve the stock-raising industry by bringing in purebred Herefords and fighting for quarantine laws to stop the importation of diseased Mexican cattle, but he used every weapon at his command to establish control over the San Rafael and adjacent lands.[12]

Soon after Cameron received the deed from Richardson, he claimed the overplus lands that the Romeros had occupied. Under the Mexican laws, a grantee could occupy lands in excess of the stipulated amount, have it surveyed, and purchase it at the price prevailing when the original grant was appraised. Accordingly, Cameron paid $1,359 to the United States Land Office at Tucson to acquire a doubtful title to the overplus surrounding the original grant. In 1885 he employed a surveyor named Lewis Wolfley, later a territorial governor of Arizona and a bitter enemy of the Cameron family, to locate Mexican deeds not yet in his hands. Recall that the citizens of the *presidio* of Santa Cruz shared the ownership of the San Rafael with Romero. For about $80 per citizen, Wolfley was able to purchase their part of the title for Cameron. Dr. Green, however, claimed to have the original *expediente* by purchase from the legal heirs of Romero and never ceased condemning Cameron for fraudulent possession of the grant. In 1886, he even wrote to President Cleveland charging Cameron with horrible crimes against settlers in the vicinity of San Rafael. Most of Green's accusations were supported by General Edward M. McCook, a former governor of Colorado and special agent sent to investigate San Rafael by Secretary of Interior L. Q. C. Lamar. After hearing witnesses, McCook reported that Cameron

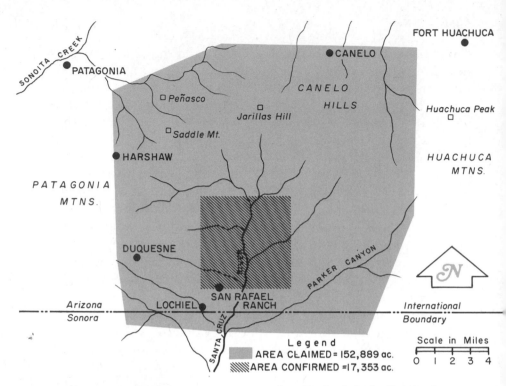

FORT HUACHUCA

SONOITA CREEK

PATAGONIA

□ Peñasco

□ Jarillas Hill

□ Saddle Mt.

CANELO

CANELO HILLS

Huachuca Peak □

HARSHAW

PATAGONIA MTNS.

HUACHUCA MTNS.

DUQUESNE

PARKER CANYON

N

Arizona
Sonora

LOCHIEL

SAN RAFAEL RANCH

SANTA CRUZ

International
Boundary

L e g e n d
AREA CLAIMED = 152,889 ac.
AREA CONFIRMED = 17,353 ac.

Scale in Miles
0 1 2 3 4

San Rafael de la Zanja Grant

Colin Cameron

Arizona Historical Society

employed the "worst class" of Mexicans to burn down the houses of homesteaders and fill up their wells. Fences had been built to enclose all of the watering places, and in 1887 Cameron was indicted by the district court grand jury in Tucson and brought to trial for unlawfully fencing the public domain.

In ordering him to remove all barriers outside the original four *sitios,* Judge William H. Barnes explained that all land grants were part of the public domain, even though they were "reserved from sale," until the claims were adjudicated. Barnes was not considering the validity of the claim in this case, but he made reference to the measurements of the San Rafael made by deputy surveyor Solon M. Allis in 1880 and concurred with the recommendation of the former surveyor general, John Wasson, that the grant be confirmed for only four square leagues. The surveyor general at the time of the trial in 1887, John Hise, was pleased. Observing that the sentiment in the territory was almost unanimous as to the justness and clarity of the decision against Cameron, he wrote, "This is the first gun in Arizona from the bench from a fearless and honest judge in opposition to what is styled 'land grabbers,' and the people hail the dawning of a brighter and happier period for our young and downtrodden territory."[13]

Hise was disappointed, however, that the evidence in this trial did not reveal the exact amount of land actually claimed by the San Rafael Cattle Company. He suspected that the claimants were concealing the magnitude of an "attempt to encompass a good slice of the public domain." And when Cameron was made a party to a suit brought by Dr. Green before the Court of Private Land Claims, evidence was unveiled which left no doubt that Hise had aptly used the term "land grabbers."

Green brought suit against the United States; and the court made all persons who claimed some interest in the San Rafael grant "parties defendant to the cause." In addition to Cameron, the defendants included Harvey L. Christie, William C. Jones, Albert Steinfeld, and sixty others. Cameron, represented by attorney Rochester Ford (until this lawyer's death while the hearings were in progress) and by Selim Franklin, filed an answer in which he denied the petitioner's claim and asserted his own. Stating that he was in possession of the tract under the grant of May 15, 1825, Cameron questioned Wasson's literal interpretation of "four square leagues." In the first place, it was alleged that the wording in the original *expediente* — "*cuatro sitios para cria de ganado mayor"* — actually meant "four leagues square," or sixteen *sitios* (69,415 acres)* instead of four (17,354 acres).[14]

Furthermore, Cameron contended that the original grant to Romero was not one of quantity (that is an exact number of *sitios*) but was a sale by "metes and bounds." By this system, the extent of the grant, including overplus lands, was determined by the natural landmarks surrounding "la Zanja," as established by the Spanish survey. Using this reasoning, the San Rafael Cattle Company claimed 152,889.62 acres, approximately 239 square miles. After hearing from all parties concerned, the court, with Chief Justice Joseph Reed presiding, confirmed the title, not for the plaintiff but for Cameron and Christie.† The size of the grant was limited to "four *sitios*, the same to be measured in a square." The "square" measurement moved the southern boundary of the San Rafael de la Zanja away from the Mexican border. Wasson's survey in 1880 had arranged the *sitios* in a reverse "L" shape with three extending north from the border and the fourth along the line to the west. In 1902, the Supreme Court affirmed the decision of the lower court in all aspects.[15]

---

*Cameron had some legal justification for claiming sixteen *sitios*. No less an authority than R. C. Hopkins explained in 1884 that Romero had paid more than enough for this amount of land ($1200 or $75 per *sitio*), since the highest rate per square league in 1822 was $60 which would be $960 for sixteen *sitios*. "This [$1200] would certainly be considered as an exorbitant price for the land," he said, "in view of the time at which the sale was made and the uninviting character of the locality which, at that time, and long prior to and after that date, was notoriously exposed to the inroads of the Apache Indians, the northern portion of the tract, as measured, being especially noted, as a lurking place for these murderous savages." See "Report of an examination on the ground, of the boundaries of the Rancho of San Rafael de la Zanja, for the purpose of ascertaining if the natural land marks, called for in the original title papers, can be identified on the ground," by R. C. Hopkins, December 15, 1884, in National Archives RG 49, GLO. The Commissioner of the General Land Office, N. C. McFarland, agreed: "The sale and conveyance having been made by the Mexican government for the sixteen square leagues and the parties having taken possession and continued such possession peaceably for so long a time," he wrote, "I do not think it competent now for this government to reduce the quantity." Letter of N. C. McFarland, Commissioner of the General Land Office, to the Secretary of Interior, S. J. Kirkwood, from Washington, D.C., April 11, 1882, in RG 49, GLO, Arizona Private Land Claim Docket #9.

† Cameron and Christie presented the original *titulo* to the court as well as the original *expediente* found in the archives of the Mexican government. Associate Justices Murray and Fuller, however, did not concur in the decision. In the dissenting opinion Murray wrote: "It has not been shown that the grant in this case was recorded in the archives of Mexico, and this court has no power to confirm it. . . . The books of the *Toma de Razon* were in evidence on the trial but there is no entry of this grant on either. . . ." See "Dissenting Opinion" in Report of U.S. Attorney Matt. G. Reynolds, CPLC, in the case of Alfred A. Green, plaintiff, vs. United States et al., defendants, San Rafael de la Zanja Grant, from Santa Fe, March 15, 1900, in RG 60: Department of Justice, National Archives.

The Cameron interests were somewhat disappointed but really had little to complain about. For twenty years they had profited from the use of a vast domain without having to pay the taxes assessed on privately owned lands. In 1903, the ranch and stock were sold for $1,500,000 to William C. Greene, and Cameron retired from ranching to live in Tucson. Greene wanted a place for breeding pure Hereford bulls to introduce on his extensive grazing ranges south of the border. His intention was to improve the low-bred Mexican cattle, but as the San Rafael and adjacent Greene ranches grew, the pure stock was also marketed in the United States. Greene and his heirs used Cameron's "6T" brand until 1922 when it was changed to "RO."

Greene was one of the most picturesque characters in Arizona history — a high-stake gambler who dreamed big dreams and an inveterate prospector who saw a potential fortune in every red-stained ridge. Born in Wisconsin, he came to Arizona in 1877 while still in his twenties and audaciously built up a multi-million dollar legacy. After searching for minerals in the Bradshaw Mountains of northern Arizona, he joined the rush to Tombstone during the boom days of that town. Working as a miner and a supplier of wood, he eventually married a widow and settled on a ranch near Hereford in the San Pedro Valley. A tragic event in his life occurred after he constructed a dam to direct water into an alfalfa patch. Someone dynamited the dam, creating a flooded river in which Greene's little daughter Ella and a playmate were drowned, and he blamed his neighbor downstream — a man named Jim Burnett who had been an unpopular justice of the peace when he served in that capacity. Greene angrily looked for Burnett and shot his unarmed victim on the street in Tombstone. The Cochise County courthouse was jammed for his three-day murder trial in December, 1897; but after B. A. Packard, a prominent and respected rancher, testified that Burnett had earlier threatened the defendant's life, the jury acquitted Greene, taking only ten minutes to deliberate on the verdict. Before the end of the century, Greene's first wife died and he went prospecting near Cananea in Mexico. Acquiring an option on the rich Cobre Grande copper mine, he flamboyantly established himself at the Waldorf in New

York and accumulated sufficient working capital to begin operations. Several years later, however, he liquidated his mining interests for about six million dollars and began devoting his energies to cattle ranching. In addition to the Ranchos de Cananea, containing approximately 700,000 acres in a fifty-mile strip south of the border, the Greene Cattle Company controlled not only the San Rafael de la Zanja, but other ranches in Arizona. Greene, the former copper magnate, had truly become cattle king of the border by the time of his death on August 5, 1911. He died of acute pneumonia that resulted from several broken ribs and other injuries sustained when his team of horses was spooked and ran away in Cananea.[16]

When Mary Proctor, his second wife — who was a Tucson *Citizen* typesetter at the time she met and married Greene — died in 1955, the huge estate was passed on to her four sons (William, Frank, Kirk, and Charles) and two daughters (Virginia Sturdivant and Florence Sharp). Mrs. Eva Greene Day, a daughter by Greene's first wife, sued for and secured a one-seventh share in 1961. By that time, in 1958, the Mexican government had seized the vast Greene ranch in Sonora in accordance with a provision in the 1917 constitution which forbade foreigners to own land within 62 miles of the border. Over 800 Mexican families were destined to be settled on the expropriated lands. As of the early 70s, the Greenes still owned ranches in Arizona, however, even though some of the holdings had been divided among members of the family. From 1958, the San Rafael de la Zanja was under operation by the San Rafael Cattle Corporation headed by Mrs. Florence Greene Sharp. Her brother, Charles H. Greene, was president of the Greene Cattle Company that controlled the huge Baca Float No. 5 and adjacent lands in the Prescott-Seligman area from 1937 to 1973.*

---

*The Greene Cattle Company transferred ownership of the San Rafael (17,474.06 acres) to the San Rafael Cattle Corporation in 1958. See Docket Book No. 12, pp. 208–10, Santa Cruz County Recorder's office, Nogales, Arizona. See also the files of the San Rafael Cattle Corporation and the Greene Cattle Company, Inc. — containing articles of incorporation and financial statements — in the Arizona Corporation Commission, Incorporating Department, Phoenix, Arizona.

San José de Sonoita

The smallest land grant in Arizona was the San José de Sonoita which stretches out along both sides of the meandering Sonoita Creek west of the town of Patagonia. The Spanish first came into contact with this area when Father Kino established a *visita* of the Guevavi mission (the Jesuits called it Los Reyes de Sonoidag) for about five hundred Sobaípuri Pimas under Chief Coro. In 1698, the Jesuits had moved from Quíburi to the Sonoita — which in Papago means "place where the corn grows" — in order to increase the distance between themselves and the Apaches. But the incursions of the Apaches continued. At the time of the Pima Revolt in 1751 there were fewer than a hundred natives living at Sonoidag. By the 1780s it was abandoned.

In 1821, a rancher and resident of nearby Tubac, Leon Herreras (spelled Herreros in some of the records), petitioned for two *sitios* of land at "a place called San José de Sonoita in the jurisdiction of Tubac" to pasture his rapidly increasing herd of cattle. The necessary survey of the land was supervised by Ignacio Elías González. Starting at a point within the walls of an old building at the *visita*, the surveyors zigzagged around rough, rocky country that the claimant did not want included in his grant. Because of many turns and angles, the measurements seemed big enough on paper to enclose more than the two *sitios* requested. So Herreras consented to a lesser amount, one and three-fourths *sitios*, to avoid any misinterpretation of the survey. After the required public auctions, he bought the land in November, 1821, at the appraised price of $105 plus fees; the grant was valued at $60 per *sitio* because it had running water and was considered to be suitable for cultivation. A title was issued in 1825 by Juan Miguel Riesgo, commissary-general of the newly combined Mexican state of Sinaloa-Sonora, called Occidente.

Like the San Rafael de la Zanja title, the Herreras title was granted by the Republic of Mexico but in accordance with the provisions of the Spanish law of 1754. A proviso was included whereby the land would revert to the public domain if abandoned for more than one year, except if invaded by Apaches. During the 1830s the Herreras family was driven

Henry O. Flipper

National Archives

away by Indian depredations. In 1857 the heirs sold out and after several transfers the grant was acquired by Matias Alsua who submitted his claim to the U.S. General Land Office for approval. After investigation, the surveyor general in 1880 recommended confirmation of 7,598.07 acres on the basis of a preliminary survey made by John L. Harris. The Court of Private Land Claims rejected the title in 1892, however, on the grounds there was no law authorizing the sale of public lands for several years following the Mexican declaration of independence on March 1, 1821 or the beginning of the provisional Mexican government on September 28, 1821.* In other words, the court ruled that the *intendente* had no power to sell lands to Herreras in November, 1821. The Court of Private Land Claims also declared that it was impossible to determine the true location of the lands because the

---

* Henry O. Flipper, the first Negro graduate of West Point and a former Army officer, made the investigations into the archival records and the location of the grant for the Court of Private Land Claims. See Report of U.S. Attorney Matt. G. Reynolds in the case of the United States vs. Santiago Ainsa, from Santa Fe, June 9, 1894, in RG 60: Department of Justice, National Archives. See also, *Arizona Enterprise* (Florence), March 31, 1894.

grant was made for a definite quantity of land within a broader area having specified natural outboundaries.

In 1898, the U. S. Supreme Court reversed the decision of the lower court, arguing that the claims court was one of equity and hence not limited to the dry, technical rules of a court of law.[17] The initial point of the survey was known and therefore the court could investigate and decide what was reasonably intended by the Mexican officials in granting the title. The Supreme Court also explained that the Mexican government made no attempt to question the validity of the Sonoita sale or to dispossess the grantee up to the time of the transfer of the Gadsden Purchase lands to the United States. It was thus the duty of the American government to respect and enforce the Herreras title. The case was remanded to the lower tribunal which still held that the Sonoita grant was "without warrant of law and invalid" but concluded that "the question has been decided by the supreme court, and is settled." The title was confirmed for 5,123.42 acres.[18] About two thousand acres overlapped the Baca Float No. 3 grant and were later awarded to the claimants of that grant.

In the 1930s the Sonoita grant became part of the Wilshaw Ranch operated northeast of Nogales by a couple from New York, Frank W. Cowlishaw and his wife. In 1931, they came to the Circle Z Ranch, adjacent to and south of the Sonoita grant, for the holidays. Their usual traveling consisted of an annual trip to Europe to buy antiques for Macy's Corner Shop managed by Mrs. Cowlishaw. They had never been west and didn't know a steer from a cow but liked what they found and within three weeks bought a cattle ranch. Applying modern merchandising methods to the livestock industry, they soon had one of the most efficiently operated spreads in the state. Their ranch house — located on the Circle Z southwest of Patagonia on State Highway 82 to Nogales — was designed by a California architect; with landscaped gardens and eighteenth century antique furniture, it became a showplace that has been publicized in national magazines. When Frank Cowlishaw died in 1945, his wife stayed on in the big home and directed the cattle operations. In 1949, however, she sold the Sonoita land grant to Mrs.

Leila H. Lewis. The Phoenix Title and Trust Company (now named the Transamerica Title Insurance Company) purchased it from Mrs. Lewis in 1960.[19] Today the huge Cowlishaw ranch is no longer intact, though the San José de Sonoita itself has not been broken up very much. Some of the land on the east portion of the grant near Patagonia has been subdivided, and the Patagonia Recreation Association, Inc. has constructed a dam that holds back a lake on nearly a square mile of land on the western end of the grant. A lot of cattle have roamed over the hills in between these projects since Don Leon Herreras drove in his first herd during the 1820s.

San Ignacio del Babocomari

The Babocomari was one of the most ideally situated grants. Stretching out more than twenty miles along a creek by the same name, it is located at about 4,000 feet elevation and the rainfall is heavier here than in most parts of southern Arizona. The boundary line between Cochise and Santa Cruz counties today splits the grant into two almost equal parts for tax purposes; several bunkhouses are in Santa Cruz, but other improvements are on the Cochise tax rolls. The modern headquarters of the ranch is on the site of the old Pima Indian village of Huachuca, after which the fort and some mountains south of the grant are named.

Father Kino and Manje first visited here in 1697, having traveled from the south through the San Rafael Valley and across the Canelo Hills west of the present-day Huachuca military reservation. The padre and his companion were welcomed by some eighty persons under Chief Taravilla ("the Prattler") and lodged in an adobe house. As did later visitors to the area through the centuries, Kino observed the moist, fertile valley and La Ciénega (the marsh) where plentiful crops were raised. Huachuca was the last village of the people whom the Spaniards called Pimas proper. Those beyond were the Sobaípuri Pimas. Leaving Huachuca, Kino went downstream to the villages of Santa Cruz and Quíburi, near the juncture of the Babocomari with the San Pedro, where the Indian neophytes were caring for 100 head of cattle.

When the Apaches became more hostile, the Pimas of this region moved westward to the Santa Cruz River and its tributaries. In 1762, one group was escorted to the settlement of San José del Tucson by Captain Francisco Elías González de Zaya, the illustrious ancestor of the Elías González family that settled at least five grants in Arizona and produced a line of famous people in Sonora — including several governors, a president of Mexico, soldiers, priests, and big landowners. In 1827, Don Ignacio Elías González and Doña Eulalia Elías González asked for a tract of eight *sitios* of land — known as San Ignacio del Babocomari — for raising large herds of cattle and horses. The land was auctioned and bought by the petitioners the following year. The appraised price was $60 for each of the six *sitios* that had running water and $10 each for two dry ones — a total of $380 for slightly more than 54 square miles of some of the best grazing land in Arizona. The customary title — which was issued at Arispe on Christmas Day, 1832 — contained a three-year abandonment clause and required the purchasers to mark the boundaries with monuments. For practical purposes, however, the usable area extended from the Santa Rita Mountains on the west to the San Pedro River on the east. For nearly twenty years the Elías livestock grazed the lush well-watered grasslands of the valley. But by the end of the 1840s the family, like the Pimas before them, left their flourishing *hacienda* to the Apaches who had already killed two Elías brothers.

In September, 1851, Boundary Commissioner John R. Bartlett camped near the ruins of the Elías ranch house where his men caught fish in the stream and observed a herd of wild horses. Bartlett recorded the following description of the deserted Mexican land grant in his diary:

> The valley of the Babocomari is here from a quarter to a half mile in breadth and covered with a luxuriant growth of grass. The stream, which is about twenty feet wide, and in some places two feet deep, winds through this valley, with willows, and large cotton-wood trees growing along its margin. Some of our men followed it about seven miles, to its junction with the San Pedro. This hacienda, as I afterwards learned, was one of the largest cattle establishments in the State of Sonora. The cattle roamed along the entire length of the valley; and at the time it was abandoned, there were not less than 40,000 head of them

besides a large number of horses and mules. The same cause which led
to the abandonment of so many other ranchos, haciendas, and villages,
in the State, had been the ruin of this. The Apaches encroached upon
them, drove off their animals and murdered the herdsmen; when the
owners, to save the rest, drove them further into the interior, and left
the place. Many of the cattle, however, remained and spread themselves
over the hills and valleys near; from these, numerous herds have
sprung, which now range along the entire length of the San Pedro, and
its tributaries."[20]

Several years after Bartlett's visit, one of Arizona's first
pioneer Indian fighters, Captain James H. Tevis, camped at
the old ranch headquarters. In his book, *Arizona in the 50s,*
Tevis wrote that the old Mexican fort at Babocomari consisted
of adobe buildings covering about an acre of ground. The
fifteen-foot wall that encircled the entire fort had a lookout
post at each corner. The only entrance was large enough to
drive a wagon through. "The first night we were there," the
Captain wrote, "we put up a regular guard, and, besides that,
we pulled one of the wagons up before the entrance, blocking
it up effectively."[21]

In 1864, the old walled fort of San Ignacio del Babocomari was occupied by a unit of the United States Cavalry.
Simply designated New Post at first, it was named Camp
Wallen two years later. From this fort, the troopers conducted
several campaigns against the Apache warriors of Cochise in
the region lying between the Huachuca Mountains and the
Chiricahuas, some eighty miles to the east. Camp Wallen was
abandoned in 1869, however, and it was eight years before a
replacement post was established at Fort Huachuca.

By 1877, Dr. Edward B. Perrin had purchased all the
rights to the Babocomari from G. H. Howard and others; he
submitted his claim to the surveyor general for approval.
Formerly a Confederate soldier from Alabama, Perrin accumulated large areas of land in California and was destined to
become one of Arizona's biggest landowners; besides the
Babocomari, he acquired possession of well over 200,000
acres of checkerboard lands along the Atlantic and Pacific in
addition to the 100,000 acre Baca Float no. 5, south of Seligman. The latter, of course, was sold to the Greene Cattle Company five years after his death in 1932. Of all his land, the

Babocomari grant seemed to be the most difficult to obtain, at least in the acreage he sought. The surveyor general recommended approval for only eight square leagues, or 34,723.028 acres, as measured by his deputy, Solon Allis. On June 23, 1881, Dr. Perrin sold the "Bavacomeri" to his brother Robert for $16,000. The latter secured a deed for eight *sitios*, which is now recorded in the Cochise County courthouse at Bisbee, but later asked the Court of Private Land Claims for about three and a half times that amount, including overplus lands.

The claim was rejected in the hearings before this tribunal because there was uncertainty about the description of the property in the Mexican *expediente*. The U. S. Supreme Court in 1898, however, reversed the judgment and remanded the case for further proceedings. "Perhaps the claimants," said the higher court, "may be able to satisfactorily identify a tract not larger than the area purchased and paid for which should equitably be recognized as the tract granted."[22] In a split decision, the Court of Private Land Claims subsequently confirmed title to approximately eight *sitios*.[23] In 1902, Robert Perrin transferred the grant back to his brother, E. B., but ten years later bought a one-sixth interest which he gave up in 1917.

The Letter of Patent, dated May 16, 1904, affirmed that $374.61 had been paid for one-half the cost of the survey and officially gave title to the land to Dr. Perrin. As the legal purchaser, he was to ". . . . have and to hold the said tract of land with the appurtenances thereunto belonging unto the said Ignacio and Eulalia Elías and to their heirs, successors in interest and assigns forever with stipulations aforesaid . . . ." The document was signed by President Theodore Roosevelt, and adorned with the seal of the General Land Office.[24]

In 1936, the Brophy family acquired a deed to the Babocomari ranch from the Perrin Properties, Inc. An undivided 2500 acres of the grant had been sold to Byron Waters in May, 1898, and transferred to Walter Vail a month later.[25] Whereas previous owners of the grant had faced the uncertainties of Apache depredations, the new owners were confronted with problems of a different nature. As in most of Arizona, the ranges of the Babocomari (or Babacomari, as it is now spelled) had deteriorated because of a half century of overgrazing. Several periods of drought had also helped to diminish the grass cover, letting the torrential summer rains wash the precious topsoil down the Babocomari Creek to the San Pedro River. A fight began to save the grasslands. Check dams were constructed in arroyos and furrows were dug on the hillsides to stop or divert the waters that were no longer absorbed gradually into grass-covered earth. Pastures were reseeded and new wells were dug. The effort paid off and Frank Cullen Brophy was able to say in the mid 1960s: "After thirty years of conservation warfare, peace has come again to San Ignacio del Babacomari."[26]

San Juan de las Boquillas y Nogales Grant

The Boquillas grant is located along both banks of the San Pedro River, extending about an equal distance from the north and south juncture of the Babocomari Creek. "Boquillas" (little mouths in Spanish) is an appropriate name because of the little streams that run into the Babocomari near its confluence with the San Pedro. Once the site of a Kino *ranchería,* this area was controlled by the Apaches in the last half of the eighteenth century. In 1827, Captain Ignacio Elías González, an active military commander on the Arizona frontier, and Nepomucino Felix applied for an elongated grant of four *sitios* — approximately three-fourths of a league wide and five and one half leagues long. The grantees paid $240 for the four *sitios;* they were issued a title in 1833 and complied with the customary provisions for occupying the lands until the Apaches drove them away.

The initial point of survey was about a half mile south of the present railroad station of Fairbank. The San Pedro Valley is broad at this point but contracts to a few hundred yards at some places. Back from the flat lands are mesas that are cut up by gorges and washes running toward the river. Above the northern boundary the Mormon town of St. David was located in 1877; on the southern end, the wild town of Charlestown bustled with rustlers, miners, and soldiers during the 1880s.

The original Mexican owners each left numerous children and heirs to the Boquillas grant. The rights of the descendants who could be found were eventually bought by George Hill Howard. There was some confusion in the transactions, however, since different members of the Mexican families were found to have the same name. Legal questions also clouded the Howard claim. Apparently one of Nepomucino's sons, Francisco María Felix, was never heard from after he left home to join the gold rush to California; his interests, and those of children he might have had, remained outstanding. Another legal technicality developed with the death of Concepción Bustamante whose mother, daughter of the original grantee Felix, was also deceased. Concepción's husband, Jesus López León, sold the rights of her three children; but apparently he had no power of attorney or authority to alienate their interests.

By 1880, however, Howard had established a sound claim to the Boquillas; he transferred half of it to his wife Janet G., and the other half to George Hearst. These two claimants petitioned Surveyor General John Wasson for recognition of their title; Wasson had the grant surveyed and recommended approval of the claim in 1881 for 17,355.86 acres, approximately the four *sitios* allowed in the original grant. Hearst — a newspaperman, mine-owner, and U. S. Senator from California in 1886 and again from 1887 until his death in 1891 — purchased Mrs. Howard's half interest in 1889.[27] Then his widow, Phoebe (also Phebe), and their famous son, William Randolph Hearst, petitioned the Court of Private Land Claims for confirmation of 30,728 acres, including overplus lands. And finally, on February 14, 1899, Chief Justice Joseph R. Reed informed the plaintiffs that their title was valid but only the four square leagues auctioned by the Mexican authorities in 1827 could be confirmed. No appeal was made to the Supreme Court and John A. Rockfellow made the official survey — 17,355.86 acres by measurement — for Surveyor General George Christ in 1899.[28]

President William McKinley's name was affixed to a patent issued January 18, 1901. In July of the same year, the

Hearst family sold the property to the Boquillas Land and Cattle Company operating out of Bakersfield, California.[29] This company faced the same range problems during the 1930s that plagued the Brophys on the Babocomari. Though excessive erosion had started later in the San Pedro Valley than in most other parts of southern Arizona, deterioration, resulting mainly from overgrazing, began during the 1880s and was quite evident on the Boquillas grant by 1892. The flat land, originally covered by high sacaton grass and groves of trees, was changed into a forest of mesquite by the arroyo-cutting process.

The Boquillas Land and Cattle Company became a subsidiary of the Kern County Land and Cattle Company which recorded a deed in its name to the Rancho San Juan de las Boquillas y Nogales in 1958. The Kern company was one of the largest ranching, farming, and landowning operations in the United States, with holdings in Oregon, California, and New Mexico, as well as in Arizona. In addition to the Boquillas grant, the Kern company acquired ownership of the San Rafael del Valle and the two grants became known collectively as the Little Boquillas Ranch. In 1967, the Kern company consolidated with Tenneco, Inc. and has done business in Arizona since 1971 as Tenneco West, Inc.[30]

San Rafael del Valle

There were two Arizona land grants in the San Pedro Valley south of the Boquillas: the San Pedro and the San Rafael del Valle. Each was a grant of four *sitios* given to Rafael Elías González who apparently also had a share of the Agua Prieta. The San Rafael del Valle, which stretches out over rolling hills on both sides of the river, north of present-day Hereford, was acquired by the grantee in 1827 for $240; he received a title five years later. Then followed the same pattern of occupation — large herds of cattle and cultivation followed by Apache raids and desertion of the land grant. When Rafael Elías died, he left a widow, Guadalupe Pérez de Elías, and three sons (José Juan, Manuel, and José María) in possession of his land grants.

In 1862, the Elías brothers and their mother gave a $12,000 mortgage on thirty-two leagues of their inheritance, including the San Rafael del Valle, in favor of the Camou brothers (Joseph, Pierre, and Pascual) of Hermosillo, Sonora. When the three year mortgage was up in July, 1865, the French army was occupying Mexico and the two parties to the loan were not in communication. José Juan Elías was killed fighting in the army of General Pesqueira, the governor of Sonora; on the other hand, the Camou brothers, being French citizens, sided with the invaders. The Camous never foreclosed their mortgage nor protested for non-payment, since their real objective was to acquire the property, not to collect their money. On March 23, 1869, the Elías lands were deeded to them by the surviving mortgagers; Bernadina — the widow of José Juan and mother of his seven children — also signed the deed. When the Camous petitioned the surveyor general for approval of their title to the San Rafael del Valle, the administrator for the estate of José Juan, one Santiago Ainsa, entered an adverse claim. He argued that the widow's signature was invalid under the laws of Arizona since she did not inherit any of the separate property of her husband. But after examination of all the papers pertinent to the claim, Surveyor General Wasson decided that the San Rafael grant was valid and recommended confirmation of a title for the Camous. He explained that the statements filed by Ainsa were not sufficiently verified and that validation of the Camou claim would not prevent adverse claimants from suing the owners to satisfy alleged interests in the grant.

Congress took no action, however, and twenty years were to elapse before the Camou family had a clear title. It took four court cases to settle their claim to the San Rafael del Valle — two in the Court of Private Land Claims and two before the Supreme Court. The lower court started the chain in 1891 by rejecting the Camou petition for 20,034 acres — more than the four leagues recommended by Wasson twelve years earlier. The judgment was based upon an edict of Dictator Santa Anna, after the Gadsden Purchase Treaty was negotiated with him, that subjected all post-1821 land grants in Mexico to review by the central government in

Mexico City. Three out of five members of the Court of Private Land Claims were of the opinion that since the government of the United States recognized Santa Anna as the head of the Mexican government while negotiating the purchase, the American courts must also recognize his declaration in respect to titles as authoritative. If titles reviewed in Mexico were rescinded, for example, then it followed that similar titles in the Gadsden area should not be confirmed. The U. S. Supreme Court reversed the decision of the lower court, however, on the grounds that the "declaration of a temporary dictator was not potent to destroy the title," especially since Santa Anna's edict providing for a review of land titles issued after 1821 was revoked by his successor.[31] The Court of Private Land Claims then subserviently bowed to the decree of the higher court and confirmed the grant for 17,474.93 acres, or approximately four *sitios*.[32] But then the United States government appealed, contending that the San Rafael del Valle grant was "a mere float within exterior boundaries containing a larger tract" and that a specific plat of four square leagues could not be identified. The Supreme Court, however, sided with the Camou family and expressed the opinion that a definite grant was located prior to the Gadsden purchase.[33]

In 1905, the San Rafael del Valle was purchased from the Camou family by Cornell Greene, then of Bisbee. The deed was signed on April 19 by the following members of the family — the large number of which illustrates the problem often encountered in clearing the title to a Spanish or Mexican land grant: Jean Pierre Camou (also known as Juan Pedro Camou, the Spanish form of his French name), a widower; Luisa Camou de Morales and Arturo Morales, her husband; Rafael Camou, a single man; Catarina Camou de Escabosa, a widow; Aglae Camou de Morales and Alfonso Morales, her husband; Guadalupe Camou and J. P. M. Camou, her husband; Eduardo Camou and Beatriz Mange de Camou, his wife — all residents of the cities of Hermosillo or Guaymas, state of Sonora, Republic of Mexico.[34]

In 1912 — after Greene's death — the San Rafael del Valle was sold by the Greene Cattle Company to the Boquillas Land and Cattle Company, which also owned the San Juan de las Boquillas y Nogales downstream.* During World War II, the United States government bought 2,000 acres on the south end of the San Rafael for $11,000.[35] The larger remaining part of the San Rafael del Valle has undergone the same changes in ownership as has the Boquillas grant. After 1958 the title was in the ·name of the Kern County Land and Cattle Company, a huge California corporation that merged with Tenneco, Inc. in 1967.

San Bernardino

Like most of the grants, the San Bernardino, located seventeen miles east of Douglas, illustrates a continuity of Spanish-Mexican-American settlement in Arizona. Here in the midst of a broad desert valley in southeastern Arizona, water flows from natural springs. Continuously from the late 1600s to the days of the California gold rush, the ranch was a crossroads of travel for military expeditions, emigrants, and stock drives. From a high mesa near the present ranch house one can see sixty miles north to the Chiricahua Mountains and almost as far south into the Bavispe Valley of Old Mexico. The high ground is called "Mesa de la Avanzada," or mesa of the advanced guard, because it is believed that an advance detachment of soldiers from the presidio of Fronteras was once stationed there. Mention is made of the San Bernardino in the *Rudo Ensayo* of 1763. And Captain Juan Bautista de Anza wrote a letter from the ranch to Mexico City when he was quartered there in 1773 while leading a campaign against the Apaches from his home fort at Tubac.

In 1820, Lieutenant Ignacio de Pérez proposed to establish a buffer state against the Apaches at San Bernardino. Petitioning for a grant, he offered to induce the Indians to settle down to a peaceful life of farming. Four *sitios* of land were

---

* *The Tucson Citizen,* April 25, 1912. The Boquillas Land and Cattle Company paid $400,000 for Greene Cattle Company rangeland and cattle. Included in the sale was the San Rafael del Valle (17,474.92 acres) and over fifty smaller ranches stretching some ninety miles south of Benson, Arizona, into Sonora. In 1958, the title to the San Rafael del Valle was transferred from the Boquillas company to its parent corporation, the Kern County Land and Cattle Company. Since 1971 the title has been in the name of Tenneco West, Inc., a subsidiary of Tenneco, Inc. that includes the former Kern company's operations. See the files of these companies in the Arizona Corporation Commission, Incorporating Department, Phoenix, Arizona.

surveyed in 1821 and witnesses testified that Pérez had enough livestock to start a ranch. The land was advertised at Fronteras and auctions held at Arispe in May, 1822. Pérez had to bid a total of $90 to get the property, though the land had been appraised for only $60 — one *sitio* with the springs at $30 and three dry *sitios* at $10 each. A record of the grant was filed but no *titulo* was ever issued to Pérez by the Spanish king, whose authority in Mexico ended in 1821. The ranch was occupied with thousands of cattle, horses, and mules until the 1830s when the Apaches were again on the warpath. The Spaniards departed hastily, abandoning a large number of cattle that reverted to being wild. Some of the animals were encountered in December, 1846, by Philip St. George Cooke and the Mormon Battalion during the Mexican War. The Mormons and other emigrants during the gold rush butchered enough of the cattle to replenish their food supply.

Boundary Commissioner John R. Bartlett visited the deserted old *hacienda* of San Bernardino in May, 1851, and described it in his diary:

San Bernardino is a collection of adobe buildings in a ruined state, of which nothing but the walls remain. One of these buildings was about one hundred feet square, with a court in the centre; and adjoining it were others with small apartments. The latter were doubtless the dwellings of the peons and herdsmen. The whole extending over a space of about two acres, was inclosed with a high wall of adobe, with regular bastions for defence. Being elevated some twenty or thirty feet above the valley, this hacienda commands a fine view of the country around. Vast herds of cattle were formerly raised here, but the frequent attacks of the Apaches led to the abandonment of the place . . . I saw a number of these cattle when riding in advance of the party, but having only my double-barrelled gun and my revolvers with me, did not dare to shoot at them. These herds were small, not more than six in each, led by a stately bull. A wounded bull would be a serious antagonist, more so, I have been told, than a buffalo. This establishment was abandoned about twenty years ago, since which time, no attempt has been made to reoccupy it . . ."[36]

In August, 1852, Bartlett was back at San Bernardino and met Colonel Gilanin García with troops from the Tucson garrison at the springs. After the Gadsden Purchase, another boundary commissioner, William H. Emory, stopped at the deserted ranch. His survey of the new international boundary put most of the ranch in Mexico. Of approximately 70,000 acres, including overplus, only 2,383 acres were found to be on the American side.*

The owner of the ranch after 1884, on both sides of the border, was John Slaughter, who came from Texas with a large herd of longhorns during the boom days of Tombstone. When Slaughter spotted the San Bernardino grant with its plentiful supply of water, he arranged to buy it from one G. Andrade of Guaymas, Mexico. His claim before the Court of Private Land Claims was for 13,746 acres north of the border, but only slightly more than a half *sitio* was confirmed and no appeal was made to the Supreme Court.[37] With the purchase of private lands and most of the water holes in the area, he was able to build up one of the largest spreads in Arizona. Until 1890, Slaughter had a partner, George W. Lang, who helped him accumulate up to 50,000 head of cattle. His brand, a "Z" on the right shoulder, was the first to be registered in Cochise County.

From 1887 to 1890, Slaughter took time from his cattle business to serve as sheriff. During the 1880s, the county seat at Tombstone and the whole of Cochise County were so infested with cattle rustlers, border bandits, gamblers, and other lawless men that it was unsafe for respectable people. When an offense occurred while Sheriff Slaughter was in office, he took to the trail and seldom returned with a live prisoner; the suspects never returned to Tombstone or anywhere else. After cleaning up the county in this frontier fashion, Slaughter concentrated on the San Bernardino where he built a rambling ranch mansion of adobe, a village for the cowboys, barns, granaries, and eventually even a schoolhouse. Artesian wells were drilled and a concrete dam was constructed to back up a lake. With extensive pastures surrounding this headquarters, John Slaughter was one of the prominent cattle kings in Arizona until his death in 1922. Two years later, his wife

---

*The Court of Private Land Claims set the figure in 1900 at 2,366.5 acres "more or less," but the official survey of John A. Rockfellow in 1901 established the size as 2,382.86 acres. See "Descriptive Notes of the Survey of the San Bernardino Private Land Grant," witnessed by Hugh Price, U.S. Surveyor General of the Territory of Arizona, June 13, 1902, in RG 49, GLO, Arizona private land claim #1.

John Slaughter

Arizona Historical Society

Viola turned the ranch over to John H. Slaughter Ranch Incorporated. In 1937, the San Bernardino was sold to Marion L. Williams, who transferred a 60-foot-wide strip stretching for three miles along the border, totaling 21.81 acres, to the U. S. government the following year. In the late 1960s the ranch was purchased by Mr. and Mrs. Paul A. Ramsower, formerly the operators of a large supermarket in Tucson.

Baca Float No. 3

The huge Baca Float No. 3, in the Santa Cruz Valley south of Tubac, was unique among the Spanish and Mexican land grants in that it was not selected as a land grant until 1863 when all of Arizona was part of the United States. Baca Float No. 3 was one of five 100,000 acre grants authorized by the Congress in 1860 for the heirs of Don Luis María Baca as compensation for the approximately 500,000 acre Las Vegas grant which they claimed in northern New Mexico. The history of the Las Vegas goes back to January 16, 1821, when Don Luis,

a descendant of the renowned Alvarado Cabeza de Vaca, petitioned the Spanish crown for a grant of land then known as
Las Vegas Grande.[38] For a number of years he had been grazing several hundred horses and mules as well as flocks of sheep
and goats near San Miguel del Bado, but his employees were
having more and more difficulty in finding good grass and
water for the animals. Hearing stories from sheepherders
about the lush pastures of the Las Vegas Grande and the Río
Gallenas that ran through it, Baca formally applied for a
Spanish land grant that was confirmed by the proper officials
at Durango on May 29. With a title in his pocket, Don Luis
moved his large family, servants, and livestock to the new
ranch, establishing his headquarters on the site of the present
city of Las Vegas, some sixty miles east of Santa Fe. He had
been given a grant by metes and bounds and had no idea
about its actual size. When the grant was measured in later
years by American surveyors, however, it was found to contain 496,446.95 acres.

The Baca family prospered on the Las Vegas Grande,
despite the theft of livestock and the harassment of field hands
by Navajo raiders. Finally, however, the Indians burned down
most of the buildings on the ranch and drove off all of the
horses, causing Don Luis to fear for the lives of his family. He
returned to San Miguel and then settled later at Peña Blanca
where he was killed in 1827 by an impatient Mexican soldier
who had been refused entrance to the Baca home to search for
furs allegedly stored there by American trappers who had been
operating illegally without Mexican licenses. After Don Luis's
death, the affairs of the huge Baca clan were taken over by his
son, Juan Antonio Baca. But when Juan was killed in an
Indian raid, the Baca family seemed to disintegrate. Apparently none of the Baca progeny attempted to return to the
Las Vegas grant and the land was abandoned until 1835 when
Mexican citizens interested in colonizing the region successfully petitioned Governor Francisco Sarracino at Santa Fe for
a grant having identical boundaries as the one given to Baca.
The reason for the governor's issuance of a conflicting title is
not clear. The conjecture, however, is that he either found no
record in Santa Fe to corroborate the previous Baca ownership
— because Don Luis's petition had been filed with Spanish offi-

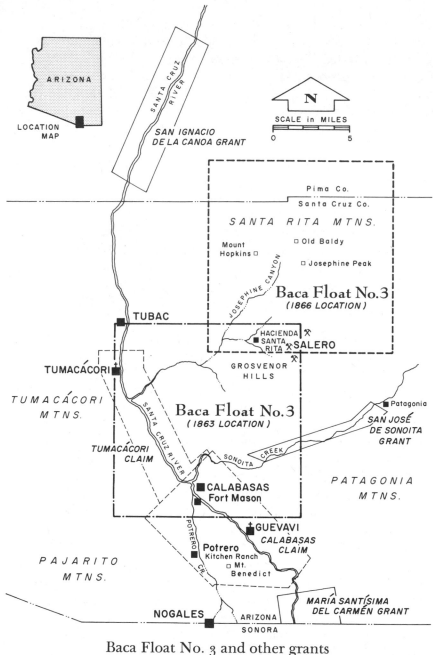

ARIZONA

LOCATION
MAP

SANTA CRUZ RIVER

SAN IGNACIO
DE LA CANOA GRANT

N

SCALE in MILES
0   5

Pima Co.
Santa Cruz Co.

SANTA RITA MTNS.

Mount
Hopkins □   □ Old Baldy

□ Josephine Peak

JOSEPHINE CANYON

Baca Float No. 3
(1866 LOCATION)

TUBAC

HACIENDA
SANTA
RITA   ✕ SALERO

TUMACÁCORI

GROSVENOR
HILLS

TUMACÁCORI
MTNS.

Baca Float No. 3
(1863 LOCATION)

SANTA CRUZ RIVER

TUMACÁCORI
CLAIM

SONOITA   CREEK

Patagonia ■

SAN JOSÉ
DE SONOITA
GRANT

PATAGONIA
MTNS.

■ CALABASAS
Fort Mason

POTRERO CR.

GUEVAVI

CALABASAS
CLAIM

Potrero
Kitchen Ranch
□ Mt.
Benedict

PAJARITO
MTNS.

MARÍA SANTÍSIMA
DEL CARMEN GRANT

NOGALES   ARIZONA
SONORA

Baca Float No. 3 and other grants
in the Santa Cruz Valley

cials in Durango — or he believed that the grant had been abandoned too long and thus, legally, had been forfeited by the Baca heirs. At any rate, the new owners moved on the land and began building the town of Las Vegas around a large plaza. By 1839 the town was a favorite stopping place for wagon trains rumbling over the Santa Fe Trail.

The Baca heirs finally protested, arguing that the colonists were squatting on the Las Vegas grant, but their pleas were ignored by the Mexican authorities. After the Mexican War, however, Surveyor General William Pelham — acting in accordance with the terms of the Treaty of Guadalupe Hidalgo whereby legitimate Spanish and Mexican titles were to be recognized by the United States — reported to Congress that both the Baca heirs and the citizens of Las Vegas had valid claims; he recommended court action by the claimants to decide the rightful ownership of the grant. But Congress was unwilling to risk the eviction of 2200 residents from the town of Las Vegas — in event that the Baca heirs won the case — and compromised the knotty problem by recognizing both claims, permitting the Baca heirs to select substitute lands elsewhere in the Territory of New Mexico.

The Bacas were given three years to pick out five rectangular tracts from the public domain, each to contain a maximum of 100,000 acres of non-mineral land. At the time this offer was made in 1860, the Territory of New Mexico included all of present Arizona and a portion of southeastern Colorado between the 37th and 38th parallels of latitude. In 1861, however, all of the Territory of New Mexico north of the 37th parallel was transferred to the new Territory of Colorado; then in 1863 Arizona was created as a territory separate from New Mexico. As a result of these boundary changes, only two of the five Baca grants wound up in the present State of New Mexico: No. 1 west of Los Alamos and No. 2 north of Tucumcari. Baca Float No. 4 is located in the northern part of the San Luis Valley in Saguachi County, Colorado. No. 3, of course, is in Arizona near the Mexican border and No. 5, also in Arizona, is west of Prescott. The guiding hand in the successful claim of the Baca heirs and in the selection of their five scattered grants was John S. Watts. A lawyer from Indiana, he came to New Mexico as part of an army of legal carpetbaggers who anticipated lucrative career's representing the litigants in land grant cases. The United States government had nearly two hundred claims to settle at Santa Fe and Watts proved to be one of the most capable of the attorneys employed by claimants. In addition to his private practice, he served as an associate justice of the territorial court of New Mexico (1851–54) and was appointed chief justice in 1868. He served one term as delegate to Congress (1861–63), succeeding Miguel A. Otero, another prominent New Mexico politician with whom he had fought a bloodless duel in 1859.

The Baca Float No. 3 site chosen by Watts in behalf of the Baca heirs was a huge, square tract in southern Arizona measuring 12 miles, 36 chains, and 44 links on each side.* This extensive area included nearly all the agricultural lands of the central Santa Cruz Valley and a mineral region on the western slope of the Santa Rita Mountains (in the northeast corner); the settlements of Tubac, Tumacácori, and Calabasas were within the boundaries to be surveyed. An attempt to survey the Baca Float was postponed, however, when the Apaches went on a rampage. Two well known Arizona pioneers — Gilbert W. Hopkins and William Wrightson — were killed in the vicinity of the Baca Float and now have twin peaks in the Santa Ritas named after them. Actually, the tract selected in 1863 was not surveyed until 1905 and was not confirmed until 1914. During the interim, the claimants to whom the interests of the Baca heirs were sold, sought a relocation of the float.

In 1866, Watts, to whom the grant had been transferred, contended that a mistake was made in the location of the initial point and asked for a corrected site north and east of the first one. The Department of the Interior discovered upon investigation that the "amended" claim of 1866 included only a small section in the northeast corner of the original selection of 1863 and was in fact a new location. Yet, from 1866 to 1899, the assignees of the Baca interests claimed the land embraced by the amended selection of 1866 and asserted no rights to the 1863 tract except where it overlapped in the northeast corner with the 1866 location. Some of the claimants unsuccessfully

---

*A surveyor's chain is 66 feet long and a link is one-hundredth of a chain, or 7.92 inches. Each side of the Baca Float was therefore slightly less than 12½ miles.

sought lieu lands in other parts of the country. In 1877, John H. Watts, the son and heir of the deceased John S. Watts, was denied a request for permission to relocate the claim on other lands. In the 1880s, John C. Robinson became an owner of Baca Float No. 3, by purchasing the deed that the Santa Rita Land and Mining Company had secured from the Baca heirs. In an application similar to that of Watts, Robinson explained that squatters had preempted the most desirable locations on the grant; lawsuits to remove them would be expensive and time-consuming "which at my time of life," he said, "with my infirmities, having but one leg, and suffering from the effects of wounds, render it impossible for me to attend . . ." Robinson's request to seek out lieu lands was approved by the acting commissioner of the General Land Office in 1885; but the following year the new commissioner overruled the decision of his predecessor.

After the U. S. Supreme Court in 1898 invalidated the Tumacácori and Calabasas grants, the government felt free to permit homesteaders and preemptors to file for patents on these lands. The Baca Float claimants were not particularly concerned that some of the entries were on the 1863 location that embraced nearly all of the Tumacácori claim and a large part of the Calabasas; as late as 1899, they repeated their request for a survey of the 1866 amended selection. But the Department of the Interior decided that this area was actually a relocation, not an amended description based upon a "mistake in the initial point," and ordered the surveyor general of Arizona to survey and investigate the claim in accordance with the description given in 1863. The survey was completed by Philip Contzen in 1905, and showed that there were a total of 30,408.83 acres of conflicting private land claims inside the boundaries of the float.

Surveyor General Frank S. Ingalls then investigated the Baca Float to determine if it had been legally selected in 1863. The statute of 1860, which permitted the Baca heirs to select lieu lands, provided that each float had to be "non-mineral" and "vacant" at the time of selection. After hearing the testimony of the oldest settlers along the Santa Cruz, Ingalls concluded that Watts must have known that the lands he selected had both occupants and valuable metal deposits; in fact, the

attorney himself once publicly described Baca Float No. 3 as
containing one of the richest mineral fields on earth. Ingalls
therefore recommended that the claim be rejected in its
entirety since it was conceived in fraud. The report was studied and emphatically endorsed by the commissioner of the
General Land Office who also heard testimony presented by
Judge J. M. Jamison of Phoenix representing some of the settlers. The assignees of the Baca lands appealed the commissioner's decision on up to the Secretary of the Interior but lost
again. In 1908, the secretary rejected the Baca Float No. 3
claim, summarizing the opinion of the surveyor general that
the lands were not legally subject to selection in 1863 because
they were occupied and contained minerals.

After the secretary's decision in 1908, the Watts heirs
finally found success when they secured an injunction from the
Court of Appeals in Washington, D. C. to restrain the land
office from receiving any more homestead applications for land
on the Baca Float. Even more important, the appeals court
also confirmed the grant for the claimants. Secretary of the
Interior Franklin Lane took the case to the U. S. Supreme
Court only to have the opinion of the Court of Appeals
affirmed.[39] The decision of the court was naturally a great disappointment to the homesteaders, especially since they soon
began receiving eviction notices issued by the federal district
court at the request of Cornelius C. Watts and James E. Bouldin — the major claimants. George W. Atkinson, who had
lived on the lands of the Baca Float No. 3 for 37 years, offered
$250,000 for the confirmed grant but the owners wanted
$400,000. Having fought the battle in the courts and lost, he
began asking Congress for a bill to help the settlers. "As for
myself, it does not matter so much," he said, "although I spent
$40,000 in one jolt to fight this case, I still have enough to
support me to the end of my days. I still have my cattle. These
cannot be taken from me . . ." But other pioneers were less
fortunate and Atkinson suggested that the government pay
the Baca Float owners for the lands of the bona fide settlers;
that way the farmers and ranchers could stay on the lands
which they had homesteaded before the government closed
the area to settlement.

Congress did come to the rescue, but with a different kind
of relief bill. The law that was passed provided that the bona

fide landholders on the Baca Float could select lieu lands in other parts of Arizona. Some of the displaced people willingly accepted substitute public land in the vicinity of Buckeye and elsewhere in the state, but others resisted. Mrs. Sarah M. Black, whose deceased husband had settled on 240 acres and built a two-room house, later expressed her feelings at Tubac: ". . . They sent for the United States Marshal to put me off," she said. "They wanted me to come off but I said 'No, I'm going to be put off like the rest' . . . My land looked like an auction yard. They put everything outdoors, the furniture and dishes and everything. It was the most brutal thing that ever happened. I don't know as I cared much, but it was pretty hard for the people who were too old to begin again . . ."[40]

The Baca Float owners had difficulty removing the settlers, but it was their neighbor on the Sonoita grant who presented the most serious obstacle to consolidation of the grant. They had to go all the way to the U.S. Supreme Court to recover about 2,000 acres of the confirmed Sonoita lands that overlapped the Baca Float.[41] With the addition of this strip along the Sonoita Creek, most of the 99,289.39 acres of the original tract were then intact. In 1918, however, Weldon M. Bailey and James E. Bouldin relinquished title to the Tumacácori National Monument land. Since that time, the Baca Float has been divided in many different and complex ways; today it has many owners, both individual and corporate. Perhaps the most famous investor in the grant was ex-Senator Joseph W. Bailey of Texas. In 1924, he and a Dallas bank bought 40,000 acres for $250,000 at a sheriff's foreclosure on the holdings of the Baca Float Land and Cattle Company.

In 1929, the Bouldin family and Wallace Bransford deeded a large tract which they had acquired to Tol T. Pendleton and F. M. Dougherty. Most of their land was in the west part of the grant along the Santa Cruz River and the Tucson-Nogales highway. In 1932, Pendleton and Dougherty formed the Baca Float Ranch Corporation in which others, including the Merryweather family of Nogales, have shared ownership. Pendleton, a graduate of Princeton who had been in the oil business in Texas, introduced the cherry-red Santa Gertrudis breed of cattle to the Baca Float and headed the operation of the ranch until it was sold to the Gulf-American Corporation of Baltimore and Florida in 1966. Gulf-Ameri-

can, which changed its name in 1969 to GAC Properties of
Arizona, bought the lands to subdivide for its multi-million
dollar Rio Rico real estate development.[42] There are still large
grazing tracts in the eastern part of the grant and several dozen
smaller parcels of land along the highway and river south of
Tubac which were once a part of Baca Float No. 3.

Baca Float No. 5

The only land in northern Arizona that can be traced
back to a Spanish or Mexican land grant is Baca Float No. 5,
the last of five floats selected for the heirs of Luis María Baca
in lieu of a 500,000 acre Mexican grant in New Mexico.
Located in Yavapai County about fifty miles northwest of
Prescott, the 99,445.2 acre grant includes some of the best
lands in Arizona. A large part of it is covered by a magnificent
growth of pine, oak, juniper, and native deciduous trees in
addition to miles and miles of excellent pasture and grazing
lands. Situated on the highest ground in the western part of
the state, the grant drains into a number of important streams
that have their sources high up on its wooded slopes: among
them are Burro Creek flowing to the south, Trout Creek to
the west, Muddy Creek to the north, and Walnut Creek to
the east across the present-day Prescott National Forest.

The original deed to this property was recorded in Santa
Ana County, Territory of New Mexico, on June 1, 1871.
Given to John S. Watts at that time and recorded in the
Yavapai County Recorder's office a year later by Recorder
Edmund W. Wells, it indicates that Baca was the progenitor
of a large family.[43] Some eighty-six of his heirs signed the
document conveying their rights to Baca Float No. 5, then
measured as being 99,289.39 acres in area. Some of the sur-
names of the children, cousins, and in-laws were Baca, López,
García, Silva, Trujillo, and Salazar — a good cross section of
Mexican-American families. Watts, who paid $6,800 for Baca
Float No. 5, did not hold on to the grant very long. In 1872
he sold it to William V. B. Wardwell for $30,000. Other
owners of the grant during the 1870s were Atwater M. Wardwell, Frederick Clay, and Peter Dean.[44]

The Yavapai County records show that the title to Baca Float No. 5 was transferred several times during the last decades of the nineteenth century. The ownership of the grant was frequently shared, several transactions involving undivided fractional shares such as 5/19ths and 5/107ths or shares identified in terms of a given number of acres — 4,000 or 4,600, for example. Interestingly enough, the grant was sometimes sold at sheriff's sale for delinquent taxes. Under the territorial law, however, the highest bidder was given only a tax collector's deed and the owner had six months to redeem his property by paying the taxes due.

Dr. Edward B. Perrin was the owner who started subdividing the grant and letting it go for taxes. However, he was also the man who eventually bought up the smaller shares, consolidated the grant, and combined it with thousands of acres of railroad checkerboard sections, private patented lands in the vicinity of Williams, and forest leases to create one of the largest ranches in the southwest.[45] A story in the *Weekly Arizona Miner*, April 16, 1880, tells about Perrin's first arrival at Prescott by stage from California with Dr. George F. Thornton. A few weeks earlier, Perrin had visited the offices of the Atchison, Topeka, and Santa Fe Railroad in New York City and been assured that a transcontinental railroad was soon to be built across northern Arizona. The Baca Float was not far south of the route selected and Perrin was willing to speculate that the railroad would increase its value. Accompanied by George Ruffner he took a buckboard to look at the grant which, at the time, was in the hands of the Merchants Exchange Bank of San Francisco. According to the Yavapai County records, Thornton bought it for the amount of the $27,500 mortgage on May 6, 1880, and transferred it to Perrin a week later for the same amount.[46] Apparently, a grass fire in the area, as well as the coming of the railroad convinced Perrin the land was valuable. "Any country that will produce feed like that grass fire burns," he said to Ruffner, "is good enough for me." To help defray the cost, Perrin sold an undivided 5/19ths share of the grant on May 17 to Burwell B. Lewis of Tuscaloosa, Alabama, for $14,000.[47]

It was some time before Perrin converted the ranch into a profitable investment, however. In fact, he let it go at sheriff's

sale on March 12, 1885, for the nonpayment of his 1884 taxes
amounting to $656.34 on an assessed valuation of $19,858.
Sheriff William J. Mulvenon advertised the sale in the Prescott
Courier and subsequently issued a tax collector's deed certificate for Perrin's Baca Float property to one P. Smith,
entitling him — as the highest bidder — to the land at the
expiration of six months unless it was redeemed. Before this
period of grace elapsed, however, Thornton purchased the
certificate from Smith and then received the deed to the grant
from Sheriff Mulvenon on December 21, 1885, upon payment
of the delinquent taxes. A short time later, on April 18, 1887,
Thornton deeded it back to Perrin and Baca Float No. 5
remained in the hands of the Perrin family until 1922 when
it was deeded to the Los Angeles Trust and Savings Company.[48] In 1934, two years after Edward Perrin died, Perrin
Properties, Inc. acquired control of the grant. Perrin's son
— Lilo M. Perrin, Jr. — was the treasurer of this California
corporation and knew the property. In 1937, however, the
Greene Cattle Company bought Baca Float No. 5 and operated it until 1973 as part of vast holdings of private and leased
lands in that part of Arizona.[49] Unlike Baca Float No. 3, the
Float in Yavapai County was kept intact by the Greenes, except
for a small parcel of 1,227 acres on the southern edge that was
sold in 1940 and became a part of the Seven-Up Ranch. Perrin's holdings outside the float in the vicinity of Williams have
been divided, however, and now comprise the Greenway, Bar
Cross, Poquette, and Cooper ranches as well as homesteads and
subdivisions.

UNCONFIRMED GRANTS
Arivaca

Arivaca, located some thirty miles west of Tubac, is
another old Arizona ranch, like the Canoa, that was owned
by Tomás and Ignacio Ortiz. With a history going back to
the early 1700s when Spaniards were attracted to the fine
grazing lands and mines in the vicinity, "La Aribac" was at
one time a *visita* of the mission at Guevavi. Abandoned after
the Pima uprising of 1751, it once again became the center of
mining activities following the Apache armistice of 1790. In
1833, the Ortiz brothers petitioned the *alcalde* at Tubac for

two *sitios* at Arivaca to be used for stockraising. They claimed to be the legal owners on the basis of an 1812 grant to their father, Augustín Ortiz, then a resident of the presidio of Tucson. Don Augustín had paid $747 and three *reales* into the treasury at Arispe after a public auction at which he was the highest bidder. There was an entry in the treasurer's book for the amount paid. But since no title or *expediente* containing a record of a survey, appraisements, and auctions could be found, the Ortiz brothers asked the Tubac *alcalde* to take the depositions of three witnesses to prove their ownership of the ranch which had been granted to their deceased father.

The official proceeded to take the requested testimony of witnesses who swore that the "Aribac" ranch had been occupied by the Ortiz family since 1812. The boundaries given for the land were vague, however, considering that the grant was for the specific quantity of two *sitios*. There were four landmarks: "the one towards the north on the high pointed hill *(divisadero)* that rises on this side of the Tagito mine and borders on the Sierra de Buena Vista; the one towards the south standing on this side of the Longorena mine on a low hill next to the cañon covered with trees; the one towards the east standing up the valley from the spring on a mesquite tree that has a cross cut in it and borders on the Sierra de las Calaberas; and the one towards the west standing at the Punta de Agua on a pointed hill opposite the Sierra del Baboquivari."[50] Despite the lack of a definite location by survey, Sonoran officials approved the Ortiz petition of 1833 and directed that a title to "two sitios of land for raising cattle and horses, which comprise the place called Aribac" be issued. But twenty years later Arivaca was made a part of the United States by the Gadsden treaty and, in 1902, the Supreme Court denied confirmation of the grant because of its uncertain location.

Long before that decision, however, the Arivaca changed hands several times. The Sonora Exploring and Mining Company, with Samuel P. Heintzelman as president, acquired all the Ortiz rights in 1856. This company was a two-million-dollar corporation made up of eastern investors organized by Charles Poston and others. It operated extensive mines near Arivaca and in the vicinity of Tubac, until the evacuation

A page from Charles D. Poston's diary

of troops from Arizona at the outbreak of the Civil War forced them to close down. The next transfer of the grant came in 1863. In that year, it was purchased by the Arizona Land and Mining Company, a Rhode Island corporation which owned mines at San Xavier and on the Sopori Ranch south of the Canoa. The company's new property was described in 1864 by J. Ross Browne, who visited Arivaca during a tour of Arizona. In addition to twenty-five closed silver mines and other valuable mineral resources not yet touched, Browne observed the rich meadow land bordering on a never-failing stream. "It is well-wooded," he wrote, "with oak, walnut, ash, cottonwood and mesquit, and is capable of sustaining a population of 5 to 6000 souls. . . . The reduction works of the Heintzelman mine was situated on the ranch for the convenience of wood, water, and pasturage, and were projected on a costly and extensive scale. Little now remains of them save the ruins of the mill and furnaces, the adobe store houses and offices and a dilapidated corral." [51]

In 1870, the Arivaca was deeded again. The new owner was Charles Poston, a stockholder in the Sonora Company whose younger brother, John Lee, was killed by Apaches at one of the mines in 1861. Even though he had no *expedientes* for the 1812 and 1833 proceedings, Poston submitted a claim to the surveyor general for confirmation. Deputy surveyor George J. Roskruge made a preliminary survey in 1881, which he admitted was "essentially arbitrary" since there was no way to exactly locate two specific *sitios* (8,676.928 acres) within the larger area of 26,508.06 acres claimed; there were no field notes or initial point from which true boundaries might be surveyed. Nevertheless, the surveyor general recommended confirmation for 8,680 acres, the approximate grant given to the Ortiz family; no overplus land was included. [52] Congress, however, took no action on the recommendation.

Even before the survey, Poston had already given notice to occupants of the grant to vacate. He even secured judgment in a territorial court against C. H. Lord, a Tucson merchant, but was not permitted to recover $266,238.23 in damages. Several years later, on December 22, 1884, he wrote an open letter, printed in the Tucson *Sunshine and Silver,* in which he vented his frustrations. He said that all the millions of dollars which he had persuaded eastern people to invest in Arizona had been stolen by thieves; he denounced the judges in no uncertain terms: "I do not mind the Apaches," he wrote, "who stole 150 head of stock from me one night and killed five of my best men, but those pesky thieves who came with a commission from Washington: they are the thieves in sheep's clothing." Continuing in the same vein, he wrote, "The decision in the Arivaca case was the most infamous I ever heard from a political tribunal. . . . Everybody in Arivaca is a thief. Nobody has paid anything for his possessions save the undersigned; and he is the rightful owner. . . . I am only 50 yards over the line, and if anybody feels aggrieved, they can have it at sunrise. . . ."[53]

Poston gave up his claim and was thus spared further setbacks by the courts over the Arivaca. His rights to the grant were acquired by the Arivaca Land and Cattle Company which asked for a hearing before the Court of Private Land Claims in 1893. The majority of this court rejected the claim because there was "such uncertainty as to the land which was intended to be granted that it is now impossible to identify it."[54] Two justices dissented, however, being of the opinion that the grant should be confirmed for two *sitios*. The case was then appealed to the U.S. Supreme Court, where the decree of the lower court was affirmed on March 24, 1902. This was exactly three months before the poverty-stricken Poston, called the "Father of Arizona," died at his dilapidated adobe house facing an alley in downtown Phoenix. The high court cited the Gadsden treaty, which provided that Spanish and Mexican grants made before September 25, 1853, were not to "be respected or be considered as obligatory, which have not been located and duly recorded in the archives of Mexico." Since the two *sitios* could not be presumed to have been properly located and surveyed within the meaning of the treaty, the court denied the grant and also refused to consider a claim to overplus lands. The effect of the decision was to remove the Arivaca from litigation and make it a part of the public domain.

El Sopori

Another unconfirmed grant, important for both its grasslands and mines, was the Sopori. The word Sopori is probably a corruption of Sobaípuri, the name applied to the Pima Indian group in southern Arizona by Father Kino. For years the Pimas had a *ranchería* at Sopori, but the place was abandoned in 1751 during the Pima uprising. The Jesuit author of the *Rudo Ensayo* described it in 1762 as a depopulated ranch more than two leagues north of the *presidio* of Tubac. There is some evidence that the Sopori ranch was inhabited again during the Spanish or Mexican periods, but not by the alleged recipient of a large grant there. Purportedly, the

wealthy Joaquín Astiazarán of Sonora was deeded 31 and
7/8ths *sitios* and a *caballería* of unoccupied grazing lands
stretching from Tubac to San Xavier in 1838. The grantee
supposedly paid $919 for this vast estate. He apparently never
occupied the land, but his heirs were able to sell their rights
to the unconfirmed grant to American interests after the
Gadsden Purchase. The principal negotiator with the Astiazarán family was Sylvester Mowry, a big stockholder in both
the Sopori Land and Mining Company and the Arizona Land
and Mining Company. In 1858, he purchased part of the
Mexican claims; two years later he and the heirs of Astiazarán
sold all their interests to the Arizona Company. Most people
in the territory were surprised to learn of the existence of
the grant, including Charles Poston who was acquainted
with both the American and the Mexican parties in the
transactions.[55]

Meanwhile the Sopori Land and Mining Company bought
out the Americans who occupied the land during the 1850s.
Among the latter were Colonel James W. Douglas, a colorful
Virginian who had served in the Mexican Army, and C. C.
Dodson. As early as 1854, these pioneers were erecting buildings, grazing cattle on the nutritious wild grasses, and farming
the rich bottomlands in the Sopori Valley. Charles Poston, who
established Tubac as the headquarters of his mining enterprises in 1856, entertained Douglas at a Christmas feast that
year; the Colonel rode over from Sopori, Poston explained,
with "a motley retinue, including a harper and fiddlers
three." Another occupant of Sopori lands was Frederick Ronstadt, one of about twenty men in the Poston party that rushed
into the Gadsden Purchase region in 1854 to develop mines.
With Poston acting as his agent for a one-fourth commission,
Ronstadt sold his doubtful claim to four square leagues of
land to the Sopori Land and Mining Company for $4,000.

The mining company took control of the Sopori ranch
in the late 1850s. Under the guidance of a superintendent,
the employees occupied the old houses at the Sopori spring,
made a survey, cultivated the land, raised cattle, and worked
a gold mine. In June, 1861, however, several hundred Apaches
swept through the Santa Cruz Valley and killed Richmond
Jones Jr., the man in charge, and drove off all the livestock,

forcing the company to close down operations. Not until the
1870s did the Apache depredations let up enough that the
Sopori could be reoccupied.

J. Ross Browne described the abandoned ranch as he saw
it in 1864:

> A delightful ride of five or six miles through a broad, rich valley
> of grass, pleasantly diversified with groves of mesquit and palo-verde,
> brought us to a narrow pass, on the right elevation of which stand the
> remains of the buildings of the Sopori Land and Mining Company.
> Little is left now save ruined adobe walls and tumbled in roofs. As
> usual not a living thing was to be seen . . . The Sopori Ranch, although
> at the present uninhabited, possesses advantages as a mining and grazing
> region which have long since given it a reputation in Sonora . . ." [56]

In 1866, the Sopori Land and Mining Company repur-
chased the interests of the Arizona Company and began the
long struggle for confirmation of a title. Their hopes were
thwarted in 1881, however, when Surveyor General John
Wasson advised rejection of the claim "on the grounds that
the original title papers are forged, ante-dated and otherwise
invalid." While attempting to adjudicate the claim, Wasson
heard the testimony of numerous witnesses, including Poston
and Pete Kitchen. Poston reacted in his usually forward
fashion when advised of the boundaries claimed for the Sopori
grant — the San Xavier mission lands on the north, Tubac
on the south, the Santa Ritas on the east, and the Baboquívari
sierra on the west. The following excerpt from the official
transcript is interesting, both for the information contained
in the context on the Sopori and as an example of the hundreds of depositions taken in all of the land grant investigations:

> Questions by the Surveyor-General to Chas. W. Poston; Ques.
> Col. Poston, please state if since you first knew of the 31-league Sopori
> title in 1858, and now under examination in this office, if you at any time
> have had reason to believe it to be genuine and ought to be confirmed
> by the U.S.?
> (The claimants respectfully object to the question because it is not
> confined to the knowledge of the witness as to facts, and asks for the
> opinion of the witness whether based upon facts within his knowledge
> or not.)

Ans. I will state the facts which first led me to form my opinion. The houses and ruins within the boundaries of the 31-league grant are much older than the date of the grant. There were several smaller grants within the boundaries [the Canoa in particular] which had been notoriously occupied and owned by other parties. I am familiar with the territory embraced in the technical boundaries of the 31-league grant. They are absurdly at variance with any practical knowledge of the locality. There was no occupation, there was no evidence of occupation, under the 31-league grant, and although I was acquainted at that time with the most intelligent sources of information in regard to Mexican titles in this Territory, neither I nor any one in my employment ever heard anything about this grant until it had been sold to the Rhode Island company, and when I reproached one of the negotiators for selling the grant, he acknowledged that it was fraudulent and asked me not to expose the transaction, or to say no more about it. These are the facts upon which I founded my opinion, and I see no cause to change it.

Ques. Are you willing to give the name of the said negotiator? —Ans. I should rather be excused from that.

Ques. Are you willing to assign any reason for not giving the name of said negotiator? — Ans. Yes, because he is dead. There were several parties of prominence in the East concerned in the negotiation whose names do not appear in the record, and at least three of them have departed this life.[57]

After completing his investigation of the Sopori claim, Surveyor General Wasson made his negative report. The Secretary of the Interior in turn submitted it to Congress where it was studied by the Senate committee on private land claims and ordered printed. But as usual no action was taken. And since the status of its title was indefinite, the Sopori Company held on to the grant without having to pay taxes on it. But its claim of 141,721.60 acres was rejected by the Court of Private Land Claims in 1895, and the U.S. Supreme Court refused to hear an appeal.[58]

Today the area of the Sopori Ranch is about half the size of the amount rejected. It sprawls out over some 124 sections of desert ranges, including both privately-owned patented and lease lands. Actually, the countryside described by Browne in 1864 has changed very little, except that the winding road, from the Nogales highway, some forty miles south of Tucson, now borders fields of cotton and forage crops. The main house is still at the head of the valley. The old adobe ruin, which had walls two feet thick and no windows — protection against marauding Apaches — was reconstructed in 1924 with a screened entrance porch, beamed ceilings, and partitions. Mr. and Mrs. Maurice Handman, who took over the ranch in 1950, have completely modernized the old structure and added new rooms. Handman developed a successful commercial cattle business. His man-made lakes and wells for the cattle that graze the extensive ranges greatly increased the value of the ranch.[59]

Tumacácori and Calabasas *

The history of Tumacácori goes back to the Jesuits, but it was not until 1784 that it became a head mission. Guevavi and Calabasas were *visitas* but were abandoned near the end of the century while Tumacácori continued to prosper. As the herds of horses and cattle increased at the mission under the direction of Fray Narciso Gutiérrez, the lands originally purchased from the natives became insufficient,† and the title papers to these lands had been lost sometime before 1806. In that year, Juan Legarra, governor of the pueblo of Tumacácori, petitioned the *intendente* of the province, Don Alejo García Condé, for an adjudication and survey of the land for the *fundo legal* (farming purposes) and the *estancia* (grazing land) to replace the old title. Complying with this request, Condé issued a royal patent to the Indians of the pueblo of Tumacácori and instructed Manuel de León, the commander of the presidio at Tubac, to measure and mark off the four square leagues to which each pueblo was entitled, plus two *sitios* of grazing lands previously occupied by the pueblo of Calabasas — a total amount that would have exceeded 26,000 acres.[60] The needed land that was actually surveyed for use by the Indians, however, was a little less than a fourth of a

---

* Calabasas has been the accepted spelling since the United States census of 1870. Calabazas, however, is the form found in most Spanish and Mexican records. See Bernard L. Fontana, "Calabazas of the Río Rico," in *Smoke Signal*, No. 24 (Fall 1971), p. 86.

† The remains of Father Narciso Gutiérrez lie beneath a stone slab in the mortuary chapel at San Xavier del Bac.

square league. The combined pueblo and *estancia* lands totaled only about 5,000 English acres.

One unusual provision in the new title was the stipulation that, in event the lands should be abandoned for a period of three years, any person might claim them. As fate would have it, Tumacácori declined during the 1830s and 1840s, as did other missions administered by the Mexican civil authorities who were given control under the laws of 1833 and 1834. The Mexicans practically abolished the peace policy previously used by the Spaniards. As a result, the Apaches returned to the plunder trail and many of the missions on the northern frontier were deserted. In 1842 the Mexican government under Santa Anna began selling abandoned church lands valued at $500 or less. By that time, Tumacácori, though not completely abandoned, had declined and was sold in 1844, along with the stock farm of Calabasas and adjacent lands, to Francisco Aguilar for $500 at a public sale. Actually, Aguilar was a stand-in for his brother-in-law, Manuel María Gándara, who got the ranch in operation for a short time during the 1850s.

A political opportunist, Gándara was governor of Sonora off and on for two decades, beginning with his appointment by the Mexican president, Anastasio Bustamente, in November, 1837. At that time, Gándara supported strong central government in Mexico City at the expense of states' rights. He was opposed on this issue by José Cosme Urrea, a Tucson-born military hero of the Texas war who was also to serve as governor of Sonora in the 1840s. The centralism versus federalism controversy divided Sonorans into two factions which waged bloody civil war in the province until 1846. Throughout this conflict the Apaches stepped up their depredations, showing contempt for an ineffective military defense line that was weakened even more by the participation of many presidio troops in *la guerra* Gándara-Urrea.

With the Apache warriors in control of the Sonoran frontier, it was 1853 before Gándara could capitalize on the land investment which he held in Aguilar's name. On December 9, 1852, he entered into a partnership with a German named Federico Hulsemann and several others to develop a *hacienda* with livestock which he supplied.* The old Calabasas church was converted into a ranch house and Mexican herdsmen were soon watching over thousands of sheep and goats. The ranch was an established operation by April, 1854, when a large band of Apaches struck, only to meet with one of their rare reverses. An Apache squaw had revealed the Indian plan of attack to Gilanin García, the Mexican commander at Tucson, and on the day of the attack García was waiting in readiness at the ranch with sixty Mexican dragoons and forty friendly Apache *mansos* from Tucson. When the Indians came to begin their attack, the Mexican cavalry charged, taking the attackers by surprise.

Peter Brady, an early Arizona pioneer who was camped nearby with the Andrew B. Gray railroad survey crew, described the ensuing battle:

> No cry of mercy was given and no quarter shown. The carnage was awful. They killed and butchered as long as there was an Apache in sight . . . there were not over three or four shots fired during the massacre, they were all killed by the Mexican Dragoon lances and their brave allies, the Apache mansos, finished the wounded. Don Gilanin and Don Federico invited us over to another part of the courtyard to show us more evidence of the slaughter. It looked first like a string of dried apples 2½ to 3 feet long, but on close inspection they were the ears of their dead foes . . .[61]

The Apaches were eventually more successful, however, and forced the abandonment of Gándara's operations several months before the arrival of United States troops under the command of Major Enoch Steen at the ranch in November, 1856. In the years following the Gadsden treaty, the enterprising Americans rushed into the newly-acquired area to seek their fortunes. Sylvester Mowry, who was busily engaged in

---

*A contract was signed by Gándara with four men (Federico Hulsemann, Luis P. Chambon, Clemente A. Payeken, and Carlos Hundhausen) representing the firm of Payeken, Hundhausen & Co. Gándara agreed to give up half ownership of the *hacienda* and furnish 5,000 sheep, 1,000 goats, 100 cows with calves, 100 brood mares, 10 yokes of oxen, 6 pack mules, and 10 horses for use. The contract is recorded in "Old Records of Pima County, Arizona, Book No. A," pp. 207–208. See Fontana, *Calabazas*, p. 77. Hulsemann stayed at Calabasas through 1855. Sometime early in 1856 he drove his livestock south where they were confiscated by the Prefect of San Ignacio. After the American occupation of the Gadsden Purchase, he eventually returned to the Santa Cruz Valley and was the postmaster at Tubac in 1859. See *The Weekly Arizonian*, March 3, 1859.

mining operations around Tubac, wrote in 1859 that the rich lands at Tumacácori and Calabasas were being cultivated by American squatters. There were enough people there the following year to have representation at a constitutional convention held in Tucson for the purpose of organizing a temporary government. But the Civil War ended the brief period of American prosperity as abruptly as it had started. With the removal of U.S. troops to New Mexico, southern Arizona was paralyzed by Apache attacks and was soon deserted. When J. Ross Browne visited the area in 1864 he described the Calabasas ranch as one of the finest in the country; its excellent pastures and farm lands were a league wide and extended for six leagues along the Santa Cruz. "At present, however," he added, "and until there is military protection in the country, it is utterly worthless, owing to incursions of the Apaches."[62]

If Browne had come a year later he would have seen soldiers from two armies at Calabasas. A detachment of Union soldiers from the California Column was bivouacked there and the army of Governor Ignacio Pesqueira, Gándara's enemy, was encamped on the plain near the elevated plateau where the ranch buildings were located. With the help of American rifles and ammunition given him by Colonel Lewis, the Governor eventually returned to Mexico, defeated the French troops of Emperor Maximilian, and regained control of Sonora.

After the Civil War, there was again an influx of American population into the Gadsden Purchase region and the value of lands steadily increased. In 1869, Aguilar formally sold the Tumacácori and Calabasas grants to Gándara for $499. Charles P. Sykes of San Francisco paid $12,500 in gold coin for the lands in 1878 and sold a 3/16ths interest the same year to John Currey, an ex-judge of the California Supreme Court, for $9,000. In 1879, Sykes and Currey transferred their interests to some Boston men for $75,000. The new owners organized the Calabasas Land and Mining Company, later the Santa Rita Land and Cattle Company. Sykes remained as director of the company and attempted to attract capital to Calabasas with exaggerated advertisements and illustrations, including one picture of a line of steamers on a river.

Long before the Gulf-American Corporation bought the same area east of the Santa Cruz in 1967, to develop the Río Rico settlement, Sykes built a two-story brick hotel, called the Santa Rita, and supplied it throughout with walnut furniture and Brussels carpet. Excellent cuisine was served to gala parties from Tucson who came on the railroad via Benson, and to distinguished visitors from as far away as England. The hotel was a beehive of activity until 1893 when business slackened and the name "Pumpkinville," which the *Tombstone Epitaph* had given the promotion scheme, became more appropriate. The Sykes heirs lived at Calabasas, which literally means "pumpkins" in Spanish, until 1915, when they moved to Nogales. The deteriorating Santa Rita Hotel was used by a rancher for storing hay until it burned down along with other buildings at Calabasas in 1927.

Meanwhile the company sought confirmation of its claim to what were called the Tumacácori, Calabasas, and Guevavi grants. The surveyor general recommended that Congress approve the titles for 52,007.95 acres — 17,363.55 acres of arable land and 34,644.40 acres of grassland.[63] The claimants asked the Court of Private Land Claims to confirm 81,350 acres, but the court refused to recognize the validity of the title issued to Aguilar in 1844. In the opinion of the judges, only the national government of Mexico could sell lands from the public domain in 1844; the treasurer of Sonora who gave a title to Aguilar did not have the authority to do so. The U.S. Supreme Court heard an appeal of the case in 1898, and upheld the decree of the lower tribunal in these words: "We concur that . . . there was a fatal want of power in the departmental treasurer to make the sale. . . . "[64] Most of the Tumacácori lands and a large part of the Calabasas grant, including Calabasas itself, were part of the Baca Float No. 3 grant that the Supreme Court validated in 1914.

Los Nogales de Elías

By the decision of the Supreme Court of the United States in the case of Ainsa vs. United States (161 *U. S. Reports*, 208), the right of the claimants of the Los Nogales de Elías private land claims was denied and their claim thereto disallowed and the lands included in said claim have been restored to the public domain.[65]

So wrote the surveyor general of Arizona, George J. Roskruge, in 1897. The grant to which he referred was located on the border between the Calabasas grant in the United States and the Sonoran ranch called "Casita." Despite the fact that the intention of the petitioners was to purchase all the vacant land between these two ranches, the Los Nogales de Elías grant was for the exact quantity of 7½ *sitios* and 2 *caballerías,* or about 32,763 acres; it was not a grant by metes and bounds whereby the grantee might legally take all the land within certain out-boundaries.

The archives of Sonora show that on January 7, 1843, a title was issued to Don José Elías and his parents, Francisco Elías González and Balvanera Redondo, the owners of the Casita and residents of the pueblo of Imuris. All the land received was classified as desert, because there was no running water, and hence was bought for $15 per *sitio,* a total of $113.12½ cents and 10 grains for the aggregate. The grant did contain some gold, silver, copper, and iron, but it was acquired originally for the purpose of raising cattle and horses on the nutritious grasses. Witnesses during the proceedings testified that Don Francisco and his wife possessed as many as 4,000 head of cattle to run on the property.

The enterprising Camou brothers of Sonora eventually secured ownership of one undivided half of Los Nogales de Elías and submitted a claim to Surveyor General John Wasson. In 1881, after having Roskruge, then a deputy, survey the grant, Wasson said that the title was properly recorded in Sonora and was perfectly valid. In his report to the Commissioner of the General Land Office, J. A. Williamson, he recommended confirmation of that part of the grant lying within the Territory of Arizona — that is to say, 10,638.68 acres, half of which belonged to the Camou brothers and the other undivided half to the legal representatives of the original grantees.[66] Congress, however, did not act upon the claim and it came before the Court of Private Land Claims in Tucson in 1894.

Separate claims were filed by Juan Pedro Camou, George Hill Howard, and Santiago Ainsa, administrator of Frank Ely. These claimants had acquired the rights to the grant and admitted to owning the lands in common, though each pleaded his own case for confirmation. On March 30, 1894, however, the court rejected the claim, explaining that the grant was clearly specific as to quantity but not as to location.* The only effect of the proceedings prior to the issuing of a title, was to designate certain out–boundaries within which the lands granted could be located. But the grantees took no subsequent action prior to the Gadsden treaty to have the limits of their grant surveyed and properly identified. The United States was therefore not bound, according to the court, to recognize the grant.[67] The residents of Nogales and settlers in that vicinity rejoiced upon hearing news of the decision since their lots and farms lay within the area claimed. The "victory for the settlers," as the *Arizona Daily Star* described the court's decree, was complete when the U.S. Supreme Court affirmed it on March 2, 1896.[68]

San Pedro Grant

"I, Don José de Jesús Pérez, resident of this capital, before your excellency, in conformity with law, and in accordance with the royal ordinances concerning land . . . state: That whereas I enjoy some property, acquired in the military service and by my own industry, without owning a place upon which to locate and bring them together. . . ." Thus began the petition in 1821 of a Spanish subject in Arispe, Sonora, to the governor *intendente* for four *sitios* of land on which to raise livestock.

Pérez asked for a grant, south of the present international line, in the depopulated area near the house of San Pedro, the ancestral home of the Elías family; this house was two or three miles northeast of the abandoned place named Las

---

* The only witness used by the United States in this case was Henry O. Flipper, a special agent employed by U.S. Attorney Matt. G. Reynolds to examine the boundaries, surveys, and location of certain private land grant claims in Arizona. Flipper was temporarily relieved of his duties while being cleared of charges of embezzling funds when he was a clerk in the Nogales post office. Earlier he had been dismissed from the Army after charges were brought against him by Colonel William R. Shafter because of a shortage of funds in his accounts when he was acting commissary at Fort Davis, Texas. Reynolds considered Flipper a most competent investigator in the land grant cases. See "Records Relating to the Army Career of Henry Ossian Flipper, 1873–1882," National Archives Microfilm Publications Microcopy No. T-1027, GSA, Washington, 1968. See also letter of U.S. Attorney Matt. G. Reynolds to the Attorney General, from Santa Fe, January 25, 1894, and letter of George H. Waterbury, P.O. Inspector, to To All Whom It May Concern, from Tucson, December 14, 1893, in RG 60, Department of Justice, National Archives.

Nutrias. Pérez wanted the survey to be made upstream (south) from the house in order that the marshy lands and better pastures would be included in the grant. But one Antunes of nearby Terrenate objected since he claimed part of the area. The dispute was compromised and the better-watered lands were divided. After the survey, appraisal, and sale, Pérez paid $190 ($60 each for three *sitios* and $10 for the fourth) plus $18 for taxes and expenses. A title to the land, which lay entirely in present-day Sonora, was finally issued in 1833 — not to Pérez but to Rafael Elías González, the owner of the San Rafael del Valle, who had bought the lands from the petitioner during the interim.

The sons and heirs of Rafael later secured overplus *(demasías)* lands in addition to the basic grant of four *sitios* *(cabida legal)*. Manuel Elías, in behalf of the Elías family, petitioned for "the overplus that may be in the ranch of San Pedro in the jurisdiction of the town of Santa Cruz in the district of Magdalena." The Mexican department of public works denied the claim in 1887 because surveyor Pedro Molera could find no monuments that would determine the limits of the ranch.* Overplus lands could not be measured unless the boundaries of the original grant were first located. But as a matter of equity, President Porfirio Díaz ordered a title given to the Elías family in 1888 for the legal area of approximately 17,350 acres (7022 hectares† or 4 *sitios*) and an overplus of about 37,150 acres (15,035 hectares).

While Manuel Elías was successfully working south of the border, his brother José María Elías was active in the Gadsden Purchase area. The *Fronterizo* of Tucson printed an account of his visit to that city in January, 1879. Reporting that Elías was making arrangements for again putting stock on the vast San Pedro ranch, the publication elaborated thusly:

---

*In a confidential report to W. A. J. Sparks, Commissioner of the General Land Office, the Surveyor General of Arizona, John Hise, wrote that all the papers in the case of the San Pedro had been examined and that his report would be adverse on the ground that the grant was located in Mexico. He delayed submitting a report until more evidence could be secured. "Senator Hearst," he wrote, "is interested in the San Juan de las Boquillas and for prudential reasons I think this investigation should be prosecuted very quietly." Hise to Sparks, from Tucson, Arizona, October 14, 1887, in RG 49, GLO, Arizona private land claim #4½.

† One hectare is equivalent to 2.471 acres.

The grant is claimed by Don José M. Elías, of Sonora; it is said to comprise 36 square miles of territory in the valley of the San Pedro river, embracing ground on both sides of the Mexican boundary line. As late as forty years ago this ranch was occupied by an immense number of cattle and horses; but the Apache Indians made repeated raids upon it, until it was finally abandoned. The lands are well-watered, have a fair proportion of arable ground, arable pasturage, and fine clumps of ash, walnut, oak and other timber. The title to this land has never been passed upon by competent authority, under U. S. laws.[69]

The claim to overplus lands, in the United States alone, actually exceeded the 36 square miles mentioned in the above article. The Reloj Cattle Company, which was incorporated in 1885, had been purchasing quitclaim deeds from the Elías heirs for two years. In a case before the Court of Private Land Claims in 1899, the company asked confirmation for 38,622.06 acres, more than 60 square miles. This was a whopping demand, considering that the Elías deeds, of doubtful validity themselves, were for only about 18,000 acres of overplus lands north of the border. The surveyor general postponed a recommendation on the company's claim but the Court of Private Land Claims permitted a hearing, despite the failure of the company to file by the March 3, 1893 deadline. The court reminded the claimants that the officials in Mexico had decided in 1880 the San Pedro had no boundaries and thus no *demasías,* or overplus; the claim sued for had been entirely satisfied and discharged by the location of the four *sitios* within the Republic of Mexico.[70] In affirming this decree in 1902, the U.S. Supreme Court said in part, "It is quite impossible to entertain the proposition that the Court of Private Land Claims should have adjudged the appellants another *cabida legal* on this side of the boundary."[71]

Agua Prieta

The Agua Prieta grant was similar in some ways to the San Pedro. Not only was it located south of the present Mexican border, but an attempt was made, after the Gadsden Purchase, to extend the grant to include overplus lands in the United States. Agua Prieta was also a part of the extensive holdings of the Elías González family. On July 21, 1831, Juan, Rafael, and Ignacio Elías González petitioned for additional land, stating that their stock had been straying to the "four points of the compass" to seek needed grass. The request was in accordance with the Mexican law, then in force, that authorized the treasurer general to grant to old breeders, "who, from the abundance of their stock need more," the quantity of land shown to be needed. The public domain, from which the Elías clan wished to select three tracts on which their cattle were already grazing, extended as far north as the Chiricahua Mountains, well beyond the present border into Arizona. Though not important in locating the lands desired at the time, the out-boundaries that were listed became important later in claims for overplus lands before the American courts.

After the initial survey and appraisal, the following advertisement for auctions to be held at Hermosillo on September 15, 16, and 17, 1836 was published:

> There are to be sold on account of the public treasury of the department eighteen *sitios* and twelve and one half *caballerías* of land for the raising of cattle and horses, comprised in the places called Agua Prieta, Naidenibacachi, and Santa Bárbara, situate in the presidio of Fronteras, in the district of this capital, surveyed at the request of the citizens of Juan, Rafael, and Ignacio Elías Gonzáles, of the town, and appraised in the sum of 432 dollars and 4 reals, as follows: The six and one half *sitios*, which compose the survey of Agua Prieta, one in the sum of 60 dollars, on account of a small spring, and the other five and one half at the rate of 15 dollars each, on account of their being absolutely dry . . .[72]

The Elías petitioners bought the three tracts for a total of $432.50, including a payment of $142.50 for the Agua Prieta, the only one which eventually involved lands in the Gadsden Purchase area. This grant was so named because the center of the survey was a lagoon or pool in the Agua Prieta Valley, south and east of the border town of Douglas. The American courts later held that the grant was one of quantity, a specific amount of 6½ *sitios,* and it was located by the original owners entirely south of the international boundary line.

The Camou brothers of Hermosillo acquired the rights to the Agua Prieta from the Elías grantees in 1862 by way of conditional sale. Then in 1880, the Camous went before the

district judge in Guaymas and asked for the overplus in addition. The Elías family, represented by Plutarco Elías, con-
tested the claim, arguing that they had transferred the *cabida
legal* to the Camous, but not the *demasías*. The final result
was an issuance of a title to the overplus to the *"Hermanos
Camou."* Already, in 1881, some 16,920 acres situated between
the Agua Prieta and the international boundary line had been
divided among three claimants: the Camou interests, one
Rochin who owned land east of the Agua Prieta, and the Elías
owners of the San Pedro grant. The Camous and their heirs
made no claim to overplus in Arizona and withdrew as early
as July, 1880, from any consideration by the surveyor general
for extension of the Agua Prieta into the Gadsden Purchase
area.

However, Santiago Ainsa, administrator for counter-claim-
ants to Agua Prieta lands, filed a petition on February 28,
1893 with the Court of Private Land Claims in Tucson. He
argued that no resurvey of the grant had been made prior to
the Gadsden treaty and that neither the original grantees nor
their successors in interest had any knowledge of their legal
entitlement, under the laws of Mexico and Sonora, to surplus
lands within the outer boundaries described in the title
papers. Ainsa tendered the sum of $600 in gold in payment
for the overplus and $200 in gold for costs, offered to pay
whatever might be adjudged due, and prayed "that upon said
payment this honorable court decree that petitioner is entitled
to and is the owner of said tract of land, as originally surveyed,
including said overplus or surplus, and that by said decree be
secured in the possession and ownership of the whole of said
tract."[73] The area delineated on Ainsa's maps, as included in
the grant claimed, was 163,797.48 acres, or nearly 256 square
miles of land. Of this claim, 68,530.05 acres were allegedly
in the United States. The Ainsa claim came before the court
in 1899 and was rejected.[74]

The case was appealed to the U.S. Supreme Court and
the decree of the Court of Private Land Claims was affirmed.
Chief Justice Fuller, in delivering the opinion of the court, on
March 17, 1902, explained that the Agua Prieta was a grant

of quantity, 6½ *sitios* clearly measured, and that the lawful area of land, including legal overplus, lay entirely south of the international boundary.

Tres Alamos

Two attempts were made during the Mexican period to colonize the lands along the San Pedro north of the Boquillas grant. In 1831, Leonardo Escalante, in the name of eight different *empresarios* (promoters) was authorized by the Congress of Sonora to occupy 58 *sitios*. The governor specified the following limits to the tract: "On the north it has the River Gila and mountains of Pinal, on the south it probably adjoins the lands taken up on the San Pedro River, to the east it extends an immense distance [probably to the Cobre Grande], and to the west it will have the common lands of Tucson."[75] Each of the promoters was given a definite number of *sitios* within the larger grant, but an Apache uprising made any attempt to occupy lands impossible. Escalante found more success as a politician, serving at one time as governor of Sonora.

After the end of the Mexican War in 1848, and before the Gadsden Purchase in 1854, the government of Mexico attempted to colonize the unoccupied frontier with Mexican citizens, hoping thereby to prevent settlement by Americans who might be tempted to seize the lands. Another objective for Mexican colonization was to create a barrier to thwart the incursion of Apaches; accordingly, the Congress of the State of Sonora passed an act on January 29, 1852, which empowered the governor to make grants of vacant and abandoned land on the frontier. Apparently only one petitioner sought to acquire a grant in Arizona under this law. In September, 1852, Don José Antonio Crespo requested ten square leagues of vacant land *(un terreno baldío)* for the purpose of stock raising and farming at a place on the San Pedro known as "Tres Alamos" (meaning "three cotton-woods"). The grant was subsequently made by Governor Fernando Cubillas. The recipient was given eight years to take possession and to settle a hundred or more Catholic families

in the area north of present-day Benson.[76] But the terms of
the grant were never fulfilled, perhaps because of Apache
hostilities.

In 1883, however, George Hill Howard sought confirmation of the grant after working out an arrangement with
Crespo's widow and her family. A clause was included in the
agreement whereby the Crespos would be compensated in
the event Howard succeeded in getting a title. They were to
receive half the proceeds of the sale of the grant, providing
the amount was not less than $20,000. If no sale were made,
Howard would hold one-half of the land in trust for the
family to handle as they wished. Surveyor General J. W. Robbins recommended on September 12, 1883, that Howard's
claim be approved for ten square leagues (over 43,000 acres).[77]
But Robbins' successor, John Hise, revoked this decision and
was hailed as a hero by the press and the American settlers in
the San Pedro Valley.

As part of his petition for a title, Howard applied for
a survey at "the ancient and well-known place of 'Tres Alamos,' situated upon the San Pedro River about seven miles
more or less down said river from the town of Benson . . . at
said place of Tres Alamos, where the ancient crossing is
found." Surveyor General Hise submitted the affidavits of
eight persons, Mexican and American pioneers who had lived
near Tucson all their lives and knew the area, to prove that
there was no Tres Alamos prior to American occupation of
the region. Testimony was given by Francisco Romero, one
of several laborers who were escorted by troops to cultivate
crops for the Tucson presidio in the San Pedro Valley in 1851.
According to him, there were at that time no roads crossing,
nor a town known as Tres Alamos north of the site of Benson.
The following affidavit of William S. Oury helped Hise to
conclude that the lands claimed by Howard had not been
located or settled by Crespo:

William S. Oury . . . a resident of the City of Tucson since 1856.
No settlement in the neighborhood of Tres Alamos from 1856 until
1861 when settlement was made by Americans. There was no wagon
road or highway crossing the San Pedro river near said Tres Alamos
except the one made by the Overland Mail Co. in the year 1858 just
below (north of) the site of the present town of Benson. Learned that

Tres Alamos was claimed under a Mexican land grant and endeavored to ascertain from the old Mexican settlers of Tucson the specific point called Tres Alamos, and from all the information received from them believe that the term 'Tres Alamos' applied to a section of country and not to any definite point.[78]

Hise's report on the Tres Alamos investigation was printed in the *Arizona Daily Star* on July 18, 1886, under the heading: "Tres Alamos, A Great Fraud Exploded — Settlers Saved!" Actually, the surveyor general didn't go so far as to call the claim a fraud. He simply concluded that the alleged grant was too indefinite and vague to permit intelligent survey and that the grantee never entered into possession of the "alleged tract of Tres Alamos" nor in any way fulfilled the requirements of the grant.

The *Tombstone Epitaph* praised the fairness of the Hise report and called him the most fearless surveyor general Arizona ever had. Commenting on the elation of the settlers, and what might have happened if the Tres Alamos grant had been confirmed, the *Epitaph* editorialized in the style of the 1880s:

> ... They would have been placed at the mercy of such villains as George Hill Howard, who has been engaged in such transactions as this the greater portion of his worthless life. The settlers along the San Pedro have labored hard to build themselves a home in this fertile valley, and, despite the numerous raids of the marauding Apaches, have succeeded in making this favored section bloom and prosper beyond the fondest expectations of the earliest settlers. ... No sooner had this been done, and the property along the river become valuable, than every alert land-grabber put in his appearance and asked the Surveyor General of Arizona to place him in peaceable possession of these lands, made valuable by the courage and industry of the men who had risked their lives and liberty in defense of their homes. ... All honor to John Hise. ... The Tres Alamos land grant fraud must go — so farewell George Hill Howard — your machinations have been in vain.[79]

Howard, however, filed a claim with the Court of Private Land Claims in 1893 for 43,384.64 acres of land stretching north from the Boquillas grant. A co-plaintiff was Francis E. Spencer, to whom Howard had sold and deeded a share of 18,500 acres in 1883. The court rejected the claim because the grant was made originally on the condition the grantee should settle one hundred families from Spain or South America on

the land, and upon several other conditions which had not
been met at the time of the Gadsden cession. The act of 1891
— establishing the Court of Private Land Claims — provided
that compliance with the conditions of a grant, prior to the
date of the treaty, was necessary before confirmation could be
given. The United States Supreme Court refused to review
the case.

El Paso de los Algodones Fraud

"The truth is that, within my personal knowledge and
that of many others, the grant was manufactured by Mexicans
subsequent to the treaty, is antedated, fraudulent, and a forgery." So wrote Charles D. Poston in 1893 after the Court of
Private Land Claims, in its first case in Tucson, confirmed
the so-called Algodones grant. Poston went on to accuse the
new court of "bribery or stupidity." He said that the people
of Arizona had endured the Apaches, famine, and thirst; some
pioneers had waited nearly forty years in the wilderness for the
government to organize a tribunal to settle land titles — "and
lo! their first act is to confirm a forgery."[80]

The government appealed the Algodones case to the
Supreme Court where the decision of the land court was
reversed in 1898. The higher court explained that the officials
in Sonora had no authority to make a grant in 1838, because
all vacant lands had become the property of the Mexican
nation by the Constitution of 1836. In a rehearing a year later,
the higher court stayed with its decision.[81]

The alleged grant was for five *sitios* along the Colorado
River between the Gila on the north and the Algodones pass
on the south. The petitioner, Fernando Rodríguez of Hermosillo, said that the lands applied for were situated in a
desert country which the Indians had made uninhabitable.
Appraisers valued the land at a relatively high $400 because
it could be irrigated with the waters of the Gila River. A
suspiciously unusual feature of this grant was the lack of a
time limit for occupation; the only requirement was that the
grantee was to settle upon the lands "as soon as the circumstances surrounding that distant and desert portion of the
state [of Sonora] may permit him to do so in view of the emi-

U. S. Surveyor General's Office,

Tucson, Arizona, *August 12* 1880.

Hon J. A. Williamson.
   Com'r Gen'l Land Office.
      Washington D.C.

Sir:

I herewith transmit, in duplicate, transcript of case (No. 6 in Docket) of the private land claim "El Paso de los Algodones," claimed by the "Colorado Commercial and Land Company," with recommendation that it be *not confirmed but rejected*, on the grounds that *the title papers are forged and ante-dated*.

There was no Exhibit F filed with the papers, and I have omitted Exhibit H from the transcript inasmuch as it is of no value for or against the claim and does not assist to define its locality, as it purports to do.

Very respectfully.
Your obt. servant,
John Wasson
U. S. Surveyor-General.

Washington National Records Center

Letter of Surveyor General John Wasson, who recommended that the Algodones claim be rejected

nent danger there on account of the savages." It was as unusual for citizens of Mexico to petition for grants of land which could not be occupied as it was for Mexican authorities to grant lands with no conditions to inhabit them.

Poston recalled that no settlement had been attempted as of 1854, when he had the original townsite of present-day Yuma surveyed. Furthermore, no one in the vicinity — including the commander of the post at Yuma, the steamboat proprietors, and the owners of the ferry — had ever heard about the Algodones land grant. According to the records in Sonora,

the rights to the grant were sold in 1845 to Juan A. Robinson
of Guaymas, and then transferred again in 1873 to the Colorado Commercial and Land Company. To satisfy the company, the government withdrew the lands from entry on
January 9, 1875 and agreed to study the claim. The investigations of Surveyor General John Wasson in 1879 showed that
the original title papers recorded in the *Toma de Razón* had
been antedated and forged. Spanish documents expert R. C.
Hopkins discovered that the signature of one José Justo Milla,
an auditor in Treasurer General José Mendoza's office was
not genuine; in one place Milla's given names were written
"José José" instead of "José Justo," a very unlikely mistake
on a document of such importance.[82]

Following up on Wasson's recommendation, the General
Land Office and the Secretary of Interior continually urged
Congress to place the lands in the public domain and open
them to settlement. Finally, a motion — made by Arizona's
delegate in Congress, Marcus A. Smith — to reject the Algodones grant as fraudulent was passed by the House Committee
on Private Land Claims. The new claimant, Earl B. Coe, presented his case before the Court of Private Land Claims and,
as mentioned above, secured confirmation for 21,692 acres,
"notwithstanding some irregularities" in the title papers.[83]
Several concessions by the successful claimant did not make
the court's decision any more palatable. The Southern Pacific
railroad was given a quitclaim deed to its right-of-way through
the Algodones, and the Yuma territorial penitentiary was left
in public hands despite being on the grant.

Immediately after this decision, the alleged owners of the
grant began selling deeds to settlers for tracts of 40 acres or
less. In return for the payment of "large and valuable considerations" the settlers believed that they had secured bona
fide titles and began constructing improvements and permanent homes. The effect of the Supreme Court 1898 and 1899
decisions reversing the Algodones claim was to restore the
lands to the public domain. Congress, however, passed an act
on January 14, 1901, to relieve the occupants. By this law, all
the lands in the grant were opened to entry on March 18 of
that year, but in anticipation of a great rush for the irrigable

acreage, the Congress gave prior rights to bona fide settlers who were on the land before the Supreme Court decision of May 25, 1898. Each person was limited to 40 acres and was required to pay $1.25 per acre after proving possession.[84] Additional land was available, however, under the homestead act. Twenty applications were presented to the land office in Tucson on March 18 and all were for 160 acres.[85]

Peralta-Reavis Fraud

Of more than eleven million acres of land claimed in Arizona under Spanish or Mexican titles, only about 120,000 acres, exclusive of the Baca Floats, were confirmed. Most of the rejected acreage was in the fraudulent claim of James Addison Reavis, a master crook who first came to Arizona about 1880 as a subscription agent for the San Francisco *Examiner*.[86] With a vivid imagination and a developed talent for forgery, Reavis nearly succeeded in pulling off one of the most gigantic swindles in history. After spending years in arduously altering, adding to, or replacing pertinent records in the official depositories of Spain and Mexico, the ex-Confederate soldier and Missouri streetcar conductor went to Tucson in March, 1883, to file a sheaf of documents with Surveyor General J. W. Robbins to prove his claim to the alleged Peralta grant.[87]

In essence, what Reavis had done was invent a family lineage starting with one Don Nemecio Silva de Peralta de la Córdoba. According to the fictitious data accumulated by Reavis, Peralta was given the title of Baron de los Colorados by King Ferdinand VI of Spain in 1748, and also an extensive grant of land in the northern provinces to go with it. To establish connection between himself and the Peralta family, Reavis explained how he acquired title to the Peralta grant from one George Willing, a mine developer from the East who was in and out of Arizona several times after 1864. Willing supposedly had purchased the deed from a descendant of the original Baron de los Colorados, a poverty-stricken Mexican named Miguel Peralta. Actually, Miguel existed only as a character in forged deeds and transfers designed to place the

Peralta grant in Reavis' possession. George Willing could not
contradict the story since he died in Prescott the day after he
recorded the deed in the Yavapai County courthouse in
March, 1874.[88]

Besides Willing, there was another character in the plot,
this one a Cinderella-like creation of Reavis' fertile imagination. To strengthen his claim, he found a Mexican orphan
girl, had her educated, and eventually made her his wife, giving her the title of Baroness of Arizona. For a man who had
forged documents on two continents, it was no great challenge
to change church birth records in California and thereby make
his bride the last surviving descendant of the Peralta family.
Before this alteration and other false documents were revealed,
the Baron and his sophisticated, probably unsuspecting lady
were to make a deep imprint on Arizona history.

The barony they sought was no ordinary land claim.
In September, 1887, Reavis applied for a survey of the fictitious
Peralta-Reavis claim. It was a large rectangle of land, stretching from a point northwest of Phoenix to the southeast corner
south of Silver City, New Mexico.[89] In addition to Phoenix, it
included the towns of Tempe, Mesa, Globe, Clifton, Solomon-
ville, Casa Grande, and Florence. The Southern Pacific Railroad crossed its southwest corner and the fabulously rich Silver
King mine was located within its bounds. Though this huge
claim had not been validated in any court, many frightened
and gullible people began to pay Reavis varying amounts for
quitclaim deeds to their homes, farms, mines, businesses, and
even schools.[90]

The fact that some brilliant, nationally famous lawyers,
including Roscoe Conkling and Robert Ingersoll, scrutinized
the fraudulent documents and found them to be good in law
and unassailable in court only increased the hysteria. And when
millionaires like Charles Crocker and Collis P. Huntington
pronounced the claim valid and financed the Baron's wanderings over the world in search of historical evidence, what could
the "little" man do? Even the editor of the *Arizona Gazette,*
Homer H. McNeill, who was urging the people to fight for
their rights, was one of the first to purchase a deed from Reavis
and have it recorded.[91] The big contributors, of course, were
the Southern Pacific, which paid $50,000, and the Silver King

*James Addison Reavis,
alias the "Baron of Arizona"*

Arizona Historical Society

*Doña Sofia Loreta Micaela de
Maso-Reavis y Peralta de la
Córdoba, the "Baroness-of Arizona"
and wife of James Addison Reavis*

Washington National Records Center

your power we would ever pray,

Respectfully,

*Doña Sofia Loreta Micaela de Maso-Reavis
y Peralta de la Córdoba*

James Addison Peralta Reavis

Tucson, Arizona Territory,

September 2nd, 1887.

Washington National Records Center

*Signatures of the Peralta Grant claimants on the "Application
for a Preliminary Survey," filed in Tucson, September 2, 1887*

mine, which gave $25,000 toward defraying the cost of the Baron's expensive tastes.[92] With this kind of income, Reavis was able to live in courtly style. He maintained homes in St. Louis, Washington, D.C., Madrid, and Chihuahua City, and traveled widely at home and abroad in a manner befitting royalty.

Meanwhile, however, the investigation of the Peralta claim was being patiently conducted by the office of the surveyor general. Robbins died of tuberculosis and was succeeded by Royal A. Johnson, the chief clerk and a well trained lawyer. The latter's sincere interest in the claim was indicated by the advice which he gave to his father, a New York attorney, to refuse a retaining fee offered by Reavis. The newspapers and citizens in general criticized Johnson for dallying but suddenly became his enthusiastic admirers when he finally released his carefully prepared exposé of the fraudulent Peralta grant in 1889. His analysis of the questioned documents disclosed several forgeries and historical inaccuracies which led him to the conclusion that the Reavis claim was spurious and should be rejected.

The scientific evidence compiled in Johnson's report reads like a detective story. Some of his observations, like the following, also show practical reasoning:

> One very noticeable feature in this case is that no will is produced in this office enumerating that the testator owned a watch, money, heirlooms, or even books, carriages, or that inseparable companion of the average Mexican, a horse. In the will of the Grantee in 1783 and the codicil of 1788, not a thing is devised but the Peralta Grant. Are we to be asked to credit a showing that a Grandee of Spain, a man of heroic deeds, and recognized merits, a man under the immediate patronage of a great King, a friend of a Viceroy and a Captain of Dragoons possessed nothing in the World that he could leave his child except this very land claim, which is so essential, should be traced in these wills.[93]

The people of Phoenix showed their appreciation of Johnson's report by giving him a gala reception in 1890. They still had five years to wait, however, before the Court of Private Land Claims in Santa Fe — Chief Justice Joseph Reed presiding — decreed the Reavis claim to be "wholly fictitious and fraudulent." The court declared that the forged documents had been surreptitiously introduced into the records and archives of Madrid, Seville, and Guadalajara, and into the baptismal and burial records of the parish of San Bernardino and San Salvador in California.

Reavis was then placed under arrest and, after a year of legal maneuvering, was convicted of conspiracy to defraud the government.[94] He was fined $5,000 and sentenced to two years in prison. As convict No. 964 in the penitentiary at Santa Fe, Reavis must have wondered if the prize which he had sought was really worth the effort. If anything can be said in his favor, it might be that his grandiose scheme at least gave Arizonans a better appreciation of the value of their lands.

THE APACHE THREAT

In retrospect it is interesting to consider how different the history of Arizona might have been if the Spanish and Mexican governments had not neglected the ranches, presidios, and missions in northern Sonora. The Mexican struggle for independence, however, occupied the attention of Spain after 1811 and the frontier garrisons were inadequately and irregularly supplied. The Apaches remained tranquil through the 1820s, waiting to see what the new Mexican government would do. When the peace policy initiated by the Spanish was allowed to deteriorate, and a liberal supply of rations was no longer furnished to them, the Indians once again took to the warpath. In 1831, the Apaches rose in rebellion, striking the settlements of Sonora and Chihuahua with great fury. They agreed to a treaty the same year, but the terms proved to be unrealistic. For one thing, the Indians were expected to work for their subsistence; they had expected a revival of the rationing system. Another objectionable provision amounted virtually to a policy of containment; western Apachería was divided into three zones and each Apache group was required to remain in its own zone. So the armistice was of short duration.

In January, 1833, the Apaches of eastern Arizona and western New Mexico once again followed their plunder trails into Sonora, leaving a bloody path of destruction. The "great stealing road of the Coyoteros" originated in the Pinal and White Mountains, passed over the Gila River above (east of)

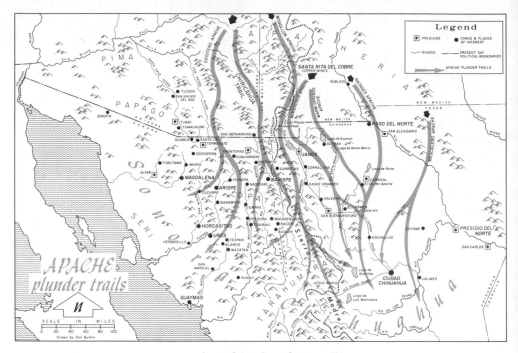

Apache plunder trails

the present-day San Carlos Lake behind the Coolidge Dam
to the Aravaipa Creek, then turned southward along the eastern side of the San Pedro Valley via the site of present-day
Bisbee and into Sonora northwest of Frontéras. There were
also diversions to the ranches along the Santa Cruz and its
tributaries. A second major route to the south was the Chiricahua Trail used by the Chiricahuas, Mimbreños, Mogollon-
eros, Tontos and other Apache bands. This route was farther
east, closer to the present Arizona-New Mexico state line; from
the Gila it paralleled the San Simon Creek, passed through the
San Bernardino Ranch, and spread out in the vicinity of the
Chihuahua-Sonora boundary line.

Many of the ranches and settlements in northern Sonora,
including Arizona, were abandoned. In 1835, Don Ignacio
Zúñiga, for several years a commander of the northern presidios, reported on the desolation of the frontier. He estimated
that at least 5,000 lives had been lost in Sonora and that another
3,000 to 4,000 settlers had been forced to flee southward.
Nothing was left in Arizona except the demoralized garrisons
of inefficient soldiers, some of whom were felons and lesser
culprits who had been assigned to presidial duty for lack of

a state prison in Sonora. Zúñiga recommended a return to Spanish policies: well-paid and disciplined troops, control of missions by the friars, and the colonization of the northern ranches by people of good character. He also proposed that some of the presidios should be moved to the Gila and Colorado rivers to protect land communication between New Mexico and California. A few campaigns were conducted against the Apaches in the 1830s and 1840s, but the reforms suggested by Zúñiga were never carried out. The key to the problem lay with the unstable government in Mexico City. Instead of sending a well equipped army under competent leadership to strengthen the presidial line and to pursue and chastise the marauding Indians, the Mexican officials viewed Sonora and the rest of the remote frontier as a kind of wasteland. The civil war involving Santa Anna's attempt to establish despotic rule also divided and weakened the government of Sonora as different factions struggled for power.

Unable to make a practical treaty or to raise sufficient money for a strong military force, the states of Sonora and Chihuahua resorted to the scalp bounty system. A hundred pesos was offered for the hair of any warrior over fourteen years of age. But scalp hunting served only to intensify the hatred for the Mexicans and also for Americans who were represented by several unscrupulous bounty seekers. The Apache incursions into Sonora continued almost unchecked until the 1850s when the Indians transferred their attention to the advancing Anglo-American pioneers.

Joseph H. Kibbey, Arizona's next-to-last territorial governor and a leader in the development of the Salt River Project, hit upon an interesting interpretation of the late Spanish and Mexican period of history when he suggested that the hostile Apaches had indirectly benefited the early American settlement of the state. Except for them, he said, the Spanish and Mexican *rancheros* would have acquired many more land grants, perhaps even a legitimate Peralta-type estate, and retarded the later development of the region. In contrast to the Rio Grande Valley in New Mexico and certain areas in California, the Salt River Valley, one of the richest agricultural regions in the Southwest, was open to settlement by the first Americans who went there.

Chapter 8

The Mountain Men

THE CHAOS ON THE FRONTIERS of New Spain set the stage for the Americanization of Arizona and the Southwest. Zebulon Pike had described the attractiveness of the Santa Fe trade in the report on his expedition into New Mexico and Chihuahua in 1806. It was not until Mexico threw off the Spanish yoke in 1821, however, that restrictions on commercial transactions with Americans were relaxed.

The isolated residents of Santa Fe eagerly welcomed the chance to trade their silver and gold bullion, mules, beaver furs, and Indian blankets for manufactured goods from the States. And American traders immediately took advantage of the new economic opportunity. One of the pioneers in this remunerative activity was a frontiersman named William Becknell who reached Santa Fe in the autumn of 1821 and returned safely to Arrow Rock, near Franklin, Missouri, plush with profits. In 1824, he organized the first of the great wagon trains to the Mexican settlements. A party of eighty-one men transported $30,000 worth of merchandise in twenty-five wagons and brought back $180,000 in gold and silver, in addition to $10,000 in furs.

Becknell did more than bring back bags of money, he opened the historic Santa Fe Trail for all who followed. Though the total volume of traffic over the route was never very large and the number of traders engaged in it probably averaged only about a hundred a year, the new trail into the Far West was of great significance. For the first time, Americans began to show interest in the Southwest. By the time Mexican dictator Santa Anna closed the trade in 1843, many people believed the whole region was manifestly destined to become a part of the United States. The Santa Fe trade itself had little direct effect in hastening the American territorial expansion, but it furnished the means by which aggressive pioneers infiltrated the Southwest. A considerable number of men became familiar with the geography and trails of this area. Most of these "first Americans" to arrive were fur trappers — better known as "mountain men" — who performed a great service in the eventual conquest of the West.

Until the mid-1830s, furs made up a considerable part of the trade carried over the Santa Fe Trail. The settlements of Taos and Santa Fe had quickly become bases from which hundreds of trappers fanned out into Mexico and as far west as the Pacific. In their search for pelts, the early trappers became the pioneer American explorers of much of the drainage basins of Utah's Green River and the Colorado River. In the early 1820s, Americans reached streams in Arizona. Between 1824 and 1832, there were hundreds of these pathfinders along the Gila, the Verde, the Salt, the San Pedro, the Colorado, and the San Francisco rivers. Fully aware that they were trespassing, the men kept scant records. Their secrecy and subterfuge in flouting the regulations of the Mexican authorities account for the obscurity of many of the trappers. It was a common practice, for example, for only one person in a party to buy the expensive trapping license, and for all the others to sell their pelts through him at the market places. The official records were therefore incomplete. Nevertheless, the Americans came. Among the more famous men who touched upon Arizona soil were Sylvester and James Pattie, Jedediah Smith, "Old Bill" Williams, Pauline Weaver, Kit Carson, Miguel Robidoux, "Peg-leg" Smith, Ewing Young, David E. Jackson, Milton Sublette, Ceran St. Vrain, Felix Aubrey, and Antoine Leroux.

The most classic contemporary report available on the adventures of the mountain men in Arizona is the *Personal Narrative of James Ohio Pattie of Kentucky*. Written by a ghost writer, Timothy Flint, and based upon Pattie's recollections after his trapping days were over, there are many details in the account which are inaccurate or vague. Yet the work is one of the first authentic books printed in the United States

which describes the Southwest at the dawn of American
civilization in this region.[1]

Pattie was only twenty years of age when he arrived at
Santa Fe in November, 1824, with his father, Sylvester, and
a caravan of traders and trappers from Missouri. Having
come to the capital city to seek a license to trap on the Gila,
the Americans found the Mexican governor reluctant to give
the party permission to set out. But fortune soon smiled on the
adventurers as the result of an exciting experience. While
waiting in Santa Fe, the Patties joined a Mexican force in
pursuit of a Comanche band which had raided some nearby
ranches and carried away several women and children. The
young Pattie personally rescued the beautiful daughter of
the former governor of New Mexico. His bravery won both the
affection of the maiden, whom he called Jacova, and the
coveted permit to trap. Spurning the girl, he set out for
the "Helay" with his father in a company that ultimately
consisted of fourteen men. En route, the party stopped at the
Santa Rita copper mines, near present-day Silver City, New
Mexico. Reaching the Gila they continued downstream to a
point where the river is joined by the Salt, southwest of
modern Phoenix.

They trapped along the various tributaries with varying
success while enduring considerable cold and hunger much
of the time. Making their way back upstream, the men came
to the virgin San Pedro River where they caught many
beavers. There, when the party was about ready to break
camp, a band of Indians crept in at night and stampeded the
grazing horses. Completely stranded, the trappers were obliged
to hide their furs and start back to the Santa Rita mines on
foot. After the ragged, exhausted wanderers reached the mines
in April, 1825, James Pattie traveled on to Santa Fe to secure
more horses and supplies. Emaciated to skin and bones by the
starvation and fatigue of the Gila expedition, the young man
must have presented a bedraggled appearance. Even in his
tattered leather garments and with matted, uncombed hair,
he was welcomed into the home of Jacova. Resisting the temptation to linger, however, Pattie completed his mission and
returned to Santa Rita to organize an expedition and search

for the buried furs. During his absence, however, the Indians had discovered the hiding place and removed the pelts. Except for a few skins in another cache, the trappers had nothing to show for so many months of danger and hardship.

Both of the Patties remained at Santa Rita for several months, overseeing the mines and protecting the settlement from the Apaches. After they leased the property, Sylvester was contented to stay put, but James — at least according to his narrative — had itching feet and joined a company of French trappers headed by Miguel Robidoux, member of a famous St. Louis fur trading family. Traveling down the Gila, the party reached a large village of Indians at the fork of the Gila and Salt Rivers.* The natives professed to be friendly, but Pattie and one other trapper distrusted them and camped outside the village while their companions stayed inside. The Indians treacherously attacked the sleeping trappers at night — the only escapees being Pattie, his friend, and a badly-clubbed Robidoux. Fortunately for them, there was another trapping party in the vicinity. This group, led by the competent Ewing Young, included such famous trappers as Tom (later called "Peg-leg") Smith, George Yount, and Milton Sublette. Joining forces, the thirty-plus men ambushed the Indians, killed many of the warriors, burned the village, and buried the dismembered and mutilated bodies of Robidoux's men. "A sight more horrible . . . I have never seen," said Pattie in his *Narrative*. "They were literally cut to pieces, and fragments of their bodies scattered in every direction."

Pattie then accompanied his new party up the Salt River, passing through the area where Phoenix is now located and beyond to the junction of the Verde with the Salt. There the company divided to follow these rivers to their sources. The Verde group went as far as the copper-rich mountains southwest of Williams. Pattie accompanied the second up the Salt into the White Mountains of eastern Arizona. The parties then returned to the juncture of the two rivers and the

---

*Pattie called the Indians "Papawars," his name for the Papagos. But George Yount, a trapper with the Young party, said that they were Pima-Maricopas. The locality and actions of the Indians would indicate that they might have been Western Apaches or Yavapais. See Clifton B. Kroeber, "The Route of James Ohio Pattie on the Colorado in 1826," *Arizona and the West*, Vol. 6, No. 2 (Summer, 1964), p. 124.

reunited company followed the Salt to the Gila and that river
to the Colorado. They found the Yumas friendly and traded
red cloth to them for dried beans. The Mojaves upstream,
however, were hostile and the trappers were involved in at
least two skirmishes while in their territory. When the company reached the vicinity of the present site of Parker Dam,
Young noticed signs of antagonism among the Indians and
directed his men to construct a breastwork of cottonwood
logs and packs of beaver pelts. His foresight paid off, for the
Mojaves attacked one day about an hour before dawn. Their
bows and arrows were no match for the rifle fire of the waiting
trappers and sixteen Indians were killed in the assault.

Up the river a few days later, however, the Mojaves
succeeded in surprising the sleeping trappers; their poisoned
arrows killed two of the men and wounded two others. Pattie
was unhurt, but he supposedly found sixteen arrows in his
blanket, two having gone through his hunting shirt. After
daybreak, the trappers followed the trail of the Mojaves,
caught and shot an unspecified number, and hanged the
corpses on trees as a warning to other natives. According to
Pattie, there was another encounter with hostile Indians,
perhaps Yavapais or Havasupais, in addition to the skirmishes
with the Mojaves. It seems that Young sent three men up one
of the tributaries of the Colorado to reconnoiter for beaver.
When the men did not return, a searching party set out to
locate them, only to find their bodies cut in pieces and
"spitted before a great fire, after the same fashion which is
used in roasting beaver." The Indians had already fled into
the mountains to avoid punishment when the searchers
arrived on this horrible scene.

By this time, the trappers were ready to return home to
Santa Fe. They had taken all the beaver pelts they could
pack. Their horses were enfeebled; the provisions and ammunition were running low. Under these circumstances, the
journey proved to be a long perilous one. It took days to
cross the rough tributary canyons that plunge down into the
great gorge at what is now the head of Lake Mead. "A march
more gloomy and heart-wearying," wrote Pattie, "to people
hungry, poorly clad, and mourning the loss of their com-

panions, cannot be imagined." George Yount, though his account of the expedition differed in some respects from Pattie's, also emphasized the hardships of the return trip across northern Arizona. "They were now threatened with starvation," he said. "They had killed their last remaining dog for meat. Only here and there could be found a poor half-starved Coyote or Porcupine which were quickly eaten entire . . . Death . . . stared them in the face . . . all were reduced to skeletons. In this condition, the party at last reached the Nation of the Sunies [Zuñis]. . . ."[2] They arrived in Santa Fe during the summer of 1826 with a fine supply of furs. Once again Pattie had only the welcoming arms of Jacova and the prosperity of his father to brighten his spirits, because the newly-appointed and anti-foreign Governor Manuel Armijo seized the furs, charging that the Americans had been trapping without a license.

Still restless, the young Pattie undertook a trading expedition into Chihuahua and Sonora. After an exciting trip during which he was supposedly almost killed by a bear — and on another occasion — by hostile Indians, Pattie again returned to Santa Fe. A short time later, he and his father joined a company of trappers and started for the Colorado River in the fall of 1827. Because of hard luck and hunger, the party eventually split up and only six of the trappers stayed with the Patties while the rest returned to New Mexico. After reaching the Colorado, the Patties were forced to improvise when the Indians stole their horses. The men constructed dugout boats from cottonwood logs and floated down the river to the Gulf of California. Hiding their furs in that vicinity, they struck out across the waterless desert to San Diego. Their suffering on this trip was exceeded only by the cruelty of the Mexican authorities once the destination was reached. At San Diego, the whole party was clamped into prison. The elder Pattie died in solitary confinement, but James secured his release and that of his friends as a reward for services as an amateur physician. Having some knowledge of a crude technique for smallpox vaccination, James was sent throughout California by Governor José María Echeandía to inoculate the inhabitants of the province.

Beginning his work in January, 1829, Pattie proceeded up the coast, vaccinating the Indians at the missions and the residents of the pueblos. There is some question about the number of people who were inoculated, but Pattie set the figure at 24,000 — including the inhabitants of the Russian settlement of Bodega across the bay from San Francisco.* Though denied the money, land, and cattle that he was promised, Pattie was granted a passport and given permission to return to the States. He boarded an American brig at Monterey on May 8, 1830, and disembarked at San Blas ten days later. From this port he and his friends traveled overland to Mexico City — where he unsuccessfully sought recompense for his work during the smallpox epidemic — and then continued on to Veracruz by stagecoach to take a boat to New Orleans which he reached on August 1. In the autumn of 1830, he arrived back at the home of his grandparents in Kentucky, a lost and impoverished man. After the publication of his remarkable narrative in 1831, he apparently disappeared into oblivion, but in six exciting, action-packed years, James Ohio Pattie had carved out a permanent niche for himself in the history of Arizona and the Southwest.[3]

While the Patties were among the first white men to cross the continent by the southern Gila route, another mountain man was one of the first to reach California by the central route through Utah. Jedediah Strong Smith was a rarity among fur trappers in that he had been fairly well educated as a youth in New York and was an outspoken Christian. Unfortunately for posterity, the journals and maps of this most widely-traveling explorer of his time were destroyed in a St. Louis fire and were never published. Before he was killed by Comanche Indians while searching for water to supply a Santa Fe Trail caravan, he traversed a large part of the trans-Mississippi West. Twice he came down by way of the Virgin River into what is now northwestern Arizona.

---

* There is good evidence that the epidemic in Alta California in 1827–28 was due to measles — not smallpox — and that Pattie's account of how he vaccinated 24,000 persons for smallpox was a "tall tale." See Rosemary K. Valle, "James Ohio Pattie and the 1827–1828 Alta California Measles Epidemic," *California Historical Quarterly,* Vol. LII, No. 1 (Spring, 1973), pp. 28–36.

In 1826, Smith and his party rested about two weeks in the Mojave villages en route westward. After trading for horses and food, they journeyed on to the coast with two native guides. Following a similar route in the summer of 1827, Smith unsuspectingly led nineteen men back to the Mojave country. The Indians appeared outwardly friendly for several days, but treacherously attacked the surprised trappers while they were crossing the Colorado on rafts. The men were at the greatest possible disadvantage, and in a few bloody minutes ten of them fell dead under the poisoned arrows and war clubs of the Mojaves.[4] The cause of this tragic episode is as much a mystery as the march of Smith and the other survivors across the hot California desert was heroic. Certainly, it was one of the more exciting events in the life of a man who had many a hair-raising experience with Indians and grizzly bears in his short life span of thirty-three years.

The story of the lives of most of the mountain men is so wrapped in legend that it is difficult to separate fact from fancy. William Shirley "Old Bill" Williams is no exception. Even though he has a mountain, a stream, and a town named after him in Arizona, he is only vaguely associated with the history of the state. His life is fairly well known from the time of his birth in North Carolina, in 1787, down to his entrance into Santa Fe in 1825, and from 1841 to the time of his death in 1849. Yet we get only an occasional glimpse of him during the intervening years when he was trapping, trading, and living among the mountain Indians in Arizona and the West.[5]

Reared a Methodist in what was then a wild and wooly St. Louis, Williams became a missionary to the nearby Osages and translated part of the Bible into the language of that tribe. While among them, he augmented his income by opening a store and trading post where he learned about all there was to know about beaver pelts. Eventually, Williams married an Indian girl named Oneida, who bore him two daughters; he also developed an admiration for the native legends, superstitions, and ceremonials. The resultant loss of his Christian faith, as well as the death of his wife, brought about a restlessness that led to the next phase of his colorful career. He literally laid aside his Bible and took up his rifle. Turning to hunting and trapping, he pitted his cunning and endurance against the nomadic tribes on the great western plains that lay between the Osages and the Rockies. In 1825, he was hired as an interpreter and guide by George C. Sibley, one of the commissioners appointed by President Monroe to mark out a road from Missouri toward Santa Fe. Williams negotiated treaties with the Osage and Kansas Indians and accompanied Sibley to Taos, New Mexico. At this point a decided break came in his life.

For the next quarter of a century, he roamed the mountains and rarely ventured eastward. His first entrance into Arizona was in 1826 with St. Vrain on an expedition down the Gila. In the next few years, he wandered across the Mogollon Plateau along the Little Colorado River, visited the Petrified Forests and the Grand Canyon, and reached the Colorado River. Mysterious and unpredictable "Old Bill" generally preferred to go it alone. An Indian of the Ute tribe, with whom he lived for some time, said that he was as solitary as "the eagle in the heavens, or the panther in the mountains." He delighted in appearing at Taos or at some rendezvous in the Rockies to confound his rivals with a profitable bundle of furs from his secret trapping grounds. His packs disposed of, Williams proceeded to drink and gamble away his fortune. Once he is said to have lost $1000 in one game of Seven Up. On another occasion, he set up a store in Taos. He soon grew tired of haggling over prices, however, and went out of business in a most unusual way. He took his stock of cloth goods into the street, where he unfurled bolts of calico worth a dollar a yard and laughed uproariously as the women of the town scrambled for the cloth. After this spectacular generosity, he departed for his solitary haunts. Like most mountain men, he needed to let off steam at intervals and would return again for more reckless sprees. Unfortunately, there were more eyewitnesses to his celebrations at the trading posts than to his exploits along the streams and with the Indians.

Though "Old Bill" probably traveled extensively in Arizona, only one contemporary record of his journeys in the state has been preserved. Another trapper, Antoine Leroux, related that in 1837, he came across Williams all alone on the river that now bears his name in northwestern Arizona. Williams told him that he had gone westward from New Mexico through the land of the Apaches to the Bill Williams Fork. After visiting with Leroux, Williams went downstream to trap, the next year unexpectedly turning up at a rendezvous in Wyoming, a thousand miles from Arizona. It is no wonder that he was regarded with a certain air of mystery.

What manner of man was Bill Williams? He signed his name and his peltry "Bill Williams, Master Trapper." Confident of his ability, he strove to be the best hunter and trapper in the West. His skill and eccentricities were so well known that most writers who visited the Rocky Mountain area during the fur trade days attempted to describe him. There is no picture of Williams in existence, but several pen sketches have been found as well as diary accounts of his appearance. Albert Pike, who was with him for nearly two months on an exploration to the headwaters of the Red River in Texas, drew a pen sketch of Williams and wrote that he was six feet one inch in height, lean but tough, red-headed, and with a weather-beaten and sun-dried face that had been deeply marked by smallpox. Another contemporary wrote that he was a dead shot with his rifle, though he shot with a double wobble; he couldn't hold the gun steady, but like many good shooters he squeezed the trigger on his muzzle-loading, long-barreled, flintlock rifle just as it swept across the target. Sure of his marksmanship, he often bet as much as a hundred dollars on a single shot.

Descriptions of his walking and riding are also revealing. On foot "Old Bill's" gait was peculiar. He staggered from side to side like a drunk but never seemed to tire. Even when well past middle age, he could run along the streams all day with six five-pound beaver traps on his back. Though an excellent horseman, he presented an unusual, Ichabod Crane-like appearance in the saddle. He used short Mexican stirrups and rode leaning forward, a position which made him look like a hunchback. His buckskin breeches were worn so that his legs were bare below the knees. In other respects the characteristics of Bill Williams were not so much eccentric as they were the ways of the Indians. Like the redman, he didn't consider it necessary to cook meat. He believed in dreams to foretell the future and said that after his death his soul would be reincarnated in the form of a buck elk.

Williams died on a mountain trail somewhere between Pueblo, Colorado, and Taos in 1849. The previous winter he had been employed by John C. Frémont to guide the latter's disastrous fourth expedition through the Rockies. Williams had given up the relative comfort of his winter quarters at Pueblo against his better judgment. Following the possible future railroad route insisted upon by Frémont, he led the party into one of the worst disasters that befell any exploring party in the history of the Rockies. The weather was too cold, the snow was too deep, and there was no known road over the selected route. Of the thirty-two men, eleven died of starvation. The remainder, including Frémont and Williams, arrived at Taos exhausted. The following spring, Williams and Dr. Benjamin J. Kern, the scientist of the expedition, were killed by Ute Indians while attempting to recover the instruments and supplies that the expedition had abandoned in the snow. Williams did not live long enough to refute the charges of incompetence, cannibalism, and premeditated treachery which were brought against him. But it is fitting justice that Richard H. Kern, brother of the scientist who accompanied him on his last expedition, should honor him. While with the Sitgreaves expedition that crossed northern Arizona in 1851, Kern and Antoine Leroux named Bill Williams Mountain and Bill Williams Fork in tribute to the old guide and trapper.

Another "lone wolf" mountain man was Pauline Weaver. He came to Arizona about 1830 and largely confined his activities to this area until his death in a lonely tent near Camp Lincoln on the Verde River in 1867.[6] Weaver was born in 1800 in White County, Tennessee, where his father had migrated before the American Revolution. His mother was the daughter of a prosperous chief of the Cherokees. Because of the strong French influence in this tribe, he was named

Paulino, later changed to Pauline. The spelling didn't matter since the boy apparently never learned to read and write. As late as 1864, he signed a mining location notice in Yavapai County with an "X." There is some doubt as to whether the "P. Weaver, 1832" inscription on a wall of the Casa Grande ruin was his writing, though he likely visited the ruin as well as the Mexican settlements of Tucson and Tubac in the early 1830s.

At an early age, he became an employee of the Hudson Bay Fur Company but soon grew tired of the cold winters in the north. After a few years of wandering through the Rockies, he settled down in what is now Arizona, occasionally finding California more attractive. Weaver seemed to be quite a versatile man. He made Arizona history in the capacities of trapper, prospector, guide, scout, and Indian negotiator. As a trapper, he found that the fur animals in the Southwest were more plentiful than in the colder regions, though the pelts were perhaps of inferior quality. Like Old Bill Williams, he preferred to remain aloof from organized companies of trappers. Roaming alone, he became very familiar with the geography of Arizona and was able to offer his service as a guide and scout to the soldiers, explorers, and travelers who came later. Although he was not a miner, Pauline did some prospecting. He is credited with having discovered the placers* along the Colorado where La Paz sprang up in 1862. He also located placer deposits up the Gila, a few miles from its junction with the Colorado. And in 1863, he guided the Abraham Harlow Peeples' party from Yuma to the mining area south of Prescott, better known as the Weaver District.

Few men in the history of Arizona were Weaver's equal as a peace-maker with the Indians. Before this area became a part of the United States, he was rewarded by the Mexican government for his work in this capacity. He received a land grant of 2800 acres in San Gorgonio Pass near the modern site

---

*A placer is a deposit of sand or gravel, in a stream bed or some other alluvium, containing heavy ore minerals (such as gold or platinum) which have been eroded from their original bedrock. The placers were the only deposits that the early Arizona pioneers could work with no equipment except a shovel and a hand pan.

of Banning, California, for negotiating a treaty between the
whites and the Indians of that region. After gold was discovered in the Prescott area, Weaver and an ex-Fort Mojave
soldier named John Moss met with representatives of several
tribes in a great council. These Indians agreed not to interfere with the passage of white men through the territory and
to show their peaceful intentions by using the passwords "Paulino, Paulino, Tobacco."

Until almost the end of his life, Weaver remained on
good terms with the Indians and was able to go among them
unharmed. In 1864, however, he lost their confidence when he
sought the aid of soldiers at Fort Whipple against a band
of Yavapais. At the time, he was living in a cabin on the
Hassayampa and cultivating a small field. While he was away
some Indian boys ravaged his crops. He first complained to
the chiefs but secured no satisfaction. Hoping to salvage his
prestige, he led the soldiers to the Indian camp, only to have
the affair get out of hand. In the skirmish that followed, the
band was wiped out, and Weaver's standing with the Indians
along with it. In a book entitled *Argonaut Tales,* Judge
Edmund Wells, who knew Weaver, described a romantic incident that grew out of this tragedy.[7]

The day after the battle, an Indian maiden named Aha-
sa-ya-mo came to Weaver's cabin and warned him of a planned
Indian ambush. In spite of the warning, he was attacked and
wounded. One flint arrowhead could not be removed and
tortured him to the end of his life. For his own safety, Weaver
attached himself to the troops at Fort Whipple and in 1866
was assigned to Camp Lincoln on the Verde. Refusing to live
at the post, he pitched his tent among the willows on the
river bottom. It was here that he was quietly cared for by an
Indian woman, perhaps Aha-sa-ya-mo, and died on June
21, 1867.

His body was buried at Fort Whipple until that post was
abandoned in 1892 and the dead moved to San Francisco. In
1929, however, his body was brought back to Prescott after
Sharlot Hall, a famous pioneer historian, collected pennies
from Arizona school children for the necessary funds. Today

one can see the large granite boulder which marks his grave on the grounds of the Old Governor's Mansion at Prescott. Part of the bronze plaque reads thus: "He was born, lived and died on the frontier of the country, always in the ever advancing westward move of civilization and was the first settler on the site of Prescott."

Perhaps no mountain man was more famous in the United States than Christopher "Kit" Carson. When he was two years old, his parents moved to the wild Missouri frontier from Kentucky, where he was born in 1809. At the age of sixteen, he was apprenticed in a saddle and harness shop in the town of Franklin, but after about a year he ran away to lead a more exciting life in the Far West.[8] While Kit was en route to Santa Fe, his employer placed an advertisement in the Franklin newspaper in which he offered a reward of one cent for the boy's return. The idea of the offer was to show the public what a worthless boy Kit seemed to be. During the next forty years, however, Kit Carson proved himself worth considerably more than that as he became the most admired trapper, guide, Indian fighter, and scout in America.

Physically undersized and too poor to provide his own outfit for trading and trapping, the youthful Carson spent three years in New Mexico doing menial tasks. He worked at the Santa Rita mines as a teamster and on wagon trains as a general roustabout. Meanwhile, he became an expert rifleman and learned enough Spanish to serve as an interpreter. His big opportunity came in 1829, when he had the good fortune to be admitted to a party of forty trappers organized by the veteran Ewing Young for an expedition into Arizona.[9] This *entrada* had two purposes: first to avenge the attack of the Apaches on a party of Young's men on their way to the Colorado River a short time before, and, second, to trap for beaver along the streams of Arizona. Young did not have a trapping license, so he attempted to deceive the Mexican authorities by leading his party northward from Taos as if bound for the United States. After awhile, he turned to the southwest and passed through Zuñi country to the headwaters of the Salt

River. In this region, the trappers ambushed a force of Indians, whom they suspected of having taken part in the attack the year before, and killed fifteen. The company then trapped down the Salt and up the Verde to its source. At this point twenty-two of the party returned to New Mexico with the furs.

The rest of the group, including Carson, set out for the Colorado River and the west coast. En route, they encountered a band of wandering Mojaves, from whom they obtained corn, beans, and a worn-out mare which they immediately killed and cooked. Young forded the Colorado near the scene of the Smith massacre two years before and reached San Gabriel Mission in early winter. Nearly starving, the men traded butcher knives for steers at the ratio of four to one and proceeded to devour the fresh beef. To avoid difficulty with the authorities, Young pushed onward to the beaver streams of the San Joaquin and Sacramento valleys. On two occasions, Carson and other trappers joined with Mexican authorities to capture Indians who had run away from the San José Mission. In retaliation, the Indians raided the trappers' camp and drove off sixty horses. Carson and twelve others followed the trail, surprised the savages, and recovered all the horses that were not turning on the roasting spits.

In September, 1830, Young started back to Arizona by way of the Pueblo de Los Angeles. There, the Mexican authorities would have arrested the trappers for not having passports if they hadn't been afraid. They did try to drown the trappers with liquor, however, and accompanied Young toward San Gabriel where they expected reinforcements to strengthen their courage. En route, one James Higgins dismounted and deliberately shot his friend, James Lawrence, with no provocation. The Mexicans were so startled by this strange incident among friends that they departed in haste for fear of what might happen if the mountain men were angered by strangers. Somewhat relieved, Young caught up with Carson, who had been sent ahead with the baggage and loose animals, and returned to the Colorado. He trapped down that river and then back up the Gila, arriving at the Santa

Kit Carson, noted Indian scout

Rita copper mines with some ten thousand pounds of beaver pelts.* Remembering his previous experience with Governor Armíjo, Young cached his furs and went on to Santa Fe where he secured a license to trade with the Indians in the vicinity of Santa Rita. He was then able to sell the beaver skins in the capital city without interference.

Kit Carson emerged from this expedition across Arizona wealthier and wiser. He had started out as an apprentice trapper and returned a full-fledged mountain man. His first-hand knowledge of the geography of this region served him well as a guide during the Mexican War. Prior to this war

---

*Christopher Carson. *Kit Carson's Own Story of His Life*. Taos, New Mexico: Santa Fe New Mexican Publishing Corporation, 1926, pp. 17–20. Near the mouth of the San Pedro, the trappers discovered a party of Indians driving some 200 horses that had been stolen from Mexicans in Sonora. After running off the Indians, the trappers took the horses that they needed for riding and packing, butchered and dried the meat of ten animals, and turned the remainder of the herd loose.

he trapped throughout the Rockies and made three exploring expeditions with John Charles Frémont. It was Frémont who made Carson a renowned figure in American history. In his own right, Carson was perhaps for forty years the greatest mountaineer and guide in the Far West. Though he belongs more to the whole nation than to any one region, he crossed Arizona several times before his death in 1868, and is part of the state's heritage during this era.

In a sense, the mountain men rediscovered the Arizona that was being deserted by the missionaries and Mexican settlers. These men brought no permanent settlement or development to the region vaguely defined as Arizona, for they were a transient and nomadic lot. They did, however, create an interest in the Gila Valley and explored trails to California. They contributed to the impatience with the Mexican rule over the Southwest, and most of all, they were the real pathfinders, the advance guard of English-speaking pioneers who would sweep westward to occupy and tame the wild lands which the United States was destined to conquer.

Chapter 9

The Mexican War

FROM 1821 TO 1848, all of Arizona was a part of Mexico. During this period, however, the United States of America was ambitiously expanding its western borders and few people doubted that the young republic would soon stretch to the Pacific. President Polk had hoped to acquire California and the intervening Mexican territory, by peaceful means. In the autumn of 1845, he sent John Slidell to Mexico to offer as much as $25 million for the desired territory, plus a satisfactory Rio Grande boundary agreement. The Mexicans, still smarting from their loss of Texas, angrily rejected Polk's offer and continued feverish preparations for war. Relations were so strained by this time that neither side could keep its powder dry much longer.

The incident which made the smouldering war official occurred in the no man's land between the Nueces and Rio Grande rivers. Each side claimed that its territory had been invaded and began fighting on April 25, 1846. Though the pretext for the clash had been found in the Texas question, the scene of conflict soon expanded. While Generals Zachary Taylor and Winfield Scott launched successful campaigns deep into the heart of the enemy country, Commodore Robert F. Stockton and Lieutenant Colonel John C. Frémont began the conquest of California. Another phase of the war more directly concerned the country in between — New Mexico, Arizona, and perhaps Chihuahua and Sonora. President Polk planned to invade this region with an army large enough to conquer the territory but small enough not to alarm the conquered.

Shortly after the President's proclamation of war on May
13, 1846, Colonel (later General) Stephen W. Kearny began
assembling the so-called "Army of the West" at Fort Leavenworth. He was instructed to occupy the weakly garrisoned
border territories of northern Mexico by peaceful persuasion
and then to join the sea-borne force in the conquest of the
Pacific coast region. An able leader, Kearny set about organizing a conglomerate group consisting of 300 regular dragoons,
over 800 mounted Missouri volunteers, and an assortment of
frontier-hardened recruits. He soon began sending the men
in detachments along the Santa Fe Trail to Bent's Fort, a
trading post in what is now southeastern Colorado. When
Kearny himself arrived at this rendezvous point, he found
that his 1700-man army had a large group of Santa Fe-bound
traders under its protection. The million dollars' worth of
merchandise, which these merchants had packed in some 400
wagons, was to be no small lure in breaking down Mexican
resistance to the advance of the army.

Colonel Kearny's confidence of success on his mission
was buoyed by knowledge that additional troops were being
raised in Missouri, and Brigham Young had promised a battalion of Mormons from Council Bluffs. Yet he hoped that the
natives of New Mexico would not resist, and on July 31,
dispatched a proclamation to them, promising civil and religious liberties in return for their submission to his superior
arms.[1] Kearny also helped to pave the way for a friendly
reception by commissioning James W. Magoffin as his advance
agent. A jovial Kentucky Irishman and influential trader,
Magoffin had many friends among his former customers in
Santa Fe and had on occasion shared a bottle with the fleshy
Governor Manuel Armíjo. He and Captain Philip St. George
Cooke were sent ahead of the main Army to Santa Fe where
they conferred secretly with Armíjo. The Governor explained
that he had neither the financial nor military resources to
resist the American invaders. And after issuing a proclamation
in which he put up a blustering display of patriotism, saying
that he was "ready to sacrifice his life and interests for his
beloved country," Armíjo prepared to desert his people.
Tradition has it that a crowd of people gathered around to

Museum of New Mexico

General Stephen W. Kearny

detain him as he mounted his horse to leave. He resourcefully distracted them by tossing coins in their midst and galloped away toward Albuquerque and Chihuahua as they scrambled for the money.*

On August 18, Kearny entered the old mud village of Santa Fe without firing a shot and was welcomed by the acting governor, Juan Bautista Vigil. In the following days, he assured the people of his peaceful intentions and accepted the pledge of allegiance from the chiefs of nearby pueblos. On September 22, he proclaimed an American civil government in Santa Fe with a code of laws, a bill of rights, and a governor. Most of Arizona was included in the province and for the first time the political institutions of the United States were applied to this area, though there were probably no Americans in Arizona to appreciate the benefits of the established gov-

---

* For a hundred years, writers and historians intimated that Magoffin bribed Governor Armíjo to offer only feigned resistance to the entry of Kearny's troops into New Mexico. See, for example, Paul I. Wellman, *Glory, God, and Gold*. Garden City, N.Y.: Doubleday & Company, Inc., 1954, p. 282. However, after studying the original sources available, including the "James W. Magoffin Correspondence and Papers, Bureau of the Budget, Washington, D.C." William A. Keleher concluded that there is no evidence to prove this contention. See William A. Keleher, *Turmoil in New Mexico*. Santa Fe, New Mexico: The Rydal Press, 1952, footnote 22, p. 114.

Governor Charles Bent. After General Kearny occupied Santa Fe during the Mexican War, he appointed Charles Bent as the first pre-Territorial American governor of New Mexico. Bent was killed by natives near his Taos home on January 19, 1847.

ernment. The first governor, Charles Bent, was the victim of an Indian rebellion. He was beheaded by a half-crazed mob of Taos natives about four months after Kearny's departure for the coast on September 25. Several hundred Indians and some Americans were also killed before Colonel Sterling Price's occupation troops could put down the uprising which had been encouraged by several proud and prominent Spanish citizens of the territory.[2]

Price's 2nd Missouri Volunteers had reached Santa Fe early in October, 1846, and relieved the 1st regiment of Missouri Volunteers under the command of Colonel Alexander W. Doniphan. The latter had accompanied Kearny as far as Santa Fe and was temporarily in command there pending the arrival of Price. Doniphan's orders were to march south to assist General John E. Wool in the conquest of

Chihuahua. This plan was delayed, however, because Kearny, now with the rank of general and en route to California, was exasperated by the raids of the Navajos on his cattle herd at Algodones, north of Albuquerque, and by their depredations upon the Mexican settlements in that area. Hoping to pacify the troublesome Indians, Kearny sent instructions to Doniphan ordering him to march into the Navajo country and make a treaty with them before proceeding to Chihuahua. With the assistance of Major William Gilpin and Colonel Congreve Jackson, whose detachments had been campaigning against the Indians since September 18, Doniphan moved his summer-clad soldiers into the rugged snow-covered country in search of Navajos on October 26. Though uncomfortable without proper clothing to ward off the inclement weather, the men rounded up approximately 500 natives for a council at Ojo de Oso (Bear Springs), near present-day Gallup, New Mexico. The Navajos could not understand why they should cease harassing the Mexicans when the Americans themselves were waging war against Mexico. Nevertheless, after a day of speechmaking, they signed a treaty on November 22. The treaty was destined to be short-lived, however, since the signatories were not the war leaders and certainly did not represent a united tribe. But Doniphan naively considered the document that bore the marks of fourteen chiefs — not one of whom could read or write any language — as "permanent" and binding.[3] After distributing gifts to the Indians and receiving much desired blankets in return, he bought sheep and cattle to be herded along toward Chihuahua, and departed for the Rio Grande. The troops were barely out of sight when the Navajo warriors, over whom the treaty signers had no authority, resumed their raids, not only on the Mexican settlements but also on the Zuñi Indians.

Meanwhile, Kearny, after a pleasant month in Santa Fe, was on his way to California with a company of 300 dragoons. South of Albuquerque, he met Kit Carson bearing the disappointing news that the war on the Pacific coast was over. After considerable resistance, Kearny persuaded Carson to give up the honor of personally delivering his dispatches to the President and to guide the Army to California. Any courier could

carry the messages to Washington, but only ex-mountain man
Carson knew the difficult terrain that lay ahead through what
is now south-central Arizona. Kearny assigned Thomas Fitz-
patrick, another mountain man, to go eastward with the
dispatches.[4] He also ordered two-thirds of the dragoons, which
were now considered to be unnecessary, to return to Santa Fe.
With a hundred picked soldiers, the wagonless Army of the
West headed for the Santa Rita copper mines, where Kearny
visited with the great Apache chieftain, Mangas Coloradas
(Red Sleeves), and then started down the Gila on October 21,
1846. In following this route, Kearny had accepted Carson's
advice to bypass Tucson, the only strong Mexican garrison in
Arizona. He clung to the Gila Trail which the beaver trappers
had used two decades earlier. The trail was passable for the
pack train of mules and horses but proved to be exasperating
for the men in charge of two twelve-pound howitzers. To these
guns, mounted on three-foot axles between wheels ten feet in
circumference, were attached viameters, used in measuring
distance. These guns and their ammunition-bearing caissons
are said to be the first wheeled vehicles to have crossed
Arizona.

The expedition was scientific as well as military and
marks the first attempt by the United States to study the
topography, Indians, plant, and animal life of the Gila Valley.
Though the force had no newspaper correspondents in the
modern sense, there were two good diarists. One was Lieutenant Colonel William H. Emory, a topographical engineer
whose records were printed in 1848 as a House of Representatives document entitled, *Notes of a Military Reconnaissance
from Fort Leavenworth, in Missouri,. to San Diego, in California.* Neither Emory nor the other diarist, Dr. John S.
Griffin — the assistant surgeon and first qualified medical man
to enter Arizona — were impressed by the country which they
observed. In early November, for example, both described
the vicinity of the juncture of the San Pedro and Gila rivers
where the town of Winkelman stands today. Dr. Griffin wrote
that the barren area was "utterly worthless" and named it
Hog River because of the wild javelinas found there. Little
did he know that in less than forty years, the famous Christmas
copper mine would be discovered a short distance away. The

Kearny's Army of the West moving slowly down the Gila Trail.
(Sketch by John Mix Stanley, 1846)

doctor went on to say that nothing grew there except cactus, some as much as fifty feet high.

This picture was also emphasized by Emory who saw Arizona for the first time through the eyes of a man from Maryland. Strolling over the hills in search of seed and geological specimens, he noted that not an animal, vegetable, or mineral in the area had anything in common with the products in the United States. A few days later, near another of the Gila's tributaries, the Santa Cruz, he further observed that four-fifths of the plain was destitute of vegetation. Not until the army reached the Pima villages near the Casa Grande ruins north of present-day Coolidge, did the men change the tune. Colonel Emory was fascinated by the ruins, pottery, and irrigation. He wrote: "To us it is a rare sight to be thrown in the midst of a large nation of what is termed wild Indians, surpassing many of the Christian nations in agriculture, little behind them in useful arts and immeasurably before them in honesty and virtue."[5] Both Emory and Griffin, however, described the scantily-dressed women as ugly and coarse-looking.

Captain Henry Smith Turner, the adjutant, also recorded his observations. "Their women, like the women of all savage nations," he wrote, "seem to perform the labor . . . The men generally have kind amiable expressions — never did I look upon a more benevolent face than that of the old chief — he is a man of about 60 years of age — spare and tall, and exhibits more of human kindness in his face, air and manner than I have ever seen in any other single individual. . . ." Turner was impressed by the Pima irrigation and prophetically commented that the valley "would be a suitable place for the Mormons to establish themselves."[6]

On November 12, Kearny moved his army farther down the Gila and made camp at the Salt River junction. After trading with the Maricopa Indians who brought more grain and vegetables to exchange for the white man's bright red cloth, knives, and beads, the expedition left the Gila. The dry, grassless route they followed was very exhausting; several mules were lost, forcing fifty of the dragoons to give up their mounts for use as pack animals. Despite the hardships encountered in crossing the Gila Bend country, through the Estrella Pass in the Maricopa Mountains where the Southern Pacific Railroad runs today, many miles were saved. The hungry and thirsty army returned to the river near the present town of Gila Bend and then struggled on to the Colorado River which was reached on November 22. At this point, the viameter attached to the howitzer wheel showed that the Army of the West had traveled 1687 miles. Nearly 500 miles were recorded along the winding Gila route from where the pack train entered Arizona near present-day Clifton. The shortest highway between Clifton and Yuma today covers less than 400 miles. Needless to say, the latter settlement has greatly changed too. Emory would likely be pleased to visit Yuma today, for he prophesied, after viewing the junction, that it "will probably yet be the seat of a city of wealth and importance. . . ."[7]

An incident occurred during the journey which tried Kearny's patience with his orders "to conciliate the inhabitants and render them friendly to the United States." A camp of Mexicans with five hundred horses was discovered by Carson and Emory a few miles north of the Gila. As it turned out, the drovers were taking the mounts to Sonora for the Mexican Army. Kearny, however, felt obligated to accept their story that they were merely herding the horses to Sonoran markets for some wealthy Californians. The herdsmen must have been surprised when they were released and permitted to go on unmolested.

Kearny was more concerned with bad news from California. Dispatches taken from a captured Mexican messenger revealed that a counterrevolution against the Americans had been successful. The red, white, and green flew over San Diego, Santa Bárbara, and Los Angeles. What an embarrassing predicament for Kearny! Here he was on the Colorado with a handful of soldiers when he needed his whole army. Yet he had no alternative but to push on across the desert. After a grueling march to the mountains northeast of San Diego, his skeleton Army of the West saw its first action in early December. Within a few minutes, a third of the weary Americans fell before a charge of the mounted Mexicans who effectively wielded lances nine feet long. The survivors were hemmed in on a hill and were saved only by the timely arrival of troops which Carson and Lieutenant Edward Beale heroically brought from Stockton's San Diego forces. After the battle, General Kearny moved his men into the coast city and cooperated in putting down the counterrevolution. The reconquest of southern California was complete when the Mexican General Andres Pico surrendered to Lieutenant Colonel John C. Frémont at Rancho Cahuenga near the site of modern Hollywood on January 13, 1847. A quarrel followed between Kearny and Frémont because the latter supported Commodore Robert F. Stockton in a dispute over authority and continued to function as governor at Los Angeles while Kearny established headquarters at Monterey. When Kearny received reinforcements from New York he arrested the "Pathfinder of the West" for insubordination and sent him east as a prisoner. Frémont, who later became territorial governor of Arizona, was convicted and sentenced to be dismissed from the service. One of the witnesses who testified against him was Captain Turner who earlier had written in his diary that both Frémont and Stockton had "behaved very

badly . . . both of them should be tried by a court-martial."
But Turner thought that Kearny had not displayed "his usual
firmness and decision of character in dealing with Frémont,"
explaining that the General's respect for Frémont's father-
in-law, the very powerful Senator Thomas H. Benton, caused
him to postpone taking the proper disciplinary measures
against the lieutenant colonel.[8] President Polk approved the
verdict of the court martial, except for a charge of mutiny,
but restored the famous Frémont to his rank. Meanwhile,
Kearny was installed as governor of California.

Kearny is probably best remembered for his activities in
New Mexico and California, but his role in establishing the
authority of the United States in Arizona is also significant.
It was most appropriate that the Kennecott Copper Company
should give his name to the new community which it began
constructing on the Gila, in 1958, near the site of its new
reduction works. Of far more importance to the future of
Arizona than Kearny's rapid march across the state, however,
was the journey of the Mormon Battalion under one of his
officers, Captain (later Lieutenant Colonel) Philip St. George
Cooke. Within a month after Kearny's dragoons left the Gila,
Cooke blazed the first practical wagon trail over the southern
Arizona deserts. Hundreds of emigrant wagon trains would
follow his route to the coast. And to a great extent, his accomplishment led to the purchase of southern Arizona from
Mexico in 1854.

Recruited mainly in Iowa, the persecuted Mormons
wanted both to demonstrate their patriotism and to secure
free passage to California. Once discharged in the West, they
hoped to locate homesites for the main body of church members. Leaving Council Bluffs in July, 1846, the battalion
reached Santa Fe in October. It was a rag-tail outfit numbering
nearly five hundred men, accompanied by twenty-five women
and some children. Cooke assumed command on October 13,
and proceeded to trim the roster by excluding some eighty-six
men who were considered physically unfit for duty, the children, and all of the women except the wives of two Mormon
captains and three sergeants. This excluded group of about
150 people, including twenty laundresses and their able-bodied

husbands, was sent north to Pueblo on the Arkansas River and the next year became part of the newly founded Mormon colony at Salt Lake City.

On October 19, the remaining 397 men — later cut to about 340 — and five women started from Santa Fe to blaze a wagon road to California. On January 21, 1847, they arrived at Warner's Ranch near San Diego after one of the most remarkable journeys in history. The route followed was farther south than the dangerous Gila Trail taken by Kearny's mule train. After leaving the Rio Grande, the battalion was guided southwest across the present international boundary by Pauline Weaver and Antoine Leroux. Turning northwest, the Mormons passed through the old abandoned ranch of San Bernardino and a week later reached the San Pedro River. This valley was grazed by wild cattle which the Apaches used very much as the Indians on the plains did the buffalo. For nearly two weeks, the battalion lived off bull meat as they tirelessly whacked their way over the rough hills of southeastern Arizona.

Moving north along the San Pedro the battalion engaged in its first and only battle — not with the Mexicans but with a herd of wild bulls. Unbelievable as it may seem, the animals attacked the wagon train. In some instances, even without provocation, they gored the mules, damaged the wagons, and injured several men. The "battle" lasted several hours because the bulls were hard to kill. Private Henry Standage, who later lived in Mesa, Arizona, wrote in his diary that "they would run off with half a dozen balls in them unless they were shot in the heart." Several dozen of the animals were felled by musket fire on the field of combat, however, before Cooke was able to reorganize his shaken battalion and move on.[9]

The Mormons went down the San Pedro and began preparing for a fight at Tucson with the Mexican army that didn't actually materialize. On December 13 — the day the battalion left the river and marched westward in anticipation of an encounter with the Mexicans — Robert S. Bliss, who wrote part of his diary in blood after running out of ink, recorded this entry in his journal: "Started early for a Spanish town fort one of our pilots [scouts] came in last night and reported they

The Mormon Battalion stopping for water
(Painting by George M. Ottinger, 1881)

had to flee to save their lives it is expected that we shall have to take the place. Marched 10 miles and encamped for Drill and Inspection drew catridges [*sic*] 20 for each man. . . ."[10]

Since Tucson was the only Mexican town and garrison left in Arizona, Cooke sent word to the *comandante,* Antonio Comadurán, that the Americans came as friends and only wished to purchase flour and other provisions. The Mexican refused to surrender, but obligingly evacuated his army from the town and all but about a hundred civilians fled south with him toward the mission of San Xavier del Bac. On December 17, 1846, the Mormon Battalion entered Tucson without firing a shot and raised the Stars and Stripes for the first time in Arizona. The Mormons were well received in the town. In the words of Private Standage: "We were kindly treated by the people of Touson [*sic*], who brought Flour, Meal, Tobacco, Quinces to the camp for sale and many of them giving such things to the Soldiers."[11] After a long march through the desert, the men also enjoyed the tortillas and pomegranates which they tasted for the first time during their short stay.

Cooke was not impressed by the adobe town and lingered only one day, just long enough to try his hand at diplomacy by writing letters of apology to Comadurán and the Governor of Sonora, Manuel María Gándara. He suggested that the real interests of the Sonorans lay with the United States and thanked his hosts for the wheat which was taken from the public granary. It is interesting to note that Lieutenant George Stoneman — then the Quartermaster for the battalion and, after 1870, the military commander in Arizona for one year — paid the citizens for supplies with War Department drafts which were written in English and redeemable only in Washington, D.C.

On the morning of December 18, the Mormon Battalion struck tents and resumed the march. After three days of constant searching to find water and grass, the Mormons reached the Gila and the next day descended that river to the Pima villages. Like Kearny a few weeks earlier, Cooke was impressed by the hospitality of these Indians. Unlike Dr. Griffin, however, he thought that the adults were good looking and the girls very pretty. He wrote these words about them in his personal narrative:

> The Pimos [*sic*] are fine-looking, seem well fed, ride good horses, and are variously clothed, though many have only the centre cloth; the men and women have extraordinary luxuriance and length of hair. With clean white blankets and streaming hair, they present mounted quite a fine figure. But innocence and cheerfulness are their most distinctive characteristics. I am told the Mexican officers used every persuasion, and promise of plunder, to excite hostility toward us.[12]

From the Pima villages, the battalion cut across the Gila Bend country. Once back on the river, Cooke decided to float some of the supplies downstream in order to lighten the load. Two wagons were lashed together end to end, between two dry cottonwood logs. "This move of the Colonel's we did not like and we had forebodings it would not be a success," wrote Henry W. Bigler in his journal on December 31. The boat leaked, but when Lieutenant Stoneman insisted that he could pole the barge down the shallow river, less than seventy miles to the Colorado junction, Cooke ordered the men to load it. Stoneman then set sail with about 2500 pounds of provisions (including flour, corn for the mules, and pork), tools, and some of Cooke's own luggage. The lieutenant reached his destination but encountered irksome snags and sand bars en route and had to discard precious supplies at various points along the banks of the Gila. Meanwhile, on January 8, 1847, Cooke and his exhausted men arrived at the mouth of the Gila with their rickety wagons and half-dead mules. Sergeant Nathaniel V. Jones gave some indication of the hardships that the men had endured when he wrote succinctly in his diary on January 5: "We had a weighing frolic. I weighed 128; weight when I enlisted, 198."[13]

After a short rest, the hard-driving commander forded the Colorado at the Yuma crossing and pushed the expedition across the California desert. On January 29, the battalion reached San Diego, having suffered much from hunger and thirst on this last lap of the journey. By the time they arrived the fighting was over in California and the Mormons were merely assigned to garrison duty in several towns until they were discharged on July 16, 1847. Cooke resigned as commander in May and hurried east to fight in Mexico. He also served in the Union Army during the Civil War, though his son, John, and his son-in-law, J. E. B. Stuart, were loyal to the Confederacy.

Cooke's pride in the accomplishments of the Mormon Battalion is shown in the order which he issued at San Diego on January 30, 1847:

> The Lieutenant Colonel commanding congratulates the battalion on their safe arrival on the shore of the Pacific Ocean, and the conclusion of the march over two thousand miles.
>
> History may be searched in vain for an equal march of an infantry. Half of it has been through a wilderness where nothing but savages and wild beasts are found, or deserts where, for want of water, there is no living creature. There, with almost hopeless labor, we have dug deep wells, which the future traveler will enjoy. Without a guide who had traversed them, we have ventured into trackless table-lands where water was not found for several marches. With crowbar and pick and axe in hand, we have worked our way over mountains which seem to defy aught save the wild goat, and hewed a passage through a chasm of living rock more narrow than our wagons. To bring these first wagons to the Pacific, we have preserved the strength of our mules by herding them over large tracts, which you have laboriously guarded without loss. The garrison of four presidios of Sonora concentrated within the walls of Tucson, gave us no pause. We drove them out, with their artillery, but our inter-

*Brigadier General
Philip St. George Cooke*

National Archives

course with the citizens was unmarked by a single act of injustice. Thus, marching half naked and half fed, and living upon wild animals, we have discovered and made a road of great value to our country . . .[14]

There had been no combat and no heroics for the battalion, but they wrote a new chapter in the conquest of the West by making the first practicable wagon road through the Southwest. Significantly for Arizona, many of them, like Henry Standage, returned to this area and helped to develop prosperous Mormon settlements.

In addition to the Kearny and Cooke visits, at least two other military expeditions came into Arizona during or shortly after the Mexican War. The Doniphan campaign to establish a "lasting peace" with the Navajos in 1846 has already been mentioned. The other *entrada* came late in 1848, after the war was over, when the heavy-drinking Major Lawrence P. Graham led a column of troops from Monterrey in Mexico to Los Angeles via Tubac, Tucson, Picacho Peak, the Pima villages, and the Gila River. For a long time, this trek was one of the least known of overland journeys by a large body of U.S. troops. *Life* magazine stimulated interest in the Graham journey in 1956, when it published abstracts from the diary of Samuel Emery Chamberlain.* He left the expedition one day's march beyond Tucson, however, and his account does not cover the final stages of the long trip across Arizona. The most complete record of the entire journey was kept by Lieutenant Cave J. Couts, an idealist of strong character who was critical of vice-ridden officers like Graham — who may have been more the rule than the exception on the frontier. Couts' devastating commentary on his superior officer was motivated by both the major's drunkenness and the route he chose to reach Tucson. "We have looked forward to Tucson with great anxiety since leaving Janas," Couts wrote on October 25, 1848. Instead of following the shorter trail blazed by Colonel Cooke down the San Pedro, the soldiers were led aimlessly over what Couts facetiously called "Major Graham's wagon route."

The column paralleled Cooke's trail westward from the Guadalupe Pass in present-day New Mexico as far as the San Pedro and then struck out for Santa Cruz in Sonora and north down the Santa Cruz Valley. "From San Bernardino," Couts wrote, "we have taken all points of the compass, and nothing but the aid of an invisible hand has brought us safely through." Couts described the various settlements along the way. At Tumacácori he observed the Pimas caring for "a very large and fine church standing in the midst of a few common conical Indian huts, made of bushes, thatched with grass, huts of most common and primitive kind." He likewise described Tubac as an Indian village since there were two Apaches for every resident of Mexican origin. He stressed the

---

Life, Vol. 41, No. 4 (July 23, 1956), pp. 68–91; Vol. 41, No. 5 (July 30, 1956), pp. 52–70; and Vol. 41, No. 6 (August, 1956), pp. 64–86. For a more complete account see Samuel E. Chamberlain, *My Confession.* New York: Harper & Brothers, Publishers, 1956. Major Graham thought that Chamberlain's sketching was a waste of time and had him tied up for drawing a picture of the presidio. Sizzling in Tucson's hot sun with him was a member of John Glanton's "Scalp Hunters," a man named Tom Hitchcock from whom Graham hoped to exact information about the trail to the Gila River. Dissatisfied with the Graham expedition, Chamberlain deserted north of Tucson and, under Hitchcock's sponsorship, joined up with the Glanton gang which had been scalping Apaches (and some Mexicans) for $50 per head.

point, however, that the Apaches — descendants of the hostiles who were settled peacefully near the presidios by the aggressive Spanish army between 1786 and 1820 — spoke the Mexican language and were treated as Mexican citizens. Farther downstream, Couts was greatly impressed by the San Xavier mission. "'Tis truly a noble and stupendous building," he said. "Its domes and spires which projected above the thick mesquite growth as we approached was of itself sufficient to guarantee a City with many churches and other large and fine buildings." He was surprised, however, to find it "standing solitary and alone, not another building nearer to it than Tucson, save the few old Indian huts of the most rude description, whose inmates (Papagos) had charge of the fine old church." [15]

On October 24, the column encamped close to the nearly dry Santa Cruz River, not far from San José de Tucson, the Pima mission at the foot of Sentinel Peak. The Mexican officer at the presidio of San Agustín planned a parade and a rousing reception for the Americans. But Major Graham was in no condition to take advantage of this opportunity to promote better relations between his country and the Mexicans. "The Comandante went out this morning at daylight to pay his respects to our commandant," wrote Couts, "But ours had already got drunk and come on into town." To the soldiers, Tucson was "no great deal after all," though it was the largest place — adding the Indians and Mexicans together — that the column had seen since leaving Chihuahua. Couts seemed to be most intrigued by the burro flour mill with which every house in Tucson was furnished at the time. A burro, blindfolded to prevent dizziness, went round and round turning a rough stone that could grind a half bushel of wheat each day.

Major Graham led his column out of Tucson on October 27, and the Gila was reached after three days of traveling. Like the earlier military visitors to the Pima villages, the Graham party considered these Pimas to be excellent farmers. But Couts could not resist mentioning their taste for alcohol. He wrote that whiskey, aguardiente, and mescal had caused an earlier golden age of Pima civilization to decline. "They gave all they had for it," he said, ". . . now they would give all that remained for the smallest quantity. Wish to get a barrel from us." Couts was probably more aware of this problem because his commanding officer apparently had the same weakness.

As the column marched slowly down the Gila from the Pima settlements, Couts commented that the pace of travel depended upon "our having water or no water, the nature of the bushes our poor animals had to live on, and the condition of the Major, whether drunk or very drunk." But the "trifling drunken sot" or "barrel of whiskey," as Couts privately called his commanding officer, somehow led the troops to the Colorado, which was reached on November 22, and then on to the "Pueblo de los Angeles." In Graham's favor, it might be said that his courage and ability had been proven in combat, first against the Seminoles in Florida and then in General Zachary Taylor's army in the early battles of the Mexican War. After leading troops under fire, the march across Mexico and Arizona to garrison duty in California must have offered little challenge to the major. His overland journey remained relatively unknown, and yet is significant because of the eyewitness accounts of Arizona in 1848 left by Couts and Chamberlain.

None of the expeditions into Arizona affected the final outcome of the Mexican War. Victory was achieved by the army of General Winfield Scott, who entered Mexico City on September 14, 1847. With their capital in enemy hands, the Mexicans entered into negotiations with President Polk's representative, Nicholas P. Trist. After some annoying delays, the war was officially ended with the signing of the Treaty of Guadalupe Hidalgo on February 2, 1848. This document was approved by the U.S. Senate and proclaimed by the President on July 4, 1848. By its terms, Mexico ceded over a half million square miles of territory. The cession included all of Arizona north of the Gila River, most of New Mexico, all of California, Nevada, and Utah, in addition to parts of Colorado and Wyoming.

In effect, the war had forced Mexico to sell this real estate on terms similar to those rejected before the conflict. The United States paid $15 million and assumed the claims which American citizens had against Mexico, a total of nearly three and a quarter million dollars.* According to the treaty, the new boundary line followed the Rio Grande to the southern line of the former Mexican territory of New Mexico, along that line to a point near the Continental Divide, northward to the Gila River, down the middle of this stream to the Colorado, and on to the Pacific along the line that divides Upper and Lower California. All but about two thousand of the Mexicans living north of this line chose to remain and thus automatically became citizens of the United States en masse. Perhaps the main criticism of the treaty was the fact that the territory south of the Gila River was conceded to Mexico, even though Cooke had demonstrated the usefulness of this area as one of the most valuable transcontinental routes to California. The mistake was corrected five years later, however, by the Gadsden Purchase Treaty and the present international boundary established. A minor adjustment in the city of El Paso in 1963, as a result of a change in the course of the Rio Grande, did not affect Arizona.

On July 4, 1848, when Arizona north of the Gila became officially a part of the United States, there were no Anglo-American settlements there. Most of the region was known only to mountain men and Indians. Virtually unchanged by the Spanish and Mexican occupation, there was little indication at the time that the so-called Great American Desert had anything but a dismal future.

---

* In accordance with the treaty, a board of commissioners was appointed by the Government of the United States to ascertain the validity and amount of those claims. The commission completed its work on April 15, 1851, allowing claims to the amount of $3,208,314.96. See "Treaty of Guadalupe Hidalgo," in Fred L. Israel (ed.) *Major Peace Treaties of Modern History, 1648–1967,* Vol. II. New York: Chelsea House Publishers, 1967, p. 742.

PART FOUR

THE 1850s AND THE CIVIL WAR

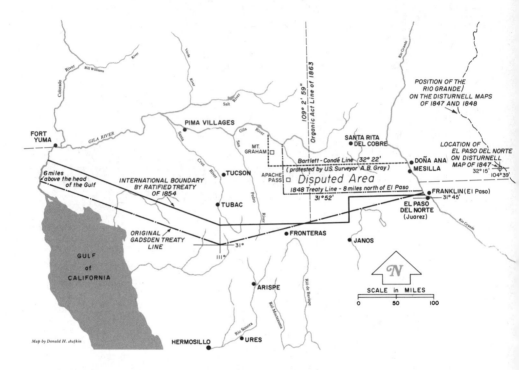

Boundary controversy — Gadsden Purchase

Chapter 10

The 1850s: Boundary Problems and the Gadsden Purchase

THE TREATY OF GUADALUPE HIDALGO provided for a survey of the southern boundary of the Mexican Cession by a Joint Boundary Commission. Mexico sent General Pedro García Condé to meet with the American representatives at San Diego in July, 1849. President James K. Polk's appointee, John B. Weller — a former Ohio Congressman with a future in California politics as governor and U.S. senator — was the first of several American commissioners. He cooperated with Condé in surveying the southern boundary of California from the Pacific Coast eastward to the Colorado River. When Zachary Taylor and the Whigs came into office in 1849, Weller was replaced by the ambitious John C. Frémont. A short time later, however, the "Pathfinder" was chosen to serve in the United States Senate and resigned as commissioner.

BOUNDARY COMMISSIONER JOHN R. BARTLETT

After that, the scholarly and colorful John Russell Bartlett of Rhode Island was selected by President Taylor and ordered to proceed to El Paso for a meeting in November, 1850, with his Mexican counterpart, General Condé. Bartlett had no particular qualifications for the job except his Whig connections. A former bookseller who had written *Dictionary of Americanisms,* published in 1848, he had a curious mixture of friends, among them Jefferson Davis, Stephen A. Douglas, and Henry B. Anthony, his brother-in-law and publisher of the *Providence Journal.* He welcomed the opportunity to give up a sedentary life in order to travel to see American Indians whom he had long admired. His annual salary was $3,000.

Bartlett's inexperience was apparent from the beginning. Once the discussions got under way at El Paso, a controversy developed. The Disturnell map, which had been designated in the treaty as the final authority, was found to be inaccurate. El Paso was located 34 miles too far north and over 100 miles too far east on this map. A compromise was necessary and Commissioner Bartlett conceded a strip of land thirty-five miles wide and over 175 miles long, including part of the Mesilla Valley just west of the Rio Grande — lands that Americans were already claiming. In Bartlett's defense, it might be pointed out that Mesilla was founded in March, 1850, by Mexicans who moved across the Rio Grande from Doña Ana and other points in Mew Mexico, as well as from Texas. They were unhappy with the transfer of their lands on the east side of the river to the jurisdiction of the United States by the Treaty of Guadalupe Hidalgo. Determined to move again if their new homes should be placed in American territory, the Mexicans celebrated enthusiastically when the boundary was established north of Mesilla. Since Bartlett was a man of some empathy, the feeling of these residents might have had bearing on his willingness to concede the Mesilla Valley to Mexico.[1] Ironically, however, Mesilla was soon to be given up by Mexico as part of the Gadsden Purchase, and become the place where the United States government formally took possession of the entire purchase on November 15, 1854.

The southern boundary of the United States, by the Bartlett-Condé Agreement of April 24, 1851, was to be as follows: up the Rio Grande to the initial point of the survey — 42 miles from El Paso, west along a line at 32 degrees 22 minutes north latitude for about 175 miles, then north at longitude 109 degrees 47 minutes to the Gila, and along that river to the Colorado. Surveyor Andrew B. Gray refused to sign the agreement, arguing that the Mesilla Strip was valuable both for the productivity of the soil and as a transcontinental railroad route. Colonel James D. Graham, the chief astronomer, agreed with Gray, as did Lieutenant Amiel Whipple, Major William Emory, and Lieutenant Ambrose E. Burnside, the quartermaster and future Civil War general. Protests from these assistants and Bartlett's unfamiliarity with conditions in the Southwest doomed him to failure as boundary commissioner. In

March, 1852, Weller, now a senator, laid an accumulation of charges against him before the Senate. Among other things, Bartlett was accused of negligence, delay, and diversion of public funds for personal junkets to Chihuahua and Sonora, and to California to view the geyscrs.

In some detail, Weller alleged that Bartlett, generously supplied with over a half-million dollars in funds, traveled with a mule-drawn ambulance, a military escort, and a supply train over the deserts and mountains of the Southwest. Perhaps no more than a fifth of the appropriations provided were actually used for the intended purpose of the surveying of the Guadalupe-Hidalgo boundary line; the rest was spent on jaunts through the countryside or wasted through mismanagement. Despite the charges against him, the refusal of Congress in 1852 to recognize the unpopular Bartlett-Condé Agreement, and the threatened outbreak of a second Mexican War over the Mesilla Strip, Bartlett was retained in his post by Taylor's successor, President Millard Fillmore. At this point, the expansionists, including Congressman Volney E. Howard of Texas, succeeded in amending the appropriations bill to hold up all funds for the boundary commission unless the Mesilla Strip was included in U. S. territory. With no more money for expenses, Bartlett had no recourse but to halt the survey in October, 1852. By this time he had gathered enough valuable material for a two-volume work which was published commercially in 1854. He was so thoroughly discredited that the Senate refused to have his report printed in the customary manner as a government publication. It has been said that his *Personal Narrative of Explorations . . .* with its pictures and maps, was one of the most expensive guidebooks ever written. Considering how much the books were later used by travelers in the Southwest, however, the government's investment in Bartlett's wanderings was definitely worthwhile. Whatever his shortcomings as boundary commissioner, he revealed information invaluable to an understanding of Arizona and the surrounding region during the 1850s.

Bartlett first came into Arizona in September, 1851, from the headquarters which he had established at the Santa Rita copper mines in New Mexico. One might expect that his chief reason for coming into this area would be to survey the Gila

River boundary. Of greater interest to him at the time, however, was the return of a pretty fourteen-year-old Mexican girl
named Inez Gonzales to her family in Santa Cruz, Sonora. On
June 27, he had rescued her at Santa Rita from itinerant New
Mexican traders who made a living trading with the Apaches
for booty and slaves captured in Mexico. Inez was kidnapped —
along with other Mexicans — by Pinal Apaches in September,
1850, while en route from Santa Cruz to a fair at Magdalena,
Sonora. She was held by these Indians to perform menial labor
during most of her captivity. Despite her months of deprivation, however, Bartlett found that the girl was "quite young,
artless, and interesting in appearance, prepossessing in manners, and by her deportment gave evidence that she had been
carefully brought up."[2]

He brought Inez's plight to the attention of General
Condé, who was camped some twenty-six miles away from the
Santa Rita mines. From Condé he learned that the released
captive's father was a respectable citizen of Santa Cruz. Condé
was going to Santa Cruz and could have escorted the girl
home, but Bartlett went to considerable trouble and taxpayers'
expense to make the delivery in person — a good deed, he said,
that "afforded a full recompense for the trials and hardships
attending our sojourn in this inhospitable wilderness."[3] Colonel Graham later reported acidly that the Gila River survey
was forgotten for forty-four days while the Commissioner
accompanied the señorita home. Leaving the survey and topographical crews of Gray and Whipple at Santa Rita, Bartlett
departed for Sonora and proceeded to get lost in the region
southeast of the Santa Rita Mountains. Graham came to the
rescue with provisions and reconnoitered the country for the
remainder of the journey up the San Pedro River. It was on
this trip that Bartlett passed through the Babocomari ranch
observing wild cattle and mustangs munching on luxuriant
grass.

Finally reaching the town of Santa Cruz, the men were
joyously received and participated in a gay fiesta. As a matter
of fact, the next few weeks were one perpetual fandango for
the homesick Americans. Bartlett extended his junket to Magdalena, Hermosillo, and other Mexican cities, supposedly in

search of mules and supplies. He was stricken ill with typhoid fever, however, and after a delay of nearly three months was taken by sea to San Diego where he arrived in February, 1852.[4] Meanwhile, the disgusted Graham returned to work and by Christmas Eve, 1851, Gray and Whipple had surveyed the Gila to a point within sixty miles of the Colorado River. Here they suspended their work for lack of provisions and hurried across the desert to San Diego which they reached ahead of Bartlett.

Not until May, 1852, did the Bartlett expedition start eastward. Before reaching the Colorado, the gallant Colonel L. S. Craig, commander of the escort, and staunch friend of the Commissioner, was shot down in cold blood by two deserters from Camp Yuma.* After burying the colonel, the saddened men resumed their nightly marches across the burning June deserts. They were welcomed at the fort by Major Samuel P. Heintzelman, who had arrived from California with two companies of infantry troops in November, 1850.† At Camp Yuma, on the California side of the crossing, the Yuma Indians wasted no time in sneaking away with fifteen of Bartlett's horses in a noiseless nocturnal raid. Lacking the time and patience to chase the thieves, the caravan crossed the river and the industrious Lieutenant Whipple resumed the interrupted boundary survey.

Bartlett once again left the work group and moved ahead to visit Indians along the Gila River. At the Cocomaricopa village — southwest of modern Phoenix near the junction of the Salt with the Gila — he was asked to lend rifles to a war party that was setting forth against the Apaches; he refused

---

*The designation Fort, rather than Camp Yuma, was first used by Bv't. Major S. P. Heintzelman in his post return of June, 1852. See "Fort Yuma, California Post Returns, October, 1850–December, 1865," on microfilm roll No. 1488 of "Returns From U.S. Military Posts, 1800–1916," National Archives Microfilm Publications, General Services Administration, Washington, D.C.

† Camp Yuma was abandoned on June 5, 1851, and reoccupied on February 29, 1852. During the interim, travelers were protected by a small guard of ten men under Lt. Thomas W. Sweeny who established "Camp Independence" downstream from Camp Yuma. See Post Returns, *ibid.* and Arthur Woodward (ed.), *Journal of Lt. Thomas W. Sweeny, 1849–1853.* Los Angeles: Westernlore Press, 1956, pp. 52–55. See also an account of Sweeny's problems with the Indians in the letter of 1st Lt. E. Murray to Bv't. Major S. P. Heintzelman, from Camp Independence, November 18, 1851, printed in the *San Diego Herald*, December 11, 1851.

this request, however, insisting that he wanted to remain neutral in the Indian fighting. Farther upstream Bartlett bought fish from the Pimas, visited the Casa Grande ruins on a 119-degree July day, and entertained one of the chiefs. This chief annoyed him, just as Mangas Colorado had done at Santa Rita, by filling his plate with seconds and passing it over his shoulder to hungry friends. The fellow wanted whiskey and wasn't convinced that the Puritan-like Bartlett didn't have any until he had sampled every bottle in camp and swallowed some bitter medicine for diarrhea.

En route from the Maricopa and Pima villages to Tucson, Bartlett was drenched by violent Arizona summer rains and met emigrants on their way to California. He found Tucson almost in a stage of siege because of Apache raids. Whereas the village once had a population of 1000, there were only some 300 left in 1852, in addition to about 300 Mexican soldiers stationed at the presidio. "The houses of Tucson are all of adobe," he wrote in the *Personal Narrative* for July 17, "and the majority are in a state of ruin. No attention seems to be given to repair, but as soon as a dwelling becomes uninhabitable it is deserted." While the party was resting, replenishing its supplies, and having new shoes put on the mules, Bartlett climbed a rocky hill west of town and sketched the Santa Cruz Valley, showing a ruined hacienda and the pueblo with the Catalina Mountains in the background.[5] Then on July 19, the men continued their southward journey by way of San Xavier mission to Tubac. Only about half of the dilapidated huts in this small presidio were occupied. Inez Gonzales, who had figured so prominently in Bartlett's experiences the year before, was living in one of them with a Captain Gómez. On this trip, however, the Commissioner went on without her, somewhat disillusioned that she was not the sweet, innocent girl he had pictured.*

The expedition passed by the desolated ruin of Calabasas, which twenty years earlier had been a prosperous ranch with cultivated fields and many cattle. Continuing through Sonora

---

*According to John C. Cremony, interpreter for the boundary commission, Gómez later married Inez and legitimatized the two sons that she bore him. After Gómez's death she married the *Alcalde* of Santa Cruz by whom she also had two children, a boy and a girl. See John C. Cremony, *Life Among the Apaches*. San Francisco: A. Roman & Co., Publishers, 1868, pp. 56–57.

Sketch of Tucson, by John Bartlett, 1852

John Russell Bartlett

and Chihuahua, the party reached El Paso del Norte in mid-August. In December, the commission moved across Texas to San Antonio where the animals and field equipment were sold. Bartlett was replaced as boundary commissioner in March, 1853, by General Robert Blair Campbell. A former commander of the South Carolina militia, member of the U. S. House of Representatives, and consul at Havana, Campbell was living in San Antonio, Texas, at the time of his appointment. Like his predecessor, he had no special qualifications for the post other than political connections. Campbell was an able administrator, however, and delegated the main responsibility for completing the boundary survey to Major Emory, the chief astronomer and surveyor. With Emory doing the work and Campbell signing the papers, the field work was completed by December, 1853.[6]

Meanwhile, Bartlett settled in his native Rhode Island where he served for fifteen years as Secretary of State and distinguished himself as a writer and bibliographer. His administration of the boundary commission was admittedly sloppy and his extensive junkets expensive. Yet the reports on his experience proved to be of inestimable value to scientists and later travelers in Arizona and the Southwest. Some of his pictures, including one of Tucson, were printed in the *Personal Narrative,* but for reasons of economy they were wretchedly engraved; the woodcuts failed to capture the detail and beauty of the originals. Already maligned as a diplomat — and for his inability to command a survey expedition of scientists, soldiers, wagoneers, and wranglers — Bartlett was also underestimated as an artist. Then in 1963, the drawings which he had given to Brown University shortly before his death in 1886 were "discovered" in the basement of the library. Most of them were reproduced in book form and publicly exhibited at art galleries in the Southwest.[7] Today he is remembered as an artist as well as for his *Dictionary of Americanisms.*

GADSDEN PURCHASE

President Franklin Pierce refused to recognize the Bartlett-Condé line as the southern boundary of New Mexico and was able to use the contradictory phraseology of the 1848 treaty to advantage in the early fifties. By that time, the United States realized that additional Mexican territory was needed in order to lay out a transcontinental railroad by way of the 32nd parallel to the Pacific. The influential Secretary of War, Jefferson Davis, favored this "southern route" and recommended that James Gadsden, a South Carolina railroad promoter, be sent to Mexico to negotiate for the necessary land south of the Gila River. Gadsden was appointed minister by President Pierce, and arrived in Mexico City in the summer of 1853 with instructions to correct the errors which had been made in the hastily-drawn Treaty of Guadalupe Hidalgo. He found President Santa Anna in need of money and fearful of both revolution and another shooting war with the United States.

President Pierce was anxious to take advantage of Santa Anna's plight and secure a liberal cession of territory. In order not to give the Mexican people an excuse to overthrow their dictator, however, the American designs were shrouded with a mantle of secrecy. When the political situation in Mexico seemed ripe for pressing negotiations, Secretary of State W. L. Marcy sent a messenger to Gadsden with memorized instructions. He could not risk having a written dispatch intercepted. By these instructions, Gadsden was authorized to make five offers, each for a different quantity of Mexican territory.

President Pierce preferred the first offer: $50,000,000 for a huge stretch of land extending from the Pacific Ocean to the Gulf of Mexico — including all of Lower California, a sea outlet on the Gulf of California, and a large slice off the northern states of Sonora, Chihuahua, Coahuila, Nuevo León, and Tamaulipas.[8] One advantage in this acquisition was that the United States would have a natural mountain and desert barrier on the south. A second offer up to a maximum of $35,000,000 could be made for 50,000 square miles that included some land south of the Rio Grande and east of the Big Bend country in Texas, as well as enough of northern Sonora and Chihuahua to give the United States a sea outlet on the Gulf of California; Lower California was not involved in the second offer, however.

A third offer up to $30,000,000 would, if accepted, give the United States 68,000 square miles — including Lower California, the head of the Gulf of California (as in all five offers), and lands south of the present Arizona and New Mexico international border, but nothing south of Texas. The fourth offer — up to $20,000,000 for 18,000 square miles — was the same as the third, minus Lower California.

In the event the first four proposals were turned down, a final offer of $15,000,000 or less was to be made for the minimal objectives of a railroad route and an outlet on the Gulf of California; for these purposes, a boundary line along the parallel 31 degrees 48 minutes north latitude running eastward from the mouth of the Colorado to the Rio Grande, was considered adequate — though a natural, more easily defensible border farther south was desired. A line even farther north along the 32nd parallel was an acceptable alternative to the fifth offer, provided it was coupled with a release from an obligation of the Treaty of Guadalupe Hidalgo. Article XI of the 1848 treaty made the United States responsible for stopping all Indian incursions into Mexico. The article had been difficult to enforce and the government wanted it rescinded.

Despite his new instructions from the President, however, Gadsden was severely handicapped in conferences with the Mexicans and nearly gave up in despair. A major hindrance was William Walker's filibustering expedition into Lower California. In November, 1853, Walker landed at La Paz with less than fifty men and proclaimed that area an independent republic. Convinced that the United States government was somehow behind the filibuster and intended to eventually annex all of Mexico, Santa Anna began seeking alliances with European powers. Only when he realized that Britain, France, and Spain would probably not come to Mexico's assistance in event of war with the United States, did Santa Anna willingly proceed to negotiate a treaty with Gadsden in order to replenish his empty treasury. Even then, he refused to give up any land except for the transcontinental railroad.

*President Antonio
López de Santa Anna*

Library of Congress

The boundary described in Article I of the document — signed on December 30, 1853 — was later changed by the United States Senate. From the juncture of the Gila and Colorado rivers at Yuma, the boundary would run 70 miles down the middle of the Colorado to a point six miles above the head of the Gulf, and then in a straight line southeast to the intersection of the 31st parallel with the 111th degree of longitude (about 21 miles south of the present border at Nogales). Then the line would run straight northeast and intersect the Rio Grande at 31 degrees 47 minutes 30 seconds, eight miles north of El Paso. This border permitted Mexico to keep its land bridge to Baja California. In exchange for the territory acquired by this provision of the treaty, the United States was to pay $15,000,000. This government was also released from all claims of Mexican citizens arising from Indian depredations, and for this concession, agreed to assume claims of Americans against the Mexican government amounting to $5,000,000. Free navigation of the Gulf and the Colorado was guaranteed to the United States.

As soon as the contents of this treaty became known in the United States, a spirited debate broke out, mainly along sectional lines. Most Northern newspapers and anti-slavery senators opposed it, while pro-slavery interests were in the forefront commending it. President Pierce was disappointed in the terms, but at the urging of Secretaries Marcy and Davis, who doubted that a better cession could be obtained peacefully, submitted the treaty to the Senate in February, 1854. This body was already divided — pro or anti-slavery — over the Kansas-Nebraska Bill, and took up the Gadsden treaty along the same battle lines. The greatest amount of discussion, of course, arose around the first article dealing with the boundary. Several amendments were offered by expansionist senators to move the line farther south, and all were defeated. Another amendment that reduced the amount of the proposed cession by 9,000 square miles and set down the boundary as it is today, was proposed by Senator James Murray Mason of Virginia, and adopted.

This boundary extends 100 miles westward from the Rio Grande along the parallel 31 degrees 47 minutes, thence south to the parallel 31 degrees 20 minutes and west along this line through modern Douglas, Arizona, to the 111th degree of longitude. At this point, instead of continuing straight west from the site of Nogales to give the United States access to the Gulf, the boundary turns northwestward to a point on the Colorado River approximately 28 miles south of the Gila junction. It continues up the middle of the Colorado to an intersection with the dividing line between Upper and Lower California. The purchase price was reduced by the Senate to $10,000,000, and the provision for assumption by the United States of $5,000,000 in claims of American citizens against Mexico was stricken. The clause abrogating Article XI of the Treaty of Guadalupe Hidalgo was retained, thereby eliminating claims of Mexicans against the United States because of Indian depredations. But even with these modifications, the

Senate refused to ratify the treaty until an additional clause guaranteeing Americans the right of transit across the Isthmus of Tehuantepec was attached.[9] Finally, on April 25, the amended Gadsden Treaty was approved by the comfortable margin of 33 to 12.

Gadsden was dissatisfied with the Senate version of his original treaty, and at first hoped that Mexico would not accept it. But Marcy convinced him that any new treaty which might be negotiated would probably be turned down by an American Senate because of the slave controversy. And as long as Santa Anna was president, the Mexican government was in no position to reject the treaty. He needed money to maintain his shaky regime in power. Besides, his minister to Washington, D.C., Juan Nepomuceno Almonte, advised the dictator that a Mexican rejection could mean war with the United States. As a highly skilled diplomat, Almonte had a hand in bringing about the altered treaty; he had effectively convinced influential senators that Mexico was entitled to a land bridge — and one wider than the six miles provided in Gadsden's original treaty — so that Lower California would not be isolated from the Mexican mainland. Except for Almonte's pleas, and the statement by Foreign Minister

Juan Nepomuceno Almonte

Library of Congress

Manuel Díaz de Bonilla that Mexico would not relinquish its land access to Baja, the Senate might have seriously considered the amendment offered by expansionist Senator James Shields of Illinois to extend the boundary line straight west from Nogales. The revised and present boundary which Almonte sold to the senators — including Senator Mason who introduced the amendment — was virtually the same boundary he had drawn in 1852 to accompany his pamphlet, *Proyecto de Leyes sobre Colonización,* urging colonization of the Indian-devastated wastelands of the northern frontier.[10] Santa Anna was satisfied with the boundary, especially since he did not consider the cession of "wild country" south of the Gila any great loss to Mexico — at least in comparison to the terms of the ignominious treaty of 1848, whereby Mexico gave up half the national property to her northern neighbor. He affixed his signature to the Gadsden Treaty on May 31, and dispatched a letter of acceptance to President Pierce.

The day after the President received the treaty document on June 20, he sent it to the House of Representatives where a bill was introduced to provide money to carry out its terms. An appropriation bill was passed on June 29 — by a vote of 103 to 62 — but only after it had again run the gantlet of debate along sectional party lines. Congressman Thomas Hart Benton, formerly a senator from Missouri from 1820 to 1850, led the opposition. Concealing his main objection, he complained that the House had not been previously consulted and argued that good routes along the 34th, 35th, 38th, and 39th parallels were already available for a transcontinental railroad. He quoted Kit Carson's description of the ceded territory as being "so desolate, desert, and God-forsaken that a wolf could not make a living on it." But Congressman Thomas H. Bayly of Virginia exposed Benton's fear that the cession of land for a southern railroad would interfere with his own pet project of a central route to the Pacific from his home state of Missouri. And the prevailing opinion was that the Gadsden Purchase was a good bargain — some 29,670 square miles (27,305 now in Arizona and the rest in New Mexico) being added to complete the continental limits of the United States, except for Alaska. Congress voted the appro-

*Etching of Senator
(later Congressman)
Thomas Hart Benton*

Library of Congress

priation and Pierce exchanged ratifications with the Mexican legation on June 30. The next day, Almonte called at the Treasury Department for a $7,000,000 draft, the first payment on the ceded real estate.* The remaining $3,000,000 installment was not due until after a survey of the new international boundary had been completed.

Major William Emory, who was in and out of Arizona over a period of ten years, was in charge of surveying the international boundary. His Mexican counterpart, Commis-

---

*The money paid was wasted on officials, speculators, hired troops and celebrations. Santa Anna himself appropriated $700,000 as a personal indemnity for the damage done to his plantations during the Mexican War. The Mexicans continued to need money and between December 19, 1854 and July 9, 1855, drafts were drawn by the Mexican government on the Treasury of the United States. It is believed that about one-third of the remaining $3,000,000 went to American bankers for advancing the money.

*General William H. Emory, who served as a boundary
commissioner in Arizona prior to his participation in
the Civil War as a Union officer*

J. Ross Browne, *A Tour Through Arizona, 1864*

*Gadsden purchase boundary marker erected in 1855 by
William H. Emory. (Sketch by Browne)*

sioner José Salazar y Larregui, met him at El Paso in December, 1854, and cooperated splendidly, partly because his government was desperately in need of cash and anxious to collect the final payment. The work of marking the boundary went on without interruption except when Salazar was temporarily imprisoned by his government as a friend of Santa Anna — deposed shortly after the Gadsden Purchase. To avoid any need for a repetition of the survey, various monuments of stone and iron were erected. As a further precaution, Emory made careful sketches of the topography in different directions from these markers. His idea was to facilitate relocation of the sites without having to make difficult calculations, in event that the Indians should succeed in destroying the monuments.

While Emory was surveying from the Río Grande, another officer, Lieutenant Nathaniel Michler, was marking the western segment from the initial point on the Colorado south of Yuma. Michler was accompanied by soldiers from Fort Yuma under the command of Lieutenant Francis Patterson. The Mexican in charge was Francisco Jiménez, who was escorted by troopers under Captain Hilarión García, remembered in Arizona history as the last presidial commander at Tucson, which was protected by a detachment of Mexican troops for several months after the end of the survey. Despite the severe summer heat, lack of sufficient water, and the presence of poisonous reptiles, Michler surveyed the diagonal boundary from the Colorado to a point near Nogales where Emory was waiting for him. All the field work was completed by October, but it was June 25, 1856, before the official maps were finished and exchanged in Washington, D.C., making Mexico eligible for the final $3,000,000 due on the purchase. And it was still another three years before all of Emory's excellent report, which included much valuable scientific data on the Southwest, was ready for printing.[11]

Mexican soldiers remained in Tucson, the principal settlement of the newly acquired territory, until March 10, 1856. In November, a detachment of United States dragoons arrived to raise the American flag and take formal possession of the only section of Arizona which had been previously settled by white men.

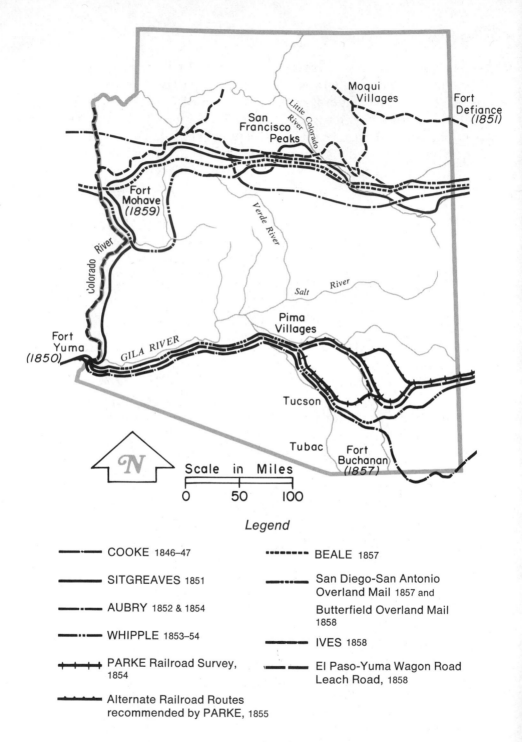

Legend

—·—·— COOKE 1846–47	▪▪▪▪▪▪ BEALE 1857
——— SITGREAVES 1851	—··— San Diego-San Antonio Overland Mail 1857 and
—·—·— AUBRY 1852 & 1854	Butterfield Overland Mail 1858
—··—··— WHIPPLE 1853–54	——— IVES 1858
+++++ PARKE Railroad Survey, 1854	— — — El Paso-Yuma Wagon Road Leach Road, 1858
┼┼┼┼┼ Alternate Railroad Routes recommended by PARKE, 1855	

Early American routes

Chapter 11

1850s: Explorations and Transportation in the New Domain

AFTER THE MEXICAN WAR, thousands of gold-seeking emigrants—sometimes called Argonauts—followed Cooke's wagon road, the Devil's Highway, and other trails across southern Arizona to California. The 1848 migration came mainly from Sonora, Chihuahua, and other Mexican states; but most of the "Forty-niners" traveled from the eastern part of the United States. When Americans read accounts of President Polk's annual message to Congress in December, 1848, verifying newspaper stories about the fabulous gold strike, a "yellow fever" mania gripped the country. The largest single westward movement in the nation's history was soon underway, and thousands of migrants passed through what is now Arizona.

ARGONAUT TRAILS

Some of the Argonauts went to California by sea, embarking from Atlantic and Gulf port cities, but the majority of them chose the cheaper and more dangerous overland trails. At first, the most popular route was the so-called Humboldt or central route through Utah. By 1849, however, the southern overland trails were receiving more publicity in such respectable newspapers as the *New York Weekly Tribune*. Texas, Arkansas, and Missouri became points of departure for many caravans which took some variation of Cooke's route through Mexican territory to the "promised land." The main divergence was between the San Pedro River and Tucson. Whereas Cooke went north down the San Pedro about fifty-five miles before turning west to Tucson, most of the Argonauts crossed this river near present-day Bisbee and reached the Old Pueblo by way of Santa Cruz and the Santa Cruz River farther west. The latter trail was not new since it had been followed by United States troops under Major Lawrence Graham in 1848.

One of the most difficult parts of the Cooke road was the stretch from Tucson to the Pima villages. John E. Durivage — a correspondent for the New Orleans *Daily Picayune* who had caught the "gold fever" — wrote about this stretch in his diary on May 31, 1849, as follows: "I consider the crossing of this *jornada* of eighty miles an era in my life and shall never forget it to the day of my death. . . . Until one has crossed a barren desert without food or water, under a burning tropical sun, at the rate of three miles an hour, he can form no conception of what misery is." [1]

Even greater difficulties were experienced on the dusty Gila Trail beyond the Pima villages. Loads had to be lightened for the animals that survived and the roadside was strewn with wagons, cook stoves, and other paraphernalia which had once been.considered necessities. A contemporary account describing the Gila Trail was written for the *Arkansas State Gazette* by Alden M. Woodruff, who crossed Arizona in late August and early September, 1849, with a group from Little Rock. He did not speak very highly of the Mexican soldiers or the Indians:

. . . We left Santa Cruz and traveled down the Santa Cruz river. We passed through one of the most beautiful vallies I ever saw. All along the banks we found deserted towns, Ranchos, and furnaces. The whole country abounds in rich gold and silver mines; but as soon as a town or rancho is built, the Apaches tear it down, and kill all the males and carry off the females. The valley is covered with "Mezquit timber," and is the finest grazing country (except Cala.) I ever saw. We traveled down the river about 100 miles to Touson where we laid by two days. There are two or three co's. of soldiers stationed here, to protect the inhabitants; but as soon as they go outside the town, the Apaches drive them in again. They are like all Mexican soldiery.

. . . It took us four or five days to make the Gila when we found what little grass there was eaten close to the ground. We found the "Pijmo" [Pima] Indians represented by Lt. Emory as the most innocent and harmless race of Indians on the continent. We camped among them one night, and next morning we were minus our lead line and almost every wagon lost some article from their wagon or harness. They might have been honest when Emory was among them, but they have learnt bad manners since.

We bought corn, fodder, wheat, melons, and such things, from the "Pijmos." They asked high prices in money, but a hickory shirt would go

as far as $5 with them. We traveled down the river three or four days
and found no grass — we had plenty of corn and wheat — but we soon
learned how to find grass; we had to swim our stock over to the bars
and islands, which were subject to overflow, and on some found plenty
of fine grass. It was on this river that my best two mules (Pol and Bill)
were ruined, by getting mired in the quicksand. After my mules were
broken down, I had to swap off both for one, leave my wagon, and pack.
We traveled about 20 days down the Gila before getting to the crossing
of the Colorado, when we crossed in a boat made by some people from
Polk Co., Ark., Burke Johnson was among them. We paid them $1.25
to cross our packs, and had to swim our mules — Pierce lost his mule in
swiming [sic].

We left the Colorado and started into the Great Desert. . . .[2]

In addition to the many natural hazards, Indians occasionally attacked small parties of emigrants, though hostilities
were still directed mainly at the Mexicans in the early 1850s.
The most notable outrage was the Oatman massacre on
February 18, 1851, which occurred at a place on the Gila
now known as Oatman Flat, about 100 miles east of Yuma.
Royse Oatman, his wife, and seven children were part of
a wagon train of fifty excommunicated Mormons — called
Brewsterites — who left Independence, Missouri, in August,
1850. They followed the circuitous Cooke route and arrived
at Tucson in February, 1851. After a short stopover, five of
the families chose to remain at "Tukjon," but after resting
awhile the Oatmans, Wilders, and Kellys pushed on to the
Pima villages. Here a disappointment awaited them. The
Pimas had no surplus food; and the discouraged emigrants
had the choice of staying at the villages, returning to Tucson,
or venturing into the desolate country toward the Colorado
with insufficient rations. The Wilders and Kellys stayed at
Maricopa Wells, but the Oatmans decided to press on to
their objective — California. Their choice was made easier
by the arrival of Dr. John Le Conte, an entomologist known
as "Dr. Bugs," who had been scouting the area for mineral
wealth with his Mexican guide. These men had just crossed
the stretch from Fort Yuma without seeing any signs of
Indians on the warpath.

About half way along the 200-mile route to Yuma, the
Oatman family was overtaken by Le Conte. He could see

that they were having a horrible journey, and would never reach the crossing without more food and fresh animals. Being on horseback, he offered to ride as rapidly as possible to Fort Yuma and ask Major Heintzelman for aid. The Oatmans were naturally overjoyed and never knew that the good doctor and his guide encountered a small group of Quechan (Yuma) a day or so after their departure. The Indians were bluffed away when faced with a cocked pistol and a long knife, but managed to steal the horses from a nearby thicket. Le Conte was worried about the Oatmans and attached a note of warning for them to a tree before continuing on to the fort on foot. Somehow, the family missed the note and trudged wearily onward, unaware that hostile natives lurked in the vicinity. By this time, the oxen were so weakened that the wagons had to be unloaded on the hills and the goods had to be carried up the steep grades. After one such day of traveling, the exhausted family camped just below the big bend of the Gila to eat their last supper of dry bread and bean soup together. Here, a party of Yavapais armed with clubs, bows, and arrows approached and professed friendship. Oatman felt confident that he could get along with the warriors. But after he passed around his pipe and tobacco the Indians demanded more food than the family could spare.

After a short consultation, the Indians turned on the family, murdered six of them within a minute or two, and left the bleeding eldest son, Lorenzo, for dead. Two sisters, Olive and Mary Ann, were carried away into captivity. Lorenzo regained consciousness and started back to the villages, helped by two friendly Pima hunters who gave him food on the trail. The Wilders and Kellys, who had decided to follow the Oatmans, finally picked him up. Startled by the bad news, these families retraced their steps to Maricopa Wells and joined other emigrants for greater safety. Once the larger party reached Yuma, the boy told his story; but Major Heintzelman could not pursue the Indians because the massacre had occurred on Mexican soil.[3]

Lorenzo spent the next five years in California trying to interest someone in helping to find his sisters. The girls were enslaved by the Yavapais and compelled to do hard work;

they were whipped when they couldn't understand what was being said to them. Providentially, they were sold after about a year to the less cruel Mojaves at the slave market price of two horses, three blankets, some vegetables, and a few pounds of beads. In the Mojave village in northwestern Arizona, the Oatman girls were tatooed on the chin with five vertical blue lines to distinguish them as Mojaves. As captive members of the tribe, they were assigned a patch of land on which to grow their own maize, melons, and corn. During a year of famine, however, Mary Ann starved to death, leaving poor Olive alone to face the ordeal of captivity. From time to time, the newspapers published rumors that a white woman was living among the Mojaves. But no one did anything about identifying her

Olive Oatman

Arizona Historical Society

until 1856. In that year, Henry W. Grinnell, a civilian carpenter at Fort Yuma, hired a Yuma Indian named Francisco to ransom the woman and bring her to the fort. For six pounds of white beads, four blankets, some trinkets and a white horse, Chief Espaniole gave up his "white daughter" over the objections of his Indian squaw who had befriended the girl. Grinnell found it difficult to believe that Olive Oatman was a white woman; she was so disguised by long exposure to the sun, paint, tattooing on her chin and arms, and Indian dress. At first she seemed dazed and did not talk. But wives of the officers took her in charge and Olive began to return to the white world, both physically and mentally.

Her sensational rescue excited the country, and especially Lorenzo. He read an account of Olive's release in the *Los Angeles Star,* and hurried to Fort Yuma for a reunion with his sister. Neither recognized the other; so much had they changed in five years. After this unusual reunion, the brother and sister went to Oregon to live with cousins. Olive told her experiences to the Reverend Royal Byron Stratton, who wrote a book entitled *Captivity of the Oatman Girls,* first published in San Francisco in 1857. The royalties from this book financed Olive's and Lorenzo's educations at the University of the Pacific. Eventually, the two of them returned to New York to visit their mother's relatives, the Sperrys. Lorenzo soon acquired a family of his own and moved to Illinois. In 1865, Olive married John Brant Fairchild, whose family had also been attacked by Indians in the Southwest. They were driving Texas longhorns to California markets in 1854, when Apaches raided their herd, driving off 200 head; the attackers also sacked the wagons and left one Fairchild dead. Olive and her husband lived for awhile in Detroit, but later settled down in Sherman, Texas, where they prospered in business. Olive died there in 1903, at the age of 66. A widely circulated story that she died of melancholia in a New York insane asylum, in 1877, has been proven unfounded.

TRANSPORTATION ON THE COLORADO

Most of the gold seeking emigrants were more fortunate than the Oatmans. The number who reached the junction of the Gila and Colorado rivers by the end of 1851 has been estimated as high as 60,000. Perhaps the first ferryman to assist travelers at the Yuma crossing was Lieutenant Cave J. Couts. This twenty-seven-year-old army officer established Camp Calhoun on the California side, at the site of the old mission founded by Garcés, in September, 1849. Though his main purpose was to protect the boundary surveyors, he aided the worn-out emigrants who arrived in the fall of 1849. Among these were the Howards whose son, named Gila, was probably the first white child born of American parents in what is now Arizona.*

One of the gold rushers — Able B. Lincoln, who had served with General Scott in the Mexican War — gained possession of Couts's business in the early part of 1850. He operated the first regular ferry at the Yuma crossing, and prospered from the very beginning. In a letter to his parents, he wrote that he had grossed $60,000 in three months. By that time, however, he had been forced into a kind of partnership with a band of murdering scalp hunters led by John Glanton.† How the noble Lincoln became associated with such a wicked wretch is still a mystery, but it is likely that Glanton "muscled in," raising prices and also abusing the Yumas who ran a competing ferry some six miles below the junction. When the Indians came to protest that their American manager — an army deserter named Callaghan — had been killed and their boat set adrift, Glanton kicked and clubbed the chief. He threatened to kill one Indian for every Mexican that the Indians carried across the Colorado.

---

* Elias H. Howard, the father, said in 1885 that Couts purchased the wagon in which his son, Gila Howard, was born and used it as a ferry-boat at the Yuma Crossing. The elder Howard also said that Gila was then living in Lake County, California. See *San Francisco Bulletin*, July 8, 1885. See also Anna Paschall Hannum (ed.), *A Quaker Forty-Niner: The Adventures of Charles Edward Pancoast on the American Frontier.* Philadelphia: University of Pennsylvania Press, 1930, p. 25. Pancoast mistakenly wrote that the baby was a girl.

† Glanton and other American desperadoes scalped Indians in Chihuahua for bounty rewards ($200 for a warrior and $150 for a squaw) offered by the state government. After the Indians became scarce, the renegade Americans began killing Mexicans and selling their scalps as Indian scalps. Once the government detected this deception, the bounties were discontinued and the Glanton gang had to move on. See "Crumbs of 49," Part 2, in "Original Journal of B. B. Harris," in Huntington Library, San Marino, California. Harris was a Forty-Niner from Virginia who went via Texas and Chihuahua to California. His journal was published in 1960. See Benjamin B. Harris, *The Gila Trail: The Texas Argonauts and the California Gold Rush.* Norman: University of Oklahoma Press, 1960, pp. 109–11.

Enraged by this treatment, the Yumas plotted revenge. On April 21, 1850, they attacked their white rivals and killed eleven ferrymen.[4] According to the three survivors, who were away cutting willow poles at the time, Glanton had just returned from purchasing supplies in San Diego and was celebrating when the massacre occurred. The Yuma chief, whom Glanton had insulted, personally sought out the desperado and split his head open with a hatchet. Meanwhile, another chief caught the sleeping Lincoln by surprise and clubbed him to death. All of the victims of the outrage were thrown into a fire, Glanton and Lincoln being singled out for a final act of cruelty; each leader's dog was tied to its master's body and burned alive. The Yumas evidently found some of the money which the ferrymen had saved, and, for some time, bought freely from passing emigrants. They paid exorbitant prices since they did not know the value of either Mexican or United States coins. As late as June 16, 1860, however, the *Daily Alta California,* a San Francisco newspaper, stated that people were still searching in the Yuma area for large sums of ill-gotten money that Glanton had supposedly hidden. "A great deal of digging has been done in places which he frequented," the paper reported, "but the hiding place, if there was any, remains a secret."

News of the massacre was printed in the California papers and aroused much excitement. Governor Peter H. Burnett ordered the enlistment of volunteers to protect American emigrants at the crossing, to punish the Yumas, and to recover the treasure taken from Lincoln and Glanton. Induced by high wages, some 142 militiamen assembled under the command of Quartermaster General Joseph C. Morehead. The "Gila Expedition" arrived at the Colorado River in late summer. After a losing skirmish with the Yumas, the troops settled down to the task of consuming their expensive rations.[5] Astounded by the cost of the Morehead fiasco, the governor recalled the idle army. It took California four years to pay the accumulated bills. Nothing was accomplished except to increase the Indian disrespect for the white man.

A company of eleven California ferrymen, including

*Louis J. F. Iaeger
(often spelled Jaeger)*

Louis J. F. Iaeger (also Jaeger),* who had reopened business at the crossing in July, 1850, welcomed the arrival of troops under the command of the capable Major Samuel P. Heintzelman.[6] On December 1, the Major selected a site for Camp Yuma about a mile below the hill where Lt. Couts had established the temporary Camp Calhoun in 1849. From the beginning, the problem of supplying the military post proved more difficult than that of controlling the angry Yumas — since food and equipment had to be transported across two hundred

---

*Iaeger's name is usually spelled "Jaeger." In the 1860 census, however, he is listed as Louis John Frederick Ieager ("ea" instead of "ae"). He was described as a Pennsylvania-born merchant, age 35, who possessed property valued at $55,000. See "Excerpt from Decennial Census, 1860, for Arizona County in the Territory of New Mexico," in *Federal Census — Territory of New Mexico and Territory of Arizona*, Senate Document No. 13, 89th Congress, 1st Session, 1965. In a claim filed with the Court of Claims, he signed his name "Iaeger." See "L. J. F. Jaeger vs. the United States and Yuma Indians," 1891, in RG 123: Court of Claims Records, Indian Depredations, Case File 1108, National Archives.

General Thomas W. Sweeny, who was stationed on the Colorado River as a lieutenant in 1851

National Archives

miles of hot desert. Heintzelman's poorly supplied men suffered from scurvy and near starvation, but finally had occasion to rejoice in January, 1851, when a water route from San Francisco was opened. Captain Alfred H. Wilcox — with a crew of thirteen — succeeded in sailing a military schooner, the *Invincible,* thirty miles up the Colorado with a cargo of provisions for the garrison. With five men, Major Heintzelman unloaded the army supplies at Howard's Point and hauled them the remainder of the way to Camp Yuma by wagon. The government was slow to follow up this first successful voyage, however, and the stock of supplies at the post was soon depleted. In March, the camp was moved to the cooler hilltop where Garcés had built his mission.* Finally, with no relief in sight, Heintzelman was ordered to fall back with his command and departed for a camp near Santa Isabel

---

* Letter of Bv't. Major Samuel P. Heintzelman to Major E. R. L. Canby, from Camp Yuma, Calif., March 23, 1851, in Heintzelman Papers, Library of Congress. Heintzelman wrote of the move: "It is a most desirable change from the dusty camp below. The point we occupy is on the plateau to the east of the remains of the old mission buildings."

(Ysabel), California on June 5 — leaving only ten men under Lt. Thomas W. Sweeny to protect the ferry company and emigrants. Sweeny moved down the river six miles below Camp Yuma, as ordered, and selected a new campsite, which he christened Camp Independence.[7]

Meanwhile, Louis J. F. Iaeger's Yuma ferry was doing a thriving business until his friend Heintzelman departed in June, 1851. Then the Indians became more troublesome. While Iaeger was in San Diego buying supplies, the natives attacked a party of Americans being transported across the river. On his return trip, Iaeger was jumped by a pack of Yuma bowmen; he dug in his spurs and raced for the safety of the Yuma stockade with at least one arrow in his left arm. A few hundred yards short of the brush fort, he was struck in the neck by a well-aimed arrow. He reached the stockade, but fell off his horse unconscious. When he regained his senses, he learned that most of the boats had been sunk and his cattle driven off. His life was saved only because his associates slipped away at night and carried him to San Diego where a surgeon removed an arrowhead from his neck.

After this tragic turn of events, Heintzelman was sent back to the crossing in February, 1852, with a strong force. The fort was permanently reestablished, and George Alonzo Johnson — one of the ferrymen who had sold out to Iaeger — secured a contract to supply the military post. On February 17, the schooner *Sierra Nevada,* with Captain Wilcox in command and Johnson on board, arrived at the mouth of the Colorado with supplies for the garrison. The load was transferred to two flatboats which were moved upstream by poles; unfortunately, one of the boats was swamped and sunk with its entire cargo.[8] It soon became evident that flatboats were not going to meet the requirements of the posts. A new contract was awarded to Captain James Turnbull, who had a river steamboat shipped to the mouth of the Colorado. In December, 1852, the paddle-wheeled steamship, christened the *Uncle Sam,* became the largest vessel that had ever navigated the Colorado as far as the crossing. It was a sixty-five-foot-long side-wheeler and carried thirty-two tons of freight. The boiler generated only twenty horsepower but blew off enough steam to frighten the Yuma Indians. Lieutenant Sweeny, a veteran of the Mexican War and later a brigadier general, was stationed at Fort Yuma when the *Uncle Sam* made its historic voyage to the post. He described the event in his diary under the entry of December 12, 1852:

> The steamer *Uncle Sam*, so long expected from below, arrived at the post on the 3d with about twenty tons of commissary stores, etc. She was fifteen days coming up the river from where the schooner *Capacity* is lying, 120 miles from the post. They found it difficult to get wood on their way up. Colorado and José, Cocopa chiefs, and a Yuma came up on her.
>
> On the 8th Captain Driscoll, of the *Capacity*, Mr. Turnbull, the contractor, and Mr. Phillips, the engineer, proposed a trip up the Rio Gila and the Colorado, provided the officers not on duty would accompany them. We started on the morning of the 8th at half-past 9 o'clock and returned about sunset. The trip was rather pleasant than otherwise, more on account of its novelty than anything else, I surmise, for we got pretty well sprinkled during the voyage. The steamer is only sixty-five long and ten or twelve feet wide. However, it was the first steamer that navigated the Gila and the Colorado.[9]

When the *Uncle Sam* went aground and sank, in the spring of 1853, Turnbull went out of the steamboat business and, for awhile, Fort Yuma was again supplied by mule teams from San Diego. Johnson then organized a navigation company and transported parts to the Colorado for a new steamer, the *General Jesup*, a 104 foot side-wheeler equipped with a seventy horsepower engine. By January, 1854, the new and bigger boat was completed. It operated without mishap until September, when the boiler exploded at Ogden's Landing below Yuma. It was December before repairs could be made, and for the second time, the fort was supplied by wagon supply trains dispatched from San Diego. The successful operation of the *General Jesup* proved that steam navigation of the Colorado was practicable. By December, 1855, the company had a stern-wheeler, the *Colorado,* in operation. This type of boat proved to be indispensable for cutting through sand bars and operating in narrow channels.

The *General Jesup,* however, was the first steamer to go up the Colorado beyond the crossing. In early 1858, the boat reached a point several miles above the future Fort Mojave, and on the return voyage, struck a rock about fifty miles north of Yuma and sank. It was rescued and placed back into service by the crew of the *Colorado Number One*. But a short time later, the boilers exploded and the ship was finally condemned in 1861. The first official exploration of the Colorado River was also made in 1858, by Lieutenant Joseph C. Ives in the *Explorer*. This fifty-four-foot iron-hull steamer had been built in Philadelphia, dismantled, and carried to the mouth of the Colorado by way of Panama. The odd-looking craft was reassembled, the weak hull being strengthened by a timber bolted on each side of the keel. Piloted by Captain D. C. Robinson of the Johnson Company, the *Explorer* finally reached the Black Canyon — though it was aground on sandbars a good part of the time. As Ives struggled upstream, he was very chagrined to meet Johnson on the *General Jesup* heading homeward. Johnson had already explored much of the territory that the *Explorer* had been sent at great government expense to examine. Ives continued with his assignment, however, and made an optimistic report on Colorado River navigation. The *Explorer*, after reaching Yuma, was sold at auction to Johnson's Colorado Steam Navigation Company. It was hardly the type of boat that the lieutenant recommended for use above the crossing. Instead, the *Explorer* was used to carry firewood on the Gila until rudder trouble caused her to drift down the Colorado into a slough. Before the crew could pull the boat out, the unpredictable stream changed course and left her landlocked.

In May, 1859, a correspondent of the *Alta California* of San Francisco took a boat ride down the Colorado from the newly established Fort Mojave and described the difficulties of transportation on the river for his readers:

I promised you in my last a description of the Colorado from Ft. Mojave, New Mexico (Arizona was part of New Mexico until 1863) to Ft. Yuma, California. . . . The difficulties attending steam navigation of the Colorado are many and great . . . the river is either too high or too low; there is no regularity of channel, which changes constantly with the day, owing to the quick sands. Spread out in places over an immense surface, the most experienced pilot cannot ascertain its true course. There is but very little timber in the valleys for the use of the steamer, and fifteen miles per day, average, is the most a steamer can make on the river from Yuma to the Mojave valley . . . the land travel is far worse in proportion to the river . . . it is impossible to discover two equally worse routes in any part of the world. . . .[10]

The steamer Cocopah, *which was launched in 1859.*
The Southern Pacific Railroad bridge in the back-
ground was built at Yuma in 1877.

Despite hardships of navigation, steamers continued to ply the river and engage in a thriving commerce. Until 1864, there was only one steam company and it had difficulty keeping pace with expanding military and mining activities which gave impetus to the river trade. Fort Mojave was established on the Colorado early in 1859. Though this post was abandoned in 1861, it was reactivated two years later because of a gold and silver strike north of the Gila and the consequent increase in traffic across Arizona and along the Colorado. Several new boats helped to relieve the need for additional river transportation. One of these, the *Cocopah,* was built at Gridiron, thirty-five miles north of Robinson's Landing — which was at the mouth of the river — and launched in September, 1859. Named in honor of the Indian tribe on the river delta, the *Cocopah* was the fifth steamer to operate on the Colorado; it was 140 feet long and had a carrying capacity of 100 tons. Another steamboat, the *Mojave,* was launched in 1863 at Yuma to replace the *General Jesup,* which had been scrapped two years earlier; the *Mojave* was shorter than the *Cocopah* but had a capacity of 192.61 tons. Even with these new boats, it still took eight days to make a round trip from the mouth of the Colorado to Yuma and about forty days for Fort Mojave. As late as 1863, freight was still piling up awaiting shipment. Dissatisfaction and impatience with this kind of service led to the founding of a rival company and a period of intense commercial rivalry on the Colorado.

EXPLORATIONS: SITGREAVES

During the 1850s, the United States government showed an interest in the "sight unseen" real estate acquired from Mexico. Several surveys were organized to explore the land, then known as New Mexico. The army's topographical engineers were assigned the task of looking for wagon roads, navigable streams, and possible railroad routes. The first expedition went across what is now northern Arizona in 1851, under the direction of Captain Lorenzo Sitgreaves. With a party of twenty, escorted by thirty soldiers, Sitgreaves spent nearly a month at the Zuñi pueblo making final preparations. He had instructions to follow the Zuñi River, the Little Colorado, and the Colorado to the gulf to learn if these waters were navigable. Circumstances, however, necessitated a change in this plan.

In September, the expedition went down the barely flowing Zuñi River to its confluence with the Little Colorado and then followed the course of this river to about the 35th parallel. At that point, Antoine Leroux, the experienced guide and trapper, advised Sitgreaves that to follow the river any longer would bring them into the Grand Canyon of the Colorado. Because of the poor condition of the pack animals and the dwindling food supply, the Captain decided to leave the river and travel west to pick up the Colorado below the Grand Canyon. The route taken approximated that traversed by Padre Garcés in 1776, and was near a line that would run through the modern towns of Winslow, Flagstaff, and Kingman to a point near which Fort Mojave was later built on the Colorado; the tracks of the Santa Fe Railroad were later laid along almost the same route.

After leaving the vicinity of Bill Williams Mountain, near modern Flagstaff, the party found rough going. They suffered from a scarcity of food and water. Though they secured some beans, grain, and pumpkins from the Mojaves, they soon found these Indians to be unfriendly. Leroux was wounded before the expedition reached the Colorado and Dr. S. W. Woodhouse, the physician and naturalist, was hit in the leg by a Mojave arrow during the march down the river. During this part of the journey, the expedition was repeatedly attacked, first by the Mojaves and then by the Yumas. Unable to obtain more food from the natives, the men killed and butchered the mules as they gave out from exhaustion. The loss of these pack animals made it necessary to discard equipment, books, saddles, and tents along the way. By the time the expedition reached Fort Yuma, the men were in deplorable condition and welcomed a temporary respite and a chance to obtain new supplies before pushing on to San Diego.[11]

The trek from Santa Fe was probably not as significant an exploration as it could have been. The trail covered only part of the direct route needed for a transcontinental road. And the report, especially the scientific supplement, was not impressive. The importance of the Sitgreaves expedition lies in the fact that it was a reconnaissance of an unknown region. The map gave a good picture of country through which a railroad could be built as far as the Colorado. The expedition not only encouraged further investigation of this region, but brought an old Spanish dream of a roadway connecting New Mexico and California one step closer to fulfillment. Lieutenant Lorenzo Sitgreaves's importance in history is commemorated today in several geographical place names. Sitgreaves Pass in Mohave County, Mount Sitgreaves in Coconino County, and the Sitgreaves National Forest in Coconino and Yavapai Counties remind us that he was the first American military man to explore a route across northern Arizona.

WHIPPLE, IVES, AND MÖLLHAUSEN

Sitgreaves's exploration was followed in 1853–1854 by another survey along the 35th parallel route for a possible railroad to the Pacific. Lieutenant Amiel W. Whipple, who first entered Arizona in 1851, as an astronomer with Bartlett's boundary commission, was in charge. Lieutenant Joseph Christmas Ives was his chief assistant and Lieutenant John M. Jones commanded the infantry escort. The expedition was well staffed with scientists, including Dr. Jules Marcou, a Swiss geologist and protegé of the renowned Louis Agassiz, and Heinrich Baldwin Möllhausen, an artist-naturalist. The party experienced some difficulty, however, in assembling the necessary instruments because of the simultaneous outfitting of other expeditions for scientific exploration in the Arctic, North Pacific, Japan, and across the northern part of the United States. Despite a shortage of portable transits, magnetometers, and barometers, Whipple completed the survey from Fort Smith, Arkansas, to Albuquerque. Here, he was joined by Ives for the most crucial part of the project and proceeded to the Zuñi pueblos to make final preparations. The primary objective of Whipple's survey was to examine more carefully the country between Zuñi and the Colorado River.

Whipple left Zuñi on November 23, 1853, guided by Leroux. The latter was inclined to retrace the trail over which he had led Sitgreaves in 1851. But the party left the Little Colorado farther south, near the site of present-day Winslow, and traveled west to San Francisco Springs past the location of modern Flagstaff and through a pass south of the San Francisco Mountains, a route which Whipple considered an improvement over the one followed by Sitgreaves. About a month was spent in search of an easier route from the high country to the Colorado, but the terrain over which Whipple finally decided to take his party — down to the Bill Williams Fork south of the Sitgreaves trail — was just as difficult. Nevertheless, an alternative route was explored and mapped. From the mouth of the Bill Williams, the expedition went up the Colorado and crossed to the California side near modern Needles on February 27, 1854. They were assisted by the previously warlike Mojaves who were described by Lieutenant Whipple under the entry of February 26 in his report:

With the chief Francisco for a guide, and José for interpreter, preceded and followed by great crowds of Indians, we continued our survey up the magnificent valley of the Mojaves. The soil, for miles from the river, seemed of exceeding fertility, and was sprinkled with patches of young wheat and fields of corn stubble. There were no acequias [canals]. Irrigation had not been resorted to; although, without doubt, the crops would have been benefitted thereby. We frequently passed rancherías surrounded by granaries filled with corn, mezquite beans, and tornillas. The houses are constructed for durability and warmth. They are built upon sandy soil, thirty or forty feet square; the sides are about two feet thick, of wicker-work and straw; the roofs thatched, covered with earth, and supported by a dozen cotton-wood posts. Along the interior walls are ranged large earthen pots filled with stores of corn, beans, and flour for daily use. In front is a wide shed, a sort of piazza, nearly as large as the house itself. Here they find shelter from rain and sun. Within, surrounding a small fire in the centre, they sleep, protected from the cold. But their favorite resort seems to be upon the top, where we usually could count from twenty to thirty persons, all apparently at home. Near the houses were a great number of cylindrical structures, with conical roofs, quite skilfully made of osier twigs. They were the granaries referred to above, for their surplus stores of corn and the mezquite fruit.

View of Mojave Indians crossing the Colorado River (From Lt. A. W. Whipple, Report of Explorations for a Railway Route)

The latter is highly saccharine, and, when ground to flour, is a favorite article of food with the Indians of the Gila and Colorado rivers. Its flavor is similar to that of pinole, and this name, taken from the Spanish, is sometimes applied to it. Among the most curious articles of household furniture noticed were the pestle and mortar for grinding flour.... Judging from the slight difference in price between grain and flour, it would seem that the labor of grinding is esteemed of little account.[12]

Another member of the Whipple expedition, Lt. David Sloane Stanley, was not at all impressed by the Mojaves and described them in his diary on February 24, 1854:

... A more degraded race of Indians does not, perhaps, exist. The men go naked, except the few rich ones who possess a few rags they have gotten from the Yumas below — and the old duds they have traded us out of. The women wear a kind of petticoat made of willow, giving them a kind of ostrich-like appearance as they shuffle along. They seem neither to hunt or fish, but depend upon the soil for their maintenance. They cultivate pumpkins, beans, corn, wheat, watermelons. Generally they are large and stalwart, the women extremely fat, and they put me much in

Heinrich Balduin (Baldwin) Möllhausen, sometimes called "the German Cooper," made three journeys into the American West. Between 1849 and 1852 he traveled independently with a German nobleman, Duke Paul of Württemberg. In 1853–54 he was an artist and topographer with Whipple's 35th parallel railroad survey expedition. In 1857–58 he accompanied Lt. Joseph Ives in exploring the Colorado River.

Arizona Historical Society

mind of an old matron sow — only they exceed that animal in dirt and disgusting appearance. The only thing we could bring our imagination down to permit us eating were their beans and pumpkins, which they could not well dirty and, as we now have nothing but meat and these articles, we are of course happy of the privilege . . .[13]

From the Colorado, the party completed the survey to Los Angeles in March, and Whipple prepared an elaborate report on his findings to Washington. It contained valuable descriptive information on the topography, flora, fauna, and Indians of northern Arizona. Published in 1856, as the third volume of the *Pacific Railroad Reports,* the work was richly illustrated with engravings and maps. While trying to be objective about the 35th parallel route, he did not entirely suppress his enthusiasm for it. He suggested that the route was not only practicable but in many respects advantageous. Not only could a railroad be built through the passes of the various mountain ranges, but the land was more adaptable to settlement than had been previously reported. Whipple was one of the first to believe that Arizona was more than a

cactus-filled desert. It is only fitting and proper that Whipple
Valley and Fort Whipple near Prescott should be named after
him. Nearly a decade after his Arizona experience, Whipple
was mortally wounded in the Battle of Chancellorsville on
May 3, 1863; he received his commission as a major general
just before he died in Washington, D.C. at the age of 47.

The Whipple expedition was the second of three ventures into the west for Möllhausen. He was encouraged in
his travels by German dignitaries, especially the great geographer, Alexander von Humboldt. A man of letters, science, and
art in his own right, Möllhausen's *Diary* was more than a
logbook; it included drawings and natural history as well as
early history which he learned from men like Antoine Leroux.
Some of his personal experiences were left for Whipple to
describe in his records. The German barely mentions, for
example, his act of heroism during the Colorado crossing
in February, 1854. When a barge capsized and William
White, one of the surveyors, and a small Mexican boy nearly
drowned, only "the exertions of Mr. Möllhausen succeeded

Major General
Amiel W. Whipple

National Archives

The Explorer, *used by Lt. Joseph C. Ives in exploring the Colorado River in 1858. (From a sketch by H. B. Möllhausen)*

in extricating them from beneath the boat." Möllhausen modestly recorded the incident by writing, "I was the only one in the party who could swim, and I had to make great exertions to get Mr. White to where he could lay hold of the tow rope."[14] After Möllhausen returned to Berlin, Humboldt secured him an audience with King Frederick William IV of Prussia. The latter appointed him custodian of the libraries in the royal residences in Potsdam, a title which Möllhausen held until his death in 1905. The job was in essence a subsidy, since Möllhausen was left free to roam and follow his inclinations. In 1857, he was invited by Lieutenant Ives to join the expedition exploring the Colorado River on the river steamer *Explorer*. He reached Yuma by way of Panama, San Francisco, and a trip across the California desert.

Möllhausen made a sketch of the now famous *Explorer*, which eventually transported the Ives party to the Black Canyon, 530 miles above the mouth of the Colorado in the early part of 1858. The Colorado was the largest western river that had not been explored by the Army Corps of Topographical Engineers; Ives's instructions were to chart the river's course, make a hydrographic survey, and to study the geology and natural history of the surrounding country. After determining the highest point of navigation, his next assignment was to organize an overland expedition to survey the Colorado and her tributaries in the canyon country. Just before leaving Fort Yuma on January 11, Ives received dispatches from his commanding officer in Washington, D. C., informing him of a hostile situation in Utah where Mormons were insisting on being governed by their own leaders rather than by carpetbag officers. The crisis was aggravated when President James Buchanan appointed a new roster of outsiders, headed by Alfred W. Cumming of Georgia as governor, to run the territorial government. Troops had already entered Utah from the east and the War Department wanted Ives to investigate the feasibility of opening a second front, in event of conflict between the Army and the Mormons, whereby military personnel could be transported on steamers to the mouth of the Virgin River. From this point the troops might march overland into Utah.

The Ives expedition did not reach the Virgin, discovering instead that the portal of the Black Canyon was the head of navigation for the Colorado. After mapping the Black Canyon area, Ives steamed downstream reaching the Mojave Indian country by mid-March. He was surprised to learn that a group of Mormons led by Jacob Hamblin, the famous missionary, had been circulating among the Indians establishing friendly alliances. The Mormons feared that Ives might be bringing an army into Utah and contrived a plan to place a spy aboard the *Explorer* to learn his intentions. Acting according to Hamblin's instructions, a Mormon named Thales Hastings Haskell posed as a renegade from Utah seeking help and was taken aboard the steamer. He was identified as a bishop in the church, however, by one of the men who claimed to have seen him in Utah. Haskell was summarily put ashore unharmed, but only after he had supposedly overheard the "treacherous Yankees" tell horrible stories about the Mormons and what they intended to do to them. Tension continued to rise as both the Mormons and Ives' party questioned the motives of the other. Möllhausen, for example, anticipated a Mormon-inspired Indian attack and overemphasized the prospect that the entire party would be killed. In a letter written to his wife, he described how the fifty-five men of the party camped in a wooded area along the river and were surrounded by two to three thousand Mojaves "who were incited by the Mormons, and who owing to their fearful painting and by their weapons of war, and the absence of their women and children and owing to the shooting of one of our mules, only too clearly gave evidence of their hostile intentions."[15]

Fortunately, however, the expedition reached the Mohave Valley — near the confluence of the present boundaries of Arizona, Nevada, and California — without being attacked by the natives. When a mule train arrived from Fort Yuma on March 18, Ives began preparing for his second assignment, the overland journey. He divided his men into two contingents, sending Captain Robinson back to Fort Yuma by boat with the crew and the hydrographers. He himself led a land party, including Möllhausen, to the Grand Canyon via Diamond Creek. Guided by Iritaba (also spelled Irataba), whom Ives praised as "the best Indian that I have ever known," and other Mojave Indians, the men rode their mules over Lieutenant Edward F. Beale's new wagon road to a point near the present site of Kingman. Turning north, they then passed through the domain of the dwarfish Walapais and descended into the Lower Granite Gorge, becoming the first white men of record to reach the floor of the canyon. Here Möllhausen had a heyday sketching scenes of the magnificent gorge and the scientists recorded their geological observations. The expedition then returned to the rim and bade farewell to the Mojave guides, after rewarding Iritaba for his loyalty with two mules in the name of the "Great Grandfather in Washington." A few days later, the party reached a tributary of the Havasu Canyon and, on April 13, attempted to descend along a trail that was less than a foot wide in places. The men and mules were stretched out along the steep path "like a row of insects crawling upon the side of a building."[16] But the mules could not accomplish the descent all the way to the bottom of the canyon and the explorers had to retrace their dizzying and weary way to the top.

From the canyon the party skirted the southern slopes of the cool San Francisco Peaks and reached the Little Colorado River in early May. Sending Möllhausen ahead to Fort Defiance with the main body of the expedition, Ives took a small detachment in a futile attempt to reach the Colorado again by way of the Hopi villages. The Hopis were unwilling to guide him to the river, but a delegation of the tribe accompanied him to Fort Defiance to seek redress for grievances caused by Navajo raids. The Navajos were showing signs of disaffection at the time of Ives' arrival at the fort and his reunited party began the journey to Albuquerque none too soon. "Only a fortnight afterwards," he later reported, "hostilities broke out between the tribe and the United States troops, which would have seriously imperilled our safety had they commenced while we were still in the Navajo territory. As it was we reached the settlements on the Rio Grande without interruption."

Ives had to return to Fort Yuma to dispose of the steamer; he took the stage from Santa Fe to El Paso, and from that place went by way of the southern overland mail route. Meanwhile, Möllhausen and the other members of the expedition went eastward over the Santa Fe Trail to Fort Leavenworth and continued on to New York and Washington. Möllhausen was back in Berlin by September 1. His travels formed the basis for a career in writing. Aptly called the "German Cooper," he wrote no less than forty-five novels or books of short stories, his western experiences giving him the original impetus for this prolific output. It was his sketches, however, that were most precious to him. Though not a great painter, Möllhausen had an opportunity to portray the primeval terrain of the Colorado River basin and the native inhabitants whose culture was still almost untouched by the white man. His drawings give us an invaluable pictorial record at a time when Anglo-Americans were just beginning to migrate into the wilds of Arizona.

PARKE

When the Corps of Topographical Engineers, Department of War, began its comparison of the relative merits of various proposed railroad routes, the lack of information available on the 32nd parallel route became apparent. Details on passes, grades, roadbeds, and resources of the country that might support a railroad were needed. Accordingly, Lieutenant John G. Parke, who had been surveying passes along both the 32nd and 35th parallels in California, was appointed to investigate a possible route between the Pima villages on the Gila and

El Paso. Receiving his orders on December 20, 1853, Parke quickly organized an expedition of 58 men and had the survey under way in January. The Gadsden Purchase Treaty was not yet consummated but Santa Anna's government gave permission for the work to proceed through Mexican territory.

Stopping in Tucson with an escort — under the command of Lieutenant George Stoneman, who served later as the commander of the Military Department of Arizona and as governor of California — Parke camped beside the Santa Cruz River which had a stream of clear running water a foot deep and six feet wide. Leaving Tucson, described as a flat-roofed adobe town of 600 inhabitants whose livelihood depended upon agriculture, the expedition started out on the approximate route of Cooke's wagon road. In order to locate a shorter route, however, the men took a cut-off over the emigrant trail known as Nugent's Wagon Road. They passed through the Chiricahua Mountains at the Puerto del Dado (Apache Pass), crossed the salt plains to the Rio Grande, and reached the town of Molino just above El Paso by a direct approach. In general, the relatively level terrain was found to be the main advantage of the 32nd parallel route. The lack of timber and water was the greatest drawback. Parke reported that there were only nine localities along the route where a permanent water supply was available and recommended that experiments be made in the drilling of artesian wells.

In 1855, he made a more detailed survey and discovered two alternate routes which had definite advantages over the one surveyed through Tucson the year before. Another pass was located north of Puerto del Dado, between the base of Mount Graham and the Chiricahua Mountains; it was 580 feet lower in elevation. From Railroad Pass, as he called it, the "Aravaipa route" skirted the base of the slopes of Mount Graham and entered the Aravaipa Valley which was followed to the San Pedro and down that river to the Gila — a distance of 345 miles from the Rio Grande to the Pima villages in comparison to 406 via Tucson. A second alternate went directly from Railroad Pass to the San Pedro and down that stream to the Gila; it was 31 miles shorter than the Tucson route. The number of summits to be crossed would be reduced from 10,

General John G. Parke

Library of Congress

by way of Tucson, to 7, via San Pedro, or 6, via Aravaipa. The maximum grade would be lowered from 93 feet per mile on the Tucson route to 60.3 feet per mile on the Aravaipa, but would be raised to 100 feet per mile on the San Pedro.[17]

Parke's report on his exploration contained an adequate description of the topography and scenery; it also included a favorable recommendation for the construction of a railroad. But 25 years were to elapse before a railroad was built across southern Arizona. Like Whipple, Parke served meritoriously in the Union Army during the Civil War and received his brevet as a major general before it was over. In 1887, he became Superintendent of the United States Military Academy at West Point.

GRAY

In 1855, Andrew Belcher Gray, who had been a controversial member of Bartlett's boundary commission, was employed by the Texas Western Railroad Company to survey a possible route across southern Arizona. This company was composed of wealthy and influential Southerners who liked the way Gray opposed the Bartlett-Condé line whereby the Mesilla Valley would have been relinquished to Mexico. The president of the board of directors was Robert J. Walker of Mississippi,

Andrew Belcher Gray

Title Insurance and Trust Company,
San Diego, California

an ex-Secretary of the Treasury under President Van Buren
and leader of the Lower California filibuster; the vice president
was Thomas B. King, ex-governor of Georgia. In 1852, these
men secured a charter from the Texas legislature, which also
gave the company sixteen sections of land for every mile of
track laid across the state to El Paso; the directors were anxious
that the first transcontinental railroad should be a southern
one. Gray's survey crew consisted of only nineteen men but
they were nearly all hardy Texas Rangers who knew how to
deal with a crisis when they faced it. Among them was Peter
R. Brady, who settled in Arizona after the railroad survey was
completed and engaged in business, stock raising, mining, and
politics. The artist of the expedition was a German named
Charles Schuchard, who sketched pictures of the Chiricahua
Mountains, Babocomari ruins, Calabasas, Fort Yuma, and
many other scenes to illustrate the places and landmarks along
the way. He made Tucson his home and was among the asso-

ciates who filed claims to several mines including the Salero and the Heintzelman.*

On the basis of his observations, Gray recommended two acceptable alternate routes — both by way of Tucson rather than via Parke's San Pedro or Aravaipa shortcuts. He explained that the route through Apache Pass and thence directly to Tucson was perhaps the most expedient. The second route was longer but also had advantages; it went through the Chiricahuas at the Pass of the Dome (south of Apache Pass and 402 feet lower in altitude) to the San Pedro River, via the cool valleys of the Babocomari and Sonoita tributaries to Tubac, and down the Santa Cruz to Tucson. The remainder of the Gray survey followed the well-trod trail to the Pima villages, Fort Yuma, and to the terminus at Los Angeles.

Despite Gray's favorable recommendation on the feasibility of building a railroad, however, the Texas Western never got around to laying rails to California. In the early 1870s, the Texas and Pacific Railroad received a Congressional land grant, 80 miles wide across the whole of Arizona for a railroad by the Gila route to San Diego. But financial problems proved insurmountable. It was the Southern Pacific, building eastward from Yuma, without a grant, that reached Tucson in 1880, and connected with the Santa Fe at Deming, New Mexico, the following year.

Like Brady, Schuchard, and several other members of the survey party, Gray came to Arizona after the expedition was finished. Settling in Tucson, he was employed to survey and mark the lines for the Indian reservations on the Gila and to locate a copper mine about twenty miles east of Florence. But when Texas seceded from the Union in February, 1861,

---

*Heintzelman mentioned Schuchard several times in his diary. For example, after describing activities at the Cerro Colorado mine in 1858–1859, including the installation of a furnace and an amalgamation works, Heintzelman made the following interesting entry for January 26, 1859: "On Sunday, after dinner (2½ p.m.) the Overland stage arrived [at Tucson] with three passengers. Mr. Schuchard & I got seats [$150 each to the railroad connection at Tipton, Missouri]. We had no trouble about our baggage, though both of us had a little over 40 pounds allowed. There were in the stage three rather hard looking characters. I afterwards learned that one was a butcher & I think a common gambler; another a broken down Fourth ward . . . politician & the third a green farmer from Arkansas, who took cattle to Calif. They did not make the most agreeable companions." See the diaries of Samuel P. Heintzelman in the Library of Congress, Manuscripts Division.

he offered his allegiance to the South. He served in the Army of the Mississippi as an engineer and helped plan the strategic defenses on Island No. 10. After the Battle of Shiloh, General Beauregard assigned Gray the task of strengthening Confederate defenses on the Mississippi. He was killed when the boiler in his river steamer exploded close to the Arkansas shore below Fort Pillow. Brady later described Colonel Gray in these words: "He was one of the most amiable and even tempered men that I ever met with. In all that trying trip I never saw him in the sulks nor down hearted . . . He was finely educated and in his profession, civil engineering, he had few if any superiors . . . I used to think he was insensible to fear, but he lacked discretion and did not seem to know what danger was."[18]

EL PASO – FORT YUMA WAGON ROAD

The first trans-territorial route built across southern Arizona for the California-bound migration was a wagon road, not a railroad. And though it was the soldiers of the Corps of Topographical Engineers of the Department of War that explored and surveyed the region, it was the civilians of the Department of the Interior who were designated to construct the road. In 1857, Congress responded to the pleas of westerners for better transportation facilities by appropriating $600,000 for four roads to the Pacific, putting the Interior department in the road building business for the first time. The Topographical Engineers had dominated the federal road building program from 1850 to 1857, but they were too slow to satisfy men like Senator John B. Weller of California. He said that the Engineers were too interested in collecting geological and botanical information to build roads, whereas private contractors would "wield shovels and pickaxes with vigor."[19] Three of the four new roads were assigned to the Department of the Interior which set up the Pacific Wagon Roads Office to coordinate the new program.

One of the roads was to run from the town of Franklin, north of El Paso, to Fort Yuma.* On the basis of his previous experience, Jesse B. Leach of Stockton, California, was appointed superintendent of construction. He had improved one

---

* At that time, Franklin was present-day El Paso and El Paso was present-day Juárez.

road in Utah under contract with the War department, built canals and railroads in Ohio and Michigan, and served as the quartermaster agent with the Doniphan expedition during the Mexican War. Appointed as his chief engineer was N. Henry Hutton, a veteran of the Whipple and Parke surveys. Lesser positions were treated as political patronage; personnel records reveal that service to the Democratic party in pivotal states was the main qualification for appointment. The selection of mechanics and foremen was left to Superintendent Leach who spent months touring the eastern part of the country, not only to hire the needed men but also to outfit the expedition with equipment, wagons, and supplies. The men and property were assembled in forty wagons at Memphis, Tennessee and then moved overland to El Paso. The first group of thirteen mule-drawn wagons was under Leach's direction and covered the 1300 miles to El Paso in 114 days, arriving on October 22, 1857. The supply-laden, ox-pulled wagons, twenty-seven in number, did not catch up with Leach at Mesilla until June 25, 1858, two days short of a full year after their date of departure from Memphis.

Not much road building was done during the interim, though the Superintendent divided the available men into working parties. He personally supervised improvements on the Franklin to Mesilla segment. Assistant Engineer N. P. Cook was directed to set up a camp in the Pima villages on the Gila to work toward Yuma while another group of laborers worked east from Yuma; Leach wisely hoped to complete much of this western sector during the cool winter months. Another main camp of sixty men, mainly Mexicans, was established on the San Pedro River to clear the brush.

Parke's railroad route was thoroughly reexamined but was abandoned in several places. Engineer Hutton left the Rio Grande farther north to pass through established watering places since not enough money was appropriated for digging all the wells needed. The engineering party also attempted to locate a road along the Aravaipa route from Railroad Pass that was surveyed by Parke, but found the canyon too narrow for a wagon road. Parke's alternate San Pedro route was selected, but with modifications. The road went through Nugent's Pass

and struck the San Pedro River, 13 miles below Parke's survey.
The right bank was followed to the mouth of the Aravaipa.
The road crossed the San Pedro at this point and ascended the
Tortilla Mountains lying between the San Pedro and the Gila;
the bank of the latter was reached 15 miles west of the mouth
of the San Pedro. The rocky spurs on the Gila were thereby
avoided, the route was shortened, and expenses in construction
were correspondingly reduced. Continuing on down the south
bank of the river to Maricopa Wells, the road, with minor
exceptions, retraced the route into Yuma, followed by Kearny
and Cooke in 1846–47. Hutton estimated that emigrants would
save 47½ miles by adhering to this route, and have the running
water and grass of the San Pedro Valley.

The road was 18 feet wide on straight stretches and 25 feet
wide on the curves. Improvements consisted mainly of clearing
away brush, boulders, and timber. An attempt was made to
smooth road surfaces and to reduce grades, particularly in the
Gila Valley. In making side cuts or in building up the road bed,
over 50,000 cubic yards of dirt and stone were excavated. The
three wells, nine tanks, and one reservoir which were constructed increased the water potential along the road by some
300,000 gallons and reduced the greatest distance between
camps to 27 miles. Hutton boasted that future emigrants would
save five-days travel time and the road would encourage settlement of the San Pedro and Gila valleys. The southern overland
Leach road cannot be compared, of course, with the super-
highways that traverse the state today, but it was at least the
equivalent of other federal wagon roads of the 1850s.

Unfortunately, however, the expedition's bookkeeping
was at best inefficient. Once the party left Memphis, Leach's
disbursing agent, M. A. McKinnon, was with the ox-train and
therefore could not countersign vouchers as required for the
purchase of needed items. Discrepancies in the accounting of
funds before the departure from Memphis were also uncovered.
An investigator from the Department of the Interior found at
least a dozen merchants who testified that the amounts they
received for supplies or animals did not coincide with the figures on the vouchers. The 65 mules bought for the expedition,
for example, in reality cost $8,612.60; they were reported by

Leach's assistant, D. Churchill Woods, to have cost $11,817. And one New York firm was paid $1,692 for shipping wagons and other property, including ten barrels of alcohol and forty boxes of wine, to Memphis, but Woods cleared $3,406.60 of government funds to pay the bill. What happened to the difference? Hoping to recover part of the expenditures, the government indicted Leach, who was bonded, for falsified and forged vouchers totaling over $10,000. The Department of the Interior, however, dropped this fraud case against Leach in the Washington, D. C. Criminal Court because the difficulty of procuring witnesses in the remote parts of Tennessee and Texas made an early trial impossible. He was still held accountable, however, for a shortage of $23,003.05 in funds. A compromise settlement of $13,400 was proposed by the Interior department to cover the shortage. All interest in the cash deficiency was terminated by the outbreak of the Civil War, however, and there is no record of any amount having been paid to the government by Leach.

Meanwhile, Secretary of the Interior Jacob Thompson — a southerner who resigned from the cabinet in April, 1861, when President Lincoln sent a ship to relieve Fort Sumter — had attempted to salvage something from the financial chaos surrounding the El Paso-Fort Yuma road. He contracted with Captain Charles P. Stone to improve a section of the road from the Pima villages on the Gila east and south to the mail station of Ojo Excavada (now in New Mexico). The amount spent by Stone on the repairs and to provision his work crew of about thirty men was $10,829.44. Thompson returned an unexpended and unstolen $3,535.60 to the Treasury surplus fund from the original appropriation of $200,000.[20] Thus the total cost of the Leach road was $196,464.40.

It is difficult to compare the Department of the Interior's 32nd parallel experiment in road building and the Army's 35th parallel wagon road located about the same time by Edward Fitzgerald Beale. The Army had more experience in such matters and was free from political influence in the selection of personnel. The Secretary of the Interior may have had the Army "know-how" in mind when he took advantage of a clerical omission in the appropriation bill for overland roads to the Pacific. The section of the law that authorized $50,000 for the construction of a road along the 35th parallel — west of Fort Defiance to the Colorado River — failed to specify which department would be in charge of the project. Secretary Thompson used the ambiguity in the law to leave construction under the direction of the Secretary of War. Actually, the new road program under the Department of the Interior continued the same federal policy under which the national government assumed the obligation of improving transportation in the territories; there was a shift only in administrative responsibility, and apparently the Secretary of the Interior was not as eager to take on the new burden as Congress was to transfer it. By securing control of construction on the 35th parallel wagon road, the Army preserved the continuity of its role as the nation's chief road builder. Beale was honored for his work and given a political appointment by President Lincoln while Leach, in the light of investigation and public scrutiny to which the Army was not subjected, was dishonored. Yet, the importance of Leach's accomplishment cannot be underestimated. The magnitude of his project — pushing across half a continent to build a road in the other half — is in itself remarkable. Part of the road was soon used by Butterfield mail coaches, emigration across the desert country was made easier, and settlement adjacent to the road followed its completion. The national hold on the Southwest was strengthened. And, ironic as it may have seemed to Thompson as he sat behind Confederate lines, the road was one of the routes over which Colonel James H. Carleton's California Column moved during the Civil War to wrest New Mexico from the grasp of the South.

AUBRY

For some time, the government had been interested in establishing a wagon road along the 35th parallel route for the benefit of emigrants going to California. The route had been recommended for both a railroad and a wagon road by François Xavier Aubry, a Santa Fe trader of French Canadian origin, who made two round-trip journeys from Santa Fe to San Francisco between November, 1852 and August, 1854. He drove sheep westward to the California market and explored the country for possible railroad and wagon roads on his eastward trips, thereby combining his private business with a project of public interest. In 1852, he took ten large wagons, about 3500 sheep, 100 mules, and a number of horses to San Francisco by way of Tucsón and Los Angeles. After returning to New Mexico across northern Arizona,

Most of Aubry's crew of sixty men remained in California and the small returning party of ten Americans, six Mexicans, and a Negro cook was an inviting target for harassment by Indians in Arizona whom Aubry called Garroteros. These natives — probably a Yuman group named by the Spaniards after their pestle-shaped war clubs, called *garrotes* in Spanish — began stalking and shooting arrows at the well-provisioned party on August 3, 1853, in or near a valley in northwestern Arizona now named for Aubry. On August 14, in the vicinity of present-day Flagstaff, the Garroteros switched tactics. They came into Aubry's camp feigning friendship by concealing all their weapons and bringing along their women, children, and babies. After milling around awhile, the Indians gathered in the camp, supposedly to depart peacefully. But then the chief signaled for a planned massacre by holding on to Aubry's hand after grasping it in a gesture of farewell. The Garroteros had intended to beat each member of the white party to death with clubs that were hidden in the animal skins wrapped around the children and babies. Nearly all of Aubry's men were wounded in the surprise attack, but they were equipped with Colt revolvers and quickly dispersed the Garroteros, killing at least twenty-five and removing a few scalps. Continuing eastward to Santa Fe, Aubry presented a gift-wrapped Garrotero scalp to the startled editor of the *Weekly Gazette* and submitted a report to Governor David Meriwether of the Territory of New Mexico. Writing optimistically, he said, "I am satisfied that a railroad may be run almost mathematically direct from Zuñi to Colorado [the river], and from thence to the Tejon pass in California."[21]

Aubry then joined with other prominent men in Santa Fe, gathering together approximately 50,000 sheep to drive to California. At Albuquerque, in October, 1853, the drovers found Lieutenant Whipple making preparations for his exploration of the 35th parallel route and Aubry furnished the inquisitive officer with a copy of the journal from his first trip. The Santa Fe party arrived in Los Angeles with its huge flock on January 10, 1854, and then continued on to San Francisco where the sheep were sold. On July 6, Aubry departed from San José in command of sixty men. He pulled a wagon to make a trail across the same route — roughly along the 35th parallel he had explored the year before — and arrived in Santa Fe on August 18, just forty-three days after his departure. During this journey, he occasionally crossed his own earlier trail and that of Whipple's.

Aubry had no sooner returned than he was involved in an altercation with Richard Weightman, a Santa Fe attorney and Mexican War veteran who favored the 32nd parallel route for a railroad. Weightman first came to New Mexico in 1846, with Kearny's Army of the West. He was present at the occupation of Santa Fe and fought with gallantry at the battle of Sacramento in Chihuahua. After New Mexico — which then included Arizona north of the Gila — was established as a territory in 1850, Weightman was elected the delegate to Congress. For a time, he edited a newspaper in Albuquerque called *Amigo Pais* and evidently had printed an article on Aubry's first trip to California that was not to the latter's liking. Weightman was in the Mercure brothers' store when Aubry entered to buy a drink and the two men exchanged insults. When the editor was accused of printing inaccurate information in the then defunct newspaper, he threw a tumbler of liquor in Aubry's face. The angered Aubry drew his pistol but was fatally stabbed in the abdomen with a Bowie knife before he could take careful aim.

After this unfortunate affair, which was ruled justifiable homicide since the victim had drawn his revolver first following a quarrel, Aubry's travel notes from his last journey were printed in the *Missouri Republican*. They contained much valuable information relative to the nature and resources of the country through which he passed. Aubry's private diaries were studied in Washington and stirred the government to make further exploration. Meanwhile, Weightman returned to Missouri where he cast his lot with the Confederacy during the Civil War.

BEALE'S WAGON ROAD

In 1857, Edward Fitzgerald Beale was chosen by Secretary of War John B. Floyd to build a road along the 35th parallel and, at the same time, to conduct an experiment with camels as beasts of burden in the Southwest. Beale had served as a young naval officer under Commodore Stockton in California during the Mexican War. Though wounded, he and Kit Carson demonstrated gallantry in action by slipping through enemy lines to bring aid from San Diego for Kearny's "Army of the West." In October, 1847, he served as a witness for John C. Frémont in the latter's court martial trial in Washington, D. C. During a period of two years he made six ocean-to-ocean journeys across the continent. On the second of these trips he brought the first authentic and official news of gold discovery in California and a bag of the precious metal to the nation's capital. During one trip to Washington, he talked with Secretary of War Jefferson Davis, Floyd's predecessor, and demonstrated enthusiasm for a novel plan of using camels to transport supplies to army posts in the Southwest.* His appointment as superintendent for the Fort Defiance to Colorado River wagon road project was partly influenced by his willingness to merge the camel experiment with the road building.

Beale left San Antonio with his wagon train and camel caravan on June 25, 1857. Two months later he was at Zuñi ready to move into the wilderness. The most direct route was south of Fort Defiance, but to comply with the Congressional stipulation that the eastern terminus be located at the fort, Beale left his train at Zuñi and rode north with twenty men through Navajo country in order to officially start the wagon road reconnaissance at the post. The legal requirements having been fulfilled, the detachment returned to Zuñi and the combined party moved westward along the 35th parallel. Occasionally crossing Whipple's trail, Beale led his expedition along a route close to the Little Colorado and turned west near the northern outlet of Devil's Canyon. The trail was

---

*Beale became interested in the possibilities of using camels in western America after reading Abbe Hue's *Travels in China and Tartary*.

Lt. Edward F. Beale, U.S.N. Disguised as a Mexican, Beale rode across Mexico with dispatches telling of the discovery of gold in California and with a sample of it. He beat the Army carrier by a month and appeared before Congress to tell his story.

marked by the wheels of the wagons and distances were recorded with an odometer. The route westward — by way of Leroux and Lewis Springs to Mount Floyd — lay north of the present towns of Flagstaff and Williams. The Colorado was reached north of the site of Needles, California, at the southernmost tip of the present state of Nevada.

The road work was kept to a minimum on this first exploratory trip, the main objective being to seek out terrain that would be passable for wagons. After crossing the river, Beale took his camels to his ranch near Fort Tejón, ninety miles north of Los Angeles. To test their resistance to cold weather, the animals were left near the summit of the Sierra Nevada where they seemed to thrive in several feet of snow.

After a brief trip to Los Angeles to recruit and refit his party, Beale returned eastward to determine if his new road could be traveled in mid-winter as well as in summer. He and twenty picked men crossed the Colorado aboard the steamboat *General Jesup* on January 23, 1858, and reached the initial campsite near Fort Defiance on February 21. The last entry in his journal summarized the trip:

A year in the wilderness ended! During this time I have conducted my party from the Gulf of Mexico to the shores of the Pacific Ocean, and back again to the eastern terminus of the road, through a country for a great part entirely unknown, and inhabited by hostile Indians, without the loss of a man. I have tested the value of camels, marked a new road to the Pacific and traveled 4,000 miles without an accident.[22]

Beale had no doubt about the practicality of a wagon road through the country along the 35th parallel. Ardently advocating improvements along the route, he submitted his journal to the House of Representatives and asked for additional appropriations. "I have written it for emigrants more than for show," he wrote in a letter to Speaker James L. Orr. "I have described things as I found them...."

... As far as the San Francisco mountain the road needs scarcely any other improvement than a few bridges. In one place alone a bridge at Cañon Diablo would save twenty-five or thirty miles of travel ... as this will inevitably become the great emigrant road to California, as well as that by which all stock from New Mexico will reach this place, it is proper that the government should put it in such a condition as to relieve the emigrant and stock drivers of as many of the hardships incident to their business as possible. For this purpose I would recommend that water dams be constructed at short intervals over the entire road. With these and a few bridges and military posts I do not doubt that the whole emigration to the Pacific coast would pursue this one line, instead of being divided and scattered over a half a dozen different routes ... I presume that there can be no further question as to the practicability of the country near the thirty-fifth parallel for a wagon road, since Aubrey, Whipple and myself have all travelled it successfully with wagons, neither of us in precisely the same line, and yet through very much the same country....

I regard the establishment of a military post on the Colorado river as an indispensable necessity for the emigrant over this road ... scattered emigrant parties with their families, and the confusion of inexperienced teamsters, rafting so wide and rapid a river with their wagons and families, would offer too strong a temptation for the Indians to withstand.

Another appropriation of $100,000, to build bridges, cut off elbows and to straighten the road from point to point, and to make other improvements and explorations, will be required for the present year.

I feel assured that the public lands, which would be brought into the market and sold within three years after the opening of this road, will repay four-fold the appropriation asked. . . .[23]

The House rejected an appropriation to complete the road and the Senate failed to take action, but the Department of War succeeded in squeezing $100,000 from the Army Appropriation Act of 1858 to complete the wagon road west of Albuquerque. Beale was retained to make the improvements needed, and soon began putting together a motley group at Fort Smith, Arkansas. His road crew, including a military escort, consisted of 130 men. There were three Indian guides and hunters: Jesse Chisholm, a half-breed Cherokee; Dick, a well-trained Delaware; and Little Axe, a Shawnee. Several mail stages and emigrant parties also joined up to secure the protection of numbers. And Beale had his Negro manservant and constant companion, Absolum, who was making his third transcontinental trip. On March 3, 1859, the expedition reached Albuquerque and rested for five days. Besides building temporary bridges on the Puerco and Little Colorado Rivers and smoothing the road, the men located water sources along the way. West of the San Francisco Mountains, the road was graded, large rocks removed, springs cleaned, and watering places provided not more than thirty miles apart.

Beale had sent a clerk to California by way of El Paso with orders to have his camels sent to the Colorado with supplies. He was delightfully surprised one day to see two of his mail-laden dromedaries approaching from the west, one ridden by Hadji Ali who had accompanied him on the 1857–1858 trip.* Fortunately for Beale, a military escort of some 700 had escorted the camel party as far as the Colorado where they were forced to engage 1000 Mojave warriors in battle near the banks of the river. On May 1, 1859, Beale and

---

* Better known as "Hi Jolly," his name is usually seen spelled Hadji Ali. He signed his name "Hadji Alli," however, in a letter written from Fort McDowell on November 6, 1871. See letter of Hadji Alli from Fort McDowell to Captain J. L. Johnston, AAQM, Tucson, November 6, 1871, in the Fort McDowell Post Correspondence, RG 98, National Archives.

thirty-five of his men marched ahead of the road building crew, anticipating possible trouble with the Indians, but instead were met by troops whose commander, Lieutenant Colonel William Hoffman, had ended hostilities by forcing the Mojaves to sign a treaty of peace. The expedition then established a camp on the west bank of the Colorado and spent the next two months improving the western end of the road between Saavedra's Spring and the river. This part of the completed roadbed was pronounced good enough for six-mule team wagons carrying 3,500 pounds.

Meanwhile, Beale had gone to California and returned with supplies for the return trip which began on July 2. Though marching rapidly, he stopped long enough at Floyd Peak (northeast of present-day Seligman) to pick mint, open a bottle of brandy brought along for snakebite, and prepare what was perhaps the first, if not the last, mint julep ever tasted on that mountain side. By July 29, the expedition was back in Albuquerque, having covered the entire distance from the Colorado River in 108 hours of traveling. His funds exhausted, Beale was unable to construct bridges and further improve the stretch of road between Albuquerque and Floyd Peak. His days as a wagon road builder at an end, he returned to his ranch in southern California and later accepted an appointment as surveyor general of California and Nevada from President Lincoln.

Throughout his survey work along the 35th parallel, Beale had recognized the importance of a wagon road on that route to prove that a railroad also could be constructed there. His work prepared the way for the chartering of the Atlantic and Pacific Railroad in July, 1866. The A and P collapsed financially during the Panic of 1873, but was incorporated into the Atchison, Topeka, and Santa Fe system. By 1883, the Santa Fe had linked Albuquerque and Needles by rail and secured the lapsed land grants of the A and P from Congress.

UNCLE SAM'S CAMELS

By far the most unusual aspect of the Beale expedition was its use of camels. The idea of using these foreign animals as beasts of burden in the Southwest was not new. But it was not until March, 1855, that Congress finally got around to appropriating $30,000 to implement the pet scheme of Jefferson Davis, then Secretary of War. Davis was enthusiastic about experimenting with camels for military purposes. He hoped that camels would solve some of the transportation problems of the Southwest, especially through the waterless desert areas and over the rugged mountains where horses and mules suffered severely. Eager to get his project underway, the Secretary commissioned Major Henry C. Wayne to purchase camels in the Near East. Some thirty-odd of the dromedaries were transported on the *Supply,* commanded by Lieutenant (later Admiral) David Dixon Porter, to Indianola, Texas, where they arrived in May, 1856.

The camels were taken to Camp Verde, about sixty miles northwest of San Antonio, where they were joined by forty-four more animals which came the following February. After a period of training and acclimatization, the camel herd was ready for the big test. About two dozen of them were assigned to Lieutenant Beale's survey expedition which left San Antonio on June 25, 1857. The caravan also included eight mule-drawn covered wagons, fifty-six men and 350 sheep. This strange procession reached New Mexico without mishap and departed from the Zuñi villages near the end of August.

Beale had nothing but high praise for his awkward-looking creatures of the desert. On September 21, 1857, he wrote this entry in his journal:

> My admiration for the camels increases daily with my experience of them. The harder the test they are put to the more fully they seem to justify all that can be said of them. They pack water for others four days under a hot sun and never get a drop; they pack heavy burdens of corn and oats for months and never get a grain; and on the bitter greasewood and other worthless shrubs not only subsist but keep fat; withal they are so perfectly docile and so admirably contented with whatever fate befalls them. No one could do justice to their merits or value in expeditions of this kind, and I look forward to the day when every mail route across the continent will be conducted and worked altogether with this economical and noble brute.[24]

Beale's experimentation showed that the animals could bear heavy loads over long distances without water and arrive at their destination in good condition. They seemed to be of

National Archives

The Beale Expedition looking for water. Note camels in the background. The original of this painting, done by Narjot in 1867, was presented to the Museum of Kingman, Arizona, by Mrs. Truxton Beale, widow of Beale's son.

inestimable value in Arizona. On one occasion, for example, the camels were used to pack water for the mules when an ignorant guide led the party more than thirty miles from the nearest spring. And they were often used on reconnaissance while the mules rested.

Despite Beale's eulogy for the camels, however, there were factors that prevented further experimentation by the government. For one thing, the men, horses, and mules did not like the strange, malodorous beasts. It was difficult to get anybody except imported camel drivers to have anything to do with them. Pack trains and wagon teams often panicked with the approach of the camels. Some reports indicate that the camels were also unsatisfactory because their soft-padded feet were literally cut to pieces by the dry, rocky ground of the Southwest. Be that as it may, however, there is no doubt that the Civil War caused a suspension of interest on the part of the government as the western roads suddenly seemed less important and were hence neglected. In the post-war period, railroads linked East and West, thus precluding any need for the dromedaries. "Operation Camel" was a romantic episode in the history of Arizona, though in retrospect we can see that its importance was dwarfed by the construction of Beale's wagon road.

Surprisingly enough, however, the Army's experiment with camels did not end the story of those noble beasts in the Southwest. Most of the animals that Beale took to his ranch near Fort Tejón in California were later transferred to the quartermaster at Los Angeles and sold at public auction.* Some of them were purchased for parks or circuses and by ranchers, who hitched them to buckboards. Eventually, however, many of the camels were abandoned to live in a wild state. All sorts of weird, fascinating, and improbable tales have been told about these roaming camels and their descendants which were encountered in Arizona. One of the more plausible stories was reported about a camel which was captured near Phoenix in 1905, and sold to a saloon keeper. One day the animal escaped from his corral and trotted through the saloon into the street. Pandemonium reigned as scared horses bolted and scattered wagon loads of farm produce over half of the town. There were many other yarns told by prospectors and desert travelers, some of them undoubtedly true.

A few of the stories concern Arizona's "happy little Turk," who was not a Turk at all, but a Syrian born in 1828. This man's Arab name was Hadji Ali, but he was known as

---

* Three of the camels were sent to Fort Mojave in 1861 to be used by Sylvester Mowry, the U.S. Commissioner in charge of surveying the eastern boundary of California. See the *Los Angeles Star,* February 2, June 22, and October 5, 1861.

*Hadji Ali
and his bride*

"Hi Jolly," a name that suited his likeable personality and willingness to work. One of the camel drivers imported to care for the "ships of the desert," he first crossed Arizona with the Beale expedition. After making the journey to California, Hi Jolly did some gold mining before settling down as a scout with the U.S. Army in Arizona. While with the Army at Tucson in 1880, he was naturalized Philip Tedro, U.S. citizen, and a short time later married Gertrude Serna of that town. His wife had to raise their two daughters, however, because Hi Jolly grew tired of married life and, in 1889, returned to prospecting. He lived in the desert around Quartzsite, about eighty miles north of Yuma, where from time to time, he captured one of his hump-backed friends, which had been turned loose on the desert, and used it on his trips. Occasionally, his earnings would enable him to settle in California for awhile.

One story is told about how his name was once left off the invitation list for a picnic sponsored by the German colony in Los Angeles. Knowing the reaction of horses to camels,

Hi Jolly vindictively harnessed two huge beasts to a cart and drove into the midst of the picnic area. When the resulting disturbance was over, the countryside was strewn with wiener-wurst, broken halters, and disabled buggies.

Hi Jolly's later life was not so exciting. He lived at Quartzsite, where he died in poverty on December 16, 1903. In spite of all his years in the service of the U.S. Army, the camel driver was ineligible for a pension since he had never enlisted. But in his declining years he was assisted by the ranchers and prospectors who knew and loved him. Since 1935, his grave has been marked by a pyramidal stone monument which is topped appropriately by a copper camel. Fittingly enough, the ashes of Topsy, the last survivor of the camel herd, repose in the monument. She was put to sleep by a Los Angeles zoo in 1934, outliving Hi Jolly by a third of a century.

OVERLAND VIA "JACKASS MAIL"

One of the earliest results of the migration of eastern people to the Pacific coast, following the discovery of gold, was an insistent demand for adequate communication between the old East and the new West. The public was not content with the monthly service of the Pacific Mail Steamship Company, via Central America. There was high hope that a railroad would someday span the continent, but meanwhile the West demanded regular mail and stagecoach services.

The first mail and passenger line that operated across Arizona to the Pacific was started in July, 1857. The route ran from San Antonio, Texas, to San Diego, California, by way of El Paso, Tucson, and the Yuma crossing — where Louis Iaeger ferried coaches, mules, and passengers across the Colorado. Designated simply as "Route 8076" in the contract given to James E. Birch, the line was derisively called the "Jackass Mail" because mules were usually used to pull the coaches and to pack the mail and passengers over the 180-mile stretch of the Colorado Desert between Fort Yuma and San Diego. The Postmaster General, Aaron V. Brown of Tennessee, apparently chose the route in anticipation of a railroad eventually to be built connecting the South to the west coast.

He awarded Birch an annual subsidy of $149,800, with the stipulation that a semi-monthly service be scheduled to leave San Antonio and San Diego on the ninth and twenty-fourth of each month — thirty days allowed for each trip.

To get the line under way, the first mail was dispatched from San Antonio on July 9, 1857, just seventeen days after the contract was signed with the government. With four men, James E. Mason traveled by horseback to El Paso. Here, the crew took a coach and had proceeded as far as Ciénega de Sauz (near the San Pedro River in southern Arizona) when they were overtaken by a second party which left San Antonio on July 24 in charge of Henry Skillman who had come in a coach the entire distance. The two parties moved on together as far as the Pima villages, finding water in three or four places in the eighty-mile desert between Tucson and the Gila. From this point, Mason took both mails and, with one companion, pushed on with pack mules, making the trip to San Diego in nine days across the worst part of the entire route. The arrival of the first two mails at noon on August 31, in the time of 54 and 39 days respectively, prompted the *San Diego Herald* to issue an "extra" edition expressing its pleasure and the satisfaction of people all along the line.[25] The service continued to improve, the fifth trip being made in 26 days and 12 hours. After the arrival of the mules on that occasion, October 6, 1857, the *Herald* announced the "complete triumph of the southern route notwithstanding the croakings of the opponents of the administration."*

Actually, however, the service of the San Antonio and San Diego Mail Line was inefficient and unsatisfactory. Although there were 87 stations listed on the original itinerary, only three of them, the two terminals and El Paso in between, had adequate buildings. The largest and most important station between El Paso and San Diego was at Maricopa Wells in Arizona — the dividing line where eastbound and westbound mails met and turned back. Like some of the other so-called station stops, it had a brush corral and an adobe

---

* *San Diego Herald*, October 10, 1857. The trip from the Pima villages to San Diego was made in 4 days and 6 hours, the shortest time on record.

OVERLAND TO THE PACIFIC.

The San Antonio and San Diego Mail-Line.

ADVERTISEMENT OF AN OVERLAND STAGE LINE
Mark Twain paid $150 for a ticket from Missouri to Nevada by another line.

Security Pacific National Bank, Los Angeles

Advertisement of the San Antonio and San Diego mail and passenger line

hut. The majority of the stations were merely camping places. Traveling by day and camping at night, or vice versa, was a slow and uncomfortable routine.

Southern politicians were hoping to popularize the route, but service was really slower than the roundabout Panama route. The people in northern California looked at the "Jackass Mail" line as a mystery. According to them, "the line ran from no place through nothing to nowhere" and might just as well have run from San Antonio to Guaymas, Mexico. An eastern traveler reaching New Orleans, for example, could take a 540-mile steamer ride to Indianola, Texas, and transfer to a four-horse carriage going 140 miles to San Antonio, where the line began. The journey to the western terminal at San Diego covered 1,476 miles. Once on the Pacific Coast, the passenger could board a California Steam Navigation Company vessel to San Francisco. Add to this indirect method of getting between populous centers of the east and west, a tiring ride by mule-back that sometimes started in Tucson, a long stretch of desert to be crossed, the lack of comfortable facilities and stations, and the threat of Indian attacks in some sections. Is it any wonder that the line failed to gain public favor? The San Antonio-San Diego Mail Line also carried the lightest mail load in the Post Office Department. Total postal earnings for the one year that the line operated over the entire route amounted to only $601.

An excellent diary, in which some of the hardships and dangers of traveling on the "Jackass Mail," are described, was kept by Phocion R. Way. A native of Ohio who was employed by the Santa Rita Mining Company of Tubac, the thirty-one year old Way rode in mule-drawn vehicles, including one called an ambulance, from San Antonio as far as Tucson between May 22 and June 11, 1858. In the entries of June 10, 11, and 12, Way described the journey through Apache country and gave a dismal picture of Tucson in the late 1850s:

Arizona Department of Library and Archives, Phoenix

Sketch of ambulance used in the mail line, drawn by Phocion R. Way

June 10th. We passed through a range of mountains yesterday — Chiricahua mountain range of Sierra Madre—in a deep and wild looking dado pass [Apache Pass]. The mountains rise on either side from 600 to a thousand feet above our heads, and in many places it presented a perpendicular wall of rock for a great height, with only just space enough for one wagon to pass between. Near the end of this pass is the Apache Spring. This is a bad place for the Indians. The spring is half a mile from the road in a canon [sic], and I and three others were appointed to stay and guard the wagon while the rest shouldered their rifles and went after the water. About 5 o'clock we passed over another range of mountains. It was a very rough passage and reminded me of Bonaparte crossing the Alps. We finally got over — wagons, mules and all — but it was a laborious task. We encamped last night in the midst of a beautiful valley between two ranges of lofty mountains. We saw Indian fires on the mountains all around us but we were not molested. The continuing howling of the wolves was the only annoyance we had to complain of.

We started at daylight this morning and are now 12 o'clock stopping at Dragon [Dragoon] Springs.... We expected some trouble at these springs as the Indians are numerous around here and very hostile. They rob and murder white men whenever they can ... We have to go a mile up a deep ravine or canon [sic] with craggy rocks and low shrubbery on either side — a fine hiding place for Indians. Our captain exhibited more anxiety here than he has done anywhere on the road. We examined our arms and prepared everything for a fight. The captain took six men and started after the water ... We picked our way to the spring, looking cautiously on every side and driving our mules before us. We were not attacked.... We are too strong a party to be in much danger.... Left Dragoon Springs about one o'clock. Saw no Indians....

We are now camping on the San Pedro river to get our suppers. It is a small, short and muddy river. It empties into the Gila. I have just been bathing in its murky waters and feel much refreshed ... We are now about 70 miles [from Tucson]. We follow this stream 6 or 7 miles and then we strike out west and leave it. If no accident happens, we will be in Tucson tomorrow night....

June 11th. Camped last night about 10 miles this side of the San Pedro. Hobbled our mules, stationed our guard, and retired to rest on the ground as usual. Started at daylight this morning. Traveled 8 miles and stopped at the de los Pimas Creek for breakfast....

June 12th. Arrived at Tucson about 6 o'clock last evening. We had heard bad reports of this town all along the route, and we were fully prepared to see a miserable place — and we were not in the least disappointed. It contains about 200 inhabitants, all Mexican and Indians with exception of about a dozen....

Col. Walker, the Indian agent here, is very much of a gentleman and highly esteemed by all classes of people. Mr. Robinson, a merchant and trader, is a good looking, generous, wholesome Kentuckian. Mrs.

Robinson, his wife, is the only American lady in this place. . . . An older brother of Kit Carson [Moses Bradley Carson] also resides here. . . . The Mail Party is here and there are some Callifornians [sic] here but they are not residents of the place. The mail company do not run their stages farther than here, and those who paid their passage through must ride over a sandy waste on mule back and furnish the mule themselves, or stay here and get the fever and ague. This is a most rascally imposition and the company will very likely have to pay for it. . . .

The houses here are all adobe and miserable ones at that. . . . The hogs wallow in the creek, the Mexicans water their asses and cattle and wash themselves and their clothes and drink water out of the same creek. The Americans have dug a well and procure tolerably good water, which they use. There are a few acres of land along the bottom cultivated by irrigation . . . if hell is any hotter than this I don't want to go there.

At present there are a number of Apache and Pimos Indians encamped near town. There are a small band of what the Indian agent calls tame Apaches. They are friendly to the whites, but the great body of the nation are at war with all the rest of mankind. . . .

There is no tavern or other accomodation [sic] here for travelers, and I (was) obliged to roll myself in my blanket and sleep either in the street or in the corral, as the station house had no windows or floor and was too close and warm. The corral is where they keep their horses and mules, but I slept very comfortably as the ground was made soft by manure. I would rather have slept in the street as a great many of the natives do, but it is hardly safe for a stranger. Someone might suppose that he had money about his person and quietly stick a knife into him in the night, and no one would be the wiser — there is no law here, or if there is it is not enforced. Might makes right.

Yesterday a dispute occurred between two men about something, when one of them shot the other dead on the spot. The man is running at large and no particular notice is taken of it . . . The murdered man's name was Batch, on his way home from California and stopping here for a few days. I guess King Alcohol was at the bottom of all the trouble. . . .

Among the native women here I believe that chastity is a virtue unknown. Some of the young girls are pretty. They are remarkable for the ease and grace of their movements and their brilliant black eyes. . . . One of our party named Beardsley seems to be a great favourite with the senorittas [sic], and has a fine looking black-eyed girl for his especial favourite. He is laying on the ground within six feet of me at this moment fast asleep, while she is setting by his side keeping the flies from disturbing him. . . .

We could not hire any kind of conveyance in this God forsaken town for Tubac. So we were compelled to send an express to Col. Poston informing him of our arrival. . . . I will not be sorry when we get off, for it is hard living. There is no place to board and not much to eat in the d — d town. There was no fresh meat to be had and we would have been in a bad fix if the mail party had not kindly invited us to eat with them. Even they could procure nothing and were compelled to live on the remains of their provisions they had on the road, a little bacon and coffee and bread so hard from age that you could not bite it. They have to do their own cooking and all travelers must do the same or hire a Mexican to do it for them. Our fare, as bad as it is, is better than the average in this town. We spread an old greasy cloth on the ground in the corral. Some of the hungry citizens watched us while we were at our meals, and when we were through they eagerly devoured the scraps. I have just learned that our captain has succeeded in buying a roast of beef. If this proves to be true, won't we have a feast today?[26]

The San Antonio and San Diego Stage Company was not responsible for the conditions that existed along its route, but no one was really pleased with the service in any respect. The company blazed the trail, however, for the more ambitious Butterfield line. And as a feat in rapid improvisation, the "Jackass Mail" is worthy of esteem. During the company's brief period of existence, it employed 65 men and accumulated fifty coaches and 400 mules. Yet, only forty trips were made along the full length of the route before it was curtailed. Financing was a problem at first, since Birch died at sea before the first trip was completed. His contract was transferred to G. H. Giddings and R. E. Doyle, however, and these men continued running the company, even after the better-organized Butterfield line commenced operations in September, 1858. The El Paso to Fort Yuma portion of the route through Arizona was the only part over which both companies operated; so in December, 1858, the San Antonio and San Diego Stage Company cut its services down to the two ends. Schedules on the shorter routes, San Antonio to El Paso and San Diego to Fort Yuma, were improved to provide weekly trips. In 1860, however, the Fort Yuma service was eliminated too, leaving the line only its Texas runs. A new mail contract was given to the San Antonio and San Diego Company after Butterfield suspended service over the southern route in the spring of 1861. The hostility of the Apaches, after the outbreak of the Civil War, however, prevented the contractors from starting up again, except for a couple of trips in the summer of 1861. The "Jackass Mail" then took its almost unheralded place in the history of pioneer transportation in the Southwest.

BUTTERFIELD OVERLAND MAIL

The first dependable well-organized transcontinental stage line was the Butterfield Overland Mail, which began operation on September 16, 1858. John Butterfield was guaranteed an annual federal subsidy of $600,000 for six years to provide semi-weekly service in each direction on a twenty-five day, or less, schedule. With the help of financiers, mainly in New York state, he organized a joint stock company with a capital of $2 million and selected a route that could make use of existing wagon roads and railroads where practical. People in the North who opposed the line called it the "ox-bow route" because of the deep southward bend which it made as it swung from the eastern terminals, St. Louis and Memphis, to San Francisco. The *Chicago Tribune* called it "one of the greatest swindles ever perpetrated upon the country by the slaveholders." But Postmaster General Aaron V. Brown made no apologies for the southern route. "The Department supposed Congress to be in search of a route that could be found safe, comfortable, and certain during every season of the year," he said. The route covered over 2700 miles, going through Texas to El Paso, westward to Tucson, down the Santa Cruz to the Pima villages on the Gila, west to Fort Yuma, and on to San Francisco by way of Warner's Ranch and Los Angeles.

The company spent a year making careful preparations. Butterfield facilitated operations by breaking the line into nine subdivisions, each in charge of a superintendent. Altogether some 750 men were employed as station attendants, stage drivers, shotgun messengers, hostlers, blacksmiths, and managers. Stagecoaches and wagons were purchased and moved to designated points so that passengers and luggage could be shifted into a fresh coach about every three hundred miles. The large Concord coach, built by Abbot-Downing Company in Concord, New Hampshire, cost about a thousand dollars and was used mainly near the eastern and western terminals of the route. It had an oval-shaped body resting on straps slung between the front and rear axles. This type of suspension enabled the body of the coach to roll rather than jerk or bounce when the wheels hit obstructions. Nine to twelve people could be seated inside, depending on the

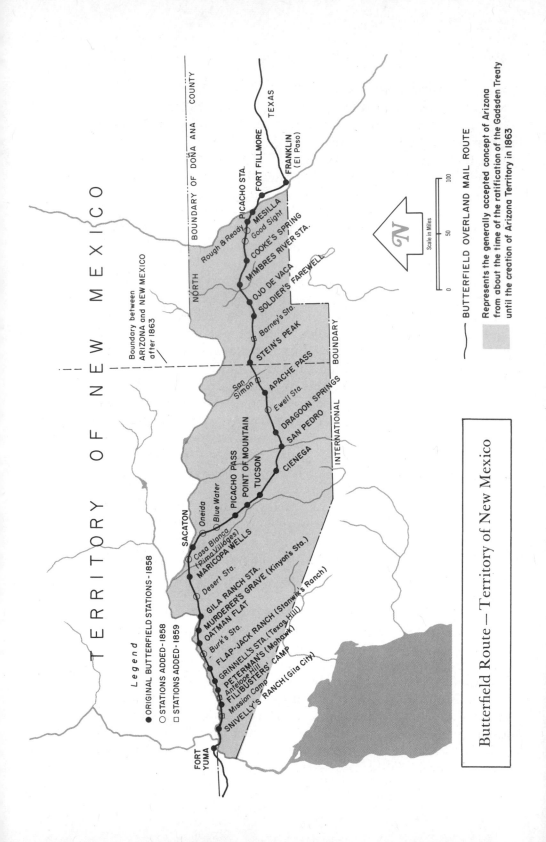

TERRITORY OF NEW MEXICO

BOUNDARY OF DOÑA ANA COUNTY

TEXAS

FORT FILLMORE

FRANKLIN (El Paso)

PICACHO STA.

Rough & Ready
MESILLA
Good Sight
COOKE'S SPRING
MIMBRES RIVER STA.
OJO DE VACA
SOLDIER'S FAREWELL
Barney's Sta.
STEIN'S PEAK
San Simón
APACHE PASS
Ewell Sta.
DRAGOON SPRINGS
SAN PEDRO
CIENEGA

NORTH

Boundary between
ARIZONA and NEW MEXICO
after 1863

INTERNATIONAL BOUNDARY

Oneida
Blue Water
PICACHO PASS
POINT OF MOUNTAIN
TUCSON

SACATON
Casa Blanca
(Pima Villages)
MARICOPA WELLS
Desert Sta.
GILA RANCH STA.
MURDERER'S GRAVE
OATMAN FLAT
Burk's Sta.
FLAP-JACK RANCH (Stanwix's Ranch)
GRINNELL'S STA. (Kinyon's Sta.)
PETERMAN'S (Mohawk)
Antelope Hill
FILIBUSTERS' CAMP
Mission Camp (Gila City)
SNIVELLY'S RANCH (Gila City)

FORT YUMA

N

Scale in Miles
0   50   100

—— BUTTERFIELD OVERLAND MAIL ROUTE

Represents the generally accepted concept of Arizona
from about the time of the ratification of the Gadsden Treaty
until the creation of Arizona Territory in 1863

Legend
● ORIGINAL BUTTERFIELD STATIONS - 1858
○ STATIONS ADDED - 1858
□ STATIONS ADDED - 1859

Butterfield Route—Territory of New Mexico

GOING WEST

Leave	Days.	Hour	Distance place to place.... Miles	Time allowed Hrs	Average miles per hour......
St. Louis, Mo., and Memphis, Tenn..................	Mon. & Thur.	8:00 AM	—	—	—
P. R. R. terminus, Mo.......	Mon. & Thur.	6:00 PM	160	10	16
Springfield, Mo.............	Wed & Sat	7:45 AM	143	37¾	8 79
Fayetteville, Ark.	Thur & Sun	10:15 AM	100	26½	3.79
Fort Smith, Ark	Fri. & Mon.	3:30 AM	65	17¼	3.79
Sherman, Texas...........o..	Sun. & Wed	12:30 AM	205	45	4½
Fort Belknap, Texas.........	Mon & Thur.	9:00 AM	146½	32½	4½
Fort Chadbourne, Texas......	Tues. & Fri.	3:15 PM	136	30¼	4½
Pecos river (Em. cross).......	Thur. & Sun.	3:45 AM	165	36½	4½
El Paso....................	Sat. & Tues.	11:00 AM	248½	55¼	4½
Soldier's Farewell...........	Sun. &.Wed.	8:30 PM	150	33½	4½
Tucson, Arizona............	Tues. & Fri.	1:30 PM	184½	41	4½
Gila river, Arizona..........	Wed. & Sat.	9:00 PM	141	31½	4½
Fort Yuma, Cal,...........	Fri. & Mon.	3:00 AM	135	30	4½
San Bernardino, Cal.........	Sat. & Tues.	11:00 PM	200	44	4½
Fort Tejón (via Los Angeles)..	Mon. & Thur.	7:30 AM	150	32½	4½
Visalia, do.................	Tues. & Fri.	11:30 AM	127	28	4½
Firebaugh's Ferry, do........	Wed. & Sat.	5:30 AM	82	18	4½
Arrive					
San Francisco..............	Thur. & Sun.	8:30 AM	163	27	6

GOING EAST

Leave	Days.	Hour	Distance place to place.... Miles	Time allowed Hrs	Average miles per hour........
San Francisco, Cal............	Mon. & Thur.	8:00 AM	—	—	—
Firebaugh's Ferry, Cal.......	Tues. & Fri.	11:00 AM	163	27	6
Visalia, Cal.................	Wed. & Sat.	5:00 AM	82	18	4½
Fort Tejón (via Los Angeles to)	Thur. & Sun.	9:00 AM	127	28	4½
San Bernardino, do..........	Fri. & Mon.	5:30 PM	150	32½	4½
Fort Yuma, do..............	Sun. & Wed.	1:30 PM	200	44	4½
Gila river, Arizona..........	Mon. & Thur.	7:30 AM	135	30	4½
Tucson, Arizona............	Wed. & Sat.	3:00 AM	141	31½	4½
Soldier's Farewell...........	Thur. & Sun.	8:00 PM	184½	41	4½
El Paso, Texas..............	Sat. & Tues.	5:30 AM	150	33½	4½
Pecos river (Em. cross)......	Mon. & Thur.	12:45 PM	248½	55¼	4½
Fort Chadbourne, Texas......	Wed. & Sat.	1:15 AM	165	36½	4½
Fort Belknap, Texas.........	Thur. & Sun.	7:30 AM	136	30¼	4½
Sherman, Texas.............	Fri. & Mon.	4:00 PM	146½	32½	4½
Fort Smith, Ark.............	Sun. & Wed.	1:00 AM	205	45	4½
Fayetteville, Ark.	Mon. & Thur.	6:15 AM	65	17¼	3.79
Springfield, Mo.............	Tues. & Fri.	8:45 AM	100	26½	3.79
P. R. R. terminus, Mo.......	Wed. & Sat.	10:30 PM	143	37¾	3.79
Arrive					
St. Louis, Mo., and Memphis, Tenn	Thur. & Sun.	—	160	10	10

Schedule of the Butterfield Overland Mail Company between St. Louis and San Francisco. (From The First Overland Mail: Butterfield Trail)

Concord coach used on the Butterfield stage line

model, and additional passengers rode on the top. Mules instead of horses and a lightweight coach called the "Celerity Wagon" were usually used on the long, hot southwestern stretches of the trail; these coaches were specially built for Butterfield by James Goold and Company of Albany, New York. They were more adaptable to rough mountain and desert travel; the seats were not upholstered and could be folded down to provide beds for the passengers.

The construction of stage stations, usually about twenty miles apart, was a major task. Various materials were used, though adobe was the most common in Arizona — where there were seventeen stops along a 437-mile trail, between Fort Yuma, California, and Stein's Peak in New Mexico. Each station was protected by a wall and several armed men. Expensive hay and corn had to be stored for the horses and mules, which numbered about 1500 in all. Finally, everything was ready and the stages rolled along the trails. Butterfield's instruction to his drivers was, "Remember boys, nothing on God's earth must stop the U.S. Mail!" This seemed to be the organization's creed. Before the line was transferred to the central

Modified Concord coach also used by Butterfield

route, by Congress at the outbreak of the Civil War in 1861, some 111 Americans and 57 Mexicans met violent deaths. Yet the stage line was late only three times at the end of the line, a most remarkable record.

The Apache war against the Overland Mail was concentrated mainly on the stealing of horses, mules, and cattle. The isolated stage stations were made to order for the Indian strategy of maximum gain for minimum risk. Preferring stealth to open confrontation as their means of acquiring plunder, the Apaches could easily keep a few men occupied while driving off the herd. In contrast to this typical pattern of operation, an attack on a stage offered only small gain for the risk involved. Yet there was always the possibility that the Apaches might try to annihilate the whites since they had little fear of the small military force stationed in Arizona. The increasing hostility of the Apaches and the uneasiness of the non-Indian population by 1860 is indicated in the following excerpt from a letter written by Thompson M. Turner, the Arizona correspondent for the *Missouri Republican* (St. Louis), on January 14:

The driver of the Overland Mail stage brought the news on his last trip that friendly Indians at Apache Pass had given intimations of extensive preparations for a total extermination of the Overland Mail line through their country, to be followed by a descent upon the settlements. Everything seems to portend lively times here for a season. Should this information prove correct, you may look for the success of their efforts in interrupting the transit of the mail which will prove a calamity not only to our sparse population but to the whole nation. If they decide upon this step, they can with ease massacre the men at the stations and seize the exchange horses. Then there remains nothing more to be done but to seize the coaches which, with proper precaution on the part of conductors, will be a more difficult task. But the temporary interruption of intercommunication may be looked for with confidence. There can be no doubt that the Apaches are unfriendly and will annoy the Americans all in their power.[27]

In earlier years, 1858 and 1859, the Chiricahuas were more friendly and even had a contract with the Butterfield company to supply wood to the Apache Pass station (near modern Bowie). Perhaps one reason why the Apaches became increasingly more hostile is that they were better armed. With weapons and ammunition that they purchased from white traders or took from their victims, the Apaches were more independent and could act more defiantly as they did in the famous "Bascom Affair" at Apache Pass, in February, 1861. This incident not only intensified the hatred of Cochise — a Chiricahua chief — for white intruders, but it dramatized the Apache hostilities that were already underway. Cochise was accused by Lt. George Bascom, a young, inexperienced lieutenant from Fort Buchanan, of stealing livestock belonging to John Ward and of kidnapping the latter's stepson. In revenge for the lieutenant's holding of six Chiricahua Apaches — three men, a woman, and two boys — as hostages, Cochise captured a stage driver named James Wallace and three men in a wagon train that was encamped west of the Apache Pass station. Eight of the men in the same train were tied to the wagon wheels and roasted alive. Wallace and the three survivors were later tortured and their bodies left for the coyotes to devour. In retaliation Bascom ordered the hanging of Indian hostages, hoping thereby to discourage the Apaches from future outrages by a policy of "an eye for an eye and a tooth for a tooth!"

Not all of the atrocities were committed by the Apaches, however. Dragoon Springs station was the scene of a triple murder perpetrated by Mexicans back in September, 1858, just a few weeks before the arrival of the first stagecoach. Dragoon Springs was forty miles west of Apache Pass in the heart of a region which became known as the Cochise Stronghold. There were six Americans stationed there: Silas St. John, James Burr, Preston Cunningham, James Laing, William Brainard, and Frank de Ruyther. The latter two were away from Dragoon Springs on the night that the three Mexican employees attempted to murder the remaining Americans. Armed with axes and a stone maul, the assailants killed Burr and so mutilated the bodies of the others that only St. John survived. Despite the fact that he had a deep axe wound in his right hip and his left arm had been partially severed, St. John drove away the Mexicans and defended his dead or dying associates from wolves and buzzards for three days before help came. The frontier status of Arizona in 1858 is well-illustrated in this episode; nine days elapsed before a doctor, Bernard J. D. Irwin, could be brought from Fort Buchanan to amputate St. John's arm. Of course, no one was able to apprehend the murderers and collect the reward offered by the Butterfield company.

Within a month after his operation, St. John rode on horseback into Tucson where the first overland mail from the east had arrived on October 2, 1858. The only "through" passenger on that historic first coach was Waterman L. Ormsby, a reporter for the *New York Herald,* who wrote about the Dragoon Springs massacre in a letter to his newspaper. In later correspondence from San Francisco, dated October 13, 1858 — after a trans-Mississippi trip lasting twenty-three days and twenty-three and a half hours — Ormsby described Tucson and his journey on to the coast. Tucson was the end of the sixth division, assigned to Butterfield's friend, William Buckley, and the beginning of the seventh division that extended to Fort Yuma. Ormsby wrote that "Tucson is a small place, consisting of a few adobe houses. The inhabitants are mainly Mexicans. There are but few Americans, though they keep the two or three stores and are elected to the town offices."[28]

After leaving Tucson, the stage stopped at Point of Mountain (or Pointer Mountain), near the present Rillito railway depot, before arriving at the Picacho Mountain station. Ormsby stated that the latter had the first desirable water in the forty-mile stretch north of Tucson. He did not mention the Blue Water station, three miles east of modern Toltec, nor Oneida, near the Signal Peak school. But he did mention Sacaton, nearly forty miles northwest of Picacho, probably because he was fascinated by the Pima Indians there. He watched them butcher a beef animal and commented on their fine physical development, little of which was obscured from view because of scanty clothing. Ormsby noted that the men were lazy, as were the squaws, and had almost as much work to drive the women to their tasks as they would to do the work themselves.

The next station, down the Gila, mentioned by the New York reporter was at Maricopa Wells. Changing from horses to a mule team at this point, the stage then crossed the "Forty Mile Desert" to the Gila Ranch station with only one stop en route. Gila Ranch was about four miles north of the present-day town of Gila Bend and was, like Tucson and Fort Yuma, a time-table station. Continuing along the south bank of the Gila, the stage stopped at stations spaced from fifteen to twenty miles apart and with such interesting names as Murderer's Grave, Oatman Flat, Flap-Jack Ranch, and Filibuster Camp. At Snivelly's Ranch (Gila City station), which was about twenty-two miles from Yuma, there was an exchange of vehicles with the east bound stage. Ormsby thought he got the worst of the deal since he was transferred to a lumber wagon. Reaching Arizona City, originally called Colorado City and now named Yuma, the stage wagon was transported across the river on Iaeger's ferry at a cost of five dollars for the four-horse team. Fort Yuma, on the California side, was the last station of the seventh division of the line.

William Tallack, an English Quaker who was traveling from California on a Butterfield stage in 1860, wrote about the 150-mile stretch along the south bank of the Gila east of Fort Yuma as follows:

Breakfasted on venison at three A.M. at Stanwick's ranche on the Gila and, by special favor of the conductor had time for a plunge in the stream. On starting we noticed hereabouts the marks of several recent Indian campfires. A month subsequently to our visit here, two overland passengers, wishing to bathe in the Gila, and not having any extra time allowed for the stage to stop, borrowed horses from the ranche, had their bath, and rode after the others, overtaking them at the next station. But on the way they were assaulted by five Indians armed with bows and arrows. In self-defense, they killed three of the Indians, and so escaped to their fellow-travelers and the stage. . . .

We took our next meal at two P.M. at Gila Bend. This station had been destroyed by the Indians only four months previously, but the inmates escaped. More than a hundred arrows were afterwards picked up around the spot. . . .

At nightfall we reached the Pimo [sic] villages, a settlement of comparatively civilized Indians. . . . Near the station our attention was called to a "sweat-house," where the Indians get rid of fevers by a vapour-bath process.

Whilst our supper was preparing we washed in an Indian bowl formed of reeds, but quite watertight. Saucepans also of reeds are here made use of. They are filled with water, which is then boiled by dropping hot stones into it . . .[29]

With the opening of the Butterfield mail route, the destiny of Arizona looked upward. Though still a part of the territory of New Mexico, this region was to be an important link in the greatest overland transportation venture ever undertaken. At last the raw desert frontier was to have a connection with civilization both east and west. Yet, two events shattered the dream. One was the faster Pony Express which was begun in April, 1860, through Utah; the other was the coming of the Civil War. It was feared that a sectional clash might disrupt transportation over the southern route, so, in March, 1861, the Butterfield Stage was shifted north to the central route through South Pass and Salt Lake City. Thus ended the most dramatic and picturesque pioneer experiment in overland passenger and mail service across the vast stretches of the American Southwest.

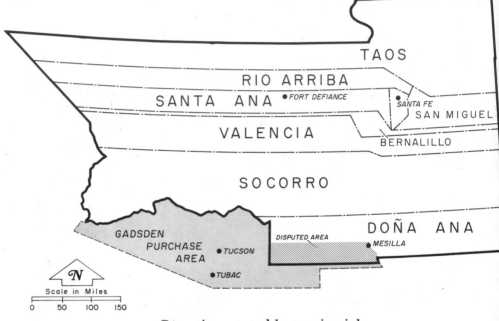

TAOS

RIO ARRIBA

SANTA ANA ●*FORT DEFIANCE*

SANTA FE

SAN MIGUEL

VALENCIA

BERNALILLO

SOCORRO

GADSDEN
PURCHASE
AREA ●*TUCSON*

DISPUTED AREA

DOÑA ANA

●*MESILLA*

●*TUBAC*

N

Scale in Miles

0   50   100   150

Counties created by territorial
legislature of New Mexico in 1852

Chapter 12

1850s: Government and Politics

ON DECEMBER 30, 1853, the Gadsden treaty was signed. Six months later, on June 30, 1854, ratifications were exchanged between President Franklin Pierce and the Mexican legation in Washington, D. C. With the completion of these negotiations, nearly thirty thousand square miles of land were acquired by the United States to fill in the now familiar profile of this country. The only bona fide settlers in the new domain, which was added to the Territory of New Mexico, were Mexicans.[1] Migration from the States to the wild country of Arizona came slowly, despite the ambitions of Southerners for a transcontinental railroad and the dreams of expansionists for another mineral bonanza. The constructive work of the few prospectors, merchants, ranchers, boundary·surveyors, road builders, and promoters who arrived seems remarkable considering the obstacles that impeded the progress of civilization. What the Apaches left undone in the categories of robbery, murder, and devastation, the renegades of Sonora and the desperate fugitives from vigilante justice in California or Texas completed. Without government, law, or strong military protection in what one traveler called the "paradise for devils," every man was armed and administered justice to suit himself. In 1855, the New Mexico legislature added the Gadsden Purchase lands to Doña Ana County for administrative purposes.* There was little evidence of any county rule in

---

*In January, 1860, the legislature of New Mexico created Arizona County from the western part of Doña Ana County. The county seat was at Tubac until January, 1861, when it was moved to Tucson. Then, in January, 1862, the lands in Arizona County were returned to Doña Ana County. See B. Sacks, *Be It Enacted*. Phoenix: Arizona Historical Foundation, 1964, p. 102, note 238.

James S. Calhoun, 1851–52

William Carr Lane, 1852–53

David Meriwether, 1853–56

Abraham Rencher, 1857–61

Henry Connelly, 1861–66

Photos Museum of New Mexico

Governors of the Territory of New Mexico prior to the separation of Arizona in 1863. Each governor, until 1857, served also as Superintendent of Indian Affairs, and was involved in matters concerning the Navajo Indians. Meriwether did not complete his term; the territorial secretary fulfilled the duties until Rencher was appointed.

what is now southern Arizona, however, except on the occasions when a criminal was sent to the county seat at Mesilla.

The political situation in this region was aptly described on March 3, 1859, by Edward E. Cross, editor of the state's first newspaper, *The Weekly Arizonian,* at Tubac:

We commence today the publication of a weekly newspaper under the above title, devoted to the interests of Arizona and the development of its resources. The territory we have selected for our home is unlike any other portion of the United States. Separated on the one hand by the broad, unsettled wastes of Texas and New Mexico from the Atlantic States and on the other from the golden sands of California, it resembles neither region in its climate, soil or resources. Attached as we now are nominally to the Territory of New Mexico, and situated many hundred miles from its seat of government, the western portion of Arizona is a region without the shadow of anything that claims to be law. The highest crimes may be committed and justice never overtake the fugitive. So far as we know, no judge or justice, either Federal or Territorial, has ever visited this portion of the country. One great object we shall have in view will be to advocate the establishment of law and government in Arizona.

It was only natural that political activity in Arizona in the late 1850s should center around agitation for civil government and for the creation of a separate territory. The territorial officials resided in far away Santa Fe. Before the Gadsden Purchase — from 1850 to 1854 — the location of the capital of the huge Territory of New Mexico made little difference, since the area north of the Gila was for the most part unsettled. Theoretically, this region was divided horizontally by the westward extension of the New Mexican counties, of which Socorro County was the largest. The only Anglo-American settlement was Fort Defiance — a military post in what is now northeastern Arizona — established in September, 1851, by Colonel Edwin V. Sumner as a base from which to operate against the hostile Navajo. Not until 1859 was another post built north of the Gila. In that year, Major L. A. Armistead located Fort Mojave on the east bank of the Colorado upon the recommendation of Lieutenant Beale. The fort served as a shelter for California-bound emigrants and as a base of operations against the Mojave Indians.

Like the Spaniards and Mexicans before them, the frontiersmen from the States were attracted to that part of Ari-

zona which lies south of the Gila. It was there that a demand
for law and order first arose. By the time the last Mexican
troops left Tucson in March, 1856, there were already a
number of Americans residing in the Gadsden Purchase.
Among the earlier arrivals were Pete Kitchen, John W. Davis,
John B. "Pie" Allen, Mark Aldrich, Hiram S. Stevens, and
Charles D. Poston.* William H. Kirkland was there when the
Mexican soldiers left; at the time of their departure, he and
two companions lashed several mesquite poles together to
make a staff for a flag — furnished by a local merchant named
Edward Miles — and unfurled the American colors over Tucson for the first time.† Some Arizonans who might have
observed the stars and stripes flying over Mile's adobe store
were Fritz and Julius Contzen, Theodore Green Rusk, Nelson
Van Alstine, William Henry Harrison "Paddy" Burke, William H. Finley, John Muncie, and V. S. Shelby as well as
Kitchen, Davis, and others. Among the prominent Mexican
citizens in Tucson at the time were Jesús Elías, Juan Santa
Cruz, Solano León, Guillermo Tellez, Ignacio Pacheco, Francisco Romero, Ignacio Sais, and Ignacio Ortiz.

By the summer of 1856, many people who lived in the
Gadsden Purchase were advocating a separate political existence. Following the example of residents in the Rio Grande
area — who met at Mesilla earlier in the year — pioneers of
the southwestern part of the New Mexico Territory, both
Anglo and Mexican, met at Tucson on August 29. Protesting
that their local needs were ignored by officials in distant
Santa Fe, and that they had no laws, no courts, no vote, and

---

*At the time the Mexican soldiers departed, Charles D. Poston, one of Arizona's
first pioneers, was in Cincinnati helping to form a company to reopen some of the
abandoned silver mines of southern Arizona. See B. Sacks, "Origins of Fort Buchanan,"
Arizona and the West, Vol. 7, No. 3 (Autumn, 1965), pp. 208–209. See also "Diary of
Charles Debrille Poston" in Sharlot Hall Museum, Prescott, Arizona (the diary is
also on microfilm, Records of the States of the United States of America, Library of
Congress, 1949, Arizona XX, Reel 1a.). John Warner Davis, the least known pioneer
on this list, came to Arizona in 1854 in the employ of Don Manuel Gándara, who
served several times as the governor of Sonora. Davis worked as a barber and as a
clerk in mercantile stores, dying in Yuma in 1884. See Hayden File in Arizona
Department of Library and Archives.

†See the William H. Kirkland File, Arizona Historical Society. Lt. Col. Philip St.
George Cooke, leader of the Mormon Battalion, may have raised the United States
flag in Tucson when he stopped there in December, 1846, but the town was then a
part of Mexico.

no representation in any legislative body, the assembled citizens drew up a memorial to Congress asking that Arizona be organized as a territory separate from New Mexico. Stretching from the Colorado River on the West to the Rio Grande on the east, the proposed territory would comprise the land south of 34 degrees 20 minutes. The memorialists also asked for the "speedy settlement of land titles . . . for the protection of mining interests, for the establishing of post routes, and the subjugation of the hostile Indian tribes that infest the territory. . . ."[2]

The president of this historic convention was Mark Aldrich of Tucson, who had arrived from California in 1855. Selling Mexican products, he was the first Anglo-American to operate a store in the Old Pueblo; he also served as the first U. S. postmaster and the first *alcalde* of that town. Other officers of the convention were James Douglass, of Sopori, vice president; G. K. Terry and Willis N. Bonner, secretaries; and Nathan P. Cook, Granville H. Oury, Herman Ehrenberg, Ignacio Ortiz, and J. D. L. Pack, members of the Committee on Resolutions and Memorials. Oury, a Virginia-born Southern sympathizer, was sent to Santa Fe as a member of the legislature and Cook was elected delegate to Congress. The latter was denied a seat, but the memorial — with 260 signatures — was introduced in the House of Representatives on December 11, 1856, by Miguel A. Otero, the delegate from New Mexico. Congress passed no legislation in response to Cook's plea, but in December, 1857, President Buchanan recommended the establishment of a territorial government for Arizona. He stressed the need for efficient protection of American citizens and property, the rich agricultural and mineral resources, and the important mail routes across the proposed territory.[3]

The problems involved in operating mines on the unprotected frontier got the leaders of the mine companies into politics.* Sylvester Mowry, for example, was already in Wash-

---

* The first issue of *The Weekly Arizonian* (Tubac), March 3, 1859, contained a report on the mines. This newspaper was established by the Santa Rita Silver Mining Company in cooperation with its parent company, the Sonora Exploring and Mining Company.

Miguel Antonio Otero

Museum of New Mexico

ington lobbying for improved transportation facilities and more soldiers to control the Apaches. In September, 1857, he was elected "delegate" by a motley group of miners, soldiers, merchants, and settlers who gathered at Tubac. The residents at Tucson also endorsed Mowry as Cook's successor. The latter, though unsuccessful in securing territorial status, did not let the grass grow under his feet. He was appointed assistant engineer on the El Paso and Fort Yuma wagon road, for which he had been lobbying.

Mowry, like Cook, was refused a seat in Congress as a delegate. Member of a prominent Rhode Island family and a West Point graduate with a reputation as a lady's man, Mowry first became interested in Arizona's mineral wealth while a lieutenant at Fort Yuma from 1855 to 1857. Prior to the Civil War, he was the most zealous lobbyist seeking recognition for Arizona.* He wrote and circulated a pamphlet entitled *Memoir of the Proposed Territory of Arizona,* in which he advocated the union of the eastern and western portions of southern New Mexico — that is, all the land between Texas and California south of the 34th parallel.[4] He argued that this region was separated from northern New Mexico by natural geographic barriers and contained a growing Anglo population that wished to be independent of the Mexican Americans who dominated the legislature in Santa Fe. Mowry freely quoted the outstanding scientists, explorers, and army officers who had visited Arizona. He was assisted in Washington, D. C. by Major Samuel P. Heintzelman, the former commander at Fort Yuma who was then on leave from his post at Newport Barracks, Kentucky. Together, on March 1, 1858, the two soldiers-turned-statesmen presented a report on the Sonora Exploring and Mining Company to the chairman of the Senate Committee on the Territories, Stephen A. Douglas — only to be told that mining is poor business.[†]

Meanwhile, a memorial signed by 500 residents of the western portion of the Gadsden Purchase was placed in the *Senate Journal,* by sympathetic Senator William M. Gwin

---

* In the summer of 1857 Mowry was accepted as a delegate to the Southern Commercial Convention; he secured the passage of resolutions endorsing territorial status for the people of the Gadsden Purchase, the construction of a transcontinental railroad via El Paso and Fort Yuma, and the acquisition of a more southern boundary with a port on the Gulf of California. See the *San Diego Herald,* October 10, 1857, for article reprinted from the Knoxville *Register* of August 15. The best work on the career of Mowry is: B. Sacks, "Sylvester Mowry: Artilleryman, Libertine, Entrepreneur," in *The American West,* Vol. I, No. 3, (Summer, 1964), pp. 14–24, 79.

† *The Weekly Arizonian,* March 3, 1859. Several mining companies were doing well in southern Arizona including the Sonora Exploring and Mining Company with Heintzelman as president and Solon H. Lathrop as superintendent. From one furnace ten inches square the company was obtaining 300 to 400 ounces of silver per week. When a $30,000 amalgamation works was in complete operation the company expected to reduce about three tons of ore per day. Over a hundred men were employed at the Heintzelman mine. Other companies that were doing satisfactorily were the Patagonia Mining Company with Col. Douglass as superintendent, the Union Exploring and Mining Company under Col. Titus, the San Xavier Mining Company with Major Allen as president, and the Santa Rita Company that was working the old Salero mine with William Wrightson as president. According to an indenture recorded in Book B of Deeds, Doña Ana County, New Mexico, pp. 613–14, Mowry bought the Patagonia mine (later called the Mowry mine) on April 9, 1860, for $22,500 and other "considerations."

of California in December, 1857. Gwin also introduced a detailed bill, with no mention of slavery, to split the New Mexico Territory horizontally with the region south of the 34th parallel comprising the new Territory of Arizona. Early in 1858, the memorial was withdrawn from the Senate and later presented to the House by Delegate Otero. In March of that year, Mowry brought a second memorial to the attention of the Senate, this one signed by nearly a thousand residents living along the Rio Grande in the eastern portion of the Gadsden Purchase. The people of this section had been active for some time in the territorial movement. In 1856, they met at Mesilla and elected William Claude Jones as their delegate to Congress from the "Territory of Mesilla." Jones's official duties as U. S. Attorney of New Mexico kept him from proceeding to Washington, however, and Mowry, therefore, spoke for all the people in his proposed territory.

In addition to the promotional pamphlets mentioned above, Mowry tried to impress the lawmakers with earnest letters from such influential pioneers as Poston, Douglass, Granville Oury, Ehrenberg, Solomon Warner, and Peter R. Brady. Nothing seemed to move Congress — not even President Buchanan's second recommendation in December, 1858. On this occasion, the President said that the people "are practically without a government, without laws, and without any regular administration of justice. Murder and other crimes are committed with impunity."[5] The refusal of Congress to act might be explained by the intersectional rivalry over slavery. Northerners suspected that the Arizona territorial movement was part of some Southern scheme.

The residents of the Gadsden Purchase area continued to urge territorial organization, however. Before Mowry returned to Arizona — with an appointment as special Indian agent to distribute $10,000 worth of gifts to the Pima and Maricopa Indians on the reservation surveyed by Andrew B. Gray — a meeting was held at Arizona City on May 7, 1859. Besides praising Mowry for his exertions in Washington, D. C., the delegates passed resolutions explaining the need for a separate government for Arizona. In the following preamble, the chaotic conditions existing in the region south of the Gila were summarized:

*General Samuel P.
Heintzelman*

Library of Congress

... We have shown that we are wholly without government, that in the entire country, from the Rio Grande to the Colorado, a distance of six hundred miles east and west ... there are no counties, no civil officers, no laws, and that crime stalks abroad in our midst in open day. We have shown that Immigrant trains have been attacked ... and that marauding parties of ruthless savages and barbarous Mexicans, infest our Territory, deluging the country in blood, driving off our herds, producing constant dread and alarm in our midst, preventing immigration, impoverishing the people, and depopulating the country....[6]

One of the authors of the resolutions was Lansford Warren Hastings, a lawyer and the local postmaster, who later threw in his lot with the South after the Civil War broke out; he presented an elaborate plan to President Jefferson Davis for adding Arizona and California to the Confederate States and was commissioned a major in the Army of the South.

Other conventions were held at Mesilla and Tucson during June and July, 1859, to reaffirm resolutions which had been passed at previous meetings in those towns. Both conventions heard optimistic remarks from Mowry and resolved to boycott New Mexican elections. The Tucson convention also supported Mowry in his condemnation of the Tubac *Weekly Arizonian* and its editor, Edward E. Cross, for opposing the organization of a separate territory. All that was needed, according to the editor, was a judicial district with adequate law enforcement, courts, and a government surveyor's office — not a new territory.[7] It seems that Cross started this controversy, even before the *Arizonian* was founded, when he dispatched a story to the St. Louis *Missouri Republican* under the pen name of "Gila," saying that President Buchanan had exaggerated in estimating the number of people living in Arizona. That was on January 30, 1859. The following July 8, after a war of words between Cross and Mowry, the two protagonists fought a bloodless duel at Tubac over Arizona's population figures. The quarrel ended when Mowry purchased the *Arizonian* and moved it to Tucson with a new editorial policy. Cross subsequently abandoned his opposition and openly advocated separate territorial status, both in articles to the *Republican* and in an interview with President Buchanan.

Despite this display of unity, however, Congress continued denying all pleas for admission of Arizona as a new territory. By the spring of 1860, ten bills for this purpose had been defeated, and five elections for delegate — one in the Mesilla Valley (W. Claude Jones) and four in the western section of the Gadsden Purchase (Cook once and Mowry three times) — had been ignored. Finally, the inhabitants of "no man's land" took matters into their own hands at a convention held in Tucson, April 2–5, 1860. Delegates from thirteen towns in the Gadsden Purchase region drew up a provisional constitution for the Territory of Arizona which was to remain in force "until Congress shall organize a territorial government and no longer."[8] The new territory was to include all of New Mexico south of 33 degrees 40 minutes and was to be divided into four counties: Doña Ana, Mesilla, Castle Dome, and Ewell. The latter was named after the commander at Fort Buchanan, Captain Richard S. Ewell, who was to serve later as a Confederate general.

Dr. Lewis S. Owings of Mesilla — physician and later the first mayor of Denison, Texas — was elected governor and authorized to appoint a roster of officials to create judicial districts and to convene a bicameral legislature consisting of

Arizona Historical Foundation
Courtesy Rex W. Strickland

*Lewis S. Owings, physician from Mesilla, was
chosen governor of the provisional Territory of
Arizona organized in Tucson in 1860.*

nine senators and eighteen representatives. Most of the citizens
selected to fill the offices of the provisional government were
southern sympathizers who later helped the Confederacy
organize a territory with the capital at Mesilla. The extralegal
government established by the Tucson convention had a
limited existence but was assured a place in history by the
first imprint in English produced on an Arizona press. This
long-titled work — *The Constitution and Schedule of the
Provisional Government of the Territory of Arizona and the
Proceedings of the Convention Held at Tucson* — was published in 1860 by J. Howard Wells, editor of the *Arizonian*
and justice of the peace in Tucson.[9]

Several bills to give legal status to this provisional territory were considered by Congress. Chairman of the Committee
on Territories, Senator James S. Green of Missouri introduced

a bill to create a temporary "Territory of Arizona." This
resulted in protracted debate over the issue of slavery in the
territories in December, 1860. Most of the discussion centered
around conflicting amendments — one, offered by Senator
Albert S. Brown of Mississippi, guaranteeing protection for
slave property in the territory, and another, by Senator Lyman
Trumbull of New York, providing for the retention of
Mexico's antislavery law in lands acquired from that country.
The slave controversy overshadowed the question of territorial
status for "Arizuma." More territories (Colorado, Dakota, and
Nevada) were created in 1861, after the Southern states began
withdrawing from the Union, but with both Mowry and
Poston in Arizona, there was no strong lobby in the capital
to plead the cause for this territory. It was the Civil War that
brought about the passage of an organic act whereby Arizona,
with its present boundaries except for the northwest corner,
was created as a Union territory. Both the North and the
South coveted the lands between Texas and California for its
potential mineral wealth and as a possible route for a transcontinental highway of commerce between the South and
ports on the Pacific.

The South appeared to have the most support in the
territory at first. Another convention was held at Mesilla in
March, 1861; the delegates who attended voted to repudiate
the "Black Republican" administration of the recently inaug-
urated Lincoln and to unite with the Confederacy. Tucson
residents supported the new government and sent Granville
H. Oury to Richmond as delegate. In the summer, Lieutenant
Colonel John R. Baylor led his Texan troops across the Rio
Grande and formally took possession of the "Territory of
Arizona," becoming military governor on August 1. The
Confederate Congress was slow in recognizing this acquisition,
but about a month after Oury addressed that body on
December 18, 1861, a bill creating the Confederate Territory
of Arizona out of the region south of the 34th parallel was
passed and signed by President Jefferson Davis. Control over
this area, however, was ultimately decided by the superiority
of Northern arms in the Southwest, not by the Southern
sympathies of leaders at the political meccas of Mesilla and
Tucson.

CRABB EXPEDITION

A few months before Sylvester Mowry was elected "delegate to Congress" from the region south of the Gila, and Hi Jolly drove his camels across the northern mountains, a famous filibustering expedition passed through the territory en route to Sonora. This group of nearly a hundred disappointed gold seekers was recruited in California by Henry Alexander Crabb for the purpose of assisting in the overthrow of Manuel María Gándara, the governor of Sonora, who had refused to relinquish that office to his federally appointed successor, Ignacio Pesqueira. Frustrated in California politics, Crabb was eager to take advantage of the family feud in Sonora; he even dreamed of conquering the north Mexican state.

A native of Nashville, Tennessee, Crabb had entered the legal profession at Vicksburg, Mississippi, in 1845. He was soon involved in politics, but after killing a man in an election duel during the campaign of 1848, Crabb joined the gold rush to California. Seeking public office again, he ran as a Whig and eventually served in both houses of the state legislature. He also married into the house of Ainsa, a large and prominent Sonoran family, most of whom were living in exile in Stockton or San Francisco. Crabb ambitiously joined the Native American or Know Nothing Party and sought unsuccessfully to unseat U. S. Senator Gwin. After this defeat, Crabb looked to Mexico for action and soon formed the "Gadsden Colonization Company" as a disguise for the conquest of Sonora. In the spring of 1856, he visited Hermosillo and, through members of the Ainsa family still residing in Sonora, apparently entered into a secret bargain with the Pesqueira faction. By this agreement, he was to bring 1000 American adventurers into Sonora, ostensibly as colonists but in reality to aid in the overthrow of Gándara. Convinced that he had driven an opening wedge into Sonora politics for himself and his Ainsa kinfolk, Crabb hastened back to California to recruit volunteers.

He was undaunted by the failure of previous filibusters in Mexico, having himself given testimony in behalf of William Walker at the latter's trial in 1854. Walker was an adventurous southerner from Crabb's home town of Nashville whose filibuster in 1853 antagonized Mexico and embarrassed

Henry A. Crabb

Arizona Historical Society

James Gadsden who was negotiating for a treaty. On this venture, Walker led an expedition of water-front rowdies from Upper California to La Paz, declared himself "President of Baja California," and proclaimed Sonora to be a part of his republic. Threatened by hostile Mexicans and prevented from receiving supplies by customs officials in San Francisco, Walker ingloriously fled across the border from his "paper republic" into the waiting arms of the U. S. Army. Brought to trial for violation of neutrality laws, he was acquitted by a sympathetic jury in San Francisco.*

Despite the failure of the Walker filibuster and similar abortive attacks against Sonora, led by a French exile named Count Gaston de Raousset-Boulbon in 1852 and 1854, Crabb

---

*Supported by southern expansionists, Walker eventually succeeded in setting himself up as a dictator of Nicaragua, only to be killed before a firing squad in 1860.

believed that the Gándara-Pesqueira struggle presented him an excellent opportunity, not only for carrying out his proposed colonization project, but also for conquering the whole state of Sonora. Leaving his crony, General John D. Cosby, to supervise the recruitment and departure of later detachments, Crabb and a brother-in-law, John Cortelyou, led a small party from San Francisco in January, 1857.[10] A few other "Gadsden emigrants" presumably sailed at intervals for Sonora, but not as a consequence of Cosby's efforts. His duties as state senator from Siskiyou County suddenly became so onerous that his interest in the enlistment of "colonists" did not extend beyond the pocketing of the funds at his disposal.

Crabb disembarked at El Monte, near Los Angeles, to begin the overland trip to the Gadsden Purchase. After buying mules to pull his wagons, he pushed on via Warner's Ranch to Fort Yuma. Many of Crabb's followers deserted at this point, wanting no part of a Sonoran filibuster. About ninety men, however, ascended the Gila Valley for forty-five miles to a point where a stage station known as Filibuster Camp was later located. From this camp, Crabb dispatched two of his "Majors," Robert N. Wood and Charles W. Tozer, to Tucson, Tubac, and Calabasas to seek more recruits among the settlers of the Santa Cruz Valley. Concerning the latter expedition, Charles Poston later wrote: "I was then at Tubac, the headquarters of the Sonora Exploring and Mining Company as manager, and had control of large quantities of arms, ammunition, horses, saddles, and transportation, with quite [about] a hundred men, so they naturally applied to me to join the expedition with my force and means."[11]

Poston refused to help, explaining that he was opening mines at the time and depended on Sonora for supplies and labor. "I not only declined," he said, "but remonstrated with them against the expedition as unlawful and calculated to disturb the friendly relations then growing up on the border."[12]

In the meantime, Crabb's main party moved southeast from Filibuster Camp toward Sonoita, just south of the Mexican line. As had many travelers before them, the Californians suffered severe hardships in the dry *Camino del Diablo* country of southwestern Arizona. One of the two wagons and most of the mules were lost. About midway, at Cabeza Prieta, the filibuster leader made a desperate decision. Leaving Captain Freeman S. McKinney to come on more slowly with the one remaining wagon and a company of twenty men — some of them disabled — Crabb hastened with sixty-eight men toward Sonoita. The separation of his force proved to be a fatal error, especially since all of the spare ammunition was in the wagon left behind with the captain. When Crabb rode into Sonoita with nine men and began purchasing food for the rest of the company, rumors spread rapidly through the border towns, but not any faster than the messengers of the frontier officials who were keeping Pesqueira informed of Crabb's activities. By this time, Pesqueira had unseated the Gándara government and was trying to unite the people of Sonora. He no longer required the services of his fellow conspirator from California and did not wish to elicit further criticism from his enemies for having invited the Americans. Appealing to the strong prejudice of the Mexicans against Anglo-Americans in the 1850s, he disavowed the entire transaction and attempted to arouse the country against the filibuster.

When Crabb learned that the prefect at Altar, José María Redondo, had been preparing a hostile reception — including the poisoning of wells and the incitement of the Papagos against the expedition — he wrote a letter of protest on March 26. Insisting that his party came with no sinister designs, in advance of 900 other friendly settlers, Crabb explained to Redondo that he had entered Mexico "in accordance with the colonization laws of Mexico and in compliance with several very positive invitations from the most influential citizens of Sonora. . . ."[13] Blaming Redondo in advance for any bloodshed that might take place, Crabb said that he intended to proceed to his destination at Altar.

Four days later, Pesqueira reacted to Crabb's communication by calling all "free Sonorans" to arms. "Show no mercy, no generous sentiments toward these hounds," he said. "Let them die like wild beasts who, daring to trample under foot the law of nations, the rights of states, and all social institutions . . . appeal to brute force alone . . . Viva Mexico! Death to the Filibusters."[14]

Notwithstanding the dangerous situation, Crabb, with the dry desert behind him and the fertile Asunción Valley ahead, resolved to advance upon Caborca, 110 miles southward, with sixty-nine followers. Leaving twenty men behind to proceed at a more leisurely pace, he moved out, hoping that 900 additional immigrants would be waiting at the port of Libertad, on the coast southwest of Caborca. He never reached Libertad and disappointment awaited him there anyway, since no reinforcements had been sent. Ambushed on the outskirts of Caborca on the morning of April 1, the Americans fought their way into town and withstood a six-day siege in low, adobe buildings across the roadway from the church.

Though outnumbered about ten to one and scorched by falling roofs which the Mexicans set on fire, some of Crabb's men wanted to sally forth and try fighting their way back to the border. Crabb prevailed upon the fifty-nine remaining men to surrender, in hope of securing safe transport back across the Arizona line. The captives gave up their weapons and allowed their hands to be bound. When all were helpless, the Americans were marched into the Mexican barracks. A few hours later they were informed through Cortelyou, who spoke Spanish, that they were to be executed at sunrise. On April 7, the men were brought out in small groups and shot in the back by firing squads refusing to face them. Crabb was reserved for last, and permitted to write farewell letters to his wife and family. His head was severed immediately after his death; it was preserved in vinegar or mescal and exhibited to an exulting populace as a trophy of victory and as proof of Pesqueira's incorruptible patriotism. Only one person, a sixteen-year-old boy named Charles Edward Evans, was spared and lived to tell the story.[15]

Though the boy did not witness the execution, he was able to visit the scene three days later and described a shocking desecration of the dead in these words:

. . . . I went to the cemetery and saw their bodies strewn about the ground, unburied. All were stripped of their clothing — even stockings. The stench arising from the bodies prevented my approaching nearer than to observe that they had been gnawed and mutilated by beasts. I saw a finger lying near me, which appeared to have been cut off — perhaps to take a ring from it. From where I stood I was able to recognize several bodies . . . I remained in Caborca fifteen days, and, up to the time of my departure, I saw no attempt made to bury them: It was a standing and exultant joke among the Mexicans that their hogs would get fat on the Yankee flesh — ready for killing next fall. I recognized the clothing of our party worn by the people around me.[16]

About the time that Evans made these observations, a sequel to the battle and "massacre" occurred. Mexican detachments met Crabb's rear guard of sixteen men under McKinney a short distance from Caborca, forced them to surrender, and marched them into town. The men were immediately shot and their bodies left unburied where they fell. With the deaths of these men, the filibuster party was nearly wiped out. Besides young Evans, four men remained alive. They were sick at the time of the Sonoran invasion and were left behind with Jesus M. Ainsa — another one of Crabb's brothers-in-law — at Edward E. Dunbar's trading post near Sonoita on the American side. On April 17, however, Mexican troops crossed over the line in violation of American territory — though this was denied by Acting Commander Hilario Gabilando — gunned down the last of the invading party, and returned home with Ainsa, then a clerk at the post, as captive.[17] Ainsa was held in jail for several months and then released after a trial in which the authorities failed to prove that he was implicated in the Crabb expedition.

Just prior to the Sonoita affair, Gabilondo summarized the Mexican attitude toward all the events surrounding the Crabb Massacre in a commendation to his soldiers. After praising the defense preparations made by the vanguard troops, he wrote:

. . . Heaven blessed our efforts, and by the sixth day, at midnight, the pirates did not exist any more, as all had fallen at our hands. You, my comrades have been witnesses to their horrible intentions. You saw their efforts to blow up the church and convent where all the families of the town had taken refuge. But they received a good lesson . . . We have given our country a day of Glory and have made an exemplary punishment of these men . . . Long live the Mexican Republic. Hail to the Conquerors of Caborca. Death to the Filibusters.[18]

La Purísima Concepción de Nuestra Señora de Caborca in 1972

When news of the massacre reached Hermosillo, the jubilant government of Pesqueira freely distributed mescal to the people, who "supposed that their country had been saved from the ravages of heretics, and that the Mexican nation was invincible."[19] Assembling in the plaza with Indians from various tribes, the residents of the town glorified the event with loud rejoicing long into the night.

To many indignant Americans, however, the violation of American territory at Sonoita by Mexican troops was grosser than Crabb's invasion of Sonora with armed followers. There was an outburst of ill feeling on both sides of the border over the Crabb affair. The two governments exchanged a series of acrimonious notes, and the Mexican authorities laid a temporary embargo on all exportation of provisions from Sonora. As a result of the latter action, Poston said that he had to send to the Pima villages for food to supply his Arizona miners. When all the diplomatic exchanges were completed, however, there was little that our Minister Plenipotentiary to Mexico, John Forsyth, could say in defense of the Crabb expedition.[20] The killing of the four men at Dunbar's post on American soil was hardly a cause for drastic action. At best, Crabb was a restless visionary who led his duped followers into a trap from which there was no escape. The severity with which the American transgressors were treated served the double historical function of firmly discouraging similar undertakings and of creating a patriotic legend for the people of the Sonora borderland. Americans, particularly Arizonans, were to speak often of the benefits to be derived from expansion, but the time for moving the boundary southward, either by force or negotiation, had passed forever.[21] Though parts of Mexico were still coveted, particularly an outlet to the sea for Arizona, the tragedy of Henry Crabb brought to a close almost a decade of territorial expansionist activities in the southwest.

Among the more disappointed people were twenty-four men of a relief expedition enlisted at Tucson and Calabasas by Tozer and Wood. The volunteers, each of whom had been promised 160 acres of land, assembled at the Sopori silver mine northeast of Arivaca on April 1. Granville Oury was elected captain and led the Arizona company toward Caborca, avoiding as many settlements as possible. A few miles from their destination they were confronted by several hundred Mexicans and Indians commanded by Captain Juan Moreno. The Arizonans, more wily to the Sonoran way of doing business than were Crabb's Californians, refused to lay down their arms. Instead, the small force took a stand in a thick willow grove adjoining the Altar River bed. After holding off an attack by Moreno's command, the Arizonans escaped on foot during the night through several miles of mesquite forest to the vicinity of Pitiquito. Here they were attacked by more than fifty National Lancers firing old muskets. The better armed Arizonans held the Mexicans at long-rifle range and succeeded in resuming the journey homeward, though four members of the Oury party were killed and two wounded.

Oury rode ahead to his ranch in Arizona and sent Dodson back with a mule load of provisions to sustain his tired and hungry companions on the return trip. Charles Poston was on hand when the footsore men made their way into Arizona. "I was at Arivaca when they returned in a terrible destitute condition — some of them wounded and nearly all needing clothes, shoes, and provisions. . . ."[22] Sergeant John G. Capron, who was to outlive all the other members of the rescue party — despite a dangerous career as a cross country mail carrier — later wrote that the men first stopped at the Oury ranch after returning. "We stayed here two days and had a good deal of pleasure in rolling each other in the sand and picking out the cactus. Our feet were in a very pitiable condition, mine especially."[23]

The surviving members of the rescue party split up and went their separate ways. Tozer and one group went to Tucson while the wounded Capron went to Calabasas where he attempted to fulfill his contract to supply hay to four troops of United States dragoons, stationed there under Major Enoch Steen. At Calabasas, Capron recovered from his wounds under the ministrations of a young merchant, Charles Trumbull Hayden. Hayden, father of former U. S. Senator Carl Hayden, was born in Connecticut and migrated to southern Arizona after engaging in commercial ventures in Independence, Missouri, and Santa Fe, New Mexico. He later moved to Tempe where he ran a grist mill and operated the first ferry across the Salt River at that city.[24]

The best official reports on the Oury rescue mission, as well as on the Crabb Massacre, were submitted by Charles B. Smith, the American vice consul at Mazatlán. In describing the running retreat from Pitiquito, Smith revealed another atrocity committed by the Sonorans. The body of John Hughes, one of the four Americans killed, was badly mutilated; the man's hands, heart, and ears were stuck on a spear and taken to the town of Altar. But Smith's protests, like those of Forsyth, were in vain. The Crabb expedition and all the events associated with it served only to intensify the ill feeling that already existed along the border.

Chapter 13

1850s: Towns and Forts

THERE WERE FEW SETTLEMENTS in Arizona during the 1850s. The principal towns were Tubac, Tucson, and Colorado City (later called Arizona City and Yuma) — all south of the Gila River. Fort Buchanan was established to protect settlers in the Santa Cruz Valley and adjacent areas. There were no Anglo-American communities north of the Gila except Fort Defiance in the northeast and Fort Mojave (Mohave), established in 1859 on the Colorado. The short-lived town of Gila City came into existence the same year.

TUBAC

Arizona's first mining boom, during the American period, began in the Tubac area in the 1850s. Easterners, with the rich gold strikes of California still on their minds, eagerly invested in corporations to develop mines in the Gadsden Purchase. Though not a place, as one promoter described it, where "the hoofs of your horse throw up silver with the dust," the region had great potential. The companies sent out engineers and mining experts — some of them educated in the best schools of Europe — to direct prospecting in the hills and to supervise the excavation of shafts and tunnels. By 1856, the newcomers from the States and workmen from Mexico were converting Tubac from a sleepy little Spanish-Mexican village with dilapidated huts and a ruined church into a thriving community. The census of 1860 showed that more than 300 people were served by the Tubac post office.

Those who came with hope of quickly striking it rich had to risk the possibility of being killed by an Apache arrow

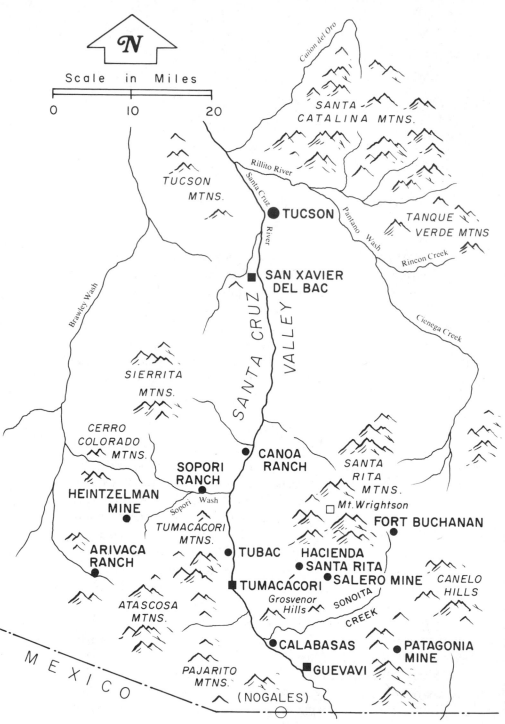

Southern Arizona in 1860

in the process of accumulating a fortune. The Indians continued to raid mines and ranches in southern Arizona, even after Fort Buchanan was established in 1857, some thirty-two miles east of Tubac. Despite the constant threat of attack, prospectors spread out in every direction from Tubac in search of gold and silver. To the east were the headquarters and mines of the Santa Rita Silver Mining Company, with H. C. Grosvenor as superintendent and Raphael Pumpelly, who later became a Harvard professor, as geologist.* Southeast, Lieutenant Sylvester Mowry developed the old Patagonia Mine into a big producer after resigning his commission in the Army. Professor W. T. Rickard of London operated the Aztec mines and there were smaller mines east of the Santa Cruz. The best-known developer of mines in the Cerro Colorado Mountains west of Tubac was Charles Poston who prospected in the vicinity of Tubac as early as 1854. He and Herman Ehrenberg, a German-born engineer, collected specimens of silver, gold, and copper in the region from Santa Cruz westward as far as present-day Ajo. Convinced of the mineral potential of the Gadsden Purchase lands, Poston, with the help of Major Samuel P. Heintzelman, promoted the Sonora Exploring and Mining Company in Cincinnati. He was appointed "managing agent" with the titles of "Colonel" and "Commandant," while Major Heintzelman served as president.

Poston outfitted the company with equipment and provisions at San Antonio, and on May 1, 1856, he set out on

---

* The Santa Rita Silver Mining Company was an offspring of the Sonora Exploring and Mining Company which was organized at Cincinnati in 1856, by Charles D. Poston and Major Samuel P. Heintzelman. In order not to draw needed money and talent away from the development of the Heintzelman Mine, the parent company formed a subsidiary to work their claims in the Santa Rita area. The Sonora company held 45 percent of the stock and sold the remaining shares at twenty dollars each, thereby bringing in $31,000 of new money. The new company quickly went into the red, however, because of the high cost of erecting a reduction works, building roads, and transporting goods from Cincinnati. The Santa Rita silver veins, where the Spanish and Mexicans had mined earlier, did not prove to be a bonanza. As a matter of fact, none of the mines of the Sonora Exploring and Mining Company or its subsidiary turned out to be the "strike" for which the pioneer entrepreneurs had hoped. The company was regularly in financial straits and never made any money on a sustained basis. See Andrew Wallace (ed.) *Pumpelly's Arizona* (An excerpt from *Across America and Asia* by Raphael Pumpelly, comprising those chapters which concern the Southwest). Tucson: The Palo Verde Press, 1965.

the 1000-mile journey to Tubac with a party of miners and
frontiersmen who were well-armed with Colt revolvers and
Sharps rifles. Traveling through Comanche country, the party
reached El Paso on July 4; they then prepared to dash across
the Apache country. At Santa Rita del Cobre, Poston established an understanding with Apache chiefs. The Indians
vowed a friendly attitude toward the Americans, providing
that their "trade" with Mexico remained unmolested. Poston
had no intention of interfering with the Apache business —
stealing stock below the border and selling it along the Rio
Grande. In hopes that the Indians would remember him and
the treaty, he distributed his tintype pictures which had been
taken in New York.

When Poston reached Tucson in August, he found the
town celebrating a festival in honor of its patron saint, St.
Augustine. He mercifully granted his travel-weary men a two-
week furlough so that "they could attend the fiesta, confess
their sins, and get acquainted with the Mexican *señoritas* who
flocked there in great numbers from the adjoining State of
Sonora."[1] While the men rejuvenated their spirits, the animals
were left at the San Xavier mission to graze under the protection of the Papagos.

After the celebration was over, Poston proceeded to
Tubac where he established his headquarters. Once it became
known in Mexico that an American company had arrived in
Tubac, Mexicans came in great numbers. Some of them were
ex-soldiers who returned to cultivate farms. Others were
skilled miners who could be employed at $15 to $25 a month
and rations. Traders from Sonora, New Mexico, and California came to exchange their supplies for bars of silver. An
unofficial census at the end of the year showed that about a
thousand people were living along the Santa Cruz River in
the vicinity of Tubac.

The ore in the Santa Rita Mountains was of too low a
grade to be worked profitably with the facilities then available. Fortunately, a vein of so-called "silver copper glance,"
which yielded $7,000 a ton, was discovered west of the Santa
Cruz and named Heintzelman — the name of both the com-

pany president and, coincidentally, the guardian spirit in German mining lore who presided over mines. The silver ore from this mine was smelted some eight miles away at the Arivaca Ranch and the bullion was sent to Guaymas for shipment to San Francisco — where it brought up to $1.32 per ounce for the Asiatic market. The first ore for the States was hauled by Santiago Hubbell, a trader from New Mexico. Hubbell arrived at Tubac in the autumn of 1857, with supplies loaded on his twelve large wagons, each pulled by twelve mules. Among other things, he delivered the first mine machinery ever brought into Arizona. While he was encamped at Tubac, Poston contracted with him to have ore in rawhide bags transported to Kansas City at 12½ cents per pound. The ore was distributed to different cities for assay and gave Arizona publicity as a producer of minerals.

The Heintzelman Mine was not the first one in the Gadsden Purchase area, however. The Arizona Mining and Trading Company was producing copper at Ajo at an earlier date. Incorporated at San Francisco in 1855, this company was headed by Robert Allen, a captain and brevet major in the Quartermaster's branch of the Department of the Pacific. It was formed after several rich specimens of copper and silver ores were brought to San Francisco by members of Colonel A. B. Gray's expedition, including Charles Schuchard and Peter R. Brady. Another favorable report by Charles D. Poston on the mineral potential of the region also influenced the Californians to organize and to send out an exploring party. Led by Edward E. Dunbar, the reconnoitering expedition located both the Ajo copper deposits and the Planchas de la Plata silver mine. The latter was in Mexican territory, however, and the party was forced by the Sonoran authorities to vacate it. Copper ore was taken from the Ajo mine in 1856 and packed to Yuma on mules owned by Iaeger. From this point, it was transported via the Gulf of California to San Francisco for transshipment to Swansea, Wales. Though the copper mine was soon abandoned, partly because of the difficulty involved in the movement of ores and supplies, several members of the exploring party — including Brady, Schuchard, and Fred A. Ronstadt — remained in the Gadsden Purchase region.*

Other companies opened mines in southern Arizona, several of them in the Tubac area. But none of the promoters became as prominent as Poston. Though only thirty-one in 1856, he was somewhat of a "great white father" to the Mexicans, a role he evidently accepted with enthusiasm. Going beyond his legal duties as deputy clerk of Doña Ana County, New Mexico, of which Tubac was then a part, he acted as mayor, justice of the peace, and — at least according to his own account — as resident priest. Poston later wrote that he performed the rites of matrimony, baptized children, granted divorces, and punished criminals. He said that Tubac became a haven for eloping couples from Sonora. Whereas the Mexican priests charged them the equivalent of $25, Poston married them for nothing and threw in a feast.[2] The marriage certificate was given some authenticity when stamped with a seal made out of a Mexican dollar. Difficulties arose with the church, however, and Father Joseph P. Machebeuf was dispatched from Santa Fe in 1858 to investigate the spiritual condition of the people. The vicar apostolic declared all of Poston's marriages, divorces, and baptisms null and void. The surprised people were terrified to learn that they were living in mortal sin. But Poston redeemed himself, at least in part, by arranging for the father to give church sanction to the questionable civil ceremonies which had been performed. The Sonora Exploring and Mining Company paid $700 for this solution to the matrimonial situation along the Santa Cruz.

Another problem Poston had to solve in Tubac was that of monetary exchange. Silver bullion was too heavy for day-by-day transactions, so Poston had pasteboard bills, known as *boletas,* printed in New York. These notes, in small denominations and about two by three inches in size, were paid to the

---

* One of the chief difficulties that confronted miners in the Ajo area was the lack of sufficient water. Also, the methods for treating low grade ores that made the Ajo mines a bonanza in the twentieth century, were unknown in the 1850s. For an interesting article written by Charles Schuchard on the Arizona Mining and Trading Company, see "Arizona Argonauts" in the *Arizona Daily Citizen,* February 15, 1894.

company's employees every Saturday. Not many of the natives could read, so the values of notes were indicated by pictures of animals. A pig on the currency meant that it was worth one bit, or 12½ cents. A calf was worth two bits, 25 cents; a rooster, 50 cents; a horse, $1; a bull, $5; and a lion, $10. The currency circulated throughout the Tubac trading area and was redeemable at the company office.

Not everyone in Tubac was illiterate, however. For a time, the town was headquarters for the most intelligent and refined inhabitants of Arizona. One sign of cultural progress was the *Weekly Arizonian,* the first newspaper ever printed in Arizona. The paper was originally published by William Wrightson as an organ of the mining interests. Edited by Edward E. Cross and printed on a hand press, the *Arizonian* first appeared on March 3, 1859. It was a decidedly neat little four-page, four-column journal. Full of advertisements about merchandise that could be shipped from Cincinnati and whiskey that was available in Tubac, the paper contained some local gossip also. In the news columns were stories about such things as Mexican politics, Indian depredations, horse stealing, cattle rustling, prospecting parties, and military deserters — all in all, a capsule history of frontier Arizona.

The issue of June 30, 1859, contained a report on a party which had returned from a disappointing search for gold in the Pinal Mountains. Casual mention was made of two members of the expedition who died from eating what was called "wild parsnip." The same edition had an article on a soldier at Fort Buchanan who was court-martialed for horse thievery and desertion. He was sentenced "to receive fifty lashes with a cowhide well laid on the bare back, to be confined at hard labor, heavily ironed, to forfeit all pay due him, to have his head shaved and to be branded with a red hot iron with the letter D, to be drummed out of the service and to receive a dishonorable discharge."[3]

Editorials on politics sometimes appeared in the *Arizonian.* Editor Cross, a veteran of the Mexican War, ardently opposed separate territorial status for Arizona. The mining company in which he owned stock was apparently battling

Sylvester Mowry's company for political control. His attack upon Mowry's population figures and arguments for a territory soon turned into personal animosity. After the two men exchanged derogatory letters, which were printed in the Eastern newspapers, Cross accepted Mowry's challenge to a duel that took place on July 8. The following account of the contest was printed in the *Arizonian*, July 14, 1859: "The parties met near Tubac, weapons, Burnside rifles, distance, forty paces. Four shots were exchanged without effect; at the last fire Mr. Mowry's rifle did not discharge. It was decided that he was entitled to his shot and Mr. Cross stood without arms to receive it. Mr. Mowry, refusing to fire at an unarmed man, discharged his rifle in the air and declared himself satisfied."[4] The antagonists shook hands and accompanied Solon H. Lathrop, managing director of the Sonora Exploring and Mining Company, to the company store. Here the last traces of ill feeling were dissipated by a few rounds of prime Monongahela whiskey.

A short time later, Mowry purchased the *Arizonian*, moved the press to Tucson, and adopted a Democratic editorial policy. The paper was published by various editors until it was closed down after the outbreak of the Civil War. Cross supported Mowry for delegate to Congress and later joined the Mexican Liberal Army in Sonora. When the Civil War broke out, however, he resigned his command and became a Union officer. He served in the 5th New Hampshire Infantry and held the rank of colonel at the time he was fatally shot in the Battle of Gettysburg, July 2, 1863.

The Civil War ended the Tubac boom. When the troops were withdrawn from Fort Buchanan and other garrisons in Arizona, the Apaches thought that their war on the white man had succeeded. As they increased their depredations, tales of carnage and horror were brought daily into Tubac. Terror-stricken miners, ranchers, and other settlers abandoned their property and only a few families were left in Tubac in July, 1861, when the Chiricahua Apaches swarmed down from the Santa Ritas to lay siege to the town. The warriors surrounded Tubac, expecting to find it easy

J. Ross Browne, *A Tour Through Arizona, 1864*

Tubac was the center of civilization in Arizona during the late 1850s but was abandoned to the Apaches by the time Browne visited there in 1864 and sketched this picture.

plunder. But the few remaining Americans put up a stiff defense for three days and managed to get a messenger through to Tucson asking for help. Granville H. Oury and some 25 volunteers responded to the pleas of the besieged inhabitants and quickly put the surprised Indians in flight. At the time of Oury's arrival, a party of 75 Mexicans, who had heard that the States were breaking up, came in from Sonora to steal anything that could be carried away. Seeing the preparations for defense at Tubac, however, they fell back on the mission at Tumacácori, which they plundered before returning south of the border.

By the end of 1861, most of the American miners and Mexican workers had departed and Tubac itself was a ghost town. J. Ross Browne found only a city of ruins in 1864:

On reaching the old Pueblo of Tubac we found that we were the only inhabitants. There was not a living soul to be seen as we approached. The old Plaza was knee-deep with weeds and grass. All around were adobe houses, with the roofs fallen in and walls crumbling to ruin. Door and windows were all gone, having been carried away by the Mexicans three years ago. Old pieces of machinery belonging to the neighboring mines lay scattered about the main building . . . At the time of the abandonment of the country in 1861, the Arizona Company had upward of $60,000 worth of machinery stored in the building attached to the old tower, every pound of which was hauled in wagons at great expense from Lavaca in Texas, a distance of twelve hundred miles. Two boilers, weighing 6000 pounds each, were hauled in the same way, one of which was taken by the Patagonia Mining Company. The other, at the time of our journey, lay on the Sonora road a little beyond the Calabasas. Some Mexicans were hauling it away when they were attacked by a band of Apaches, who killed two of the party, took the teams, burned the wagon, and left the boiler on the road-side, where it lay when we passed.

. . . Tubac is now a city of ruins — ruin and desolation wherever the eye rests. Yet I cannot but believe that the spirit of American enterprise will revisit this delightful region. . . .[5]

TUCSON

Argonauts, boundary surveyors, stage travelers, soldiers — all described Tucson during the 1850s as a one-story adobe Mexican town. The census of 1860 showed 650 people living in Tucson; this number was one-fourth of the white population of Arizona or ten percent of the total of 6,482 that included 2,421 whites, 4,040 Indians, and 21 Negroes. The inhabitants of the town were predominantly of Mexican origin, though most of the well-to-do men were Anglo-American merchants: Mark Aldrich had possessions valued at $52,000; Charles Trumbull Hayden, $20,000; Palatine Robinson, $12,800; and John G. Capron, $12,000. The prosperity of the Tucson businessmen could be compared favorably with the success of other American entrepreneurs, many of whom had been in Arizona for a longer time. One of the wealthiest men, according to the 1860 census, was Solon H. Lathrop of Tubac who was credited with the property of the Sonora Exploring and Mining Company valued at $70,000. Herman Ehrenberg, then of the same town, was worth $25,000. Louis Iaeger (Jaeger) of Fort Yuma, California, listed his possessions at $55,000. The properties of merchant George F.

Mark Aldrich

Arizona Historical Society

Hooper and steamboat operator George A. Johnson of Arizona City were reported at $9,000 and $16,000 respectively.[6]

The American businessmen made a sturdy and resourceful group. Not only did they prosper in business but also became involved in civic and political matters in Arizona during territorial days. The first Anglo-American to open a store in Tucson and to take part in community affairs was Mark Aldrich. A native of Illinois — where he served in the legislature during the 1830s with Abraham Lincoln and Stephen A. Douglas — Aldrich came to Arizona by way of California. He was soon chosen *alcalde* and given the responsibility of keeping the peace and punishing evil-doers. With only a handful of English-speaking people in town, Aldrich's problem of dealing with cut-throats and vagrants who swarmed

into town from south of the border was not an easy one. Since
there was no jail, the *alcalde* sentenced offenders to be flogged
at a whipping post in the public plaza. His constable, an
efficient and muscular Mexican, would administer half the
lashes announced in the penalty and then Aldrich would ask
the culprit to return the following day for the remainder
of the punishment. Before the appointed time, the man was
far away as it was intended he would be. This system of
administering justice was so successful the people of Tucson
asked Aldrich to serve as Judge of the Criminal Court after
a Provisional Territorial Government, separate from New
Mexico, was set up at the rump convention in Tucson in
1860. Aldrich accepted the position, but with the understanding that the people would support him. Two months
later, however, he resigned in disgust and submitted the following letter of explanation, dated November 1, 1860:

To the Citizens of Tucson, N. M.
Gentlemen:
    On the 26th day of August last, a mass meeting of the citizens was
held in Tucson for the purpose of adopting a Code of Laws for the
suppression and punishment of crime and to give security to its citizens
in the employment of life, liberty and property.
    The Code of Laws presented to the meeting by the committee
appointed for that purpose were unanimously adopted by the people.
By the laws adopted, it was incumbent upon the people to elect a Judge
of the Criminal Court, to try all persons brought before the court upon
complaint of some citizen, *under oath* — the citizens at the same time
subscribing their names to a resolution pledging themselves to sustain
the officers and to see that the laws were faithfully executed and enforced.
But what has the sequel shown?
    With the exception of a few cases for stealing (and the accused were
Mexicans) where public whipping was inflicted, not a single complaint
has ever been made for the arrests and punishment of persons, who do
not hesitate, for any offense (either supposed or real) to violate and set
at defiance the law by shooting at each other in the streets and saloons,
endangering the lives of other citizens in their immediate vicinity.
    But yesterday a man was shot dead in the street, in open day-
light, in the presence of a number of citizens and not a word is said
about arresting the person who committed the deed, or seeing the laws
enforced.

If the time has arrived when the law-abiding portion of the community, either through fear of giving offense or for want of moral
courage, fail to make the necessary complaint for the arrest and trial
of those who commit a breach of the peace, I think they have no use
for *Judge* or *Court,* and as Judge of the Criminal Court of Tucson, I
resign the same.

[s] M. Aldrich*

Lawlessness continued in Tucson after Aldrich's resignation. Since it was the center of trade with Sonora and was
located on the road between the Rio Grande and Fort Yuma,
the town became a mecca, not only for traders, but also for
speculators, gamblers, horse-thieves, and murderers. Law-
breakers, made uncomfortable by California vigilantes, found
the mild climate of Tucson congenial. "If the world were
searched over," said J. Ross Browne, "I suppose there could
not be found so degraded a set of villains as then formed the
principal society of Tucson. Every man went armed to the
teeth, and street-fights and bloody affrays were of daily occur-
rence."[7] Law and order was not established until the California Volunteers under Colonel James H. Carleton arrived
in 1862.

Meanwhile, the pioneers from the States slowly migrated
to Tucson. Mark Aldrich was the first storekeeper in Tucson,
but Solomon Warner was the first to stock his shelves with
American goods. He arrived in Tucson in March, 1856, just
a few days after the Mexican troops departed; his merchandise was transported from Fort Yuma on the backs of thirteen
mules. An advertisement in Arizona's first newspaper, the
Tucson *Arizonian,* dated November 10, 1859, would indicate
that he did a thriving business. His stock consisted of a "general assortment of dry goods, groceries, clothing, blankets,
hardware, tobacco, hats, boots, and shoes."[8] Warner's General
Store was the shopping center for southern Arizona even
though the prices were high because of expensive transportation from the sources of supply. Goods had to be shipped
from San Francisco to Yuma and then by freight wagons or

---

*The last four paragraphs here were combined into one in the letter. See Mark A.
Aldrich File, Arizona Historical Society.

Solomon Warner

Arizona Historical Society

mules to Tucson. Mexican goods were brought from Santa
Cruz, Sonora, but at great risk because of attacks by Mexican
bandits and Indians. Despite these business handicaps, Warner prospered until his goods were confiscated by Captain
Sherod Hunter of the Confederacy in 1862. Given the choice
of joining the rebels or leaving town, Warner departed for
Santa Cruz where he was even more successful than in Tucson. Engaging in business, cattle raising, and farming, he also
ran a flour mill, freighted between Guaymas and Hermosillo,
and supplied Camp Wallen, Arizona, with corn. In the 1870s
he returned to Tucson and operated a flour mill on the
eastern slope of Sentinel Peak. In his later years, prior to his
death in 1899, Warner spent much of his time trying to invent
a perpetual motion machine.[9]

Another merchant among the early arrivals was John B. "Pie" Allen who came to Arizona in 1857. He lived in the Yuma area and also participated in the placer mining excitement at Gila City before moving to Tucson. Nearly penniless, he accumulated capital for opening a mercantile business by baking delicious dried apple pies which he sold to the soldiers at a dollar each. His interests soon expanded to other towns. In the early 1860s, he pre-empted 160 acres of land at Maricopa Wells where he was also the pioneer merchant at the important stage station between Tucson and Yuma. He had another store adjoining Camp Lowell, then seven miles northeast of Tucson, and built the first substantial building in Tombstone — during the mining boom — to house a mercantile business. Eventually, however, his ranching and agricultural enterprises were more important than his business activities. Allen was also active in politics and served in the territorial legislature where he was influential in getting the capital moved from Prescott to Tucson in 1867. As the territorial treasurer, he was responsible for putting the territory in the black with his financial reforms. In the 1870s, he was appointed adjutant-general of Arizona, thereby acquiring the title of "General," and in the following decade was mayor of Tucson. In the latter capacity he started the town's first street-sweeping system, consisting of prisoners wielding brooms made from long mesquite branches.

One of the streets that ran through what is now the civic center in downtown Tucson was named after Charles H. Meyer, an ex-soldier who entered Arizona with the Army Hospital Corps. In 1858, Meyer settled in Tucson and soon opened a drugstore. A native of Germany, he amused customers with his thick accent. Like Aldrich and Allen, he was interested in politics and became famous in territorial days as the justice of peace who instituted the chain-gang system in Tucson.

Another prominent merchant-public official was Hiram S. Stevens who came to Arizona in 1854, following a tour of duty in the Southwest with the U.S. Army. Settling on a ranch in the Santa Cruz Valley near Sentinel Peak, Stevens suc-

Charles H. Meyer

Arizona Historical Society

ceeded in numerous enterprises. He sold hay and beef to the government, ran a store at Sacaton, profited as a post trader at Fort Buchanan and Camp Crittenden, and in 1876, formed a partnership with Sam Hughes to engage in mining, merchandising, and cattle trading. Stevens was purportedly worth $150,000 by 1882 — a considerable amount for the time and region. A good politician, Stevens served in the territorial legislature and as a delegate to Congress. He married into the prominent Santa Cruz family as did Hughes.

Samuel Hughes was probably the first American to come to sunny Arizona for his health. Born in Wales, he reached the Old Pueblo in 1858, after experiencing success as a cook, hotel keeper, and prospector in the California gold fields. Advised to seek a warmer climate because of a chest injury, Hughes stopped in Tucson en route to Texas and stayed there until 1917. He and several other travelers camped close to an irrigation ditch a short distance from the presidio gate. In one of his notebooks he later gave the following interesting account of his first day in Tucson, March 12, 1858:

As we were unhitching, a gentleman wearing a plug hat and a swinging cane walked toward our camp and introduced himself as Palatine Robinson, a South gentleman, and gave us all the news we could stand on an empty stomach. As it had been our custom to take an antidote about this time in the morning for scorpions, tarantulas, and centipedes, I asked him to join us, and he did.

About this time the women commenced coming for water for the day. They carry all they use in *ollas* on their head. The *ollas* were of all sizes from a pint to five gallons; and [it was a sight] to see about two hundred and fifty or three hundred women coming and going with *ollas* on their heads. But the worst of it was we could not see any of the women's faces, as they all wore *rebosos* or a piece of manta over their face, and only had one eye so they could see; and they all looked as cunning as a fox.

After breakfast we took a stroll to see the town. It did not take us long, as all the town was inside of what we now call Court Plaza — but few houses on the outside. On what is now called Pearl Street, there were three stores. Aldrich and Warner . . . and Mexicans the other. There were two blacksmith shops but neither one could weld a tire. The anvils were pieces of meteorite. One of them is now in the Smithsonian at Washington, and the other in San Francisco, California. . . .

So the day was passed in answering questions about California; and along in the evening we heard the fiddle and drum going from place to place. Asking what it meant, we were told we was to have a reception in the shape of a *baile* that evening. So off we all started and put on our Sunday clothes, so we could see those curious faces we had been looking at all day. The drums and fiddle was still going the rounds. We finally got to the place, and all the town was there. It looked more like a big family than a dance. The musicians sat on a log, and all the ladies sat round on poles of wood, there for that purpose; and the older ones sat on sheepskins and rawhide. There was no chairs I could see. [Everybody came] — old men and women, and all the children and Papagos and Apaches turned out in full force.[10]

Soon after his arrival, Hughes went into the butchering business and made money hand over fist selling grain and meat to the Overland Stage Company. He supplied stage stations between Apache Pass and Maricopa Wells until the Civil War broke out. Like Warner, Peter Brady, and other good Union men, he was given the choice of leaving Confederate-occupied Tucson or being shot. Hughes departed for California but returned shortly thereafter with Carleton's

Union forces. Always interested in community affairs, Hughes supported Governor A.P.K. Safford in efforts to establish a public school system; it was very appropriate that an elementary school in Tucson should be named after him. Because of his civic activities and widespread business affairs, it is said that Samuel Hughes was the best-known man in the Gadsden Purchase prior to the Civil War — with the exception of Charles Poston.

Hughes found very few Americans in Tucson when he arrived in 1858. In addition to the above, he later listed Palatine Robinson (a southern sympathizer whose wife was perhaps the most charming lady in town), Granville H. Oury, William S. Oury (the first agent for the Overland Mail Company in Tucson), Edward Miles, William M. and Alfred M. Rowlett, Joe Cummings, Alfred Friar, Asa McKinzie, Theodore Green Rusk and a handful of others. Whereas these people stayed to develop the country, most of the travelers from the States just came and went.

Phocion R. Way, who arrived on the "Jackass mail" stage in 1858, wrote that "there is no tavern or other accommodations here for travelers and I was obliged to roll myself in my blanket and sleep either in the street or the corral, as the station house has no windows or floor and was too close and warm."[11]

And six years later, J. Ross Browne described it in these words:

... a city of mud-boxes, dingy and dilapidated, cracked and baked into a composite of dust and filth; littered about with broken corrals, sheds, bake ovens, carcasses of dead animals, and broken pottery.... Adobe walls without whitewash inside or out, hard earth-floors, baked and dried Mexicans, sore-backed burros, coyote dogs, and terra-cotta children; soldiers, teamsters, and honest miners lounging about the mescal-shops, soaked with the fiery poison; a noisy band of Sonoranian buffoons, dressed in theatrical costume, cutting their antics in the public places to the most diabolical din of fiddles and guitars ever heard; a long train of Government wagons preparing to start for Fort Yuma or the Rio Grande — these are what a traveller sees ... the best view of Tucson is the rear view on the road to Fort Yuma.[12]

Browne's description assuming it is accurate, does serve to emphasize the accomplishments of pioneers who came into a wild country and crude surroundings to develop an oasis in the desert. Tucson grew because it was a center of trade with Sonora and the Southwest. The stage line was also a contributing factor to the town's development, as was the mining activity in the mountains around Tubac.

COLORADO CITY (ARIZONA CITY)

The first Anglo-American town to be located where modern Yuma stands today was surveyed in July, 1854, and named "Colorado City." The circumstances under which this town was laid out by Charles Poston were most unusual. Shortly after the Gadsden treaty was signed in Mexico City on December 30, 1853, Poston, who was then an employee of the customhouse in San Francisco, organized an exploring company to look for minerals in the newly acquired lands. His party, which included the German-educated engineer, Herman Ehrenberg, traveled to the west coast of Mexico on the British brig *Zoraida*, and then went overland from Guaymas to the Gadsden Purchase. Searching the hills west of Tubac and Tucson, the men eventually discovered that copper in paying quantities existed in the vicinity of present day Ajo. Elated over the find, Poston eagerly set out for California to raise capital for a copper company.*

En route, he and Ehrenberg stopped at the Colorado River and surveyed a townsite within the area of modern Yuma. Though Louis Iaeger, the ferry operator, probably cooperated as a partner in the laying out of "Colorado City," Poston made him a dupe in an embellished account of the event. According to the often repeated romantic version of the town's founding, the mine exploration party was penniless by the time it reached the river and Poston hit upon a novel

---

* Once he reached San Francisco, Poston gave the mineral specimens to Edward E. Dunbar, who, with the help of a group of interested men, organized Arizona's first copper company, the Arizona Mining and Trading Company. From San Francisco Poston went east to confer with capitalists in New York, Philadelphia, and Washington. Concentrating on obtaining financial support to open silver mines in Arizona, he met with no success until Major Samuel P. Heintzelman came to his aid and arranged for conferences with Ohio investors — including William and Thomas Wrightson. It was then that the Sonora Exploring and Mining Company was organized in Cincinnati with Heintzelman as president on March 24, 1856. See B. Sacks, "Charles Debrille Poston: Prince of Arizona Pioneers," *The Smoke Signal*, No. 7 (Spring, 1963), Tucson Corral of Westerners, 1963, pp. 4–5.

plan to pay for the transportation of his men and equipment across the river. To arouse the curiosity of Iaeger, he set Ehrenberg and a crew of men to working with survey instruments. Iaeger was attracted by all the activity amidst a great display of stakes and signal staffs and took the bait. He was especially enthusiastic when he looked at a hastily drawn townsite map and noticed that some water front lots had been set aside for a steam ferry. Convinced that a thriving trade mecca was in the making, Iaeger quickly agreed to transport the Poston party to the California side of the river as partial payment for a lot in the embryo city.* After reaching San Diego, the nearest American seat of government at the time, Poston had the plat of Colorado City recorded. His subsequent correspondence from San Francisco indicated that Colorado City was more than an expedient scheme to pay for ferriage at the Yuma crossing.

Called the "founder of Yuma" as well as the "father of Arizona," Poston wrote a report in which he forecast a great future for the Yuma area.[13] Emphasizing the mineral potential of the Southwest, the opening of navigation on the Colorado to the Mormon settlements, the thousands of migrants who had gone west by the southern route since 1849, and the projected continental railroad through the Gadsden Purchase, Poston explained that he had located land immediately below the junction of the rivers, containing about one thousand acres, and laid out a town called "Colorado City." He suggested that the money being paid out for ferriage charges at the crossing would go a long way toward defraying the cost of constructing a bridge across the river. He also mentioned several people then living in the area — including Sarah E.

---

*This oft-repeated account, which has never been completely verified, was first related in Raphael Pumpelly, *Across America and Asia*. See 3rd edition, New York: Leypoldt and Holt, 1870, p. 60. See also the *Yuma Sentinel*, February 16, 1878, and Sacks, "Charles Debrille Poston: Prince of Arizona Pioneers," p. 4. Lt. Nathaniel Michler visited the area in 1854 and wrote that the surveyed "city on paper" had a commercial future; see William H. Emory, *Report of the United States and Mexican Boundary Survey*, Senate Executive Document No. 108, 34th Cong., 1st Sess., 1855–56, Washington: A. C. P. Nicholson, Printer, 1857, p. 102. Poston only had a one-twentieth interest in the 936 acre tract that became the site of present-day Yuma. See Wallace, *Pumpelly's Arizona*, p. 118, note 19 and "Diary of Charles Debrille Poston," in the Sharlot Hall Museum, Prescott, Arizona (also on microfilm, Records of the States of the United States of America, Library of Congress, 1949, Arizona XX, Reel 1a).

*Poston's certificate of ownership to a
one-twentieth part of Colorado City*

Bowman, who operated a wayside house, "just outside the line for the new city," where travelers could get food and lodging.

Then called the "Great Western," and now also known as the "first citizen of Yuma," Mrs. Bowman arrived in the area in the early 1850s to cook for the garrison at Fort Yuma.*

---

* The census data of 1860 showed Sarah Bowman to be a resident of Arizona City, illiterate, Tennessee-born, 47 years of age, and in possession of real estate worth $2000. The census taker described her in a footnote as the "Heroine of Ft. Brown" and the "Great Western of Mexican War celebrity." Her husband at the time was a 32 year old upholsterer from Brunswick, Germany, who had $600 worth of property. See *Eighth Decennial U.S. Census (1860):* County of Arizona, New Mexico Territory. Mrs. Bowman's maiden name and her exact place of birth are unknown. She was a woman of many aliases and many amours. She first came to national attention at Fort Texas (renamed Fort Brown in 1846) when she served hot coffee and soup to soldiers who were engaged in an artillery duel with Mexican troops across the Rio Grande at Matamoros. Over six feet tall with red hair and blue eyes, the redoubtable Sarah subsequently accompanied General Taylor's Army to Mexico City, serving as a nurse and occasionally as a restaurant operator. Since the military had a requirement that a woman must be married to one of the soldiers to obtain permission to travel with the Army, Sarah simply signed on with any man who took her fancy — thus the reason for the numerous "married" names by which she was known. Today her remains lie in the San Francisco National Cemetery, having been transferred in 1890 from the Fort Yuma graveyard where she was buried on December 23, 1866. See Arthur Woodward, *The Great Western: Amazon of the Army.* San Francisco: Johnck & Seeger, 1961.

About 1853, she laid claim to a Mexican *alcalde* grant containing the site of modern Yuma, but a title to this land in the Gadsden Purchase was never issued to her by the United States. Raphael Pumpelly, who accompanied Poston to the Great Western's "dirt-roofed adobe house" for breakfast one day — when en route from Arizona to California following the outbreak of the Civil War — described Mrs. Bowman in these words: ". . . and in breakfasting — with the exception of the proprietress — our party formed the entire population of a city eight years old. Our landlady . . . no longer young, was a character of a varied past. She had followed the war of 1848 with Mexico. Her relations with the soldiers were of two kinds. One of these does not admit of analysis; the other was angelic, for she was adored by the soldiers for her bravery in the field and for her unceasing kindness in nursing the sick and wounded. . . ."[14]

There were other residents in Colorado City in the late 1850s. Poston, in his 1854 report, mentioned a new store that had been started by "Colonel Hooper" to sell goods "for consumption in the vicinity and in Northern portions of Sonora and Chihuahua." George F. Hooper's partner in this store — the first to be established by Anglo-Americans in what later became the Territory of Arizona — was Dr. George McKinstry. The two men had operated the sutler's store at Fort Yuma since 1852, and expanded their business activities to a building located at or near the southwest corner of Main and First Streets in present-day Yuma.* McKinstry sold his interest to Francis (Jack) Hinton and the new firm of Hooper and Hinton erected a larger building on Main Street near the steamboat landing where they kept a well-stocked store. The firm gave some substance to Poston's optimistic prediction in 1854 for the town that he founded: "Having now made a reconnaissance of the coast from the mouth to the head of the Gulf of California and a larger portion of both the Gila and Colorado rivers, I freely offer Colorado City as the best

---

* This leased building was the adobe house built by the "Great Western." George's brother, Major William B. Hooper, joined the firm of Hooper and Hinton in 1866. George lived most of his time in California where he purchased goods for the store and became president of the National Gold Bank of San Francisco. When William retired in 1875 he left the management of the firm in the hands of James M. Barney. See Arthur Woodward (ed.), *Journal of Lt. Thomas W. Sweeny, 1849–1853.* Los Angeles: Westernlore Press, 1956, p. 263, note 113.

and only point suitable for the location of a city in the territory in this vicinity and capable of becoming the point of supply for the extensive territories of Utah and New Mexico, portions of Sonora, Chihuahua, and California."[15]

By 1858, the town was called "Arizona" by the post office department and "Arizona City" by the journalists. The latter name was used in the 1860 census when a population of 85 was counted.[16] The year before, a newspaper reporter of the San Francisco *Weekly Alta California* mentioned Arizona City as one of several "incipient cities" in the growing Fort Yuma area.

He described it as a "flourishing" town "containing some half dozen respectable adobe houses, including two stores, two saloons, and a post office." * As an indication that Arizona City was "improving," the correspondent noted that "at least two houses, one of them a storehouse, are in course of erection. . . ." There was another settlement at the time about a mile below the fort where the Colorado Ferry and the Overland Mail depot were located. There the reporter observed "two stores, several buildings of the Overland Mail Co., two blacksmith shops, several dwellings and a house where the inner man may find grub and comfort. . . ."[17]

Like Poston, the San Francisco newspaperman was enthusiastic about the possibilities of the Yuma area and wrote accordingly to his editor: "I warn you, after this, not to let me hear a word against the supposition that the elements of a future great, and mighty empire are at work here, which will resolve themselves into shape and tangibility when Arizona is an independent republic, or when Dr. [Oliver M.] Wozencraft turns the waters of the Colorado over the sandy wastes of the desert."[18]

The town's progress was slow, however, and was nearly washed away by a flood in January, 1862. The waters of the

---

* The first postmaster at Colorado City was a clerk named John Blake Dow, who was appointed on December 2, 1857. The following March 17th Dow was reappointed and his postmark was changed to "Arizona." The office of his successor, Lansford Warren Hastings, was also designated "Arizona." Hastings served from July 17, 1858, until he cast his lot with the Confederates during the Civil War. The post office was officially discontinued on June 8, 1863, and then reopened with the name "Yuma" on October 1, 1866. From October 28, 1869, to April 14, 1873, however, the post office was known as "Arizona City" again. See John and Lillian Theobold, *Arizona Territory, Post Offices and Post Roads*. Phoenix: Arizona Historical Foundation, 1961, pp. 75, 76, and 138.

Gila and Colorado rivers jumped the banks and devastated the whole country in the vicinity of the junction. Only the houses of George Hooper and Captain George Alonzo Johnson were left standing. The rivers rose so suddenly that Hooper and Hinton were able to save only a portion of their goods. Their competitor, Sam Wells, lost his store and most of his wares. The town's billiard and ten-pin alley was entirely destroyed and the steamboat company's machine shop and store met the same fate. After the flood subsided, however, the town was rebuilt and became a thriving center of commercial activity after the Territory of Arizona was organized in 1863. The census ordered by Governor John N. Goodwin in 1864 showed a population of 151 in Arizona City, in comparison to 352 in La Paz, the first county seat of Yuma County. But by 1871, the sixth territorial legislature recognized that Arizona City had surpassed La Paz in importance and enacted a law removing the county seat.[19] The county sheriff, O. Frank Townsend, supervised the moving of the records, property, and officials down the Colorado to Arizona City on the steamer *Nina Tilden* commanded by Captain Isaac Polhamus, Jr. — a unique transporting of a desert county seat by water. The county seat continued to be known as Arizona City until February 3, 1873, when the Seventh Legislative Assembly meeting at the territorial capital (then Tucson) changed the name to Yuma.[20]

GILA CITY

In 1858, Arizona's first wild and wicked gold-rush town was born. Known as Gila City, the settlement sprang up after gold was discovered on the Gila River some twenty miles upstream from Arizona City.[21] The pioneer prospector who discovered the placer mines was Jacob Snively, a former secretary to Sam Houston in the Lone Star Republic of Texas and a veteran of the Mexican War. Snively's find stimulated the imaginations of other Americans who hurried to the Yuma area with visions of striking it rich. Within a year, approximately a thousand people rushed in to pan for the coarse gold that could be found in the alluvial deposits near the stream. The center of activity was Gila City, which was never more than a village of tents and brush shanties. In December,

1858, however, a post office was established in the town with Henry Burch as postmaster.

The influx of population was not surprising considering the glowing reports which came from the Gila "diggings." Sylvester Mowry, who visited the placers in November, 1858, wrote that he saw more than twenty dollars worth of gold washed out of eight shovelfuls of dirt by an inexperienced miner. He talked to several men who were making $30 to $125 per day. Newspaper correspondents were also writing optimistic accounts concerning the mineral potential of the region. One reporter from California wrote from Fort Yuma on October 21, 1858, after visiting the mines:

Gold has been found for a distance of three miles on each side of the river, varying from a quarter to half of a mile from the banks. No point has yet been prospected that has not yielded paying dirt. The lowest yield, per pair, 5 cents; the highest $8. The Rev. Mr. Riddle, of Texas, on his way to California, stopped there some four weeks since; he has already cleared $600. Mr. Weinenger, an old miner, two miles up, has discovered a claim which yields him $40 per day.

What is now wanted to develop these rich mines are the necessary implements for working them — such as tools, lumber and means of transporting the earth from the gulches to the river. It would be advisable for any one coming to bring necessary supplies, as there is but one store here, and everything, consequently, at the most enormous rates. This point is very readily reached by land or water. By land twice a week from San Francisco, by stage; by water, by sail or steamboats, to the mouth of the Colorado river, thence to this point by two steamers now plying on the river. The road from this point to the mines is capital.[22]

Actually the boom did not last long, but the reporter was at least right about the high prices. The town's baker charged a dollar a loaf for bread made from flour that he purchased from the commissary at Fort Yuma. Old rusty mess pork and worm-eaten dried apples each cost seventy-five cents per pound. Beans were fifty cents a pound, and flour, when available, sold for a dollar a pound. A good canteen brought as much as ten dollars and the drinking water which Mexicans hauled from the mountains cost from fifty to sixty cents per gallon. At these prices, many of the miners barely made ends meet. Hank Smith, a typical miner who made a record of his Arizona experiences, wrote that the men

in his party averaged only about ten dollars per day. That
was not very much, considering the labor involved, the hot
weather, and the constant danger of Indian attack. The dirt
had to be transported by burro from the dry "diggings" to
the river where the gold was washed out. Smith said that the
claims had to be guarded because the Mexicans started stealing
the pay dirt. After the Indians attacked the camp and drove
off every horse and pack animal, the dirt had to be packed
on the miners' backs.[23] Despite all the hard work, the mines
began to play out and Smith was happy to get a job with the
Overland Mail hauling hay from the Pima villages to the Gila
Bend station for $80 a month.

By 1859, the short-lived bonanza was finished.[24] After
about two million dollars worth of gold had been panned,
the yield was no longer sufficient to justify carrying the dirt
down to the river for washing. Gila City, instead of being
made the capital of the territory, became a ghost town and the
flood of 1862 destroyed what was left of the town.

J. Ross Browne, who camped on the site of Gila City
in 1864, summarized the rise and decline of the town in these
words:

> . . . Gold was found in the adjacent hills a few years ago, and a
> grand furor for the "placers of the Gila" raged throughout the Territory.
> . . . The earth was turned inside out. Rumors of extraordinary discov-
> eries flew on the wings of the wind in every direction. Enterprising men
> hurried to the spot with barrels of whiskey and billiard-tables; Jews
> came with ready-made clothing and fancy wares; traders crowded in
> with wagon-loads of pork and beans; and gamblers came with cards and
> monte-tables. There was everything in Gila City within a few months
> but a church and a jail, which were accounted barbarisms by the mass
> of the population. . . .[25]

The boom collapsed almost as abruptly as it had started.
At the time of Browne's visit, the "promising Metropolis of
Arizona consisted of three chimneys and a coyote."[26]

FORT BUCHANAN AND THE APACHES

When Lieutenant John G. Parke of the Topographical
Engineers reported on a proposed railroad route along the
32nd parallel from the Rio Grande to the Pima villages, he
said that the Gadsden Purchase was rich in minerals and that

the construction of a rail or wagon road, and the establishment of frequent military posts, would serve to speedily develop the immense resources.[27] But it was the fall of 1856 before four companies of mounted dragoons were transferred from present-day New Mexico by Secretary of War Jefferson Davis to protect the early pioneers in southern Arizona. The commander of these troops, Major Enoch Steen, was directed to take possession of the military installations formerly occupied by the Mexican garrison in Tucson, if they were not privately owned, and to occupy them.[28]

Steen led his command — which included blacksmiths, carpenters, laundresses, and other personnel needed to establish a permanent military post — over the route surveyed by Lieutenant Parke two years before. Arriving at the San Xavier Mission in mid-November, the Major set up a temporary camp and rode into Tucson. Dissatisfied with the "miserable huts" in the old pueblo and the lack of adequate grass and grain in the vicinity for the horses, he reconnoitered the country and chose a site on the Calabasas Ranch about sixty miles up the Santa Cruz Valley from Tucson. The ranch, only ten miles from the Mexican border, afforded good grazing and an abundance of water, as well as easy access to supplies of grain and beef in Sonora. Manuel M. Gándara, the ex-governor of that state and claimant to the Calabasas Ranch, was willing to lease land for the post. And his successor as governor, Ignacio Pesqueira, was soon permitting quartermaster wagons to pass into Sonora to haul supplies to Camp Moore, as the new post was called. This trade with Mexican merchants did not last long, however, partly because of the Crabb filibustering invasion of Sonora — which caused Pesqueira to ban all exports to the United States — and partly because Major Steen began ordering his flour and other provisions from the Rio Grande and from American merchants then doing business in Arizona.

Steen's choice of a site for a permanent post was not accepted by the acting departmental commander in Santa Fe, Colonel Benjamin Louis Eulalie Bonneville, who directed that the post be moved closer to Tucson. Steen was prejudiced against the latter town; he said that the settlers of the Sonoita valley would have to abandon their mines and ranches if not furnished protection, while only "whiskey peddlers" would suffer if the soldiers were stationed away from Tucson.[29] Besides, no suitable site for a military post could be found near Tucson, and Steen recommended a site located by Captain Richard S. Ewell about twenty miles northeast of Calabasas in the Sonoita Valley.

Bonneville approved the new site at *Ojos Calientes,* so called because of the thermal springs in the area, and a company of Steen's dragoons was detached there early in June, 1857, to begin construction of a post to be named after the new president, James Buchanan. The residents of Tucson were no more pleased with the new location, however, than they were with the one at Calabasas. In a petition of protest to the departmental commander at Santa Fe, they explained that Fort Buchanan, by the usual route of travel, was even more remote from Tucson than was Camp Moore; and their lives were in greater danger than before because the Apaches, in by-passing the new fort, would come closer to Tucson en route to Sonora.[30] The petitioners (Mark Aldrich, Granville H. Oury, Frederick and Julius Contzen, Alfred M. and William M. Rowlett, and fifteen others) also accused Major Steen of making farmers out of his soldiers instead of using them to fight Apaches.

In May and June, 1857, however, a large detachment under the command of Captain Richard S. Ewell was in the field as one of the three columns directed by Colonel Bonneville to encircle and crush the Mogollon, Gila, and Coyotero Apaches. Following Bonneville's comprehensive plan to concentrate upon the Apaches along the Gila River, near the present Arizona-New Mexico line, Ewell pushed eastward to join with Colonel William W. Loring's Northern Column from Albuquerque and the Southern Column from Fort Thorne under Colonel Dixon S. Miles. "It is expected," instructed the acting commander of the Department of New Mexico, "that the troops will remain in that country till late in fall, or longer if necessary, so that these Indians may be thoroughly chastised, and their band broken up so that they will not be heard of again as a distinct people."[31] For weeks the detachments searched through the extremely rugged country, the Western Column scouting mainly in the Chiracahua

Richard S. Ewell

Arizona Historical Society

Mountains. Corn fields were destroyed and a few prisoners taken, but it was June 27 before the only big battle of 1857 campaign was fought. In an engagement on the Gila, about thirty-five miles north of Mount Graham, the Army fell upon a band of Apaches, killing at least twenty braves and capturing a number of women and children.

Bonneville, whose Indian fighting exploits in the Rocky Mountains during the 1830s were popularized in the writings of Washington Irving, was hailed as the hero of the "Gila Expedition." He was later criticized, however, for a ghastly campaign which did not accomplish any lasting effects. Lieutenant (later Colonel) John Van Deusen Du Bois, a participant in the June 27 engagement, was quicker than most in recognizing Bonneville's shortcomings. The day after the battle on the Gila he wrote in his diary:

In camp all day. The dead were counted as they lay on the field. Twenty-four were killed and twenty-six taken prisoner, the latter women and children. One fine looking Indian brave was captured & by Col. Bonneville's desire, or express command, was taken out with his hands tied & shot like a dog by a Pueblo Indian — not thirty yards from camp. May God grant that Indian fighting may never make me a brute or harden me so that I can act the coward in this way. Humanity, honor, a soldier's pride, every feeling of good in me was & is shocked by this one act. . . .

Walked over the field today. It was a sad sight. I could not avoid asking myself why we had killed these poor harmless savages. It is not pretended that they ever did any harm to us, never coming to the Rio Grande, & robbing only from the Mexicans of Sonora.[32]

The battle of June 27, which Lieutenant DuBois so angrily observed, did not go far toward fulfilling Bonneville's plan to crush the power of the Apaches forever. The expedition was not successful, despite glowing official reports by Bonneville and others to the contrary. The Apache problem was just as great as ever in July when the soldiers were dispersed to various posts in the district. The highly-praised Arizona-based troops were led to Fort Buchanan in the Sonoita Valley by the gallant Captain Ewell whom Bonneville described as his "active man on all occasions."[33] Ewell had been placed in command of the detachment from Camp Moore when it took the field in May because Major Steen was ill with malaria at the time.

This disease plagued most of the soldiers in southern Arizona, especially after Fort Buchanan was located in the Sonoita Valley. Experience with the summer heat at Fort Yuma probably influenced the selection of a cooler site for Buchanan in the high country of southern Arizona where the best year round climate in the Gadsden Purchase could be found. In support of the Sonoita Valley site, the military men argued that this location was as good as any from which to police the region containing the greatest concentration of non-Indian settlers and friendly Indian tribes. Unfortunately, however, the presence of marshy *cienegas* of stagnant water, where fever-spreading mosquitos bred, more than offset the ideal climate and shady groves of oaks and junipers in the region. In fact, the fevers came to be feared almost as much as the Apache. Assistant Surgeon Bernard J. D. Irwin reported that the only occupants of the fort to remain free of malaria in 1858 were the employees of the sutler's store, which was separated from the nearby marshes by a knoll, and an elderly black servant of Captain Ewell.[34] The soldiers who lived in buildings constructed out of decaying oak in the proximity of swamps and quagmires were more subject to disease. Their insect-infested living quarters were made even more dangerous to health by the presence of huge piles of manure and filthy pigpens nearby.

The structures used as barracks for the men, as well as most of the officers' quarters, the laundry rooms, and the workshops were little more than temporary *jacals* (crude huts), scattered without order over a distance of half a mile. The buildings were constructed of pickets placed perpendicular to the ground, the chinks filled up with mud and the roof covered with the same material. The chinking quickly dried and fell out; and during wet weather the mud roofs served little purpose except to give "dirty shower baths to the unhappy occupants. . . ."[35] In 1858, the officers in charge of the department at Santa Fe seriously considered abandoning Fort Buchanan, but the post was continued as the base for varying numbers of soldiers under a succession of commanders until after the outbreak of the Civil War in 1861. Major Steen was succeeded by Captain E. H. Fitzgerald on April 12, 1858. Ewell also served as the post commander for awhile in 1858 and was in charge off and on in the following years. In March, 1859, he was superseded by Brevet Lt. Colonel I.V.D. Reeve. At that time, a company of the 8th Infantry arrived to replace Company D of the mounted Dragoons which was transferred to Fort Fillmore.

When the change was ordered, the editor of the *Weekly Arizonian,* Col. Edward Cross, wrote a seething article in which he questioned the effectiveness of infantry in pursuing Apaches. "They never would come in sight of Indians, still less capture them," he wrote. ". . . Mounted men are indispensable at Fort Buchanan at this time, and in the name of the people of the Territory whose lives and property are at

stake, we protest against the withdrawal of a single man."[36]
He went on to say that it was unjust and vitally injurious to
the local citizens to have soldiers stationed at the post who
were of little use except to stand guard and consume rations.

Even the one remaining company of Dragoons was ill-
equipped. There were only fifty-six horses, many of them
worn-out steeds left over from the Mexican War, for the
ninety-three soldiers. With some of the men on these decrepit
horses and others on mules, the company presented a ludi-
crous appearance when mounted. No two men carried the
same weapon; variations of eight different kinds of firearms
had been issued. Most of the ammunition, however, was of
one kind and thus some of the guns were useless for lack of
the proper bullets.[37] There was definitely a need for a well-
equipped cavalry to pursue and punish Indian marauders.

The settlers were pleased when Company D of the
Dragoons, led by Lt. R.S.C. Lord, was ordered back to Fort
Buchanan and arrived at the post in May, 1860. Company B
of the 8th Infantry left the same month to establish "Fort
Arivaipa" (renamed Fort Breckenridge in honor of Vice President John C. Breckinridge — whose name is correctly spelled
with an "i" instead of "e" in the second syllable — in August,
1860), just below the junction of the Arivaipa and San Pedro
rivers. Dissatisfied with the frequent shifting of cavalry and
infantry units, Captain Ewell, who commanded Buchanan
during most of 1860, fully expected that the War Department
would carry out its plans to increase the number of companies
to six. When the census was taken in August, however, the
total personnel at the post consisted of only 107 white males;
the families of some of the soldiers added twelve white females
and five children to the population. As in most of the frontier
Army units, there were a number of alien troops, thirty from
Ireland and nine each from England and Germany, making
the military contingent in Arizona a veritable melting pot.
The men, though led by dedicated career officers, were for
the most part young and reckless — both the emigrants and
native Americans — and had joined the Army for adventure
or to escape financial or social disappointments.

The morale of the troops was low, partly because of the
appalling accommodations at Fort Buchanan; the post, in

fact, hardly deserved the designation of fort since it was little more than a collection of scattered huts through which the Apaches often prowled at night. And the soldiers were dejected because no system of troop rotation had been worked out. The men were required to put in long periods of hazardous duty without relief because the number of soldiers allotted for policing the border country was limited. Attempts to persuade the government to change this policy of neglect were of no avail. Even though Secretary of War John B. Floyd approved a plan devised by Sylvester Mowry to hem in the Apaches above the Gila River with a string of forts similar to the old Spanish presidial line, Congress took no action. The American military force remained small and had little success in stopping the Indian marauding. The Apaches soon learned that there was little to fear from Fort Buchanan.

The limited military forces made it difficult for the Army to enforce treaties that were negotiated with the Apache tribes. An example was the Pinal treaty worked out by Dr. Michael Steck. As Indian agent, he secured several peace agreements, including one with the Chiricahuas near Apache Pass in December, 1858, whereby these Indians agreed not to molest traffic on the Overland Mail route. In hopes of persuading the Pinals to end their depredations on the settlers of Arizona, Steck and Captain Ewell, who was accompanied by troops from Fort Buchanan, met with some three hundred Pinals at Cañon del Oro, about thirty miles northeast of Tucson.[38] This historic meeting in March, 1859, was the first friendly face-to-face confrontation between the Pinals and their white counterparts and resulted in the signing of a treaty in which the people had little confidence. Expressing the viewpoint of many settlers, the editor of the *Weekly Arizonian* questioned the sincerity of the Indian promise to remain at peace. Reminding his readers of the crafty, rapacious reputation of the Pinals, he went so far as to call the treaty a "contemptible farce." Not begrudging these natives a supply of corn and beef at federal expense, however, providing they actually gave up their hunting grounds and desisted from thievery, the editor urged that they be "thoroughly and lastingly whipped into good behavior" if they commenced plundering again.[39]

In nearly every issue during the summer and fall of 1859, the *Arizonian* printed stories of treaty violations. When Col. Bonneville inspected Fort Buchanan in May, the editor wrote an article, for the Colonel's benefit, in which the need for a larger force at the post was emphasized. "We do not understand the policy of keeping five companies at Forts Bliss and Fillmore where the country is well settled and Indians scarce," he said, "while only two companies are allowed to all the vast region between Fort Fillmore and Fort Yuma."[40]

No additional troops were added, however; as a matter of fact, as mentioned above, the mobility of the garrison had been actually diminished between March, 1859, and May, 1860, during which time one of the two companies of Dragoons was replaced by an 8th Infantry company. And the essence of Edward Cross's parting shot on July 21 as editor of the *Arizonian* was "I told you so." He explained that the Pinals had received $4,000 worth of goods and 2500 pounds of corn for signing the treaty in March and took advantage of the ensuing period of ostensible peace to traverse the territory, taking account of the stock and spying out the ground for the future plundering expeditions. In the same issue, Cross reported that a party of about twenty Apaches suddenly appeared at Arivaca on July 16, and drove off the entire herd of ninety-three horses and mules belonging to the Sonora Exploring and Mining Company. Hoping to add to their plunder, the Indians stopped at the Canoa ranch. Here, however, they were surprised by Americans led by Richard Doss and Pete Kitchen. Alarmed by the presence of these men, the Apaches departed quickly for the Pinal country, abandoning more than half the animals stolen at Arivaca. The Canoa settlers pursued them but lost the trail.

Stressing this episode, as well as the stopping of an Overland Mail coach by a war party of Apaches, the *Arizonian* editor wrote:

> ... This is an illustration of the wretched policy of these blanket and calico treaties, made with the Apaches. They should be made to beg for *peace*, and to keep it without pay or bribery. If the Apache tribes commence depredations on a large scale, the whole western portion of this territory is liable to be devastated and depopulated, the overland mail destroyed, and all mining operations broken up....[41]

The Apaches feared punishment from a company of local rangers that was being formed, however, and turned over the remaining animals taken at Arivaca to the soldiers at Fort Buchanan — with the excuse that "they thought they were on the other side of the line!"[42] In late September, however, Apaches again raided the herd of the Arivaca Ranch and drove off twenty head of the fleetest horses.[43] Other depredations in the Santa Cruz Valley in October caused the ranchers to begin corralling their livestock. Even this did not thwart the marauders. The occupants of the Cullumber Ranch, for example, were driven away on the twenty-sixth. Upon returning home, the Cullumbers discovered that the Apaches had taken all their personal possessions, killed the fattest ox in celebration, and left a cross "surmounted by a white flag in token of their being *Christianes* and *amigos.*"[44] In November, when Lt. Col. Reeve commanded a combined expedition of about two hundred mounted men from Fort Buchanan and the Rio Grande into the mountain fastnesses of the roving Indians in the Gila country of eastern Arizona, the *Arizonian* again voiced the feelings of most people in southern Arizona: "We look upon this effort, although long delayed . . . to punish those thieving Apaches for their continued robberies, as one of great importance to our citizens. . . . It is only by fear that we may look for any cessation of their thefts, and to produce that, our Government should establish new posts in this section and continue a campaign against them. . . ."[45]

The pioneers in Arizona in the late 1850s were not themselves always above reproach, however. The heaviest depredations of the Apaches were in Sonora and the American miners and ranchers who cooperated were usually bypassed by the Indian raiding parties headed for the border. The owners of the Patagonia mine, just twelve miles south of Fort Buchanan, followed others in paying for protection by provisioning Apache parties that stopped there. Sylvester Mowry, formerly a lieutenant at Fort Yuma who purchased the Patagonia mine in the 1860s, wrote that "the Apache Indian is preparing Sonora for the rule of a higher civilization than the Mexican" and argued that the United States would eventually — when the time was ripe — take possession of a depopulated

J. Ross Browne, *A Tour Through Arizona, 1864*

The Mowry Mine, discovered in 1857 and known at first as the Patagonia, was purchased by Sylvester Mowry in 1860. Ore was transported in primitive carts to a nearby smelter. (Sketch by Browne)

Sonora.[46] Mowry's protagonist in the famous duel at Tubac on July 8, 1859, Edward Cross, took a different view on the Sonoran raids, however, calling them "legalized piracy upon a weak and defenseless State, encouraged and abetted by the United States government." And in a similar vein, Herman Ehrenberg, the well-known mine operator, pointed out that the American failure to restrain the Apache, whether by private protection or official treaty, resulted in bitter feelings all along the border and caused Mexicans to retaliate by stealing back their plundered stock.[47]

Any understanding that may have existed between some of the Apache Indians and certain American settlers was strained by an event at Apache Pass in February, 1861. George N. Bascom, a young lieutenant fresh out of West Point, accused Cochise, chief of the Chiricahuas, of a crime that could have been as easily committed by the Coyoteros or Pinals. In January, 1861, some Apaches raided John Ward's ranch in the Sonoita Valley a few miles from Fort Buchanan and ran off some oxen and horses. When Ward reported the incident at the fort, he charged that the depredators also kidnapped Feliz Martínez, the twelve-year-old son of his common-law Mexican wife.* Thinking that Cochise's Chiricahuas were responsible, Ward asked Lt. Col. Pitcairn Morrison, who was post commander at the time, to send troops to Apache Pass to retrieve his losses. Accordingly, on February 1, Lt. Bascom was dispatched with 54 enlisted men, mainly infantrymen mounted on mules.[48] Accompanied by Ward and an interpreter, the lieutenant had instructions to contact Cochise and demand the return of the boy and the stock, using force if necessary.

Wishing to throw Cochise off guard, Bascom told the stationkeeper of the Overland Mail in Apache Pass, Charles W. Culver, that he was marching eastward to the Rio Grande. He then camped less than a mile from the station to await Cochise who, as expected, concluded that the troops were on a routine mission and not looking for him. The chief voluntarily approached Bascom's tent and entered. There are conflicting stories about what happened next.

According to second-hand accounts passed on by soldiers and citizens who were not present, the lieutenant first accused Cochise of stealing Ward's property and kidnapping the boy. The angered chief then ran from the tent and escaped through a cordon of soldiers stationed outside, whereupon the lieutenant seized six Apaches as hostages. Bascom, however, did not mention any attempt to hold Cochise as a captive. He reported that the Indian leader denied having the Ward boy

---

*Feliz Martínez later became a famous scout for General George Crook under the name of Mickey Free. Other members of the family, as listed in the 1860 census, were John Ward (male, age 54), Jesus Martínez (female, age 30), Teodora Martínez (female, age 10), and Mary Ward (female, age 5 months). See Eighth Decennial Census (1860), County of Arizona, New Mexico Territory, *Senate Executive Document No. 13*, 89th Cong., 1st Sess., Washington, 1965, p. 31. See also Constance Wynn Altshuler (ed.), *Latest From Arizona: The Hesperian Letters, 1859–1861*. Tucson: Arizona Historical Society, 1969, pp. 165–66 and 227. It has never been proved that the Apaches took the boy and the stock from Ward's ranch.

George Bascom

Arizona Historical Society

but promised to get him from the Coyoteros if Bascom would wait ten days at Apache Pass. The lieutenant added that he took the Indian hostages simply as a bond pending the return of Feliz.[49] Whether Cochise escaped or simply concluded his parley and departed hastily does not seem particularly important, however, in the light of subsequent events.

The next day, February 5, Cochise led a large band of warriors to the stage station under a flag of truce but attempted to seize the three men who trustingly came out for a conference. James F. Wallace, a stage driver, was taken prisoner; Charles Culver evaded capture by running; and his assistant, Frank Welch, was accidentally killed by one of the soldiers, who had returned to the station after striking camp.

The elusive Cochise departed and, on February 6, attacked a surprised eastbound wagon train that was encamped a few miles west of the station. Eight of the men were tortured and killed, but three — Frank Brunner, a German teamster;

Sam Whitfield; and William K. Sanders, a half-breed Chero-
kee — were taken as hostages.[50] The names of these men were
obtained from Wallace who was brought with a rope around
his neck to a parley near the station. Here, Cochise offered
to exchange Wallace and sixteen Government mules, but not
the other captives, for the six Indians held by Bascom. When
the lieutenant insisted upon the return of the boy as part
of the exchange of hostages, the warriors departed with their
white captives.

After failing to stop the eastbound stage from Tucson
by obstructing the road and shooting the lead mule, Cochise's
braves concealed themselves in the brush near the spring,
some 700 yards east of the station, and opened fire when the
mules were driven there from the corral for watering. The

Mickey Free (Feliz Martinez) as a government scout and interpreter. This photo was taken at Willcox, Arizona.

National Archives

Entrance to the Cochise Stronghold in southeastern Arizona

Indians killed one Overland Mail employee, Moses Lyon, and wounded several soldiers; they also made off with twelve company mules and forty-two Army mules.

Meanwhile, A. B. Culver, conductor of the westbound stage from Mesilla and brother of Charles Culver, was sent to Tucson to obtain troops from Fort Breckenridge and escort his stage out of Chiricahua country.* At the same time, another courier was dispatched to Fort Buchanan by Lt. Bascom to bring supplies and medical assistance. En route from the latter post, Assistant Surgeon Bernard J.D. Irwin and his small escort recovered some stolen stock from Coyotero Apaches in the Sulphur Springs Valley and captured three warriors which they took to Apache Pass. Culver relayed his message to William S. Oury, the Butterfield agent at Tucson, who in turn sent a rider to Fort Breckenridge requesting troops from the new commanding officer, 1st Lt. Isaiah N. Moore, to meet him at Ewell's station, some fifteen miles west

---

*Culver was dispatched to Tucson by William F. Buckley, the superintendent of the Tucson to El Paso division of the Butterfield Company; he had arrived at Apache Pass on the east-bound stage. See Robert M. Utley, "The Bascom Affair: a Reconstruction," *Arizona and the West*, Vol. 3, No. 1 (Spring, 1961), p. 66. See also Altshuler, *Latest From Arizona*, pp. 171–73.

of Apache Pass. Dragoons under 1st Lt. Richard S.C. Lord arrived at the designated rendezvous point ahead of Oury.* Leaving a message for him, they continued on to the Pass which was reached shortly after Irwin arrived from Buchanan.

The day after the troops from Forts Buchanan and Breckenridge reached the Overland Mail station, Lt. Moore led the dragoons and forty infantrymen in search of Cochise. The Indian chief had departed but the Army detachment did find the mutilated bodies of the murdered Wallace (identified by his gold teeth) and several other whites who were tortured and killed near the burned wagon train. In retaliation, Bascom and Moore hanged the adult Apache captives on trees near the massacre site on February 19, and then started for their respective posts.† Bascom reached Buchanan on February 23, and Moore arrived at Breckenridge on the same day.

Historians of the Bascom incident have usually condemned the Lieutenant for precipitating a reign of Apache terror against white settlers in Arizona. In all fairness, however, it should be pointed out that Bascom was instructed to issue an ultimatum to Cochise and was praised for his conduct at Apache Pass by his commander, Lt. Col. Pitcairn Morrison.[51] The Bascom incident may have sparked vengeance on the part of the Indians, but it is quite likely that full-scale warfare launched by the Apache bands at the outbreak of

---

* 1st Lt. Moore assumed command at Fort Breckenridge on February 3, 1861. He commanded Co. "G" of the 1st Dragoons. 2nd Lt. Richard S. C. Lord was in charge of Co. "D," 1st Dragoons at the same post. An assistant surgeon and 127 enlisted men completed the roster of military personnel at the post. See "Post Return of Fort Breckenridge, N. Mex., commanded by Lieut. I. N. Moore, 1st Dragoons, for the month of February, 1861," in *Returns From U.S. Military Posts, 1800–1916*, Roll 143, National Archives Microfilm Publications. Moore first arrived in Arizona in 1856 with Major Steen's command. Both he and Lord were members of the group headed by Richard S. Ewell that purchased the Patagonia Mine from a Mexican herder in 1857. Notification of Moore's promotion to captain in 1861 arrived at Fort Breckenridge in the same mail as orders to evacuate that post after the outbreak of the Civil War. The captain led his dragoons to New Mexico where he died in defense of Fort Craig on January 16, 1862. Lord also served in the Union Army as a captain and was breveted major for gallant service in the Battle of Gettysburg. See Altshuler, *Latest From Arizona*, pp. 250, 260, and 265.

† Accounts written by Bascom, Irwin, Oury, Moore, and others differ as to the exact number hanged. The figures range from three to six dead on each side. Bascom reported that the three Chiricahua men were hanged but the woman and two boys were taken to Fort Buchanan and later released. The three Coyotero captives were hanged, too.

the Civil War would have come anyway. Regardless of the cause, Cochise kept the pressure on the Arizona frontier for more than a decade, finally agreeing to a peace treaty with General O.O. Howard in 1872.

The troops stationed at the military posts in Arizona were supposed to protect the settlers from Apache depredations but had difficulty at times in guaranteeing the security of the posts. And after the South seceded and the Confederate government of Jefferson Davis attempted to annex the Territory of New Mexico, the soldiers at Buchanan and Breckenridge were withdrawn altogether; they were needed on the Rio Grande to help repel a Confederate invasion from Texas. It was explained that soldiers could not be everywhere in the vast Southwest and Lincoln's administration gave the war effort priority over the economic development of the Gadsden Purchase. The first shift in troops came in June, when the two companies of the Second Dragoons were transferred from Fort Breckenridge to Fort Buchanan to replace the 7th Regiment of Infantry which moved to Fort Fillmore. On June 30, the military authorities in Santa Fe completed the evacuation by ordering the abandonment of Buchanan too. After burning supplies of considerable quantity and value which could not be transported, Captain Moore pulled down the flag and marched out of the post to the solemn beat of the drums on July 21, 1861. The Indians and Mexicans soon swarmed in to cart off anything usable that remained.

Knowing nothing of the fratricidal war which gripped the country, the Apaches regarded the withdrawal of troops from the Arizona posts as a sign of defeat. Assuming that the whites had become panicky, and, no longer fearing punishment, the Indians swept out of the hills and began a renewal of plunder and murder which brought the promising beginnings of economic life in the Gadsden Purchase to a temporary halt.[52] Most individual ranchers and prospectors were either killed or forced to leave. Pete Kitchen was one of the few settlers to hang on in the Santa Cruz Valley; his fortified ranch house was the only safe place between Tucson and Magdalena, Sonora. So sudden and complete was the desolation that Kitchen's phrase, "Tucson, Tubac, Tumacácori, and to Hell," to describe the road to Sonora seemed most appropriate. The Tucson *Arizonian* gloomily summarized the general situation in the territory in these words:

Our prosperity has departed. The mail is withdrawn; the soldiers are gone, and their garrisons burned to the ground; the miners murdered and the mines abandoned; the stockraisers and farmers have abandoned their crops and herds to the Indians, and the population generally have fled, panic struck and naked in search of refuge. From end to end of the territory, except alone in Tucson and its immediate vicinity, there is not a human habitation.[53]

FORT DEFIANCE AND THE NAVAJOS

Four military posts were established in the Arizona part of the Territory of New Mexico prior to the withdrawal of United States troops in this area. Besides Buchanan and Breckenridge south of the Gila, there were two posts in the unsettled country north of the river. The first was Fort Defiance, located in 1851, on Bonito Creek — in what is now Apache County in the northeastern part of the state.

Since their first contact with the Navajos in 1846, American troops had been trying by peaceful means to win the allegiance of the Navajo Indians to the United States. In August of that year, General Kearny issued a proclamation promising Anglo-American military protection to the Mexican populace of the Southwest. The ink on this document was scarcely dry when the Navajos, occupying the red rock country on both sides of the present Arizona-New Mexico boundary, staged a series of raids against their traditional enemies, the Mexicans and the Pueblo Indians. The first of a long list of officers to march into Navajo country to pacify the natives was Colonel Alexander W. Doniphan, left by General Kearny to defend Santa Fe. At Bear Springs, some fifteen miles east of present-day Gallup, New Mexico, he concluded a treaty with the Navajos — an agreement which proved to be a worthless scrap of paper.

The Navajo outrages against the peaceful inhabitants of the territory grew increasingly more bold and the Army was forced to take the field time and again in an effort to quell their depredations. In 1848, Colonel E.W.R. Newby secured a second treaty from the Diné — as the Navajos called themselves — and his successor, Colonel John M. Washington,

reached a settlement with them at a conference in the Canyon
de Chelly in 1849. What the military leaders failed to see,
however, was that the political unit of the Navajos was the
clan, not the tribe, and that any treaty was binding only on
the individual Indians who signed. Also, the liberal and
humanitarian policy of the military expeditions sent against
them was regarded by the Navajos as a sign of weakness and
only served to increase their contempt for the soldiers of the
United States. The Navajo attitude was clearly summarized
by James S. Calhoun, the first Indian agent (and later governor) in New Mexico who was sent out by the Commissioner
of Indian Affairs in 1849 to gather data that might lead to
an intelligent understanding of the Indian problems of the
region: "The wild Indians of the country have been so much

*General Edwin V. Sumner first came to the South-
west during the Mexican War as a Major in charge
of an advance force of 300 dragoons sent ahead of
Kearny's army. In 1851, when commander of the
Ninth Military Department, he established Fort
Defiance. He later fought in the Civil War as a
Union general.*   Museum of New Mexico

Museum of New Mexico

Colonel John M. Washington, who made a peace treaty with the Navajos in 1849 while he was serving as governor of New Mexico.

more successful in their robberies since General Kearny took possession of the country," he said, "they do not believe we have the power to chastise them."[54]

Conditions in New Mexico went from bad to worse. The Navajos continued their raids as if no treaty existed. The white population was decreasing — some American migrants returning East or moving on to California. Though property losses could not be accurately determined, the thefts of thousands of sheep and hundreds of cattle were reported. Travel on the Santa Fe Trail was dangerous. Mails were robbed. The territorial government was powerless. These were the circumstances that finally prompted the Secretary of War to reorganize the defenses of the territory. In 1851, the experienced Colonel Edwin Vose Sumner, who later became a Union general in the Civil War, was appointed commander of the Ninth Military Department. Immediately upon taking charge, he moved the military headquarters from Fort Marcy in "that sink of vice and extravagance," Santa Fe, to Fort Union and discharged all civilian officials. Inactive garrisons in the settled communities of New Mexico were regrouped and transferred to new frontier outposts to place the cavalry within shorter striking distance of the Indians. Fort Union was erected to protect the Santa Fe trade, Fort Fillmore to restrict the Apaches, Fort Conrad to stop the Indian aggression against Valverde, and Fort Defiance to hold back the Navajos.

Sumner established Fort Defiance while he was on a punitive expedition into the Navajo stronghold, Canyon de Chelly, during August and September. His strategy was to impress the recalcitrants with an overwhelming display of force — four companies of mounted troops, one company of artillery, and two of infantry — but the wily Indians were too deceptive for the Army. They lined the sides of the canyon, rolling down rocks on the troops and shooting arrows and bullets at them. Unable to draw the natives into decisive battle, the Colonel retreated to Cañon Bonito, some six miles north of present-day Window Rock. Here, on September 18, he authorized the construction of Fort Defiance, with Major Electus Backus in command.[55]

The narrow canyon, a hundred yards wide and a half mile long, was selected because of nearby water and grass. From the military viewpoint, however, the site was not ideal logistically, being vulnerable to attack on three sides and isolated from the main transportation routes. Actually it was a "fort" in name only. There were no stockades, trenches, blockhouses, or other fortifications. Except for sentries, it was accessible to anyone. The Navajos were not only given free entry but were also provided with overnight accommodations. Nicknamed "Hell's Gate" by the soldiers, the post was situated in one of the loneliest corners of the United States. What was more important, it was near the heart of enemy country. It was sixty miles north of Zuñi, thirty miles south of Canyon de Chelly, and fourteen miles west of a deep, cool lake called Laguna Negra — all favorite haunts of the Navajos. Though remote from civilization, Fort Defiance was to exert a strong influence in reducing the number of incursions into New Mexico. By the end of the year, the restraining

Fort Defiance, Arizona, in 1852. Established in 1851 by Colonel Edwin V. Sumner, and located in the Navajo Indian country about 280 miles west of Santa Fe, the fort was abandoned during the Civil War. (From a sketch by Lt. Col. J. H. Eaton)

effect of the military post in Cañon Bonito was being felt by the Navajos. The presence of a fort in the enemy's homeland brought more results than all the Spanish or Mexican armies and the abortive Anglo-American expeditions had been able to accomplish. For several months after Sumner returned to Santa Fe, the Navajos sent delegations to him requesting peace. In response to these pleas, he and Governor Calhoun held a parley with the headmen of the Diné at the pueblo of Jémez on Christmas Day, 1851. At this council, Sumner severely reprimanded the Indians for their depredations and warned them that "the troops at Fort Defiance could and would prevent them from raising a single field of grain, unless they remained at peace."

Over Sumner's objections, Calhoun distributed several thousand dollars worth of agricultural implements, calico, brass wire, and other assorted items; for their part, the Indians once again pledged to stay off the plunder trail. The Colonel felt that the good effect of placing his soldiers in the Navajo country was being sabotaged by a policy of appeasement.[56]

After a winter of relative quietude on the frontier, however, Sumner himself gave sheep and seed to the Navajos. The allotment system became a permanent national policy as a means of establishing permanent friendship with the Indians. In 1854, Congress appropriated $30,000 for treaties with the Navajos, Apaches, and Utes. Accordingly, Sumner's successor, Colonel John Garland, and Governor David Meriwether held a conference at Laguna Negra which was attended by several thousand Navajos. The chiefs accepted specific boundaries for their nation and agreed to cultivate the soil while living in peace. As compensation for these concessions, they were promised annuities for twenty years. The treaty was never ratified by Congress, but this was incidental, since the Indians apparently felt that their strength exceeded that of the "Big Chief" in Washington. After a few years, "the plundering went on," as one writer facetiously said, "just as though the treaty were in full force."[57] For about three years, however, the Navajos were kept in check by Captain Henry Linn Dodge, an Indian agent who lived among them until killed by Apaches in November, 1856. And even without his influence, 1857 was comparatively quiet — an occasional robbery or plunder but no major flareups. The government helped by issuing more annuity goods than ever before; but this liberality was soon forgotten. The rich, influential men in the tribe desired peace but were unable to control the "ladrones."

One cattle-rich Navajo asked Major (later Colonel) Henry L. Kendrick, commander of Fort Defiance, for permission to run his livestock with the guarded herd belonging to the post to prevent his own people from killing them. But even military property was not safe. On October 17, 1858, in the midst of another Navajo outrage, the Indians boldly attacked the post herd, killing two soldiers and wounding five. Sixty-two mules and three horses were driven off. After this raid the Navajos once again agreed to remain at peace; and another treaty was negotiated and signed at Fort Defiance on Christmas Day, 1858. A new feature of this document concerned the matter of collective responsibility for the actions of tribal members; the headmen selected Herrero Delgadito ("Little Iron Worker") as their chief and agreed to acknowledge him as the central authority for the entire tribe. No matter how good their intentions might have been, however, the headmen could never vouch for the conduct of the greater portion of the tribe. Even though they turned over some captives and stolen livestock in good faith, some of their people were plundering again by late spring of 1859.

During that year, Fort Defiance became the base for two important explorations into Navajo country under Captain John G. Walker and Major Oliver L. Shepherd. The object of these expeditions was to secure information on the topography and size of the tribe so that a successful campaign could be planned. The Army hesitated to launch a major offensive, even though Navajo depredations had been stepped up and a large military force was ready to take to the field. It was a brazen attack on Fort Defiance itself, on April 30, 1860, that brought about military operations on a full scale. An estimated 1000 Indians were able to approach the fort from three sides and surround it. About 4 A.M. the warriors poured through the corrals. The small force of less than 150 infantrymen held off the attackers and had them scurrying up the hillside at the break of dawn two hours later. There was no cavalry available to pursue the Navajos, who had nothing to show for well-timed attack except one dead and two wounded soldiers.

Fort Defiance became a beehive of activity as the new department commander, Colonel Thomas T. Fauntleroy, organized a large punitive expedition to chastise the Navajos in October, 1860. A contingent of 3,000 men began crisscrossing the Navajo country, but little was accomplished except the killing of a large number of Indian cattle. After four months, the Navajos, who had by this time become skillful diplomats, sued for peace and were granted an armistice. Meanwhile, 1500 soldiers crowded into Fort Defiance, which had been constructed for only about 250. The men built make-shift "dugouts," half below the ground and half above, for housing. Then on April 25, 1861, after the outbreak of the Civil War, all the troops were withdrawn except two units stationed at Fort Fauntleroy, east of present-day Gallup at Bear Springs.

The Navajos interpreted the troop exodus as evidence of the white man's admission of defeat and as a signal to become more aggressive. Raiding up and down the Rio Grande

Valley, they defied any attempt to pursue them into their strongholds centering around the magnificent Canyon de Chelly. Their plundering days were numbered, however, when Colonel Kit Carson was appointed in 1863 by General James H. Carleton to organize an expedition against them. Determined to remove the Navajo threat to white civilization, Carleton notified the Indians that they had until July 20, 1863, to surrender and go to the Bosque Redondo Reservation in New Mexico. After that date, every Navajo male capable of bearing arms was to be killed. The Indians who had often heard "big talk" that meant nothing, were surprised when Carson arrived at Fort Defiance in the Territory of Arizona on July 20.

At the fort, a band of Ute Indian scouts, anxious to fight their traditional enemies, the Navajos, joined the more than seven hundred troops in Carson's command. The armed Utes proved to be good marksmen and were very skilled in tracking and killing the Navajos, some of whom they scalped. So effective were Carson's encircling attacks that by the end of November, all the Navajos outside the snow-choked entrances to Canyon de Chelly had either surrendered, been killed, or fled southward. All means of livelihood were destroyed as the soldiers tore up cornfields and slaughtered thousands of sheep, leaving them in piles to rot. All that remained to subdue the tribe completely was an invasion of the canyon itself. This stronghold had long been regarded as impregnable, even in summertime. But Carson chose to strike in mid-winter. With a force of 375 men and 14 officers, he moved to the west end of the canyon in January.[58]

A detachment of New Mexico Volunteers under Captain Albert Pfeiffer entered from the east and marched through ice and snow to unite with Carson's force. En route, the Volunteers were welcomed by Navajos who skillfully moved along the high ledges like mountain cats, yelling, cursing in Spanish, and throwing rocks on the soldiers. Next, Captain Asa B. Carey retraced Pfeiffer's route from west to east with another detachment. After these maneuvers, Colonel Carson returned to his field headquarters at Fort Canby, a supply depot that he had established at a place called Pueblo Colorado, some twenty-one miles west of Fort Defiance. The

National Archives

Canyon de Chelly. The name "De Chelly" is a Spanish corruption of the Navajo word "Tsegi," which means roughly "rock canyon." Awesome canyons like this one sheltered prehistoric Indians whose dwellings still can be found below towering cliffs or perched on ledges. About 1700, Canyon de Chelly became a stronghold of Navajos, who previously had been concentrated in northern New Mexico. (Photo by Ben Wittick, about 1890)

immediate results were insignificant; but by the end of February, the fighting spirit of the Navajos seemed to be broken. By that time, there were several thousand Indians at Fort Canby awaiting a trip to Bosque Redondo. And on January 4, 1865, Carleton reported that 8,354 Navajos had taken the "long walk" to the reservation.

Southern New Mexico did not prove to be good country for them, however. In the first place, they were interned with several hundred Mescalero Apaches, their traditional enemies. Tribal jealousies were aggravated when the reservation authorities forced the Mescaleros to give up cultivated lands to the more numerous Navajos. Even when the disappointed Apaches sneaked away from the reservation early in 1865, there was still insufficient land to sustain the Navajo population. The soil was unproductive, wood scarce, and the water unhealthy. Without the livestock and the grasslands that had supported them in their own country, the Indians made a half-hearted attempt to farm. Yet, because of several crop failures due to cutworms and bad irrigation practices, and because there were no subsistence berries and roots to be found as in their homeland, the Navajos were forced to become expensive wards of the federal government. Although they submitted to the daily counting and accepted the rations, they refused to look upon the Bosque Redondo as a permanent residence and longed for the day when they could return to their own territory. Demoralized by a smallpox epidemic that took the lives of over 2000 of their people in 1865, and by the neglect of corrupt agents who were in charge of doling out rations and blankets, the Indians began quarreling with the soldiers.

Finally, after four years of dismal failure, the Department of War realized that Carleton's plan for relocating the Navajos needed to be reconsidered. In May, 1868, two Peace Commissioners, General William T. Sherman and Colonel Samuel F. Tappan, were sent to the Bosque Redondo to investigate. Satisfied that the Navajos would never be self-supporting on the New Mexico reservation, these men entered into a treaty agreement with the Indian leaders — one of whom, Barboncito, had previously made a trip to Washington, D. C., to report on conditions at Bosque Redondo. The Navajos were permitted to return to a defined portion of their former lands and were provided with liberal federal assistance to get them back on their feet. Fort Defiance became the site of the Navajo agency with Major Theodore Dodd as agent. Under his guidance the Navajos began to change from a band of paupers to a nation of industrious, nearly self-sustaining people.

FORT MOJAVE (MOHAVE) AND THE
MOJAVE INDIANS*

Lieutenant Edward Fitzgerald Beale had good reason in 1857 for recommending that a military post be established on the east bank of the Colorado River as a haven for California-bound emigrants and as a base of operations against the Mojaves. These Indians had lived for centuries along the Colorado and deeply resented any encroachments on their territory by the white man. As early as the 1820s, the Indians attacked Jedediah Smith and other trappers. In 1851, they killed a member of the Sitgreaves expedition and wounded several others. Though outwardly amicable to the large Whipple survey party, the Mojaves were actually indignant because these intruding outsiders came to map their lands.

Beale's request for a fort proved to be prophetic in the summer of 1858, when the Indians attacked a wagon train from Iowa and Missouri that had traveled over the 35th parallel road. Several scattered groups totaling 123 men, 33 women, and 47 children were approaching the Colorado in late July. The Mojaves were appalled that all these white people had so easily moved into their homeland, bringing cattle and equipment, setting up camp, chopping down trees for firewood, and looking as if they intended to stay. On August 30, the Indians attacked a party that was preparing to cross the river. Two white leaders who survived, Leonard

---

*The words Mojave and Mohave are used interchangeably, with Mohave often appearing in place names such as Mohave County, Mohave Valley, and Mohave Indian Reservation. The Mojave Tribal Council, however, has adopted the "j" form as the official spelling. The Mojaves accept the white man's version of their name, by either spelling, because it comes close to what they actually call themselves — *Aha macave*. The English translation of *aha* is water, and *macave* means along or beside — hence, people along the water. See Lorraine M. Sherer, *The Clan System of the Mojave Indians*. Los Angeles: The Historical Society of Southern California, 1965, pp. 6 and 71, note 2. Mojaves do not accept the commonly cited explanation of their name that was given by Frederick W. Hodge. He said that Mohave is derived from *hamok avi*, meaning "three mountains" and referring to the mountains south of Needles, Calif., in the homeland of the Mojaves. See Frederick W. Hodge, *Handbook of American Indians North of Mexico*. New York: Pageant Books, Inc., 1960, Vol. 1, pp. 919–21. The fort has undergone name changes. Known as Fort Mohave in the early post returns starting with the one of April, 1859, it was listed as Fort Mojave from July, 1859, until November, 1866. It was then known as Camp Mojave. See "Fort Mojave, Arizona, April 1859 — December, 1872," Returns From U.S. Military Posts, 1800–1916, Roll 787, National Archives Microfilm Publications Microcopy 617.

J. Rose and John Udell, later published descriptions of the
bloody event. The following passage is an excerpt from Rose's
story written for the November 29, 1858 edition of the
Missouri Republican:

> . . . the Indians came running from every quarter, out of the brush,
> completely surrounding the camp, and attacked us. They came within
> fifteen feet of our wagons and they evidently expected to find it easier
> work than they did, for I have no doubt they expected to massacre us.
> But we were well armed and the men that were in camp ready to receive
> them. A short time afterward, all of the men came in except two, whom
> I had sent to see if they could find Mr. Bentner and family; and some
> of the enemy being killed they retired to a safe distance. They kept up
> a continued shooting of arrows for near two hours, and part of them
> having driven off all the stock except for a few near the wagons, they all
> left. During this time, the two men had returned and reported of having
> found Miss Bentner killed, her clothes torn off and her face disfigured.
> They knew that it was unsafe for them to make any further search, and
> made for camp. From this and the fact of an Indian from the other side
> of the river shaking some scalps at us, which he had fastened on a pole,
> we supposed that they had all been killed. Mr. Brown was also killed,
> dying in camp without a struggle. We buried him in the Colorado, and
> its waters will never close over a nobler or better man, for to know him
> was to like him. Eleven more were wounded, who have all since recov-
> ered or nearly so. There were about twenty-five men in the fight.[59]

Under cover of darkness, the emigrants began retracing
their steps along the Beale wagon road. On the retreat eastward, they nearly starved since the Indians had stolen most
of their 400 head of cattle. They had to leave five loaded
wagons behind because all but about a dozen of their 37
horses were also in the hands of Mojave rustlers. A messenger
sent ahead could not reach Fort Defiance because of warring
Navajos, but did succeed in bringing help from Albuquerque.
An escort of soldiers came out, with three wagonloads of provisions, to assist the wagonless and wounded members of the
party. After the destitute emigrants were back in Albuquerque
for awhile, they held a meeting and passed several resolutions
which were sent to various newspapers and to prominent
military and civil officials. In one resolution, they made an
emphatic demand for a strong military post to be located
on the Colorado in the heart of the Mojave nation. News of

the tragedy had already reached Washington, however, and the Department of War directed Brevet Brigadier General N.S. Clarke, in charge of the Department of California, to dispatch two companies of infantry to establish a post at Beale's crossing.

Clarke had learned about the Indian attack even earlier. Anticipating the wishes of the War Department, he had instructed Lieutenant Colonel William Hoffman, a West Point classmate of Robert E. Lee, to lead four companies of the Sixth Infantry to establish a post in a suitable position to hold the Mojaves and other nearby Indians in subjection.[60] Hoffman left his infantry to establish a depot, named Camp Banning, at the entrance of Cajon Pass, and took a company of dragoons across the Mojave Desert in California to the Colorado to reconnoiter for a favorable location. In the vicinity of Beale's crossing he was forced into a skirmish by a large band of Mojaves and Paiutes; his plans upset by this opposition, he returned to San Francisco without selecting a site. General Clarke then decided to chastise the Indians and increased the force under Hoffman's command to seven companies and a detachment of artillery. "These tribes," directed Clarke, "and all others who may assume a hostile attitude, must be brought to submission. Do not temporize; if a blow must be struck, let it be effective."[61]

On February 16, 1859, Hoffman left San Francisco with four companies of infantry on the steamboat *Uncle Sam*. He stopped at San Diego to pick up another company and reached a point 25 miles from the mouth of the Colorado on February 27. The schooner *Monterey* took the troops with their cargo part way upstream and transferred them to the *General Jesup* and the *Colorado,* which in turn transported them to Fort Yuma. The two companies from Camp Banning had been waiting and were anxious to move upstream where their wool uniforms might be comfortable. Eugene Bandel, a soldier in the Banning group, wrote down some of his observations of the Fort Yuma area in a letter to his parents in Prussia. Describing the cool adobe houses and quarters which made the hot weather bearable for white inhabitants he said, "Still, though the post is but seven years old and is garrisoned by only two companies, a well-filled graveyard gives mute testimony of a most unhealthful climate for others than natives." On the Arizona side, he saw some fine specimens of silver and copper ore as well as gold from the Gila mines. "Some few earn ten dollars a day by washing gold," he said, "while many lose all they have in their eagerness to acquire riches quickly." From what Bandel saw of Arizona, however, he thought it had no value except for its minerals. And the following passage from the letter to his parents would indicate that he was certainly unimpressed by the Yuma tribe:

Indians are exceedingly numerous in the neighborhood. All belong to the Yuma tribe. As is the case with all Indians, intercourse with the whites has only made them worse. Formerly they lived by fishing in the river, and, following the yearly overflow of the river valleys, they also planted melons, pumpkins, etc. But now they live by begging, on the left-overs of the meals of the whites, and by profits of an infamous trafficking in their wives and daughters. While many of them, to be sure, now wear a shirt or even occasionally trousers, instead of merely a belt of bark as formerly, and while some speak Spanish and a few are able to swear in English, still I fail to see that civilization has profited them anything. So long as they can live by begging, they are too lazy to fish. With them, each day must provide for itself.[62]

The march up the Colorado turned out to be a grueling trip, even for veteran soldiers who had been in the field almost continuously since the close of the Mexican War. Each man carried most of his belongings in a knapsack. Tents and all excess baggage were left behind. Roasting by day and freezing by night, the troopers used their brush hooks and axes to cut a road along the river. About 120 miles north of Fort Yuma, they were transported to the Arizona side by the *General Jesup,* which had slowly puffed its way upstream, while the mules and pack trains had to swim. On the east bank, the men found the going just as rough. The road took them through sandy hills, dense willow thickets of the bottom lands, and across alkali plains. Guided by David McKenzie and the famous old mountain man, Joseph Reddeford Walker — who continued to lead gold seekers into the mountains of Arizona well into the 1860s — the party finally reached Beale's crossing after eighteen days of tough soldiering.

The Mojaves were overawed by the size of the expedition and agreed to a parley. Iritaba and five other chiefs, including his best friend, Kairook,* appeared at the encampment of soldiers with approximately 500 of their people. Kairook was dressed in an old shirt and beads; he wore a bell around his neck and carried a knife and a pair of scissors in his belt. The other leaders were similarly clad, with feathers in their hair and paint on their faces. All of the natives were suspiciously uneasy, especially after the soldiers quietly extended a cordon around the camp. It was a strange council, because neither side could speak the other's language. Captain James Benton translated Hoffman's words into Spanish for a Diegueno Indian named José María who spoke in Yuman to Pascual, a prominent Yuma leader who had accompanied Hoffman. Pascual in turn addressed the assembled tribe in the Mojave tongue. Through this roundabout communication, Hoffman informed the Mojaves that he came in peace to build a fort. He warned the Indians that he would hunt them down like so many coyotes if they chose war. Contrary to the testimony of survivors, the chiefs blamed the Walapais for the attack on the emigrant train, but readily assented to Hoffman's terms.

"They said the country was mine," the Colonel later reported, "and I might do what I pleased with it: all they asked was that they might be permitted to live in it. . . . Their whole demeanor, from the time I entered their country until I left it, was that of a subdued people asking for mercy."[63]

The Mojaves promised to respect the lives and property of all white men and assigned nine of their people to stay with the soldiers as hostages in evidence of their good faith. Although the agreement was of doubtful value, it terminated the Mojave expedition. Despite orders to establish a post on the California side of the river, Hoffman found the ground on that bank too low and marshy. He built Camp Colorado, soon renamed Fort Mojave, on the Arizona side and left Major L.A. Armistead in charge, with two companies of infantry and a detachment of artillery.[64] The remainder of the

---

* There are variant spellings of Kairook.

force was split, part of it going to Fort Yuma and others crossing the desert to San Bernardino. In his report on the expedition, Hoffman praised the officers and men of his command. No less appreciative, General Clarke wrote to the Department of War that these "troops were scarcely halted after a march across the continent, when they were called on for new labors — a tedious sea voyage, a long and painful march. Cheerfully they began their labors, and manfully they did their work."[65]

Fort Mojave was located at Beale's crossing, some seven miles above the point at which Highway 66 crosses the Colorado today. The quarters, constructed of cottonwood pickets placed upright and chinked with mud, with dirt floors and roofs, were about as comfortable as the climate would permit. The post trader at the fort in 1859 was Peter Brady who had come to Arizona from Texas with the Gray survey party.* With the help of two army officers, Bryant and Milhau, Brady published the *Mohave Dog Star*. Though this short-lived news sheet was undertaken chiefly for pastime, it was nevertheless the first publication in northern Arizona. On May 28, 1861, the post was abandoned by orders of Brigadier General Edwin V. Sumner. There was some fear at the time that the Confederacy planned to capture all the Arizona posts, men, and supplies, so the buildings at Fort Mojave were burned down and the soldiers transferred to California. Brady, however, contrived to save the post library by wrapping the books in tarpaulins and burying them under the commissary building. A supply of whiskey and several cases of fine wines were also hidden in the same hole and covered with earth. Finally the building was set afire and ashes concealed the cache. Though Brady never returned for his valuables, he maintained to his death in 1902 that they were where he left them. Needless to say, the aged vintages and rare old books would be very much in demand if discovered today.

---

*The post sutler must have done a good business. Cap't. R. B. Garrett, the post commander, wrote that his men were paying forty cents per pound for crackers because the Army-issue hardbread baked in and sent from San Francisco was "exceedingly hard, stale, and insipid." See letter of Garrett to Major W. W. Mockall, from Fort Mojave, New Mexico, February 2, 1860, in Letters Sent, 1859–61, RG 393, National Archives.

In May, 1863, the fort was garrisoned again — this time by two companies of the 4th California Infantry — and renamed Camp Mojave. Life at the post was difficult, as in earlier years. Besides watching for Indians, the troopers had to contend with supply shortages, bad weather, and snakes. All supplies came from Fort Yuma by steamer, but during certain seasons when the water in the river was low, the vessels would go aground. On one occasion, according to one of the California soldiers, Edward Carlson, the garrison had no food except "beans, coffee, sugar, and flour — and such flour! The heat had developed weevils, which multiplied to such numbers that it was hard to know which predominated, flour or weevils. . . ."[66] To escape the hot summer weather the men slept in the open air near the bank of the river. "Before turning in," Carlson said, "we would wet the ground thoroughly, then jump into the water for a good bath, and dripping wet as we came out, lie down and go to sleep." Isolation from the outside world was another problem. Mail service was cut down to one arrival per month. "True, travelers came sometimes from the settlements," according to Carlson, "but they had generally been so long on the road that they did not know much more than we did. O, with what a wistful eye did we watch, on the day we expected the mail-rider. . . . As for newspapers, they were read and re-read until we were familiar with every part of the paper, advertising matter and all."[67]

The Indians seemed to abide by their earlier agreement with Colonel Hoffman. On one occasion, however, the natives grew sullen. Their head chief, Iritaba (also spelled Irataba), was given a trip to Washington, D. C., by way of a steamer from San Francisco to New York. Because of his long absence, the Mojaves began to think that he had been taken away to be murdered. The troops feared an outbreak, especially since about half the company had been sent to quell trouble at the mining camp of La Paz. Fortunately, Iritaba returned before any disturbance could begin. He was dressed in the full cast-off uniform of a major general, except for the sword which he had traded off in San Francisco for a Japanese one. The military shoes hurt his feet and were worn tied to a string around his neck. His people must have been impressed, not only by his uniform but by what he had to tell them about the "great white father" in Washington. As a result, the danger of an Indian outbreak subsided.

In 1866, the troops at Camp Mojave were given the responsibility of protecting the Mojave and Prescott Road that ran to the territorial capital of Arizona. Fort Mojave, as it was again called after 1879, remained in existence until 1890, when it was turned over to the Indian Service. The buildings were finally torn down in 1942.

Chapter 14

The Civil War Era

THE TERRITORY OF NEW MEXICO — which until 1863 included the area that is now the states of Arizona and New Mexico — played a significant role in the power struggle between the North and the South. Jefferson Davis wished to annex California to the Confederacy and fully appreciated the importance of New Mexico as the connecting link between seceded Texas and the Golden State. Not only did Davis want a sea outlet on the Pacific Coast to weaken the Union blockade, he also coveted the precious minerals in California and the present states of Arizona, Nevada, and Colorado in order to bolster the South's inflated currency. Finally, conquest of the vast Southwest would strengthen trade and diplomatic relations with European nations, from whom Davis hoped to win recognition for the Confederate States as an independent nation.[1]

The reasons for invasion of the western territories were substantial and the chances for success were encouraging. The Confederate strategists in Richmond had cause to believe that many of the citizens of New Mexico were pro-Southern. In 1856, for example, the territorial legislature in Santa Fe had passed an act restricting free Negroes and, three years later, enacted a slave code. Several territorial newspapers, including Sylvester Mowry's Tucson *Arizonian,* were sympathetic to Southern principles.[2] And on March 16, 1861, shortly after Lincoln was inaugurated as President, a secession convention met at Mesilla, a town on the Rio Grande in southern New Mexico. Claiming to represent the people of "Arizona," the name then generally applied to the Gadsden Purchase region, the convention repudiated the "Black

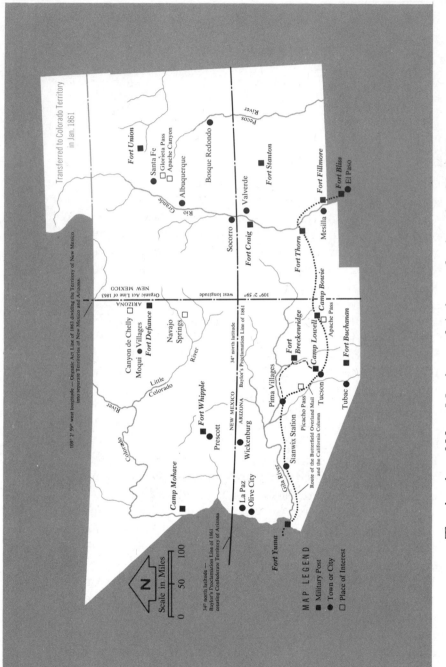

Territories of New Mexico and Arizona during the Civil War

Republican Administration" and attached "Arizona" to the Confederate States of America.[3] The South was pleased by this demonstration of support, even though the territorial government in Santa Fe ultimately decided to remain loyal to the Union, preferring to follow the hesitant "wait and see" policy of Missouri. Northern New Mexico depended on trade with Missouri and was also held in check by the presence of federal troops, most of whom remained loyal to the North.

The effectiveness of the United States Army in New Mexico was diminished, however, by the defection of many of its officers to the Confederacy.[4] Even the Departmental Commander, Colonel William W. Loring, "took the Texas route." Others who resigned their commissions in 1861 were Lieutenant Joseph Wheeler, Colonel George B. Crittenden, Major James Longstreet, Captain Richard S. Ewell, and Captain Cadmus M. Willcox — all to become Southern generals.

The commander at Fort Union, Major Henry H. Sibley, was another officer who ended a long career in the U. S. Army by tendering his services to the South. He returned to New Mexico, however, as a brigadier-general in command of troops to be known as the Confederate States of America Army of New Mexico. Following his resignation, Sibley had traveled to Richmond, where he convinced President Davis that New Mexico was the natural gateway for an expedition that could eventually conquer not only that territory but also Colorado and possibly California. Arriving at San Antonio in August, Sibley organized three regiments of the Texas Volunteer Cavalry and made preparations for the New Mexico campaign.

The actual invasion had already begun, however. On July 1, Lieutenant-Colonel John R. Baylor reached and occupied the deserted Fort Bliss (near El Paso, Texas) with a regiment of rough, tough, and determined Texas riflemen. These men were recruited ostensibly "to hunt buffalo on the plains" and furnished their own horses, saddles, guns, and ammunition. On July 25, the Texans took possession of the town of Mesilla where they were welcomed by Southern sympathizers. Major Isaac Lynde advanced with several companies of federal troops toward the town from nearby Fort

Fillmore, but retreated after a brief and indecisive skirmish. On July 27, the panicky Lynde abandoned the fort and started northeast toward Fort Stanton.

The soldiers did not have an adequate water supply and by the time Baylor caught up with the thirsty stragglers they were quite willing to surrender in exchange for a drink. Pushing on in hot pursuit, the Confederates cut the main body off at San Augustine Pass in the Organ Mountains. There, Major Lynde cowardly and disgracefully surrendered his entire command without firing a shot.* As a result of his capitulation, Fort Stanton was also abandoned, and the South had won its first territory with little opposition.

Flushed with victory, Baylor, on August 1, 1861, proclaimed the Confederate Territory of Arizona with the capital at Mesilla and himself as the military governor.[5] The territory was to comprise all of the New Mexico Territory south of the 34th parallel — an east-west line that passes near present-day Socorro, New Mexico, and Wickenburg, Arizona. Thus, Confederate Arizona extended from Texas to California and lay generally south of the Gila River in the southern parts of what are now Arizona and New Mexico. The Confederate Congress passed an enabling act on January 18, 1862, and on February 14, President Jefferson Davis formally proclaimed the Arizona Territory to be a part of the South.[6]

Baylor had given Tucson some recognition — on paper, that is — by making it the seat of the second judicial district, the first being at Mesilla. About the same time as the issuance of his proclamation, some sixty-eight Americans assembled in Tucson and passed an ordinance of secession. The Stars and

---

* Letter of Major Isaac Lynde to Acting Assistant Adjutant-General, from Fort Craig, New Mexico, August 7, 1861, in *War of the Rebellion*, Series I, Vol. 4, pp. 5–7. See also "Report of Lieut. Col. John R. Baylor, C.S. Army, spent from Doña area to headquarters of his commander at San Antonio, Texas, September 21, 1861," pp. 56–61, in Major James Cooper McKee, Surgeon, U.S. Army, *Narrative of the Surrender of a Command of U.S. Forces at Fort Fillmore, New Mexico, in July, A.D., 1861 With Related Reports by John R. Baylor, & Others.* Houston: Stagecoach Press, 1960. There is no evidence to support the story that Lynde's soldiers filled their canteens with high quality brandy and medicinal whiskey from the hospital stores at Fort Fillmore. This explanation for the thirst and the passive surrender of Lynde's command apparently appeared first in Horace Greeley's "hit the streets" history of the Civil War. See Blake Brophy, "Fort Fillmore, N.M., 1861: Public Disgrace and Private Disaster," paper presented at the Ninth Annual Historical Convention, Tempe, April 19–20, 1968. Copy in Arizona Collection, Hayden Library, Arizona State University, Tempe.

Colonel John R. Baylor, governor of the Confederate Territory of Arizona. (From a painting in the Alamo, San Antonio, Texas)

Stripes were tossed away to the summer breezes, as Granville Oury was selected territorial delegate to the Confederate Congress and Jefferson Davis was petitioned for troops.[7] This sympathy for disunion can be traced partly to the Southern origin of many of the residents. The abrupt departure of Union troops in July, however, was perhaps the strongest factor. Suddenly abandoned to the Apaches and lawless desperadoes, the people were willing to accept protection from any government.

The evacuation of troops from Forts Breckenridge and Buchanan, in the southern part of present-day Arizona, had been ordered by the military headquarters in New Mexico when Baylor invaded the territory. The Union officers had decided it would be best to destroy the Arizona posts rather than risk losing them to the South. Breckenridge was abandoned on July 10, after its supplies and buildings were burned. Joining with the force at Buchanan, the entire command of some four hundred departed for Fort Fillmore on July 21, with Captain Isaiah N. Moore in command. Distant columns of smoke were still rising from deserted Buchanan when

Granville H. Oury, Arizona delegate to the Confeder-ate Congress. Like his brother William S., "Grant" was prominent in early Arizona politics, serving more than once as Speaker of the Territorial Assembly and as dele-gate to Congress.

General Albert Sydney Johnston passed through Tucson the following day en route from California to join the Confed-eracy at Richmond. By the time Johnston reached the Rio Grande a week later, Baylor had captured Fort Fillmore. The soldiers from the forts in Arizona had been warned in time, however, to bypass Fillmore; they joined Colonel Edward R.S. Canby, then the Union commander in New Mexico, at Fort Craig, located on the Rio Grande about halfway between El Paso and Santa Fe.

Several months later, on February 21, 1862, the first major conflict of the Civil War in the Southwest was fought at Valverde, a few miles up the Rio Grande from Fort Craig. Canby's Union forces engaged Texas Volunteers under Gen-eral Sibley, who had assumed command of Southern troops in the area the previous December. After a fierce struggle which included several hand-to-hand encounters, the Texas sharpshooters succeeded in routing the Federals. "Kit" Carson, however, distinguished himself in the battle as his New Mexico Volunteers stood firm in the Union center and repulsed a charge of yelling Rebels armed with double-barreled shotguns, squirrel rifles, revolvers, and lances. But another spirited Texas charge on the Union left overwhelmed the defenders along the river. Theophilus Noel of the Texas cavalry wrote that "in this charge we carried everything before us, routing the enemy, we drove them to the river, where they 'took water,' on short notice, more like a herd of frightened mustangs than like men."[8]

Canby retreated to Fort Craig and let the Confederates march up the valley to capture Albuquerque and Santa Fe without much opposition. The Texans largely subsisted "on the country" but soon ran low on supplies because of their own vandalism and the indifference of the majority of the New Mexicans. On March 25, Sibley ordered an advance on Fort Union with the dual objectives of capturing military stores and removing the last obstacle to the South's possession of nearly all of New Mexico. Three days before the departure of the Confederates, however, more than 1300 Colorado Volunteers under Colonel J.P. Slough left Fort Union, following the Santa Fe Trail. Known as "Pike Peakers," these men had been resting at the fort after a cold mid-winter journey of over four hundred miles from Denver. They were a hardy breed of frontiersmen, a good match for the tough Texans.

The two armies clashed about twenty miles southeast of Santa Fe in the "Gettysburg of the West." Engagements at Apache Canyon on March 26, and at Glorieta Pass on March 28, proved to be the turning point in the war in saving this area for the Union. One Texan wrote that instead of meeting "Mexicans and regulars," they had encountered "regular demons, upon whom iron and lead had no effect." Major J.M. Chivington, a Bible-pounding preacher who had turned soldier, is given credit for assuring a Union victory by maneuvering to flank and surprise the Texas rear guard.[9]

His charging column swooped down upon the Confederate camp, burned the supply train, and bayoneted several hundred horses and mules which could not be driven over the rugged mountains to the Federal lines.

The tired, hungry, and demoralized Texan army retreated and probably would have been quickly wiped out had Canby permitted Slough to follow up the advantages won at Glorieta. Canby had no intention of risking his own army by attempting to annihilate the enemy, however, and allowed Sibley to lead the remnant of his column back into Texas. The desperate retreat route veered west of the Rio Grande through the San Mateo Mountains, where there was less chance of harassment by Union Troops. Struggling through difficult country, the troopers suffered terribly. One Confederate soldier, the above-mentioned Theophilus Noel, said that they "walked and staggered along like the reeling hungry, thirsty wretches" they were. Everything that the men could not personally carry was abandoned, including the sick and lame. The bloodthirsty Dog Canyon Apaches scalped the unfortunate boys whose blistered feet and weariness caused them to falter. Finally, the ill-fated expedition reached Fort Bliss in early May, a third to one-half of the original force of 3,700 having been left behind — killed, wounded, or captured.

Heroes when they marched northward two months before, the men were now released to find their way back to Texas any way they could. The attitude of the soldiers concerning Sibley's leadership was expressed by a Private George M. Brown, who wrote to his wife on April 30, 1862, that he hoped General Sibley would soon be hanged. Noel even expressed regret that the often-intoxicated general had escaped starvation during the retreat. There may be some doubt as to whether the general's addiction to alcohol and his personal cowardice had anything to do with the outcome of the New Mexican campaign. Certainly his failure to conquer the upper Rio Grande doomed Baylor's Confederate Territory of Arizona and the other strategic schemes which hinged upon the possession of New Mexico.

Meanwhile, as war raged along the Rio Grande, the region that is now Arizona became more directly involved in the war. When General Sibley was preparing to march upstream during January, 1862, he detached a company of mounted rifles under Captain Sherod Hunter to take possession of friendly Tucson for the Confederacy. The purpose of the expedition was to protect the South's growing interest — chiefly mineral — in western Arizona and to open communications to southern California. Hunter's cavalrymen encountered no opposition as they rode into the chief town of Arizona on February 28, and ran up the Confederate Stars and Bars.[10] Union sympathizers who had not already departed were given the choice of swearing allegiance to the Confederacy or leaving the territory. Solomon Warner, the storekeeper whose goods were confiscated by the troopers, was one of those who left for Sonora.

A party of Confederates also went south of the border, but for a different reason. Colonel James Reily, traveling from Chihuahua to Sonora on a diplomatic mission, happened to stop in Tucson shortly after Hunter arrived. After making a speech and participating in a formal flag-raising ceremony in the town plaza, Reily departed for Hermosillo with his escort of twenty men under Lieutenant James H. Tevis. Carrying a letter of introduction from Sibley, he was to negotiate with Governor Don Ignacio Pesqueira in behalf of the Confederacy. Reily later reported to the Southern leaders that he had made a favorable treaty; yet he actually accomplished very little, except to obtain permission to purchase supplies in gold or silver — the Mexicans refusing to accept Confederate currency.[11]

Unfortunately for the South, an enterprising reporter for the *San Francisco Bulletin* had managed to steal copies of Reily's letter of introduction and other notes, which he sent to General George Wright, the commander of the Army of the Pacific. Any inclination that Pesqueira might have had to cooperate with the Confederate States was soon forgotten with the arrival of a Union gunboat off Guaymas. In a letter containing veiled threats of invasion, Wright congratulated the governor for having refused Reily. The show of force was effective, for Pesqueira promised, in a letter dispatched to Wright on August 29, that he would consider the presence of any Southern force on Mexican soil as "an invasion by force of arms." By this time, of course, the Southwest had been saved for the Union. The struggle might have been prolonged, however, if Pesqueira had placed his weight behind the rebels.

Just as Reily's mission was devoid of results, so was Captain Hunter's occupation of Tucson. The soldiers lived off the country as Sibley's force was doing in the Rio Grande Valley. Using Tucson as a base they confiscated food, animals, and other property, including some mines owned by Northerners. On March 3, the same day that Reily left for Sonora, Hunter led his command over the old emigrant trail to the Pima Indian villages on the Gila River. There, he arrested Ammi M. White, a miller and federal purchasing agent who had been buying grain, forage, and other supplies for use by the Union troops on their eastward advance from California. Among the articles confiscated were 1,500 sacks of wheat. "This," Hunter reported to Baylor, "I distributed among the Indians, as I had no means of transportation, and deemed this a better policy of disposing of it than to destroy or leave it for the benefit (should it fall in their hands) of the enemy."[12]

While at the Pima villages, Hunter learned that every station of the old Butterfield Overland Mail between that place and Fort Yuma had been provided with hay for use of the Union troops. His raiding parties burned six of these stations, and the Rebel scouts came within a few miles of the Colorado River. Fort Yuma on this river was of great concern to Hunter because it was the planned base of operations for the California Volunteers, or California Column as they were generally called. In March and April, 1862, the infantry and cavalry were concentrating for an invasion of Arizona. Even before leaving Los Angeles, Colonel (later General) James H. Carleton, the energetic commander, had been informed of Hunter's activities, and dispatched Captain William McCleave with a squad of cavalry to learn the strength and disposition of the Confederate forces.

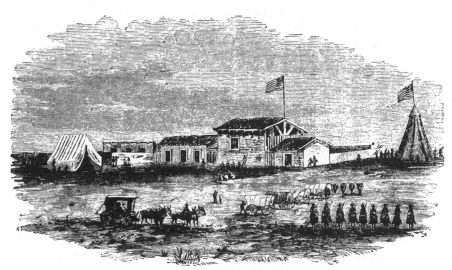

J. Ross Browne, *A Tour Through Arizona, 1864*

*Grist mill and home of Ammi White, located near the Pima villages
where he obtained his grain. White's mill, sometimes called Casa Blanca,
was on the south side of the Gila River west of present-day Florence. The
Confederates captured the mill for a short time in 1862. (Sketch by
Browne)*

McCleave's personal orders from Carleton were to stop
at the Pima villages and construct a building in which to
store the wheat and flour from Ammi White's mill. He was
also to reconnoiter Tucson and to take the town by surprise,
capturing "Mr. Hunter and his band of renegades and
traitors." As it turned out, however, the Union soldiers were
the victims of clever strategy. McCleave and his advance guard
of nine picked men were sighted by Confederate scouts in
time for a trap to be laid at the villages. Unaware that White
had been arrested, McCleave knocked on his door and was
greeted by Captain Hunter posing as the miller. In the meantime, the Confederates gathered around and easily made the
Yankees prisoners. McCleave and White were eventually
escorted to General Sibley's headquarters on the Rio Grande
by Lieutenant Jack Swilling, a man who was to reappear
often in Arizona history.

When news of McCleave's capture reached Fort Yuma, the officers and men were eager to find out what was going on in Arizona. Captain William P. Calloway was dispatched with a Union vanguard of 272 men, consisting of California infantry, cavalry, and a battery of two twelve-pound howitzers. Plans called for the establishment of a base at the Pima villages and a hasty dash toward Tucson to recapture McCleave before he could be taken east to Mesilla. Near Stanwix Station, one of the Butterfield Overland posts about eighty miles from Yuma, Calloway's men encountered some Texan troopers destroying hay stored there. Shots were exchanged and a Californian was wounded.* The Confederates then succeeded in eluding Captain Nathaniel J. Pishon's cavalry detachment which was sent in pursuit. Though hardly a battle of the magnitude of a Gettysburg or Bull Run, this action was the westernmost skirmish of the Civil War.†

Upon reaching the Pima villages, the Federals learned that some Confederate soldiers were in the vicinity. Calloway directed Lieutenant James Barrett to circle about in a flanking movement and to strike the Confederates from the east with a dozen cavalrymen. The main body under Lieutenant Ephraim Baldwin would attack on the front. On April 15, 1862,

---

*The wounded man was Private (later Corporal) William Semmilrogge (Company A, 1st Regiment of Cavalry). See Brig. Gen. Richard H. Orton, *Records of the California Men in the War of Rebellion, 1861–1867.* Sacramento, California: State Office, 1890, pp. 69 and 91.

† Actually, Arizona's Civil War annals can be extended west of Stanwix Station to La Paz on the Colorado River. No battle or skirmish was fought there, but blood was shed in May, 1863, when Union soldiers from Fort Yuma were ambushed in front of a store in which Michael Goldwater — grandfather of U.S. Senator Barry Goldwater — was then a clerk and later the proprietor. Under the command of Lt. James A. Hale, the soldiers were part of a detachment of men who were assigned to the *Cocopah*, a steamer that was chartered from the Colorado Steam Navigation Company to transport supplies to the regarrisoned post of Fort Mojave. Since boats were not navigated on the Colorado River at night, the *Cocopah* tied up at La Paz on the return trip and the men came into town, which was some distance from the river, to buy supplies. Privates Ferdinand Behn (Company H, 4th Infantry) and Wentworth Truston (Company K, 4th Infantry) were killed and another soldier wounded by an assailant identified as William "Frog" Edwards. A native of Arkansas, Edwards was free after having been imprisoned for several months — first at Camp Wright and then at Fort Yuma. He had been arrested along with other members of the Showalter Party — a band of Southern sympathizers in California led by Dan Showalter who had hoped to join the Confederate cause. Edwards fled the scene of his murders at La Paz and headed toward Sonora, dying on the desert near Ajo according to the official military report. Bert M. Fireman, "How Far Westward the Civil War?" The 1963 *Brand Book* of the Denver Posse of the Westerners, 19th annual edition, 1964, pp. 163–70. See also Orton, *California Men in the War of Rebellion*, pp. 652 and 667.

Barrett unexpectedly caught up with the Southerners at Picacho Pass, about forty-five miles northwest of Tucson. Ordered to charge, the Yankees forced the Texans into the chaparral where a few minutes of fierce fighting ensued. Lieutenant Barrett was hit in the neck and died instantly. Two Union privates, George Johnston and William S. Leonard, were also killed and three others were wounded. All the Confederates escaped except for two wounded and three who were taken prisoner. Known as the "Battle of Picacho Peak," this engagement is traditionally described as the westernmost action of the Civil War, though, as we have seen, there was an earlier conflict nearly a hundred miles farther west.

Neither side actually won the skirmish and each withdrew from the area. The Confederates fell back to Tucson; Calloway ordered a retreat to Stanwix to join with a larger advance unit of Federals under Colonel Joseph R. West. The united Union force continued on to the Pima villages which were reached near the end of April. Fort Barrett was constructed there and named in memory of the lost lieutenant. Little more than an "earthworks thrown around a trading post," near present-day Sacaton, the fort served as a resting place while the troops prepared for the advance on Tucson. Supplies that Colonel West expected to purchase from the Pimas were furnished only in limited quantities. He had nothing to offer the Indians for forage and wheat except "promises" to deliver *manta,* a kind of white cloth. Thus only trifling day-to-day rations of hay, wheat, and *pinole* (ground corn) were produced by the Pimas. As a result, Colonel West did not have a large store of supplies when he left the villages for Tucson near the middle of May.

He traveled by way of the deserted Fort Breckenridge and reestablished that post on April 18. The United States flag was hoisted as the soldiers cheered. When Carleton arrived at the Pima villages a few days later, he ordered that Fort Breckenridge be renamed Fort Stanford in honor of the Governor of California and stationed Colonel Edward E. Eyre's First California Cavalry regiment there. Meanwhile, on May 20, West occupied Tucson without a shot being fired. His advance cavalry detachment under Captain Emil Fritz

charged into town from three directions only to find that it
had been abandoned by the Confederates. Hunter had evacuated on May 4, leading his Texan troopers and several
Southern sympathizers toward the Rio Grande. While en
route, the party was attacked near Dragoon Springs — some
fifty miles east of Tucson — by Apaches who killed four men
and drove away a number of horses and mules. Hunter can
hardly be criticized for giving up the idea of holding Arizona.
His small band was no match for the approaching California
Column of 1800 volunteers.

Colonel Carleton himself reached Tucson on June 7,
1862, having delayed his arrival so that Lieutenant John B.
Shinn's artillery battery would get there first to fire a salute
in his honor. Carleton wasted no time in asserting the authority of the Federal government. On June 8, he declared Arizona
a territory of the United States, designated himself military
governor, and proclaimed martial law until such time as the
President of the United States would otherwise direct. He
contended that an assertion of military authority was necessary
because Arizona was in a chaotic state with no civil officers
to protect life and property.

The proclamation contained certain rules and regulations
which were to be rigidly enforced. All citizens of legal age
were compelled to take an oath of allegiance to the United
States. No unpatriotic words or acts would be tolerated. Every
man who remained in Arizona was required to have some
legitimate means of livelihood. And, in the absence of civil
courts, provision was made for the conduct of trials before
a military commission in cases involving either minor or
capital offenses.

Carleton let his axe fall on Confederate sympathizers as
well as on the desperadoes. Among the political prisoners was
Colonel Palatine Robinson, who had recruited troops for the
South. The most notable man arrested, however, was Sylvester
Mowry, the man who had resigned his position as the com-
manding officer at Fort Yuma to engage in mining speculation
and to work for the creation of a separate territory for Arizona.
In 1860, Mowry purchased a silver mine in the Patagonia
Mountains, some seven miles from the Mexican border, and

J. Ross Browne, *A Tour Through Arizona, 1864*

Headquarters and smelter of the Mowry Silver-Lead Mine.
Mowry's property was under federal control when J. Ross
Browne made this sketch in 1864.

immediately began developing the property. The Mowry
Silver Mine was soon prosperous, supporting a camp of some
four hundred inhabitants by 1862.

After Carleton arrived in Tucson, he received a letter,
marked Mowry Silver Mine and signed by "T. Scheuner,
Metallurgist, M.S.M." In the letter, Mowry was accused of
having aided the Confederate cause by selling percussion caps
to the Rebel forces and of having boasted that with twenty
Southerners he could whip a hundred Northerners. On the
basis of this information, Carleton sent Colonel Eyre with
a detachment of 128 men to arrest Mowry and confiscate his
silver mine on June 13, 1862. Mowry was brought to Tucson,
his entourage including his private secretary, his personal
servant, and his mistress. A board of officers headed by
Colonel West quickly convened to hear witnesses and to

examine documentary evidence. The board reached the opinion that Mowry was "an enemy to the Government of the United States, and that he has been in treasonable correspondence and collusion with well-known secessionists."* On July 2, Carleton confirmed the findings of the board and directed that the prisoner be confined at Fort Yuma where he remained until November 4.

Mowry was held "for aiding and abetting the enemy." He consistently claimed absolute innocence, however, of any treasonable actions, insisting that he was a non-participant in the Civil War and that he had asked both the North and the South for protection from the hostile Apaches. Well-liked by the officers at Fort Yuma, he was often taken for rides and furnished with choice bourbon that had been confiscated in Kentucky. After his case was investigated by General Wright, commander of the Department of the Pacific, Mowry was acquitted and given his unconditional release since the charges against him were not supported with sufficient evidence. But the matter did not end there. The bitter Carleton-Mowry feud continued until the latter's death in 1871. Convinced that Mowry was a secessionist, Carleton went beyond military arrest, court martial, and imprisonment. By a United States District Court order obtained in Albuquerque, he confiscated Mowry's property and had it sold at public auction on July 18, 1864, for a mere $2,000. The properties of W.S. and Granville H. Oury, Southern sympathizers beyond doubt, were sold on the same date.

---

* Typescript of "Proceedings of a Board of Officers Convened at Tucson, Arizona Territory, June 17, 1862," copy in Arizona Collection, Hayden Library, Arizona State University, pp. 34–35. The transcript of the board's proceedings filled sixty-eight typescript pages and included the testimony of many of Mowry's employees. His private secretary, John B. Mills, presented the most damaging evidence on July 6, four days after Mowry's fate had already been decided. Having earlier testified during the proceedings that Mowry had written to both General Edwin V. Sumner, the Union commander in California, and to Captain Hunter, for protection against the Apache Indians, Mills belatedly added that he had addressed letters for Mowry to Jefferson Davis and to members of the Cabinet and Army of the Southern Confederacy. Mills said, under oath: "I am convinced that Mr. Mowry wished very much for the success of the Southern arms, and sympathized entirely with the Rebellion against the Government of the United States, and that he rendered such assistance to the Southern Confederacy as he could. There can be no qualification of his position, in my opinion he was thoroughly identified with the rebellion in sympathy and action." See "Proceedings," pp. 65–66. For a good analysis of the Mowry arrest see Bert Fireman, "What Comprises Treason?" *Arizoniana*, Vol. I, No. 4 (Winter, 1960), pp. 5–10.

Arizona Historical Society

General James H. Carleton, commander of the California Column that occupied Tucson and restored it to the Union. He proclaimed martial law and confiscated the property of those he thought were Confederate sympathizers, including Sylvester Mowry.

Meanwhile, Mowry wrote letters to influential people, published newspaper articles, and sought vindication through legal channels. In December, 1862, he filed damage claims for more than a million dollars against Carleton and others in California's Fourth District Court. Eventually, in 1868, he received approximately $40,000 from the federal government, but his reputation was never completely redeemed. A Senate resolution — a formal gesture that was introduced in 1864 calling for a Congressional investigation — received scant attention. Mowry was consoled, however, by another resolution that was passed by Arizona's First Territorial Legislature.[13] In this resolution, the legislature censured General Carleton for expelling Mowry and for subsequently ordering his arrest the moment he arrived back in Arizona. The lawmakers were partially motivated by a desire to hasten the development of the mineral resources in this region. Along this line, Mowry went to London to raise money for refinancing his Arizona properties. While there, he became ill and died in October, 1871. Commenting upon his death, the *Arizona Miner* said, "This is sad news for Arizona. In the death of Mr. Mowry this Territory has lost as faithful a friend as it ever had in the person of one man."[14]

In addition to Mowry and Robinson, about twenty other political prisoners were arrested by Carleton and sent to California during the summer of 1862. At the same time, some of the Union sympathizers who had fled from the Confederates to Sonora, returned to Tucson and found that Carleton was reestablishing orderly government within the town itself. As the self-appointed military governor of Arizona, Carleton instructed Lieutenant Benjamin Clarke Butler, his secretary of state for the territory, to levy a tax on all business establishments in Arizona. Only concerns selling forage, subsistence stores, fruits, and vegetables were exempted. Merchants whose monthly sales amounted to $500 or less were taxed $5 per month. Another dollar was assessed for each additional $100 in sales. Gambling houses were obliged to pay $100 per month for each table in operation. Every keeper of a bar was charged $100 per month for the privilege of selling liquors. Violation of the provisions of the license-tax order subjected the gambling and liquor dealers to a fine and the seizure of all equipment and stocks upon the second offense. All money collected was earmarked exclusively for the hospital fund established for the benefit of the sick and wounded soldiers of the California Column.

While bringing some semblance of order to the frontier community of Tucson, Carleton was mainly occupied with preparations for the next leg of the army's eastward advance. The column had to be provisioned for the journey to Mesilla and contact made with the Union forces in New Mexico under Canby. For the latter purpose, Carleton sent an express rider named John Jones, Sergeant William Wheeling, and a Mexican guide known as Chávez. Only Jones escaped the Apache's scalping knife, and he was captured by the Confederates under the command of Colonel William Steele at Mesilla. Jones did manage, however, to smuggle word to Canby that Carleton was in Tucson.[15]

On June 21, six days after Jones's departure, a reconnaissance guard of 140 men under Lieutenant Colonel Edward Eyre started from Tucson for the Rio Grande. Following the route used by the Overland Mail stages before the war, the detachment had to travel about three hundred miles under a broiling sun and over a country destitute of water for distances ranging from thirty-five to sixty miles. While watering and grazing their horses at Apache Pass the troopers were approached by a mounted party of about a hundred well-armed Indians carrying a white flag of truce. The warriors asked for and were given food and tobacco, promising in return not to molest either the soldiers or the horses. Three men, however, who disobeyed orders and wandered off, were killed and stripped of their clothing and firearms. And that evening, the Indians fired into the Union camp, wounding Acting Assistant Surgeon R. W. Kittridge. Proceeding without further Indian trouble, Eyre reached the Rio Grande on the Fourth of July. Appropriate to the occasion and day, the Stars and Stripes were unfurled amid the wild cheers of the volunteers. This was the first time that Old Glory had floated over the Rio Grande south of Fort Craig since the occupation of New Mexico by Confederates nearly one year before.

On July 5, the detachment marched down the river and occupied the gutted ruins of old Fort Thorn, which had been abandoned by the Rebels. Eyre was eager to engage the Confederates under Colonel Steele. In defiance of orders from General Canby, Eyre crossed the flooding Rio Grande on July 17 in a small boat and pursued the retreating Southerners as far as Las Cruces. Meanwhile, however, Steele had evacuated Mesilla on July 8, and El Paso on July 12. In a letter written on the latter date to the Confederate government in Richmond, he explained that he could not hold the Territory of Arizona with four hundred men against the combined forces of some three thousand soldiers under Canby and Carleton. Into Texas with Steele went the dream for a transcontinental Confederacy. Southern authority along the

Rio Grande had evaporated and the Union had only to solidify its jurisdiction to be in complete control.

The second detachment of the California Column left Tucson on July 10. Under the command of Captain Thomas S. Roberts, the 126 men, twenty-two wagons and two howitzers proceeded via the Butterfield route toward Mesilla. About noon on July 15, the advance troops were ambushed near Apache Pass by Indians led by two of the most feared of all Apaches, Mangas Coloradas and Cochise. After a sharp skirmish, the Indians were driven off. But when the main body of troops moved into the pass approaching a spring for water, the Apaches began firing from behind rocks along the rim of the canyon. The "Battle of Apache Pass" that followed was one of the largest engagements ever fought between Federal troops and Apache Indians in Arizona history.

After a stubborn resistance, the Apaches were finally dislodged by bursting howitzer shells which were fired from the mysterious "wagons on wheels." By late afternoon, Roberts gained control of the water and sent Sergeant Titus B. Mitchell with five men back to warn Captain John C. Cremony, who was guarding the supply wagons with part of the cavalry. These couriers were attacked a few miles from the pass, but managed to reach the supply train. Private John Teal had to walk the last eight miles, however. After his horse was shot from under him he crouched behind the carcass and shot a big chief of the circling Apaches with his breech loading rifle. Little did he know at the time that he had hit the great Mangas Coloradas. After the attackers departed with their wounded leader, Teal frugally picked up his saddle and walked to Cremony's camp.

The next day, Roberts grouped his entire command and forced his way through the pass, again having to use his howitzers and sharpshooting riflemen. The Battle of Apache Pass was regarded as a victory for the troops since their casualties consisted of only two killed and three wounded, while estimates of Indian losses vary from ten to sixty-eight. It was also significant in that it focused the attention of Carleton on the importance of controlling the strategic Apache Pass. On July 27, 1862, he gave orders for the establishment

Fort Bowie, Arizona, in 1886

of a military camp there. It was named Fort Bowie in honor of General George W. Bowie of the Fifth California Cavalry. For years to come, the garrison at this post was to give protection to travelers, wagon trains, and stagecoaches passing through the Apache danger zone.

Meanwhile, the main body of the California Column started from Tucson on July 17, 1862. Because of the scarcity of water, 1,400 men were separated into sections to march one or two days apart. Several garrisons were left in Arizona with Major David Fergusson at Tucson in charge. Brigadier General Carleton, who had been promoted from colonel in June, left on July 23, 1862, confident that he had brought law and order to Arizona during his two months' sojourn in Tucson. He reached the Rio Grande on August 7, and the last units arrived about a week later. On September 18, 1862, Carleton replaced Canby in command of the Department of New Mexico. It had taken him nine months to move the California Column across the hot, dry desert and to occupy Arizona, southern New Mexico, and western Texas. With the Confederate danger removed, his most pressing problem during the next four years was to subdue the Indians of New Mexico and Arizona.

The Indians saw in the Civil War an opportunity to slaughter the white intruders or to expel them entirely from the land of the red man. So complete was the death and destruction carried to the mines, ranches, and settlements, that Southern and Union leaders alike considered the Indian menace a major obstacle to the occupation of the Southwest. Colonel Baylor, the Governor of Confederate Arizona, had very early decided upon a policy of extermination and on March 20, 1862, he wrote a most infamous order to Captain Helm in command of the Arizona Guards at Tucson. He urged Helm to use all available means of persuasion, including whiskey, to bring the Indians in for peace talks. Then, all grown Indians were to be killed and the children sold to defray expenses of the operation. There is no evidence that the order was obeyed, however, and Baylor was stripped of his command when President Davis learned of the incident.

Baylor was not alone, however, in supporting a policy of extermination. The Union officers followed a similar course of action. On October 12, 1862, just a few weeks after Federal troops had been forced to fight a coalition of Apaches under Mangas Coloradas and Cochise at Apache Pass, General Carleton ordered that all Indian men were to be killed whenever and wherever they could be found. He was determined to keep the lines of communication open to the west coast at all costs. After first conducting a relentless campaign to subdue the Apaches in New Mexico, Carleton extended his military protection westward into Arizona, which officially became a territory separate from New Mexico on February 24, 1863.

Brigadier General Joseph R. West, who was placed in command of the military district that included Arizona, sent expeditions from Mesilla to fight the Apaches. In January, a detachment under Edward D. Shirland induced the feared Mangas Coloradas to enter the camp of Joseph Walker, the leader of a party of gold seekers en route to Arizona. At the camp — near present-day Silver City in New Mexico — the huge Apache chief was treacherously killed under circumstances that have been described as everything from attempted escape to cold-blooded murder. His successor, Cochise, enraged by what he believed was American perfidy, swore that a hundred whites would die for every Apache killed. Holding religiously to this Indian oath, Cochise murdered, tortured, and pillaged his chosen enemies almost to the end of his own life in 1874. The influx of American miners and ranchers after 1863 gave him plenty of opportunity to wreak vengeance.

One of the main objectives of General Carleton's extermination policy was to encourage prospecting parties to develop the gold deposits which had been discovered in 1863, in the mountains of central Arizona. Though the government's policy now called for peace agreements, neither the military nor the settlers seemed to have any scruples about ejecting the red man from his homeland. The rush of several hundred miners and ranchers to the new diggings led to the establishment of Fort Whipple, in the new military district known as Northern Arizona.[16] Originally located in the Little Chino Valley about twenty-two miles north of Prescott, the fort was occupied in December, 1863, by two companies of California Volunteers. Major Edward B. Willis immediately negotiated a peace treaty with a local band of some three hundred Tonto Apaches who lived in the vicinity. Unfortunately, the soldiers who were escorting the officials of the recently organized Arizona Territory to Fort Whipple attacked and slew twenty of the bewildered Indians.

Following this engagement, the Tontos went on the warpath and threatened to end the white occupation of the territory. Ranches were swept bare of stock and miners were killed at work as the Indians made raids through the Peeples, Hassayampa, and other valleys of north-central Arizona. The men who were erecting the buildings for the new capital of Prescott went armed, and feared to venture beyond the town limits. Not all the Indian fighting was done by the soldiers, however. Hardly a week passed during 1863–1864 without an encounter between the settlers and the Apaches. The frontiersmen mobilized under the leadership of King S. Woolsey, a prominent rancher who had accompanied the Walker party on its prospecting tour in the Prescott area. Though a leader in territorial politics, ranching, and business, Woolsey is best remembered as an Indian fighter who believed that the only good Indian was a dead one.

In January, 1864, Woolsey led an expedition of settlers and friendly Maricopas in pursuit of Apaches who had stolen livestock in the Peeples Valley. Coming upon a large concentration of Indians near the present site of Miami, Arizona, he arranged a peace council with about thirty chiefs. After the conferees were seated in a circle, Woolsey touched his hat as the signal for his aides to draw pistols and start shooting the chiefs who sat next to them. The fight then became general as Woolsey's men fired upon the Indians in the nearby hills. The actual number of Apaches killed in this treacherous episode is not a matter of record — though there must have been at least twenty-four since the Maricopas brought back that many scalps.

The punishment administered to the Apaches in the so-called "Massacre at Bloody Tanks" temporarily slowed but did not end the Indian hostilities. The Indians and settlers continued to return bloody deed for bloody deed. The first Arizona Legislative Assembly, meeting in the new town of Prescott in 1864, commended Woolsey and bestowed the rank of colonel upon him. It also called for a war of extermination and authorized the raising of a regiment of voluntary infantry for this purpose.[17]

Conditions were equally bad in the southern and eastern parts of the territory. The military annals contain accounts of many expeditions sent out to punish the Apaches for their depredations. Two examples illustrate the type of activity in which the soldiers engaged. In May, 1863, Captain T. T. Tidball, in command of California Volunteers and some civilians from Fort Bowie, trailed a band of Aravaipa Apaches to Aravaipa Canyon in southeastern Arizona and killed fifty Indians with the loss of only one soldier. The men had traveled steadily at night for five days, over ground previously untrodden by whites, in order to surprise the Indians. Almost a year later, on April 7, 1864, Captain James H. Whitlock led sixty-one California Volunteers in pursuit of Chiricahua Apaches. Some 250 Apaches were routed from their camp near Grey's Peak in present-day Greenlee County. In his report on this episode, Whitlock wrote:

King S. Woolsey, commander of the territorial militia, rancher, miner, and legislator

... just as the savages were awakening from their slumbers, between daylight and sunup, I charged their camp. The fight lasted about one hour, at the end of which I had in my possession their entire "Campoody," with all its property, including forty-five head of horses and mules and the dead bodies of twenty-one Indians. I am satisfied that as many as thirty were killed in this fight. Some of my men fired as many as eighteen shots from their minie muskets. I could form no idea how many of those wretches went away with holes in their hides, but suffice it to say, a great many.[18]

These expeditions were typical of a considerable number of military and civilian forays in 1863, 1864, and 1865 to carry out General Carleton's extermination order. For the most part the campaign was ineffective and, at the end of the Civil War, the Apaches remained unsubdued in their mountain fastnesses. The desolation they caused was so complete in southern Arizona that no man's life was safe outside the walled pueblo of Tucson.

Of all the mines and ranches in the Santa Cruz and San

Pedro valleys, only Pete Kitchen's remained occupied. His fortified home on Potrero Creek, about six miles north of the border in the upper Santa Cruz Valley, was the only safe place between Tucson and Magdalena, Sonora. The Apaches killed his employees, drove his stock away, and filled his famous pigs — so much in demand in Tucson — with arrows. Yet, he stayed on as the one spark of civilization that could not be extinguished.

Despite the Indian turmoil of the Civil War era, however, prospectors came to northern Arizona in search of precious metals. Early in 1862, Pauline Weaver and others struck pay dirt on the Colorado ten miles north of the future site of Ehrenberg, where Michael Goldwater opened a business in the late 1860s. The discovery of gold placers brought people flocking to the spot. La Paz, as the new town was named, became Arizona's chief city, with a population of probably 1,500 living in tents or houses made of brush and logs. The newly established territorial government, to be described below, had hardly begun to consider La Paz as a possible site for the capital, however, when the boom was over. The collapse that came in 1864 was due mainly to the difficulty of extracting the gold, and the high prices charged by merchants for dry goods and liquor. Within a few years, most of the residents drifted away and La Paz became a mere shell of a place.

In 1863, there was great mining activity in north-central Arizona around present-day Prescott and Wickenburg. Famous pioneers like Pauline Weaver, Joseph Walker, Jack Swilling, and Henry Wickenburg located placers and veins of gold and silver along the Hassayampa, Big Bug, Lynx and Weaver creeks. The first organized group of white men to invade Arizona with the gold fever was the party of more than thirty hardy frontiersmen led by Captain Joseph R. Walker. From a point on the north bank of the Hassayampa — about five miles south of the present city of Prescott — the men explored the surrounding country and experienced "booming times" in panning gold and killing Indians. A lot of gold was also picked up on the surface in the mountains. Jack Swilling, who had joined the Walker party following his sojourn in the Confederate Army, sent two specimens of pure gold to General Carleton. The general, envisioning "vast gold fields" in the area, forwarded the samples to Secretary of Treasury Salmon P. Chase in September, 1863, for presentation to President Lincoln.[19]

Another party was guided from California to the Prescott region in May, 1863, by Pauline Weaver. Organized by Abraham H. Peeples, this group followed the Colorado River to La Paz and crossed over to the creek which they named Weaver Gulch in honor of their guide. A nearby mountain, some eighty-five miles northwest of present-day Phoenix, was named Antelope Peak because the party killed several antelope on its slope. The miners struck gold in both the creekbed and in the mountains. Just east of the creek, nugget gold was found barely beneath the surface in a small saddle-back of a mountain which was soon called Rich Mountain. Within a few months, the prospectors were able to gather thousands of dollars worth of gold, using no more than knives to force out the metal. Needless to say, newcomers came from all directions to investigate reports of the discoveries made by the Walker and Peeples parties.

Perhaps the richest deposit was the Vulture mine, which was located in 1863 by Henry Wickenburg some ten miles south of the town which now bears his name. Wickenburg, who had arrived in Arizona the year before, seemed especially suited to prospecting by virtue of geological and mineralogical studies in his native Austria. Acting on a tip from Colonel Woolsey that gold ore had been seen in the Harquahala Mountains, Wickenburg left his land in Peeples Valley and struck it rich. Supposedly, he named his mine after the turkey buzzards which hovered above the region. Within a year after the discovery of the Vulture, probably two hundred people were living at the new town of Wickenburg where the ore was hauled to the Hassayampa's waters. Along with some eighty miners who worked for Wickenburg, there were the usual saloonkeepers, gamblers, and gunmen who flocked into the mushrooming town.

Unfortunately, the "vast gold fields," about which Carleton wrote to officials in Washington, proved to be a mirage. In the years following the Civil War, copper, not gold, was the important mineral in Arizona's economy. Discovery of gold, however, was a factor that helped influence Congress to create Arizona as a territory separate from New Mexico. The Union government badly needed gold and was anxious that the potential mineral wealth of this region not fall into Confederate hands. The Arizona Organic Act was introduced on March 12, 1862, by Congressman James H. Ashley of Ohio. Already, a crosswise version of Arizona, approximating the southern parts of present-day Arizona and New Mexico, had been admitted to the Confederacy. Ashley's bill called for a vertical division of the New Mexico Territory along the meridian 109°2'59". Lively debate followed the introduction of the measure. Proponents contended that Arizona's white population of 6,500 and the 4,000 civilized Indians were entitled to civil government.

The opposition argued that all but about 600 of the estimated 6,500 whites were Mexicans, and that the loyal American population had probably been driven out by the Confederates. Opposing orators also claimed that the act was intended to benefit office seekers and would serve only to divert monies from the war effort. The bill squeaked through the House, however, by a narrow vote on May 8, 1862, though it was not until February of the following year that Senator Benjamin F. Wade of Ohio was able to guide it through the Senate. Final action followed the deletion of a clause which designated Tucson as the capital. Arizona became a territory when President Lincoln signed the bill on February 24, 1863.[20]

One of the main lobbyists for the bill was Charles D. Poston. The extent of his influence in bringing about the passage of the measure is uncertain, though his account of what happened is interesting. In his *Reminiscences* he wrote:

At the meeting of Congress in December, 1862, I returned to Washington, made friends with Lincoln, and proposed the organization of the Territory of Arizona. Oury was in Richmond cooling his heels in the ante-chambers of the Confederate Congress without gaining admission as a delegate from Arizona. Mowry was a prisoner in Yuma, cooling his head from the political fever that had afflicted it, and meditating on the decline and fall of a West Point graduate. There was no other person in Washington, save General Heintzelman, who took any interest in Arizona affairs. They had something else to occupy their attention, and did not even know where Arizona was. Old Ben Wade, Chairman of the Senate Committee on Territories, took a lively and bold interest in the organization of the Territory, and Ashley, Chairman of the Com-

Charles D. Poston, called the "Father of Arizona," because of his work in helping to bring about the creation of Arizona as a Territory separate from New Mexico. (The original of this photo is in the Brady Collection of the National Archives.)

mittee of the House, told me how to accomplish the object. He said there were a number of members of the expiring Congress who had been defeated in their own districts for the next term, who wanted to go west and offer their political services to the "galoots," and if they could be grouped and a satisfactory slate made, they would have influence enough to carry the bill through Congress. Consequently an "oyster supper" was organized, to which the "lame ducks" were invited, and then and there the slate was made, and the territory was virtually organized. So the slate was made and the bargain concluded, but toward the last it occurred to my obfuscated brain that my name did not appear on the slate, and in the language of Daniel Webster, I exclaimed, "Gentlemen, what is to become of me?" Gurley promptly replied, "O, we will make you Indian agent." So the bill was passed and Lincoln signed all the commissions, and the oyster supper was paid for, and we were all happy, and Arizona was launched upon the political sea.[21]

This silver inkstand was presented to President Abraham Lincoln by Charles D. Poston in commemoration of the signing of the Organic Act creating Arizona as a separate territory. The inkstand has been placed in the Library of Congress.

Poston probably assumed too much glory for himself. Sam Heintzelman, who had served as commander of Fort Yuma and founded a large mining company in Arizona, worked with certain Cincinnati mining investors to bring pressure on Ohio congressmen, who, with the able assistance of Delegate John S. Watts of New Mexico, were influential in pushing the Organic Act through Congress. Regardless of who deserves the greatest praise, however, it is certain that Poston played an active part.

To dramatize the event, Colonel Poston designed a massive inkstand which he intended to present to Lincoln with the request that it be used in affixing his signature to the Organic Act. Made by Tiffany's, and purportedly costing $1,500, the gift was fashioned from the purest Arizona silver. In the center was the dome of the capitol building which covered the inkwell itself. On one end was the figure of an

Indian woman — which has since been described as Comanche-type and hence not typical of Arizona tribes. On the other end was the figure of a frontiersman with rifle in hand. "Abraham Lincoln" was inscribed on one side of the base. The inscription on the other side, "From Charles D. Poston, Arizona — 1865" would indicate that the gift was about two years too late for the signing ceremony. Lincoln was privileged to use it for only about a month before his assassination. A prized item today, the inkstand is in the possession of the Library of Congress.

The officers of the new territory were mostly defeated "lame-duck" politicians.[22] Ohio Congressman John A. Gurley headed the slate as governor, but he became ill, delaying the

John A. Gurley, the first appointee as governor of the Territory of Arizona. Although he died before he could assume his post, both a street in Prescott and Gurley Mountain in Yavapai County are named for him.

Arizona Department of
Library and Archives

Some of the officials of the Territory of Arizona. Seated (left to right)
are Associate Justice Joseph P. Allyn, Governor John N. Goodwin, and
Secretary Richard C. McCormick; standing (left to right) are the Gov-
ernor's private secretary Henry W. Fleury, U.S. Marshal Milton B. Duf-
field, and U.S. District Attorney Almon P. Gage.

departure of the appointees for Arizona. Gurley died on
August 18, and John N. Goodwin of Maine was promoted
from chief justice of the Arizona Supreme Court to governor.
Richard C. McCormick of New York was appointed secretary
of the territory. William F. Turner of Iowa became chief
justice, with William T. Howell of Michigan and Joseph P.
Allyn of Connecticut as his associate judges. The other officers
were: District Attorney Almon Gage of New York, Surveyor-
General Levi Bashford of Wisconsin, United States Marshal
Milton B. Duffield of New York, and Superintendent of Indian
Affairs Charles D. Poston of Kentucky and Arizona. Reverend
Hiram W. Read, who had been a missionary in New Mexico
in 1855, accepted the position of postmaster for the new terri-
tory, hoping that he might be useful in the evangelical field.

Poston did not travel with the main party of Arizona officials. He crossed the continent to Sacramento via stagecoach, which he boarded in Kansas City. From Sacramento, he took a river steamer to San Francisco. There he met an old friend, J. Ross Browne, agent for the Department of Interior, who agreed to accompany him to Arizona. Browne described their boat trip to Los Angeles and the overland journey to Tucson, where they arrived in January, 1864, in his book, *A Tour Through Arizona in 1864*. Poston guided Browne through southern Arizona and distributed presents to various Indian tribes before joining the other officials at Prescott.

Browne revealed in a letter to his wife Lucy that Poston was paying him to publicize the mines of Arizona. ". . . As this is an enterprise of considerable hazard," he wrote from Tucson on January 16, 1864:

> I determined to have an understanding before going any further. I told Poston that I had a large family to support and could not risk my life without something certain in hand to provide for them in case of misfortune. He has agreed to give me $5000 in cash (drafts) for a year's services to the Mines; that is, to aid him for a few months in Arizona and write up the result on my return to San Francisco, which I hope will be about the 1st of May. The compensation, unfortunately is in greenbacks, and will not realize over about $3,500 in gold. He promises me, however, enough more in mining-stocks to make up probably ten thousand dollars, and I have the chance of investments in the Placer mines at Weaver's (?) and Walker's diggings. In addition to this, I shall receive pay for all my work for the Harpers and work out the $1,000 due gov't., which will make altogether at least $10,000 for my visit to Arizona. It is a great risk I have undertaken, my dear Lucy, and I may like hundreds of others fall sacrifice to my sense of duty; but I can only hope for the best. . . .[23]

Except for Marshal Duffield and his deputy, Robert F. Greely, who accompanied Poston, the rest of the territorial government party traveled from Washington to Fort Leavenworth — located on the Missouri River — and then over the historic Santa Fe Trail to Santa Fe, where they were welcomed on November 26. Until that time, the exact destination in Arizona was not certain, some members of the party even expecting that Tucson would be the new capital. General Carleton, however, argued against a location where Mexican

Appointed "Superintendent of Indian Affairs" for Arizona by President Lincoln and returned in 1863. Crossing the plains in Coaches via Salt Lake City to San Francisco, and thence to Los Angeles, Yuma, and Arizona. An account of this journey may be found in a book called "Wanderings in the Apache Country" by J. Ross Browne my companion & friend

In 1864. I was elected Delegate to Congress from Arizona. ——

It was a matter of Some pride to be elected the first Delegate to Congress from a Territory which I had had So much to do with Creating, and was the principal man in Organizing—Moreover the Mileage was $7.200: and the Salary $5000? Which all went in expenses &c

This page from Charles D. Poston's diary would indicate that he was not modest in summarizing his early political career in the Territory of Arizona.

Marker at Navajo Springs where the first officials of the Territory of Arizona took the oath of office and formally established the territorial government.

and secessionist influences were strong. He favored Chino Valley, near the geographical center of the 126,141 square miles of territory, and where a miniature gold rush had drawn several hundred miners. In October, the general had sent troops ahead under Major E. B. Willis to protect the miners and give security to property pending the arrival of the civil officers of Arizona. A military post, known as Fort Whipple, was established and became the first capital of the Arizona Territory.

The Goodwin party reached the fort after following the 35th parallel route which had been pioneered by Spanish conquistadores and U.S. Army explorers. Sometime on December 27, 1863, the officials crossed the eastern boundary of Arizona with their military escort. To make certain that they were in Arizona territory, the wagon train traveled for two more days before creaking to a halt beside a waterhole called Navajo Springs, just south of the present town of Navajo on Highway 66. There, on the snowy afternoon of December 29, 1863, the Territory of Arizona was formally established.[24]

PROCLAMATION.

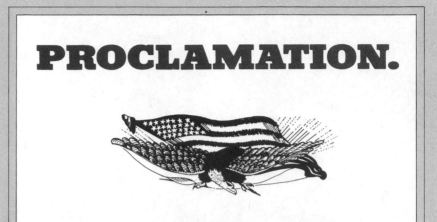

TO THE PEOPLE OF ARIZONA:

I, JOHN N. GOODWIN, having been appointed by the President of the United States, and duly qualified, as Governor of the TERRITORY OF ARIZONA, do hereby announce that by virtue of the powers with which I am invested by an Act of the Congress of the United States, providing a temporary government for the Territory, I shall this day proceed to organize said government. The provisions of the Act, and all laws and enactments established thereby, will be enforced by the proper Territorial officers from and after this date.

A preliminary census will forthwith be taken, and thereafter the Judicial Districts will be formed, and an election of members of the Legislative Assembly, and the other officers, provided by the Act, be ordered.

I invoke the aid and co-operation of all citizens of the Territory in my efforts to establish a government whereby the security of life and property will be maintained throughout its limits, and its varied resources be rapidly and successfully developed.

The seat of government will for the present be at or near Fort Whipple

JOHN N. GOODWIN.

By the Governor:

RICHARD C. M'CORMICK,

Secretary of the Territory.

Navajo Spring

FORT WHIPPLE, ARIZONA

December 29th 1863—

Governor John Goodwin's proclamation that officially established the territorial government of Arizona

After Reverend Read opened the ceremony with a prayer, Governor Goodwin and the other officers took the oath of office. Secretary McCormick delivered a brief but stirring oration and hoisted the Stars and Stripes. He also read the Governor's Proclamation which announced that a census would be taken, judicial districts formed, and an election held for members of a legislature. In his own handwriting, Goodwin specified that "the seat of government will be for the present at or near Fort Whipple." Nearly a month elapsed before the territorial officials reached the provisional capital on January 22, 1864.[25] The Territory of Arizona, which was to last until statehood was achieved in 1912, had been established in the name of the Union.

REFERENCE SECTION

Notes
Bibliography
Index

Notes to the Chapters

CHAPTER TWO

1. Emil W. Haury, "The Naco Mammoth," *The Kiva*, Vol. 18, Nos. 3–4 (Nov.–Dec., 1952), pp. 2–19.

CHAPTER THREE

1. See Harold S. Gladwin, Emil W. Haury, E. B. Sayles, and Nora Gladwin, *Excavations at Snaketown, Material Culture*. Tucson: University of Arizona Press, 1965, for a detailed account of the Snaketown project. An excellent article on the same subject is: Emil W. Haury, "The Hohokam: The First Masters of the Desert," *National Geographic Magazine*, Vol. 131, No. 5 (May, 1967), pp. 670–95.
2. For a description of Los Muertos, another pueblo of the Classic Period located south of Tempe, and a comparison with the Casa Grande, see Emil W. Haury, *The Excavation of Los Muertos and Neighboring Ruins in the Salt River Valley, Southern Arizona*. Based on the work of the Hemenway Expedition of 1887–1888. *Papers* of the Peabody Museum of American Archaeology and Ethnology, Harvard University, Vol. XXIV, No. 1, 1945, p. 14 *et seq.*
3. See H. M. Wormington, *Prehistoric Indians of the Southwest*, Denver, Colorado: The Denver Museum of Natural History, 1961, pp. 27–117, or Charles A. Amsden, *The Ancient Basketmakers*. Los Angeles: Southwest Museum Leaflets No. 11, 1939.
4. Charles A. Amsden, *Prehistoric Southwesterners From Basketmaker to Pueblo*. Los Angeles: Southwest Museum, 1949, pp. 54–57.
5. James H. Kellar, *The Atlatl in North America*. Indiana Historical Society, Indianapolis, Vol. III, No. 3 (June, 1955), pp. 302–308.
6. Amsden, *Prehistoric Southwesterners*, pp. 79–80.
7. Andrew E. Douglass, "The Secret of the Southwest Solved by the Talkative Tree-rings," *National Geographic Magazine*, Vol. 56, No. 6 (December, 1929), pp. 737–70.
8. Emil W. Haury, *Excavations in the Forestdale Valley, East-Central Arizona*. University of Arizona *Bulletin*, Vol. XI, No. 4 (October 1, 1940), p. 7 *et seq.*
9. Harold S. Colton, *The Sinagua: A Summary of the Archaeology of the Region of Flagstaff, Arizona*. Flagstaff: Northern Arizona Society of Science and Art, 1946, pp. 267–73. Drawings of Sinaguan houses are included.
10. Harold S. Colton, "The Patayan Problem in the Colorado River Valley," *Southwestern Journal of Anthropology*, Vol. 1, No. 1 (Spring, 1945), pp. 114–21.

CHAPTER FOUR

1. Cleve Hallenbeck, *Álvar Núñez Cabeza de Vaca, The Journey and Route of the First European to Cross the Continent of North America, 1534–1536*. Glendale, California: The Arthur H. Clark Company, 1940, pp. 220–28.
2. Adolph F. Bandelier (ed.), *The Journal of Álvar Núñez Cabeza de Vaca*. New York: A. S. Barnes & Co., 1905. Translation from Vaca's own narrative by Fanny Bandelier. (Reprinted at Albuquerque, New Mexico: Rio Grande Press, 1964, pp. xi–xii.)

3. "Fray Marcos' *Relación*," in Percy M. Baldwin, "Fray Marcos de Niza and His Discovery of the Seven Cities of Cibola," *New Mexico Historical Review*, Vol. I, No. 2 (April, 1926), pp. 201–23 or "Narrative of Fray Marcos," in Cleve Hallenbeck, *The Journey of Fray Marcos de Niza*. Dallas: Southern Methodist University, 1949, pp. 15–37.

4. "Castañeda's History of the Expedition," in George P. Hammond and Agapito Rey (eds.) *Narratives of the Coronado Expedition, 1540–1542*. Albuquerque: University of New Mexico Press, 1940, p. 200.

5. "Translation of the Narrative of Castañeda," in George W. Winship, *The Coronado Expedition, 1540–1542*. Reprinted in Chicago: Rio Grande Press, Inc., 1964, pp. 202–203.

6. "Castañeda's History of the Expedition," in Hammond and Rey, *Narratives of the Coronado Expedition*, p. 214.

7. See "Charges Against Coronado Resulting From the Investigation into the Management of the Expedition, September 3, 1544," in Hammond and Rey, *Narratives of the Coronado Expedition*, pp. 393–97.

8. George P. Hammond and Agapito Rey (translators and editors), *Expedition into New Mexico Made by Antonio de Espejo, 1582–1583 As Revealed in the Journal of Diego Pérez de Luxán, A Member of the Party*. Los Angeles: The Quivira Society, 1929, pp. 95–108; see also Antonio Espejo, "Account of the Journey to the Provinces and Settlements of New Mexico, 1583," in Herbert E. Bolton (ed.), *Spanish Exploration in the Southwest, 1542–1706*. New York: Barnes and Noble, Inc., 1963, pp. 185–89.

9. Katherine Bartlett, "Notes Upon the Routes of Espejo and Farfán to the Mines in the Sixteenth Century," *New Mexico Historical Review*, Vol. XVII, No. 1 (January, 1942), pp. 23, 30.

10. Don Juan de Oñate, "Discovery of the Mines," in George P. Hammond and Agapito Rey, *Don Juan de Oñate, Colonizer of New Mexico*. Albuquerque: University of New Mexico Press, 1953, pp. 408–15.

CHAPTER FIVE

1. "List and memorial of the religious whom the Indians of New Mexico have killed, 1680," in Charles W. Hackett, *Revolt of the Pueblo Indians of New Mexico and Otermin's Attempted Reconquest, 1680–1682*. Albuquerque: University of New Mexico Press, 1942, Vol. I, pp. 108–11.

2. Translated correspondence relative to this expedition can be found in Lansing B. Bloom (ed.), "A Campaign Against the Moqüi Pueblos Under the Leadership of Governor and Captain-General Don Phelix Martínez, Beginning August 16th, 1716 . . . ," an annotated translation by the late Ralph E. Twitchell. *New Mexico Historical Review*, Vol. VI, No. 2 (April, 1931), pp. 158–226.

3. Jay J. Wagoner, *History of the Cattle Industry in Southern Arizona, 1540–1940*. Tucson: University of Arizona Press, 1952, pp. 10–17.

4. Herbert E. Bolton (ed.), *Kino's Historical Memoir of Pimería Alta: A Contemporary Account of the Beginnings of California, Sonora, and Arizona, by Father Eusebio Kino S.J., 1683–1711*. Cleveland: Arthur H. Clark Company, 1919, Vol. I, pp. 122–23.

5. "Diary of Lieutenant Cristóbal Martín Bernal," pp. 35–47, and "The Observations of Kino and Three Captains, November, 1697, and September, 1698," pp. 68–75, in Fay Jackson Smith, John L. Kessell, and Francis J. Fox, S.J., *Father Kino in Arizona*. Phoenix: Arizona Historical Foundation, 1966.

6. Harry J. Karns (translator). *Luz De Tierra Incógnita by Captain Juan Mateo Manje*. Tucson: Arizona Silhouettes, 1954, pp. 51–59.

7. Bolton, *Rim of Christendom*, pp. 379–84; see also *Relación Diaria* in Smith, Kessell, and Fox, *Father Kino in Arizona*, pp. 47–50.

8. Ronald L. Ives, "The Quest of the Blue Shells," *Arizoniana*, Vol. II, No. 1 (Spring, 1961), pp. 3–7.

9. Bolton, *Rim of Christendom*, pp. 483–84.
10. Bolton, *Kino's Historical Memoir of Pimería Alta*, Vol. I, pp. 234–35.
11. John L. Kessell, *Mission of Sorrows, Jesuit Guevavi and the Pimas, 1691–1767*. Tucson: University of Arizona Press, 1970; see also Smith, Kessell, and Fox, S.J., *Father Kino in Arizona*, pp. 91 and 104.
12. Bolton, *Rim of Christendom*, p. 513.
13. *Ibid.*, pp. 425, 504–505, and Bolton, *Kino's Historical Memoir of Pimería Alta*, Vol. I, p. 205.
14. Bolton, *Kino's Historical Memoir of Pimería Alta*, Vol. I, p. 241.
15. *Ibid.*, Vol. I, p. 373.
16. Ernest J. Burrus, *Kino's Plan*. Tucson: Arizona Historical Society, 1961, pp. 32–33; see also Bolton, *Rim of Christendom*, pp. 574–79.
17. Bolton, *Kino's Historical Memoir of Pimería Alta*, Vol. 2, pp. 229–75.
18. *Ibid.*, Vol. 2, pp. 265–66.
19. See Padre Luis Velarde's *Relación of Pimería Alta*, 1716, in *Luz De Tierra Incógnita*, pp. 262–63.
20. *Acceptance of the Statue of Eusebio Francisco Kino*. Washington, D.C.: Government Printing Office, 1965.

CHAPTER SIX

1. Theodore E. Treutlein (translator and annotator), "Document: The Relation of Philipp [Phelipe] Segesser," *Mid-America*, Vol. 27, No. 3 (July, 1945), p. 142.
2. *Ibid.*, pp. 139–64.
3. *Ibid.*, p. 146.
4. *Ibid.*, p. 150.
5. *Ibid.*, pp. 146–47.
6. *Ibid.*, p. 149.
7. John L. Kessell, *Mission of Sorrows: Jesuit Guevavi and the Pimas, 1691–1767*. Tucson: University of Arizona Press, 1970, pp. 57–59.
8. "*Relación*, 1746," in Peter M. Dunne (translator and annotator), *Jacobo Sedelmayr: Missionary, Frontiersman, Explorer in Arizona and Sonora*. Tucson: Arizona Historical Society, 1955, pp. 23, 33.
9. See "Biographical Sketch," in *Jacobo Sedelmayr*, pp. 1–11.
10. "*Relación*, 1746, in *Jacobo Sedelmayr*, pp. 15–42.
11. Letter of Jacobo Sedelmayr, Visitor of Pimería Alta, et al., to the Viceroy, from Tubutama in Pimería Alta, June 25, 1751, in *Jacobo Sedelmayr*, pp. 77–80.
12. "*Derrotero*" [journey], of the ensign of the soldiers (unsigned), who accompanied Sedelmayr, in *Jacobo Sedelmayr*, p. 72.
13. "Biographical Sketch," in *Jacobo Sedelmayr*, pp. 9–11.
14. See Edward H. Spicer, *Cycles of Conquest*. Tucson: University of Arizona Press, 1962, pp. 129–30; see also Kessell, *Mission of Sorrows*, pp. 116–17.
15. Russell C. Ewing, "Investigations into the Causes of the Pima Uprising of 1751," *Mid-America*, Vol. 23, No. 2 (April, 1941), pp. 139–40.
16. Russell C. Ewing, "The Pima Outbreak in November, 1751," *New Mexico Historical Review*, Vol. XIII, No. 4 (October, 1938), pp. 339–40.
17. *Ibid.*, p. 108.
18. Ewing, "Investigations into the Causes of the Pima Uprising of 1751," pp. 149–51.
19. Kessell, *Mission of Sorrows*, pp. 139–42.
20. *Ibid.*, pp. 146–47.
21. Letter of Father Middendorff to Father Balthazar, from Tucson, March 3, 1757, in *Kiva*, Vol. 22, No. 4 (June, 1957), pp. 1–10.
22. Quoted in Henry F. Dobyns. *Pioneering Christians Among the Perishing Indians of Tucson*. Lima, Peru: Editorial Estudios Andinos, 1962, pp. 14–15.
23. J. Augustine Donohue, S.J., "The Unlucky Jesuit Mission of Bac, 1732–1767." *Arizona and the West*, Vol. 2, No. 2 (Summer, 1960), p. 137.

24. Ignaz Pfefferkorn, *Sonora, A Description of the Province*. Translated and anno-
     tated by Theodore E. Treutlein. Albuquerque: University of New Mexico Press,
     1949.
25. "Anza's Return Diary" in *Anza's California Expeditions*, Vol. II. Translated
     from the original Spanish manuscripts by Herbert Eugene Bolton. New York:
     Russell and Russell, 1966, pp. 230–31.
26. "Garcés Return Diary," in *Anza's California Expeditions*, Vol. II, p. 387.
27. "Anza's Return Diary," in *Anza's California Expeditions*, Vol. II, p. 240.
28. *Font's Complete Diary: A Chronicle of the Founding of San Francisco*. Translated
     from the original manuscript by Herbert Eugene Bolton. Berkeley: University
     of California Press, 1931, pp. 32–33.
29. *Font's Complete Diary*, p. 121.
30. *On the Trail of a Spanish Pioneer: The Diary and Itinerary of Francisco Garcés
     in His Travels Through Sonora, Arizona, and California, 1775–1776*. Translated
     and edited by Elliott Coues. 2 vols. New York: Frances P. Harper, 1900,
     pp. 388–91.
31. A copy of the last page of Chief Palma's petition, written by Anza, to Viceroy
     Bucareli, November 11, 1776, is in "Correspondence," in *Anza's California
     Expeditions*, Vol. V, p. 377.
32. Alfred B. Thomas (translator and editor). *Teodoro de Croix and the Northern
     Frontier of New Spain, 1776–1783*. From the Original Document in the Archives
     of the Indies, Seville. Norman: University of Oklahoma Press, 1941, pp. 219–23.
33. Thomas, *Teodoro de Croix*, pp. 59–60, 238.
34. See "Fages Diary" in Ronald L. Ives (ed.), "Retracing the Route of the Fages
     Expedition of 1781," Part I, *Arizona and the West*, Vol. 8, No. 1 (Spring, 1966),
     pp. 65–68.
35. "Fages Diary," Part II, *Arizona and the West*, Vol. 8, No. 2 (Summer, 1966), pp.
     162–67; see also Clarence Cullimore, "A California Martyr's Bones," *California
     Historical Society Quarterly*, Vol. XXXIII, No. 1 (March, 1954), pp. 13–21. On
     July 19, 1794, the remains of the four Yuma martyrs (Padres Garcés, Barreneche,
     Díaz, and Moreno) were reburied at the College of Santa Cruz, Querétaro, Mexico.
36. Cameron Greenleaf and Andrew Wallace, "Tucson: Pueblo, Presidio, and Ameri-
     can City, A Synopsis of Its History," *Arizoniana*, Vol. 3, No. 2 (Summer, 1962),
     p. 23.
37. Sidney B. Brinckerhoff, "The Last Years of Spanish Arizona, 1786–1821," *Arizona
     and the West*, Vol. 9, No. 1 (Spring, 1967), p. 8.
38. Dispatch from the Commandant General (Neve) of the Frontier Provinces of New
     Spain to the King's minister (José de Galvez), No. 76, 26 January, 1784, in Henry
     F. Dobyns, *Lance Ho! Containment of the Western Apaches by the Royal Spanish
     Garrison at Tucson*. Lima, Peru: Editorial Estudios Andinos, 1964, p. 32.
39. Dispatch of Neve to Galvez, April 5, 1784, in Dobyns, *Lance Ho!* pp. 34–35.
40. "The Royal Regulations of 1772," in Brinckerhoff and Faulk, *Lancers for the
     King*, pp. 21–23.
41. The report of Colonel Roque de Medina, Revista del Presidio de Tucson, October
     10, 1785, now in the Archivo General de Indias, Seville, Spain. See Max L.
     Moorhead, *The Apache Frontier: Jacobo Ugarte and Spanish-Indian Relations
     in Northern New Spain, 1769–1791*. Norman: University of Oklahoma Press,
     1968, pp. 90–91.
42. Bernardo de Galvez, *Instructions for Governing the Interior Provinces of New
     Spain, 1786*. Translated and edited by Donald E. Worcester. Berkeley: The
     Quivira Society, 1951, pp. 48–49.
43. *Ibid.*, p. 47.
44. George P. Hammond, "The Zúñiga Journal, Tucson to Santa Fe: The Opening
     of the Spanish Trade Route, 1788–1795," *New Mexico Historical Review*, Vol. VI,
     No. 1 (January, 1931), pp. 40–65.

45. Bernard L. Fontana, *Biography of a Desert Church: The Story of Mission San Xavier del Bac. The Smoke Signal,* No. 3 (Spring, 1961), p. 9. This excellent study by Fontana contains a quote from a description of San Xavier found in the report of Francisco Iturralde who visited San Xavier del Bac in September, 1797. A copy of Iturralde's report is on file at Mission San Xavier, Tucson.
46. Brinckerhoff, "The Last Years of Spanish Arizona, 1786–1821," p. 17.

CHAPTER SEVEN

1. *Report of the Commissioner of the General Land Office to the Secretary of Interior, 1869.* Washington, D.C.: Government Printing Office, 1870, pp. 150–51.
2. *Report of the Commissioner of the General Land Office to the Secretary of Interior, 1871.* Washington, D.C.: Government Printing Office, 1873, p. 202.
3. *Report of the Commissioner of the General Land Office to the Secretary of Interior, 1884.* Washington, D.C.: Government Printing Office, 1884, pp. 152–53.
4. *Report of the Commissioner of the General Land Office, 1887.* Washington, D.C.: Government Printing Office, 1887, p. 524.
5. Fred L. Israel (ed.), *The State of the Union Messages of the Presidents, 1790–1966.* Vol. II. New York: Chelsea House-Robert Hector, Publishers, 1966, p. 1645.
6. Charles Poston, *Building a State in Apache Land,* pp. 93–96.
7. *Arizona Weekly Citizen,* January 5, 1884.
8. *Deeds of Real Estate,* Book No. 19, pp. 451–54, in the Santa Cruz County Recorder's office, Nogales, Arizona.
9. *Ibid.,* Docket No. 18, p. 36.
10. *Ibid.,* Docket No. 104, p. 261.
11. *Ibid.,* Docket No. 113, p. 537.
12. A good account of Cameron's career in Arizona is Jane Wayland Brewster, "San Rafael Cattle Company," *Arizona and the West,* Vol. 8, No. 2 (Summer, 1966), pp. 133–56.
13. *Report of the Commissioner of the General Land Office.* Washington, D.C.: Government Printing Office, 1887; see also *Arizona Daily Star,* June 21, 1887.
14. Alfred A. Green, Plaintiff, vs. U.S.A., R. R. Richardson, Colin Cameron, Wm. C. Jones, Harvey L. Christie and 61 others, including Albert Steinfield. Case #2 before the Court of Private Land Claims, January, 1899, in Court of Private Land Claims Dockets, RG 49, GLO. See also *Arizona Enterprise* (Florence), April 4, 1891.
15. *U.S. vs. Green et al.,* 185 *U.S. Reports,* pp. 256–70.
16. *Tombstone Epitaph,* Sunday edition, August 6, 1911.
17. *Ely's Administrator vs. United States,* May 31, 1898, 171 *U.S. Reports,* pp. 220–41. See also Decree of Confirmation of the San José de Sonoita Grant, the U.S., plaintiff, vs. Santiago Ainsa, administrator of the estate of Frank Ely (deceased) et al. U.S. Court of Private Land Claims, Tucson, Arizona, September 1, 1902, RG 49, GLO, Arizona private land claim #8.
18. "Description Notes of the Survey of the San José de Sonoita Private Land Claim," Santa Cruz County, Arizona, witnessed on October 31, 1903, by Frank S. Ingalls, U.S. Surveyor General for the Territory of Arizona, RG 49, GLO, Arizona private land claim #8.
19. *Deeds to Real Estate,* Book No. 30, pp. 286–87, and Docket 27, p. 355, in Santa Cruz County Recorder's office, Nogales, Arizona. The Cowlishaws sold a portion of the Sonoita grant to the Baca Float Ranch, Inc., in 1938, and Mrs. Lewis transferred some acreage to the town of Patagonia in 1951. Other small portions have also been sold.
20. John R. Bartlett, *Personal Narrative of Explorations and Incidents....* New York: D. Appleton & Co., 1854, pp. 396–97.

21. James H. Tevis, *Arizona in the '50s*. Albuquerque: University of New Mexico Press, 1954, p. 76.

22. *Perrin vs. United States,* 171 *U.S. Reports,* p. 292.

23. See Report of U.S. Attorney Matt. G. Reynolds, CPLC, Arizona District, in the case of Robert Perrin, plaintiff, vs. United States et al., defendants, San Ignacio del Babocomari Grant, from Santa Fe, May 10, 1900, in RG 60: Department of Justice, National Archives. Associate Justices Murray and Fuller dissented, opposing confirmation on the grounds that the eight *sitios* granted were never definitely located within the exterior boundaries containing approximately 35 *sitios*. The amount finally surveyed and granted was 33,792.20 acres, less than eight *sitios* by approximately a thousand acres and considerably less than the 123,068.87 acres claimed in the suit of 1899. See Confirmation of the San Ygnacio del Babocomari Grant, Robert Perrin, plaintiff, vs. the United States et al., United States Court of Private Land Claims, Tucson, Arizona, February 10, 1902, RG 49, GLO, Arizona private land claim #4. See also "Descriptive Notes of the Survey of the Babocomari Private Land Claim, Situated in Cochise and Santa Cruz Counties, Territory of Arizona," witnessed April 12, 1904, by Frank S. Ingalls, U.S. Surveyor General for the Territory of Arizona, in RG 49, GLO, Arizona private land claim #4.

24. The patent is recorded in *Deeds, Real Estate,* Book 31, pp. 244–45, Cochise County Recorder's office, Bisbee, Arizona. See also *Deeds of Real Estate,* Book 3, pp. 556 and 606, and Docket 57, p. 84, Santa Cruz County Recorder's office in Nogales, Arizona.

25. See *Deeds, Real Estate,* Book 123, p. 19, Cochise County Recorder's office, for the Brophy deed. The Perrin to Waters deed is in Book 12, pp. 621–22. In 1922, the Los Angeles Trust and Savings Company gained control of the grant, except for the 2500 acres, for awhile.

26. Frank Cullen Brophy, "San Ignacio del Babocomari," *Arizona Highways,* Vol. XLII, No. 9 (September, 1966), pp. 2–5, 9–17.

27. "Petition of Janet G. Howard and George Hearst for Confirmation of Rancho San Juan de la Boquillas y Nogales," Filed December 11, 1880, John Wasson, Surveyor General, and "Deed, Janet Howard to George Hearst," October 2, 1889, Miscellaneous Papers in the Case of San Juan de las Boquillas y Nogales Grant, Court of Private Land Claims. Case No. 42, U.S. Department of Interior, Bureau of Land Management, Phoenix, Arizona, microfilm in the Arizona Department of Library and Archives.

28. Decree of Confirmation of the Rancho San Juan de las Boquillas y Nogales Grant, W. R. Hearst and Phebe A. Hearst, plaintiffs, vs. the United States et al., in U.S. Court of Private Land Claims, Tucson, Arizona, February 14, 1899, and "Descriptive Notes of the Survey of the San Juan de las Boquillas y Nogales Private Land Claim," witnessed by George Christ, U.S. Surveyor General for the Territory of Arizona, in RG 49, GLO, Arizona claim #42. See also Report of U.S. Attorney Matt. G. Reynolds, CPLC, to the Attorney General on the San Juan de las Boquillas y Nogales grant, from Santa Fe, June 15, 1899, in RG 60, Department of Justice, National Archives.

29. *Deeds, Real Estate,* Book 14, pp. 473–86, Cochise County Recorder's office, Bisbee, Arizona; *Docket* Books No. 195, p. 176, and No. 198, p. 561, in the same office.

30. Docket No. 738, p. 400, in Cochise County Recorder's office. See also the files of the Boquillas Cattle Company and Tenneco West, Inc., in the Arizona Corporation Commission, Incorporating Department, Phoenix, Arizona. Tenneco West, Inc., was chartered in Delaware in 1968. When the Kern company first merged with Tenneco West, Inc., in Texas in 1970, there were already several component companies of Tenneco in the corporation.

31. *Camou vs. United States,* 171 *U.S. Reports,* pp. 277–97.

32. See "Descriptive Notes of the Survey of the San Rafael del Valle Private Land Claim," witnessed on July 14, 1902, by Hugh L. Price, U.S. Surveyor General for the Territory of Arizona, in RG 49, GLO, Arizona private land claim #3. See also Decree of Confirmation of the San Rafael del Valle claim, Juan Pedro Camou, plaintiff, vs. the United States, U.S. Court of Private Land Claims, Tucson, Arizona, June 2, 1899, in RG 49, GLO, Arizona private land claim #3, and Report of Matt. G. Reynolds to the Attorney General on the San Rafael del Valle grant, from Santa Fe, January 2, 1900, in RG 60, Department of Justice, National Archives.

33. *U.S. vs. Camou*, 184 *U.S. Reports*, p. 572 *et seq.*

34. *Deeds, Real Estate*, Book 36, p. 636, Cochise County Recorder's office, Bisbee.

35. *Deeds, Real Estate*, Book AJ3, No. 79.

36. John R. Bartlett, *Personal Narrative* . . . , Vol. 1, pp. 255–56.

37. Decree of Confirmation of the San Bernardino Grant, John H. Slaughter vs. the United States, in the U.S. Court of Private Land Claims, Tucson, Arizona, February 10, 1900, in RG 49, GLO, Arizona private land claim #1. Associate Justices Murray and Fuller opposed confirmation on the ground that the grant was not recorded within the meaning of the Gadsden Treaty. See Report of U.S. Attorney Matt. G. Reynolds for the case of John H. Slaughter, plaintiff, vs. United States, defendant, San Bernardino Grant, from Santa Fe, March 15, 1900, in RG 60, Department of Justice, National Archives.

38. "Tomás Cabeza de Baca and Town of Las Vegas Grant," Report No. 20, File No. 6, in Records of Private Land Claims Adjudicated by the U.S. Surveyor General, 1855–1890. (Also on Reel 15, Microfilm Papers Relating to New Mexico Land Grants) in Archives Division, State of New Mexico Records Center, Santa Fe; see also Guy M. Herstrom, "Pygmy Among the Giants," 1959 *Brand Book* of the Denver Posse of Westerners, Vol. XV, pp. 237–45; see also 12 *U.S. Statutes at Large*, 1860, Chap. 167, p. 72.

39. *Lane vs. Watts*, 234 *U.S. Reports*, pp. 525–42.

40. Story of Mrs. Sarah M. Black as related to Mrs. George Kitt and Charles M. Wood, February 14, 1926, copy in Arizona Historical Society.

41. *Watts vs. Ely Real Estate Investment*, 254 *U.S. Reports*, p. 862 et. seq.

42. Docket No. 109, p. 275, in Santa Cruz County Recorder's office, Nogales, Arizona.

43. *Deeds*, Yavapai County Recorder's office, Prescott, Territory of Arizona, Book No. 5, pp. 200–206. For a copy of the patent signed by President William McKinley on October 6, 1898, as well as the notes and map of the survey by Surveyor General John Wasson, dated April 7, 1877, see *Deeds*, No. 47, pp. 240–54. The Wasson survey — made by his deputy, C. Burton Foster — measured the grant for 99,445.2 acres, whereas the original survey was for 99,289.39 acres.

44. *Deeds*, Yavapai County Recorder's office, Index No. 1, p. 569; Book No. 6, p. 67; Book No. 7, pp. 481–83; Book No. 8, pp. 313–27; and Book No. 20, pp. 426–29.

45. See Andrew C. Hargrove to E. B. Perrin, November 5, 1884, 5/107ths share in Baca Float No. 5, in *Deeds*, Yavapai County Recorder's office, Book No. 20, p. 419; Rose G. Lewis, wife of deceased Burwell B. Lewis, to E. B. Perrin, *Deeds*, No. 28, p. 335; John Vickers to E. B. Perrin, December 19, 1891, 4,000 acres, *Deeds*, No. 30, p. 516; and Hilary A. Herbert to E. B. Perrin, March 11, 1895, 46/1,000ths of Baca Float, *Deeds*, No. 37, p. 77. See also, copy of Warranty Deed, Atlantic and Pacific Railroad Company to Edward B. Perrin, March 10, 1894, in *Deeds*, Book No. 36, pp. 494–513. In this one transaction, Perrin paid $165,083.32 for extensive acreage in the three counties of Yavapai, Coconino, and Mohave. The list of sections acquired from the railroad fill sixteen pages in the Yavapai County Recorder's *Deeds* book.

46. *Deeds*, Book No. 14, pp. 24–30.

47. See E. B. Perrin to Burwell B. Lewis, May 17, 1880, undivided 5/19ths of Baca Float No. 5, in *Deeds*, Book No. 19, p. 613. Lewis, in turn, sold shares in the grant.

See Lewis to L. H. Davis, May 31, 1880, 4600 acres for $2,500, in *Deeds,* Book No. 17, p. 405; Lewis to Alonzo Hill, July 7, 1880, 5/107ths undivided interest for $2,500, in *Deeds* No. 19, p. 616; and Lewis to Andrew C. Hargrove, July 7, 1880, 5/107ths undivided interest for $2,500, in *Deeds,* No. 19, p. 618.

48. *Deeds,* No. 21, pp. 203–204; No. 102, pp. 312–13; and No. 125, pp. 529–35. As late as 1904 Baca Float No. 5 was in the hands of a receiver and was sold at public auction. The grant stayed in the family, however, when Lilo Perrin submitted the highest bid, a million dollars, to acquire title to the ranch. See *Deeds,* No. 71, p. 351.

49. Warranty deed given by Perrin Properties (J. F. Resleure, president, and Lilo M. Perrin, Jr., treasurer) to Greene Cattle Co., May 4, 1937, *Deeds,* No. 168, pp. 468–70.

50. *Arivaca Land and Cattle Company vs. United States,* March 24, 1902, in 184 *U.S. Reports,* p. 650.

51. J. Ross Browne, *Adventures in Apache Country.* New York: Harper and Brothers, 1869. Re-edition, University of Arizona Press, 1974, p. 271.

52. *Report of the Commissioner of the General Land Office to the Secretary of the Interior.* Washington, D.C.: Government Printing Office, 1888, p. 395. Poston was not pleased with the report made by the U.S. Surveyor General for the Territory of Arizona, John Wasson, on January 21, 1881. See RG 49, GLO, Arizona private land claim #15.

53. Open letter of C. D. Poston from Nogales, Arizona, December 22, 1884, quoted in A. W. Gressinger, *Charles D. Poston, Sunland Seer.* Globe, Arizona: Dale Stuart King, Publisher, 1961, pp. 167–68.

54. 184 *U.S. Reports,* p. 650; see also, *The Arizona Republican,* June 6, 1915.

55. "El Sopori Land Claim in Arizona," *Sen. Ex. Doc.* No. 93, 48th Cong., 1st Sess., p. 74.

56. Browne, *Adventures in Apache Country,* p. 260.

57. "El Sopori Land Claim in Arizona," *Sen. Ex. Doc.* No. 93, 48th Cong., 1st Sess., p. 73.

58. See RG 49, GLO, Arizona private land claim #14.

59. *The Arizona Daily Star,* February 16, 1958.

60. 171 *U.S. Reports,* pp. 244–45; *Senate Executive Document* 207, 46th Cong. 2nd Sess. (Serial #1886); and RG 49, GLO, Arizona private land claim #8.

61. Peter R. Brady, "In the Early Days," *Arizona Daily Citizen,* June 17, 1898. For a more detailed account of this incident, see "The Reminiscences of Peter R. Brady of the A. B. Gray Railroad Survey, 1853–54," in L. R. Bailey (ed.), *The A. B. Gray Report.* Los Angeles: Westernlore Press, 1963, pp. 209–14.

62. Browne, *Adventures in the Apache Country,* p. 154.

63. "Opinions and Recommendations of Surveyor General John Wasson in the Tumacácori, Calabasas, and Huehavi [Guevavi] land claims," Tucson, Arizona, January 7, 1880, in RG 49, GLO, Baca Float No. 3 Land Claim. Wasson also traced the history of Spanish missions and pueblos in this document.

64. *Faxon vs. United States,* 171 *U.S. Reports,* pp. 244–60.

65. Letter of Surveyor General George J. Roskruge of Arizona to Commissioner of the General Land Office, from Tucson, May 12, 1897, in Records of the General Land Office, Record Group 49, National Archives.

66. Letter of Wasson to Williamson, from Tucson, March 3, 1881, in RG 49, GLO; see also *Arizona Weekly Citizen,* March 6, 1881.

67. Report of United States Attorney Matt. G. Reynolds, CPLC, in the Rancho los Nogales de Elias Grant, Arizona, United States, Plaintiff, vs. Santiago Ainsa, Administrator, et al., Defendants, from Santa Fe, February 26, 1894, in RG 60, Department of Justice, National Archives.

68. *Ainsa vs. United States,* 161 *U.S. Reports,* pp. 208–34.

69. Reprinted in *The Arizona Sentinel* (Yuma), January 25, 1879.

70. See Decree of the Court of Private Land Claims, November 27, 1899, and the opinion written by Associate Justice Thomas Fuller, in Report of U.S. Attorney Matt. G. Reyonlds, CPLC, Arizona District, Reloj Cattle Company, plaintiff, vs. United States of America and E. J. Roberts, defendants, San Pedro Grant, from Santa Fe, December 15, 1899, in RG 60, Department of Justice, National Archives.
71. *Reloj Cattle Company vs. United States,* 184 *U.S. Reports,* pp. 624–39.
72. *Ainsa vs. United States,* 184 *U.S. Reports,* p. 643.
73. *Ibid.,* p. 641.
74. The unanimous opinion of the court was written by Associate Justice William W. Murray. See transcript in Report of U.S. Attorney Matt. G. Reynolds, CPLC, Arizona District, in the case of Santiago Ainsa, Administrator and Trustee, Plaintiff, vs. United States of America and Hugh H. Whitney, Defendants, Agua Prieta Grant, from Santa Fe, December 23, 1899, in RG 60, Department of Justice, National Archives.
75. *Arizona Daily Star,* July 18, 1886 and Arizona Court of Private Land Claims Dockets, Records of the General Land Office, Record Group 49, National Archives.
76. See letters of José Antonio Crespo to the Governor of the State of Sonora, from Guaymas, September 10, 1852; decree of Governor Fernando Cubillas, at Ures, Sonora, September 13, 1852, and a translation of the *titulo* authenticated by Governor Cubillas at Ures, Sonora, September 20, 1852, in Report of U.S. Attorney Matt. G. Reynolds, CPLC, Arizona District, Francis E. Spencer and George Hill Howard, plaintiffs, vs. United States, et al., Defendants, Tres Alamos Grant, from Santa Fe, June 20, 1899, in RG 60, Department of Justice, National Archives.
77. "Transcript of Proceedings before the U.S. Surveyor General of Arizona [J. W. Robbins] in the matter of the Grant of Rancho of Tres Alamos, José Ant. Crespo, original grantee, George H. Howard, present claimant," in RG 49, GLO, Arizona private land claim #17. See also *Opinion and Report of U.S. Surveyor General for Arizona, Tres Alamos Grant.* Washington, D.C.: Gibson Brothers, 1884, 7 pp. Robbins includes a report by R. C. Hopkins who studied the title and concluded that it was genuine. The title specifically described the grant as being for ten leagues *riberanos* (along the river) on the San Pedro.
78. Affidavit of William S. Oury quoted in report of John Hise to the General Land Office, *ibid.* The full text of Oury's testimony on June 15, 1886, can be found in the Arizona Court of Private Land Claims Dockets, Records of the General Land Office, Record Group 49, National Archives.
79. *Tombstone Epitaph,* quoted in the *Arizona Daily Star,* July 22, 1886.
80. Open letter from Charles D. Poston, printed in *The Arizona Daily Gazette,* March 4, 1893.
81. *United States vs. Coe,* May 23, 1898, 170 *U.S. Reports,* pp. 681–702 and *United States vs. Coe,* May 22, 1899, 170 *U.S. Reports,* pp. 578–79.
82. *House Report* No. 1585, 51st Cong. 1st Sess., 1890, pp. 1–5. (Serial # 2811). See also Report on the El Paso de los Algodones Private Land Claim, John Wasson, Surveyor General, August 12, 1880, in RG 49, GLO, Arizona private land claim #6.
83. Report of U.S. Attorney Matt. G. Reynolds, CPLC, in case of Earl B. Coe, plaintiff, vs. United States, defendant, Rancho El Paso de los Algodones Grant, from Santa Fe, April 21, 1893, in RG 60, Department of Justice, National Archives.
84. Letter of Commissioner of the General Land Office Binger Herman to U.S. Land Office (Milton R. Moore, Register, and John R. Bauman, Receiver), from Washington, D. C., January 29, 1901. Printed in *Arizona Daily Star,* February 7, 1901. See also 56 *U.S. Statutes at Large,* 56th Cong. 2nd Sess., 1900–1901, pp. 729–30.
85. *Arizona Daily Star,* March 19, 1901.
86. *Arizona Gazette,* May 9, 1881.
87. See Donald M. Powell, *The Peralta Grant* (Norman: University of Oklahoma Press, 1960), for a full, documented account of the Reavis fraud.

88. *Weekly Arizona Miner,* March 20, 1874.
89. "Order of Location by the Viceroy," and application of James Addison Peralta Reavis and Doña Sofia Loreta Micaela de Maso-Reavis y Peralta de la Córdoba for a preliminary survey of the "Peralta Grant," to the U.S. Surveyor General, Tucson, Arizona, September 2, 1887, in RG 49, GLO, Washington National Records Center (National Archives depository).
90. *In the Court of Claims of the United States . . . J. A. Peralta Reavis and Doña Sofia Loreta Micaela de Maso-Reavis y Peralta de la Córdoba, His Wife, and Clinton P. Farrell, Trustee vs. The United States of America, Petition of Claimants* [*No. 16,719*] (Washington, D.C.: Gibson Brothers, 1890).
91. *Arizona Gazette,* July 26, 1888.
92. *Petition of Claimants* [*No. 16,719*], p. 19.
93. "Report of Royal A. Johnson, U.S. Surveyor General for Arizona, adverse to the alleged 'Peralta Grant,' recommending that it not be confirmed," Tucson, Arizona, October 10, 1889, in RG 49, GLO, Private Land Claims Docket #18, Washington National Records Center. The report can also be found in Royal A. Johnson, *Adverse Report of the Surveyor General of Arizona Upon the Alleged "Peralta Grant," a Complete Exposé of Its Fraudulent Character* (Phoenix, Arizona: Gazette Book and Job Office, 1890).
94. Report of U.S. Attorney Matt. G. Reynolds to the Attorney General in the matter of the prosecution of James Addison Peraltareavis, from Santa Fe, New Mexico, July 28, 1896, in Correspondence of Matthew G. Reynolds, RG 60, Department of Justice, National Archives.

CHAPTER EIGHT

1. Timothy Flint. *The Personal Narrative of James Ohio Pattie of Kentucky.* Cincinnati: John H. Wood, 1831. [Reprinted in paperback edition in New York: Lippincott, 1962.]
2. Charles L. Camp (ed.), *George C. Yount and His Chronicles of the West.* Denver, Colorado: Old West Publishing Co., 1966, pp. 37–38.
3. A good summary of Pattie's life is: Ann W. Hafen, "James Ohio Pattie," in LeRoy R. Hafen (ed.). *The Mountain Men and the Fur Trade of the Far West,* Vol. IV. Glendale: The Arthur H. Clark Co., 1966, pp. 231–50.
4. See "A brief sketch of accidents, misfortunes, and depredations committed by Indians, etc., on the firm of Smith, Jackson & Sublette . . ." in letter to General William Clark, in Dale L. Morgan, *Jedediah Smith and the Opening of the West.* Lincoln: University of Nebraska Press, 1969, Appendix A, pp. 337–38 and note 7, p. 422.
5. A good account of the life of Williams based on primary sources is Alpheus H. Favour. *Old Bill Williams: Mountain Man.* Norman: University of Oklahoma Press, 1962.
6. Sharlot M. Hall. *First Citizen of Prescott: Pauline Weaver, Trapper and Mountain Man.* Prescott, Arizona, n.p., 1932.
7. Edmund W. Wells, *Argonaut Tales.* New York: The Grafton Press, 1927, pp. 263–78.
8. Christopher Carson. *Kit Carson's Own Story of His Life.* Taos, New Mexico: Santa Fe New Mexican Publishing Corporation, 1926, pp. 9–17.
9. Harvey L. Carter, "Ewing Young," in Hafen (ed.). *The Mountain Men and the Fur Trade of the Far West,* Vol. II, 1965, pp. 379–401.

CHAPTER NINE

1. "Proclamation to the citizens of New Mexico, by Colonel Kearny, commanding the United States forces," from Camp at Bent's Fort, on the Arkansas, July 31, 1846," in *House Executive Document* No. 60, 30th Congress, 1st Session, 1847–48 (Serial #520).

2. Report [No. 13] of Colonel Sterling Price, Commanding the Army in New Mexico, to the Adjutant General of the Army, Washington, D.C., from Santa Fe, New Mexico, February 15, 1847, pp. 520–26, in "Documents Accompanying the President's Message at the Commencement of the First Session of the Thirtieth Congress," *Senate Executive Document* No. 1, 30th Congress, 1st Session, 1847–48 (Serial #503).

3. Report [No. 11] of A. W. Doniphan, Commanding 1st Reg't. Missouri Mounted Volunteers, to Brig. Gen. R. Jones, Adjutant General from Headquarters, Detachment of the Army of the West, City of Chihuahua, March 4, 1847, in *Senate Executive Document* No. 1, 30th Congress, 1st Session, 1847–48, p. 496. (Serial #503). Major Gilpin, who served with Doniphan, later became the first territorial governor of Colorado by appointment of President Lincoln in 1864.

4. Christopher Carson. *Kit Carson's Own Story of His Life.* Taos, New Mexico: Santa Fe New Mexican Publishing Corporation, 1926, pp. 77–79.

5. Lt. Col. W. H. Emory. *Notes of a Military Reconnaissance....* House Executive Document No. 41, 30 Cong. 1 Sess., 1848, p. 84.

6. Dwight L. Clarke (ed.), *The Original Journals of Henry Smith Turner.* Norman: University of Oklahoma Press, 1966, pp. 108–109.

7. Emory, *Notes of a Military Reconnaissance . . .*, p. 95.

8. Clarke, *Journals of Henry Smith Turner*, pp. 154–55.

9. A song was written by one of the Mormons about this encounter. See "The Bull Fight on the San Pedro" by Levi W. Hancock in Sgt. Daniel Tyler, *A Concise History of the Mormon Battalion in the Mexican War, 1846–1847.* Chicago: Rio Grande Press, 1964, pp. 221–23. See also, "Report of the Secretary of War Communicating . . . a copy of the official journal of Lieutenant Colonel Philip St. George Cooke, from Santa Fe to San Diego, etc.," in U.S. Senate *Public Documents,* No. 2, March 5, 1849, 31st Congress, Special Session, 1849, p. 37. (Serial #547).

10. "The Journal of Robert S. Bliss With the Mormon Battalion," *Utah Historical Quarterly,* Vol. 4, No. 3 (July, 1931), p. 80.

11. Frank A. Golder, *The March of the Mormon Battalion . . . Taken from the Journal of Henry Standage.* New York: The Century Company, 1928, pp. 195–96.

12. Philip St. George Cooke, *The Conquest of New Mexico and California: An Historical and Personal Narrative.* New York: G. P. Putnam's Sons, 1878, pp. 161–62.

13. Nathaniel V. Jones, "The Journal of Nathaniel V. Jones, with the Mormon Battalion," *Utah Historical Quarterly,* Vol. 4, No. 1 (January, 1931), p. 10.

14. Cooke, *The Conquest of New Mexico and California . . .*, p. 197. See also, U.S. Senate *Public Documents,* No. 2, March 5, 1849, 31st Congress, Special Session, 1849, pp. 84–85.

15. Henry F. Dobyns (ed.), *Hepah California! The Journal of Cave Johnson Couts.* Tucson: Arizona Pioneers Historical Society, 1961, p. 61.

CHAPTER TEN

1. John R. Bartlett, *Personal Narrative of Explorations and Incidents . . .*, Vol. 1, New York: D. Appleton & Co., 1854, pp. 212–15.

2. *Ibid.*, p. 306.

3. *Ibid.*, p. 303.

4. *San Diego Herald,* February 14, 1852.

5. Bartlett, *Personal Narrative . . .*, Vol. 2, opposite p. 292.

6. Major William H. Emory. *Report of the United States and Mexican Boundary Survey.* House Doc. No. 135, 34th Congress, 1st Session, 1855–56, Vol. 1, pp. 15–22.

7. Robert V. Hine. *Bartlett's West: Drawing the Mexican Boundary.* New Haven, Conn.: Yale University Press, 1968.

8. J. Fred Rippy, "The Negotiation of the Gadsden Treaty," *Southwestern Historical Quarterly*, Vol. 27 (July, 1923), pp. 17–18.

9. See Article VIII of "The Gadsden Treaty Between the United States and Mexico," in Bill Tate (publisher). *Guadalupe Hidalgo Treaty of Peace 1848 and The Gadsden Treaty With Mexico 1853*. Reprinted from the New Mexico Statutes, 1963 Annotated, Vol. One. Truchas, New Mexico: Tate Gallery, 1967.

10. Odie B. Faulk (editor and translator), "Projected Mexican Colonies in the Borderlands, 1852," *The Journal of Arizona History*, Vol. 10, No. 2 (Summer, 1969), pp. 115–28.

11. Major William H. Emory, *Report of the United States and Mexican Boundary Commission, Senate Executive Document* 108, 34th Cong. 1st Sess., 2 vols. [Reprinted at Chicago: Rio Grande Press, 1967.] Same as House Executive Document 135, 34th Congress, 1st Session, 1855–56.

CHAPTER ELEVEN

1. "Letters and Journal of John E. Durivage," in Ralph P. Bieber. *Southern Trails to California in 1849*. Glendale, Calif.: The Arthur H. Clark Co., 1937, p. 213.

2. *Arkansas State Gazette,* April 26, 1850. Quoted in Grant Foreman, *Marcy and the Gold Seekers*. Norman: University of Oklahoma Press, 1939, pp. 281–83.

3. Letter of Brevet Major Samuel P. Heintzelman to Major C. S. Merchant in New San Diego, California, from Camp Yuma, California, March 27, 1851, in Copies of Army Service Letters, 1850–1854, Heintzelman Papers, Library of Congress. Later, the U.S.-Mexico relationship was such that border crossings could be made for rescues, but not at the time of the Oatman tragedy.

4. *Daily Alta California* (San Francisco), May 21, 1850 and June 16, 1860.

5. *Daily Alta California,* November 27, 1850.

6. See the "Fort Yuma, California, Post Returns, October 1850–December, 1865," on microfilm roll No. 1488 of "Returns from U.S. Military Posts, 1800–1916," National Archives Microfilm Publications, General Services Administration, Washington, D.C. See also letter of Bv't. Major Samuel P. Heintzelman to Major E. R. L. Canby, (Ass't. Adjutant-General, Bernicia, Calif.), from Camp Yuma, November 27, 1850, in the Heintzelman Papers, Library of Congress.

7. Arthur Woodward (ed.), *Journal of Lt. Thomas W. Sweeny, 1849–1853*. Los Angeles: Westernlore Press, 1956, pp. 52–55. See also, letter of Heintzelman to Lt. T. W. Sweeny, from Camp Yuma, Calif., June 4, 1851, and letter of Heintzelman to General R. Jones (Adj. Gen., Washington, D.C.), from Camp Yuma, June 5, 1851, in Heintzelman Papers, Library of Congress. Heintzelman wrote in his diary, on May 26, 1851, while at San Diego: "...I was surprised last evening on my arrival to learn that my command was ordered to San Isabel, on account of the great expence and want of means to supply us."

8. *San Diego Herald,* April 3, 1852.

9. Woodward (ed.), *Journal of Lt. Thomas W. Sweeny, 1849–1853*. pp. 187–88.

10. "Description of a Trip Down the Colorado," from Fort Yuma, May 17, 1859, in *Daily Alta California,* May 26, 1859.

11. *San Diego Herald,* December 18, 1851.

12. *Reports of Explorations and Surveys to Ascertain the Most Practicable and Economical Route for a Railroad from the Mississippi River to the Pacific Ocean ...,* 1853–54. House Executive Document No. 91, 33rd Cong. 2nd Sess., Vol. 3, pp. 115–16. Serial #793 or #760.

13. Diary of Lt. (later a Maj. Gen.) David Sloane Stanley, 2nd U.S. Dragoons, of an expedition overland from Fort Smith, Arkansas, to San Diego, Calif., from July 24, 1853, to March 26, 1854. Original in the Huntington Library, San Marino, Calif.

14. Baldwin Möllhausen. *Diary of a Journey from the Mississippi to the Pacific with a United States Government Expedition*. Vol. 2. London: Longman ..., 1858, p. 271.

15. See David H. Miller, "The Ives Expedition Revisited: A Prussian's Impressions," *The Journal of Arizona History*, Vol. 13, No. 1 (Spring, 1972), p. 21.

16. Lt. Joseph Ives. *Report on the Colorado River of the West Explored in 1857 and 1858* ... in House Executive Document No. 90, 36th Cong. 1st Sess. Washington: Government Printing Office, 1861, p. 104 and p. 131.

17. Lt. John G. Parke. *Report of Explorations for Railroads ... From the Pimas Villages on the Gila to the Rio Grande Near the 32nd Parallel of North Latitude* pp. 20–28, in *Reports of Explorations and Surveys to Ascertain the Most Practicable and Economical Route for a Railroad to the Pacific Ocean*, 1853–6, Vol. VII. Senate Executive Document No. 78, 33rd Cong. 2nd Sess., 1853–54.

18. "The Reminiscences of Peter R. Brady of the A. B. Gray Railroad Survey, 1853–1854," in L. R. Bailey (ed.), *The A. B. Gray Report*. Los Angeles: Western-lore Press, 1963, p. 223.

19. *Congressional Globe*, Vol. XXV, Part 2, 34th Cong. 1st Sess., 1856, p. 1298.

20. "Appropriation for the Interior Department," *Senate Executive Document* No. 13, 37th Cong. 2nd Sess., 1861–63 (Serial #1121), p. 13.

21. Ralph Bieber (ed.), *Exploring Southwestern Trails, 1846–1854*. Glendale, Calif.: The Arthur H. Clark Co., 1938, p. 55. See also Donald Chaput, "Babes in Arms," *The Journal of Arizona History*, Vol. 13, No. 3 (Autumn, 1972), pp. 197–204.

22. *Wagon Road from Fort Defiance to the Colorado River*, House Executive Document No. 124, 35th Cong. 1st Sess., 1857–1858 (Serial #959), p. 87.

23. *Ibid.*, pp. 2–3.

24. "The Report of the superintendent [Beale] of the Wagon Road from Fort Defiance to the Colorado River," House Executive Document No. 124, 35th Cong. 1st Sess., 1857–1858, p. 61.

25. *San Diego Herald*, September 5, 1857. Reprinted in the *Evening Bulletin* (San Francisco), September 12, 1857. See also, Roscoe P. Conkling and Margaret B. Conkling, *The Butterfield Overland Mail, 1857–1869*, Vol. 1. Glendale, California: The Arthur H. Clark Company, 1947, pp. 92–96.

26. "Diary of Phocion R. Way," in William A. Duffen (editor), "Overland Via Jackass Mail in 1858," Part 2, *Arizona and the West*, Vol. 2, No. 2 (Summer, 1960), pp. 157–62. The original diary is now in the Arizona Department of Library and Archives.

27. Constance Wynn Altshuler (ed.), *Latest From Arizona: The Hesperian Letters, 1859–1861*. Tucson: Arizona Historical Society, 1969, pp. 26–27.

28. Waterman L. Ormsby. *The Butterfield Overland Mail*. San Marino, California: The Huntington Library, 1960, p. 96.

29. William Tallack, "The California Overland Express, the Longest Stage-Ride in the World," *Historical Society of Southern California Quarterly Publication*, Vol. XVII, No. 2 (June, 1935), pp. 64–65.

CHAPTER TWELVE

1. See "An Act Declaring the Southern Boundary of New Mexico," August 4, 1854, *U.S. Statutes at Large*, Vol. X, 33rd Cong. 1st Sess. 1853–54, p. 575.

2. Copy of original memorial in B. Sacks, *Be It Enacted*. Phoenix, Arizona: Arizona Historical Foundation, 1964, pp. 118–19; see also *House Report* 117, 34th Cong. 3rd Sess., 1856–57 (Serial #912).

3. President James Buchanan, "First Annual Message," December 8, 1857, in Fred L. Israel (ed.), *The State of the Union Messages of the Presidents, 1790–1966*, Vol. 1. New York: Chelsea House–Robert Hector, Publishers, 1966, p. 962.

4. Sylvester Mowry, U.S.A., Delegate Elect. *Memoir of the Proposed Territory of Arizona*. Washington, D. C.: Henry Polkinhorn, Printer, 1857. See also "The Position of the People," in *The Weekly Arizonian* (Tucson), August 4, 1859, and *The Geography and Resources of Arizona and Sonora: An Address Before the American Geographical and Statistical Society by Sylvester Mowry*, New York, February 3, 1859. San Francisco and New York: A. Roman & Co., 1863.

5. *House Executive Document* 2, 35th Cong. 2nd Sess., 1858–59, p. 19; or President James Buchanan, "Second Annual Message," December 6, 1858, in Israel (ed.), *The State of the Union Messages of the Presidents, 1790–1966,* Vol. 1, p. 986.

6. *San Diego Herald,* May 23, 1859; see also *The Weekly Arizonian,* May 12, 1859.

7. *The Weekly Arizonian,* June 30, 1859.

8. The credentials committee seated the following delegates, names spelled as in the minutes of the convention: Tucson (Wm. S. Oury, Col. Palatine Robinson, John Capron, J. Howard Wells); Tubac (J. Dean[e] Alden, R. M. Doss); Arivaca (Rees Smith); Sonoita (W. C. Wordsworth); Gila City (B. F. Neal, Thos. J. Mastin); Picacho (Jose MaChavis) [José María Chaves]; Amoles (Jose MaGarcia) [José María García]; Santa Rita del Cobre (Leonada Liqueras [Leandro Siquieros], T. J. Thibault); Las Cruces (Frank DeRuyther, Samuel B. Ford); Doña Ana (Pablo Melendres, Pedro Aguirre); La Mesa (T. J. Miller, G. W. Putnam); Santo Tomas (Ramon Sanchez); and Mesilla (James A. Lucas, Ygnacio Orrantia, Raphael Ruelas, S. W. Cozzens, Edward McGowan, L. S. Owens [Owings], S. G. Bean, T. J. Bull. See Sacks, *Be It Enacted,* p. 133. The pamphlet, *The Constitution and Schedule of the Provisional Government of the Territory of Arizona, and the Proceedings of the Convention Held at Tucson* (Tucson: J. Howard Wells, Publisher, 1860), is reprinted in Sacks, pp. 131–54.

9. The first book printed in Arizona by Wells was *Carta Pastoral Del Obispo De Sonora,* a twenty page pamphlet in Spanish contracted by the Bishop of Sonora, Pedro Loza y Pardavé, in 1859. See Andrew Wallace, *The Image of Arizona.* Albuquerque: University of New Mexico Press, 1971, p. 89.

   Besides Owings, the other officers of the provisional territory were: lieutenant governor, Ygnacio Orrantia; chief justice, Granville H. Oury; associate justices, S. W. Cozzens and Edward McGowan; secretary, James A. Lucas; treasurer, Mark Aldrich; marshal, Samuel G. Bean; adjutant general, Palatine Robinson; major general of militia, William C. Wordsworth; and delegate to Congress, Sylvester Mowry. The latter resigned as unofficial delegate to accept an appointment as the commissioner to run the eastern boundary of California and Judge Edward McGowan was elected in November, 1860 to replace him as a lobbyist in Washington, D.C., but did not go to the capital. See Sacks, *Be It Enacted,* pp. 36, 40.

   For a good account of the life and career of McGowan, who left San Francisco in 1859 to escape justice at the hands of the vigilantes, see Altshuler, *Latest From Arizona,* pp. 261–64.

10. A complete list can be found in "Execution of Colonel Crabb and Associates," *Senate Executive Document* No. 64, 35th Cong. 1st Sess., 1857–58 (Serial #955), p. 71.

11. "Another Chapter of the Crabb Massacre as told by Chas. D. Poston," in the *Arizona Daily Star,* August 4, 1886, p. 4.

12. *Ibid.*

13. Letter of Henry A. Crabb to Don Josè María Redondo, from Sonoyta, March 26, 1857, in "Execution of Colonel Crabb and Associates," *Senate Document 64,* 35th Cong. 1st Sess., 1857–58 (Serial #955), pp. 30–31; see also Robert H. Forbes. *Crabb's Filibustering Expedition Into Sonora, 1857.* Tucson: Arizona Silhouettes, 1952, pp. 14–15.

14. Proclamation of Ignacio Pesqueira, Substitute Governor for the State and Commander of the frontier, to his fellow citizens, from Ures, March 30, 1857, in *Senate Document 64, ibid.,* pp. 32–33 or Forbes, *Crabb's Filibustering Expedition, ibid.,* pp. 15–16.

15. *Daily Alta California,* August 3, 1857.

16. Forbes, *Crabb's Filibustering Expedition,* pp. 29–30.

17. *Ibid.,* pp. 23 and 38–39. There is conflicting evidence about Ainsa's capture. For an account by his son, see Joseph Y. Ainsa, *History of the Crabb Expedition into Northern Sonora:* Decapitation of the State Senator of California, Henry A. Crabb

and massacre of ninety-eight of his friends, at Caborca and Sonoita, Sonora, Mexico, Phoenix, 1951.

18. "Gabilondo's Commendation to His Soldiers," in Forbes, *Crabb's Filibustering Expedition*, p. 37.

19. *Daily Alta California*, August 3, 1857.

20. Correspondence and enclosures of John Forsyth to Honorable Lewis Cass in *Senate Document 64;* see also Rufus K. Wyllys. "Henry A. Crabb — A Tragedy of the Sonora Frontier," *Pacific Historical Review*, Vol. IX, No. 2 (June, 1940), pp. 192–94.

21. Address of Acting Governor Richard C. McCormick in *Journals of the Second Legislative Assembly of the Territory of Arizona, 1865.* Prescott: Office of the Arizona Miner, 1866, p. 44.

22. *Arizona Daily Star*, August 4, 1886.

23. See John G. Capron's account of the relief party in the *Arizona Daily Star,* February 4, 1906 and December 11, 1910.

24. Carl Trumbull Hayden, *Charles Trumbull Hayden: Pioneer.* Tucson: The Arizona Historical Society, 1972, pp. 1–52.

CHAPTER THIRTEEN

1. Charles D. Poston. *Building a State in Apache Land*, (John Myers Myers, ed.). Tempe, Arizona: Aztec Press, 1963. (Originally published in the *Overland Monthly*, July, August, September, and October, 1894), pp. 69–70.

2. Poston, *Building a State in Apache Land*, pp. 75–77. See also copy of a marriage certificate signed by Poston, Deputy for James A. Lucas, Clerk and Recorder, Probate Court of Doña Ana County, New Mexico, in "Records of the States of the United States of America," Library of Congress microfilm, Arizona D. 2, Reel 1a, 1856–1909.

3. *The Weekly Arizonian,* June 30, 1859.

4. *Ibid.,* July 14, 1859.

5. J. Ross Browne, *A Tour Through Arizona, 1864.* Tucson: Arizona Silhouettes, 1950, pp. 147–49.

6. *Decennial Federal Census of 1860, For Arizona County in the Territory of New Mexico,* in *Senate Document 13,* 89th Cong. 1st Sess. Washington: Government Printing Office, 1965, pp. 37–48.

7. Browne, *A Tour Through Arizona, 1864,* p. 134.

8. *The Weekly Arizonian,* November 10, 1859.

9. Obituary in the *Arizona Daily Star,* November 16, 1899.

10. Quoted in Frank C. Lockwood. *Life in Old Tucson, 1854–1864.* Los Angeles: Ward Ritchie Press, 1943, pp. 200–202.

11. "Diary of Phocion R. Way," in William A. Duffen (editor), "Overland Via Jackass Mail in 1858," Part 2, *Arizona and the West*, Vol. 2, No. 2 (Summer, 1960), pp. 160–61.

12. Browne, *A Tour Through Arizona, 1864,* pp. 131–33, 138.

13. See excerpts from a report by Charles D. Poston to T. Butler King of Georgia, from San Francisco, September 15, 1854, in the *Yuma Daily Sun,* Centennial Edition, Section B–10, October 27 and 28, 1954.

14. *Yuma Daily Sun,* Centennial Edition, Section B–10, October 27 and 28, 1954.

15. *Ibid.*

16. "Decennial Census, 1860, for Arizona County in the Territory of New Mexico," in *Federal Census, Territory of New Mexico and Territory of Arizona*, Senate Document 13, 89th Cong. 1st Sess. Washington: Government Printing Office, 1965, pp. 2–3.

17. Letter from Colorado Ferry, June 28, 1859, entitled "Incipient Cities Near Fort Yuma," in *Weekly Alta California*, July 30, 1859.

18. *Ibid.*
19. "Decennial Census, 1860 . . . ," *Senate Document 13*, pp. 233–46, and 250–53, and *The Compiled Laws of the Territory of Arizona Including the Howell Code and the Session Laws from 1864 to 1871*, p. 35. A change in the course of the Colorado River in 1869 brought commercial disaster to La Paz. The new city of Ehrenberg had a better steamboat landing.
20. *Acts, Resolutions and Memorials*, Seventh Legislative Assembly, 1873, p. 39.
21. *New York Times*, April 15, 1857.
22. *Evening Bulletin* (San Francisco), October 30, 1858.
23. Hattie M. Anderson, "Mining and Indian Fighting in Arizona and New Mexico, 1858–1861: Memoirs of Hank Smith," in *Panhandle Plains Historical Review*, Vol. 1, No. 1, 1928, pp. 71–75.
24. *The Weekly Arizonian*, March 3, 1859.
25. Browne, *A Tour Through Arizona, 1864*, pp. 76–77.
26. *Ibid.*, p. 77.
27. Lt. John G. Parke, *Report of Explorations for Railroads . . . From the Pimas Villages on the Gila to the Rio Grande Near the 32nd Parallel of North Latitude*, pp. 19–42, in *Reports of Explorations and Surveys to Ascertain the Most Practicable and Economical Route for a Railroad to the Pacific Ocean*, 1853–6, Vol. VII. Senate Executive Document No. 78, 33rd Cong. 2nd Sess., 1853–54.
28. B. Sacks, "The Origins of Fort Buchanan, Myth and Fact," *Arizona and the West*, Vol. 7, No. 3 (Autumn, 1965), pp. 214–15.
29. *Ibid.*, p. 221.
30. *Ibid.*, p. 224.
31. George P. Hammond (ed.), *Campaigns in the West, 1856–1861, The Journal and Letters of Colonel John Van Deusen Du Bois.* Tucson: Arizona Historical Society, 1949, p. viii.
32. *Ibid.*, pp. 29–30.
33. Report of Col. B. L. E. Bonneville to Major W. A. Nichols, Assistant Adjutant General in Santa Fe, from Depot on the Gila, New Mexico, July 14, 1857, in *House Executive Document 2*, 35th Cong. 1st Sess., 1857–1858 (Serial #943).
34. "Sanitary Report — Fort Buchanan (Arizona)," *Statistical Report on the Sickness and Mortality in the Army of the United States . . .* , *Senate Executive Document 52*, 36th Cong. 1st Sess., 1859–1860 (Serial #1035).
35. *Ibid.*, p. 210.
36. *The Weekly Arizonian*, March 10, 1859.
37. *Ibid.*, September 15, 1859.
38. Ralph H. Ogle. *Federal Control of the Western Apaches, 1848–1886*. Albuquerque: University of New Mexico Press, 1940, pp. 41–42.
39. *The Weekly Arizonian*, March 31, 1859.
40. *Ibid.*, May 26, 1859.
41. *Ibid.*, July 21, 1859.
42. *Ibid.*, August 11, 1859.
43. *Ibid.*, October 6, 1859.
44. *Ibid.*, November 3, 1859.
45. *Ibid.*, November 17, 1859.
46. Sylvester Mowry, *Arizona and Sonora, the Geography, History, and Resources of the Silver Region of North America*, 3rd ed., New York: Harper and Brothers, 1864, p. 35.
47. *The Weekly Arizonian*, June 2, 1859.
48. B. Sacks, "New Evidence on the Bascom Affair," *Arizona and the West*, Vol. 4, No. 3 (Autumn, 1962), p. 273.
49. Altshuler, . . . *The Hesperian Letters*, pp. 224–25.
50. *Ibid.*, p. 177.
51. Brigadier General B J. D. Irwin. "The Apache Fight" and "The Chiricahua Apache Indians: A Thrilling Incident in the Early History of Arizona Territory,"

Infantry Journal, April, 1928 (reprint in Arizona Department of Library and Archives, p. 7).

52. Mowry, *Arizona and Sonora,* p. 56.

53. Quoted in Douglas D. Martin. *Yuma Crossing.* Albuquerque: University of New Mexico Press, 1954, p. 215.

54. James S. Calhoun. *The Official Correspondence of James S. Calhoun While Indian Agent at Santa Fe and Superintendent of Indian Affairs in New Mexico, 1849–1852.* (A. H. Abel, editor). Washington, D.C.: Government Printing Office, 1915, p. 32.

55. Fort Defiance was first garrisoned by Company G, 1st Dragoons; Company K, 2nd Dragoons; Company B, 2nd Artillery; and Company F, 3rd Infantry. Records of the U.S. Army Commands (Army Posts), RG 393, National Archives.

56. Calhoun, *Official Correspondence . . .,* p. 488.

57. James P. Dunn, *Massacres of the Mountains.* New York: Harper and Brothers, 1886.

58. Jay J. Wagoner. *Arizona Territory, 1863–1912: A Political History.* Tucson: University of Arizona Press, 1970, pp. 24–25.

59. Letter of Leonard J. Rose to the *Missouri Republican,* from Albuquerque, October 28, 1858. Cited in Appendix IV, "Massacre on the Colorado," pp. 306–315, of Robert G. Cleland. *The Cattle on a Thousand Hills.* San Marino, Calif.: The Huntington Library, 1941. See also John Udell, *Journal of John Udell Kept During a Trip Across the Plains Containing an Account of the Massacre of a Portion of His Party by the Mohave Indians in 1859* [1858]. Jefferson, Missouri: Ashtabula Sentinel Steam Press Print, 1868 [Reprinted as *John Udell Journal* with introduction by Lyle H. Wright. Los Angeles: N. A. Kovach, 1946, pp. 45–46.

60. Report of the Secretary of War, in *Senate Executive Document* 2, 36th Cong., 1st Sess., 1859–60, Part 2, pp. 387–422 (Serial #1024).

61. *Ibid.,* pp. 407–8.

62. Letter of Eugene Bandel to his parents, from Fort Yuma, California, March 8, 1859, in Eugene Bandel. *Frontier Life in the Army, 1854–1861.* Glendale, Calif.: The Arthur H. Clark Company, 1932, pp. 259–64.

63. Bandel, *Frontier Life in the Army,* pp. 409–13.

64. The fort was established by companies F and I, 6th Infantry, and a detachment of the 3rd Artillery. Records of United States Army Commands (Army Posts), RG 393 (formerly RG 98), National Archives microfilm T-912.

65. Bandel, *Frontier Life in the Army,* p. 407.

66. Edward Carlson, "The Martial Experiences of the California Volunteers," *The Overland Monthly,* Vol. VII (2nd Series), No. 41 (May, 1886), pp. 489–90.

67. *Ibid.,* p. 491.

CHAPTER FOURTEEN

1. Jay J. Wagoner. *Arizona Territory, 1863–1912: A Political History.* Tucson: University of Arizona Press, 1970, pp. 3–33.

2. *Weekly Arizonian* (Tucson), March 9, 1861.

3. Letter of James A. Lucas, President of the Convention, to Dr. Lorenzo Labado, from Mesilla, New Mexico, June 14, 1861, in U.S. War Department, *The War of Rebellion: A Compilation of the Official Records of the Union and Confederate Armies,* Series I, Vol. 4, p. 39.

4. Ray C. Colton. *The Civil War in the Western Territories.* Norman: University of Oklahoma Press, 1959, p. 8.

5. "Proclamation to the People of the Territory of Arizona," signed by John R. Baylor, Governor and Lieut. Col., Commanding Mounted Rifles, Confederate States Army, Mesilla, August 2, 1861, in *Confederate Victories in the Southwest: Prelude to Defeat.* Albuquerque, N. Mex.: Horn and Wallace, 1961, pp. 37–39.

6. *War of the Rebellion,* Series I, Vol. 4, pp. 853, 859, and 930.

7. *Ibid.,* Vol. 4, pp. 1–45.

8. Theophilus Noel. *Autobiography and Reminiscenses of Theophilus Noel.* Chicago: Theophilus Noel Company Print, 1904.

9. Report of Major John M. Chivington, First Colorado Infantry to Brigadier General E. R. S. Canby, U.S. Army, Commanding Department of New Mexico, March 26, 1862, in *Union Army Operations in the Southwest: Final Victory* (from *Official Records*). Albuquerque, N. Mex.: Horn and Wallace, 1961, pp. 20–21.

10. Letter of Captain Sherod Hunter to Col. John R. Baylor, from Tucson, Arizona, April 5, 1862, in *Confederate Victories,* pp. 200–201.

11. *War of the Rebellion,* Series 1, Vol. 4, pp. 167–74; Vol. 9, p. 708; and Vol. 50, Part 1, pp. 944–45 and 1047–48.

12. Letter of Hunter to Baylor, in *Confederate Victories,* pp. 200–201.

13. "Concurrent Resolution Relative to Sylvester Mowry," *Acts, Resolutions, and Memorials,* First Legislative Assembly, Arizona, 1864, p. 70.

14. *Arizona Miner,* October 19, 1871.

15. Report of Brigadier General James H. Carleton, U.S. Army, San Francisco, Calif., from Tucson, Arizona, July 22, 1862, *Union Army Operations,* pp. 40–41.

16. Assistant Adjutant-General Ben C. Cutler, *General Orders No. 27,* from Santa Fe, N. Mex., October 23, 1863, *War of the Rebellion,* Series I, Vol. 50, Part 2, pp. 653–55.

17. *Acts, Resolutions and Memorials,* First Legislative Assembly, Arizona, 1864, pp. 69–70.

18. Letter of Captain James H. Whitlock to Captain C. A. Smith, Ass't. Adjutant-General, District of Arizona, from Camp Miembres, N. Mex., April 13, 1864, in *War of the Rebellion,* Series I, Vol. 50, Part 2, pp. 827–29.

19. U.S. Bureau of Indian Affairs, *Report of the Commissioner of Indian Affairs,* 1867, p. 140.

20. *U.S. Statutes at Large,* Vol. XII, 37th Cong. 3rd Sess., 1863, Chap. LVI, pp. 664–65.

21. Charles D. Poston, *Building a State in Apache Land* (John M. Myers, ed.). Tempe, Arizona: Aztec Press, 1963, pp. 112–13 (originally in *Overland Monthly,* Vol. 24, October, 1894, p. 404).

22. *New York Times,* March 10, 1863.

23. Lina Ferguson Browne (ed.), *J. Ross Browne: His Letters, Journals, and Writings.* Albuquerque: University of New Mexico Press, 1969, pp. 290–91.

24. Letter of Secretary Richard C. McCormick to President Abraham Lincoln, from Prescott, Arizona Territory, December 1, 1864, Record Group 59, Territorial Papers: Arizona, Vol. 1. Secretary McCormick eventually replaced Goodwin as governor after the latter defeated Judge Joseph P. Allyn and Charles Poston for delegate to Congress in 1865. See the *Arizona Miner,* October 4, 1865. Poston was the first delegate.

25. *Arizona Miner,* March 9, 1864; see also, letter of Jonathan Richmond, a member of Governor Goodwin's party, to his parents, from Navajo Springs, Arizona, December 29, 1863. The original letters written by Richmond on this trip are in the Arizona Department of Library and Archives in Phoenix. The Arizona "capital on wheels" was established at Prescott in 1864. The territorial legislature moved it to Tucson in 1867 and back to Prescott ten years later. In 1889, Phoenix was made the seat of government for Arizona. See Jay J. Wagoner, *Arizona Territory, 1863–1912: A Political History.* Tucson: University of Arizona Press, 1970.

Bibliography

1. Geographical Background

Arizona Highways. Contains hundreds of pictures and articles pertaining to the geography of Arizona.

Baker, Simon and Thomas J. McClenaghan. *An Arizona Economic and Historical Atlas.* Tucson: University of Arizona and Phoenix: Valley National Bank, 1966. This atlas is a good source of "mappable" information about Arizona.

Barnes, Will C. *Arizona Place Names.* (Revised and enlarged by Byrd H. Granger). Tucson: University of Arizona Press, 1960.

Corle, Edwin. *The Gila: River of the Southwest.* New York: Rinehart & Company, 1951.

DeRoos, Robert. "Arizona: Booming Youngster of the West," *National Geographic,* Vol. 123, No. 3 (March, 1963), pp. 299–343.

Hastings, James R. and Raymond M. Turner. *The Changing Mile.* Tucson: University of Arizona Press, 1965.

Hoover, J. Wenger. *The Geography of Arizona.* Boston: Ginn and Co., 1936.

————. *Physiographic Provinces of Arizona.* Des Moines, Iowa: Geological Publishing Co., 1936.

Humphrey, Robert R. *The Desert Grassland.* Tucson: University of Arizona Press, 1968.

Irish, F. M. *Arizona.* New York: The Macmillan Co., 1907.

Manning, Reg. *What Is Arizona Really Like?* Phoenix: Reganson Cartoon Books, 1968.

McKee, Edwin D. *Ancient Landscapes of the Grand Canyon Region.* 24th ed. Flagstaff, Arizona: Northland Press, 1966.

McKee, Edwin D., Richard F. Wilson, William J. Breed, and Carol S. Breed (eds.), *Evolution of the Colorado River in Arizona.* Flagstaff: Museum of Northern Arizona, 1967.

Mowry, Sylvester. *Arizona and Sonora: The Geography, History, and Resources of the Silver Region of North America.* 3rd ed. New York: Harper, 1864. Originally issued in 1859.

O'Kane, Walter C. *The Intimate Desert.* Tucson: University of Arizona Press, 1969.

Robinson, Dorothy F. *Geographical Background of Arizona.* Phoenix: Western Bookbinding Service, Inc., 1963.

United States Department of Interior. *The Natural Resources of Arizona*. Washington, D.C.: Government Printing Office, 1963.

University of Arizona Faculty. *Arizona: Its People and Resources*. 2nd ed. Tucson: University of Arizona Press, 1972.

Watkins, T. H. and Contributors. *The Grand Colorado: The Story of a River and Its Canyons*. n.p.: American West Publishing Company, 1969.

Wyllys, Rufus K. "The Historical Geography of Arizona," *The Pacific Historical Review*, Vol. XXI, No. 2 (May, 1952), pp. 121–27.

Zierer, Clifford M., ed. *California and the Southwest*. New York: John Wiley & Sons, Inc., 1956. A regional geography which includes Arizona.

2. Prehistoric Animals and Early Men

Arizona Republic, August 11, 1957; February 4, 1959; August 17, 1961; and January 13, 1962.

Barnett, Lincoln. "An Arizona Hunt," *Sports Illustrated*, Vol. 5, No. 16 (October 15, 1956), pp. 52–60. Though popularly written, this article contains the essential information on the discovery and excavation of the Lehner Ranch mammoth site where prehistoric Llano man (pre-Cochise) hunted. The article contains a good painting by Eric Mose and pictures of artifacts.

Breed, William J. *The Age of Dinosaurs in Northern Arizona*. Flagstaff: Museum of Northern Arizona, 1968.

Colbert, Edwin H. "The Beginning of the Age of Dinosaurs in Northern Arizona," *Plateau*, Vol. 22, No. 3 (January, 1950), pp. 37–43.

Colton, Harold S. *Black Sand: Prehistory in Northern Arizona*. Albuquerque: University of New Mexico Press, 1960.

Haury, Emil W. "The Naco Mammoth," *The Kiva*, Vol. 18, Nos. 3–4 (November-December, 1952), pp. 2–19.

———. "A Possible Cochise-Mogollon-Hohokam Sequence," *Proceedings of the American Philosophical Society*, Vol. 86, No. 2 (February, 1943), pp. 260–63.

———. *The Stratigraphy and Archaeology of Ventana Cave*. Tucson: University of Arizona Press and Albuquerque: University of New Mexico Press, 1950.

Haury, Emil W., Ernst Antevs, and John F. Lance. "Artifacts With Mammoth Remains, Naco, Arizona," *American Antiquity*, Vol. 19, No. 1 (July, 1953), pp. 1–24.

Haury, Emil W., E. B. Sayles, and William W. Wasley. "The Lehner Mammoth Site, Southeastern Arizona," *American Antiquity*, Vol. 25, No. 1 (July, 1959), pp. 2–30. Articles by Ernst Antevs, pp. 31–34, and John F. Lance, pp. 35–42, are in the same volume. A good bibliography relevant to the Lehner mammoth site is on pp. 39–42.

Martin, Paul S., John B. Rinaldo, and Ernst Antevs. *Cochise and Mogollon Sites, Pima Lawn Valley Western New Mexico.* Fieldiana: Anthropology, Vol. 38, No. 1, Chicago Natural History Museum, April, 1949.

Martin, Paul S., George I. Quimby, and Donald Collier. *Indians Before Columbus.* Chicago and London: The University of Chicago Press, 1947.

Phoenix Gazette, May 8, 1962.

Sayles, E. B. and Ernst Antevs. "The Cochise Culture," *Medallion Papers,* No. XXIX. Globe, Arizona: Privately printed for Gila Pueblo, June, 1941, pp. 1–81.

3. Prehistoric Indian Cultures

Amsden, Charles A. *The Ancient Basketmakers.* Los Angeles: Southwest Museum Leaflets No. 11, 1939.

———. *Prehistoric Southwesterners From Basketmaker to Pueblo.* Los Angeles: Southwest Museum, 1949.

Arizona: Its Place in Time. Phoenix: The Arizona Republic, 1960.

Caywood, Louis R. and Edward H. Spicer. *Tuzigoot:* The Excavation and Repair of a Ruin on the Verde River Near Clarkdale, Arizona. Mimeographed publication. Field Division of Education, National Park Service, Berkeley, California, July, 1935.

Colton, Harold S. "The Patayan Problem in the Colorado River Valley," *Southwestern Journal of Anthropology,* Vol. 1, No. 1 (Spring, 1945), pp. 114–21.

———. *The Sinagua: A Summary of the Archaeology of the Region of Flagstaff, Arizona.* Flagstaff: Northern Arizona Society of Science and Art, 1946.

Cummings, Byron. *First Inhabitants of Arizona and the Southwest.* Tucson: Cummings Publication Council, 1953.

DiPeso, Charles C. *The Babocomari Village Site on the Babocomari River, Southeastern Arizona.* Dragoon, Arizona: The Amerind Foundation, Inc., 1951.

Dittert, Alfred E., Jr. "They Came From the South," *Arizona Highways,* Vol. XLVIII, No. 1 (January, 1972), pp. 34–39.

Douglass, Andrew E. "The Secret of the Southwest Solved by Talkative Tree-Rings," *National Geographic,* Vol. 56, No. 6 (December, 1929), pp. 737–70.

Gladwin, Harold S. *Men Out of Asia.* New York: McGraw-Hill Book Company, Inc., 1947.

Gladwin, Harold S., Emil W. Haury, E. B. Sayles, and Nora Gladwin. *Excavations at Snaketown, Material Culture.* Tucson: University of Arizona Press, 1965.

Haury, Emil W. *The Excavation of Los Muertos and Neighboring Ruins in the Salt River Valley, Southern Arizona.* Cambridge, Massachusetts: *Papers* of the Peabody Museum of American Archaeology and Ethnology, Harvard University, Vol. XXIV, No. 1, 1945.

―――. *Excavations in the Forestdale Valley, East-Central Arizona.* University of Arizona *Bulletin,* Vol. XI, No. 4 (October 1, 1940).

―――. "The Hohokam: The First Masters of the Desert," *National Geographic,* Vol. 131, No. 5 (May, 1967), pp. 670–95.

―――. *The Mogollon Culture of Southwestern New Mexico.* Medallion Papers No. XX. Globe, Arizona: Privately printed for the Medallion, Gila Pueblo, April, 1936.

―――. *Painted Cave in Northeastern Arizona.* Dragoon, Arizona: The Amerind Foundation, Inc., 1945.

―――. *Roosevelt: 9: 6: A Hohokam Site of the Colonial Period.* Medallion Papers No. XI. Globe, Arizona: Privately printed for The Medallion, Gila Pueblo, 1932.

Haury, Emil W. and E. B. Sayles. *An Early Pit House Village of the Mogollon Culture, Forestdale Valley, Arizona.* Tucson: University of Arizona Press, 1947.

Kellar, James H. *The Atlatl in North America.* Prehistory Research Series, Indiana Historical Society, Indianapolis, Vol. III, No. 3 (June, 1955).

Klinck, Richard E. *Land of Room Enough and Time Enough.* Albuquerque: University of New Mexico Press, 1958.

Lister, Florence C. and Robert H. Lister. *Earl Morris and Southwestern Archaeology.* Albuquerque: University of New Mexico Press, 1968.

McGregor, John C. *The Cohonina Culture of Northwestern Arizona.* Urbana: University of Illinois Press, 1951.

―――. *Culture of Sites Which Were Occupied Shortly Before the Eruption of Sunset Crater.* Flagstaff, Arizona: Museum of Northern Arizona *Bulletin* No. 9, October, 1936.

―――. *Southwestern Archaeology,* 2nd ed. Urbana: University of Illinois Press, 1965.

Martin, Paul S., George I. Quimby, and Donald Collier. *Indians Before Columbus.* Chicago: University of Chicago Press, 1947.

Midvale, Frank. "Prehistoric Irrigation of the Casa Grande Ruins Area," *The Kiva,* Vol. 30, No. 3 (February, 1965), pp. 82–86. A map showing the locations of prehistoric irrigation canals in the Gila River Valley is included.

―――. "Prehistoric Irrigation in the Salt River Valley, Arizona," *The Kiva,* Vol. 34, No. 1 (October, 1968), pp. 28–32. A map is included.

Pinkley, Edna T. *Casa Grande, the Greatest Valley Pueblo of Arizona.* Arizona Archaeological and Historical Society, 1926.

Schroeder, Albert H. and Homer F. Hastings. *Montezuma Castle*

National Monument. National Park Service Historical Handbook Series No. 27. Washington, D.C., 1958.

Weaver, Kenneth. "Magnetic Clues Help Date the Past," *National Geographic,* Vol. 131, No. 5 (May,, 1967), pp. 696–701.

Wheat, Jo Ben. *Mogollon Culture Prior to* A.D. *1000.* American Anthropological Association, Vol. 57, No. 2, Part 3, Memoir No. 82, April, 1955.

————. *Prehistoric People of the Northern Southwest.* 2nd ed. Grand Canyon: Grand Canyon Natural History Association, 1959.

Wormington, H. M. *Prehistoric Indians of the Southwest.* Denver, Colorado: The Denver Museum of Natural History, 1961 edition.

4. Spanish Explorers in the 1500s

Bandelier, Adolph F. (ed.). *The Journal of Álvar Núñez Cabeza de Vaca.* New York: A. S. Barnes & Co., 1905. Translation from Vaca's own narrative by Fanny Bandelier. (Reprinted at Albuquerque, New Mexico: Rio Grande Press, 1964.)

Bartlett, Katharine. "Notes Upon the Routes of Espejo and Farfán to the Mines in the Sixteenth Century," *New Mexico Historical Review,* Vol. XVII, No. 1 (January, 1942), pp. 21–36.

Bolton, Herbert E. *Coronado: Knight of Pueblo and Plains.* New York: Whittlesey House, a division of McGraw-Hill Company, 1949, and also Albuquerque: University of New Mexico Press, 1949.

————. (ed.). *Spanish Exploration in the Southwest, 1542–1706.* Original Narratives of Early American History. New York: Barnes and Noble, Inc., 1963.

Day, A. Grove. *Coronado's Quest.* Berkeley and Los Angeles: University of California Press, 1940.

Hallenbeck, Cleve. *Álvar Núñez Cabeza de Vaca: The Journey and Route of the First European to Cross the Continent of North America, 1534–1536.* Glendale, California: The Arthur H. Clark Co., 1940. Hallenbeck traces Vaca's route through New Mexico and Arizona. See his map on p. 223.

————. *The Journey of Fray Marcos de Niza.* Dallas: Southern Methodist University Press, 1949.

Hammond, George P. *Coronado's Seven Cities.* Denver, Colorado: W. H. Kistler Stationery Co., 1940.

Hammond, George P., and Rey, Agapito. *Don Juan de Oñate: Colonizer of New Mexico, 1595–1628,* 2 vols. Albuquerque: University of New Mexico Press, 1953.

———— and ————. *Expedition Into New Mexico by Antonio de Espejo, 1582–1583:* as revealed in the Journal of Diego Pérez de Luxán, a member of the party. Los Angeles: The Quivira Society, 1929.

———— and ————. (eds.). *Narratives of the Coronado Expedition, 1540–1542.* Albuquerque: University of New Mexico Press, 1940.

Hanke, Lewis. *The Spanish Struggle for Justice in the Conquest of America*. Boston: Little, Brown and Co., 1965.

Hodge, Frederick W., and Theodore H. Lewis (eds.). *Spanish Explorers in the Southern United States, 1528–1543*. New York: Charles Scribner's Sons, 1907. Contains "The Narrative of Álvar Núñez Cabeza de Vaca," pp. 3–126, and "The Narrative of the Expedition of Coronado, by Pedro de Casteñeda," pp. 281–387. (Reprinted at New York: Barnes & Noble, 1953.)

Ives, Ronald L. "Melchior Díaz — The Forgotten Explorer," *The Hispanic American Historical Review*, Vol. 16, No. 1 (February, 1936), pp. 86–90. Contains map for the Díaz expedition of 1540.

Jones, Paul A. *Coronado and Quivira*. Lyons, Kansas: Lyons Publishing Co., 1937.

Marcos de Niza, Fray. *His Own Personal Narrative of Arizona Discovered by Fray Marcos de Niza Who in 1539 First Entered These Parts On His Quest for the Seven Cities of Cíbola* (from the original Spanish). Topawa, Arizona: Bonaventure Oblasser, O.F.M., 1938.

Mecham, J. Lloyd. "Antonio de Espejo and His Journey to New Mexico," *New Mexico Historical Review*, Vol. XXX, No. 2 (October, 1926), pp. 114–38.

————. "The Second Expedition to New Mexico, An Account of the Chamuscado-Rodríquez Entrada of 1581–1582," *New Mexico Historical Review*, Vol. 1, No. 3 (July, 1926), pp. 265–91.

Simpson, Brevet Brigadier General J. H. "Coronado's March in Search of the 'Seven Cities of Cíbola' and Discussion of Their Probable Location," *Annual Report of the Board of Regents of the Smithsonian Institution, 1869*. Washington: Government Printing Office, 1871.

Terrell, John Upton. *Estevanico the Black*. Los Angeles: Westernlore Press, 1968.

Villagrá, Gaspar Pérez de. *History of New Mexico* (translated by Gilberto Espinosa). Los Angeles: Quivira Society, 1933. A history of New Mexico in verse written by one of Oñate's officers.

Wagner, Henry R. "Fray Marcos de Niza," *New Mexico Historical Review*, Vol. IX, No. 2 (April, 1934), pp. 184–227.

————. *The Spanish Southwest, 1542–1794: An Annotated Bibliography*. Albuquerque: The Quivira Society, 1937.

Winship, George P. "The Coronado Expedition, 1540–1542," Bureau of Ethnology, *Fourteenth Annual Report*, Part 1, pp. 339–613. Washington: Government Printing Office, 1896. (Reprinted in Chicago: Rio Grande Press, Inc., 1964.)

5. Missionaries in the 1600s

Acceptance of the Statue of Eusebio Francisco Kino.
House Document No. 158, 89th Cong. 1st Sess. Washington: Government Printing Office, 1965.

Bartlett, Katharine. "Spanish Contacts With the Hopi, 1540–1823," *Museum Notes*, Vol. 6, No. 12 (June, 1934), pp. 55–60. Also in the Museum of Northern Arizona Reprint Series No. 2, Flagstaff, January, 1951, pp. 1–5.

Benavides, Fray Alonso de. *Benavides Memorial of 1630*, translated by Peter P. Forrestal, C.S.C. Washington, D.C.: Academy of Franciscan History, 1954.

——. *Fray Alonso de Benevides' Revised Memorial of 1634*, With Numerous Supplementary Documents Elaborately Annotated. Frederick W. Hodge, George P. Hammond, and Agapito Rey (eds.). Albuquerque: University of New Mexico Press, 1945.

Bloom, Lansing B. "Fray Estevan de Perea's *Relación*," *New Mexico Historical Review*, Vol. VIII, No. 3 (July, 1933), pp. 211–35.

Bolton, Herbert E. *Kino's Historical Memoir of Pimería Alta*. Berkeley: University of California Press, 1948. Originally published as 2 vols. in Cleveland: Arthur H. Clark, 1919.

——. "The Mission As a Frontier Institution in the Spanish-American Colonies," *American Historical Review*, Vol. XXIII, No. 1 (October, 1917), pp. 42–61.

——. *The Padre on Horseback*. San Francisco: The Sonora Press, 1932. Reprint in John Francis Bannon, S.J. (ed.). *The American West*, Chicago: Loyola University Press, 1963.

——. *The Rim of Christendom*. New York: Russell & Russell, 1960.

Bucher, Rev. Mark, O.F.M. "Mission San Xavier del Bac, Tucson, Arizona," *The Hispanic American Historical Review*, Vol. 16, No. 1 (February, 1936), pp. 91–93.

Burrus, Ernest J., S.J. *Kino and the Cartography of Northwestern New Spain*. Tucson: Arizona Historical Society, 1965.

——. *Kino Reports to Headquarters: Correspondence of Eusebio F. Kino, S.J., From New Spain With Rome*. Original Spanish text of Fourteen Unpublished Letters and Reports with English Translation and Notes by Ernest J. Burrus, S.J., Rome, Italy: Institutum Historicum Societatis Jesu, 1954. These letters pertain mainly to Kino's part in the Jesuit efforts to found missions in California.

——. (translator and annotator). *Kino's Plan for the Development of Pimería Alta & Upper California: A Report to the Mexican Viceroy*. Tucson: Arizona Historical Society, 1961.

DiPeso, Charles C. *The Sobaipuri Indians of the Upper San Pedro River Valley, Southeastern Arizona*. Dragoon, Arizona: The Amerind Foundation, Inc., 1953.

——. *The Upper Pima of San Cayetano del Tumacácori*. Dragoon, Arizona: The Amerind Foundation, Inc., 1956.

Eckhart, George B. "A Guide to the History of the Missions of Sonora, 1614–1826," *Arizona and the West*, Vol. 2, No. 2 (Summer, 1960), pp. 165–83.

Engelhardt, Fr. Zephyrin, O.F.M. *The Franciscans in Arizona*. Harbor
    Springs, Michigan: Holy Childhood Indian School, 1899.
Hackett, Charles W. (ed.), *Revolt of the Pueblo Indians of New Mexico
    and Otermin's Attempted Reconquest, 1680–1682*, Parts 1 & 2.
    Translations of the Original Documents by Charmion Clair
    Shelby. Albuquerque: University of New Mexico Press, 1942.
Hastings, James R. "People of Reason and Others: The Colonization of
    Sonora to 1767," *Arizona and the West*, Vol. 3, No. 4 (Winter,
    1961), pp. 321–40.
Heald, Weldon F. "Eusebio Kino, Southwest Pioneer," *Desert*, Vol. 23,
    No. 12 (December, 1960), pp. 14–17.
Hunt, Frazier and Robert. "Father Kino's Mustangs," *Arizona High-
    ways*, Vol. XXVIII, No. 1 (January, 1952), pp. 32–35.
Ives, Ronald L. "Navigation Methods of Eusebio Francisco Kino, S.J."
    Arizona and the West, Vol. 2, No. 3 (Autumn, 1960), pp. 213–43.
————. "The Quest of the Blue Shells," *Arizoniana*, Vol. II, No. 1
    (Spring, 1961), pp. 3–7.
Kessell, John L. *Mission of Sorrows: Jesuit Guevavi and the Pimas,
    1691–1767*. Tucson: University of Arizona Press, 1970.
Lockwood, Frank C. *With Padre Kino on the Trail*. Tucson: University
    of Arizona Press, 1934.
McDermott, Rev. Edwin J., S.J. "The Saga of Father Kino," *Arizona
    Highways*, Vol. XXXVII, No. 3 (March, 1961), pp. 6–35.
Manje, Juan Mateo. *Luz de Tierra Incógnito: Unknown Arizona and
    Sonora, 1693–1721*. Translated by Harry J. Karns and associates.
    Tucson: Arizona Silhouettes, 1954.
Montgomery, Ross G., Watson Smith, and John O. Brew. *Franciscan
    Awatovi*: The Excavation and Conjectural Reconstruction of a
    17th Century Spanish Mission Establishment at a Hopi Indian
    Town in Northeastern Arizona. *Papers* of the Peabody Museum
    of American Archaeology and Ethnology, Harvard University,
    Vol. XXXVI, Cambridge, Mass., 1949.
Morrisey, Richard J. "Early Agriculture in Pimería Alta," *Mid-
    America*, Vol. XXXI, No. 2 (April, 1949), pp. 101–108.
Murphy, James M., "The Discovery of Kino's Grave," *The Journal of
    Arizona History*, Vol. VII, No. 2 (Summer, 1966), pp. 89–95.
Polzer, Charles, S.J. *A Kino Guide*. Tucson: Southwestern Mission
    Research Center, 1968.
Scholes, Frances. "Documents for the History of the New Mexican
    Missions in the Seventeenth Century," *New Mexico Historical
    Review*, Vol. IV, No. 1 (January, 1929), pp. 45–58.
Smith, Fay Jackson, John L. Kessell, and Francis J. Fox. *Father Kino in
    Arizona*. Phoenix: Arizona Historical Foundation, 1966.
Smith, Watson. *Seventeenth-Century Spanish Missions of the Western
    Pueblo Area*, in *The Smoke Signal*, No. 21 (Spring, 1970), The
    Tucson Corral of Westerners.

Stoner, Victor R. "Original Sites of the Spanish Missions of the Santa Cruz Valley," *The Kiva,* Vol. 2, Nos. 7 and 8 (April and May, 1937), pp. 25–32.

―――. "The Spanish Missions of the Santa Cruz Valley," M.A. thesis, University of Arizona, 1937.

Velarde, Luis, S.J. "Padre Luis Velarde's *Relación* of Pimería Alta, 1716," (edited by Rufus Kay Wyllys). *New Mexico Historical Review,* Vol. VI, No. 2 (April, 1931), pp. 111–57.

Wagoner, Jay J. *History of the Cattle Industry in Southern Arizona.* Tucson: University of Arizona Press, 1952.

Wyllys, Rufus K. "Kino of Pimería Alta, Apostle of the Southwest," *Arizona Historical Review,* Vol. V, No. 1 (April, 1932), pp. 5–32; No. 2 (July, 1932), pp. 95–134; No. 3 (October, 1932), pp. 205–25; and No. 4 (January, 1933), pp. 308–26.

―――. *Pioneer Padre.* Dallas, Texas: The Southwest Press, 1935.

6. Missionaries and Soldiers in the 1700s
Relations With the Pimas, Yumas, Apaches, and Hopis

Bents, Doris W. "The History of Tubac, 1752–1948." M.A thesis, University of Arizona, 1949.

Bolton, Herbert E. (translator). *Anza's California Expeditions, Opening a Land Route to California.* Diaries of Anza, Díaz, Garcés, and Palóu. Translated from the original Spanish manuscripts by Herbert Eugene Bolton. Vol. 2. New York: Russell & Russell, 1966.

―――. *Font's Complete Diary, a Chronicle of the Founding of San Francisco.* Translated from the original Spanish manuscript by Herbert Eugene Bolton. Berkeley: University of California Press, 1931.

―――. *Outpost of Empire.* New York: Alfred A. Knopf, 1939. (This volume is also in Herbert E. Bolton's *Anza's California Expeditions,* Vol. 1.)

Bowman, J. N. and Robert F. Heizer. *Anza and the Northwest Frontier of New Spain.* Highland Park, Los Angeles: Southwest Museum, 1967.

Brinckerhoff, Sidney B. "The Last Years of Spanish Arizona, 1786–1821," *Arizona and the West,* Vol. IX, No. 1 (Spring, 1967), pp. 5–20.

Brinckerhoff, Sidney B. and Odie B. Faulk. *Lancers for the King.* Phoenix: Arizona Historical Foundation, 1965. Contains the Royal Regulations of 1772 in both Spanish and English.

Burrus, Ernest J., S.J. (ed.). *Diario Del Capitan Commandante Fernando de Rivera.* Madrid: Ediciones Jose Porrua Turanzas, 1967. The introduction has a good biography of Rivera in English. The diary is in Spanish.

Carranco, Lynwood. "Anza's Bones in Arizpe," *Journal of the West,* Vol. VIII, No. 3 (July, 1969), pp. 416–28.

Coues, Elliott (ed.). *On the Trail of a Spanish Pioneer: The Diary and Itinerary of Francisco Garcés in His Travels Through Sonora, Arizona, and California, 1775–1776.* Translated and edited by Elliott Coues, 2 vols. New York: Francis P. Harper, 1900.

Cullimore, Clarence. "A California Martyr's Bones," *California Historical Society Quarterly,* Vol. XXXIII, No. 1 (March, 1954), pp. 13–21.

Dobyns, Henry F. "Indian Extinction in the Middle Santa Cruz Valley, Arizona," *New Mexico Historical Review,* Vol. XXXVIII, No. 2 (April, 1963), pp. 163–81.

———. *Lance Ho! Containment of the Western Apaches by the Royal Spanish Garrison at Tucson.* Lima, Peru: Editorial Estudios Andinos, 1964.

———. *Pioneering Christians Among the Perishing Indians of Tucson.* Lima, Peru: Editorial Estudios Andinos, 1962.

Donohue, J. Augustine, S.J. "The Unlucky Jesuit Mission of Bac, 1732–1767," *Arizona and the West,* Vol. 2, No. 2 (Summer, 1960), pp. 127–39.

Dunne, Peter M. (translator and annotator). *Jacobo Sedelmayr: Missionary, Frontiersman, Explorer in Arizona and Sonora.* Tucson: Arizona Historical Society, 1955. Contains four original manuscript narratives, 1744–1751, translated and annotated by Dunne.

Engelhardt, Fray Zephrin, O.F.M. *The Franciscans in Arizona.* Harbor Springs, Michigan: Holy Childhood Indian School, 1899.

Ewing, Russell C. "Investigations Into the Causes of the Pima Uprising." *Mid-America,* Vol. 23, No. 2 (April, 1941), pp. 138–51.

———. "The Pima Outbreak in November, 1751," *New Mexico Historical Review,* Vol. 13, No. 4 (October, 1938), pp. 337–46.

Fontana, Bernard L. *Biography of a Desert Church: The Story of Mission San Xavier del Bac,* in *The Smoke Signal,* No. 3 (Spring, 1961), Tucson, Arizona: Tucson Corral of Westerners, 1961.

Galvez, Bernardo de. *Instructions for Governing the Interior Provinces of New Spain, 1786.* Translated and edited by Donald E. Worcester. Berkeley: The Quivira Society, 1951.

García, Luis Navarro. *Don José de Galvez y la Comandancia General de las Provincias Internas del Norte de Nueva España.* Sevilla: Publicaciones de la Escuela de Estudios Hispano-Americanos de Sevilla, 1964.

Gardiner, Arthur D. (ed.) "Letter of Father Middendorff, S.J., Dated from Tucson, 3 March, 1757," *The Kiva,* Vol. 22, No. 4 (June, 1957), pp. 1–10. Contains copy of the original in Latin as well as the English translation.

Greenleaf, Cameron and Andrew Wallace. "Tucson: Pueblo, Presidio, and American City: A Synopsis of Its History," *Arizoniana*, Vol. 3, No. 2 (Summer, 1962), pp. 18–38.

Habig, Marion A., O.F.M. "The Builders of San Xavier del Bac," *The Southwestern Historical Quarterly*, Vol. 41, No. 2 (October, 1937), pp. 154–66.

Hammond, George P. "Pimería Alta After Kino's Time," *New Mexico Historical Review*, Vol. 4, No. 3 (July, 1929), pp. 220–38.

————. "The Zúñiga Journal, Tucson to Santa Fé: The Opening of the Spanish Trade Route, 1788–1795," *New Mexico Historical Review*, Vol. VI, No. 1 (January, 1931), pp. 40–65.

Holterman, Jack. "José Zúñiga, Commandant of Tucson," *The Kiva*, Vol. 22, No. 1 (November, 1956), pp. 1–4.

Ives, Ronald L. "Enrique Ruhen, S.J. — Borderland Martyr," *The Kiva*, Vol. XXIII, No. 1 (October, 1957), pp. 1–10.

————. (ed.). "Retracing the Route of the Fages Expedition of 1781," 2 parts, *Arizona and the West*, Vol. VIII, No. 1 (Spring, 1966), pp. 49–70; and Vol. VIII, No. 2 (Summer, 1966), pp. 157–70. The September 16 to December 30, 1781, period of the Fages diary is included.

Kessell, John L. (ed.). "Anza Damns the Missions: A Spanish Soldier's Criticism of Indian Policy, 1772," *The Journal of Arizona History*, Vol. 13, No. 1 (Spring, 1972), pp. 53–62.

————. (editor and translator). "Anza, Indian Fighter: The Spring Campaign, 1766," *Journal of Arizona History*, Vol. IX, No. 3 (Fall, 1968), pp. 155–63.

————. (editor and translator). "Father Eixarch and the Visitation at Tumacácori, May 12, 1775," *The Kiva*, Vol. XXX, No. 3 (February, 1965), pp. 77–81.

————. "The Making of a Martyr: The Young Francisco Garcés," *New Mexico Historical Review*, Vol. XLV, No. 3 (July, 1970), pp. 181–96.

————. *Mission of Sorrows: Jesuit Guevavi and the Pimas, 1691–1767*. Tucson: University of Arizona Press, 1970.

————. (editor and translator). "San José de Tumacácori — 1773: A Franciscan Reports from Arizona," *Arizona and the West*, Vol. VI, No. 4 (Winter, 1964), pp. 303–12.

Kinnaird, Lawrence (editor and translator). *The Frontiers of New Spain, Nicolas de Lafora's Description, 1766–1768*. Berkeley, California: The Quivira Society, 1958.

Matson, Daniel S. and Albert H. Schroeder, "Cordero's Description of the Apache — 1796," *New Mexico Historical Review*, Vol. XXXII, No. 4 (October, 1957), pp. 335–56.

Miller, Joseph. "Mission San Xavier del Bac: Christendom's Glorious Shrine," *Arizona Highways*, Vol. XV, No. 12 (December, 1939), pp. 6–9, 42.

Mills, Hazel E. "Father Jacobo Sedelmayr, S.J.: A Foreign Chapter in Arizona Missionary History," *Arizona Historical Review*, Vol. VII, No. 1 (January, 1936), pp. 3–18.

Moorhead, Max L. *The Apache Frontier: Jacobo Ugarte and Spanish-Indian Relations in Northern New Spain, 1769–1791.* Norman: University of Oklahoma Press, 1968.

Newhall, Nancy. "Mission San Xavier del Bac," *Arizona Highways*, Vol. XXX, No. 4 (April, 1954), pp. 12–35.

Park, Joseph F. "Spanish Indian Policy in Northern Mexico," 1765–1810," *Arizona and the West*, Vol. IV, No. 4 (Winter, 1962), pp. 325–44.

Pfefferkorn, Ignaz. *Sonora, A Description of the Province.* Translated and annotated by Theodore E. Treutlein. Albuquerque: University of New Mexico Press, 1949. Pfefferkorn was the missionary at Guevavi (in present-day Arizona) in 1763.

Pradeau, Albert Francisco. "Nentuig's Description of Sonora," *Mid-America*, Vol. XXXV (24 in New Series), No. 2 (April, 1953), pp. 81–90.

Priestley, Herbert I. *José de Galvez Visitor General of New Spain, 1765–1771.* Berkeley: University of California Press, 1916.

Rosbach, Virginia H. "The History of the Mission Period of Pimería Alta to 1828," M.A. thesis, University of Texas, 1953. Copy in Special Collections, University of Arizona.

Rudo Ensayo. This book was written by an anonymous Jesuit padre in 1763 and republished at Tucson: Arizona Silhouettes, 1951. The author is now known to have been Father Juan Nentuig (also Nentvig).

Sedelmayr, Jacobo. *Jacobo Sedelmayr: Missionary, Frontiersman, Explorer in Arizona and Sonora. Four Original Manuscript Narratives, 1744–1751.* Translated and annotated by Peter M. Dunne. Tucson: Arizona Historical Society, 1955.

Spicer, Edward H. *Cycles of Conquest: The Impact of Spain, Mexico, and the United States on the Indians of the Southwest, 1533–1960.* Tucson: University of Arizona Press, 1962.

Thomas, Alfred B. *Teodoro de Croix and the Northern Frontier of New Spain, 1776–1783.* From the original document in the Archives of the Indies, Seville. Norman: University of Oklahoma Press, 1941.

Treutlein, Theodore E. "The Economic Regime of the Jesuit Missions in Eighteenth Century Sonora," *The Pacific Historical Review*, Vol. VIII, No. 3 (September, 1939), pp. 289–300.

————. "Father Gottfried Bernhardt Middendorff, S.J., Pioneer of Tucson," *New Mexico Historical Review*, Vol. XXXII, No. 4 (October, 1957), pp. 310–18.

————. "Father Pfefferkorn and His Description of Sonora," *Mid-America*, Vol. 20, No. 4 (October, 1938), pp. 229–52.

————. "The Jesuit Missionary in the Role of Physician," *Mid-America*, Vol. 22, No. 2 (April, 1940), pp. 120–41.

————. (translator). *Missionary in Sonora: The Travel Reports of Joseph Och, S.J.* San Francisco: California Historical Society, 1965.

————. (translator). "The Relation of Philipp [Phelipe] Segesser," *Mid-America*, Vol. 27, No. 3 (July, 1945), pp. 139–87, and No. 4 (October, 1945), pp. 257–60.

Yates, Richard. "Locating the Colorado River Mission San Pedro y San Pablo de Bicuner," *The Journal of Arizona History*, Vol. 13, No. 2 (Summer, 1972), pp. 123–29.

7. Spanish and Mexican Land Grants

Almada, Francisco R. *Diccionario de Historia, Geografia, y Biografia Sonorenses.* Chihuahua, Chihuahua, Mexico: privately published, 1952.

Annual Report of the Commissioner of the General Land Office. Washington, D.C.: Government Printing Office, 1870 through 1892. Includes reports of the surveyor general of Arizona.

Arizona Court of Private Land Claims Dockets, Records of the General Land Office, U.S. Department of Interior, in Records of the Bureau of Land Management. Record Group 49, National Archives. Microfilm copy of the dockets in the Arizona Historical Society. Microfilm copies of the court proceedings are in the Arizona Department of Library and Archives.

Arizona Daily Citizen (Tucson), May 1, 1880 and June 17, 1898.

Arizona Daily Star (Tucson), July 18 and July 22, 1886; June 21, 1887; February 7 and March 19, 1901; and February 16, 1958.

Arizona Enterprise (Florence), April 4, 1891 and March 31, 1894.

Arizona Gazette (Phoenix), May 9, 1881; July 26, 1888; and March 4, 1893.

Arizona Private Land Claims Records in RG 49; Records of the General Land Office, National Archives (deposited in the Washington National Records Center, Suitland, Maryland).

Arizona Republican (Phoenix), June 6, 1915.

Arizona Sentinel (Yuma), January 25, 1879.

Arizona Weekly Citizen (Tucson), March 6, 1881 and January 5, 1884.

Bartlett, John Russell. *Personal Narrative of Explorations and Incidents in Texas, New Mexico, California, and Chihuahua.* 2 vols. New York: D. Appleton & Co., 1854. [Reprinted in Chicago: Rio Grande Press, 1965.]

Black, Mrs. Sarah M. "Story of Mrs. Sarah M. Black as told to Mrs. George Kitt and Charles M. Wood, February 14, 1926." Copy in Arizona Historical Society.

Bolton, Herbert E. *Rim of Christendom.* New York: Russell and Russell, 1960.

Brewster, Jane Wayland. "The San Rafael Cattle Company," *Arizona and the West,* Vol. 8, No. 2 (Summer, 1966), pp. 133–56.

Brophy, Frank Cullen. "San Ignacio del Babacomari," *Arizona Highdays,* Vol. XLII, No. 9 (September, 1966), pp. 2–5, 8–9, 11–12, 16–17.

Browne, J. Ross. *Adventures in Apache Country.* New York: Harper and Brothers, 1869. [Reprinted in Tucson: Arizona Silhouettes, 1950.]

County records (Cochise, Pima, Santa Cruz, and Yavapai) in the offices of the respective county assessors and county recorders. Contain information on land holdings, assessments, taxes, and property transfers.

Deeds of Real Estate, Santa Cruz County Recorder's Office, Nogales, Arizona. Book Nos. 3, 19, and 30, and Docket Nos. 18, 27, 57, 104, 109 and 113.

Deeds, Real Estate, Books 12, 14, 31, and 123, in Cochise County Recorder's Office, Bisbee, Arizona.

Deeds, Records, Yavapai County Recorder's Office, Prescott, Arizona, Book 5.

Dobyns, Henry F. "Tubac Through Four Centuries: A Historical Resumé and Analysis," 3 vols. Manuscript. Tucson: Arizona State Museum, 1959.

Docket Books 195 and 198, Cochise County Recorder's Office, Bisbee, Arizona.

Erwin, Allen A. *The Southwest of John H. Slaughter.* Glendale, California: The Arthur H. Clark Company, 1965.

Flipper, Henry O. "Records Relating to the Army Career of Henry Ossian Flipper, 1873–1882," National Archives Microfilm Publications Microcopy No. T-1027, GSA, Washington, D.C., 1968.

Fontana, Bernard L. *Calabazas of the Río Rico,* in *The Smoke Signal,* No. 24 (Fall, 1971), pp. 66–88.

Gressinger, A. W. *Charles Poston — Sunland Seer.* Six Shooter Canyon, Globe, Arizona: Dale Stuart King, Publisher, 1961.

Herstrom, Guy M. "Pgymy Among the Giants," 1959 *Brand Book* of the Denver Posse of Westerners, Vol. XV, pp. 233–78.

House Reports and Senate Documents as cited in footnotes.

Johnson, Royal. *Adverse Report of the Surveyor General of Arizona Royal A. Johnson Upon the Alleged "Peralta Grant," a Complete Exposé of Its Fraudulent Character.* Phoenix: Arizona Gazette Book and Job Office, 1890. (Also published at Tucson: Tucson Citizen Print, 1889). Copy in RG 49: General Land Office Records, National Archives.

Lounsbury, Frank. "Mexican Land Claims in California," mimeographed publication in the National Archives, RG 60; Department of Justice, National Archives.

Mattison, Ray H. "Early Spanish and Mexican Settlements in Arizona," *New Mexico Historical Review,* Vol. XXI, No. 4 (October, 1946), pp. 273–327.

————. "The Tangled Web: The Controversy Over the Tumacácori and Baca Land Grants," *The Journal of Arizona History,* Vol. 8, No. 2 (Summer, 1967), pp. 71–90.

Minutes of the U.S. Court of Private Land Claims, July 1, 1891–April 13, 1904, Bureau of Land Management, Record Group 49, Federal Records Center, Bell, California.

Mowry, Sylvester, *Arizona and Sonora.* New York: Harper and Brothers, 1864.

New York Times, June 14, 1891.

Poston, Charles D. *Building A State in Apache Land.* John M. Myers, ed. Tempe, Arizona: Aztec Press, 1963. (Originally published as four articles in *Overland Monthly* in 1894.)

Powell, Donald M. *The Peralta Grant: James Addison Reavis and the Barony of Arizona.* Norman: University of Oklahoma Press, 1960.

Proyecto de Microfilmación en archivos históricos del Estado de Sonora, Mexico, Mayo, 1966. Instituto Nacional de Antropología e Historía, Departmento de Investigaciones Históricas, Mexico, D.F. Dr. Wigberto Jiménez Moreno, Director, in collaboration with the Arizona Historical Society, Librarian Andrew Wallace, Tucson, Arizona. Document selection by Dr. Jiménez and Father Kieran McCarty. Contains some valuable documents on the Apache wars.

Register of Documents Filed in the U.S. Court of Private Land Claims, February, 1892–June, 1899, Federal Records Center, Bell, California.

Reynolds, Matthew G., U.S. Attorney, Court of Private Land Claims, Correspondence of. RG 60: Department of Justice, National Archives.

Robbins, J. W. *Opinion and Report of U.S. Surveyor General for Arizona, Tres Alamos Grant. Washington, D.C.:* Gibson Brothers, 1884.

Smith, Ralph A. "The Scalp Hunter in the Borderlands, 1835–1850," *Arizona and the West,* Vol. 6, No. 1 (Spring, 1964), pp. 5–22.

Stevens, Robert C. "The Apache Menace in Sonora, 1831–1849," *Arizona and the West,* Vol. 6, No. 3 (Autumn, 1964), pp. 211–22.

————. "Mexico's Forgotten Frontier: A History of Sonora, 1821–1846." Ph.D. dissertation, University of California, Berkeley, 1963.

"Tomás Cabeza de Baca and Town of Las Vegas Grant," Report No. 20. File No. 6, in Records of Private Land Claims Adjudicated by the U.S. Surveyor General, 1855–1890. (Also on Reel 15, Microfilm Papers Relating to New Mexico Land Grants), in Archives Division, State of New Mexico Records Center, Santa Fe.

Tombstone Epitaph, August 11, 1911.

Transcript of Letters Written During the Examination of Titles to Private Land Claims in Arizona, Sêptember 1, 1879–July 29, 1882, Federal Records Center, Bell, California.

Tucson Citizen, April 25, 1912.

U.S. Court of Claims. *In the Court of Claims of the United States . . . J. A. Peralta Reavis and Doña Sofia Loreta Micaela de Maso-Reavis y Peralta de la Córdoba, His Wife, and Clinton P. Farrell, Trustee, vs. The United States of America, Petition of Claimants* [No. 16,719]. Washington, D. C.: Gibson Brothers, 1890.

U.S. Court of Private Land Claims, Santa Fe District. *James Addison Peraltareavis and Doña Sofia Loreta Micaela de Peraltareavis, née Maso y Silva de Peralta de la Córdoba, Husband and Wife, Petitioners, vs. The United States, Respondent,* 1895.

U.S. Reports, U.S. Supreme Court cases as cited in the footnotes.

U.S. Statutes at Large, U.S. laws as cited.

Wagoner, Jay J. *Arizona Territory, 1863–1912: A Political History.* Tucson: University of Arizona Press, 1970.

————. *History of the Cattle Industry in Southern Arizona, 1540–1940.* Tucson: University of Arizona Press, 1952.

Weekly Arizona Miner, March 20, 1874, and April 16, 1880.

8. The Mountain Men

Camp, Charles L. *George C. Yount and his Chronicles of the West.* Denver, Colorado: Fred A. Rosenstock, Old West Publishing Company, 1966.

Carson, Christopher. *Kit Carson's Own Story of His Life,* (edited by Blanche C. Grant). Taos, New Mexico: Santa Fe New Mexican Publishing Corporation, 1926.

Cleland, Robert G. *This Reckless Breed of Men: The Trappers and Fur Traders of the Southwest.* New York: Alfred A. Knopf, 1952.

Favour, Alpheus H. *Old Bill Williams, Mountain Man.* Chapel Hill, N.C.: University of North Carolina Press, 1936. [Reprinted in Norman: University of Oklahoma Press, 1962.]

Flint, Timothy. *The Personal Narrative of James Ohio Pattie of Kentucky.* Cincinnati: John H. Wood, 1831. [Reprinted in paperback edition in New York: Lippincott, 1962.]

Hafen, LeRoy R. (ed.). *The Mountain Men and the Fur Trade of the Far West,* 7 vols. Glendale, California: The Arthur H. Clark Co., 1965–69.

Hall, Sharlot M. *First Citizen of Prescott: Pauline Weaver, Trapper and Mountain Man.* Prescott, Arizona, n.p., 1932.

Hill, Joseph J. "Antoine Robidoux, Kingpin in the Colorado River Fur Trade, 1824–1844," *The Colorado Magazine,* Vol. VII, No. 4 (July, 1930), pp. 125–32.

————. "Ewing Young in the Fur Trade of the Far Southwest, 1822–1834," *The Quarterly of the Oregon Historical Society,* Vol. XXIV, No. 1 (March, 1923), pp. 1–35.

————. "Free Trapper: The Story of Old Bill Williams . . .," *Touring Topics (Westways),* Vol. XXII, No. 3 (March, 1930), pp. 18–27.

————. "New Light on Pattie and the Southwestern Fur Trade," *Southwestern Historical Quarterly,* Vol. XXVI, No. 4 (April, 1923), pp. 243–54.

Kroeber, Clifton B. "The Route of James O. Pattie on the Colorado in 1826," *Arizona and the West,* Vol. 6, No. 2 (Summer, 1964), pp. 119–36.

Lockwood, Frank C. "American Hunters and Trappers in Arizona," *Arizona Historical Review,* Vol. II, No. 2 (July, 1929), pp. 70–85.

Marshall, Thomas M. "St. Vrain's Expedition to the Gila in 1826," *Southwestern Historical Quarterly,* Vol. XIX, No. 3 (January, 1916), pp. 251–60.

Morgan, Dale L. *Jedediah Smith and the Opening of the West.* Lincoln: University of Nebraska Press, 1969. [Reprint from Bobbs-Merrill edition, 1953.]

Ruxton, George F. *Life in the Far West,* (LeRoy R. Hafen, editor). Norman, Oklahoma: University of Oklahoma Press, 1951.

Sabin, Edwin L. *Kit Carson Days, 1809–1868,* 2 vols. New York: The Press of the Pioneers, Inc., 1935.

Smith, Alson J. *Men Against the Mountains: Jedediah Smith and the South West Expedition of 1826–1829.* New York: The John Day Company, 1965.

Wells, Edmund W. *Argonaut Tales.* New York: The Grafton Press, 1927.

9. The Mexican War

Bieber, Ralph (ed.). *Exploring Southwestern Trails, 1846–1854.* Glendale, Calif.: The Arthur H. Clark Co., 1938.

Bigler, Henry W. "Extracts from the Journal of Henry W. Bigler," (edited by Adelbert Bigler), *Utah Historical Quarterly,* Vol. 5, No. 2 (April, 1932), pp. 35–64.

Bliss, Robert S. "The Journal of Robert S. Bliss, with the Mormon Battalion," *Utah Historical Quarterly,* Vol. 4, Nos. 3 and 4 (July and October, 1931), pp. 67–96, 110–28.

Carson, Christopher. *Kit Carson's Own Story of His Life,* (edited by Blanche C. Grant). Taos, New Mexico: Santa Fe New Mexican Publishing Corporation, 1926.

Calvin, Ross. *Lieutenant Emory Reports.* Albuquerque: University of New Mexico Press, 1951. This book is a reprint of Lieutenant W. H. Emory's *Notes of a Military Reconnaissance.*

Chamberlain, Samuel E. (Roger Butterfield, editor). *My Confession.* New York: Harper & Brothers, 1956. Parts of this journal were printed in *Life* magazine, July 23, July 30, and August 6, 1956.

Clarke, Dwight L. *Stephen Watts Kearny, Soldier of the West*. Norman, Oklahoma: University of Oklahoma Press, 1961.

Cooke, Philip St. George. *The Conquest of New Mexico and California: An Historical and Personal Narrative*. New York: G. P. Putnam's Sons, 1878. [Reprinted at Chicago: Rio Grande Press, 1964.]

Couts, Cave Johnson. *Hepah California: The Journal of Cave Johnson Couts...1848–1849* (edited by Henry F. Dobyns). Tucson: Arizona Historical Society, 1961.

Cutts, James M. *The Conquest of California and New Mexico...1846 & 1847*. Albuquerque: Horn & Wallace, Publishers, 1965.

"Documents Accompanying the President's Message at the Commencement of the First Session of the Thirtieth Congress," *Senate Executive Document* No. 1 (Serial #503). Contains reports by A. W. Doniphan, Commanding the 1st Regiment, Missouri Mounted Volunteers, and Colonel Sterling Price, Colonel Commanding the Army in New Mexico.

Emory, Lt. Col. William H. *Notes of a Military Reconnaissance From Fort Leavenworth, in Missouri, to San Diego, California*. House Executive Document No. 41, 30th Cong. 1st Sess., 1848, pp. 7–416.

Gibson, George R. *Journal of a Soldier Under Kearny and Doniphan*. (Ralph P. Bieber, editor). Glendale, Calif.: The Arthur H. Clark Co., 1935.

Golder, Frank A. *The March of the Mormon Battalion from Council Bluffs to California: Taken from the Journal of Henry Standage*. New York: The Century Co., 1928.

Griffin, Dr. John Strothers, "A Doctor Comes to California: The Diary of John S. Griffin, Assistant Surgeon with Kearny's Dragoons, 1846–47" (edited by George Walcott Ames, Jr.), *California Historical Society Quarterly*, Vol. 21, No. 3 (September, 1942), pp. 193–224; Vol. 21, No. 4 (October, 1942), pp. 333–57; and Vol. 22, No. 1 (March, 1943), pp. 41–66.

Hughes, John T. (First Regiment of Missouri Cavalry). *Doniphan's Expedition Containing An Account of the U.S. Army Operations in the Great American Southwest*. Chicago: The Rio Grande Press, Inc., 1962. [Reprint of book published in Cincinnati: J. A. and U. P. James, 1848.]

Israel, Fred L. (ed.). *Major Peace Treaties of Modern History, 1648–1967*, Vol. II. New York: Chelsea House Publishers, 1967.

Jones, Nathaniel V. "The Journal of Nathaniel V. Jones, with the Mormon Battalion," *Utah Historical Quarterly*, Vol. 4, No. 1 (January, 1931), pp. 3–24.

Layton, Christopher. *Christopher Layton* (edited by Myron W. McIntyre and Noel R. Barton). Salt Lake City: privately published, 1966. Chapters 5 and 6 deal with the march of the Mormon Battalion in Arizona and include songs composed along the route.

"Messages of the President of the United States with the Correspondence, Therewith Communicated, Between the Secretary of War
and other Officers of the Government, on the subject of. the
Mexican War," *House Executive Document* No. 60, 30th Cong.
1st Sess., 1847–48. (Serial #520).

Peterson, Charles; John F. Yurtinus; David E. Atkinson; and A. Kent
Powell. *Mormon Battalion Travel Guide*. Salt Lake City: Utah
Historical Society, 1972.

"Report of the Secretary of War [George W. Crawford] Communicating
. . . a copy of the official journal of Lieutenant Colonel Philip St.
George Cooke, from Santa Fe to San Diego, etc.," Senate *Public
Documents*, No. 2, March 5, 1849, 31st Cong. Special Sess., 1849,
85 pp. (Serial # 547).

Robinson, Jacob S. *A Journal of the Santa Fe Expedition Under Colonel
Doniphan*. Princeton: Princeton University Press, 1932.

Turner, Henry Smith. *The Original Journal of Henry Smith Turner:
With Stephen Watts Kearny to New Mexico and California,
1846–47* (edited by Dwight L. Clarke). Norman: University of
Oklahoma Press, 1966.

Tyler, Daniel. *A Concise History of the Mormon Battalion in the
Mexican War, 1846–1847*. n.p., 1881. [Reprinted in Chicago: Rio
Grande Press, 1964.] Tyler, a sergeant in the Mormon Battalion,
compiled this history from "diaries written during service and
numerous letters and statements from surviving members of that
valiant corps."

Young, Otis E. *The West of Philip St. George Cooke, 1809–1895*. Glendale, Calif.: The Arthur H. Clark Co., 1955.

10. 1850s: Boundary Problems and the Gadsden Purchase

Bartlett, John R. *Personal Narrative of Explorations and Incidents in
Texas, New Mexico, California, Sonora, and Chihuahua, During
the Years 1850, '51, '52, and '53*. 2 vols. New York: D. Appleton
& Co., 1854.

Cremony, John C. *Life Among the Apaches*. San Francisco: A. Roman &
Company Publishers, 1868. [Republished at Tucson: Arizona
Silhouettes, 1951.] Cremony was the interpreter for the U.S.
Boundary Commission headed by John R. Bartlett.

Emory, William H., "Report of the United States and Mexican Boundary Commission," *Senate Executive Document* 108, 34th Cong.
1st Sess., 2 vols. Reprinted at Chicago: Rio Grande Press, 1967.

Faulk, Odie B. (editor and translator), "Projected Mexican Colonies in
the Borderlands, 1852," *The Journal of Arizona History*, Vol. 10,
No. 2 (Summer, 1969), pp. 115–28.

———. *Too Far North: Too Far South*. Los Angeles: Westernlore
Press, 1967.

"Fort Yuma, California Post Returns, October, 1850–December, 1865,"
on microfilm roll No. 1488 of "Returns from U.S. Military Posts,
1800–1916," National Archives Microfilm Publications, General
Services Administration, Washington, D.C. Copy in Arizona
Historical Society Library, Tucson.

Garber, Paul N. *The Gadsden Treaty.* Gloucester, Mass.: Peter Smith,
1959.

Hine, Robert V. *Bartlett's West: Drawing the Mexican Boundary.* New
Haven, Conn.: Yale University Press, 1968.

Rippy, J. Fred. "The Negotiations of the Gadsden Treaty," *Southwestern Historical Quarterly,* Vol. 27 (July, 1923), pp. 1–26.

Schmidt, Louis B. "Manifest Opportunity and the Gadsden Purchase,"
Arizona and the West, Vol. 3, No. 3 (Autumn, 1961), pp. 245–64.

Tate, Bill (publisher). *Guadalupe Hidalgo Treaty of Peace 1848 and
the Gadsden Treaty with Mexico 1853.* Reprinted from the New
Mexico Statutes, 1963 Annotated, Vol. One. Truchas, New
Mexico: Tate Gallery, 1967.

Woodward, Arthur (ed.). *Journal of Lt. Thomas W. Sweeny, 1849–1853.*
Los Angeles: Westernlore Press, 1956.

11. Explorations and Transportation in the New Domain

Altshuler, Constance Wynn (ed.). *Latest From Arizona: The Hesperian
Letters, 1859–1861.* Tucson, Arizona: Arizona Historical Society,
1969.

Aubry, Francois Xavier, "Diaries of Francois Aubry, 1853–1854," in
Ralph P. Bieber and Averam B. Bender (eds.). *Exploring South-
western Trails, 1846–1854.* Glendale, California: The Arthur H.
Clark Co., 1938, Vol. 7, pp. 353–83.

Bailey, L. R. *The A. B. Gray Report.* Los Angeles: Westernlore Press,
1963.

Bandel, Eugene (Ralph P. Bieber, ed.). *Frontier Life in the Army.*
Glendale, California: The Arthur H. Clark Co., 1932.

Barrows, H. D. "A Two Thousand Mile Stage Ride," *Annual Publica-
cation of the Historical Society of Southern California,* 1896,
pp. 40–44.

Beale, Edward F. "The Report of the Superintendent [Beale] on the
Wagon Road from Fort Defiance to the Colorado River," in
Wagon Road from Fort Defiance to the Colorado River, House
Executive Document No. 124, 35th Cong. 1st Sess., 1857–1858.
(Serial #959).

Bieber, Ralph P. (ed.). *Southern Trails to California in 1849 (South-
west Historical Series,* Vol. V). Glendale, California: The Arthur
H. Clark Co., 1937. Contains "Letters and Journal of John E.
Durivage," pp. 159–255.

Bonsal, Stephen. *Edward Fitzgerald Beale.* New York and London:
G. P. Putnam's Sons, 1912.

Chaput, Donald. "Babes in Arms," *The Journal of Arizona History,* Vol. 13, No. 3 (Autumn, 1972), pp. 197–204.

Conkling, Roscoe P. and Margaret B. *The Butterfield Overland Mail, 1857–1869.* 3 vols. Glendale, California: The Arthur H. Clark Co., 1947.

Cosulich, Bernice. *Tucson.* Tucson, Arizona: Arizona Silhouettes, 1953.

Crosby, Alexander L. (ed.). *Steamboat Up the Colorado.* From the Journal of Lieutenant Joseph Christmas Ives, United States Topographical Engineers, 1857–1858. Boston: Little, Brown and Company, 1965.

Cross, Jack L. "El Paso — Fort Yuma Wagon Road: 1857–1860," *Password,* published by the El Paso Historical Society. Vol. IV, No. 1 (January, 1959), pp. 4–18 and Vol. IV, No. 2 (April, 1959), pp. 58–70.

Duffen, William A. (ed.). "Overland via 'Jackass Mail' in 1858: The Diary of Phocion R. Way," 4 parts in *Arizona and the West,* Vol. 2, No. 1 (Spring, 1960), pp. 35–53; No. 2 (Summer, 1960), pp. 147–64; No. 3 (Autumn, 1960), pp. 279–92; and No. 4 (Winter, 1960), pp. 353–70.

Faulk, Odie B. (ed.). *Derby's Report on Opening the Colorado, 1850–1851.* From the Original Report of Lt. George Horatio Derby. Albuquerque: University of New Mexico Press, 1969.

Floyd, Dr. William P. "Journal kept by the surgeon of Edward Fitzgerald Beale's wagon road expedition, describing his trip from Virginia to Fort Smith, and thence to the Colorado River, September 27, 1858, to May 15, 1859." Original in the Huntington Library, San Marino, Calif.

Foreman, Grant. *Marcy and the Gold Seekers.* Norman: University of Oklahoma Press, 1939.

Fowler, Harlan D. *Camels to California.* Stanford, California (Palo Alto): Stanford University Press, 1950.

Goetzmann, William H. *Army Exploration in the American West, 1803–1863.* New Haven, Conn., and London: Yale University Press, 1965.

Hammond, George P. and Edward H. Howes (eds.). *Overland to California on the Southwestern Trail: Diary of Robert Eddleston.* Berkeley and Los Angeles: University of California Press, 1950.

Harris, Benjamin B. *The Gila Trail: The Texas Argonauts and the California Gold Rush* (edited by Richard H. Dillon). Norman: University of Oklahoma Press, 1960. Original journal of Harris, a Virginian, is in the Huntington Library, San Marino, Calif.

Heintzelman, General Samuel Peter. Correspondence and notebooks, 1822–1880. Six portfolios and ten volumes of diary, 1825–1872. Library of Congress, Manuscripts Division.

Hoffman, Velma Rudd. "Lt. Beale and the Camel Caravans Through Arizona," *Arizona Highways,* XXXIII, No. 10 (October, 1957), pp. 6–13.

Ives, Lt. Joseph C. *Report Upon the Colorado River of the West, 1857–1858.* House Executive Document No. 90, 36th Cong. 1st Sess., 1859–1860. Washington: Government Printing Office, 1861.

Jackson, W. Turrentine. *Wagon Roads West.* Berkeley and Los Angeles: University of California Press, 1952.

Jaeger, (Iager), Louis J. F. "Diary of a Ferryman and Trader at Fort Yuma, 1855–57," *Annual Publication of the Historical Society of Southern California,* Vol. XIX, Part I (1928), pp. 89–128 and Part II (1929), pp. 213–42.

"Journal of Isaiah C. Woods on the Establishment of the San Antonio and San Diego Mail Line," (Noel M. Loomis, ed.) in Ray Brandes (ed.), *Brand Book Number One, The San Diego Corral of Westerners,* n.p., 1968, pp. 94–125. Good bibliography on stagecoaching, pp. 142–44.

Judd, B. Ira. "The Overland Mail," *Arizona Highways,* Vol. XXXIV, No. 10 (October, 1958), pp. 8–13, 38–39.

Lammons, Frank B. "Operation Camel: An Experiment in Animal Transportation in Texas, 1857–1860," *The Southwestern Historical Quarterly,* Vol. LXI, No. 1 (July, 1957), pp. 20–50.

Lang, Walter B. (ed.). *The First Overland Mail: Butterfield Trail, St. Louis to San Francisco, 1858–1861.* Washington, D.C.: n.p., 1947. Contains the contemporary accounts of three men who traveled on the Butterfield stage: Waterman Ormsby, J. M. Farwell, and William Tallack.

Leavitt, Francis H. "Steam Navigation on the Colorado River," *California Historical Society Quarterly,* Vol. 22 (1943), No. 1, pp. 1–25 and No. 2, pp. 151–74.

Lesley, Lewis (ed.). *Uncle Sam's Camels: The Journal of May Humphreys Stacey Supplemented by the Report of Edward Fitzgerald Beale* (1857–1858). Cambridge, Mass.: Harvard University Press, 1929.

Lockwood, Frank C. *Life in Old Tucson, 1854–1864.* Los Angeles: The Ward Ritchie Press, 1943.

Martin, Mabelle (ed.). "From Texas to California in 1849: Diary of Cornelius C. Cox," *The Southwestern Historical Quarterly,* Vol. XXIX, No. 1 (July, 1925), pp. 36–50; No. 2 (October, 1925), pp. 128–46; and No. 3 (January, 1926), pp. 201–23.

Miller, David H. "The Ives Expedition Revisited: A Prussian's Impressions," *The Journal of Arizona History,* Vol. 13, No. 1 (Spring, 1972), pp. 1–25, and Vol. 13, No. 3 (Autumn, 1972), pp. 177–96. In this narrative, Miller has used excerpts from Balduin Möllhausen's account of the Ives expedition, *Reisen in die Felsengebirge Nord-Amerikas bis zum Hoch-Plateau von Neu-Mexico, unternommen als Mitglied der im Auftrage der Vereinigten Staaten ausgesandten Colorado Expedition,* 2 vols. (Leipzig: H. Costenoble, 1861) that have never been published in English.

Möllhausen, Baldwin. *Diary of a Journey from the Mississippi to the Pacific with a United States Government Expedition* (Introduction by Alexander Von Humboldt and translation by Mrs. Percy Sinnett), 2 vols. London: Longman, Brown, Green, Longman, and Roberts, 1858.

Ormsby, Waterman L. *The Butterfield Overland Mail* (edited by Lyle H. Wright and Josephine M. Bynum). San Marino, California: The Huntington Library, 1955.

Pearce, Basic C. "The Jackass Mail: San Antonio and San Diego Mail Line," *The Journal of San Diego History,* Vol. XV, No. 2 (Spring, 1969), pp. 15–20.

Pettid, Rev. Edward F. "The Oatman Story," *Arizona Highways,* Vol. XLIV, No. 11 (November, 1968), pp. 4–9.

"Report of Mr. Beale Relating to the Construction of a Wagon Road from Fort Smith to the Colorado River," (1859), in *Wagon Road — Fort Smith to the Colorado River,* House Executive Document No. 42, 36th Cong. 1st Sess., 1859–60. (Serial #1048).

"Report of the Secretary of War (John B. Floyd), 1859," 2nd part, in *Message from the President of the United States to the Two Houses of Congress at the Commencement of the First Session of the Thirty-Sixth Congress,* Senate Document No. 2, 36th Cong. 1st Sess., 1859–60. (Serial #1025). Contains a report on the "San Antonio and San Diego" and the "Great Overland Mail," pp. 1410–12.

Report Upon Pacific Wagon Roads. House Executive Document No. 108, 35th Cong. 1st Sess., 1858–59, pp. 9–11. (Serial #1008).

Reports of Explorations and Surveys to Ascertain the Most Practicable and Economical Route for a Railroad from the Mississippi River to the Pacific Ocean (Pacific Railroad Reports), 1853–54. Vol. 3 (Whipple survey) in House Executive Document No. 91, 33rd Cong. 2nd Sess., 1854–1855. (Serial #760 or #793); Vol. 7 (Parke) in Senate Executive Document No. 78, 33rd Cong. 2nd Sess., 1854–1855. (Serial #758).

Sitgreaves, Captain Lorenzo. *Report of an Expedition Down the Zuni and Colorado Rivers, 1851.* Senate Executive Document No. 59, 32nd Cong. 2nd Sess., 1852–1853. (Serial #668). Reprinted at Chicago: Rio Grande Press, 1962.

Stratton, Royal B. *Captivity of the Oatman Girls.* 3rd ed. New York: privately published by the author, 1858.

Taft, Robert. "The Pictorial Record of the Old West: Heinrich Baldwin Möllhausen," *Kansas Historical Quarterly,* Vol. XVI, No. 3 (August, 1948), pp. 225–44.

Tallack, William. "The California Overland Express, the Longest Stage-Ride in the World," *Historical Society of Southern California Quarterly Publication,* Vol. XVII, No. 2 (June, 1935), pp. 33–78; No. 3 (September, 1935), pp. 83–114.

Wallace, Edward S. *The Great Reconnaissance: Soldiers, Artists and Scientists on the Frontier, 1848–1861*. Boston: Little, Brown, and Company, 1955.

Way, Phocion, R. "Diary of a Trip to Arizona and of a Residence at Santa Rita Within the Gadsden Purchase," ms. at Lafayette College. Also see W. Clement Eaton. "Frontier Life in Arizona, 1858–1861," *Southwestern Historical Quarterly*, Vol. XXXVI, No. 3 (January, 1933).

Winther, Oscar O. "The Southern Overland Mail and Stagecoach Line, 1857–1861," *New Mexico Historical Review*, Vol. XXXII, No. 2 (April, 1957), pp. 81–106.

————. *Via Western Express and Stagecoach*. Stanford University, California: Stanford University Press, 1945.

Woodward, Arthur. *Feud on the Colorado*. Los Angeles: Westernlore Press, 1955.

————. (editor). *Journal of Lt. Thomas W. Sweeny, 1849–1853*. Los Angeles: Westernlore Press, 1956.

12. 1850s: Government and Politics

Ainsa, Joseph Y. *History of the Crabb Expedition Into Northern Sonora: Decapitation of the State Senator of California, Henry A. Crabb and massacre of ninety-eight of his friends, at Caborca and Sonoita, Sonora, Mexico*. Phoenix: privately published, 1951.

Capron, John G. "The Story of the Trials and Incidents of the Relief Party, by John G. Capron, the Only Surviving Member of the Party," in the *Arizona Daily Star*, February 4, 1906; "The Crabb Massacre — An Exciting Episode in the Early History of Arizona," *Arizona Daily Star*, December 11, 1910.

"Diary of Charles Debrille Poston," in Sharlot Hall Museum, Prescott, Arizona (also on microfilm, Records of the States of the United States of America, Library of Congress, 1949, Arizona XX, Reel 1A.

Forbes, Robert H. *Crabb's Filibustering Expedition Into Sonora, 1857*. Tucson: Arizona Silhouettes, 1952.

Hayden, Carl T. *Charles Trumbull Hayden: Pioneer*. Tucson: The Arizona Historical Society, 1972.

Hunsaker, William J. "Lansford W. Hastings' Project for the Invasion and Conquest of Arizona and New Mexico for the Southern Confederacy," *The Arizona Historical Review*, Vol. IV, No. 2 (July, 1931), pp. 5–12.

Israel, Fred L. (ed.). *The State of the Union Messages of the Presidents, 1790–1966*, Vol. 1. New York: Chelsea House — Robert Hector, Publishers, 1966.

Lamar, Howard R. *The Far Southwest, 1846–1912, A Territorial History*. New Haven and London: Yale University Press, 1966.

Mowry, Sylvester. *The Geography and Resources of Arizona and Sonora: An Address Before the American Geographical and Statistical Society by Sylvester Mowry*, New York, February 3, 1859. San Francisco and New York: A. Roman & Co., 1863.

————. *Memoir of the Proposed Territory of Arizona*. Washington: Henry Polkinhorn, Printer, 1857.

"Official information and correspondence in relation to the executions of Colonel Crabb and his associates," in *Senate Executive Document* 64, 35th Cong. 1st Sess., 1857–1858, 84 pp. (Serial #955).

Poston, Charles D. "Another Chapter of the Crabb Massacre as Told by Chas. D. Poston," in the *Arizona Daily Star*, August 4, 1886.

Sacks, B. *Be It Enacted: The Creation of the Territory of Arizona*. Phoenix: Arizona Historical Foundation, 1964. This book is the best work on the government and politics of pre-territorial Arizona.

————. "Sylvester Mowry: Artilleryman, Libertine, Entrepreneur," in *The American West*, Vol. I, No. 3 (Summer, 1964), pp. 14–24, 79.

Stephens, B. A. "A Biographical Sketch of Louis J. F. Iaeger [Jaeger]," *Annual Publication of the Historical Society of Southern California, 1888–89*. Los Angeles, Calif.: Frank Cobler, the "Plain Printer," 1889, pp. 36–40. [Reprinted for Dawson's Book Shop, 1965.]

Wallace, Andrew (ed.). *Pumpelly's Arizona* (An excerpt from *Across America and Asia* by Raphael Pumpelly, comprising those chapters which concern the Southwest). Tucson: The Palo Verde Press, 1965.

Weekly Arizonian, March 3, 1859.

Wyllys, Rufus K. "Henry A. Crabb — A Tragedy of the Sonora Frontier," *Pacific Historical Review*, Vol. IX, No. 2 (June, 1940), pp. 183–94.

13. 1850s: Towns and Forts

Acts, Resolutions and Memorials, Seventh Legislative Assembly, Territory of Arizona, 1873.

Altshuler, Constance Wynn. *Latest From Arizona! The Hesperian Letters, 1859–1861*. Tucson: Arizona Historical Society, 1969.

Anderson, Hattie. "Mining and Indian Fighting in Arizona and New Mexico, 1858–1861: Memoirs of Hank Smith," in *Panhandle Plains Historical Review*, Vol. 1, No. 1, 1928, pp. 67–115.

Annual Report of the Secretary of War, *House Executive Document* 2, 32nd Cong. 1st Sess., 1851–1852, Part 1 (Serial #634); and *Senate Executive Document* 2, 36 Cong. 1st Sess., 1859–1860, Part 2 (Serial #1024).

Arizona Daily Star, November 16, 1899.

Bailey, L. R. *The Long Walk: A History of the Navajo Wars, 1846–68*. Los Angeles: Westernlore Press, 1964.

Bandel, Eugene. *Frontier Life in the Army, 1854–1861* (edited by Ralph P. Bieber and translated by Olga Bandel and Richard Jente). Glendale, Calif.: The Arthur H. Clark Company, 1932.

Barney, James M. *Yuma.* n.p.: Charter Oak Insurance Co., 1953. Barney's father was the Treasurer of Yuma County when the county seat was moved from La Paz to Arizona City (Yuma). He was also the first postmaster of Ehrenberg and the first mayor of Arizona City.

Bents, Doris W. "The History of Tubac." Unpublished master's thesis, University of Arizona, Tucson, 1949.

Brandes, Ray. *Frontier Military Posts in Arizona.* Globe, Arizona: Dale Stuart King Publisher, 1960.

Browne, J. Ross. *A Tour Through Arizona, 1864, or Adventures in the Apache Country.* Reprinted at Tucson: Arizona Silhouettes, 1950.

Calhoun, James S. *The Official Correspondence of James S. Calhoun While Indian Agent at Santa Fe and Superintendent of Indian Affairs in New Mexico, 1849–1852* (Annie H. Abel, editor). Washington, D.C.: Government Printing Office, 1915.

"Camp Breckenridge, New Mexico, Post Returns, August, 1860–June, 1861," Records of the Adjutant General, Record Group No. 94, National Archives. Microfilm copy at the Arizona Historical Society.

Carlson, Edward. "The Martial Experiences of the California Volunteers," *The Overland Monthly,* Vol. VII (2nd Series), No. 41 (May, 1886), pp. 480–96.

Cleland, Robert G. *The Cattle on a Thousand Hills.* San Marino, Calif.: The Huntington Library, 1941. The appendix, pp. 306–315, contains an eyewitness account of the Mojave attack on an emigrant wagon train in 1858.

Cosulich, Bernice. "Three Centuries of Tubac History," *Arizona Highways,* Vol. XVIII, No. 10 (October, 1942), pp. 14–19, 40–41.

———. *Tucson.* Tucson: Arizona Silhouettes, 1953.

Decennial Federal Census of 1860, For Arizona County in the Territory of New Mexico, in *Senate Document* 13, 89th Cong. 1st Sess. Washington: Government Printing Office, 1965, pp. 37–48.

"Diary of Charles Debrille Poston" in Sharlot Hall Museum, Prescott, Arizona (also on microfilm, Records of the States of the United States of America, Library of Congress, 1949, Arizona XX, Reel 1A).

Dobyns, Henry F. "Tubac Through Four Centuries: An Historical Resume and Analysis." 3 binders. Unpublished report for the Arizona State Parks Board, 1959.

Dunn, James P. *Massacres of the Mountains.* New York: Harper and Brothers, 1886.

Emory, William H. *Report of the United States and Mexican Boundary Survey,* 1857, Vol. 1. *Senate Executive Document* 108, 34th Cong. 1st Sess., 1855–1856. Washington, D.C.: A.O.P. Nicholson, Printer, 1857.

Evening Bulletin (San Francisco), October 30, 1858.

"Fort Buchanan, New Mexico, November, 1856–May, 1862, Returns from U.S. Military Posts, 1800–1916," National Archives Microfilm Publication, Roll 156. Washington, D.C., 1965. Copy at the Hayden Library, Arizona State University.

"Fort Mojave: Letters Sent, 1859–1861." Record Group 393: Department of War, in the National Archives.

Gressinger, A. W. *Charles W. Poston: Sunland Seer.* Globe, Arizona: Dale Stuart King Publisher, 1961.

Hammond, George P. (ed.). *Campaigns in the West, 1856–1861, The Journal and Letters of Colonel John Van Deusen Du Bois.* Tucson: Arizona Historical Society, 1949.

Irwin, Brigadier General Bernard John D. "The Apache Fight" and "The Chiricahua Apache Indians: A Thrilling Incident in the Early History of Arizona Territory," *Infantry Journal,* April, 1928. [Reprint in Arizona Department of Library and Archives.]

Letherman, Jonathan, assistant surgeon of the U.S. Army, "Sketch of the Navajo Tribe of Indians, Territory of New Mexico," Smithsonian Institution, *Tenth Annual Report.* Washington, D.C.: Cornelius Wendell, Printer, 1856, pp. 283–97.

Lockwood, Frank C. *Life in Old Tucson.* Los Angeles: The Ward Ritchie Press, 1943.

Lockwood, Frank C. and Captain Donald W. Page. *Tucson — the Old Pueblo.* Phoenix: The Manufacturing Stationers, Inc., 1930.

Mowry, Sylvester. *Arizona and Sonora, the Geography, History and Resources of the Silver Region of North America.* New York: Harper Brothers, 1864.

New York Times, April 15, 1857.

Ogle, Ralph H. *Federal Control of the Western Apaches, 1848–1886.* Albuquerque: University of New Mexico Press, 1940. [Reprinted in 1970.]

Parke, Lt. John G. *Report of Explorations for Railroads . . . From the Pimas Villages on the Gila to the Rio Grande Near the 32nd Parallel of North Latitude,* in *Reports of Explorations and Surveys to Ascertain the Most Practicable and Economical Route for a Railroad to the Pacific Ocean,* 1853–6, Vol. VII. Senate Executive Document 78, 33rd Cong. 2nd Sess., 1853–54.

Poston, Charles D. *Building A State in Apache Land* (John M. Myers, ed.) Tempe, Arizona: Aztec Press, 1963.

————. Papers of Charles Debrille Poston in the Arizona Historical Society.

Pumpelly, Raphael. *Across America and Asia*. New York: Leypoldt and Holt, 1870.

Records of the U. S. Army Commands (Army Posts), R. G. 393, National Archives microfilm T-912.

Report of Col. B. L. E. Bonneville to Major W. A. Nichols, Assistant Adjutant General in Santa Fe, from Depot on the Gila, New Mexico, July 14, 1857, in *House Executive Document* 2, 35th Cong. 1st Sess., 1857–1858. (Serial #943).

Sacks, B. "Charles Debrille Poston: Prince of Arizona's Pioneers," *The Smoke Signal*, No. 7 (Spring, 1963). Tucson Corral of Westerners, 1963.

———. "New Evidence on the Bascom Affair," *Arizona and the West*, Vol. 4, No. 3 (Autumn, 1962), pp. 261–78.

———. "The Origins of Fort Buchanan, Myth and Fact," *Arizona and the West*, Vol. 7, No. 3 (Autumn, 1965), pp. 207–26.

"Sanitary Report—Fort Buchanan (Arizona)," *Statistical Report on the Sickness and Mortality in the Army of the United States* . . . in *Senate Executive Document* 52, 36th Cong. 1st Sess., 1859–1860.

[Schuchard, Charles]. "Arizona Argonauts," in *Arizona Daily Citizen*, February 15, 1894.

Serven, James E. "The Military Posts on the Sonoita Creek," *The Smoke Signal*, No. 12 (Fall, 1965). Tucson, Arizona: Tucson Corral of the Westerners, 1965.

Theobold, John and Lillian. *Arizona Territory, Post Offices and Post Roads*, Phoenix: Arizona Historical Foundation, 1961.

Udell, John. *Journal of John Udell Kept During a Trip Across the Plains Containing An Account of the Massacre of a Portion of His Party By the Mohave Indians, in 1859* [1858]. Jefferson, Missouri: Ashtabula Sentinel Steam Press Print, 1868. Copy in Huntington Library. [Reprinted as *John Udell Journal* with introduction by Lyle H. Wright, Los Angeles: N. A. Kovach, 1946.]

U. S. Department of War. "Expedition Against the Navajo Indians, January 6–21, 1864," Vol. 34, Part 1, pp. 69–80, of *The War of Rebellion: A Compilation of the Official Records of the Union and Confederate Armies*, Series I.

Utley, Robert M. "The Bascom Affair: A Reconstruction," *Arizona and the West*, Vol. 3, No. 1 (Spring, 1961), pp. 59–68.

Wagoner, Jay J. *Arizona Territory, 1863–1912: A Political History*. Tucson: University of Arizona Press, 1970.

Walker, Captain John G. and Major Oliver L. Shepherd (L. R. Bailey, editor). *The Navajo Reconnaissance: A Military Exploration of the Navajo Country in 1859*. Los Angeles: Westernlore Press, 1964.

Wallace, Andrew (ed.). *Pumpelly's Arizona*. Tucson: The Palo Verde Press, 1965.

Way, Phocion R. "Diary of Phocion R. Way," in William A. Duffen (ed.), "Overland Via Jackass Mail in 1858," Part 2, *Arizona and the West*, Vol. 2, No. 2 (Summer, 1960), pp. 147–64. The original diary is now in the Arizona Department of Library and Archives.

Weekly Alta California (San Francisco), July 30, 1859.

Weekly Arizonian (Tubac and Tucson), March 3, 1859 *et. seq.*

Woodward, Arthur. "The Founding of Fort Mohave," *Pony Express Courier* (Placerville, California), May, 1937.

———. *The Great Western: Amazon of the Army*. San Francisco: Johnck & Seeger, Printers, 1961, pamphlet, 3 pp.

——— (ed.). *Journal of Lt. Thomas W. Sweeney, 1849–1853*. Los Angeles: Westernlore Press, 1956.

Yuma Daily Sun, Centennial Edition, October 27 and 28, 1954.

Yuma Sentinel, February 16, 1872. Contains a report on a visit to the Yuma vicinity in 1854 by Lieutenant Nathaniel Michler.

14. The Civil War Era

Arizona, Territory of. *Acts, Resolutions and Memorials,* First Legislative Assembly, 1864, at Prescott.

Arizona Miner, 1864 and October 19, 1871.

Brandes, Ray. *Frontier Military Posts of Arizona*. Globe, Arizona: Dale Stuart King, Publisher, 1960.

Brophy, Blake. "Fort Fillmore, N. M., 1861: Public Disgrace and Private Disaster," paper presented at the Ninth Annual Historical Convention, Tempe, April 19–20, 1968. Copy in Arizona Collection, Hayden Library, Arizona State University, Tempe.

Browne, J. Ross. *Adventures in the Apache Country*. New York: Harper and Brothers, 1869. [Re-edition. Tucson: University of Arizona Press, 1974.]

Colton, Ray C. *The Civil War in the Western Territories*. Norman: University of Oklahoma Press, 1959.

Confederate Victories in the Southwest: Prelude to Defeat (from the U. S. Department of War, *Official Records*). Albuquerque, New Mexico: Horn & Wallace, Publishers, 1961.

Conner, Daniel E. *Joseph Reddeford Walker and the Arizona Adventure*. Norman: University of Oklahoma Press, 1956.

Cremony, John C. *Life Among the Apaches*. San Francisco: Roman and Company, Publishers, 1868.

Fireman, Bert M. "How Far Westward the Civil War?" The 1963 *Brand Book* of the Denver Posse of the Westerners, 19th annual edition, 1964, pp. 163–70.

———. "What Comprises Treason? Testimony of Proceedings Against Sylvester Mowry," *Arizoniana*, Vol. I, No. 4 (Winter, 1960), pp. 5–10.

Hollister, Ovando J. *Boldly They Rode: A History of the First Colorado Regiment of Volunteers.* Lakewood, Colorado: The Golden Press, 1949. [Reprint of book published in 1863.]

Hunt, Aurora. *The Army of the Pacific: Its Operations . . . 1860–1866.* Glendale, Calif.: Arthur H. Clark Co., 1951.

Lindgren, Raymond E. (ed.). "A Diary of Kit Carson's Navaho Campaign, 1863–1864," *New Mexico Historical Review,* Vol. XXI, No. 3 (July, 1946), pp. 226–46.

Lockwood, Frank C. *Life in Old Tucson, 1854–1864.* Los Angeles: The Ward Ritchie Press, 1943.

McKee, Major James Cooper, Surgeon, U. S. Army, *Narrative of the Surrender of a Command of U. S. Forces at Fort Fillmore, New Mexico In July, A. D., 1861 with Related Reports by John R. Baylor, & Others.* Houston, Texas: Stagecoach Press, 1960.

Mesilla Times, May 11, 1861.

Mowry, Sylvester. *Memoir of the Proposed Territory of Arizona.* Washington, D. C.: Henry Polkinhorn, Printer, 1857. [Reprinted in Tucson: Territorial Press, 1964.]

New York Times, March 10, 1863.

Noel, Theophilus. *Autobiography and Reminiscences of Theophilus Noel.* Chicago: Theophilus Noel Company Print, 1904.

Orton, Brig. Gen. Richard H. *Records of California Men in the War of the Rebellion, 1861–1867.* Sacramento: State Office, 1890.

Poston, Charles D. *Building A State in Apache Land.* John M. Myers, ed. Tempe, Arizona: Aztec Press, 1963. (Originally published as four articles in the *Overland Monthly* in 1894.)

"Proceedings of a Board of Officers Convened at Tucson, Arizona Territory, June 17, 1862," 68 pp., typescript in Arizona Collection, Hayden Library, Arizona State University, Tempe, Arizona.

Record Group 59: General Records of the Department of State, Territorial Papers, Arizona (April 4, 1864–February 3, 1872) and Territorial Papers, New Mexico (January 2, 1861–December 23, 1864).

Richmond, Jonathan. Letters of Jonathan Richmond, a member of Governor John Goodwin's party, to his parents, 1863–64. Originals in the Arizona Department of Library and Archives, Phoenix.

Sacks, Benjamin. "Sylvester Mowry," *The American West,* Vol. 1, No. 3 (Summer, 1964), pp. 14–24 and 79.

Santee, J. F. "The Battle of Glorietta Pass," *New Mexico Historical Review,* Vol. 6, No. 1 (January, 1931), pp. 66–75.

Speech of John A. Bingham of Ohio, *U. S. Congressional Globe,* 36th Cong. 2d Sess., January 22, 1861, Appendix, p. 83.

Union Army Operations in the Southwest: Final Victory (from the U. S. Department of War, *Official Records*). Albuquerque: Horn and Wallace, Publishers, 1961.

U. S. Bureau of Indian Affairs. *Annual Report of the Commissioner of Indian Affairs to the Secretary of Interior,* 1867.

U. S. Department of War. *The War of Rebellion: A Compilation of the Official Records of the Union and Confederate Armies.* Series 1, Vols. 4; 9; 34, Part 1; and 50, Parts 1 and 2.

U. S. Senate. *Message of the President of the United States,* 38th Cong. 1st Sess., 1863–64, Senate Document No. 49, pp. 1–3. Contains material relative to Sylvester Mowry's arrest as a Confederate sympathizer.

U. S. Statutes at Large, Vol. XII, 37th Cong. 3d Sess., 1863, Chap. LVI. Contains the Organic Act which created the Territory of Arizona.

Wagoner, Jay J. *Arizona Territory, 1863–1912: A Political History.* Tucson: University of Arizona Press, 1970.

Walker, Charles S. "Causes of the Confederate Invasion of New Mexico," *New Mexico Historical Review,* Vol. 8, No. 2 (April, 1933), pp. 76–97.

Watford, W. H. "Confederate Western Ambitions," *The Southwestern Historical Quarterly,* Vol. 44, No. 2 (October, 1940), pp. 161–87.

Weekly Arizonian, March 9, 1861.

Woody, Clara T. "The Woolsey Expeditions of 1864," *Arizona and the West,* Vol. 4, No. 2 (Summer, 1962), pp. 157–76.

Index